国际法双语教学试用教材

上海市教育委员会重点学科建设项目——国际法（J51103）
上海市教育高地第三期建设子项目

"十二五"普通高等教育本科国家级规划教材

International Commercial Arbitration
国际商事仲裁

刘晓红 袁发强 主编

北京大学出版社
PEKING UNIVERSITY PRESS

图书在版编目(CIP)数据

国际商事仲裁/刘晓红,袁发强主编.—北京:北京大学出版社,2010.1
(国际法双语教学试用教材)
ISBN 978-7-301-16447-1

Ⅰ.国… Ⅱ.①刘…②袁… Ⅲ.国际商事仲裁-高等学校-教材 Ⅳ.D997.4

中国版本图书馆 CIP 数据核字(2009)第 227335 号

书　　　名:	国际商事仲裁
著作责任者:	刘晓红　袁发强　主编
责 任 编 辑:	朱梅全　王业龙
标 准 书 号:	ISBN 978-7-301-16447-1/D·2519
出 版 发 行:	北京大学出版社
地　　　址:	北京市海淀区成府路205号　100871
网　　　址:	http://www.pup.cn
电　　　话:	邮购部 62752015　发行部 62750672　编辑部 62752027
	出版部 62754962
电 子 邮 箱:	law@pup.pku.edu.cn
印　刷　者:	三河市博文印刷有限公司
经　销　者:	新华书店
	730 毫米×980 毫米　16 开本　29.25 印张　557 千字
	2010 年 1 月第 1 版　2022 年 3 月第 4 次印刷
定　　　价:	54.00 元

未经许可,不得以任何方式复制或抄袭本书之部分或全部内容。
版权所有,侵权必究
举报电话:010-62752024　电子邮箱:fd@pup.pku.edu.cn

编 者 说 明

在教育部要求推动法律专业课程双语教学的形势下,华东政法大学国际法学院在数年教学实践摸索的基础上尝试编写国际商事仲裁法学的双语教材。

关于双语教学,各地高校都在摸索过程中,许多院校以中文教材为学生学习用书,另指定一些英文文章为参考资料。在课堂讲授过程中,对于外语基础比较好的学生采取全外语授课方式,而对于外语基础一般的本科学生则以中文讲授为主,以学生自学外文参考资料为辅的方式进行。总体上看,由学生自学外文参考资料不过是形式上的"双语"教学,实际没有体现外语的作用;而完全采用外文方式难以适应本科学生的外语水平,也不符合"双语"的要求,更难以反映某些国内法的内容,有形式上的法律课程、实际上的外语课程之嫌。因此,编写既适合本科学生英语水平又能反映课程知识全貌的教材成为双语教学急需解决的问题。

双语教学的目的自不待言,有利于与国际社会接轨,然而不同法律专业课程的特点和内容不同,使用外语教授本国法律理论和司法实践不仅对于授课老师来说难度很大,而且对于学生而言,也存在理解上的困难。仲裁法学是少数受国内法影响较小的部门法学,从法律文化因素上看,更多地带有"舶来品"的色彩;同时,商事仲裁的国际化或者说非本地化倾向一直存在,并且影响到国际商事仲裁法学理论和知识的发展。因此,国际商事仲裁法学与国际贸易法学等部门法学是可以通过双语教学方式使学生获得更多知识的课程,也是学生能够不完全依赖国内法理念就可以掌握的课程。为此,我们特意选择以此作为编写双语教材的起点。

本教材使用对象为大学本科学生,包括法律专业学生和选修该课程的其他专业学生,如外语专业、商业经济、国际贸易、工商管理专业学生等。

目前,国内七百多所大学中有近六百所大学开设有法律专业。一般政法性院校还设置有其他专业,这些专业学生都有选修法律课程的要求和计划。因此,本教材使用面极宽。

在多数高等院校中,国际商事仲裁法学是作为选修课性质安排教学计划的,因而课时量一般不超过36学时。这样,我们在编写教材时,没有追求大而全的编写方式,而是根据课时量选取主要内容组织编写。考虑到仲裁法学是一门实践性很强的课程,在本科阶段不宜作过多理论探讨,应侧重能力培养和实践需要,因而教材篇幅不宜太长,选取精练内容,辅以部分阅读材料比较合适。

作为教材，应当以有利于学生掌握知识的方式组织编写，不能为了追求理论或体系的严谨而牺牲可读性。故本教材避免从概念入手介绍仲裁知识的模式，即使有需要掌握的名词，也多以描述的手法进行解释，对于存在理论争论的问题，设"阅读与思考"部分介绍。每章不刻意追求每节之间的内在逻辑联系，而是按照需要介绍的知识分布情况撰写相关内容。

在内容的编写上，我们采取了与其他教材不同的方式，按照需要讲授的内容和知识，在书中分别以中英文表述。从语言表述看，跳跃性较大，但有利于学生掌握系统的法学知识内容，以免遗漏部分内容。相对于其他部门法学而言，国际商事仲裁法学的外文专著和教材在英语语言上没有特别晦涩难懂的词汇和语法结构，但仲裁实践中使用英语的可能性很大。这个特点要求我们在编写双语教材时给予充分考虑，不能刻意缩减英文部分内容，而是要精选或编写与中文部分密切相关的英文材料。在阅读材料方面，保持节选文章的英文原貌，帮助学生在理解正文知识的基础上提高专业英语阅读能力，适应英语原版教材的风格，熟悉有关专业词汇和语法。

本教材由刘晓红和袁发强担任主编，王冠、马莉君、李俊美、姚竞燕、胡君、张永飞、陆雅丽、史忠辉、张雪、李海跃、葛丽霞、孙笑、倪鑫、方美玲、洪一帆、李晓蕾等承担了本书的编写工作。杨玲、范铭超、黄志瑾承担了本书的校对工作。

编写这样的双语教材是我们的初步尝试，虽然几经审稿和校对，书中仍可能存在错误和不当的地方，希望能够得到读者和同行的批评指正，为今后编写类似教材提供有益经验。

编　者

2009 年 9 月 14 日

目　　录

第一章　国际商事争议概述 ……………………………………………… 1
第一节　争议及争议解决方式 …………………………………………… 1
第二节　国际民商事争议解决方式 ……………………………………… 6
第三节　国际商事仲裁 …………………………………………………… 13
第四节　国际商事仲裁的发展趋势 ……………………………………… 23
阅读材料 ………………………………………………………………… 32
思考题 …………………………………………………………………… 37

第二章　有关仲裁的法律与规则 ………………………………………… 38
第一节　国内立法 ………………………………………………………… 39
第二节　国际立法 ………………………………………………………… 63
第三节　仲裁规则 ………………………………………………………… 75
阅读材料 ………………………………………………………………… 86
思考题 …………………………………………………………………… 91
推荐阅读 ………………………………………………………………… 91

第三章　国际商事仲裁的法律适用 ……………………………………… 93
第一节　国际商事仲裁程序的法律适用 ………………………………… 94
第二节　国际商事仲裁实体问题的法律适用 …………………………… 108
第三节　国际商事仲裁裁决撤销与执行中的法律适用 ………………… 119
案例 ……………………………………………………………………… 131
阅读材料 ………………………………………………………………… 139
思考题 …………………………………………………………………… 141
推荐阅读 ………………………………………………………………… 142

第四章　国际商事仲裁协议 ……………………………………………… 143
第一节　国际商事仲裁协议概述 ………………………………………… 143
第二节　国际商事仲裁协议的表现形式 ………………………………… 149
第三节　国际商事仲裁协议的法律要件 ………………………………… 151

第四节　国际商事仲裁协议的继受 ································ 162
　　阅读材料 ··· 169
　　案例 ··· 172
　　思考题 ··· 178
　　推荐阅读 ··· 178

第五章　仲裁员与仲裁庭 ··· 180
　　第一节　仲裁员的资格与选任 ···································· 180
　　第二节　仲裁庭组成 ··· 190
　　第三节　仲裁庭的管辖权 ·· 201
　　第四节　仲裁庭的权力（利）和义务 ······························ 215
　　案例 ··· 229
　　阅读材料 ··· 233
　　思考题 ··· 236
　　推荐阅读 ··· 237

第六章　国际商事仲裁程序 ······································· 238
　　第一节　国际商事仲裁程序概述 ·································· 238
　　第二节　国际商事仲裁程序启动 ·································· 240
　　第三节　国际商事仲裁审理过程 ·································· 248
　　阅读材料 ··· 262
　　思考题 ··· 269
　　推荐阅读 ··· 270

第七章　国际商事仲裁裁决 ······································· 271
　　第一节　国际商事仲裁裁决概述 ·································· 271
　　第二节　国际商事仲裁中的临时性保全措施 ······················· 280
　　第三节　国际商事仲裁裁决的效力与撤销 ························· 289
　　案例 ··· 302
　　阅读材料 ··· 307
　　思考题 ··· 316
　　推荐阅读 ··· 316

第八章　国际商事仲裁裁决的执行 ································ 317
　　第一节　概述 ··· 317
　　第二节　涉外仲裁裁决的执行 ···································· 322
　　第三节　外国商事仲裁裁决的执行 ································ 328

第四节　我国区际仲裁裁决的执行 ································· 339
　　案例 ··· 348
　　阅读材料 ··· 352
　　思考题 ··· 359
　　推荐阅读 ··· 360
附录　仲裁法律与规则 ·· 361
　　一、国际法制部分 ··· 361
　　二、国内法制部分 ··· 400
　　三、仲裁规则部分 ··· 422

第一章　国际商事争议概述

第一节　争议及争议解决方式

一、什么是争议

在漫漫的历史长河中,我们一直向往一个没有争议、没有纠纷,人人富足、宁静祥和的桃花源式的社会。但现实生活中的真实情况总是与我们理想中的情景相去甚远,生活中总是存在各种各样的争议。而争议的产生又总是给人们的生活带来种种的烦恼与不便。这样,问题便产生了:争议是从人类产生那一天起便有的么? 争议是如何产生的呢?

争议也称为争端、争执,是有关当事人各方对于相互之间的权利、义务有不同的主张。争议的产生可以归结为两种原因:利益冲突和认识分歧。这两种原因是从两个角度进行分析的,一个是物质层面的,另一个是精神层面的。在物质层面上,各方存在利益冲突,资源的有限性和人们需求的增长产生冲突,争议也就无法避免;在精神层面上,各方也可能存在认识分歧,对某个问题各方会有不同的见解,这些不同的见解也会导致争议的产生。

首先我们讨论物质层面的利益冲突。经济利益(或称为物质利益)是利益这个大概念中的核心内容,人们的活动都是围绕经济利益进行的,政治利益也是用来实现经济利益的手段。经济利益冲突的根源在于社会财富不丰裕,社会财富的有限性和经济资源的稀缺性与人们不断增长的需要产生了矛盾,使得利益冲突成为一种必然。所以,只有在社会财富极端丰富,而且在人们的需求得到满足的情况下,争议才有可能减少或者避免。但这种说法也不绝对。上述情况下只可能避免物质层面上由利益冲突引起的争议,另一种精神层面的争议则不能避免,因为不同的人看待问题的角度不同,不同的人由于自身经验、认识水平以及客观条件的限制,对同一个问题会有不同的看法,由此会导致认识上的分歧,这种分歧所导致的争议是纯粹的、观念上的争议。比如在中世纪,由于科学技术和人们认识水平上的局限性,有的人认为天是圆的,地球是方的;也有人认为天是方的,地球是圆的。这种认识分歧都是与经济或物质利益无关的、单纯的观念上的不同,无论生产力发展到何种程度,无论社会资源多么丰富,这种观念上的认识分歧都是无法避免的。所以说,争议产生的两大方面原因便是利益冲突和认识分歧。

The question, "what is a dispute?" should be understood as, "what are the various phenomena that can be thought of as a dispute?" Because the idea of dispute implies something in contention, "dispute" and "problem" are not synonymous. This following will articulate some conceptions of "dispute." They are not mutually exclusive, and any contentious situation is likely to be a dispute in multiple senses.

1. Conflicts of Wills (Desires, Intentions). Considering two children quarreling over a toy. Depending on their development, they may rationalize their positions by claims of right, but the underlying matter is a conflict of "wants." Conflicts of wills are resolved when disputants' wills are modified or when circumstances effect a disengagement (for example, the children are sent to their rooms). A definitive resolution of a question of legal rights may not resolve parties' conflict of wills.

2. Argument/Disagreement. For example, "when does life begin?" or "what is 'the right to bear arm'?" It is this sense of dispute that dominates dictionary definitions.

3. Unsettled Relationships. Marital and labor management disputes are, only most obviously, likely to be this kind of dispute in some of their aspect.

4. Conflicting Views/Intentions Regarding Future Relations. In this conception, a version of unsettled relations, the dispute may be formal (for example, in contract negotiation) or informal (for example, a dating couple breaking up because only one of them wants to continue).①

利益冲突和认识分歧可以导致争议的产生，此时的争议是通常意义上的纠纷或争执，并没有上升为法律争议。一种简单的争议上升为法律争议是需要特定条件的。例如，夫妻间的吵架只是简单的争议，可能是由于双方感情不和而引起的小纠纷，此时的争议并不是法律争议，但当吵架变得严重，一方主张离婚时，这种争议就上升为法律争议了，特别是离婚时要涉及财产分割和子女抚养的情况下，即涉及双方权利义务的产生、变更以及消灭时，这种法律争议便需要通过合适的方式进行解决，较为常用的争议解决方式包括协商、调解、诉讼以及仲裁等方式。

---

① See Edwin H. Greenebaum, Lawyers' Agenda for Understanding Alternative Dispute Resolution, Indiana Law Journal, Summer, 1993.

二、什么是民商事争议

民商事争议又称为民商事纠纷,是指发生于平等主体之间,以民商事权利义务为内容的社会纠纷。一般而言,民商事争议是因某一方或者双方当事人违反了民商事法律规范或者约定而引起的。当事人认为对方违反规定或约定的行为,侵害了自己的民事权益,从而采取行动要求得到某种形式的弥补,这样,民商事争议就产生了。

民商事争议的主要特点在于:首先,它发生在平等的民商事主体之间,包括自然人与自然人之间、自然人与法人之间或者法人与法人之间。其次,这种争议是限于特定范围内的,可以由民商事法律规范予以调整的争议。在各种各样的社会关系中,有很多是法律所不能踏足的领域。比如说对于那些同乡、同学、恋人之间的人际关系,还有宗教团体内部的各种联系,法律就显得无能为力。最后,民商事争议是以某一民商事权利义务关系为焦点的。争议的内容往往就是针对谁应该享有哪些民事权利,谁又应该承担哪些民事义务的争论。

民商事争议可以通过两种渠道解决:一种是争议主体依靠自身的力量自行解决民商事争议,比如通过和解、协商等方式,这类解决方式又称为私力救济;另一种是争议主体依靠社会或国家的力量解决争议,维护自己的权益,比如通过诉讼、仲裁等方式,这类解决方式又称为公力救济。私力救济作为一种古老的纠纷解决方式,起源于人类趋利避害的本能和初民社会无政府状态。在国家和法律出现之前,私力救济是人们解决纠纷的唯一手段。随着人类社会的不断发展,在权利救济与制裁当中,国家公权力逐渐强化,公力救济逐步取代了私力救济而占据了主导地位。但是,私力救济在现代社会中依然大量存在。这两种渠道中的某些方式日渐式微,而某些方式又方兴未艾。在现代社会,民商事争议主要通过四种方式得到解决:协商、调解、仲裁、诉讼。这其中,以仲裁方式解决民商事争议在世界范围内得到普遍承认和运用。

三、什么是国际民商事争议

从字面理解,国际民商事争议的特点体现在"国际"二字上,如民商事争议的主体在不同国家,或者主体之间权利义务的产生、变更、消灭的事实发生在不同国家,或者主体间交易的标的物在国外等。国际民商事争议的主体位于不同国家仅仅是从住所或经营场所来划分的,当事人的国籍并不是主要参考因素。对于一项民商事争议,在当事双方位于一国国内时,它仅仅是国内的民商事争议;倘若当事双方位于两个不同国家,民商事争议便发展为国际民商事争议。当今的世界,人们享受着高科技所带来的便利,活动范围已经不是前人可以比拟的了。人口流动的速度与广度空前加大,民商事交往不再局限于单一的国家,而是趋向于国际性,国与国、一国国民与他国国民之间的交往增多,在这些纷繁复杂且密切的合作与交往中,逐渐形成了一定的游戏规则。这些规则中,有些已经被大多数国家制定为法律,有的则是在国际民商事交往和合作中新产生的并为国际社会所认同。有规则就应遵守,当然也会有破坏规则的现象发生。这种破坏行为或者出于故意,或者出于对规则理解的不一致,或者该问题本身还没有规则进行规制,但是无论如何,有破坏,争议就会随之而来。这些争议有的能够受到法律评价(包括广义的国际惯例、公约、各国有关法律规范等),有的不能受到法律评价,这主要取决于各国和国际社会的价值观念、利益要求以及对该问题的重视程度。我们将这种发生在国际民商事领域的,能够受到法律评价的纠纷称为国际民商事争议。

不同国家间民商事交往的形式和内容多种多样,包括民事交往,如婚姻、抚养等;也包括经济交往,如货物买卖、服务提供等。在国际商事实践中,大多数国际商事交易行为能够顺利完成,但事实上,相当多的交易会发生争议或纠纷,虽然产生争议或纠纷的原因各有不同。各国无不采取措施减少或解决这种争议或纠纷,以维护交易人的正当合法权益。国际商事争议是纷繁复杂的,解决的方式也多种多样,但比较广泛采用的还是诉讼、仲裁以及 ADR 等方式。

International commercial disputes occur for a number of reasons. Most, however, stem from difficulties in communication. Although miscommunication is possible in any business relationship, domestic or international, when parties come from different countries the risk of communication failure increases exponentially. This is because of the added cultural component.

The more dissimilar their cultures of origin, the greater the potential for inaccurate perceptions, strong emotions and misunderstandings between parties when they attempt to form a relationship or negotiate a dispute. Culture, including language, is the acquired knowledge that members of a given community use to subconsciously interpret their surroundings and guide their interaction with others. Individuals from the same culture use their shared background to decipher each other's statements and actions. The overall disparity between Japanese and American cultures makes it especially hard for commercial parties from these nations to understand each other. As a result, the potential for the eruption of disputes between them is substantial.[1]

---

[1] See Andrew Sagartz, Resolution of International Commercial Disputes: Surmounting Barriers of Culture without Going to Court, Ohio State Journal on Dispute Resolution, 1998.

国际民商事争议与国内民商事争议相比,其根本特点在于它的国际性。由此衍生而来的特点是:

第一,冲突的国际关注性。由于国际民商事争议涉及两个甚至多个国家的自然人或法人,如果得不到妥善解决,私人之间的纠纷很有可能导致国家政府之间结怨,甚至产生国际争端。因此,国际范围内的关注在所难免。

第二,调整规范的多元性。当一个国际民商事争议需要得到解决时,往往会适用国际条约和国际惯例。另外,冲突规范也起到指引作用。在法律适用的选择中,当事人的意愿受到重视。

第三,救济手段的多样性。国际民商事争议的当事人可以选择诉讼、仲裁以及ADR等方式解决争议。由于国际商事仲裁固有的程序简便、保密、操作快捷等特点,它在商人们中间有相当大的影响力。除此之外,当事人还可以通过调解或者自行和解等ADR方法解决争议。这种由当事人协商的方式虽然出自不同当事人的不同动机,可能还包含当事人企图回避审判等情况,但仍不可忽视这些诉讼外争议解决方式的重要性,这一点在下文将有详细论述。

四、争议解决处理方式多元化

解决国际民商事争议的方式多种多样,概括起来主要有协商、调解、仲裁和诉讼四种:

1. 协商和调解方式:这样两种方式在程序上基本一致,而且它们的主要精神都在于友好谈判,互谅互让。协商是指有争议的双方当事人签订协议之后,心平气和地商量解决问题,在这个过程中,有可能有第三方的参与,而这个第三方只是在某些环节中提出一些建议或者缓和一下现场气氛,总之是一种间接的促进作用。而调解的不同之处在于调解人会提出解决方案。在调解中,第三方协调是最为重要的解决争议的步骤,双方当事人达成的协议中承认了第三方的这种更为主动的参与方式。

2. 仲裁:指纠纷主体根据双方协议,将争议提交第三方,由第三方居中裁决的一种方式。仲裁有着比诉讼更为悠久的历史。如果当事人双方不愿协商、调解,或者协商、调解不成的,可以根据双方当事人在合同中的仲裁条款或者事后达成的书面仲裁协议,提交常设仲裁机构或临时仲裁庭,以解决双方的纠纷。下文将对仲裁作具体阐述。

Arbitration is a device whereby the settlement of a question, which is of interest for two or more persons, is entrusted one or more other persons—the arbitrator or arbitrators—who derive their powers from a private agreement, not from the authorities of a State, and who are to proceed and decide the case on the basis of such an agreement.①

3. 诉讼：其实质是由特定的国家机关，在纠纷主体的参加下，处理特定的社会纠纷的一种最权威最有效的机制。诉讼的特点主要包括：一是国家强制性，诉讼是法院凭借国家审判权确定纠纷主体双方之间民商事权利义务关系，并以国家强制执行权迫使纠纷主体履行生效的判决和裁定。二是严格的规范性，诉讼必须严格地按照法律规范进行。

When an international commercial dispute arises, litigation is usually the least appealing method to resolve the conflict. The extensive, well-documented problems with litigation of ordinary commercial disputes include high cost, the likelihood of injury to the underlying commercial relationship and the uncertainty of the outcome. International transactions, however, carry an additional set of interrelated problems, such as forum shopping, procedural complexities, enforcement, added costs and sovereign immunity.②

第二节 国际民商事争议解决方式

在国际民商事关系中，由于不同的当事人或当事方有着不同的人身或者经济利益，同时不同的当事人处在不同的地理位置，拥有不同的文化背景、价值观念和法律观念，特别是从民商事关系的产生、实施，再到完成，有一个主客观情况不断变化的过程，国际民商事争议由此而产生。为了维护当事方合法的和正当的权益，为了保障国际民商事活动的正常进行，为了促进国际社会经济文化关系的不断发展，各国法律、各国政府及有关国际组织等，都积极鼓励有关当事人通过适当途径和方式解决国际民商事争议。国际民商事争议的解决方法一般而言有四种，即协商、调解、仲裁、诉讼。这四种不同的方式具有各自不同的特点、作用和效果。

一、诉讼

诉讼是一种常见且古老的争议解决方式。当私有制发展到一定程度，为了保护新的社会关系，缓和日益激烈的阶级斗争，国家便应运而生，进而体现国家意志的法律被制定出来，为了保障社会秩序的稳定，法院等国家强制机构也建立起来，诉讼也就随之产生。

---

① See Rene David, Arbitration in International Trade, Kluwer Law and Taxation Publishers, 1985, p.5.
② See Andrew Sagartz, Resolution of International Commercial Disputes: Surmounting Barriers of Culture without Going to Court, Ohio State Journal on Dispute Resolution, 1998.

对于大多数的国内争议,当事方都会选择诉讼的方式来解决。诉讼方式在解决国内争议方面的优势在于,法院对案件审判并作出公正的判决,这种审判具有权威性,能够产生拘束力而得以执行,可以保证当事双方权利义务的实现。而在国际民商事争议中,选择诉讼方式的较少,其主要原因也是在于裁决的执行上存在问题。对于国际民商事争议,若选择了诉讼的解决方式,当一国法院作出判决后,往往会存在判决需要在另一国进行执行的问题。但由于各国法律体系以及政治、文化等方面存在诸多差别,且国际层面并不存在民商事判决自由流通的条约机制,因此一国的民商事判决在他国并不一定能够得到承认和执行,这就给当事方权利义务的实现带来极大困难。所以在国际民商事交往中,当事人通常会考虑到诉讼解决争议可能带来的风险。

国际民商事诉讼是解决跨国争议的一种方式,但不是唯一的方式,其他诸如仲裁、调解等方式也占有举足轻重的地位。国际民商事诉讼可以分为国际民事诉讼和国际商事诉讼两部分。国际民事诉讼是解决跨国民事争议的一种方式,跨国民事争议包括由跨国婚姻关系、跨国抚养关系等引起的争议,解决这类争议的诉讼被称为国际民事诉讼;国际商事诉讼是解决跨国商事争议的一种方式,跨国商事争议包括由国际货物买卖、国际服务提供等商业行为引起的争议,解决这类争议的诉讼被称为国际商事诉讼。国际民事诉讼和国际商事诉讼在处理国际争议的早期起着同样重要的作用,但随着国际交流的发展和国际贸易的强化,国际民事诉讼和国际商事诉讼在处理两类争议时的地位发生了变化。在当今世界,国际民事诉讼在处理跨国民事争议时仍占据重要地位,跨国民事争议的当事方在争议发生时仍会较多地选择诉讼这种争议解决方式;而国际商事诉讼在处理跨国商事争议时的地位则显得不那么重要,跨国商事争议的当事方在争议发生时不会单一地倾向诉讼这一解决方式,他们可能会选择协商、调解的方式,更多地则会选择仲裁这种解决方式。造成这种现象的原因有很多种,主要的原因在于仲裁这种方式给予当事方很大的自由度,当事方可以自己选择仲裁规则,可以自己选择仲裁员,可以自己选择仲裁所适用的法律,同时仲裁裁决的执行也存在一定的便利性,各国一般都不排斥仲裁裁决的执行,仲裁的这些优势博得了当事方的青睐,使得仲裁超过了诉讼,成为解决国际商事争议的最重要解决方式。

二、替代性争议解决方式

替代性争议解决方式这一术语是由英文 Alternative Dispute Resolution 而来,简称为 ADR。这一名称源于美国,而后在欧洲大陆各国、日本、韩国、澳大利亚等国广为盛行。它原来是指 20 世纪逐步发展起来的各种诉讼外纠纷解决方式,现已引申为对世界各国普遍存在着的、民事诉讼制度以外的非诉讼纠纷解决程序或机制的总称。这一概念既可以根据字面意义译为"替代性(或代替性、选择性)纠纷解决方式",亦可根据其实质意义译为"审判外(诉讼外或判决外)纠纷解决方式"或"非诉讼纠纷解决程序"或"法院外纠纷解决方式"等。ADR 观念的广泛传播始于 20 世纪 70 年代,但运用 ADR 解决纠纷的思想古已有之,如我国儒家的"礼"治思想即可追溯到春秋战国时期。当今国际社会比较常见的替代性纠纷解决方式包括协商、调解、微型审理以及监察员制度等。下面对重要的 ADR 方式作简要的介绍。

(一)协商(Negotiation)

协商是指在国际经济交往活动中发生纠纷时,由争议双方当事人在自愿互谅的基础上,直接进行磋商,自行解决纠纷,不需要任何第三者的参与,在不损害双方关系的基础上,互谅互让地解决争议。在这种方式下,双方通过谅解和让步,最终达到双方都可以承受或接受的结果,是一种较为理想的争议解决方式。

(二)调解(Mediation)

调解是指第三者应争议双方当事人的请求,通过尽量协调双方的分歧,而不是作出有约束力的决定的方式解决当事人之间争议的方法。调解是 ADR 中较为常见和重要的一种形式。

Among the various alternative dispute resolution methods, mediation stands out as particularly advantageous. Mediation has several special features, including its informality, its flexibility and its completely voluntary and non-binding nature, that make it preferable not only to litigation but often to other alternative means of dispute resolution as well.①

(三)微型审理(Minitrials)

微型审理一般是由第三方以及争议双方各自指派的一人组成微型审理小组。各方就这一过程的根本规则达成协议,严格限制提交的文件数目以及各方准备陈词和陈述意见的时间。在指定的听证日期(一般不超过两天),先由双方分别陈述意见,再由分别代表争议双方的人员(如各自的法律顾问)自行碰头力图达成协议。当事方如有要求,中立方将就争议若进入诉讼阶段最可能产生的结果给出口头意见。在此基础上,争议双方再度进行磋商以寻求解决方案,整个过程是非公开的。微型审理有时又被称为妥协谈判,带有模拟诉讼的特点。

A minitrial can be an effective way for large institutions to resolve disputes. A minitrial's main advantage is that it forces senior officials in institutions to focus on a dispute and settle it early, thus saving the parties a significant amount of money.

In a minitrial, each attorney engages in a truncated discovery process and then

---

① See Kenneth R. Feinberg, Mediation—A Preferred Method of Dispute Resolution, Pepperdine Law Review, Spring, 1989.

presents a summary case to a specially constituted panel. The panel consists of a neutral advisor and a senior official from each party's organization who has not been involved in the underlying dispute and who has the authority to settle the dispute.

After hearing both sides of the case, the senior officials try to negotiate a settlement. If they reach an impasse, the neutral advisor may try to mediate a resolution. If unsuccessful, the advisor might advise the parties of the likely outcome if the case were to go to court. With this additional information, the senior officials would continue to negotiate. If they again reach an impasse, the parties may suspend any litigation for an additional cooling-off period and if no settlement is reached, turn back to the courts for resolution. But, the parties are now much further along in preparing for trial.①

(四) 简易陪审团审判(Summary Jury Trial)

简易陪审团审判发源于英美法系,它通过民事陪审团的介入促进在司法审判中解决争议。目前,简易陪审团审判在美国是相当普通的司法实践。在这种解决争议的模式中,陪审团在任何官方听证会举行之前,听取各方当事人的简要陈述,并作出一个建议性的裁决(Advisory Verdict)。该裁决可能会构成当事人进行谈判磋商的基础,从而使当事人免于陷入冗繁费时的法院诉讼。

Summary jury trials can be effective in cases in which parties differ substantially in how they think juries will react. Like minitrials, summary jury trials consist of abbreviated discovery and summary presentations of cases. However, the cases are heard by real juries in real courtrooms under the supervision of real judges. The jury even renders a verdict though a non-binding one.

Like minitrials, summary jury procedures also force parties to focus on cases and settle them early, saving the parties considerable money. This occurs because new information and insights are generated early which the parties can factor into ongoing negotiations. The information and insights are generated when the parties are preparing their summary presentations, observing the reactions of the jury and evaluating the jury's non-binding verdict.

The procedures for a summary jury trial were developed by Judge Thomas Lambros of the Northern District of Ohio in 1980 and have since been used in several states including Ohio, Michigan, Massachusetts and Florida. To the best of my

---

① See Harold I. Abrahmson, A Primer on Resolving Disputes: Lessons from Alternative Dispute Resolution, New York State Bar Journal, March/April, 1992.

knowledge, they have not yet been used in New York State.①

ADR 不仅仅局限于上述几种方式,还包括租借法官(即雇请或租借退休法官处理私人案件)、早期审理评议(Early Trial Evaluation)、最后报价仲裁(Final Offer Arbitration)等,甚至包括仲裁这一方式。一般来说,狭义的 ADR 仅指协商、调解等方式,并不包括仲裁;而广义的 ADR 则包括了仲裁等诸多非诉讼的争议解决方式。实际上,仲裁方式也是替代诉讼解决争议的一种重要方式,但它与其他非诉讼方法(协商、调解等)有明显的不同之处,即除了具有很强的灵活性和自主性之外,还具有一定的强制性,比如仲裁裁决的执行便具有一定的强制性,如果一方当事人不愿履行裁决,另一方当事人可向法院申请强制执行。鉴于仲裁的特殊性,本书中所称的 ADR 采取狭义的解释,不包括仲裁。

ADR 制度理论实践的重大成就几乎都是首先出现在美国,但是在 1925 年以前,美国司法系统对于 ADR 一直都予以排斥,这种状况到了 70 年代才有所改善。直至 1998 年克林顿总统签署了《替代性纠纷解决法》,ADR 才得到美国社会的全面认可。事实上,在进入 20 世纪 90 年代后,英美 ADR 呈现出一个重要的发展特点和趋势,即日益呈现出程式化特征。所谓程式化特征,体现在大量 ADR 机构的出现,也体现在 ADR 适用规则的制定以及 ADR 专业人员的培训上。这不仅为运用 ADR 实现实体正义提供了重要的程序保障,也为把 ADR 程序的正式化作为赋予 ADR 以法律效力提供了必要的实践基础。

The purpose of ADR, which in its primitive phase is older than any judicial system, is to provide an alternative to litigation within a national court system. Modern international ADR, more specifically in its arbitration form, developed as part of the growth of internationalism after World War Ⅰ with the creation of arbitral decisional bodies. These became known as institutional ADR providers and included the International Chamber of Commerce ("ICC") and the American Arbitration Association ("AAA"). In time, the London Court of International Arbitration ("LCIA"), which prior to World War I acted as a decisional body in Great Britain for both domestic and international arbitral disputes, changed its name and purpose while at the same time limiting the right of judicial appeal from its decisions. Following the creation of the World Bank after World War Ⅱ, the International Centre for Settlement of Investment Disputes ("ICSID") was established for the purpose of arbitrating or mediating private international investment disputes between states and nationals of other states. The main focus was upon resolving disputes

---

① See Harold I. Abrahmson, A Primer on Resolving Disputes: Lessons from Alternative Dispute Resolution, New York State Bar Journal, March/April, 1992.

between developing nations as debtors and foreign enterprises, especially contractors. Subsequently, the Arbitration Institute of the Stockholm Chamber of Commerce ("SCC") changed from a solely onshore institution to the role of an offshore provider. The foregoing international ADR institutions, together with certain trade associations based in London, are the major providers of international ADR services in the world.

Following the adoption in 1958 of the United Nations Convention on the Recognition and Enforcement of Foreign Arbitral Awards, better known as the New York Convention, the number of international arbitration cases grew rapidly. The Convention is currently applicable to over 130 ratifying independent nations. By precluding litigation in national courts when parties are legally bound to arbitrate their disputes and providing that arbitral decisions be directly enforceable by the judiciary within any of the signatory jurisdictions, it caused international commercial arbitration to come of age.

International arbitral ADR provides several distinct advantages over litigation. In addition to simplified extra national enforcement, it allows for reduction in costs, control over selection of neutrals with expertise in the subject of the dispute, confidentiality, limited delaying tactics such as discovery and pre-hearing pleadings, and reduction in the length of proceedings.[①]

三、仲裁

仲裁制度是指民商事争议的当事人达成协议,自愿将争议提交选定的第三者根据一定程序规则或公正原则作出裁决,并自愿受到裁决约束的一种法律制度。仲裁通常为民间活动,是一种私人行为,即私人裁判行为,而非国家裁判行为。尽管如此,仲裁行为仍依法受到监督,法院对仲裁的监督包括审查仲裁协议的效力、仲裁程序的制定以及仲裁裁决的撤销和执行几个方面。

Arbitration is a method of dispute resolution "involving one or more neutral third parties who are agreed to by the disputing parties and whose decision is binding." The arbitration proceeding is distinct from litigation and its underlying purpose is to "encourag[e] dispute resolution without resort to the courts." Arbitration is an attractive form of dispute resolution because it "leads to the efficient resolution of

---

① See Robert Bennett Lubi, Reducing Costs and Inconveniences in International Commercial Arbitration and Other Forms of Alternative Resolution through Online Dispute Resolution, Hans Smit and Juris Publishing, Inc., 2006.

disputes without resort to the time and expense of litigation."

Arbitration is one of several alternative processes that parties can use to resolve disputes. The main reason parties agree to arbitrate is to avoid the time and expenses that often accompany the litigation process. Furthermore, unlike litigation, arbitration is private, and thus appeals to those wishing to keep their disputes out of the public eye. Arbitration can be defined as a private process where one or more neutrals render a decision after hearing arguments and reviewing evidence. Generally, in arbitration, the neutral's decision is binding unless the parties contract in such a way as to allow for an appeal of the decision. However, most often arbitration is used as a binding dispute resolution procedure.[1]

可仲裁的范围是有一定限度的。我国《仲裁法》规定可以进行仲裁的包括平等主体的公民、法人和其他组织之间发生的合同纠纷和其他财产权益纠纷,而涉及人身权益的纠纷,如婚姻、收养、监护、扶养、继承纠纷则不能仲裁。此外,依法应当由行政机关处理的行政争议也不可以提交仲裁。

The advantages of arbitration are readily apparent. Firstly, arbitration allows the parties to keep private the details of their dispute. Secondly, as the parties can choose their own rules of procedure, there is greater scope for minimizing acrimony, keeping costs low and electing the times and places at which hearings may be held. Thirdly, the ability of the parties to choose their own "judge" permits the choice of an expert in the field who may have knowledge or skills not possessed by the ordinary courts and who is more able to view the dispute in its commercial setting. Finally, it is possible for the arbitrator to establish a rapport with the parties and thus to obtain greater insights than might otherwise be possible.

Arbitration in international business fulfills largely the same function that litigation performs in the domestic fields, providing a neutral forum to fairly decide a dispute. In addition, the opportunity to choose the arbitrators, the confidentiality of the arbitral proceedings and the arbitral award, the chance of saving time and money and the easy enforcement of arbitral awards are advantages that can hardly be overestimated in the practice of settling international commercial disputes. Arbitration is a "fundamental service" for international trade.[2]

---

[1] See Nickolas J. McGrath, McCauley v. Halliburton Energy Services, Inc.: Treatment of a Motion to Stay Proceedings Pending an Arbitrability Appeal, Denver University Law Review, 2006.

[2] See Christian Buhring-Uhle, Lars Kichhof, Gabriele Scherer, Arbitration and Mediation in International Business, Kluwer Law International, 2006, p.10.

第三节 国际商事仲裁

一、什么是仲裁

就字面而言,"仲"为居中,"裁"为评断。二字连用,意即居中公断。作为一项法律制度,仲裁是指根据当事人之间的协议,双方当事人将其发生的争议,提交给仲裁机构或者临时组成的仲裁庭居中作出具有约束力的裁决,以解决当事人之间的争议,确定当事人的权利义务关系。较之诉讼,仲裁出现的时间更早,它作为当事人自愿选择的争议解决手段,逐渐呈现出灵活性、自主性、一裁终局性等特点。

Arbitration has long been a popular method of settling business disputes arising out of a contractual relationship. It is used extensively in the settlement of international trading and maritime disputes and in the construction industry. The terms of a contract invariably require that disputes be referred for settlement to one of a number of institutions, such as the Court of Arbitration of International Chamber of Commerce or the London International Arbitration Center. The rules of these bodies provide a framework of procedure, which if adopted, can avoid lengthy disputes on the operation of the arbitration. On the other hand, the contract may simply provide for the appointment of a single arbitrator or arbitration panel, to be agreed by the parties.[①]

二、什么是国际商事仲裁

国际商事仲裁,是指在国际商事活动的当事人在合同中订立仲裁条款或纠纷发生后达成仲裁协议,自愿把他们之间的商事争议交付常设仲裁机构或临时仲裁庭进行评断和裁决。仲裁庭或仲裁机构作出的裁决是对各方当事人均具有拘束力的终局裁决,当事人有主动履行仲裁裁决的义务。"国际商事仲裁"缺乏统一的被普遍接受的明确界定的概念,各种界定的不同主要是因为对"国际"和"商事"存在着不同解释。有的国家把当事人的国籍、住所或居所、法人注册地等作为区分是否为"国际"仲裁的标准;而有的国家则以当事人间的争议是否存在国际性作为标准。至于何为"商事",更是几乎没有国家给出明确定义。对国际商事仲裁概念解释的不同,并不是什么小问题,它直接关系到仲裁裁决是否可以得到他国法院的承认和执行。当一个争议涉及多个国家,而有的国家认为属

[①] See Robert Bradgate, Nigel Savage, Commercial Law, Butterworths, 2000, p.603.

于国际商事仲裁,有的国家则认为不属于国际商事仲裁时,问题也就出现了。

(一)关于"国际"的含义

大多数国家明确区分国内仲裁与国际仲裁,并在立法与实践中给予不同的待遇。例如,大多数国家都给予国际商事仲裁更多的自由,更多地体现当事人自己的意志,并且相对而言施加较少的司法干预。理由如下:第一,除了仲裁程序在内国发生之外,国际仲裁的主体环节通常与进行仲裁的国家没有实质关系;第二,国际商事仲裁的当事人通常是经济实体或者是公司,而不是个人,那么所涉国家有可能对此类仲裁采取更加宽松的态度。相比较而言,国内仲裁通常为个人所提起,此类请求金额虽小,但是对于所涉当事人却是相当的重要。在此,国家的控制体现出了更多的对于本国公民的保护。① 因此,一项仲裁是"国际"的还是"国内"的,意义重大。

The principal legal significance of arbitration is that a number of countries, such as France, Italy, and Switzerland, apply more different legal regimes to "international" arbitration than they do to those, which are domestic. (Since domestic arbitration only involve a state's own domiciliary and nationals, a state is likely to wish to maintain a closer control of the arbitration procedure in such arbitrations than it would for those arbitrations in which one or more foreigners seek to have a dispute settled by arbitration.) If arbitration looks as if it might be "international" in character, one must alert to the fact that special rules (differing to a greater or lesser extent from those applicable to domestic arbitrations) may be applied to it by the legal system of the country under consideration.

As is so often the case when the laws and practices of two or more countries have to be looked at, there is no generally accepted definition of "international" and, in each case, the relevant system of law (usually being that of the country in which the arbitration is to take place) will have to be considered.②

大体上,各国区分商事仲裁是否属于"国际"的准则有两种:

1. 以实质性连结因素(Material Connecting Factors)为认定标准:在一些国家,认定仲裁的国际性是以实质性连结点为根据的。这些连结点包括仲裁的地点,当事人的国籍、住所或惯常居所,法人注册地或者管理中心地等。采用此标准的有英国、丹麦、瑞典、瑞士等欧洲国家以及埃及、叙利亚等中东国家。1988年瑞士《联邦国际私法法规》第176条第1款规定,即使仲裁庭在瑞士,但在缔结

---

① 参见〔英〕艾伦·雷得芬、马丁·亨特等:《国际商事仲裁法律与实践》,林一飞、宋连斌译,北京大学出版社2005年版,第13页。

② See Mark Huleatt-James & Nicholas Gould, International Commercial Arbitration: A Handbook, LLP, 1996, p.8.

仲裁协议时有一方当事人在瑞士既无住所也无惯常居所的仲裁也为国际仲裁。这种方法明确、易辨，但是其缺陷也是非常明显的。例如，它排除了某些仅仅具有少量涉外因素的争议仲裁的国际性。当两个具有同一国籍的当事人基于位于他国境内的标的物发生争议的仲裁，按照瑞士《联邦国际私法法规》第 176 条第 1 款的标准便被列为国内仲裁，但是这种争议具有明显的国际因素。因此，实质性连结因素标准固然简单、明确，但是过于粗线条，不符合当今国际商事交易多样性的状况，缺陷明显。

2. 以争议的国际性质为认定标准：由于实质性连结因素标准显而易见的缺陷，争议性质标准逐渐产生。该标准是指如果争议某一环节涉及"国际商事利益"，那么就将此仲裁视为国际仲裁。例如，法国 1981 年《民事诉讼法》第 1492 条规定，"凡……涉及国际商事利益的仲裁是国际仲裁"。争议性质标准有利于满足复杂的国际经济活动的需要，但它的缺点正是实质性连结因素标准的优点，即不够简单、明确。因此在实践中，判断仲裁的国际性质时，往往仍要综合考虑国籍、住所等具体的连结因素。1985 年《联合国国际贸易法委员会国际商事仲裁示范法》①（以下简称《示范法》）即采取了综合性的多重判断方法。

In this book the approach taken by the draftsmen of UNCITRAL when preparing the Model Law on International Commercial Arbitration has been adopted and the arbitrations that are regarded as "international" are those：

（1） which involve parties which have their places of business in different countries, or

（2） which deal with disputes

（a） arising out of obligations to be performed, or

（b） connected with subject matter

（c） in a different country from the place of business of at least one of the parties.

上述定义中的第（1）项和第（2）(a)项是以当事人的营业地和仲裁地为认定标准，而第（2）(b)和(2)(c)项则是依照争议涉及的"国际商事利益"为判定标

---

① 《联合国国际贸易法委员会国际商事仲裁示范法》(UNCITRAL Model Law on International Commercial Arbitration)，于 1985 年 6 月 21 日由联合国国际贸易法委员会主持制定，1985 年 12 月 11 日联合国大会通过批准该示范法的决议，其宗旨是协调和统一世界各国调整国际商事仲裁的法律。建议各国从统一仲裁程序法的愿望和国际商事仲裁实践的特点出发，对该示范法予以适当的考虑。该示范法公布后，对各国的仲裁立法产生了巨大影响，对规范国际商事仲裁起到了积极的推动作用。2006 年 7 月 7 日，联合国国际贸易法委员会第 39 届会议通过了对 1985 年《示范法》的修订。美国的许多州、加拿大、澳大利亚、俄罗斯、意大利、新西兰、英国以及中国的香港地区等，都以该示范法为蓝本稍加修改或直接移植使用。中国 1994 年的《仲裁法》在起草过程中也参考了该示范法。

准的。① 同时,《示范法》的规定还显示了将当事人的意思作为确定仲裁"国际"性标准的倾向。《示范法》出台以后,接受或效仿其确立自己的仲裁制度的国家不在少数,并且数十个著名的国际仲裁机构也开始采用其中规则或愿意担任该规则所规定的"任命机构"。② 由此可见,《示范法》的上述规定体现了国际商事仲裁发展的一种趋势,即对"国际"作广义理解,在立法方式上采用两种界定方法相结合,既有明确的连结点又有概括的性质归纳的方法。另外,《示范法》在国内法院可以干预仲裁程序的程度上,规定了严格的限制。其第5条规定:"本法管辖事项,法院不应干预,除非本法规定。"许多国家,包括比利时、巴西、哥伦比亚、法国、尼日利亚、新加坡、瑞士和其他一些国家,已经采纳了单独的法律制度来管辖国际商事仲裁,即承认不同的考虑因素可以适用于此类仲裁。

我国立法从未对国际商事仲裁的"国际"一词作过明确的解释。根据2007年修订的我国《民事诉讼法》与1994年《仲裁法》,"涉外经济贸易、运输和海事中发生的纠纷"的仲裁属于涉外仲裁的范畴。而中国国际经济贸易仲裁委员会(又称"中国国际商会仲裁院")2005年《仲裁规则》第3条关于"管辖范围"的规定中,除国内争议外,则将国际的或涉外的争议案件及涉及香港特别行政区、澳门特别行政区或台湾地区的争议案件等包括到仲裁委员会的受案范围内,与"国内"案件相对而言,似乎对"国际"作了隐含的、非常宽泛的解释。从这两点看,我国采用的应该是争议性质标准,对"国际"的理解相当灵活。

(二) 关于"商事"的含义

"商事"一般是指贸易活动或与贸易相关的财产性活动,国际商事纠纷一般也就是财产性的纠纷,而财产性的纠纷一般会采取仲裁等私力救济的方式,很少采用诉讼的方式。大多数国家的法律都将非商事性质的争议排除在仲裁管辖的范围之外。因此,确定一项争议是否属于商事争议,是仲裁制度中的先决事项,它关系到争议能否以仲裁方式解决,以及裁决作出后能否得到本国或外国法院的承认和执行问题。

对于商事的概念,各国的定义是不一致的,这就为在国际层面上确定商事的含义带来了困难。例如,1997年7月1日生效的新西兰《仲裁法》规定消费争议不属于可仲裁的事项。1996年9月23日通过的巴西《仲裁法》明确规定,家庭和有关身份的争议不能仲裁解决。此外,有不少国家在参加1958年联合国《承认和执行外国仲裁裁决公约》(以下简称《纽约公约》)时,提出了"商事保留",即声明保留的缔约国仅承认和执行在其他缔约国境内作出的具有商事性质的仲

---

① 参见陈治东:《国际商事仲裁法》,法律出版社1998年版,第16页。
② See Gerold Hermann, The UNCITRAL Model Law on International Commercial Arbitration: Introduction and General Provisions, Essays on International Commercial Arbitration, edited by Petar Sarcevic, Graham & Trotman Marimus Nijhoff, 1989.

裁裁决，其他性质的裁决不在此列。该公约也未对"商事"一词作出解释，而将此问题留给各缔约国依照各自的国内法来处理。对此，《示范法》也没有给其以准确的定义，只采取列举的方式对其进行限定。

Article 1—Scope of application

1. This Law applies to international commercial arbitration, subject to any agreement in force between this State and any other State or States.

2. The provisions of this Law, except articles 8, 9, 35 and 36, apply only if the place of arbitration is in the territory of this State.

3. An arbitration is international if:

(a) the parties to an arbitration agreement have, at the time of the conclusion of that agreement, their places of business in different States; or

(b) one of the following places is situated outside the State in which the parties have their places of business:

(i) the place of arbitration if determined in, or pursuant to, the arbitration agreement;

(ii) any place where a substantial part of the obligations of the commercial relationship is to be performed or the place with which the subject-matter of the dispute is most closely connected; or

the parties have expressly agreed that the subject-matter of the arbitration agreement relates to more than one country.

4. For the purposes of paragraph (3) of this article:

(a) if a party has more than one place of business, the place of business is that which has the closest relationship to the arbitration agreement;

(b) if a party does not have a place of business, reference is to be made to his habitual residence.

5. This Law shall not affect any other law of this State by virtue of which certain disputes may not be submitted to arbitration or may be submitted to arbitration only according to provisions other than those of this Law.①

上述第1条第1款的注释中对"商事"一词加以说明，并列举了一系列被视为商事关系的交易事项。该注释指出：对"商事"一词应该作广义解释，使其包括不论是契约性或非契约性的一切商事关系所引起的种种事情。商事性质的关系包括但不限于下列交易：供应或交换商品或劳务的任何贸易关系；销售协议；商事代表或代理；代理；租赁；建造工厂；咨询；工程；设计；许可证；投资；银行；保

---

① UNCITRAL Model Law On International Commercial Arbitration (1985).

险;开发协议或特许权;合营或其他形式的工业或商业合作;货物或旅客的航空、海上、铁路或公路的运输。

The UNCITRAL Model Law envisages that it should "be given a wide interpretation so as to cover matters arising from all relationships of a commercial nature, whether contractual or not". The commercial nature of a dispute is of particular importance when an attempt is made to enforce an arbitration agreement, or recognition or enforcement of an award is sought, pursuant to the provisions of the New York Convention on the Recognition and Enforcement of Foreign Arbitral Awards of 1958. A large number of countries have availed themselves of the reservation permitted by the Convention that they need only apply the provisions of the Convention to disputes which are regarded as commercial by their own internal system of law. This makes it clear that, as with the term "international", there is no generally accepted definition of "commercial". Appendix 1 contains a list of the signatory states to this Convention, and indicates those countries which rely on the "commercial reservation".

但一般来说,大多数国家都认为应当给予商事性以广义解释。根据我国最高人民法院《关于执行我国加入的〈承认与执行外国仲裁裁决公约〉的通知》(1987年4月10日)第2条规定,我国仅对按照我国法律属于"契约性或非契约性商事法律关系"所引起的争议适用《纽约公约》。所谓的"契约性或非契约性商事法律关系"具体是指由于合同、侵权或者有关法律规定而产生的经济上的权利义务关系,如货物买卖、财产租赁、工程承包、加工承揽、技术转让、合资经营、合作经营、勘探开发自然资源、保险、信贷、劳务、代理、咨询服务、产品责任、环境污染、海上事故和所有权争议以及海上、民用航空、铁路、公路的客货运输等,但不包括外国投资者与东道国政府之间的争端。显然,我国关于"商事"的解释也是很广义的。

三、仲裁与诉讼的不同

仲裁与诉讼是当今最为重要,也是最为常用的两种争议解决方式。我们有必要将两者进行比较,以便于当事人在清楚了解各种方式的特点后轻松进行选择。仲裁与诉讼主要存在以下五个不同点:

1. 性质不同:诉讼是国家司法机关行使国家司法权力的表现,是公法救济行为,这种行为只能由国家司法机关行使。仲裁则属于私法救济行为,是根据当事人约定而授予仲裁机构或仲裁庭行使的。有人将仲裁称为准司法,在法律意义上是一种并不确切的说法。

2. 管辖不同:诉讼一般为法定管辖(除少数情况下当事人可以选择管辖的

法院外），只要一方向具有管辖权的法院提起诉讼，法院就应当受理，也有权强制另一方当事人参加诉讼并作出判决。仲裁则需要当事双方提交协议，属于约定管辖。双方必须在争议发生之前或之后达成书面的仲裁协议，一方将协议提交仲裁庭后，仲裁庭才有权对争议进行裁决。

3. 审级制度不同：我国《民事诉讼法》规定了两审终审制，当事人如果对一审判决不服，在收到判决书后的 15 天内可以提出上诉，超出上诉期后，判决生效。上诉之后的二审判决为终审判决。仲裁为一审终审，仲裁裁决在法律上具有终局性，裁决一旦作出，任何一方当事人均不得向原仲裁机构或向法院提出再审或者上诉的请求。

4. 组庭原则不同：在法院诉讼中，审理案件的合议庭是由法院依职权指定的法官组成，当事人无权选择审判员。而在仲裁程序中，当事人可以根据案件的性质选择相应的仲裁员。

5. 到国外执行方面不同：法院的判决如果要到国外执行，则必须根据司法互助条约或互惠原则才有可能实现。而根据 1958 年《纽约公约》，只要国际商事仲裁裁决作出国与执行地国都是公约的成员国，当事人就可以向执行地国法院提出承认和执行的申请。

此外，在一些细节程序中，两者也有很多区别，比如仲裁还具有不公开审理、程序相对简便、气氛比较友好等特点。

The comparison of the legal frameworks of international arbitration and transnational litigation shows that with a properly drafted arbitration agreement, the legal framework of international commercial arbitration:

——ensures a competent tribunal and excludes competing procedures practically on a worldwide scale;

——permits to flexibly adjust the procedure to the needs of the parties while guaranteeing the neutrality of the tribunal, a minimum standard of procedural fairness and the confidentiality of the procedure; as well as to achieve a reasonable degree of discovery and to limit judicial review to the most basic question;

——achieves results that are final and enforceable on a global scale; the enforceability of awards has the indirect effect of encouraging voluntary compliance or even an amicable settlement eliminating the need for a decision by the tribunal.

Obviously these advantages do not materialize in every arbitration, but the framework of international commercial arbitration makes it possible to ensure a high probability that they will.①

四、仲裁与调解等其他争议解决方式的不同

ADR 意指替代性纠纷解决方法,泛而言之,它是一切诉讼外纠纷解决方法的总称。ADR 既可适用于国内民事纠纷的解决,也适用于国际民商事争议的解决。

Generally speaking, all mechanisms for settling dispute other than by judicial process may be referred to as "alternative dispute resolution" or "ADR". In recent times the phrase has tended to be regarded as excluding arbitration and instead as relating to a wide variety of techniques designed to allow the parties to resolve their disputes speedily, cheaply, without prejudice to their continuing commercial relationship, and in a manner which does not necessarily reflect the technical legal rights and wrongs of their respective positions. ADR may be proved for in the agreement between them has arisen: the decision to attempt ADR may be a voluntary one by the parties, or it may be in effect forced upon them by the case management powers of the English courts.②

There are three basic types of ADR: negotiation, mediation, and arbitration. Negotiation, the most frequently used alternative dispute resolution process, is commonly defined as "communicat[ing] ... with another to arrive at the settlement of some matter." Negotiation serves as the foundation for other ADR processes, particularly mediation. Mediation is essentially facilitated negotiation, in which a mediator helps the parties in a neutral fashion to engage in negotiation and cooperative problem solving. Mediation is particularly useful in cases involving ongoing relationships and emotional concerns. Finally, in arbitration, parties can select a decision maker or panel of decision makers, often with subject matter expertise. Parties agree on rules and procedures and decide whether the decision will be binding or merely advisory. Arbitration is the ADR process that most resembles traditional litigation. Each of these processes can be combined or modified to form a myriad of hybrid ADR processes.③

狭义来讲,仲裁是被排除在 ADR 之外的一种争议解决方式。但是在采用仲

---

① See Christian Buhring-Uhle, Lars Kichhof, Gabriele Scherer, Arbitration and Mediation in International Business, Kluwer Law International, 2006, p.63.

② See Robert Merkin, Arbitration Law, Informa Legal Publishing, 2004, p.165.

③ See Amy S. Moeves & Scott C. Moeves, Two Roads Diverged: A Tale of Technology and Alternative Dispute Resolution, William and Mary Bill of Rights Journal, April, 2004.

裁方式解决争议的实践中,协商、调解等 ADR 方式也往往会穿插应用于仲裁之中,这些 ADR 方式有助于双方达成满意的仲裁结果,所以仲裁与其他 ADR 方式存在着密切的联系。下面仅就仲裁与调解的关系作简要分析:

Mediation can be helpful when parties are having difficulty negotiating among themselves. Mediating a dispute simply means negotiating with the assistance of a third party called a mediator. A mediator is an expert in helping people negotiate. A mediator should be impartial, neutral, and acceptable to the parties and should have no decision-making power.

Professional mediators are of course much more sophisticated; they have received extensive training in how to intervene in disputes. A professional mediator approaches a dispute with a formal strategy consisting of a method of analysis, an opening statement, recognized stages of mediation and an array of tools for breaking impasses and facilitating a resolution.①

首先,就事先协议的约束而言,调解比仲裁更显随意。在调解的过程中,任何一方当事人可以随时退出调解,调解人也不得强行继续调解。而在仲裁程序中,由于双方都受到仲裁协议的束缚,即使被申请人不出庭参加仲裁程序,仲裁程序仍将进行并最终作出裁决。其次,就争议解决的程序而言,调解有着更强的灵活性。调解可以按照调解机构制定的程序进行,也可以按照当事人或调解人认为的合适的程序进行。而仲裁的程序一般需按照双方约定的仲裁程序规则进行,任何一方不能违背仲裁规则。再次,就第三人的作用而言,调解员和仲裁员有很大的不同。调解员在调解程序中主要起到协调和促进作用,促使双方互谅互让,达成协议。而仲裁员的职责远不止于此,不仅要起到协调和促进的作用,更要独立、公正地裁决。最后,就争议解决后文书效力而言,调解书和裁决书也有很大不同。在中国,除了在诉讼程序中或者仲裁程序中达成的调解协议外,一般而言,调解协议只具有合同的约束力而没有强制执行的效力。相比来说,仲裁裁决是终局的,如果应当履行的一方不自动履行仲裁裁决中的事项,另一方当事人可以向有管辖权的法院申请强制执行。

五、仲裁在解决国际商事争议中的优势

仲裁一直是解决商事争议的首选方式。和其他争议解决方式相比,仲裁具有以下优点:

(一) 裁决作出者的公正性(Impartiality of the Decision Maker)

One of the reasons that arbitration is a preferred method for settling international

---

① See Harold I. Abrahmson, A Primer on Resolving Disputes: Lessons from Alternative Dispute Resolution, New York State Bar Journal, March/April, 1992.

business disputes is that it offers a neutral tribunal which neither party may be able to find in the country of the other. The parties choose "the judge and the jury," rather than being assigned finders of fact and law as is the case in court proceedings. A properly drafted arbitration clause will also allow the parties to designate the law to be applied as well as the place and the language to be used. Such a forum for the resolution of international commercial disputes helps satisfy the business manager's need for assurance that a potential dispute will be decided fairly.

（二）保密性（Confidentiality）

仲裁案件不公开审理，从而可以有效地保护当事人的商业秘密和商业信誉。

A peculiarity of both arbitration proceedings and awards is that they are normally carried out privately. Indeed, the rules of several arbitration institutions require that proceedings be confidential unless the parties to the dispute direct otherwise. Confidential arbitration awards have a distinct advantage over court adjudication in that both court proceedings and judgments are public. Because commercial relationships often involve confidential information such as trade secrets, neither party desires such confidential matters be available to third parties. In addition, because many international commercial relationships are, in fact, of long standing, it would hinder the ongoing relationship to have "dirty linen" aired in public.

（三）仲裁员的专业性（Technical Expertise）

Many commercial relationships involve products, services or technology that are technologically complex. For a tribunal to resolve a dispute regarding those products, services or the transfer of technology from one party to the other, the arbitrator or judge must have a considerable amount of technical knowledge concerning the subject matter in dispute. The parties, by choosing arbitrators who are technically knowledgeable, are more likely to have a "judge" with the specialized competence needed to properly evaluate technical claims.

（四）费用的经济性（Expense）

Arbitration can be a much less expensive means of resolving a dispute than a court proceeding. If either of the parties to a dispute is a small company or the amount in controversy is small, litigation may be too expensive and, therefore, not practical for resolving disputes. If there is a sole arbitrator available, known to the parties, and with technical knowledge in the area, the dispute could be resolved readily so that the parties can go on about their business, often without any significant rancor existing between them.

(五) 解决争议的迅捷性 (Expeditious Resolution)

Arbitration can also be a faster and more expeditious means of resolving a dispute. Again, in contrast to litigation, arbitration allows the parties the flexibility to obtain an impartial arbitrator and quickly submit a dispute which cannot be resolved by negotiation. With a properly worded arbitration clause, the parties can establish a time frame within which a dispute must be resolved. A rapid resolution of the dispute allows parties to continue to do business, without being subjected to protracted court proceedings involving expensive and time consuming discovery.

(六) 仲裁裁决的可执行性 (Enforceability)

1958年《纽约公约》是涉及仲裁裁决承认与执行的一个重要公约。迄今为止,世界已有一百多个国家批准了该公约,根据该公约,仲裁裁决可以在这些缔约国得到承认和执行。此外,仲裁裁决还可根据其他一些有关仲裁的国际公约和条约得到执行。《纽约公约》于1987年对中国生效,中国在加入《纽约公约》时作出了商事保留和互惠保留。

The enforceability of awards makes binding arbitration a much more predictable way of resolving disputes than adjudication by courts of either country. Enforceability as an element of predictability cannot be underestimated. The businessman dislikes uncertainty above almost all other risks of doing business. The New York Convention, which lessens uncertainty that an agreement to arbitrate will be enforced, coupled with a well structured arbitration procedure, such as the New York Convention or the Panama Convention, adds assurance that support will be provided by the courts of either Mexico or the United States for the enforcement of an award rendered pursuant to arbitration.[①]

第四节　国际商事仲裁的发展趋势

一、国际商事仲裁的发展历史

仲裁作为一种处理当事人之间的民商事纠纷的争议解决方式,有着悠久的历史。公元前621年,古希腊的成文法律制度中就包含有仲裁的内容,城邦之间发生争议,常常采用仲裁方式解决。公元前5世纪,古罗马共和国时代的《十二铜表法》中对仲裁多有记载,后来由于受到高卢族的入侵,《十二铜表法》被毁,但仲裁这种争议解决方式却得以保存下来。随着古罗马城市和商业经济的发

---

① See Hope H. Camp, Jr., Binding Arbitration: A Preferred Alternative for Resolving Commercial Disputes between Mexican and U.S. Businessmen, Saint Mary's Law Journal, 1991.

展,仲裁的重要性日益显现出来。由于当时的社会封建经济仍处于主导地位,商业活动仍受到封建经济及封建制度的压制,所以商业活动所产生的争议并不能直接到古罗马的法院得到解决,法院对商业纠纷采取抵制态度,不予受理。在这种情况下,争议双方的商人们便共同选择彼此信任的第三者来居中裁断,裁断的结果为仲裁双方自觉履行,并且一裁终局。这种仲裁的一大缺点在于仲裁裁决的执行需要当事双方自愿,缺乏法律执行力。

当然,无论是乡间的居间裁断还是古希腊和古罗马时代的商人间的居中裁判,都还只是仲裁的早期阶段,那时的仲裁从形式到内容都比较简单,主要用来解决简单的乡间民事纠纷或者商人间的债权债务争议,并未形成制度。直至14世纪,瑞典才确认仲裁是解决民商事纠纷的有效制度,英国则于1697年率先颁布了第一个仲裁法案,并于1889年制定了第一部仲裁法。时至16—18世纪,随着大机器、大生产、大消费的产生,世界市场得到了迅速发展。世界市场在推动世界经济迅猛发展的同时,跨国纠纷亦随之大量出现。仲裁作为解决国际商事争议的作用越来越为众多国家所重视。近代以来,仲裁从形式到内容都产生了极大的变化。从范围上看,仲裁逐步由一国国内的民商事仲裁扩展到国际经济贸易仲裁、海事仲裁、解决国家间争端的仲裁。就裁决的执行而言,早期是单纯依靠当事人自动履行,后来则因各国通过仲裁立法对仲裁法律地位予以确认,仲裁裁决的执行有了保障。就仲裁形式看,从单纯的临时仲裁发展到机构仲裁和临时仲裁共存的阶段。从仲裁机构的发展阶段看,从纯粹的国内仲裁机构发展到具有世界影响的国际仲裁中心。以上种种正是仲裁的影响力逐步扩大的佐证。

Arbitration is not a new concept by any means. Arbitration is a form of dispute resolution that was implemented by the Greek city-states as early as the sixth century B. C. Others trace the roots of arbitration "at least as deep as the British Law Merchant. 'The Law Merchant was an outgrowth' of business disputes and an attempt by commercial industry to settle disputes through their industries, custom and/or trade." Historically, arbitration offered several advantages to merchants when compared to adversarial litigation. First and foremost, arbitration offered merchants a speedy resolution to their disputes. In addition, arbitration was less costly and less destructive to business relationships than traditional adversarial litigation.[①]

It is not known exactly when formal non-judicial arbitration of disputes first

---

① See Brent S. Gilfedder, "A Manifest Disregard of Arbitration?" An Analysis of Recent Georgia Legislation Adding "Manifest Disregard of The Law" to the Georgia Arbitration Code as a Statutory Ground for Vacatur, Georgia Law Review, Fall, 2004.

began but it can be said with some certainty that arbitration, as a way of resolving disputes predates formal courts. Records from ancient Egypt attest to its use especially with high priests and their interaction with the public. Arbitration was popular both in ancient Greece and Rome.

Under English law, the first law on arbitration was the Arbitration Act 1697, but when it was passed arbitration was already common. The first recorded judicial decision relating to arbitration was in England in 1610. The noted Elizabethan English legal scholar Sir Edward Coke referred to an earlier decision dating from the reign of Edward IV (which ended in 1483). Early arbitrations at common law suffered from the fatal weakness that either party to the dispute could withdraw the arbitrator's mandate right up until the delivery of the award if things appeared to be going against them (this was rectified in the 1697 Act).

The Jay Treaty of 1794 between Britain and the United States sent unresolved issues regarding debts and boundaries to arbitration, which took 7 years and proved successful.

In the first part of the twentieth century, many countries (France and the United States being good examples) began to pass laws sanctioning and even promoting the use of private adjudication as an alternative to what was perceived to be inefficient court systems.

The growth of international trade, however, brought greater sophistication to a process that had previously been largely ad hoc in relation to disputes between merchants resolved under the auspices of the lex mercatoria. As trade grew, so did the practice of arbitration, eventually leading to the creation of a variant now known as international arbitration, as a means for resolving disputes under international commercial contracts.

Today, arbitration also occurs online, in what is commonly referred to as Online Dispute Resolution, or ODR. Typically, ODR proceedings occur following the filing of a claim online, with the proceedings taking place over the internet, and judgment rendered on the basis of documentation presented. www.net-arb.com is the world's leader in Internet Arbitration.

二、中国国际商事仲裁的发展历史

仲裁这种争议解决方式在中国古代社会便有了萌芽。中国古代社会一个重要特征在于社会结构是一种复合式的二元结构，除了保障中央集权的法律体制外，乡规民约在地方乡绅和长老的权威的保证下也得到人们心甘情愿的执行。

当这个地区出现某种纠纷时,人们往往寄希望于他们,指望他们说一句公道话。而他们的调解或是裁决将会受到尊重与执行。这种现象一旦被国家法律所正式承认,就会被吸收为国家纠纷解决体制的一部分,如汉代的"三老制"、明朝的"申明亭"。当然,在大多数情况下,家族村落解决内部纠纷的机制是独立于国家法律体制之外的,而它也一直受到封建统治者的尊重与认同。那时的这种居间裁决的方式便是仲裁的早期阶段,无论从形式到内容都比较简单,主要用来解决简单的乡间民事纠纷或者商人间的债权债务争议,并未形成制度,裁决的执行也主要依赖当事人对裁决者的信赖和道德观点的约束而自行履行,不受法律的调整。

明清之际,地方的纠纷多由里老乡长处理。那时的里老已有类似今日仲裁员的权力。仲裁员由类似政府管理部门选定,他们会选择族里德高望重之人对纠纷作出裁断,裁断在族中会得到严格执行,里老的权威不容冒犯,不执行者会遭到族人的唾弃,这亦体现了里老裁断的权威性,也是仲裁强制执行力的体现。

时至清朝后期,在资本主义萌芽状态出现的百年内,封建制度走向衰弱,传统的"重农抑商"的思想受到很大的冲击。与商业的繁荣同时出现的是商事纠纷的频繁发生。商事纠纷的特殊性促使着一种新的争议解决机构——商会的产生。随后,商会的公断职能得到了政府的承认。这种公断事实上就是一种商事仲裁[①]。清末《奏定商会简明章程》的制定,充分肯定了商会这种民间组织具有受理纠纷诉讼的权利。民国时期,为了进一步规范商会的商事裁判行为,司法、工商两部门于1913年1月28日颁布了《商事公断处章程》,对公断处的主旨、组织、职员之选举及任期、公断处的权限等作了详细的规定,明确规定商事公断处为商会的附属机构,"对于商人间商事之争议,立于仲裁地位,以息讼和解为主旨"。其主要受理以下两类案件:"未起诉先由两造人同意自行申请者"与"起诉后由法院委托调处者"。可见,近代意义上的商事仲裁至少在清末民初已经出现。

Since officially "opening its doors" to international trade in 1979, the People's Republic of China (PRC) has become one of the world's major trading countries as well as one of the largest recipients of foreign investment. Corresponding to such rapid growth in international trade and transactions has been an increase in the number of international commercial disputes between Chinese and foreign parties.

In the PRC, as in many other countries, there are typically four ways to resolve

---

[①] 事实上,对于中国古代的商会的性质,有不少学者持不同见解。有的认为纯属民间组织,有的又认为是准司法性质。笔者认为,这恰恰证明了中国古代商会公断具有仲裁性质。人们现在对于仲裁性质的争论同样也是介于此间的。

disputes. They are: negotiation, mediation or conciliation, arbitration, and litigation. Negotiation and mediation often are unenforceable, and litigation can be time consuming and very expensive. Many parties, therefore, consider arbitration to be the most efficient manner to resolve commercial disputes.[①]

In 1912, the then Chinese government promulgated the Constitution for Business Arbitration Office, followed by the Working Rules for Business Arbitration Office in 1913, which made provisions for the parties to a business dispute to submit their dispute to the Business Arbitration Office for settlement. The rules, however, also provided that an arbitration award would not become legally binding without the consent of the disputing parties. In circumstances where the consent of the disputing parties could not be obtained, a disputing party was at liberty to file civil proceedings in court. The successful reception of this development may have formed the basis for the positive attitude shown today towards the consensus-building mediation and conciliation services available within the Chinese arbitral framework.[②]

1930年,国民政府颁行了《劳资争议处理法》,在解决雇佣方和受雇方争议过程中推行了协商和仲裁程序。1949年,天津市政府颁行了《天津市调解仲裁委员会暂行组织条例》,其中规定了争议调解和仲裁的组成、受理权限以及工作原则。随着中华人民共和国的建立,中国逐步建立了包括国内仲裁和涉外仲裁的两套仲裁体系,其中包括劳动仲裁、经济合同仲裁以及不动产仲裁等。

People's Republic of China ("PRC") has a relatively recent history of conducting international commercial arbitrations. The Foreign Trade Arbitration Commission was renamed as the Foreign Economic and Trade Arbitration Commission (FETAC) in 1980. In 1988, the State Council further renamed FETAC as the China International Economic and Trade Arbitration Commission (CIETAC). CIETAC has exclusive jurisdiction in respect of arbitration arising out of international or "foreign related" economic or trade transactions and the China Maritime Arbitration Commission (CMAC) has a similar jurisdiction in relation to maritime disputes. CIETAC is perhaps the busiest arbitration center in the world. It received 778 references to arbitration during 1996. However, many CIETAC arbitrations arise from arbitration clauses in standard from documents for trade with Chinese state

---

① See Alexander Lourie, International Commercial Arbitration in China: History, New Developments, and Current Practice, John Marshall Law Review, Spring, 1995.
② See Jingzhou Tao, Arbitration Law and Practice in China, Kluwer Law International, 2004, p.1.

enterprises, which are, in effect, non-negotiable. ①

The principal sources of arbitration law in the PRC are the Arbitration Law of 1995 and the Civil Procedure Law of 1991. The Arbitration Law primarily governs domestic arbitrations but does contain provisions relating to the enforcement of CIETAC and CMAC awards. The Civil Procedure Law contains provisions that require the PRC Courts to give effect to arbitration agreements and for the enforcement of the awards of foreign arbitral bodies.

As noted, CIETAC and CMAC have an effective monopoly over the conduct of arbitrations in the PRC. Until very recently CIETAC would only apply its own rule, although the parties can now choose to adopt the rules of another institution.

Although CIETAC has stated that it has no objection to other arbitral institutions supervising arbitrations in the PRC, international arbitrations in the PRC under the rules of a foreign institution are in practice discouraged by the absence of any legal mechanism for the enforcement of awards other than those made by CIETAC and CMAC arbitrators. Thus, whilst the PRC court will give effect to an ICC or LCIA arbitration award made, for instance, in London or Paris, they would not recognize an LCIA award made in the PRC itself.

Similarly, ad hoc arbitration is not recognized in the PRC. Arbitration clauses which do not name a specific institution to administer the arbitration have been rejected as defective by the PRC Courts. The courts have refused to give effect to an arbitration clause which provided for arbitration pursuant to the rules of the ICC in Paris on the grounds that the clause failed to state that the arbitration would be administered by the ICC. ②

综上所述,仲裁这种争议解决方式在新中国的发展历史还较短,但随着中国经济的迅速崛起,与世界各国贸易往来的加深,仲裁的优越性越发体现出来,越来越多的中外经贸纠纷采用了仲裁的方式解决,这不但减轻了法院的受案负担,而且有利于争议双方采取更具灵活性的方式解决纠纷。中国国际经济贸易仲裁委员会(以下简称"CIETAC")经过五十多年的努力,目前已经成为国际上主要国际商事仲裁中心之一,受案数量已居世界第二位。案件的当事人涉及四十多个国家,并在上海、深圳设有分会,这两个分会是中国国际经济贸易仲裁委员会的分支机构,使用同一仲裁规则和仲裁员名单。CIETAC 作为中国主要的仲裁

---

① See Stefan N. Frommel and Barry A. K. Rider, Conflicting Legal Cultures in Commercial Arbitration: Old Issues and New Trends, Kluwer Law International, p.67.
② Ibid., p.68.

机构,每年处理的案件数量逐步攀升,随着贸易的发展,其毫无疑问将在中外贸易纠纷解决中扮演更为重要的角色。然而,从上述分析中我们可以了解到,CIETAC 在某些方面还和一些国际著名仲裁机构存在差距,这些都是其需要在未来进行完善的。

三、国际商事仲裁的发展趋势

国际商事仲裁在实践中起着举足轻重的作用,越来越多地被争议双方所采用。近年来,随着国际商事仲裁实践的发展,其主要呈现出下述几种趋势:

(一) 仲裁法的现代化

The last decade brought a wave of modernization of arbitration laws, and in particular widespread acceptance of the UNCITRAL Model Law. It is highly probable that more states will follow the example and incorporate the Model Law in their national laws. The ensuing modernization and homogenization of arbitration laws can be perceived as one of the major trends in the field.

上述《示范法》是在联合国的倡议和主持下制定并于 1985 年通过的,联合国在推动仲裁法的统一化过程中还制定了另外两个重要的有关仲裁的公约或规则,它们分别是于 1958 年通过的《纽约公约》以及 1976 年制定的《联合国国际贸易法委员会仲裁规则》。

(二) 仲裁所适用的程序和实体法律非国内化趋势加强

在当今的国际商事仲裁实践中,仲裁所适用的程序规则和实体法律不再局限于仲裁庭当地或本国的法律,而是更富灵活性,出现了强烈的"非国内化"或"非本地化"的趋势。在国际商事仲裁的程序规则适用方面,仲裁庭可以基于当事人的约定确定仲裁规则进行仲裁,而不必使仲裁规则局限于受仲裁庭本国法支配。例如,CIETAC 1995 年《仲裁规则》以及在此之前的所有规则都规定:凡当事人同意将争议提交 CIETAC 仲裁的均视为按 CIETAC 仲裁规则仲裁,但 1998 年《仲裁规则》、2000 年《仲裁规则》第 7 条将这一规定修改为:"凡当事人同意将争议提交仲裁委员会的,均视为同意按照本仲裁规则进行仲裁。但当事人另有约定且仲裁委员会同意的,从其规定。"这一修改显示了我国涉外仲裁制度"非国内化"的发展趋向。在仲裁实体法律适用方面,仲裁庭一般根据当事双方协议选择的法律进行仲裁,当事人可以选择仲裁庭所在国法律,也可以选择任何其他国家的法律,甚至包括国际公约、习惯法以及一般法律原则等,这体现了国际商事仲裁实体法律适用的巨大的灵活性。

(三) Multi-party constellation

International transactions increasingly involve multiple parties and multiple contracts. Since drafters of arbitration clauses occasionally have been (and still are) unaware of the additional risks and uncertainties resulting from multiparty constellations, and since many international commercial arbitration laws and rules do not regulate multi-party disputes sufficiently, problems are common.

One basic challenge in multi-party arbitration is to ensure consistency of decisions. Ideally, the tribunal should have jurisdiction to deal with all disputes arising between all parties. Four main types of multi-party arbitration have been developed: unified multi-party arbitration and consolidated arbitration, concurrent bilateral arbitration as well as parallel bilateral arbitration. The arbitration clause should explicitly name the form of multi-party arbitration to be conducted.

A significant problem in multi-party arbitration arises from the inherent right of each party to nominate its own arbitrator. Two possible solutions shall be briefly indicated: Firstly, the arbitration clause may provide that all parties on one side of the arbitration, the joint claimants or joint respondents, shall make a joint nomination of one arbitrator; they may also authorize the selected arbitration institution to appoint at its discretion one arbitrator for the party that disagrees. Alternatively, the arbitration clause may provide that all arbitrators shall be appointed by the governing arbitration institution.

（四）法院对仲裁的干预或控制日益减弱

法院的诉讼和仲裁庭的仲裁是两种不同的争端解决方式，在某种程度上可以认为二者是平行或互补的，然而，这两种相对独立的争端解决方式却有着紧密的联系。有的学者认为，法院对仲裁的干预是仲裁这种相对缺少强制性的解决方式得以维持和延续的保障，离开了法院对仲裁积极的干预或支持，现代意义上的仲裁则不能存在。当前的实际情况是，除解决投资争端国际中心（ICSID）仲裁外，无论是英美法系内的仲裁还是大陆法系内的仲裁，均无法摆脱内国法院的司法干预。但就目前的趋势看，国际上要求法院减少对仲裁干预的呼声甚高，各国法院在实践中对仲裁的干预也呈弱化趋势，而且这种干预多局限于程序上的问题。《纽约公约》规定了承认和执行仲裁裁决的程序和实体事项，这些规定一方面肯定了法院对仲裁进行干预的必要性，另一方面也限制了法院的干预范围，使得法院不能滥用这种权力，进而保证了仲裁裁决的执行性。《示范法》第5条也规定："由本法管辖的事情，任何法院不得干预，除非本法另有规定。"该规定显得更为强硬。

（五）Focus on evidence

International arbitration laws and rules tend to give relatively little guidance on the crucial question of the admissibility and taking of evidence. The reason may be two-folded: firstly, the arbitrators and parties are in charge of conducting the arbitration procedure, thereby making the procedure as flexible as possible; and secondly, there is a desire to maintain a neutral stance in the competition between the influence of Civil Law and Common Law.

This has generated an intense debate in the field of international commercial arbitration on the following issues: What evidence is admissible, how and what stage of the procedure it must be taken and how should it be presented to the arbitral tribunal? In an effort to fill the procedural gap, the IBA has published "Rules on the Taking of Evidence in International Commercial Arbitration". The Rules have been relatively well received and widely used and are likely to shape the future practice.

(六) 常设仲裁机构数量增加

在国际商事仲裁领域内临时仲裁与机构仲裁是并存的,从国际商事仲裁的发展历史看,是先有临时仲裁,后有机构仲裁。早期的国际商事仲裁多为临时仲裁,而如今,随着经济贸易的发展,仲裁需求的日益增长,许多国家商会或非政府间的行会则相继成立了常设的仲裁机构。这些常设的仲裁机构较之临时仲裁有着自身的优势,包括有固定的仲裁场所、稳定的仲裁员构成,并且制定了各自的仲裁规则,而且常设仲裁机构一般对仲裁员的选定、仲裁庭的组成方式、仲裁员的回避等事项都有最后的决定权。这些优势是临时仲裁所无法替代的。虽然当前通过临时仲裁机构解决的国际商事争议仍多于通过常设仲裁机构解决的,但机构仲裁的快速发展确有超过临时仲裁之势。

(七) Increasing role of alternative settlement techniques

Alternative Dispute Resolution (ADR)—which has formed an integral part of the legal system in the United States several decades ago—has become a significant element of the judicial landscape in many other countries in Europe and beyond, and statistics show that the use, for example, of commercial mediation services is rising rapidly. It is no longer considered as misconduct for an arbitrator to go beyond his traditional mandate and structures the process to facilitate settlement. Instead, the discussion now focuses on whether it is a matter of good practice or even a duty of the arbitrator to actively encourage settlement.

Evidently, there is also increasing awareness of the various practical ways in which the arbitrator can re-orientate the process in a direction increasing the chances of settlement. Processes like mediation and conciliation as well as methods like mini-trial or dispute review boards have entered the mainstream discussions and practice, and more and more arbitral institutions offer particular rules on mediation, conciliation or mini-trials.

(八) Rising empirical work on ICA

The body of empirical work on Internet arbitration is growing. This trend is fostered by academic and practitioners' interest in the subject, the activity of organizations like the Global Center for Dispute Resolution and an increasing openness of both arbitrators and arbitration institutions with regard to figures and proceedings. A number of investigations into the inner workings of international commercial arbitration have begun to increase the transparency of the field.①

现代社会,随着国际经济贸易交往的逐步加深,国际商事仲裁被越来越多的贸易当事方广泛采用。仲裁作为解决纠纷的最古老的方式之一,得以延续的优势在于它的灵活性和适应性。商事仲裁根源于早期的居间裁判,是民间自然而发的一种争议解决方式,随着社会客观环境的变化,又融入了新的内容和特点,它的适应性使其能够不断迎合社会的需要,最终成为各国广泛采用的一种纠纷解决方式。仲裁在解决国际商事争议方面具有司法诉讼无可比拟的优越性,因此一直受到贸易当事方的广泛青睐,并已发展成为当代世界各国解决国际商事争议最为普遍的方式之一。

阅读材料

1. Is arbitration a part of ADR?

Can arbitration really be considered a part of the ADR scenario? Historically, arbitration was indeed born as an alternative to the submission of disputes to the ordinary courts of justice, both domestically and under international law.

But what is the situation today, particularly in trade and business matters? Domestically, at any rate in the United States and the United Kingdom, arbitration is generally considered a form of ADR. Internationally, however, the answer is not quite so clear. The International Chamber of Commerce Amicable Dispute Resolution system (ICC-ADR), for example, excludes arbitration. But other institutions in the field, such as the London Court of International Arbitration (LCIA), do not seem to take the same view and both arbitration and ADR appear to be considered as alternatives, albeit each with its own characteristics.

The answer probably lies in the path that arbitration is likely to follow. It has been noted that arbitration has evolved towards more structured forms that make the

---

① See Christian Buhring-Uhle, Lars Kichhof, Gabriele Scherer, Arbitration and Mediation in International Business, Kluwer Law International, 2006, p.101.

differences with court adjudication less meaningful. In point of fact, many times the strategy pursued by lawyers litigating in arbitration is not too different from that used in the ordinary courts of justice. Sometimes arbitrators tend to approach the procedure in a similar manner.

Should this approach prevail in the future, then it is probable that ADR will become an alternative not only to the courts but also to arbitration as it is characterized by a greater degree of flexibility and fewer formalities. ①

2. Our system of justice can be seen as having passed through at least two distinct phases

During the middle ages, disputes were resolved in a system based on a belief in divine intervention. This evolved during the industrial revolution to produce our current adversarial system, which is based on competition. It is my belief that we are now witnessing a transition to a third phase. We are finding that dispute resolution in this third phase is based largely on economic and fiscal considerations.

The basis of our current adversarial system was developed in England in the high middle ages. It was preceded in the early medieval period by three separate forms of trial: trial by battle, trial by ordeal and wager of law. In trial by battle, disputants or their agents engaged in physical combat until one side yielded, or in some cases was slain. In trial by ordeal, the litigant was put through an ordeal, such as being scalded by a red hot iron. If the litigant's wound did not fester after a prescribed period, he was found innocent. Wager of law required the litigants to produce a certain number of witnesses, known as compurgators, to testify for them under oath. A litigant won if the correct number of compurgators testified under oath in the proper fashion. The central theme behind all forms of medieval trial was that God would always intercede in a correctly administered trial and vindicate an innocent party.

The 12th century began to see the decline of these forms of trial and by 1215 the Fourth Lateran Council prohibited church involvement in trials by ordeal. By the mid-thirteenth century trials by battle, ordeal and wager of law had fallen into disfavor. By that time, the jury system had begun to be used to resolve disputes. Early juries bore little resemblance to the neutral fact finding jury of today. At first, juries heard no evidence and apparently sought only divine assistance to render their decision. Eventually, juries were allowed to "certify" themselves by talking to some litigants

---

① See Francisco Orrego Vicuña, Dispute Resolution Mechanisms in the International Arena: The Roles of Arbitration and Mediation, American Arbitration Association Inc., 2002.

and witnesses prior to trial. Nevertheless, at the close of the middle ages, divine intervention was still the central precept of Anglo Saxon jurisprudence.

England then saw great social change during the years of the Renaissance, the Reformation and the Industrial Revolution. By the 1700s, England was undergoing an economic revolution. The old baronial system, which had overseen a stable social order throughout the middle ages, was losing its control as economic competition and social change became the order of the day. This led to radical new ideas by such theorists as John Locke and Adam Smith. ①

3. Arbitration

Arbitration, perhaps because of its resemblance to already familiar domestic litigation, is the most popular method of resolution of international commercial disputes and allows parties to avoid many of the problems associated with litigation. "Differences between legal systems have traditionally made arbitration attractive: it is by its essence the most international means of settling disputes." Arbitration is also the most formal and oldest method of ADR in international commerce.

The merits of arbitration of international commercial disputes are well-documented. "Arbitration provides a neutral forum away from either party's home jurisdiction, protecting against real and imagined prejudices and unfamiliar legal practices." Use of arbitration also reduces legal expenses and time needed to settle disputes. Arbitration allows the parties to customize the arbitral procedure, including the choice of location, language of the proceedings and applicable law, as well as to maintain privacy. Finally, there are rarely problems with arbitration-clause enforcement; and, more importantly, an arbitral award provides a binding solution enforceable at law.

Depending upon the nature of the dispute and countries of origin of the disputants, however, arbitration may not be advisable. "Zealous and opportunistic litigation practices are increasingly supplanting courtly manners in international commercial arbitrations. As a practical matter, claims that arbitration is faster and cheaper than litigation appear increasingly ungrounded." This is especially true when a lot is at stake. Moreover, the need for interim protective measures such as temporary injunctions, evidence from unwilling third parties or joinder of others may greatly complicate arbitration. Finally, it is often difficult to get international parties

---

① See Bradley L. Brown, The Evolution of Our System for Dispute Resolution, Oregon State Bar Bulletin, December, 1997.

to reach an accord on important steps of the arbitral proceedings.

The disadvantages of arbitration listed above are common to all international parties. For arbitrations between Asian and Western parties, however, there is an added cultural drawback. Many Asian cultures, including Japan, detest such a confrontational form of dispute resolution. They prefer face-saving, mutually agreeable compromises rather than edicts proclaiming one party's rights. As a result, Asian parties may oppose clauses that immediately send disputes to arbitration.

Although Japanese courts recognize the validity of arbitration awards rendered in foreign countries and agree to enforce them, the Japanese do not like arbitration for many of the same reasons that other Asians find it distasteful. The Japanese business community, for example, rarely resorts to arbitration to resolve domestic commercial disputes. At home, the Japanese favor conciliation. To resolve conflicts arising out of international business transactions, however, the Japanese do utilize arbitration. The seemingly strange preference of conciliation for domestic matters but arbitration for international commercial disputes may be because foreign parties are unfamiliar with conciliation. The Japanese recognize that their own preference, unmatched by support from the other side, is not enough. Both sides must agree to conciliation for the method to be successful. Arbitration provides the next best alternative.

In sum, "the West with its law consciousness and its inclination towards ... arbitration seems to have dominated the transnational business system." Thus, arbitration may continue its position of primacy for some time. Given their own choice, however, the Japanese and others would probably not choose arbitration. [1]

4. A brief history of arbitration

Just as government is a monopoly of the legitimate means of coercion, courts in civilized societies might be defined as a government-created monopoly on the legitimate and enforceable means of dispute resolution. However, courts have at best held only an imperfect monopoly on dispute resolution. The courts themselves have disavowed monopolist status or tacitly acknowledged their inability to obtain it by setting reasonably broad parameters on self-help, and almost always condoning if not overtly approving informal, non-judicial settlement. Occasionally, other means of resolving disputes arise and gain popularity as an alternative to the courts.

Arbitration proved to be one of the more popular and enduring alternatives, with

---

[1] See Andrew Sagartz, Resolution of International Commercial Disputes: Surmounting Barriers of Culture without Going to Court, Ohio State Journal on Dispute Resolution, 1998.

roots at least as deep as the British Law Merchant, a specialized set of rules governing commercial disputes in England during the Eleventh Century. The Law Merchant was an outgrowth of manufacturers' and traders' attempts to arrange for expedited resolution of their disputes in accordance with the customs of the trade. Admiralty matters were often determined by the Law Merchant. For many decades, the Law Merchant was administered—and decided—by non-lawyers. Eventually, the Law Merchant ceased to exist as a separate entity and cases formerly decided by it were adjudicated in the English courts of common pleas. The doctrines and principles of the Law Merchant in effect became precedent applied by the official English courts.

Although the historical record is not clear, it seems likely that the absorption of the Law Merchant into the official British Courts during the late Eighteenth Century begot the rise and popularity of commercial arbitration as the more formal courts eroded much of the Law Merchant's speed, inexpensiveness and informality, thus creating a market in the business community for an alternative forum. In any event, merchants began to provide for arbitration of their contractual disputes in significant numbers during the Nineteenth Century.

Even in more important matters evidenced by written agreements there was often no formal agreement to arbitrate but rather an implied understanding that questions involving delayed delivery, quality of merchandise, or terms of payment would be decided by a third party with knowledge of the trade. It appears that arbitration initially meant presenting the dispute to a selected third party merchant or group of merchants and asking the third party for an oral ruling. If one of the disputants failed to abide by the decision, the other side's chief remedy was adverse publicity and ostracism, undoubtedly a weak reed where the difficult adversary was a "one-shot" player whose principal operations lay within another merchant community. [1]

5. Introduction of CIETAC

Currently, CIETAC is the sole organization in the PRC authorized to hear non-maritime commercial arbitrations between Chinese and foreign parties. CIETAC has become one of the largest commercial arbitration centers in the world.

CIETAC's growth as an international commercial arbitration center can be attributed to a number of factors. First, as stated, the Chinese government has authorized CIETAC as the sole international commercial arbitration center in China.

---

[1] See Jeffrey W. Stempel, Pitfalls of Public Policy: The Case of Arbitration Agreements, Saint Mary's Law Journal, 1990.

Second, a number of regulations and provisions under Chinese law specifically recommend that Chinese and foreign parties involved in certain transactions send their disputes to CIETAC for arbitration. Third, not surprisingly, along with the dramatic increase in international transactions in China has come a corresponding increase in the number of arbitrable disputes. Finally, Chinese parties, who generally have little experience with international business practices, are not very familiar with other international arbitration forums such as the International Chamber of Commerce in Paris or the Arbitration Institute of the Stockholm Chamber of Commerce. Consequently, Chinese parties dealing with foreigners often attempt to include a standard arbitration clause in their contracts naming CIETAC as the venue for arbitration. As CIETAC gains experience in international arbitration matters and educates more arbitrators in the field of international arbitration, more foreign parties appear willing to name CIETAC as the designated arbitration commission.

Currently, more than fifty percent of the arbitration cases which CIETAC accepts relate to international trade disputes. Approximately one-third are equity and contract joint venture disputes. Most of the remaining cases involve disputes over intellectual property, construction contracts, processing production, or compensation. In the near future, a sharp increase is expected in the number of arbitrations relating to securities and real estate matters.

In addition to CIETAC's headquarters in Beijing, there are two sub-commissions located in Shanghai and in the Shenzhen Special Economic Zone.①

思考题

1. What will be the status of international arbitration in the future system of dispute resolution?
2. Please briefly analyze the history of dispute resolution.
3. What is the advantage and disadvantage of arbitration in comparison with litigation?
4. What is the trend of international arbitration?

---

① See Alexander Lourie, International Commercial Arbitration in China: History, New Developments, and Current Practice, John Marshall Law Review, Spring, 1995.

第二章 有关仲裁的法律与规则

国际商事仲裁协议的订立、仲裁程序的有序进行、仲裁裁决的执行和监督等都需要一定的法律和规则对其加以规制。细心的读者可以发现,此处我们不仅讲到了法律,而且提到了规则,这就是仲裁与诉讼很大的不同。规制仲裁整个过程的,不仅仅有仲裁法律法规,而且还有仲裁机构的仲裁规则。可以说,它们两者的地位是同样重要、缺一不可的。因此,在研习国际商事仲裁的过程中,我们不仅要关注涉及仲裁的法律法规,而且要着眼于仲裁规则。[①]

For arbitration to exist and succeed there must be a regulatory framework that controls the legal status and effectiveness of arbitration in national and international legal environment. The sources of international arbitration are of both public and private origin.

调整国际商事仲裁活动的法律与规则大体上分为三个部分:(1)国际商事仲裁的国内立法;(2)国际商事仲裁的国际立法;(3)国际商事仲裁规则。

The first and second parts constitute the public source of international arbitration, which consist of rules enacted or simply proposed by relevant national authorities acting in a domestic or international context. In addition, the growth of international arbitration as a means of settling disputes has led to the increasing of inter-governmental conventions and instruments drawn up by international organizations.

国内立法方面,最常见的就是各国制定的仲裁法。除此之外,根据各国所属法系/法域的不同,如相关的判例、我国的司法解释,都是仲裁中会适用到的国内法。国际立法方面,则包括涉及国际商事仲裁的公约和条约,如1927年《关于执行外国国际仲裁裁决的日内瓦公约》(以下简称"1927年《日内瓦公约》")、双边投资协定(Bilateral Investment Treaties,即所谓的"BITs")中的有关仲裁的规定等。此外,有必要提及《示范法》。《示范法》仅起示范作用,并不以直接产生法律效力的方式在仲裁实践中适用,其在各国的表现形式和作用形式不完全相同,各国的一般做法是,通过国内立法,将《示范法》条文规定下来,并加以适用。

[①] 在许多国际商事仲裁的教材和专著中都有"仲裁制度的法律渊源"的提法。上文已经提到,仲裁的过程中还涉及仲裁规则的适用(尤其在临时仲裁中),不能简单地将仲裁规则归入法律渊源之中。因此,本书不采用"法律渊源"这一说法。

As to private sources of international arbitration, institutional arbitration rules are of great importance. The binding nature of arbitration rules is not derived from the acts of one or more public authorities. Therefore, we categorized it into the third part. "Arbitration rules" indicates a set of provisions intended to govern arbitral procedure and drafted by an arbitral institution or other organization. It has the feature of diversity and flexibility which satisfies the varying requirements under the international commercial environment.

仲裁规则,则是由各仲裁机构制定或由当事人合议订立的(多见于临时仲裁中),仲裁机构和有关仲裁当事人在进行具体的商事仲裁活动过程中适用的程序规则。它直接制约着仲裁活动的进行,甚至影响着仲裁裁决的效力,因此,仲裁规则在仲裁中的地位不容忽视。一个好的仲裁规则,能提高仲裁的效率,能为仲裁机构赢得良好的声誉。本章第三节中将介绍一些主要仲裁机构的仲裁规则。

第一节 国内立法

商事仲裁作为国际社会所普遍承认的解决商事争议的常用方式,在19世纪中期以后,被赋予了法律上的意义,从而成为一种法律解决方式,并使得商事仲裁制度成为一种程序法律制度。随着商品经济的日益发达,商事仲裁这种争议解决的有效方式也得到了很大发展,并开始受到更为普遍的接受和欢迎。于是,各国立法都开始顺应时代的要求,纷纷制定了仲裁法。

It might be thought that international commercial arbitrations would be governed by international law; and indeed, from time to time this is so. For example, an arbitration between two sovereign states, even if the matters in dispute are concerned with commercial rather than with the more usual political issues, will be governed by international law. The same is true of arbitrations relating to investment disputes under the provisions of the Washington Convention, where only one of the parties is a state and the other is a private investor.

For the most part, however, international commercial arbitration depends for its full effectiveness upon the support of different systems of law and in particular domestic laws.

仲裁虽由当事人的仲裁协议而起,但却无法存在于法律真空之中,仲裁必须受特定国家的法律及相关国际条约的调整。仲裁协议的效力、仲裁裁决的承认与执行等,均受特定国家仲裁法的支配。当事人和仲裁庭所享有的高度自治权,只能在仲裁法规定的范围内行使。为了保证国家把守好仲裁的最后一道关,各国法律均规定了拒绝承认与执行裁决或撤销裁决的条件与程序;为了保证仲裁事项、仲裁程序符合本国基本的道德、法律准则和公正观念,各国仲裁法均规定了一些当事人不能违反的强制性规则和公共政策规则,无论是当事人确定的仲裁规则,还是仲裁机构制定的仲裁规则,均不得与这些规则相抵触。因此,可以说,国内仲裁立法对国际商事仲裁的影响是至关重要的。

国际贸易的蓬勃发展促进了仲裁制度的国际化。国际商事仲裁作为解决国际商事争议的一种有效方式,其地位日益重要。仲裁的国际立法不断推动着各国国内相关仲裁法律的制定。各国政府纷纷制定或修改仲裁法,以求解决逐年增多的国际商事争议。几乎每一个国家都制定有自己本国的仲裁立法,但基于各国法律传统的不同,不同国家的商事仲裁法律制度具有不同的立法体例。德国、法国、日本等大陆法系国家主要在民事诉讼法典中专章规定有关商事仲裁程序的内容;而英国、美国等英美法系国家则采取单行法的形式规范商事仲裁法律制度;再有,如印度,采取仲裁与调解合并的立法例。不过,越来越多的大陆法系国家也逐渐开始采取专门立法的形式,对仲裁法律制度作出规定,如1999年《韩国仲裁法》、2004年《日本仲裁法》。

It should be noted that most developed trading states (and many other countries) have enacted national arbitration legislation. These national laws provide for the enforcement of international arbitration agreements and awards, limit judicial interference in the arbitration process, authorize specified judicial support for the arbitral process, affirm the capacity of parties to enter into valid and binding agreements to arbitrate future commercial disputes, provide mechanisms for the enforcement of such arbitration agreements, and require the recognition and enforcement of arbitration awards. In addition, most modern arbitration legislation restricts the interference of national courts in the arbitration process, when arbitral proceedings are pending or in reviewing ultimate arbitration awards. Some domestic legislation even authorizes limited judicial assistance to the arbitral process. Such judicial assistance can include selecting arbitrators or arbitral situses, enforcing a tribunal's orders with respect to evidence taking or discovery, and granting provisional relief in aid of arbitration.

下面对各国的仲裁立法逐一介绍。

一、外国国内立法

从发展上看,各国的国内立法都有着明显的有利仲裁的发展趋势。自19世纪商人团体使用仲裁条款始,其法律效力一直未得到承认。直至1925年12月31日,法国在其国内立法中首次承认了仲裁条款的法律效力,芬兰也于1928年

2月4日将仲裁程序的规定纳入其民事诉讼法中。瑞典紧随其后,于1929年6月14日制定了本国的仲裁法,对国内和涉外仲裁等事项加以规定。西班牙也于1953年12月22日制定了仲裁法。

In recent years, there have been numerous legislative reforms worldwide, with each country seeking to make international arbitration on its own land more attractive. The competition between the traditional international arbitration locations and the ambitions of a number of other countries can be clearly seen from an examination of a number of legal systems. As follows, we may choose the legislations in England, America, France, Germany, Switzerland, Singapore, Japan, and Korea to have a review.

(一) 英国

英国有着悠久的仲裁实践历史。早在15世纪初期,普通法院极为苛刻的诉讼程序,致使商事纠纷不能得到及时有效的解决,仲裁作为一种较为灵活的纠纷解决方式应运而生。到了19世纪80年代中期,英国已成为世界主要的贸易国。贸易的发展带来了商事纠纷的增加,从而使得商事仲裁的实践进一步发展。为了更好地规范仲裁行为,除有关法律,如《1854年普通法程序法》包含仲裁规定外,英国还于1889年至1934年之间专门制定了多部仲裁法,为仲裁制度构建了基本框架。这期间的英国仲裁法的基本特征之一是法院在仲裁程序中具有很大的权力,而这一特征也成为英国仲裁法日后历次改革中重点修订的方面之一。在此之后,英国又先后制定了《1950年仲裁法》、《1975年仲裁法》和《1979年仲裁法》。

进入20世纪80年代,在国际商事仲裁全面发展的背景下,英国再度将仲裁制度改革提上了议程。1985年联合国大会通过了由联合国国际贸易委员会(UNCITRAL)起草的《示范法》,《示范法》的通过对世界上很多国家的仲裁立法产生了影响,这其中最典型的就属英国。英国政府专门成立了一个咨询委员会(Departmental Advisory Committee, DAC),研究英国采用《示范法》的必要性。经研究,该委员会的最终报告指出:英国有必要制定一部新的仲裁法,新法在可能情况下应体现《示范法》的发展,但全盘照搬《示范法》是有害的。

在《示范法》的影响下,1990年新的仲裁法开始起草;1996年,新仲裁法通过;1997年1月31日起,新法开始施行。该法生效后,《1950年仲裁法》、《1975年仲裁法》和《1979年仲裁法》同时废止。

The Arbitration Act of 1996 is probably the most radical piece of legislation in the history of English arbitration law. It contains an almost complete statement of principles relating to the law of arbitration. It uses straightforward and logical language to explain those principles and presents them in chronological format starting with the principles affecting the arbitration, the seat of the arbitration, the formation of the arbitral tribunal and ending with the recognition and enforcement of an award. Although at its conception it was agreed that the Arbitration Act of 1996 would not enact the UNCITRAL Model Law without modification it is clear from the use of language and format that the UNCITRAL Model Law has played a major part in the shape that the Arbitration Act has taken.

The 1996 English Arbitration Act has significantly reformed English arbitration law and consolidated changes made by recent judicial decisions in England. Notable among the features of the new Act is the primacy it grants to the autonomy of the parties to an arbitration. The Act stipulates, as one of its general principles, that "the parties should be free to agree how their disputes are resolved, subject only to such safeguards as are necessary in the public interest." This provision is remarkable because historically English arbitration law had been characterized by extensive judicial intervention in the arbitral process.

上述当事人意思自治的原则性规定体现了《1996年仲裁法》弱化法院干预的倾向。除此之外,该倾向还具体体现在很多方面。首先,有效的仲裁协议可排除诉讼管辖权。根据英国《1996年仲裁法》第9条和第4条,对于诉讼程序启动之后产生的纠纷,当事人申请终止诉讼的,法院倾向于终止诉讼程序。其次,弱化法院干预还广泛体现在仲裁程序进行中。例如,《1996年仲裁法》第38条规定,除非当事人另有约定,命令当事人提供费用担保的权力属于仲裁庭。这一规定与《1950年仲裁法》把该权力授予法院截然不同。在这一点上,英国仲裁法显然借鉴了《示范法》的精神。

另外,弱化法院干预也体现在法院对仲裁活动的监督上。例如,法院针对仲裁裁决中涉及的法律问题实施司法监督是英国仲裁法的传统实践,当事人可以就法律问题向法院提起上诉。

The 1979 English Arbitration Act was designed in part to curtail the level of judicial intervention in the arbitral process. Some of the significant reforms introduced by the 1979 Act were the abolition of the stated case procedure of judicial review of arbitration and the granting to parties to an international contract a limited right to exclude review on the merits of the award. However, the 1979 Arbitration Act did create a right of appeal before the High Court on "any question of law arising out of an award" and allowed the parties to put a "preliminary point of law" arising during the arbitration before the courts. Further, the legislation did not make it easy for the parties to agree to exclude these statutory rights of recourse in international disputes.

《1996年仲裁法》则更加深入地强调了上诉权的有限性。该法第69条第3

款规定,法院应该允许上诉的情形包括:对有关法律问题的决定将实质性地影响一方或多方当事人的权利;有关法律问题是仲裁庭根据当事人请求作出决定;根据裁决中所发现的事实,仲裁庭对法律问题的裁决存在明显错误,或该法律问题具有普遍的公共重要性且仲裁庭的裁决至少引发严重疑问;虽然当事人约定通过仲裁解决纠纷,但无论如何由法院对该问题作出判决是公平和适当的。值得注意的是,根据该法第69条第1款的规定,当事人可以通过约定排除上诉权。

However, the tradition of judicial intervention remains in certain respects: the powers of the court remain substantial; there are numerous mandatory provisions; the powers of the court to determine a preliminary point of law and to hear an appeal of a point of law are maintained where English law is applicable to the merits, even if they can be excluded by agreement of the parties. Finally, there remains an impressive list of "serious irregularities affecting the tribunal, the proceedings or the award" which allow a party to challenge the award.

除此之外,在实践中,法院并没有真正地实现立法中关于减少对仲裁裁决上诉的意图。实际上,如果说 Diplock 伯爵在案例中确定的指导原则仅仅将允许上诉的门打开了一道窄缝的话,那么 2002 年上诉法院的做法是将允许上诉的大门打得更宽了一点。自从《1996 年仲裁法》颁布以来,仲裁案件上诉的数量一直保持不变,与该法颁布前一年的数量大致持平。

除了弱化法院干预这一趋势外,《1996 年仲裁法》还首次明确制定了仲裁法的三大基本原则,即仲裁法的目的所在、当事人自治原则和减少法院干预。同时,根据 1996 年 DAC 报告,该法中如有任何模糊之处,基本原则将具有最高效力。

(二) 瑞典

与英国仲裁相似,瑞典的仲裁制度也具有悠久的历史。由于政治上的中立性,瑞典在国际仲裁中具有重要的地位,许多国际商事合同选择在瑞典进行仲裁。瑞典关于仲裁的成文法规定最早可追溯至 14 世纪中期。1887 年,瑞典制定第一部《仲裁法》,1919 年作出重要修订。1929 年,在 1919 年修订的 1887 年《仲裁法》的基础上,新法制定而成。另外,作为加入 1927 年《日内瓦公约》的结果,瑞典还在 1929 年制定了《涉外仲裁协议与仲裁裁决法》。1929 年的两部法律均在其后的 1971、1976 和 1981 年进行过一些修订。1999 年,新的《仲裁法》颁布。在 1999 年《仲裁法》制定前,1929 年的仲裁立法及其后的修订构成瑞典主要的仲裁法律制度,并发挥着重要的作用。除此之外,案例法在解释成文法和成文法未规定的其他方面以及发展仲裁原则方面也起着重要作用。

In 1999, a reform was taken in Sweden. Sweden found that a reform was important for two reasons. Firstly, the arbitration of commercial disputes, especially between large companies, has become more and more frequent on the domestic level in Sweden when compared with most other countries. Secondly, the past two decades have witnessed a steadily increasing number of international arbitrations in which Sweden is the selected venue. The latter trend is attributable in part to Sweden's policy of neutrality. This trend is also attributable to the fact that Sweden is a signatory state without reservations to the aforementioned 1958 New York Convention. In light of the increasing interest in and use of arbitration in Sweden on the national as well as the international plane, the Committee proposed the creation of "an efficient, up-to-date and easily comprehensible legislative framework for the arbitral resolution of disputes."

On April 1, 1999 the New Arbitration Act entered into force in Sweden and the New Act replaced the foresaid two 1929 arbitration laws, i.e. domestic and foreign. It is of great significance that the New Arbitration Act, albeit not a replica of the Model Law, was drafted so as at least to conform with the most important principles of the Model Law.

The new Act applies to both domestic and international arbitration. However, certain provisions relate specifically to "international matters" and to the recognition and enforcement of foreign awards. One of the most important new provisions is that allowing parties with no links to Sweden to waive their right to bring an action before the Swedish courts to set aside an award made in Sweden. This was inspired by Swiss law, but a liberal line of Swedish cases concerning international arbitration had already paved the way. The 1999 Swedish Arbitration Act, which entered into force on April 1, 1999, is also based to a large extent on the Model Law. All continents and all legal traditions are represented, reflecting the universality of the text.

(三) 美国

美国在殖民时期即已传承了英国普通法有关仲裁的立法,也是较早发展仲裁法的国家之一。但是,在1925年美国《联邦仲裁法》(Federal Arbitration Act of 1925)通过前,对于仲裁案件均承袭英国的仲裁理念,法院对仲裁始终抱有相当的敌意,并不承认一个已生效的仲裁协议的法律效力,也不能将仲裁裁决交付强制执行。这是由普通法系国家认为的一切私权争议都应由专属法院管辖,不得由当事人以约定排除的观念所决定的。

在介绍美国1925年《联邦仲裁法》之前,有必要提及1920年的《纽约州仲裁法》,它在美国仲裁法的历史中占有很重要的地位,是美国第一个州仲裁立法。该法首次提出了"仲裁条款对于当事人间未来产生的一切争端均有强制执行性及不可撤回性",更显著影响了《联邦仲裁法》的制定,同时也促使了美国第一个具独立性、永久性的仲裁机构——美国仲裁协会(AAA)的建立。继1920年《纽约州仲裁法》制定后,全美各州,除佛蒙特州(Vermont)外,都相继制定了类似的州仲裁法。现全美有36个州依据1956年修正的《统一仲裁法》,制定了各州的仲裁法规,虽有些细微差异,但大多与1925年美国《联邦仲裁法》相同。

在美国法律系统之下,凡是有关地方色彩的仲裁争议,均由州法律来规范,而但凡牵涉到州际间、国际间的商务争端以及一切有关海商法的问题则由美国《联邦仲裁法》来规范。

1925年制定的《联邦仲裁法》涵盖层面广阔,诸如商事和海商运送仲裁,不仅赋予法院对海商运送仲裁裁决的强制执行权,而且规定了仲裁的指导原则,对仲裁的意义、管辖、违约行为及赔偿事项等都作了界定。然而,该法对仲裁程序并未明确规定,而由几个独立的仲裁机构及仲裁协会作补充规定。

美国《联邦仲裁法》的通过,标志着美国仲裁进入了一个新的时期。在此之前,仲裁合意依据普通法理论是可得撤销、无法强制执行的。而依《联邦仲裁法》,仲裁条款是有效、不可单方撤销和可交付强制执行的。此外,在 Marine Transit Corp. v. Dreyfus[①] 一案中,联邦最高法院的判决肯定了《联邦仲裁法》未违反美国《宪法》的规定,从而在判例法上为仲裁裁决的强制执行开了先例。

美国于1970年9月正式签署加入《纽约公约》。为配合《纽约公约》的施行,国会修订了《联邦仲裁法》,增订了第201—208节。

As early as 1925, the United States adopted a modern federal law, known as the Federal Arbitration Act (FAA) or United States Arbitration Act (USAA), which draws no distinction between domestic and international arbitration. Chapter 2 of the Act, which was added on July 31, 1970, introduced the New York Convention into federal law and thus deals with international arbitration and non-US awards.[②] Since the enactment of this legislation, the United States federal courts have proved to be substantially in favor of arbitration, seeking to give it full autonomy and a very wide scope. The liberal policy underlying this approach (on grounds including the easing of the courts' caseload) has not always met with unanimous approval. In international arbitration, after confirming the principle of the autonomy of arbitration agreements, the United States Supreme Court took a broad view of the arbitrability of disputes, despite the existence of compulsory legislation concerning securities law and antitrust issues in particular. In domestic arbitration, the Supreme Court now accepts not only that an action for securities fraud is arbitrable, in spite of the applicability of

---

① 284 U.S. 263, 52 S. CT. 166 (1932).
② See 9 U.S.C.A. §§ 201-08.

mandatory rules, but also that arbitrators are empowered to award punitive damages.

However, the liberalism of federal case law does not go far enough, in particular as regards the recognition in the United States of international arbitral awards. In addition, the jurisdiction of arbitrators to determine their own jurisdiction has still not been fully accepted. The desire to serve as a competitive international arbitration venue is leading some U.S. states to enact new laws on international commercial arbitration. Some states reproduce the UNCITRAL Model Law in full, or adapt it slightly, while others merely draw inspiration from it or make altogether less ambitious reforms.

(四) 德国

按照德国的立法体例,有关仲裁的规定存在于《民事诉讼法》之中,即《民事诉讼法》第十编对仲裁程序作了具体规定。该法自 1877 年生效以后,在仲裁方面几乎没有任何实质性的改进。1930 年和 1986 年的两次小修改,均无法适应国际经济贸易发展的需要。民主德国于 1975 年制定的《仲裁法》相对而言较为先进,但随着两德的统一,法律技术上的处理使得该法在 1990 年以后再无适用的余地。

当时立法的滞后程度,正如某些学者所指出的:"德国《民事诉讼法》第十编中规范的仲裁程序法很大程度上仍然是上一个世纪(19 世纪)的产物"①,这种状况不可避免地影响了德国作为国际仲裁地的声誉,并因此引发了德国学术界人士对改革仲裁法以符合时代要求并与现代发展相适应的呼吁。1990 年德国组建"仲裁程序法革新委员会",经过 7 年的讨论,终于在 1997 年 12 月颁布了《仲裁程序修正法》。

Until 1997, the German legislature had made only a few alterations to the 1879 Code of Civil of Procedure (ZPO), which covered arbitration in Articles 1025 to 1048. A law dated July 25, 1986, which reformed German private international law, eliminated a number of overly restrictive rules concerning international arbitration.

This "mini-reform" disappointed many German arbitration practitioners. They were frustrated that their country played only a very modest role as an international arbitration situs and had therefore sought a more spectacular reform designed to make Germany and attractive place for arbitration. To meet their concerns, a draft statute was prepared in 1994. In 1996, a slightly modified draft was put before the *Bundestag* and it was enacted on December 22, 1997.

---

① 《联邦议院公报》第 13/5274 号(BT-Drucks. 13/5274),第 1 页。转引自孙珺:《德国仲裁立法改革》,载《仲裁与法律通讯》1998 年第 3 期。

1998 年 1 月 1 日生效的《仲裁程序修正法》,对《民事诉讼法》第十编规定的仲裁程序进行了修订,与诉讼程序相比,用仲裁程序解决纠纷更为便捷。德国新仲裁法①在许多方面较之旧的规定都有重大的变动。立法者在这次改革中大胆地摒弃了一些落后的、不尽完善的做法,并作了许多符合国际和时代发展需要的规定。对"可仲裁性"重新定义,使得可提交仲裁的争议大幅扩张,改革者期望仲裁程序在解决国内争议方面大有作为,从而减轻法院的重负,这是此次仲裁程序改革的一项宗旨。

The new statute modifies a number of provisions of the Code of Civil Procedure and completely revises its Book X (Arts. 1025 to 1066). It is essentially based on the UNCITIAL Model Law and does not distinguish, in principle, between domestic and international arbitration.

从总体上看,德国新仲裁法体现了如下三个特点:

1. 充分尊重了当事人的意思自治。1998 年《仲裁程序修正法》明确规定当事人可以自行规定或者援引仲裁规则,当事人可以对仲裁庭的组成、仲裁的法律适用以及仲裁裁决的作出等问题进行协商。其对"仲裁协议"的要求甚至比英国《1996 年仲裁法》还要宽松,更是体现了这一特点。

2. 加强了司法对仲裁制度的支持。例如,根据德国仲裁法改革之前的判例,基于当事人的授权,仲裁庭有权对自己是否享有案件的管辖权作出终局决定,而新法通过时则采纳了《示范法》第 16 条第 3 款的规定,将最终的决定权交给法院,当事人不能随意排除法院的监督,这一规定无疑有利于保障仲裁制度健康有序地发展。

3. 内容更加详细和完备,增强了稳定性和可预见性。这有益于当事人对自己的行为有一定的预期,从而保障仲裁程序的顺利进行。

(五) 法国

在法国进行商事仲裁具有良好的法律环境。法国加入了所有有关仲裁的国际公约,如 1923 年《关于仲裁条款的日内瓦议定书》(以下简称"1923 年《日内瓦议定书》")和 1927 年《日内瓦公约》、1958 年《纽约公约》。法国仲裁法②也作出了有利于仲裁的规定,法官对国际仲裁、国际贸易的特殊规则也都比较熟悉,对仲裁采取支持的态度,尤其是尊重仲裁条款。法国最高法院在 1981 年改革之

---

① 德国立法者没有将仲裁程序的规定从《民事诉讼法》中抽出来形成一部形式意义上的《仲裁法》,而是继续把仲裁程序的规定放在《民事诉讼法》第十编中。在这点上,德国仲裁立法与中国仲裁立法是有区别的。不过,德国学术界经常会直接使用"仲裁程序法"或"仲裁法"这两个术语,这实际上指的就是实质意义上的仲裁法,即《民事诉讼法》第十编关于仲裁程序的规定。本文下面提及德国仲裁法时,也是从这个意义上说的。

② 与德国仲裁立法体例一样,法国的仲裁法内容也规定于其《民事诉讼法典》(The Code of Civil Procedure)中。

前已作出有利于仲裁的判决,如承认合同中仲裁条款的独立性,即使合同无效,其仲裁条款也有效。此外,还承认公共事务也可诉诸仲裁。

France was one of the first countries to modernize its arbitration legislation. French law is considered by many to be, if not a model, then at least an essential point of reference. Although before 1981, there were no statutory rules relating to international arbitration alone, the courts laid the foundations of French international arbitration law without the support of any legislation.

The major two-stage reform of arbitration law in France took place in the early 1980s. In 1980, domestic arbitration law was brought up to date; one year later, specific rules were enacted governing international arbitration. This affirmation of the specific nature of international arbitration is one of the most significant features of French law.

1981年对民事诉讼程序进行改革后,法国将国际仲裁定性为商业经济性质,并承认国际仲裁规则。之后,由于有大量判例,使得整个国际仲裁的执行拥有了相当的法律基础。

No further upheavals have occurred in French arbitration law since the enactment of the New Code of Civil Procedure. On the whole, the courts have encountered no particular difficulties in applying the new provisions. All the major cases since the reform have shown that the courts have properly understood and implemented the spirit of the new law.

在法国进行仲裁,当事人可选择任何国家的法律、语言、仲裁员、程序规则,也可选择由仲裁员不仅依据法律也可依据公平原则进行仲裁。在法国,裁决的强制执行程序非常简单,只需在裁决书上加盖法院的执行章,该裁决便可在全法国得到承认和执行。法院对裁决采取有限度的监督,其依据是《纽约公约》。法国仲裁委员会的秘书长还设想,依据中国CIETAC的仲裁规则在巴黎进行仲裁是完全可能的,唯一的限制是不能违反法国的公共秩序。秘书长还反复强调了在法国仲裁与伦敦仲裁相比的优势是收费低廉、程序快捷。

(六) 日本

在过去,仲裁由日本旧《民事诉讼法典》规范。该法典于1890年实施,最终在1998年被新《民事诉讼法典》所取代。新《民事诉讼法典》保留了旧《民事诉讼法典》中有关公告和仲裁程序方面的规定,并将其命名为"公告程序和仲裁程序法"(即《旧法》)。

1988年《日本仲裁法草案》以《示范法》为蓝本起草,其基本结构与《示范法》大同小异,所依据的基本原则也十分接近。

2003年8月1日,经日本议会通过的《日本仲裁法》(即《新法》)最终颁布,并于 2004 年 3 月 1 日开始实施。它替代了旧《民事诉讼法典》遗留的那部分《旧法》。《新法》独立于《民事诉讼法典》,并且规定了一个独立的综合性仲裁制度。这意味着,日本新的仲裁制度不再是民事审判的补充了。

早在 2001 年 12 月下旬,日本首相小泉纯一郎直接领导下的日本政府司法体制改革促进办公室就成立了一个《新法》专家研究组,开始修改仲裁法。专家们对仲裁法的研究修改以《示范法》的国际商事仲裁内容为基础,并于 2004 年 3 月结束研究工作。此前,在 2003 年 3 月 14 日,改革办公室已就《新法》向议会提交了议案。

《新法》在实体和形式上均仿照《示范法》。《旧法》仿照的是 1897 年生效的德国《民事诉讼法》中的仲裁法部分。这部过时的《旧法》已有一百多年没有修改过,对其进行修改并发挥日本在国际仲裁中积极作用的呼声日益增多。随着以《示范法》为基础的《新法》的通过,日本现在已加入到国际仲裁行列中来了。

(七) 新加坡

Singapore amended its 1953 Act in 1980 to reflect the English 1979 Arbitration Act, and ratified the New York Convention in 1986, simultaneously adopting a number of specific provisions governing international arbitration. Then, in 1994, it adopted the UNCITRAL Model Law.

二、中国国内立法

在香港、澳门已经回归和两岸终将统一的背景下,在我国领域内同时并存着四个不同的法域,是一个多法域国家,即出现"一国两制四法域"的格局。在大陆、香港、澳门和台湾四个法域,仲裁法律的立法体例有所不同,因此,我们将对大陆立法和港、澳、台立法分别进行介绍。

(一) 大陆地区

与其他国家和地区不同的是,大陆地区的仲裁立法始于涉外仲裁制度的建立。1954 年 5 月 6 日,中央人民政府政务院第 215 次政务会议正式通过《中央人民政府政务院关于在中国国际贸易促进委员会内设立对外贸易仲裁委员会的决定》。1958 年 11 月 21 日,国务院全体会议第 82 次会议通过《中华人民共和国国务院关于在中国国际贸易促进委员会内设立海事仲裁委员会的决定》。上述两个决定,为我国涉外仲裁立法奠定了基础。此后,《经济合同法》、《技术合同法》、《涉外经济合同法》、《著作权法》、《铁路法》、《民事诉讼法》等也对仲裁作了规定。但是,以上述法律、法规为依据而建立的仲裁制度存在着两个重要问题:一是仲裁机构过多,且不健全;二是仲裁规则不统一,在仲裁程序、仲裁管辖、审裁关系上各不相同,且其中许多规定违背仲裁的基本性质,与社会主义市场经济体制的要求不相符。例如,《仲裁法》实施前的国内仲裁无须仲裁协议,国内仲裁机构可以根据地域管辖和级别管辖原则行使仲裁管辖权,当事人对仲裁内容不服的,可重新向人民法院起诉。因此,这种仲裁实则是一种行政性质的仲裁,这不仅违背了仲裁的独立性、自愿性、快捷性等特点,也与仲裁最根本的、区别于诉讼的性质相去甚远。

Prior to August 1994, in Mainland China there were fourteen laws, eighty administrative regulations and nearly two hundred local regulations that contained clauses on arbitration. However, many of these laws and regulations were contradictory in nature. Apparently, the government of Mainland China recognized a comprehensive and uniform arbitration law governing both domestic and international arbitration is urgently needed. Therefore, on August 31, 1994, Mainland China adopted the Arbitration Law of the People's Republic of China (1994 Arbitration Law). Recognizing different treatment for domestic and international arbitration, the 1994 Arbitration Law codified these two types of arbitration into a single law.

1994年8月31日《仲裁法》的颁布,是我国仲裁制度发展史上的一个里程碑,标志着一个适应市场经济体制要求的、基本符合国际通行做法的仲裁法律体系的诞生。它表明大陆在建立符合国际标准的仲裁制度方面迈出了实质性步骤。该法有三个突出特点:(1)立法体例上维持了国内仲裁与涉外仲裁的二元立法体例;(2)仅对争议事项中的商事争议部分进行调整,通过排除法扩大了可仲裁的争议范围;(3)统一设立独立的仲裁机构。此后,大陆还颁布了一系列与仲裁相关的行政法规、规章以及司法解释。

The primary law regulating arbitration today is the Arbitration Law of the People's Republic of China (CAL). In addition, the Civil Procedure Law, Uniform Contract Law, Sino-Foreign Equity Joint Venture Law, Sino-Foreign Co-operative Joint Venture Law, and other laws contain some provisions concerning arbitration or enforcement of arbitral agreements and awards.

当代中国大陆法律制度,整体上奉行的是大陆法系(民法法系)法律理论及其相应制度。以《宪法》为核心的各种制定法是主要的法律渊源。就仲裁而言,其法律渊源主要有:1994年《仲裁法》、1991年《民事诉讼法》、1999年《合同法》等。此外,最高人民法院《关于执行我国加入的〈承认及执行外国仲裁裁决公约〉的通知》、《关于认真贯彻〈仲裁法〉依法执行仲裁裁决的通知》、《关于人民法院处理与涉外仲裁及外国仲裁事项有关问题的通知》等有关仲裁的司法解释,也构成仲裁法的渊源。

At the present time, China's main statutes governing arbitration include the Arbitration Law 1994 and the Civil Procedure Law 1991. The Arbitration Law 1994, by itself evidence of China's public policy favoring arbitration, aimed at fostering use of arbitration as an effective way to resolve disputes in business transactions. There is no specific law on international commercial arbitration. Special provisions on international commercial arbitration are contained in Chapter 7 of the Arbitration Law 1994.

In addition, the Supreme People's Court has promulgated judicial interpretations regarding arbitration in the form of regulations, explanations or replies to questions raised by lower courts. Those judicial texts also have binding legal force.

1. 1995 年《仲裁法》(CAL)

该法共 8 章 80 条。《仲裁法》的颁布,结束了我国没有仲裁法典的历史,确立了仲裁法律制度在我国法律体系中的重要地位,恢复了仲裁制度的本来面目,标志着我国仲裁制度的进一步完善。该法在制定过程中,充分考虑了我国建立社会主义市场经济体制的要求,借鉴了国外仲裁制度的有益经验和国际上通行的做法,特别是《纽约公约》和《示范法》。总体而言,《仲裁法》是一部水平较高的符合国际通行做法的仲裁法。

The Arbitration Law of the People's Republic of China was enacted by the National People's Congress on August 31, 1994 and became effective on September 1, 1995. The Arbitration Law provides for the organization of both domestic and international arbitration bodies in the PRC, and for the procedures to be followed in conducting both domestic and international arbitration. The law drew upon international arbitration legislation and practices, especially provisions in the New York Convention on Recognition and Enforcement of Foreign Arbitral Awards (New York Convention) and the Model Law on International Commercial Arbitration (UNCITRAL Model Law), promulgated by the United Nations Commission on International Trade Law (UNCITRAL) in 1985.

随着《仲裁法》的颁布,大陆真正建立起了现代意义上的商事仲裁法律制度。《仲裁法》对仲裁的案件范围、仲裁机构、仲裁的基本原则和制度、仲裁协议、仲裁程序、申请撤销仲裁裁决、仲裁裁决的执行和涉外仲裁等问题作了详细规定,并且在仲裁机构的性质和法律地位、仲裁协议以及仲裁裁决的法律效力等方面,都作了与现代商事仲裁法律制度的要求基本一致的规定。《仲裁法》第一次将仲裁机构从国家行政机关的体制下独立出来,明确规定了商事仲裁机构的民间性质,确立了商事仲裁机构独立于其他任何机构或部门的法律地位;强调了仲裁协议所具有的确定仲裁机构的管辖权和排除法院诉讼管辖权的法律效力;明确规定了仲裁条款的独立性,确立了或裁或审、一裁终局等制度。

As the first unified and relatively complete law on arbitration in the PRC, the

Arbitration Law brings welcome advances for the systems and procedures of arbitration in China. The reforms brought by the Arbitration Law are the culmination of three years of drafting and the consolidation of thirty years of experience in arbitrating foreign-related business disputes in the PRC. Most changes introduced by the Arbitration Law are procedural in nature and do not directly affect the nature or proceedings of international arbitration organizations, such as CIETAC. We summarize below the most significant aspects in the Arbitration Law.

(1) 该法体现了当事人意思自治原则(Promoting Party Autonomy)

从根本上讲,意思自治是一种法哲学理论,即人可以依其自身的意志创设自己的权利义务。因此,当事人的意志不仅是权利义务的渊源,而且是其行为发生的根据。意思自治原则是国际私法上合同制度中的一项基本原则,也是目前各国在处理涉外合同的法律适用问题上普遍采用的主要原则。它是仲裁与诉讼的重要区别,也是仲裁最根本和最显著的特点之一。这项原则的适用,有利于保持当事人法律关系的稳定和及时有效地解决争议,因而为多数国家所采纳,并在仲裁法中作为一项基本原则予以确认。该原则包括双方当事人自愿选择仲裁方式解决争议、自愿选择仲裁机构和仲裁员、自愿选择仲裁规则等内容。这一制度原来只在我国涉外仲裁中实行,虽然后来也被《涉外经济合同法》、《技术合同法》以及修改后的《民事诉讼法》和《合同法》所确认,但这些法律对此作出的规定是分散的、不完整和不彻底的。而《仲裁法》对此作出了全面、完整的规定。

Promoting party autonomy is one of its primary goals, although in alignment with building a socialist market system.① Parties must agree to arbitrate "of their own accord" before an arbitration institution can exert jurisdiction; if there is a valid agreement to arbitrate, Chinese courts cannot assert jurisdiction over the dispute and an arbitration provider cannot accept a dispute if there is no valid agreement to arbitrate. Parties can choose a particular arbitration institution (e.g., the Beijing Arbitration Commission, CIETAC or a provider institution outside of China) and can select the arbitrator(s). During the arbitration procedure, the parties remain free to agree to settle their dispute through negotiation or conciliation.

---

① Article 1 of the CAL states: "The law is formulated with a view to ensure fair and timely arbitration of economic disputes, reliable protection to legitimate rights and interests of parties concerned and a healthy development of the socialist market economy."

(2) 明确了仲裁机构的设置和法律地位(Establishment of Independent Arbitration Commissions)

The Arbitration Law establishes the institutional framework for the creation of Arbitration Commissions that are administratively independent from the Chinese Government.[①] The Arbitration Law also calls for the creation of the China Arbitration Association, a non-governmental, self-regulating organization of the Arbitration Commissions. Additional provisions describe the requirements for the establishment of Arbitration Commissions, the composition of the Arbitration Commissions, and the qualifications for appointment of arbitrators. These provisions together legitimize arbitration as a process of adjudication that is recognized by, but independent of, the Chinese Government. These advances for domestic arbitration do not have any direct effect on international arbitration. Nevertheless, advances for domestic arbitration may hold some important consequences for foreign investors who unwittingly end up before domestic tribunals.

《仲裁法》不单单是一部仲裁程序法,而且还是一部仲裁机构组织法。《仲裁法》第二章专门规定了仲裁委员会和仲裁协会,规定了仲裁委员会应当具备的条件、仲裁委员会的组成、仲裁员的产生及其应当具备的条件,以及仲裁协会的性质、任务及组成。之所以在《仲裁法》中对仲裁机构作专门规定,就是为了要建立与现代仲裁制度相适应的仲裁组织体系。

(3) 该法确立了或裁或审和一裁终局制度

仲裁的优势之一是快速、及时地解决纠纷,这一优势主要通过或裁或审和一裁终局制度来实现。过去我国的国内经济合同仲裁和其他纠纷仲裁长期实行"裁审混合"、"一裁二审"甚至"二裁二审"的制度。这种又裁又审、裁后再审的做法,既不利于发挥仲裁制度的作用,又拖延了解决纠纷的时间,不符合社会主义市场经济体制的要求,也与仲裁本身的性质相背离。尽管其后制定的《涉外经济合同法》、《技术合同法》等对仲裁的规定已实行或裁或审和一裁终局,但就我国整体仲裁体制而言,并未发生根本改变。或裁或审和一裁终局制度是目前国际上普遍实行的仲裁制度,国际公约和绝大多数国家的仲裁法都确立了这两项制度。我国《仲裁法》明确规定了各类仲裁,除劳动争议和农业集体经济组织内部的农业承包合同纠纷的仲裁以外,均统一适用或裁或审和一裁终局制度,确

---

① Article 14 of the law makes all "arbitration committees independent from the administrative organs, and they are not subject to any administrative organs and neither are they affiliated to each other." Hierarchical relationships between arbitration commissions and administrative authorities are also prohibited, and Article 8 provides that arbitration shall be conducted independently according to the law and shall not be subject to interference from governmental entities, social organizations, or individuals.

立了我国仲裁与审判脱钩的基本格局,与国际上的通行做法相一致。该项制度的实行,有利于充分体现仲裁制度快捷的优点和发挥仲裁制度的作用,对于充分体现当事人的意思自治,提高解决纠纷的效率,都起着决定性的作用。

The powers of the PRC courts in relation to arbitration proceedings are defined: to rule on the validity of the arbitration agreement; to offer measures for the preservation of property or for the interim protection of evidence, and to grant or reject an application for setting-aside the arbitration.

(4) 对涉外仲裁进行特别规定(Special International Issues)

《仲裁法》统一了涉外仲裁和国内仲裁。基于涉外仲裁自身的特点,《仲裁法》以专章对涉外仲裁的特定事项作出了有别于国内仲裁的特别规定。[①] 包括涉外仲裁机构的设立、仲裁员资格、采取保全措施的法院、涉外仲裁裁决的撤销与不予执行等。与此同时,为使现有的涉外仲裁机构的仲裁规则与《仲裁法》保持一致,两大涉外仲裁机构都对其仲裁规则进行了修改,即1995年9月通过的《中国国际经济贸易仲裁委员会仲裁规则》和《中国海事仲裁委员会仲裁规则》,这两个规则于同年10月1日起正式实施。从此,《仲裁法》可以被名副其实地称为"统一仲裁法"。

Another significant aspect of the Arbitration Law is the inclusion of "special provisions" that relate to the "arbitration of disputes involving a foreign element and trade, transport and maritime interests." The significance of these provisions is two-fold. First, reference to a "foreign element" legitimizes CIETAC's expanded jurisdiction specified in Article 2 of the CIETAC Arbitration Rules. Second, by designating special provisions governing foreign-related arbitrations, the Arbitration Law affirms that the two types of arbitration are distinct enough to require some separate provisions, although China is harmonizing domestic and foreign-related arbitration.

Before the enactment of the Arbitration Law, arbitration law distinguished between domestic and international. Foreign-relate disputes were governed by the China International Economic and Trade Arbitration Commission (CIETAC) and the China Maritime Arbitration Commission (CMAC) only. With the enactment of the Arbitration Law, international and domestic laws were governed by the same legislation.

---

① 我国《仲裁法》第七章专门规定了"涉外仲裁的特别规定"。

2. 2007年《民事诉讼法》(The 2007 Civil Procedure Law)中的相关规定

除了《仲裁法》对商事仲裁作了系统的规定外,其他法律中也有关于仲裁的规定。

2007年修订的《民事诉讼法》①在第十二章"第一审普通程序"、第二十章"执行的申请和移送"、第二十七章"仲裁"和第二十八章"司法协助"的有关条款中,就仲裁机构的管辖权、仲裁程序以及仲裁裁决的承认与执行方面的问题作了规定。

A number of Articles on arbitration can also be found in Chapter XXVIII, Part Four of the Civil Procedure Law 2007. As indicated by the title of Part Four, "Special Provisions for Civil Procedure of Cases Involving Foreign Elements", the chapter only deals with foreign related arbitration.

该法第111条第2项规定,依照法律规定,双方当事人对合同纠纷自愿达成书面仲裁协议向仲裁机构申请仲裁、不得向人民法院起诉的,人民法院应当告知原告向仲裁机构申请仲裁。第213条规定,对依法设立的仲裁机构的裁决,一方当事人不履行的,对方当事人可以向有管辖权的人民法院申请执行。受申请的人民法院应当执行。被申请人提出证据证明仲裁裁决有法定情形之一的,即当事人在合同中没有订有仲裁条款或者事后没有达成书面仲裁协议的、裁决的事项不属于仲裁协议的范围或者仲裁机构无权仲裁的、仲裁庭的组成或者仲裁的程序违反法定程序的、认定事实的主要证据不足的、适用法律确有错误的,以及仲裁员在仲裁该案时有贪污受贿、徇私舞弊、枉法裁决行为的,经人民法院组成合议庭审查核实,裁定不予执行。该法第二十七章是专门规范涉外商事仲裁的一章,其中包括对于涉外经济贸易、运输和海事中发生的纠纷当事人可以提交仲裁,涉外仲裁程序中财产保全申请由人民法院裁定,当事人可以申请法院执行涉外仲裁裁决,法院不予执行涉外仲裁裁决的法定情形等内容。第二十八章还对我国仲裁机构裁决在国外的承认和执行,以及国外仲裁机构裁决在我国的承认和执行作了规定。

In April 1991, the NPC adopted the Civil Procedure Law② to replace the 1982 Civil Procedure Law. The Civil Procedure Law confirms the consensual nature of China's foreign-related arbitration and reaffirms that in cases where an arbitration agreement exists no party may institute an action in a People's Court. Court actions are only permitted when the parties have neither included an arbitration clause in their contract nor subsequently reached a written arbitration agreement. The Civil

---

① 2007年修订后的《民事诉讼法》与1991年颁行的《民事诉讼法》在这一部分内容没有变化。
② Adopted at the 4th Session of the 7th NPC and effective from April 9, 1991.

Procedure Law also recognizes the finality of arbitral awards. When a foreign-related arbitral institution renders an arbitral award, the parties are thereafter barred from submitting the same dispute for determination by a People's Court. If one party fails to honor its obligations under such an award, the other party may initiate judicial proceedings for the enforcement of the award. The Civil Procedure Law lays down rules for the enforcement of arbitral awards rendered by China's foreign-related arbitral bodies. The conditions set down for such enforcement empower the People's Court to examine the procedural aspects of the arbitration proceedings from which the arbitral award stems.

3. 有关仲裁的司法解释

在我国的法律体系中,最高人民法院司法解释的作用不容忽视。司法实践中为便于法律的实际操作,最高人民法院往往针对司法实践过程中提出的问题作出司法解释。最高人民法院的司法解释在实践中一般并不公开引用,但却是司法实践中指导各级法院的重要文件。有关仲裁的司法解释,主要是最高人民法院为使《仲裁法》及相关法律能够得到正确实施所作出的规定和解释。

本来最高人民法院的司法解释只对各级人民法院具有约束力,仲裁委员会作为民间机构不受其约束,但由于法院的监督和保障是仲裁的一个基本原则,仲裁环节中不可避免地涉及仲裁裁决的撤销问题、仲裁过程中的财产保全问题、仲裁裁决的承认与执行等问题,这些都需要法院的介入。因此,司法解释对仲裁的影响可以说带有一定的强制性,构成仲裁法律制度的一个重要渊源。①

Following China's accession to the New York Convention, and particularly after the Arbitration Law took effect, the Supreme People's Court issued a great number of judicial interpretations concerning both foreign-related and international arbitration. The content of these numerous interpretations indicates that the Supreme People's Court has interpreted the Arbitration Law in a rather purposeful and flexible manner, attempting to ensure that the development of international arbitration in China follows international norms and standards. These interpretations have been particularly helpful in relation to recognition and enforcement in China of foreign-related and international arbitral awards. In consequence, when handling foreign-related arbitration cases, it is now mandatory for the Intermediate People's Courts to report to and obtain the consent of the Higher People's Court, and, ultimately, the Supreme People's Court for any decision that would revoke a foreign-related award, deny enforcement of a foreign-related award, or would deny recognition and enforcement of

---

① 司法解释作为法律渊源在理论界是存在一定争议的。

an international award.

Each of the foregoing interpretations issued by the Supreme People's Court is aimed at filling much of the vacuum left by the Arbitration Law. For example, the Regulations of the Supreme People's Court Regarding the Recognition by the People's Courts of Civil Judgments Rendered by Relevant Courts of Taiwan Region has made it possible for the People's Courts to recognize and enforce both arbitral awards and civil judgments rendered by Taiwanese Courts. Such decision has served to significantly improve economic cooperation with Taiwan by eliminating the legal uncertainties that previously existed with respect to the mutual enforcement of arbitral awards.

多年来,为了贯彻实施我国参加的有关仲裁的国际公约或条约及《仲裁法》,最高人民法院作出的有关司法解释数量众多,其中比较重要的有:

(1)《关于执行我国加入的〈承认及执行外国仲裁裁决公约〉的通知》

该通知由最高人民法院于1987年4月10日发布实施,共5条,主要内容是就执行该公约的几个问题向各级法院作了通知。这几个问题是:a. 我国在加入该公约时所作的互惠保留声明;b. 我国加入该公约时所作的商事保留声明;c. 有权申请我国法院承认和执行外国仲裁裁决的主体,以及我国有权受理该申请的法院;d. 我国法院对外国仲裁裁决承认及执行的情形和拒绝承认及执行的情形;e. 我国作出的只承认和执行我国加入本公约之后在外国作出的仲裁裁决的声明。

(2)《关于适用〈中华人民共和国民事诉讼法〉若干问题的意见》

该意见由最高人民法院于1992年7月14日发布,主要是就《民事诉讼法》中的有关规定,包括有关商事仲裁的法律规定作了更为具体的解释和规范。该意见涉及商事仲裁的条款为第48条、第145—148条、第156条、第277条、第278条、第305条、第313—317条。

(3)《关于适用〈中华人民共和国仲裁法〉若干问题的解释》

2006年8月23日公布、同年9月8日施行的最高人民法院《关于适用〈中华人民共和国仲裁法〉若干问题的解释》(以下简称《仲裁法解释》)共31条,几乎涉及仲裁法的各个主要方面。该解释整合了我国自《仲裁法》颁布实施以来的仲裁实践,以及以往最高人民法院作出的相关通知、批复、意见等,是《仲裁法》颁布实施以来涉及面最广、内容最全面的关于仲裁法的司法解释。该解释总体上体现出的支持仲裁的特点,不仅使《仲裁法》中的一些原则性规定更加明确化和具体化,增强了《仲裁法》的可操作性,而且突破了一些传统解释的障碍,加大了支持仲裁的力度。《仲裁法解释》无疑已经成为仲裁实践中最重要的法律依据之一。

（4）最高人民法院在实施《仲裁法》过程中作出的其他司法解释

除《仲裁法解释》外，最高人民法院为正确实施《仲裁法》，还发布了一系列的通知、复函、批复。如最高人民法院《关于认真贯彻仲裁法依法执行仲裁裁决的通知》、《关于同时选择两个仲裁机构的仲裁条款效力问题给山东省高级人民法院的函》、《关于涉蒙经济合同未直接约定仲裁条款如何认定案件管辖权给内蒙古自治区高级人民法院的复函》、《关于仅选择仲裁地点而对仲裁机构没有约定的仲裁条款效力问题的函》、《关于实施〈中华人民共和国仲裁法〉几个问题的通知》、《关于人民法院裁定撤销仲裁裁决或驳回当事人申请后当事人能否上诉问题给广西壮族自治区高级人民法院的批复》、《关于审理当事人申请撤销仲裁裁决案件几个具体问题的批复》、《关于确认仲裁协议效力几个问题的批复》、《关于我国仲裁机构作出的仲裁裁决能否部分撤销问题的批复》、《关于内地与香港特别行政区相互执行仲裁裁决的安排》、《关于人民检察院对不撤销仲裁裁决的民事裁定提出抗诉人民法院应否受理问题的批复》、《关于仲裁协议无效是否可以裁定不予执行的处理意见》、《关于内地与澳门相互认可和执行仲裁裁决安排》等。在本书附录中，我们会列举几个较新、较重要的司法解释。

(二) 港澳台立法

1. 我国香港地区的商事仲裁立法

香港法律属普通法系(英美法系)。其法律渊源有普通法、衡平法、条例、附属立法和习惯法。因此，对于香港现行的商事仲裁制度来说，主要由成文法性质的经过多次修改的《香港仲裁条例》(Arbitration Ordinance)和判例法性质的各种商务仲裁判例组成。由于香港还是采用《示范法》(虽然该《示范法》所反映的内容和体例在香港曾被修改)的地区，因此，《示范法》也是其仲裁制度必不可少的组成部分之一。

In addition to the legal system established by Hong Kong domestic law, international treaties form an integral part of Hong Kong arbitration law. The 1958 New York Convention on the Recognition and Enforcement of Foreign Arbitral Awards, to which Hong Kong became a party through the United Kingdom in 1977, is the most important of these international treaties. Under the New York Convention, a party to an arbitration may seek enforcement in Hong Kong courts of an arbitral award rendered in another party country.

香港于1963年7月5日颁布了香港第一部仲裁法——《香港仲裁条例》。该条例从内容到文字几乎完全照搬了英国《1950年仲裁法》。随着1979年英国对仲裁法进行重大修改，香港亦在1982年，以英国《1950年仲裁法》为蓝本，对其仲裁条例进行了大幅度的修改。1982年新的《香港仲裁条例》不再是照搬照抄，它既汲取了英国《1979年仲裁法》的精华，又有许多创新和发展，如增加了调解,适用联合国国际贸易法委员会仲裁程序等。

In many ways, the 1982 Arbitration Ordinance represented the beginning of Hong Kong's movement away from English arbitration practice. In order to make Hong Kong a more attractive venue for international arbitrations, the 1982 Arbitration Ordinance adopted many features desired by the international legal and business communities. One of the changes is the 1982 Arbitration Ordinance abolished the special case procedure. In addition, the 1982 Arbitration Ordinance distinguished domestic arbitrations and international arbitrations and permitted foreign counsel to handle international arbitrations in Hong Kong. The 1982 Arbitration Ordinance also, for the first time, listed conciliation as an alternative means of dispute resolution and permitted a conciliator to continue to serve as an arbitrator if the conciliation failed.

On the other hand, the 1982 Arbitration Ordinance remained the parties with the right to appeal an arbitration award to a court for judicial review and the jurisdiction of the court to determine any question of law arising in an arbitration. The 1982 Arbitration Ordinance, however, permitted parties to waive their right to appeal questions of law to the courts by inserting an exclusion or "vouching out" clause in their arbitration agreements. The provisions of the 1982 Arbitration Ordinance still apply to domestic arbitrations in Hong Kong.

此后,随着经济的发展和实际需要,香港又分别在 1984 年、1985 年、1987 年、1989 年、1990 年和 1996 年对有关条文作了修改和增减。尤其是 1996 年新的《香港仲裁条例》,进行了诸多重要修改,如放宽了对仲裁协议形式的要求、明确给予仲裁员责任豁免、授权仲裁员来判断应由谁承担仲裁费用等等。2000 年 1 月及 6 月,《香港仲裁条例》再次被修订,以适应香港回归之后的新情况。

Among those modifications, it is necessary to specify the 1990 Arbitration Ordinance, which is another substantial modification of Hong Kong arbitration law and further departure from English practice. Following the recommendation of Hong Kong's Law Reform Commission, the 1990 Arbitration Ordinance adopted the United National Commission on International Trade Law Model Law on International Commercial Arbitration ("UNCITRAL Model Law") as applicable law for international arbitrations. For domestic arbitrations, the 1990 Arbitration Ordinance kept the legal system established by earlier statutes. Thus, the 1990 Arbitration Ordinance created separate arbitration regimes for domestic and international arbitrations. However, the two regimes are interchangeable. Parties to a domestic arbitration can agree to follow the UNCITRAL Model Law to settle their dispute, and parties to an international arbitration can elect to follow the domestic arbitration system.

香港商事仲裁制度及立法产生背景特殊,它经历了由单一临时仲裁形式到临时仲裁与常设机构仲裁并存,由判例法到成文法,由本地仲裁到国际仲裁,由本地立法到国际条约的演变过程。这一演变过程是迅速而巨大的。正因为如此,其商事仲裁立法体现出了其独有的特点。这些特点集中表现在以下几个方面:

第一,立法的指导思想和立法技术受到英国法深远的影响,在具体规范上留有英国法明显的印记;

第二,东西方文化交融的特点明显,是一部高度国际化、现代化的仲裁立法;

第三,以高度意思自治及高效率为追求。

2. 我国澳门地区的商事仲裁立法

澳门自16世纪中叶开埠以来,逐渐成长为一个繁荣的商业社会,并一直在东西交流中起着桥梁作用。我国实行改革开放后,澳门在南中国地区经济圈中的重要地位得到进一步加强。如今,澳门与外界商业交往频繁,与内地、香港和台湾乃至世界各国均有广泛的商业联系。在这种背景下,在澳门产生的各种民商事纠纷自然会日益增多。过去,澳门的民商事纠纷除了通过中国传统的民间方式加以解决外,主要通过诉讼解决,尽管在澳门施行的《葡萄牙民事诉讼法典》第四卷中也有仲裁制度的规定,但长期有名无实。如果澳门仍然固守自己的传统,仅依赖司法诉讼途径去解决民商事争议,显然不能满足实际的需要。因此,澳门有必要建立自己的民商事仲裁制度,并设立自己的仲裁机构。

早在1962年,《葡萄牙民事诉讼法典》第四卷关于仲裁制度的规定已经延伸适用于澳门,但是此制度又随着葡萄牙的民事诉讼改革而在1986年被废止。直到1991年8月29日第112-91号法律所通过的《澳门司法组织纲要法》第5条第2款中规定:"得设立仲裁庭,并得设非司法性质之方法及方式,以排除冲突。"

然而,上述规定也仅仅是纲要性质,还不是一套完整的仲裁法律制度。直到1996年,立法会才在《澳门司法组织纲要法》的基础上制定了《仲裁法律制度》(即第29/96/M号法令,于1996年9月15日开始生效),为自愿仲裁的进行创造了必要的法律条件。考虑到以机构形式长期进行仲裁工作,将对当事人利用自愿仲裁解决争议更加有利,澳门政府又于同年7月制定了第40/96/M号法令,从而确立了机构自愿仲裁的法律制度。

澳门的商事仲裁,主要以澳门政府《核准仲裁制度》(1996年6月11日澳门政府法令第29/96/M号颁布)和《涉外商事仲裁专门制度》(1998年11月13日核准,澳门政府法令第55/98/M号颁布)为依据。前者共分3章44条,较为系统地规定了仲裁的标的、适用的法律、仲裁协议的形式、仲裁庭的组成、仲裁员的指定、仲裁员与参与人的报酬、仲裁的程序、裁决及上诉等。后者共9章38条，几乎完全参照了1985年《示范法》，只是为了使仲裁标的及拒绝执行仲裁裁决的依据与《葡萄牙民事诉讼法典》规定一致，而对《示范法》第7条第1款及第36条第1款作了细微的修改。第55/98/M号法令的发布标志着澳门仲裁制度的最终确立。

从整体上审视澳门的仲裁立法，不难看出，它与世界上的许多国家和地区的做法基本一致，因而不失为一个较为成功的糅合中西方法律文化、适应本地实际和国际发展趋势的立法例。概言之，澳门现行仲裁立法有如下特点：

第一，本地仲裁与涉外仲裁分别立法。在澳门，本地仲裁制度由第29/96/M号法令规范，已于1996年建立；涉外仲裁制度由1998年11月公布的第55/98/M号法令规范。澳门法律对于本地仲裁和涉外仲裁有不同的规定，例如，对于仲裁协议的内容及形式的要求，虽然两部法令均要求具备书面形式，但第29/96/M号法令对于仲裁协议的内容有强制性规定：要求单独订立的仲裁协议应明确争议事项，并指定仲裁员，或者指出选定仲裁员的方式；而存在于合同中的仲裁条款应明确可能发生的争议所涉及的法律关系，否则，仲裁协议无效。又如，对于仲裁裁决的撤销、执行程序以及不执行裁决的理由，第29/96/M号法令和第55/98/M号法令也有不同规定。

第二，充分但有限制地尊重当事人的意思自治。当事人意思自治是澳门地区两部仲裁法令的首要原则，在许多条款中都得到了充分的体现。当事人可以通过协议将争议（即使是法院正在审理的争议）提交仲裁解决；当事人可以约定指定仲裁员的程序、仲裁地点和仲裁程序。对于仲裁中的很多事项，法令都规定应当首先遵从当事人的约定，在当事人没有约定时，才可按照法令执行。所谓的"限制"主要体现在第29/96/M号法令中，除规定自愿仲裁外，还规定某些争议实行强制仲裁；对于仲裁庭根据当事人的授权意思所作出的仲裁裁决，任何利害关系人或检察官公署均可随时主张无效，法院也可依职权随时宣告无效。

第三，承认临时仲裁，并以其为主要形式。两部法令均规定仲裁包括临时仲裁和机构仲裁，第55/98/M号法令第2条"定义及解释规则"中甚至更为明确地指出仲裁系指任何仲裁，而不论仲裁是否交给一个常设的仲裁机构进行。然而事实上，除了澳门消费委员会依照第29/96/M号法令所设立的，通过调解及仲裁方式解决在澳门地区发生的、涉及金额不高于澳门币5万元的消费争议的消费争议仲裁中心外，澳门并未成立一个常设的仲裁机构，因而澳门的仲裁主要是以临时仲裁的形式存在。

3. 我国台湾地区的商事仲裁立法

台湾地区现代商事仲裁制度肇始于20世纪60年代。1961年1月20日,台湾地区颁布了"商务仲裁条例"(下称"条例"),但其内容颇为简单,且仲裁的适用以商事争议为限。70年代末以来,随着外向型经济的发展,涉及外国仲裁裁决申请在台执行的案件逐年增加,但"条例"却缺乏此类规范。为适应经济发展的需要,台湾地区分别在1982年6月和1986年12月,对"条例"作了两次修正,增订承认与执行外国仲裁裁决,以及当事人得以书面形式约定仲裁裁决可进行强制执行,无须法院来执行裁定等。同时规定仲裁裁决应在三个月内作出;仲裁裁决经法院撤销后,当事人可以就争议事项提起诉讼;仲裁裁决前的和解与仲裁裁决具有同等效力等。

随着各国仲裁制度的相互借鉴,尤其是《示范法》的制定,大大推动了各国仲裁制度的趋同化进程,"条例"已经落后于时代潮流。此外,有关方面还认为,仲裁对解决两岸经贸争议的作用将不断加强,在大陆已经颁布《仲裁法》的情况下,台湾地区应尽快完成"条例"的第三次修正,以利两岸经贸交流。

Therefore, Taiwan has revised its arbitration law to bring the arbitration system in Taiwan more in line with the international arbitration standard as reflected in the UNCITRAL Model Law on International Commercial Arbitration adopted by United Nations Commission on International Trade Law on June 21, 1985 ("UNCITRAL Model Law"). The revised Taiwanese version, simply called the "Arbitration Law", was passed on May 29, 1998 by the Legislature, and became fully effective on December 24, 1998.

这次"仲裁法"的修正,强调了"国际化与自由化",并加强了对仲裁当事人权益的保障、尊重当事人自治、确保仲裁人与仲裁程序的公正性。与大陆《仲裁法》不同的是,该法不采"国内仲裁"与"涉外仲裁"的二元立法模式,而且把可仲裁事项从商事争议扩大到"民事诉讼法"规定的所有"得为和解"的事项。该法不仅广泛借鉴英、美、德、日等国的仲裁制度,而且注重吸收《示范法》的先进立法经验,其立法思想和具体规范基本符合国际仲裁制度的最新发展趋势,尤其确立了效率优先的基本价值取向,既注重扩大当事人意思自治的范围与程度,又赋予仲裁庭较大的权力,把仲裁机制中权利与权力的平衡推向新的高度,保障并促进了仲裁程序的便捷进行。总体看,1998年台湾"仲裁法"是一项比较成功的立法成果。

纵观此部"仲裁法"的基本内容,主要体现了以下特点:

第一,尊重当事人的意思自治,尊重当事人的权益,同时强调国际化与自由化;

第二,不但广泛吸纳了西方先进商事仲裁制度,同时又借鉴、吸收了《示范

法》中先进的立法理念,从立法指导思想到立法技术和具体规范均与商事仲裁制度的最新发展成果相吻合;

第三,赋予了仲裁庭更大权力,减少法院的干预性监督,同时又强调法院的"协助"功能;

第四,实行任意仲裁制度及机构仲裁与临时仲裁并存,以机构仲裁为主的制度。

第二节 国际立法

随着国际贸易的蓬勃发展,国际商事争议的增多,如何更加便捷有效地解决国际商事争议,引起了国际社会的思考和关注。国际商事仲裁作为解决国际商事争议的一种有效方式,其重要性正日益凸显出来。但是,仲裁制度的国际化并非一蹴而就。

一方面,在国际投资比较发达的国家或地区之间,仲裁条款可见诸各国之间签订的投资协定中。① 这种协定包括双边投资协定(Bilateral Investment Treaties, BITs)和多边投资协定(Multilateral Investment Treaties, MITs),其中许多都包含国家之间的一种约定,即将东道国和另一国投资者之间的争议通过仲裁解决。

另一方面,各国仲裁立法的不统一,促使国际社会通过推动仲裁国际公约的制定和执行进行协调。仲裁重要性的提升促使各国政府纷纷制定或修正本国仲裁法,以求解决逐年增多的国际商事争议。但是由于历史上有的国家已形成自己的仲裁规则,有的大国凭借其在世界贸易中的龙头地位不断扩大本国仲裁规则的影响,由此造成了国际商事仲裁的不统一。为促进国际商事仲裁的协调发展,国际社会做出了种种努力,最有效的方式就是通过全球范围内的普遍性国际公约。国际公约将国内法律制度连接入各种法律构成的网络,对成员国的国内法院执行仲裁协议或仲裁裁决作出了规定。此外,还有许多区域性条约也都对国际商事仲裁的发展产生了影响。

除了上述投资协定和国际公约外,国际商事仲裁的国际立法还包括一系列"软法"。这些软法一般是由一些国际组织起草的,不具有强制性。其中,1985年UNCITRAL制定的《示范法》,对统一国际商事仲裁内国法律及程序规则产生了重要影响。

---

① 由于"投资协定"只起到约定仲裁的作用,并不规范仲裁,因此本节不作进一步介绍。

一、全球性的国际公约

仲裁这种解决争议的方式自产生以来的一个重要趋势就是越来越国际化。正如前文所述,仲裁的国际化并非一蹴而就,在仲裁的国际化过程中最重要的体现和驱动力当属国际公约。国际公约是国际商事仲裁法最为重要的渊源,这些国际公约有一些是旨在统一各国的仲裁立法,另外一些则主要是为了确保仲裁协议及仲裁裁决具有可执行性,其中后者尤为重要。

Unlike bilateral or multilateral agreements, the most important conventions concern exclusively arbitration. We will nevertheless briefly examine those multilateral conventions which may have an incidental impact on arbitration or which contain ancillary provisions concerning arbitration.

协调国际商事仲裁的思想在1923年和1927年的《日内瓦议定书》和《日内瓦公约》中第一次为国际社会所接受。《日内瓦议定书》和《日内瓦公约》得到了国际商会的倡导和推动,因而在国际范围内执行仲裁裁决的思想得到联合国的采纳。1958年的《纽约公约》是二战后制定的国际公约中最有影响力的公约。另外,1965年的《华盛顿公约》建立了解决投资争议国际中心(ICSID)。

(一) 1923年《日内瓦议定书》和1927年《日内瓦公约》(The Geneva Protocol of 1923 and the Geneva Convention of 1927)

虽然这两大公约的内容后来大都为《纽约公约》的规定所取代,但在承认国际商事仲裁对于发展国际贸易的重要性方面,却是标志性的第一步。两个公约都是在国际商会的主持下缔结的,二者具有的特点仍保留于《纽约公约》及以其为基础的其他公约和UNCITRAL制定的《示范法》。

The world's business community established the International Chamber of Commerce (ICC) in 1919. The ICC was directly involved in the promotion and adoption of the Geneva Protocol on Arbitration Clauses of 1923 and the Geneva Convention on the Execution of Foreign Awards of 1927.

1923年《日内瓦议定书》于1923年9月24日通过,于1924年7月28日生效,有33个国家批准或加入了该议定书,除此之外它还适用于一些前殖民地国家和地区。1923年《日内瓦议定书》是关于国际商事仲裁的第一个真正意义上的国际性公约。该公约有两个目的:第一个并且是主要的目的,是确保仲裁条款在国际上是可执行的,这样任何仲裁协议的当事人都须通过仲裁解决争议,而不是通过法院;第二个目的是次要目的,即确保依据此类仲裁条款作出的仲裁裁决在其作出国境内可以执行。

Although the Protocol is brief, containing only four articles covering the validity and effect of arbitration clauses, it nevertheless had a decisive impact on the future of arbitration throughout the world.

The Geneva Protocol of 1923 was limited in its range and effect. It applied only to arbitration agreements made "between parties subject respectively to the jurisdiction of different contracting states"; and it could be further limited by states availing themselves of the "commercial reservation". So far as the enforcement of arbitration awards was concerned, each contracting state agreed to ensure the execution under its own laws of awards made in its own territory pursuant to an arbitration agreement which was covered by the Protocol.

1927年9月26日，又一部关于外国仲裁裁决执行的公约即1927年《日内瓦公约》在日内瓦通过了，该公约生效于1929年7月25日，有27个国家批准或加入，同样也适用于一些前殖民地国家和地区。该公约旨在扩大《日内瓦议定书》的适用范围，规定根据议定书作出的仲裁裁决可在缔约国境内承认与执行，而非仅仅在裁决作出国境内。但是，该公约在适用过程中产生了许多问题，除了其适用范围的局限性之外，依照该公约，寻求执行的当事人需要证明执行所必要的条件，为了表明裁决在其作出国是终局的，胜诉方在执行地法院执行裁决前，常需在仲裁进行地国的法院寻求宣告，表明裁决在该国是可执行的。这就是所谓的"双重标准"(double-exequatur)问题。

However, the Geneva Convention usefully excludes any review of the merits of the award, and some of its terms are presented in the form of substantive rules that constitute universal conditions governing the international validity of awards. These include the parties' right to a fair hearing and the respect of the limits of the arbitrator's brief.

Despite their limitations, the two Geneva Treaties have a well-deserved place in the history of international commercial arbitration as a first step on the road towards international recognition and enforcement of international arbitration agreements and awards. However, after 1958, the Geneva Protocol and Geneva Convention have been almost entirely superseded by the New York Convention.

（二）1958年《纽约公约》(The 1958 New York Convention)

各国仲裁立法的不同，使得在国际范围内承认和执行其他国家作出的仲裁裁决十分不便和困难。为了解决这一问题，1958年6月10日在纽约召开的联合国国际商事仲裁会议上，通过了《纽约公约》，该公约于1959年6月7日生效。《纽约公约》是目前世界范围内缔约国最多的公约之一，也是目前国际社会在商事仲裁方面一个最具普遍性的国际公约。到目前为止，有超过140个国家签署了该公约。① 我国于 1986 年 12 月 2 日第六届全国人大常委会第十八次会议上通过了关于我国加入该项条约的决定,公约自 1987 年 4 月 22 日起对我国生效。

从《纽约公约》的全称可以看出,该公约的内容主要涉及外国仲裁裁决的承认与执行。它主要规定了各缔约国应当承认与执行仲裁协议和依据有效的仲裁协议作出的仲裁裁决,以及拒绝承认与执行外国仲裁裁决的条件。该公约对于统一各缔约国承认与执行外国仲裁裁决的条件,发挥了积极的作用。该公约的成功意义并非在生效之初就表现出来,而是在几十年后逐渐发挥出其重要作用的,原因在于直到 20 世纪七八十年代,包括美国、英国、加拿大、中国等一些重要的国家才对其作出批准决定。

According to the Convention on the Recognition and Enforcement of Foreign Arbitration Awards, as long as there is a written agreement to arbitrate, courts of contracting states are required to enforce that agreement by referring the parties to arbitration, "unless it finds that the said agreement is null and void, inoperative or incapable of being performed." Recognition and enforcement of an arbitration agreement or award may only be refused upon limited grounds.

As to the foreign arbitration awards, the New York Convention identifies five grounds on which recognition and enforcement of a Convention award may be refused at the request of the party against whom it is invoked. If the opposing party can prove: (1) the incapacity of the parties or invalidity of the arbitration agreement; (2) improper notice or other lack of due process; (3) an award beyond the scope of the agreement to arbitrate; (4) improper arbitral procedure or composition of the arbitral board; or (5) that the award has been set aside or suspended or is otherwise not binding, then recognition or enforcement may be refused. In addition, Article V (2) of the Convention provides that recognition or enforcement may be refused if the subject matter of the dispute is not capable of settlement by arbitration under the enforcing state's laws or if recognition or enforcement would be contrary to the public policy of that state.

除了对拒绝承认与执行的理由进行限制外,与 1927 年《日内瓦公约》相比,《纽约公约》的进步还表现在对证明责任的分配上,即如一方提交了仲裁协议和仲裁裁决请求承认与执行,则反对执行的另一方有义务证明裁决不应被执行的理由(见公约第 5 条)。另外,《纽约公约》还有一个重要特征,即承认当事人在组成仲裁庭和确定仲裁程序中的意思自治。

---

① 资料来源:http://www.uncitral.org/uncitral/en/uncitral_texts/arbitration/NYConvention_status.html,2009 年 7 月 10 日访问。

The New York Convention is by far the most important international treaty concerning international commercial arbitration. With over 140 signatory countries, its primary objective is the recognition and enforcement of foreign arbitration awards as between signatory states. The Convention specifies the foresaid very limited grounds on which recognition and enforcement can be refused, in the absence of which the courts of signatory states are required to recognize and enforce the foreign award. However, the implementation of the Convention in each country depends upon effective local implementing legislation.

该公约的成功之处可归结为以下三点:第一,缔约国家非常多。如上文所述,有超过140个国家签署了该公约,这是在国际商事领域得到极为广泛适用的为数不多的公约之一。第二,为了更加准确地解释和适用该公约,许多国家的法院主动了解其他缔约方法院如何适用公约具体条款作出裁决。这样,虽然外国法院的裁决对其本国没有直接的约束力,但是在如何适用公约概括原则上,各国之间却能够产生直接影响,从而推动国际商事仲裁法律与实践的发展,也同时使《纽约公约》不分国界地对当事人、仲裁员以及内国法院产生了影响。第三,承接以上两点,在当今国际商事仲裁界,仲裁协议和裁决已经能够得到大多数国家的承认与执行。支持和鼓励仲裁的态度已在大多数国家开始推广。

值得注意的是,虽然公约概括地要求,在任何外国国家作出的仲裁裁决都应该得到缔约方的承认与执行,但是公约同时又允许缔约方在批准该公约时作出保留,即缔约方可以声明,仅承认和执行在另一缔约方境内作出的仲裁裁决,以及仅承认和执行对缔约方本国法律所认为的"商事"争议作出的裁决。这就是所谓的互惠保留和商事保留。

The first reservation had been made, as of March 31, 1999, by sixty-five of the contracting states. Although it complicates the implementation of the Convention, and despite the fact that its effectiveness is sometimes questionable, it proved impossible to require contracting states to be more open at the time the Convention was adopted. If the influence of the UNCITRAL Model Law continues to grow, and if national legislative reforms continue to relax the conditions governing the international enforcement of arbitral awards, the progress made in the New York Convention will eventually lose its importance.

各国立法中对"商事"的理解和规定是有差异的,这就导致在实践中声明了商事保留的缔约国,可以以本国法律不认为某一外国裁决解决的争议是商事争议为由,拒绝承认与执行该外国裁决。这也是《纽约公约》受到一些学者批评的地方之一。但是我们应该看到,这其实是国际社会为了追求国际商事仲裁的统一与协调而采取的权宜之计,从对整个公约的制定、通过与执行上讲,是利大于弊的,对各国承认与执行外国或者国际仲裁裁决起积极作用。需要指出的是,我国对上述两个事项均声明了保留。

The New York Convention was a substantial improvement upon the Geneva Convention of 1927, since it provided a simple and effective method of obtaining recognition and enforcement of foreign awards. The New York Convention has been described as "the single most important pillar on which the edifice of international arbitration rests" and as a convention which, perhaps could lay claim to be the most effective instance of international legislation in the entire history of commercial law.

《纽约公约》推动了外国仲裁协议和裁决的承认与执行,确立了国际商事仲裁崭新的法律制度。在现代国际商事仲裁形成的过程中,《纽约公约》跨出了极为重要的一步。迄今为止,没有任何其他公约能有同样的效果。

(三) 1965 年《华盛顿公约》(The 1965 Washington Convention)

另外一个比较有影响的国际公约,是 1965 年 3 月 18 日在世界银行的倡导和主持制定下,有关国家在美国华盛顿签署的《解决国家与他国国民之间投资争议的公约》(以下简称《华盛顿公约》)。该公约于 1966 年 10 月 14 日起生效。截至目前,签署该公约的国家已达 156 个,其中 144 个国家已经向解决投资争议的国际中心交存了批准书。① 我国已于 1990 年 2 月 9 日正式签署了该公约,1993 年 1 月 7 日批准了该公约,并于 1993 年 2 月 6 日正式加入该公约。

In the late 1950s and 1960s many of the former colonial countries achieved their independence and were looking to take over ownership and control of major concessions owned by foreign companies. Therefore, upon the promotion of the World Bank, the Washington Convention on the Settlement of Investment Disputes between States and Nations of other States was signed on March 18, 1965 and came into effect on October 14, 1966. It created an institutional arbitration mechanism specially adapted to foreign investment disputes: the International Center for Settlement Investment Disputes (ICSID).

以此公约为基础,建立的解决投资争议的国际中心仲裁体制专门负责解决一国与他国国民之间的投资争议。《华盛顿公约》并非一个专门针对国际商事仲裁的国际公约,事实上,它仅仅是一个为了以法律方式解决私人国际投资者与东道国之间发生的投资争议而制定的国际公约。然而,该公约所详细规定的解决争议方式之一的仲裁制度属于国际商事仲裁的类型之一,即专门规范私人国际投资者与东道国之间的商事争议的仲裁制度。这种在某一国际公约中涉及国

---

① 资料来源:http://icsid.worldbank.org/ICSID/FrontServlet? requestType = CasesRH&actionVal = ShowHome&pageName = Memberstates_Home,2009 年 10 月 27 日访问。

际商事仲裁制度的立法形式,是国际商事仲裁立法向纵深发展的表现,是国际商事仲裁制度进一步细化、分工化和专业化的反映,是国际商事仲裁体系进一步成熟和完善的例证。

The popularity of ICSID arbitration has grown since its inception in 1966. There are presently 144 contracting states to the ICSID Convention, with another twelve states as signatories. Additionally, advance consents to submit investment disputes to ICSID arbitration are found in about twenty national investment laws, in over 900 BITs, and under four recent multilateral trade and investment treaties: the North American Free Trade Agreement, the Energy Charter Treaty, the Cartagena Free Trade Agreement and the Colonia Investment Protocol of Mercosur.

Obviously, Arbitration minimizes direct hostility between the parties that is inherent in a more adversarial judicial process. Moreover, all ICSID Contracting States, whether parties to the dispute or not, are required by the Convention to recognize and enforce any ICSID arbitral awards "as if it were a final judgment of the courts" of that state (Art. 54 (1)). The recognition of an award is the formal confirmation by the State that the award is authentic and has full legal effect.

在中国与上百个国家签订的双边投资协定(BITs)中,一般都规定案件的责任部分由中国法院管辖,只是在确定责任后才把赔偿金额的高低交给 ICSID 仲裁。但是,自 2005 年下半年以来,这一情况有了变化。在与荷兰及德国的 BITs 中,中国同意所有投资争议都提交给 ICSID 仲裁。另外,BITs 中常有涉及最惠国待遇与国民待遇的条文,如英国与埃及 BITs 的条文中规定:"Neither Contracting Party shall in its territory subject investments or returns of investors of the other Contracting Party to treatment less favorable than that which it accords to investment or returns of its own nationals or companies or to investments or returns of nationals or companies of any third State."这表示中国今后再也不能在其他 BITs 中坚持责任问题由中国法院先审理,而是应该全部交给 ICSID 仲裁。

二、区域性国际公约

区域性的国际公约有很多,其中,1889 年在乌拉圭首都蒙得维的亚举行的统一拉美各国冲突法会议上所签署的《关于国际民事诉讼程序法的公约》是涉及仲裁的第一个区域性国际公约。此外,区域性国际公约还包括 1961 年通过的《关于国际商事仲裁的欧洲公约》、1966 年签订的《统一仲裁法的欧洲公约》(European Convention Providing a Uniform Law on Arbitration)、1975 年签订的《美洲国家间关于国际商事仲裁的公约》、1979 年签订的《美洲国家间关于外国判决和仲裁裁决域外效力的公约》(即《蒙得维的亚公约》),以及 1987 年签订的《阿曼阿拉伯国家商事仲裁公约》等。

There are a number of regional conventions on international arbitration, many of which were established after the introduction of the New York Convention. However, only certain of these regional conventions have made significant progress when compared to that achieved by the New York Convention. As follows, we choose some of them to give you a bird's-eye view of them.

(一) 1961 年《关于国际商事仲裁的欧洲公约》(The European Convention on International Commercial Arbitration)

1961 年《关于国际商事仲裁的欧洲公约》(以下简称《欧洲公约》)由联合国欧洲经济委员会主持制定,于 1961 年 4 月 21 日由欧洲各国在日内瓦签署,1964 年 1 月 7 日生效,西欧某些国家如英国、荷兰没有参加该公约。该公约的目的在于补充 1958 年《纽约公约》,尽可能排除欧洲各国的自然人或法人相互之间在有关国际商事仲裁的组织工作中的困难,特别是在临时仲裁的情况下仲裁程序规则的问题,以期推动欧洲贸易的发展。该公约仅在当事人居住于缔约国时对其适用。

The European Convention is one of the few regional conventions to have sought to go further than the New York Convention, and to have succeeded in doing so. Its proponents recognized that international commercial arbitration was obstructed, in the stages prior to enforcement of the award, in a number of ways. They provided original solutions to those problems, often based on specific substantive rules and underling the independence of international arbitration from national laws.

Commentators of the European Convention are unanimous in the view that it has made an important contribution to the development of international commercial arbitration law, through both its method and its content. As far as its method is concerned, the European Convention was the first international instrument to treat international commercial arbitration as a whole, and consequently to provide it with rules directly governing all of its various stages. The content of the Convention is quite varied, and its empiricism and novelty are striking. However, it does focus on arbitration in European, and above all on East-West arbitration.

The European Convention applies to international arbitrations to settle trade disputes between parties from different states, whether European or not. However, the European Convention of 1961 failed to meet its objectives. First, its approach was theoretical rather than practical. More importantly, it did not deal with the recognition and enforcement of awards. This is left to other conventions such as the New York Convention to which the European Convention may fairly be seen as a supplement.

In fact, there is another European Convention with its full name as the European Convention Providing a Uniform Law on Arbitration. It was developed through the Council of Europe and signed on January 20, 1966. This convention was aimed at providing a uniform national and international arbitration law. It was signed by Austria and Belgium and ratified only by the latter. It has never come into force.

(二) 1975年《美洲国家间关于国际商事仲裁的公约》(Inter-American Convention on International Commercial Arbitration)

1975年1月30日在巴拿马召开的国际私法特别会议上通过了《美洲国家间关于国际商事仲裁的公约》(以下简称《巴拿马公约》),该公约于1976年6月16日生效,它是由美洲国家组织主持制定的拉美国家的区域性商事仲裁公约。该公约有两点值得注意:一是没有规定仲裁协议的强制执行;二是规定如果当事人未能就仲裁程序规则达成一致,则适用美洲国家间商事仲裁协会适用的程序规则。

The Inter-American Convention on International Commercial Arbitration (or "*Panama Convention*") is based on the New York Convention and is primarily concerned with the recognition and enforcement of arbitration agreements and awards but it is territorially restricted to the area of America. It opens new avenues for enforcement of foreign arbitral awards in a number of Latin American countries that have not ratified the New York Convention.

Within that regional context, the Convention makes significant progress as compared to the 1958 Convention, adding substantive rules concerning the organization of the arbitration (Arts. 2 and 3), in the same way as the 1961 European Convention. The substantive rules are simpler and less radical than those in the European Convention. The Panama Convention is thus both innovative and of some importance, and its application by the courts of signatory states is now the subject of regular commentary.

由于《巴拿马公约》只适用于通过仲裁解决各缔约国相互之间有关商业交易中发生的商事争议,为了保证该组织成员国作出的所有仲裁裁决的域外效力,1979年5月8日美洲国家组织各成员国在蒙得维的亚又签订了《美洲国家间关于外国判决和仲裁裁决域外效力的公约》,并将其适用范围扩大到所有未被1975年《巴拿马公约》包括在内的争议事项的仲裁裁决。

(三) 1991年《南方共同市场国际商事仲裁公约》(Mercosur Agreement)

The Mercosur Agreement on International Commercial Arbitration of 1998 was created by the Treaty of Asuncion in March 1991. The Mercosur Agreement was singed on July 27, 1998 but only Argentina has ratified it as of 2002. The Agreement is a complete code of arbitration the object of which is "the regulation of arbitration as an alternative private means for the solution of disputes arising from international commercial contracts between natural or legal persons of private law." It covers situations where there is an arbitration agreement made by entities located or domiciled in more than one member state or if there is a contract with an objective connection, whether legal or economic, with a Mercosur state.①

(四) 1987 年《阿曼阿拉伯国家商事仲裁公约》(Amman Arab Convention)

1987 年 4 月 14 日,由 14 个阿拉伯国家在约旦首都阿曼签署了《阿曼阿拉伯国家商事仲裁公约》。该公约的目的在于建立统一的阿拉伯国家商事仲裁规则。根据该公约,在摩洛哥的拉巴特成立了常设的阿拉伯商事仲裁中心。

The Center will handle a dispute if an arbitration clause or submission agreement refers disputes to it. The only applicable objective condition is that one of the parties must be a subject of a country bound by the Convention. The Convention governs the constitution of the arbitral tribunal and the arbitral procedure, and it stipulates that the only available means of setting aside an award is by an action before the Center itself. Enforcement of the award in member states is a matter for the Supreme Court of each state, which may only refuse enforcement on the ground that public policy has been violated.

三、1985 年《示范法》

"示范法",顾名思义,是为各国立法提供借鉴意义的软法,它不同于国际条约,并非经由若干国家制定、加入和批准而形成,而是由国际组织或有关专家制定的、供各有关国家的立法机关在制定本国法律时单方面采纳的非强制性的规范性文件。各国在采用示范法时,一般可以根据本国的具体情况对其进行修订和补充。又由于示范法一般均由国际组织起草,同时得到世界上众多国家的参考和借鉴,因而理应属于国际立法范畴。于是,在本节中,我们在国际公约外单列示范法,以示其特殊性和重要性。

在国际商事仲裁领域,由 UNCITRAL 主持制定的 1985 年《示范法》(UNCITRAL Model Law on International Commercial Arbitration)具有重要意义。《示范法》于 1985 年 6 月 21 日由 UNCITRAL 在维也纳召开的第 18 届会议上通过。制定《示范法》,是为了进一步协调世界各国规范国际商事仲裁的国内立

---

① See Julian D. M. Lew, Loukas S. Mistelis and Stefan M. Kroll, Comparative International Commercial Arbitration, Kluwer Law International, 2003, p.24.

法,进一步统一世界各国有关国际商事仲裁的程序,并使国际社会的商事仲裁不再集中于伦敦、巴黎等几个有限的城市,为各国制定和修改其本国的仲裁立法提供一个统一的范本。2006 年 7 月 7 日,UNCITRAL 第 39 届会议通过了对 1985 年《示范法》的修订。

The modern legislative trend in international arbitration law is embodied in the Model Law on International Commercial Arbitration. The Model Law was drafted under the auspices of the United Nations with the intention that if enacted by member States, the law would contribute to the harmonization and modernization of national laws on international commercial arbitration. The Model Law covers virtually all aspects of arbitration. Drafted by arbitration experts and representatives from various countries and international agencies, it has been described as the "most remarkable development and influential accomplishment in the field of commercial arbitration in the eighties."

与公约或条约相比,《示范法》虽然不具备严格意义上的法律效力,但是对于国际商事仲裁体系的建立和完善具有重要意义。《示范法》的出现对世界上很多国家的仲裁立法产生了深刻影响,目前很多国家已经参照《示范法》修订了本国的仲裁立法和仲裁规则。加拿大、新加坡等多国根据《示范法》制定了符合世界潮流的国内仲裁法,无形中使国际商事仲裁制度趋向统一,弥补了因各国法律制度迥异所造成的国际仲裁实践中的障碍,提升了以仲裁制度解决国际贸易纠纷的效率。

The authors of the Model Law paid due regard to the fact that its text ought to be edited in such a way as to conform to the provisions of the New York Convention on Recognition and Execution of Foreign Arbitral Awards of 1958, the European Convention on International Commercial Arbitration of 1961 and the UNCITRAL Arbitration Rules of 1976.

As opposed to multilateral international conventions and uniform laws, the Model Law offers its potential users texts, whose adoption and enforcement depends on a unilaterally expressed will of the national legislators who, in their respective statutes, may emulate the patterns offered in the Model Law. They can, at their own discretion, adopt these texts integrally or partially, or they may significantly modify them, on the basis of an evaluation of their specific position in the international community and according to the interests they attempt to protect.

《示范法》在世界范围内为各个国家及地区提供了一个现代仲裁立法的范本,得到了大多数国家及地区的认可。加拿大是世界上第一个采纳《示范法》的国家。除加拿大外,还有澳大利亚、保加利亚、塞浦路斯、中国香港、尼日利亚、马来西亚、新加坡、俄罗斯等国家和地区,或者完全采纳了《示范法》,或者稍加修改后采用。在一国境内的很多州、省也采用了《示范法》,如美国的加利福尼亚州、康涅狄格州、俄勒冈州和得克萨斯州,英国的苏格兰等。① 埃及、芬兰、匈牙利、爱尔兰、肯尼亚、新西兰、秘鲁等国也在积极考虑采用《示范法》。此外,在1986年以后颁布的仲裁法,如1986年荷兰《仲裁法》,都或多或少地受《示范法》的影响。日本于2004年3月1日起生效的《仲裁法》就是以《示范法》的国际商事仲裁内容为基础,对旧《仲裁法》进行修改,其实体和形式均仿照《示范法》,所依据的基本原则也十分接近。我国在1991年修订《民事诉讼法》和1994年颁布《仲裁法》时,也都参考了《示范法》。可以预见,在不久的将来,会有更多的国家依据《示范法》进行仲裁立法或对已有的仲裁法进行审查修改。

Today, forty-seven individual jurisdictions from all parts of the world have adopted the Model Law. Some countries have adopted the Model Law as both their domestic arbitration law and their international arbitration law, while others prefer two separate regimes of law. Even in those nations that decided not to adopt the Model Law, consideration of the UNCITRAL approach has influenced the shape and contents of the non-uniform legislation that was enacted, as evidenced by the English Arbitration Act of 1996.

《示范法》的特点集中体现在两个方面:

第一,给当事人的意思自治以法律效力,限制内国法院的作用,以实现国际商事仲裁的自由化。《示范法》在以下几个方面给予当事人意思自治的权利:仲裁庭的人数、仲裁员的国籍、指定仲裁员的程序、仲裁庭进行仲裁的程序、仲裁地点、仲裁使用的语言以及适用于争议的实体规则。另外,根据《示范法》,当事人可以协商确定仲裁规则,并可以在现有某一仲裁规则允许的情况下,对之加以修改、补充,以满足案件的特定需要。

第二,通过仲裁制度的非本土化趋势,促进仲裁的国际化。非本土化趋势在《示范法》中表现在以下几个方面:首先,在当事人没有就仲裁的有关事项达成协议时,仲裁庭可以适用补充规则或者由仲裁员自由裁量。其次,通过当事人意思自治原则摆脱了传统的本地程序法干预。最后,非本土化还表现在对法院干预的限制上。②

The Model Law is particularly significant because it embodies those principles of arbitration law that worldwide experts believed were the core elements of the law of arbitration. The Model Law establishes the basic substantive rules for regulating

---

① 而在欧洲,至今只有苏格兰在立法中采用了《示范法》。
② 《示范法》第5条规定:"由本法管辖的事情,任何法院均不得干预,除非本法另有规定。"

arbitration.

In addition, the Model Law has fulfilled its objective in an increasing number of national jurisdictions. It was designed to provide States with a highly advanced statutory framework of arbitration law—in effect, to make it possible, especially for developing States, to become instantly supportive of arbitration and thereby able to participate in trans-border commerce. It is an architecture of law that transcends national and regional differences and codifies a truly global approach to international commercial dispute resolution. While the system is not without its flaws and idiosyncracies, and even has some noticeable disabilities, it nevertheless has significantly advanced international uniformity and unity in matters of arbitration.

UNCITRAL《示范法》通过"示范法"的这一形式开创了仲裁法国际统一的现实途径,为国际社会和多法域国家实现仲裁法律的统一提供了有益的经验。另外,《示范法》还规定了国际仲裁与国内仲裁相比应受到较少的限制,确保机构仲裁和临时仲裁都能发挥作用等,这些都体现了国际商事仲裁的发展趋势,对各国仲裁立法有较大的指导作用。

第三节　仲　裁　规　则

仲裁机构和有关的仲裁当事人以及仲裁活动的其他参与人,在进行具体的仲裁活动时,除了遵守特定的仲裁法外,还必须遵循一定的规范和准则,以保证仲裁程序的有序进行,这就是所谓的仲裁规则。

In spite of the abundance of public sources of international commercial arbitration law, international companies, professional organizations and their lawyers need other rules to supplement national or international laws or to exclude aspects of those laws which they consider to be inappropriate. To achieve the resolution of their disputes in a manner adapted to their needs, they opt for international arbitration. Naturally, they want to be able to determine the rules governing that arbitration as freely as possible.

仲裁规则又可称为仲裁程序规则,它为具体的仲裁活动提供了行为准则和程序指引,直接制约着仲裁活动的进行,无论是仲裁机构、仲裁庭,还是仲裁员、仲裁当事人,都必须遵照仲裁规则行事,否则会影响到仲裁裁决的效力。同时,仲裁规则得当与否,对仲裁效率的提高至关重要,是外界衡量仲裁机构影响力的一个重要标志。因此,在实践中,仲裁机构、仲裁员和当事人以及相关的法院都十分重视仲裁规则的作用。

The somewhat ambiguous expression "arbitration rules" denotes a series of provisions intended to govern arbitral procedure and drafted by an arbitral institution or other organization. Arbitration rules are known as a private source of international arbitration because their binding nature is not derived from the acts of one or more public authorities. Of course, we must go beyond this initial, negative definition and establish the legal value of these instruments and their role in the creation and development of international arbitration law.

在介绍具体仲裁规则之前,有必要对仲裁规则和仲裁法这两个概念作一下区分和比较。

一、仲裁规则与仲裁法的关系

仲裁规则和仲裁法是规范和约束国际商事仲裁活动的两种主要表现形式。在理论和实践中,这两者是既有着非常密切的联系,又有着本质区别的两个概念、两种制度和两种程序规则。

两者之所以有着密切联系,是因为一般来说,仲裁法都是制定仲裁规则的依据,仲裁规则是其所依据的仲裁法的细化。同时,对于当事人在仲裁规则中没有明确约定的事项,仲裁法又能自动起到补充作用。仲裁规则和仲裁法都是仲裁程序中的各有关仲裁当事人、仲裁机构、仲裁庭进行商事仲裁活动的行为规范。在某一具体的商事仲裁活动中,各有关方面既不能违反仲裁规则的规定,更不能违反有关国家的仲裁法的规定。

然而,仲裁规则和仲裁法两者也存在着明显的区别,主要表现在如下几个方面:

1. 制定主体不同。仲裁规则是由各种仲裁机构、各类民间团体或组织制定的,或由仲裁当事人合意确定,或者由仲裁庭决定的(因而属于 private source 的范畴);仲裁法则是世界各国通过国内立法或国际立法的方式,单独或者集体制定的(属于 public source 的范畴)。

2. 内容范围不同。仲裁规则主要规范仲裁的内部运作过程,即主要约束和支配仲裁庭的具体仲裁活动,包括仲裁申请的提出、仲裁员的指定、仲裁庭的组成、答辩的方式、仲裁的审理、仲裁裁决的作出以及裁决的效力等内容;而仲裁法则具有更为广泛的内容,它除了调整仲裁庭的内部运作程序外,还规范和确定与仲裁活动有关的外部运作程序的内容。例如,法院对于仲裁协议的效力认定和强制执行、法院强制证人作证和协助采取保全措施、仲裁地国法院撤销仲裁裁决以及相关法院对于仲裁裁决的承认和执行问题等。

3. 性质不同。仲裁规则不是法律,只有在当事人合意选择或确定该仲裁规则后,才对特定的仲裁当事人具有约束力,因此契约性是仲裁规则的本质特征。仲裁规则是当事人之间对于仲裁活动如何进行的一种共同意思表示,但一经确定,即对当事人、仲裁机构及仲裁员产生约束力,甚至法院也必须尊重合乎法律规定的仲裁规则。而仲裁法,其本身包括任意性规则和强制性规则两类,对于任意性规则当事人可以选择排除适用,而对于强制性规则仲裁当事人则必须适用。

4. 效力不同。虽然仲裁规则和仲裁法都是规范仲裁活动的规则,但是两者的效力存在较大差别。仲裁规则的效力只及于相关的仲裁机构、仲裁员、当事人以及其他仲裁参与人;而仲裁法却具有普遍性的法律效力。仲裁规则一般是根据该国仲裁法的内容和原则制定的,并且当事人依据仲裁规则所进行的仲裁活动不得违反或规避仲裁地国的仲裁法,否则会导致仲裁裁决被撤销,或者无法被承认或执行。例如,1976年《联合国国际贸易法委员会仲裁规则》第1条第2款规定,仲裁应受本规则支配,但是本规则的任何规定,如与双方当事人必须遵守的适用于仲裁的法律规定相抵触时,应服从该法律的规定。

5. 在司法程序中的作用不同。仲裁规则只是法院干预商事仲裁时需要考虑的因素,即主要是依据仲裁规则的执行情况来对仲裁程序进行监督;而仲裁法则是管辖法院干预商事仲裁的依据。

二、主要仲裁规则介绍

由于程序问题直接影响到实体问题,为确保仲裁程序的顺利进行,防止产生分歧,当事人在订立仲裁协议时,一般应明确规定有关仲裁所应适用的仲裁规则。在仲裁协议没有选定仲裁规则的情况下,选择仲裁规则的一般原则是:将争议提交某一常设仲裁机构解决就意味着适用该仲裁机构的仲裁规则。但有一些仲裁机构,除适用自己的仲裁规则外,还允许当事人选择其他仲裁规则。在这一部分,我们将主要介绍国际上一些主要的仲裁规则。

The organizations which draft and publish arbitration rules are mainly arbitral institutions. Therefore, institutional arbitration plays a dominant role in international arbitral practice. Given that ad hoc arbitration inevitably remains confidential, a statistical assessment of the respective importance of these two forms of arbitration is impossible. However, it is apparent that over the past twenty years, the well-established arbitral institutions have witnessed a significant growth in their activity, and a number of newly established arbitral institutions have opened for business. It is true that many of the new institutions have yet to have a substantial impact on the international commercial arbitration market, and also many may never do so.

随着国际商事仲裁的发展越来越迅速,1958年联合国通过了《纽约公约》,1961年欧洲一些国家签订了《关于国际商事仲裁的欧洲公约》,然而,这两个国际公约在仲裁程序方面并没有给予足够的重视。

The earliest arbitration rules contained in optional instruments of the United

Nations were drafted by two United Nations regional economic commissions. The first of these were the Arbitration Rules of the United Nations Economic Commission for Europe, adopted in 1963, together with an annex containing a List of Chambers of Commerce and other institutions. These Rules were officially published in 1966. The second set of rules was that prepared by the United Nations Economic Commission for Asia and the Far East, through its Centre for Commercial Arbitration, also published in 1966.

Of far more importance, however, are the Arbitration Rules produced by the United Nations Commission on International Trade Law (UNCITRAL).

（一）1976 年《联合国国际贸易法委员会仲裁规则》(UNCITRAL Arbitration Rules)

在众多国际商事仲裁规则中,最为著名、最有影响的无疑是 1976 年《联合国国际贸易法委员会仲裁规则》[①]。联合国国际贸易法委员会 1968 年成立后不久便开始进行委员会仲裁规则的起草工作,八年后即 1976 年 4 月 28 日,仲裁规则制定完成,并于同年 12 月 15 日在第 31 届联合国大会上正式通过,然后推荐各国采用。

《联合国国际贸易法委员会仲裁规则》充分考虑到了工业发达国家和发展中国家企业之间的关系,被广泛应用于临时仲裁,并且世界上许多常设仲裁机构也都采用了这一规则,或在适用时仅作少量的修改,如瑞典斯德哥尔摩商会仲裁院、中国香港国际仲裁中心、美国仲裁协会、美洲国家商事仲裁委员会等,都允许当事人选择这一规则。该规则甚至对各国国内仲裁立法产生了很大影响。

The UNCITRAL Arbitration Rules were prepared in consultation with lawyers from many countries and were published in final form in 1976. The key points to remember about these rules are the following:

(a) They were designed for use in ad hoc arbitrations (i.e. those arbitrations in which the parties devise their own procedures in which the parties have agreed to conduct their arbitration under the aegis, and in accordance with the arbitration rules, of an institution such as the ICC or the LCIA). However, some institutions such as the LCIA and the AAA are prepared to administer arbitrations which are conducted in accordance with the UNCITRAL Arbitration Rules, rather than their own rules, if the parties so agree.

(b) They provide a framework for an arbitration which ensures that those matters which must be dealt with in any ad hoc arbitration agreement are dealt with.

---

① 至于该仲裁规则的具体内容,此处不详述,在本书附录中,附有该仲裁规则全文。

Nevertheless they leave the parties with considerable flexibility as to how the proceedings are to be conducted.

(c) Because they were prepared in consultation with lawyers from many different backgrounds, they should prove acceptable to any bona fide party contemplating ad hoc arbitration, no matter what the legal background of that party is.

在该仲裁规则中,有两方面内容特别值得注意:

(a) If the parties fail to agree upon how the arbitrator is to be appointed, or how challenges to him are to be dealt with, the Rules provide that one of the parties must request the Secretary-General of the Permanent Court of Arbitration at the Hague to designate an appointing authority (Articles 6(2) and 12(1) respectively). This could lead to some delay in getting the proceedings going. The problem can be avoided if the parties agree at the outset on an appointing authority.

(b) When there are three arbitrators, the award must be made by a majority (Article 31(1)). This differs from the position under the ICC and LCIA rules which gives the chairman of the tribunal the power to make the award on his own if there is disagreement between all three arbitrators. The UNCITRAL Arbitration Rules can result in delay whilst the chairman negotiates agreement with the arbitrator whose views most closely approximate to his own.

The Rules may be modified by agreement between the parties, thus providing the parties with an opportunity to avoid these potential problems.

(二) 仲裁机构仲裁规则

除了《联合国国际贸易法委员会仲裁规则》外,众多处理国际商事争议的常设仲裁机构通常都制定有自己的仲裁规则。例如,国际商会(ICC)仲裁院、瑞典斯德哥尔摩商会仲裁院、伦敦国际仲裁院、阿拉伯国家仲裁中心、日本东京海事仲裁委员会、中国国际经济贸易仲裁委员会和中国海事仲裁委员会、美国仲裁协会以及解决投资争议国际中心等。

An institutional arbitration is one entrusted to a major arbitration institution. The best known of these institutions include the International Chamber of Commerce, the London Court of International Arbitration, and the American Arbitration Association. It is important to note that these are not the only arbitral institutions. Each of these arbitral institutions, as well as the others, has enacted one set or sets of procedural rules that apply where parties have agreed to arbitration pursuant to such rules.

Institutional arbitration plays a main role in international arbitral practice. There are more than one hundred institutions which are truly active in the field of international arbitration, and each has their own sets of arbitration rules with distinctive feature. Hence, we will not try to describe the content of the various institutional rules here, some of which will be covered in the annexes of this book, particularly by the most important institutions, such as the ICC, the LCIA and the AAA. What we do here is to outline some of the most influential institutions and their rules.

1. 国际商会仲裁院1998年《国际商会仲裁规则》(ICC)

国际商会仲裁院1932年成立,总部设在巴黎,是国际商会下设的具有国际性的仲裁机构。① 国际商会仲裁院本身不直接受理仲裁案件。具体的仲裁案件由商会在各国聘任的仲裁员受理。国际商会仲裁院的主要任务是:(1)保证仲裁院所制定的仲裁规则和调解规则的适用;(2)指定仲裁员或确认当事人所指定的仲裁员;(3)决定对仲裁员的异议是否成立;(4)批准仲裁裁决的形式。

The International Chamber of Commerce (ICC) is the world's leading arbitral institution. The ICC's International Court of Arbitration (the Court), established in 1923, currently boasts membership from over eighty nations. The ICC remains a pioneer in the development of international arbitration and its Rules of Conciliation and Arbitration (ICC Rules) are used extensively. Since its inception, the Court has handled more than 13,000 cases, and in 2003 about 580 new matters involving 123 jurisdictions were filed with the Court.

国际商会仲裁院现行的仲裁规则即《国际商会仲裁规则》,于1998年1月1日生效。这套规则言简意赅,注重普适性。

The ICC Arbitration Rules have been revised on several occasions, and the most recent reform is one of the most important. The revision process began in 1995 and involved two years of discussion within the ICC's International Arbitration Committee. The new rules were adopted in April 1997 by the ICC Council and entered into force on January 1, 1998. The ICC International Court of Arbitration will apply the new rules to all arbitrations beginning on or after that date unless otherwise agreed by the parties.

The ICC Rules are the result of very extensive experience of international arbitration. They are therefore particularly representative of the private sources of international arbitration law and have had considerable influence on the rules and practice of other institutions. They are known as the flexibility of their procedural provisions, for the powers conferred on the parties, the arbitrators and the Court itself, and for their complete independence, since 1975, from the procedural law of

---

① 我国现已成为国际商会仲裁院成员。

the set of arbitration.

依据该规则,当事人约定将争议提交该院仲裁时,可以通过其所属国的国际商会国家委员会或直接向该院秘书处提交仲裁申请书。当事人可约定选择1名仲裁员进行独任仲裁,也可以约定选择3名仲裁员组成仲裁庭进行仲裁。如果约定实行独任仲裁时,双方当事人可以协商提名仲裁员并经仲裁院确认。如果在申请人的仲裁申请书通知另一方当事人之日起30日内,或在秘书处许可的延长期内,当事人未就独任仲裁员的提名达成协议,则由仲裁院委任。如果约定由3名仲裁员组成仲裁庭进行仲裁,当事人应分别在其申请书和答辩书中各提名1名仲裁员报仲裁院确认。如果其中有一方当事人未委任仲裁员,也可由仲裁院代为委任。第三名仲裁员原则上由仲裁院委任,并担任首席仲裁员,除非当事人另有约定,但此第三名仲裁员亦应报仲裁院确认。仲裁院委任的独任仲裁员或首席仲裁员,原则上应由不具有当事人国籍的人士担任。仲裁庭一经组成且秘书处收到该阶段需要缴纳的费用后,案卷将尽快移交仲裁庭。仲裁员在着手处理案件前,应根据当事人提交的文件或双方当事人到场表示的意见,拟定一项被称为"审理范围书"的文件,以说明当事人名称和基本情况、当事人的请求及争议要点、待决问题清单、仲裁员姓名和基本情况、仲裁地点、仲裁应适用的程序规则等等,由当事人及仲裁庭签署后送交仲裁院,如一方当事人拒绝参与拟定或签署审理范围书,则审理范围书须提交仲裁院批准。审理范围书经签署或批准后,仲裁将继续进行,仲裁庭应在对审理范围书签名(或仲裁院批准)之日起6个月内作出裁决。仲裁庭在签署裁决前,应将裁决稿提交仲裁院核阅,以便就裁决的形式问题提出修改,并在不影响仲裁庭自主决定权的情况下,亦可建议仲裁庭注意裁决中的某些实体问题。在裁决书经仲裁院批准前,仲裁庭不得作出裁决。凡裁决书对当事人均有拘束力。

Pursuant to the ICC Rules, the ICC is involved extensively in the administration of individual arbitrations. This role includes, but is not limited to, the following: (1) determining whether there is a prima facie agreement to arbitrate, (2) deciding on the number of arbitrators, (3) appointing arbitrators in the event one party defaults or the parties cannot agree, (4) deciding challenges against arbitrators, (5) ensuring that arbitrators are conducting the arbitration in accordance with the ICC Rules and replacing the arbitrators if necessary, (6) determining the place of arbitration, (7) fixing and extending time-limits, (8) determining the fees and expenses of the arbitrators, (9) setting and collecting payments on account of costs, (10) reviewing the "Terms of Reference" which define the issues to be arbitrated, and (11) scrutinizing arbitral awards.

2. 英国伦敦国际仲裁院1998年《伦敦国际仲裁院仲裁规则》

英国仲裁历史悠久,但其仲裁制度于1697年才正式被英国国会承认。1892年11月23日,伦敦仲裁会(London Chamber of Arbitration,LCA)正式成立,1903年4月2日改名为伦敦仲裁院(London Court of Arbitration)。该仲裁院于1981年开始改用现名伦敦国际仲裁院(London Court of International Arbitration,LCIA)。

伦敦国际仲裁院是目前英国最主要的国际商事仲裁机构。该仲裁院于1981年制定了《伦敦国际仲裁院仲裁规则》。仲裁院的裁决是终局裁决,但当事人可以根据英国《1979年仲裁法》的规定,请求法院对仲裁中的法律问题作出裁定。为此,当事人还可以通过排除协议的方式,排除法院对仲裁中法律问题的裁定或审查。

Founded in 1892, the London Court of International Arbitration (LCIA) is an important player in international commercial arbitration. It is mainly viewed as an English institution, despite its efforts to revamp this image. The LCIA administers a set of arbitration rules, the London Court of International Arbitration Rules (LCIA Rules), which were extensively revised in 1998. In contrast with the ICC Rules, the LCIA Rules do not contain Terms of Reference procedure and do not provide for review of arbitral awards. The LCIA is not as involved in the arbitration process as the ICC. Nevertheless, the LCIA does have the power to order discovery and security for legal costs.

过去,英国法院对仲裁干预较多。《1979年仲裁法》对法院的干预进行了限制,当事人可以通过签订协议排除法院对仲裁案件的法律问题以及裁决的审查。但仲裁仍受到法院的较多影响,如法院有权更换因行为失当或未以应有的速度进行仲裁和作出裁决的仲裁员,并有权撤销仲裁协议等。因此,这个老牌的仲裁机构曾走下坡路,每年受案数量由以前的世界第一位逐步下滑。为改变这一局面,加强伦敦作为国际仲裁中心的地位,英国颁布了《1996年仲裁法》,规定法院对仲裁应给予较为适度的干预,进一步强化了自由仲裁的政策。根据该法,伦敦国际仲裁院制定了新的仲裁规则,自1998年1月1日起开始实施。

3. 美国仲裁协会2003年《美国仲裁协会国际仲裁规则》

美国仲裁协会(American Arbitration Association,AAA)是美国主要的国际常设仲裁机构。1926年设立,总部在纽约。该协会分支机构遍布美国的主要城市。协会受理的仲裁案件主要是货物买卖合同、代理合同、工业产权、公司的成立与解散,以及投资等方面的争议。海事仲裁案件由专门的海事仲裁机构受理。

美国仲裁协会制定有多套仲裁规则,其现行国际仲裁规则是1991年3月1日生效并经2003年7月1日修改的《美国仲裁协会国际仲裁规则》。

The most active arbitral institution in the US is the American Arbitration Association (AAA). This arbitral institution has promulgated numerous arbitration rules for specialized types of international commercial disputes. The most extensively used are the AAA Commercial Arbitration Rules. The AAA handles roughly 400 international disputes on an annual basis. In 1991, the AAA promulgated the AAA International Arbitration Rules designed specifically for international arbitrations. The rules "are based principally on the UNCITRAL Arbitration Rules, and were intended to permit a maximum of flexibility and a minimum of administrative supervision." They were recently revised in July 2003. Under the 2003 version, the AAA International Arbitration Rules provide the applicable set of AAA arbitration rules in "international" disputes.

按照该仲裁规则的规定,在国际性仲裁案件中,当事各方未在协议中明确仲裁员人数的,应委任1名仲裁员,除非协会根据案件的情况自行决定3名仲裁员是适宜的。当事人可以共同约定委任仲裁员的程序,并将此程序通知协会;如当事人未达成此等协议,协会应根据任何一方当事人的书面请求,委任仲裁员并指定首席仲裁员;如当事人约定了委任仲裁员的程序,但一方当事人未按照协议行事,协会得应任何一方当事人的请求,行使约定程序规定而尚待履行的所有职权。在选任仲裁员时,协会应尽量征求当事人的意见,委任合适的仲裁员,并得应当事人的要求或自行决定,委任与各方当事人国籍不同的一国国民为仲裁员;仲裁员应是公正独立的。如一方当事人对仲裁员的公正性或独立性有合理怀疑而提出异议时,协会应通知其他当事人,其他当事人可以同意接受回避要求,在此种情况下,被异议的仲裁员应当离职;若无此类同意,被要求回避的仲裁员也可以离职。在这两种情况下,离职并非意味着要求回避的理由是有效的。如其他当事人不同意回避要求,或者该仲裁员未离职,协会应自行单独对回避请求作出决定。仲裁庭在遵守正当程序的情况下,可自行决定案件的审理方式,以便快速解决争议。协会一般都是按自己的仲裁规则进行仲裁,但当事人可以协议对规则作出修改。

In comparison to the ICC, the AAA administrative staff plays less of a role in the arbitration process. Besides playing a less significant role in setting the arbitrators' fees, the AAA does not receive or serve initial notices or requests for arbitration, nor does it require or review a Terms of Reference, nor does it review draft awards.

美国仲裁协会受理的国际商事仲裁案件,在裁决上实行终局裁决制。根据美国《联邦仲裁法》的规定,法院对仲裁的干预较少,只有在仲裁员被指控有受贿、欺诈、明显偏袒一方的情况时,法院才可以撤销仲裁裁决,法院对仲裁员在仲裁中有关事实和法律适用上是否错误不予过问,体现了很强的仲裁独立性。

4. 瑞典斯德哥尔摩商会仲裁院 1999 年《斯德哥尔摩商会仲裁院仲裁规则》

商事仲裁在瑞典有着悠久的历史。早在 1359 年就有一部地方法典把仲裁作为解决纠纷的手段,1669 年瑞典通过立法赋予了仲裁裁决书司法上的强制执行力。1887 年,瑞典通过了第一部《仲裁法》。现在瑞典的民事纠纷,95% 都是通过调解或仲裁解决的,只有 5% 的纠纷由法院判决,由此可见仲裁对当地的社会生活具有相当大的影响力。在瑞典所有仲裁机构中,斯德哥尔摩商会仲裁院(SCC)是最有影响的一个。该院成立于 1917 年,最初只处理国内仲裁。1970 年初"冷战"双方美国和苏联政治上对立,军事上对抗,法律和文化上的差异较大,因而经济往来难免会产生纠纷,于是美国和苏联就基于瑞典政治上的中立和斯德哥尔摩商会仲裁院的高素质,一致推荐它作为处理东西方两大阵营之间经济纠纷的主要仲裁机构。从此以后,SCC 就走上了国际化的道路,受到东西方各国的认可。它每年受理的与瑞典无关的仲裁案件都占全部案件的绝大部分,如 2003 年受理的 167 个案件中,就有约 105 个案件和瑞典没有丝毫关系。

该仲裁院从 1999 年 4 月 1 日起适用新的仲裁规则。按照新的仲裁规则,该仲裁院受理世界上任何国家当事人所提交的商事争议。当事人如若要将争议事项提交该仲裁院仲裁,则必须向该院提交仲裁申请书。经仲裁院审查,认为有管辖权且当事人及时缴纳了立案费的,即协助筹组仲裁庭。该仲裁院没有固定的仲裁员名单,当事人在指定仲裁员时,可以不受国籍的限制,但必须同当事人没有利害关系。如果当事人未约定仲裁员人数,则仲裁庭人数应为 3 人。如当事人已约定仲裁员人数,除非当事人另有约定,独任仲裁员应由仲裁院任命,其他情况,则由当事人各指定人数相同的仲裁员,然后由仲裁院指定一名仲裁员担任首席仲裁员。如果一方当事人没有委任仲裁员,或者所委任的仲裁员辞职,或者由于资格不合格或未能履行其职责等原因而被解职时,该仲裁院在与有关当事人磋商后,可代为或重新指定仲裁员。仲裁地点,除当事人已有约定外,一般都由仲裁院决定。仲裁庭在进行仲裁时,既可适用该仲裁院的规则,也可适用当事人选择的其他规则。

SCC 仲裁规则最主要也最重要的一个特征就是灵活性。比如说语言方面,当事人可以自行选择用何种语言来进行仲裁程序;又比如仲裁方式及进程方面,当事人可以建议不开庭,由仲裁庭经书面审理后直接裁决。事实上,在 SCC 的仲裁实践中,仲裁程序通常都是灵活的或者说是不正式的,仲裁庭时常准备接受双方关于如何进行材料交换、开庭和适用何种规则等方面的建议。

5. 中国国际经济贸易仲裁委员会 2005 年《中国国际经济贸易仲裁委员会仲裁规则》

我国的仲裁制度发展较慢。新中国成立以后,我国建立了国内仲裁制度和涉外仲裁制度。涉外仲裁机构由民间性商会即中国国际贸易仲裁促进会组建。中国国际商事仲裁机构设立在中国国际经济贸易促进委员会(即中国国际商会)内,分为中国国际经济贸易仲裁委员会和中国海事仲裁委员会,总部设在北京。

中国国际经济贸易仲裁委员会[1](China International Economic and Trade Arbitration Commission,CIETAC)是中国国际贸易促进委员会根据政务院 1954 年 5 月 6 日《中央人民政府政务院关于在中国国际贸易促进委员会内设立对外贸易仲裁委员会的决定》,于 1956 年 4 月设立的。当时的名称为"对外贸易仲裁委员会",并制定了《仲裁程序暂行规则》。1980 年改名为"对外经济贸易仲裁委员会",现在的"中国国际经济贸易仲裁委员会"是在 1988 年定名的。该仲裁委员会于 1988 年在原来的《仲裁程序暂行规则》的基础上制定了其仲裁规则,1994 年进行了全面的修改。《仲裁法》实施后,CIETAC 根据《仲裁法》的规定,分别于 1995 年、1998 年、2000 年对仲裁规则又进行了相应的修改。现行的仲裁规则于 2005 年 1 月 11 日经中国国际贸易促进委员会通过,2005 年 5 月 1 日起施行。

新规则扩大了当事人选择仲裁员的权利和范围,加强了仲裁庭对程序的管理权,明确了仲裁的审理方式,增加了行业仲裁和专业仲裁的规定等。它更加尊重当事人的意思自治,符合当事人的商业需要,程序更加灵活高效,规则也更加透明开放。该仲裁规则在现有法律框架下,充分体现了仲裁的本质特点,有利于商事争议得以独立公正地解决。

6. 其他仲裁机构仲裁规则

此外,其他著名的国际商事仲裁机构的仲裁规则还包括:瑞士苏黎世商会仲裁院(Court of Arbitration of the Zurich Chamber of Commerce,ZCC)1985 年《苏黎世商会仲裁规则》[2]、新加坡国际仲裁中心(Singapore International Arbitration Center,SIAC)2007 年《新加坡国际仲裁中心仲裁规则》、德国仲裁协会(DIS)1998 年《德国仲裁协会仲裁规则》、荷兰仲裁协会(Netherlands Arbitration Institute,NAI)2003 年《荷兰仲裁协会仲裁规则》、日本商事仲裁协会(Japan

---

[1] 自 2000 年 10 月 1 日起同时启用名称"中国国际商会仲裁院"。
[2] 2004 年 1 月起,《瑞士国际仲裁规则》生效。此前,包括苏黎世商会在内的瑞士六家商会各自拥有不同的仲裁规则,用于解决国际商事纠纷。为了促进瑞士的机构仲裁并统一当前的仲裁规则,苏黎世商会以及巴塞尔商会、伯尔尼商会、日内瓦商会、提契诺商会、沃州商会采纳了统一的《瑞士国际仲裁规则》,并以此规则取代各商会以往的国际仲裁规则。

Commercial Arbitration Association，JCAA)2006年《日本商事仲裁协会仲裁规则》等。

阅读材料

1. Reforming Chinese Arbitration Law

The dramatic growth in commercial transactions between Chinese and non-Chinese parties in recent decades has been accompanied by a remarkable growth in China's law and processes governing international commercial arbitration. Not surprisingly, some conflicts surfaced during this era of growth and change, but all the issues highlighted above can be addressed to keep Chinese law and practices evolving in conformity with international norms. While Chinese arbitration law and practices are generally in agreement with UNCITRAL Model Law and international arbitration practices, we suggest that future reform of arbitration legislation and practices should center on the following items.

First, the arbitration legislation should allow for ad hoc arbitration in China and abroad. Parties should be allowed to select a particular qualified person as an arbitrator. An award issued in ad hoc arbitration should have the same binding force as that made by the arbitration tribunal under an arbitration commission.

Second, the importance of party choice and autonomy needs to be reinforced with some significant procedural changes. Conditions for the validity of the arbitration agreement should be relaxed and the court's role in supporting the validity of agreements to arbitrate, even when particular commissions are not specified by the parties, should be strengthened. After the arbitration tribunal is established, if a party challenges the validity of the arbitration agreement, the commission should allow the tribunal to rule on the validity of the arbitration agreement and its own jurisdiction, as contemplated by Article 6(1) of the CIETAC 2005 Rules, with some appeal to the courts available. The present panel system, unique to each individual arbitration commission, should be reformed and a unified panel registration for qualified arbitrators should be established. The names of qualified arbitrators could be published on the Internet, making them available for both the parties' and commissioners' selection and appointment. Arbitrators should have greater authority to award interim relief to parties who make the appropriate showing. Alternatively, as in Article 6(1) of the CIETAC 2005 Rules, parties should be able to appoint an arbitrator, by agreement, whose name is not included in the panel list in some circumstances, subject to the approval of the commission administering the arbitration.

Finally, Chinese Arbitration Law and the related Civil Procedure Law provide two different standards of review for awards involving only domestic parties and awards involving foreign parties or elements. The review accorded the latter by Chinese courts is much more deferential and mirrors international arbitration norms. Recent clarification of these laws by the Chinese Supreme Court affords the more deferential standard of review to all arbitration awards involving foreign parties or elements, regardless of whether the arbitration tribunal issuing the award was an international or domestic arbitration commission.

Chinese arbitration law and practice has made significant strides to manage the rapidly increasing caseload associated with a period of amazing growth in economic interactions between Chinese and non-Chinese parties. The reforms suggested here would continue that development, making arbitration within China a more appealing alternative for both Chinese and foreign parties by ensuring efficiency, finality, and party autonomy.

【Zhao Xiuwen, Lisa A. Kloppenberg, Reforming Chinese Arbitration Law and Practices in the Global Economy, 31 University of Dayton Law Review 421.】

2. The Principles in Arbitration Law

The desire of commercial parties to international contracts, as well as governments, for a neutral and reliable method of dispute resolution has led to a remarkable confluence of international arbitration law and practice. Governments seeking to encourage international commerce and investment have long recognized the attraction of reliable dispute resolution. This, and the requirements of international business, have produced a steady trend towards the harmonization of arbitration law and practice internationally.

The principle instruments of this trend have been the 1958 Convention on the Recognition of Foreign Arbitral Awards (the "New York Convention"), and subsequent measures of the United Nations Commission on International Trade Law (UNCITRAL) including a model set of ad hoc arbitration rules, the well-known UNCITRAL Arbitration Rules (1976); the UNCITRAL Model Law on International Commercial Arbitration (1985) (or "Model Law"), as well as Notes on Organizing Arbitration Proceedings (1996).

The New York Convention is by far the most important international treaty concerning international commercial arbitration. With over 120 signatory countries, its primary objective is the recognition and enforcement of foreign arbitration awards as between signatory states. The Convention specifies the very limited grounds on which recognition and enforcement can be refused, in the absence of which the courts of signatory states are required to recognize and enforce the foreign award. However, the implementation of the Convention in each country depends upon effective local implementing legislation.

The UNCITRAL Model Law was adopted by a U. N. resolution which recommended that "... all States give due consideration to the Model Law ... in view of the desirability of uniformity of the law of arbitral procedures and the specific needs of international commercial arbitration practice. " The Model Law is therefore a very deliberate attempt to achieve international harmonization of arbitration laws. Its primary objectives are to provide a reliable and familiar procedural arbitration framework; to limit the role of the local courts in arbitration allowing parties to agree to resolve their disputes by arbitration, and to establish the core arbitration principles of fairness, equality of treatment and due process. The provisions of the Model Law closely reflect the related provisions of the New York Convention (which pre-dates it), particularly as to requirements for enforcement of arbitration awards.

Arbitration, and the jurisdiction of the arbitral tribunal, is based principally upon agreement between the parties, usually as to the agreed rules of arbitration procedure and the place of arbitration. The chosen arbitration rules may be ad hoc or institutional, the latter being administered by one of the numerous arbitration centers or institutions. The agreed place of arbitration will normally determine the procedural law of the arbitration. The parties will also usually expressly agree a choice of governing or proper law of the contract, which will determine their substantive contractual rights and obligations.

Once an arbitration award is obtained, its validity and enforcement will be determined partly by the law of the place where it was given (the "seat" of the arbitration) and of the law of the place where the award is sought to be enforced.

Thus, the applicable law of an international arbitration may be diverse. An international commercial arbitration will take place within the framework of any applicable international treaty or convention; the proper law of the contract; the procedural law of the place of arbitration; any supervening national laws and public policy, and in accordance with the arbitration rules and procedures that may have been agreed between the parties.

【David J. Howell, An Overview of Arbitration Practice in Asia, International Arbitration Law Review, Vol. 4, No. 5, 2001, p. 143.】

3. CIETAC's Prospering Institutional Reputation and Status

In addition to enhancement of the Arbitration Law, other trends bode well for the continued and expanding prosperity of CIETAC as an arbitral institution. CIETAC arbitral awards are generally enforced outside of China. CIETAC's caseload has continued to increase rapidly, reaching an estimated 600 cases in 1996. At present, CIETAC has more arbitration cases than any other arbitration body in the world. The CIETAC list of potential arbitrators has expanded to include younger arbitrators who have some exposure to foreign legal systems and are more inclined than the senior bureaucrats they replace to find "legal" rather than "practical" resolutions to disputes. Other major breakthroughs are CIETAC rule changes that permit foreign arbitrators to be included in the Panel of Arbitrators and foreign parties to use their own non-Chinese attorneys. These changes have helped to bring the CIETAC Arbitration Rules more in line with recognized international standards. These developments, along with an emerging track record, have led many to remark that CIETAC arbitration has become much more sophisticated than in earlier days.

In addition to CIETAC's institutional composition, on September 4, 1995, the China Chamber of International Commerce ("China CIC") adopted significant amendments to the CIETAC Arbitration Rules. While many of the changes adopted by the amendments are too subtle to warrant comment in this Essay, other changes are likely to have important consequences for international arbitration in China.

One of the more interesting changes is the expansion of CIETAC's jurisdiction. This amendment was introduced in response to designation of CIETAC by the Chinese Securities Supervision as the official arbitration institution for handling securities disputes arising between or among China's securities firms and the securities exchange agency. One observer expects a "sharp increase" in the number of securities related matters brought before CIETAC, probably as a result of the expanded securities jurisdiction.

Another significant change conforms the CIETAC Arbitration Rules to the Arbitration Law. The amendments stipulate that any objection to the validity of an arbitration agreement or to the jurisdiction of the Arbitration Tribunal shall be raised before the initial hearing of the Arbitration Tribunal or in the initial substantive defense. When the parties dispute the validity of the arbitration agreement and raise the issue both before the Arbitration Tribunal and a People's Court, the decision of the People's Court will prevail if the Arbitration Tribunal's conclusion is different. This amendment conforms the CIETAC Arbitration Rules to the Arbitration Law, which contains virtually identical provisions.

[Fredrick Brown & Catherine A. Rogers, The Role of Arbitration in Resolving Transnational Disputes: A Survey of Trends in the People's Republic of China, 15 Berkeley Journal of International Law, 1997, p.329.]

4. Significant Revision of Most Major Sets of International Arbitration Rules

Since 1996, the major independent arbitral organizations, including the International Chamber of Commerce (ICC), the London Court of International Arbitration (LCIA), and the American Arbitration Association (AAA), have all redrafted their international arbitration rules. Increasingly, they are being joined by specialized institutions like WIPO in fashioning specialized regimes for arbitration in specific industries. With these widespread changes, the use of international commercial arbitration is likely to increase. It is important to consider how these arbitral regimes compare with each other, and what effect the revised regimes will have on uniformity and predictability in the settlement of international commercial disputes.

The changes are taking place primarily in rules governing administered arbitrations, that is, arbitrations under rules established by an institution which will manage or supervise the arbitration—to a greater or lesser extent, depending upon the institution. This practice is in contrast to ad hoc arbitration, where the individual parties operate the arbitration under procedures fashioned by individual negotiation and agreement on programs, or by adoption of an established set of arbitration rules by agreement of the parties. In selecting an established set of rules for their ad hoc arbitration, the parties might choose, for example, the UNCITRAL Model Rules (which are not administered), or the parties might choose the rules of an arbitral institution without also choosing to have their arbitration administered by the arbitral institution.

As a result, the arbitration rules of institutions like the ICC, the AAA, and the LCIA, have an influence beyond the arbitrations that they administer because their rules may be borrowed by ad hoc arbitrations. More broadly, they serve as significant models and sources of inspiration for other arbitral institutions and for individual parties seeking draft language for contractual clauses concerning arbitration.

Many of the revisions to the ICC, AAA and LCIA rules appear to be modest technical changes to operational provisions. However, seen in context, these changes represent the effects of the increasing globalization of commerce. Christopher Drahozal has pointed out: "competition among countries to serve as arbitral sites has accelerated. Increasingly, countries are adopting specialized international arbitration statutes to replace ... previous statutes that [were] ... designed principally for domestic arbitrations."

So also with the revisions to the arbitration rules, competition among arbitration institutions for the growing number of international commercial arbitrations has moved their respective technical details closer to conformity. While differences still remain among these rules, the differences tend to relate to variances in fundamental institutional policy. For example, there remain differences in the degree to which each institution may actively supervise individual arbitrations under its rules, with the ICC International Court of Arbitration still taking the most active role among the three major institutions.

【Michael P. Malloy, Current Issues in International Arbitration, 15 Transnational Law 43 (2002).】

思考题

1. 最高人民法院《关于适用〈中华人民共和国仲裁法〉若干问题的解释》对我国仲裁制度和仲裁实践有哪些作用？
2. 普遍性国际公约和区域性公约在国际商事仲裁过程中的地位和作用是什么？
3. 《示范法》在各国实践中是如何得到适用的？
4. 仲裁规则在仲裁过程中如何发挥其作用？

推荐阅读

1. 〔法〕菲利普·福盖德、伊曼纽尔·盖拉德、贝托尔德·戈德曼：《国际商事仲裁》，中信出版社2004年版，第63—196页。
2. 〔英〕艾伦·雷德芬、马丁·亨特等：《国际商事仲裁法律与实践》，林一飞、宋连斌译，北京大学出版社2005年版，第66—79、470—476页。

3. Andrew Tweeddale and Keren Tweeddale, Arbitration of Commercial Disputes, International and English Law and Practice, Oxford University Press, 2005.

4.《北京仲裁》第 60 辑,中国法制出版社 2007 年版,第 1—104 页。

5. 谢石松主编:《商事仲裁法学》,高等教育出版社 2003 年版,第 78—107 页。

第三章 国际商事仲裁的法律适用

国际商事仲裁具有鲜明的国际性。与国内仲裁不同,它涉及各个国家的国内法,还涉及国际条约和国际习惯。无论在程序问题上还是在实体问题上,都存在着法律适用的问题。法律的适用对仲裁的进行过程和当事人的权利义务关系有非常重要的影响。国际商事仲裁中法律适用问题的重要意义体现在下述三个方面:

Firstly, compared to national court proceedings, international commercial arbitration is a more flexible and speedy way to resolve international commercial disputes. To safeguard its reputation of speed and flexibility, the choice of law offers the parties quite a large degree of freedom in deciding how the arbitration procedures shall be conducted.

Secondly, the parties want to predict the outcome of the arbitration. Such expectations may be more easily achieved if a valid choice of the proper law has been made by the parties themselves. In particular, by doing this the parties will have the advantage of knowing where they stand and what rights and obligations they have by choosing the proper law of the contract themselves.

Finally, the choice of the proper law has a critical importance at the stage of recognition or enforcement of the arbitral awards. An award made by arbitrators who failed to observe or respect the parties' express choice of law not only can be successfully challenged by the losing party but also most national courts will refuse to enforce such an award. ①

本章讨论国际商事仲裁过程中可能出现的法律适用问题:

首先要关注的是仲裁协议的法律适用。有效的仲裁协议是进行国际商事仲裁的基础。那么,判断仲裁协议有效性的标准是什么?一般而言,仲裁协议所适用的法律,首先由当事人确定;如无法确定当事人的意思,则适用仲裁地

---

① See Hong-lin Yu, Choice of Laws for Arbitrators: Two Steps or Three, International Arbitration Law Review, International Arbitration Law Review, Vol. 4, No. 5, 2001, pp. 152—163.

的法律。①

其次,仲裁开始前,还要决定仲裁进行的程序。为此,我们要讨论仲裁程序的法律适用。

再次,程序确定后,就要开始具体分析案件的法律关系。那么,应当依据何种法律来确定当事人的权利和义务呢?这需要研究仲裁实体问题的法律适用。

最后,仲裁裁决作出后,需要得到有关国家的承认与执行,在此过程中,又涉及法律的适用问题。

第一节 国际商事仲裁程序的法律适用

西方法谚有云:正义不但要实现,而且要以看得见的方式实现。只有经过合法的审理程序而得出的仲裁裁决才能让当事人信服,并得到法院的承认与执行。正当的仲裁程序能够保证当事人充分主张自己的权利,有利于仲裁庭更好地查明事实,得出结论。那么,什么才是合法的仲裁程序呢?换言之,仲裁程序应当依据什么法律?这就必然要求我们探讨仲裁程序的法律适用问题。

一、仲裁程序法的含义

(一)仲裁程序法的概念和范围

仲裁程序法是一切调整仲裁程序的法律规范的总称。它不是仅仅指以"仲裁法"命名的法律规范。仲裁程序法一般被规定在各国的仲裁法和民事诉讼法当中。在普通法系国家,其渊源还包括司法判例。也有学者为了强调其在审理程序中的突出作用,称其为"仲裁审理程序法"②。

至于仲裁程序法所调整的范围,各国法律的规定有所不同,一般认为仲裁程序法的范围主要包括以下事项:争议的可仲裁性、仲裁协议的效力、仲裁庭的管辖权、仲裁庭的组成、对仲裁员的异议、仲裁程序必须遵守的最低标准、法院对仲裁的支持与协助、仲裁程序上的与实体上的法律适用及裁决的形式、效力与终局性等等。

---

① 在 Japan Educational Corporation (Japan) v. Kenneth J. Feld (US)案(High Court, Tokyo, 30 May 1994. See ICCA Yearbook, 1995, pp 745—749)中,关于仲裁协议的适用法律,法院认为:"仲裁协议是使某些涉及权利义务或者法律关系的争议最终由仲裁在法院外解决的协议。仲裁协议应规定进行仲裁的各种必要事项,包括哪些争议由仲裁解决。当事人对这些事项的协议所适用的法律,涉及就争议解决方式达成的协议,但这仍属当事人意思自治的范围内。因此,该适用法律由当事人自己进行确定。如果当事人的意思不明确,由于规定特定地点的特定程序是仲裁协议的性质,因此,我们必须假设,当事人希望仲裁程序进行地的法律得以适用。没有足够的事实推翻该假设。"

② 谢石松主编:《商事仲裁法学》,高等教育出版社2003年版,第216页。

(二) 区分几个易混淆的概念

学习仲裁程序法,首先需要厘清几个容易混淆的概念:仲裁法、《仲裁法》、仲裁地法、仲裁程序法、仲裁规则。它们相互间有严格的区分。

首先,仲裁法(arbitration law)是一个广义的概念,它不仅仅指有关商事仲裁审理程序的法律规范,也包括仲裁机构的建立、仲裁裁决的承认与执行等内容。实际上,所有与仲裁活动有关的法律规范、司法解释乃至司法判例都在仲裁法的范围内。仲裁法是一国立法机构针对仲裁制定的专门法律,如前所述,尽管它常常包括了最主要的仲裁规范,但是它并不是仲裁法的唯一渊源。例如,在我国,仲裁法就不仅仅指1995年《仲裁法》,它还包括《民事诉讼法》当中有关仲裁裁决的承认与执行、仲裁裁决的撤销、仲裁协议的效力等内容。此外,我国是《纽约公约》和《华盛顿公约》的缔约国,这两个公约中关于仲裁的大量规定也是我国仲裁法的内容。

其次,仲裁程序法与仲裁地法(law of arbitral situs / lex loci arbitri)既密切联系又互相区分。各国一般规定仲裁地法对仲裁的许多方面有监督作用,在当事人没有对仲裁程序法作出明确选择时,仲裁庭往往会适用仲裁地法。但是,这不意味着仲裁程序法等同于仲裁地法。

It is clear that the law of procedure applied to an arbitration need not be that of the place of arbitration. Whilst parties (or arbitrators) may choose to adopt the procedural law of the place of arbitration for the sake of convenience, there is no mandatory requirement to do so. In fact, parties to an arbitration are expressly permitted to choose their own procedural law, whether that law be the procedural law of the situs, or another country, or even a-national rules of procedure which are selected by the parties.

另外,即使当事人选择了仲裁地法以外的其他法律,仲裁地法也仍然发挥着作用。一般认为,尽管当事人可以依据意思自治原则选择仲裁程序法,但是仲裁程序仍然不得违背仲裁地的强行法(mandatory law)。否则,依照这种程序作出的裁决可能被仲裁地法院撤销,从而面临在其他国家无法得到法院承认和执行的危险。

最后,在仲裁审理程序中直接发挥作用的往往不是仲裁程序法,而是仲裁规则(arbitration rules)。仲裁程序法是由国家制定的,与之不同,仲裁规则既可以是常设仲裁机构为其所进行的机构仲裁而拟定的,也可以是当事人临时约定的,不具备法律的强制效力。仲裁规则主要用于规范仲裁程序的内部运作,而仲裁程序法还包括与仲裁有关的外部运作规则,如法院对仲裁的监督等等。

It is common for parties to nominate a set of procedural rules of arbitration which have been established by international institutions or arbitration bodies, such as the

UNCITRAL Arbitration Rules or the International Chamber of Commerce ("ICC") Rules of Arbitration. These Rules specify many of the laws of procedure necessary for an international arbitration, but are not exhaustive. For example, the UNCITRAL Rules include provisions relating to the appointment and replacement of arbitrators, the place and language of the arbitration, the statements to be provided by parties, the making of awards and the distribution of costs.①

由于仲裁规则一般是仲裁机构制定的或当事人约定的,所以它有很大的灵活性。在一定条件下,仲裁机构有较大的自由裁量权来处理程序问题。例如,《联合国国际贸易法委员会仲裁规则》(UNCITRAL Arbitration Rules)第15条第1款规定,只要是为了平等对待当事人,给予他们充分表达意见的机会,仲裁庭就可以依据他们认为恰当的方式进行仲裁。②《国际商会仲裁规则》第15条也作出了类似规定。③

(三) 仲裁程序法的独立性

在过去很长的一段时间里,人们一直认为适用于仲裁程序的法律体系和适用于仲裁实体问题的法律体系应该是同一的,没有把仲裁程序的法律适用当做一个独立的问题来对待。这是因为过去的商事仲裁主要是国内性质的。随着国际商事仲裁的出现,人们逐渐意识到不仅在实体问题上可能会适用非仲裁地法,在程序问题上也可能有别的选择。法律适用问题的复杂性导致实体问题与程序问题适用不同的法律成为可能,甚至成为必然。

It has long been established that the law of procedure in arbitration need not necessarily be of the same nationality as the substantive "proper law" governing the merits of the dispute. In the English case of James Miller Ltd. v. Whitworth Street Estates,④ the House of Lords found that a Scottish arbitration, which applied English law as the substantive law of the contract, was not bound by English procedural law. In that case, the court upheld the Scottish arbitrator's refusal to submit his award in the form of a "case stated" to the English High Court, which was, at that time, a remedy available to parties under English procedural law. The court found that the

---

① See Pippa Read, Delocalization of International Commercial Arbitration: Its Relevance in the New Millennium, American Review of International Arbitration, 10 Am. Rev. Int'l Arb. (1999), p.177.

② Article 15 (1) of UNCITRAL Arbitration Rules: "Subject to these Rules, the arbitral tribunal may conduct the arbitration in such manner as it considers appropriate, provided that the parties are treated with equality and that at any stage of the proceedings each party is given a full opportunity of presenting his case."

③ Article 15 "Rules Governing the Proceedings" of Rules of Arbitration of ICC: "The proceedings before the Arbitral Tribunal shall be governed by these Rules, and, where these Rules are silent by any rules which the parties or, failing them, the Arbitral Tribunal may settle on, whether or not reference is thereby made to the rules of procedure of a national law to be applied to the arbitration."

④ [1970] 1 All E.R. 796 (H.L.).

arbitration was governed instead by Scottish procedural law, as Scotland was the place of arbitration.

在上述案例中,虽然案件在实体上适用的是英格兰法,但是仲裁员认为仲裁地位于苏格兰,从而在程序上应适用苏格兰的仲裁程序法。在当代,仲裁程序法与仲裁实体法相互独立已经是一个受到广泛认同的理念。

仲裁程序法的独立性还表现为它独立于仲裁地法。如前所述,仲裁程序法与仲裁地法是有区别的。长期以来,人们一直认为仲裁程序必须适用仲裁地的法律。这种观点是把仲裁和诉讼的性质混为一谈了。当事人选择仲裁地点并不当然意味着他们选择适用仲裁地的程序法。特别是国际商事仲裁,当事人考虑的是仲裁的便利和对仲裁机构的信赖,而与仲裁地所在国的法律无关。争议本身和仲裁地国家很可能没有任何联系。因此,现代商事仲裁理论和实践认为,当事人双方完全有权通过协议选择自己希望适用的仲裁程序法。在著名的 SEEE v. Yugoslavia 案[①]中,法官表达了如下观点:

The court held:

—that the law of the place of arbitration does not always and necessarily govern the arbitral proceedings;

—that the "procedural law" that governs the arbitration may equally be another national law or the agreement of the parties.

此外,《纽约公约》和《示范法》都表达了仲裁程序法相对于仲裁地法的独立性:

Under the New York Convention, the law of the situs of the arbitration is not necessarily determinative on either the enforcement or recognition of the award. Thus, the Convention provides "potent support for the view that the applicable law is not necessarily the rex-loci arbitri."[②]

The UNCITRAL Model Law effectively separates the procedural rules governing international arbitration from the domestic rules of the situs state. The procedural law of arbitration is not necessarily the law of local state even there is not agreement on the applicable law. Article 19, "Determination of rules of procedure", provides that:

1. Subject to the provisions of this Law, the parties are free to agree on the procedure to be followed by the arbitral tribunal in conducting the proceedings.

2. Failing such agreement, the arbitral tribunal may, subject to the provisions of

---

① (Paris TGI, 8.7.70) 98 JDI 131 (1971).
② Jay R. Sever, The Relaxation of Inarbitrability and Public Policy Checks on US and Foreign Arbitration: Arbitration out of Control? 65 Tul. L. Rev. 1661 (1991).

this Law, conduct the arbitration in such manner as it considers appropriate. The power coffered upon the arbitral tribunal includes the power to determine the admissibility, relevance, materiality and weight of any evidence.

二、仲裁程序法的确定

与其他争议解决机制相比,国际商事仲裁有其自身的特点,因此它的程序法律适用具有独特之处。另外,仲裁员在决定仲裁程序法时要处理的情况也更为复杂。

Unlike a judge, an arbitrator in any international arbitration faces the threshold question of which procedural law should govern the arbitration process. This question does not arise in judicial proceedings because of the universally recognized principle that procedural issues are governed by the lex fori, law of the forum, whereas substantive issues may be governed by either forum or foreign law. Although the line between substance and procedure is not always clear, the distinction between the two categories is as old as the law of conflict of laws.

Assuming that in international arbitration the lex causae may, or should be, segregated from the lex arbitri[①], the second question that an arbitrator faces is which law should govern the proceedings: the law of the situs of arbitration, the law of the country of which the arbitrator is a national, or another law. Commentators and arbitrators have responded to this question differently, and their responses are discussed next.

(一) 当事人选择的仲裁程序法

1. 当事人意思自治的意义

国际商事仲裁的当事人自由选择法律具有重要的实践意义。首先,与法院诉讼不同,国际商事仲裁的特点在于它的灵活和快捷。因此,当事人自由选择适用于他们的便捷的程序规则显得极为重要。其次,当事人选择仲裁的意图不仅仅是解决争端,而且是以他们可以预见的方式来解决争端。[②] 通过选择程序法,他们可以事先就预知各自在仲裁中有何种程序性权利和义务。最后,在裁决的承认与执行上,《纽约公约》第5条第1款d项规定"仲裁机关之组成或仲裁程

[①] Hereby the "lex causae" refers to the substantive law governing the merits problem in the arbitration while "lex arbitri" refers to the procedural law of arbitration. See Vitek Danilowicz, The Choice of Applicable Law in International Arbitration", 9 Hastings Int'l & Comp. L. Rev. (1986), p.177.

[②] See Hong-lin Yu, Choice of Laws for Arbitrators: Two Steps or Three, International Arbitration Law Review, Vol.4, No.5, 2001, pp.152—163.

序与各造间之协议不符"①是法院拒绝执行仲裁裁决的一个理由。

Within certain limitations, the parties' freedom in choosing the proper law of the contract is well recognized in international commercial arbitration cases. As Rabel states:"The practice of allowing parties to determine the law applicable to their contractual relations... for centuries has been applied by courts throughout the world with slight dissent."② Once their intention is found, it is compulsory for the arbitrators to apply this choice of law in order to decide the substantive issues arising from the main contract between the parties.

Unlike a judge, an arbitrator often conducts proceedings in a country other than his or her own. Often, the parties choose one country as the place of arbitration and then nominate an arbitrator from a different country; on other occasions the arbitrator may choose an arbitration seat not located in his or her home country. In either situation, the arbitrator may not be familiar with the procedural law of the place of arbitration; therefore, the rationale for applying the lex fori is not compelling. In fact, considerations of convenience suggest the opposite result: that the arbitrator or the parties should have the freedom to choose a procedural law other than the law of the place of arbitration.

2. 立法实践

当事人在选择仲裁程序法方面的意思自治原则已经得到了大量的国际性文件(包括国际公约、国际商事仲裁机构的仲裁规则等)和国内立法的确认。

1988年《斯德哥尔摩商会仲裁院仲裁规则》第16条规定,仲裁庭在决定进行仲裁程序的方式时,应遵循当事人在仲裁协议中的约定及该规则的规定,并应考虑当事人的意愿。③ 最为典型的是1985年《示范法》第19条"Determination of rules of procedure"规定:"Subject to the provisions of this law, the parties are free to agree on the procedure to be followed by the arbitral tribunal in conducting the proceedings."

国内立法也存在大量关于当事人选择仲裁程序法的规定。例如,法国《民事诉讼法》第1494条规定:"仲裁协议可以通过直接规定或援引一套仲裁规则来明确仲裁应遵循的程序;它也可以选择特定的程序法作为准据法。"1989年瑞士《联邦国际私法法典》第182条规定,当事人可以直接或按照仲裁规则确定仲裁程序,他们也可以按其选择的程序法进行仲裁程序。英国《1996年仲裁法》赋

---

① 这里以联合国中文译本作准本。其原文为:"The composition of the arbitral authority or the arbitral procedure was not in accordance with the agreement of the parties."
② Rabel, Comparative Conflicts, Vol.I, 2nd ed., 1958, p.90.
③ 参见杨树明主编:《国际商事仲裁法》,重庆大学出版社2002年版,第138页。

予了仲裁当事人广泛的自由,如"自由约定仲裁程序被视为开始的时间","自由约定委任仲裁员包括首席仲裁员和公断人的程序",约定程序及证据事项,"自由约定仲裁庭关于仲裁程序可行使的权力",约定仲裁庭是否有权作出临时裁决,甚至约定仲裁庭决定自己是否具有管辖权的权力。① 1998 年德国《民事诉讼法》第 1042 条第 3 款规定:"除非本编有强制性规定,当事人得自由决定或援引一套仲裁规则而决定仲裁程序。"

3. 当事人选择仲裁程序法的限制

依据意思自治原则,当事人有权选择可适用的仲裁程序法,但是这种选择一般要受到仲裁地强行法的限制。例如,根据意大利《民事诉讼法》第 2 条的规定,意大利本国人不得协议排除意大利法院的管辖权。德国法律规定,当事人选择仲裁程序法的范围不是任意的,而是限于依据国际公认的一般原则对案件有管辖权的国家的仲裁程序法。

The specific mandatory provisions of procedural law will obviously differ amongst jurisdictions but the most prevalent mandatory laws of procedure relate to matters of public policy and procedural fairness. It may be against the public policy of the forum to permit specific types of disputes to be arbitrated, or to permit the rendering of awards which breach certain norms, for example an award enforcing a contract which breached national boycott laws. Fundamental standards of procedural fairness, such as arbitrator impartiality and the requirement that both parties have an equal opportunity to present their cases, will also be mandatory in most jurisdictions.②

The attitude taken by national law with respect to the parties' choice of the lex arbitri reflects the sovereign's understanding of its interests in regulating arbitration proceedings. The crucial question is not whether the arbitration is jurisdictional or contractual in nature, but to what extent the sovereign controls, or should control, the proceedings. Recent developments in international arbitration indicate that, at least in the most developed countries, the state's interest in promoting commerce prevails over its interest in subjecting arbitral proceedings to national law. As a result, parties and arbitrators are given more freedom to choose the lex arbitri. Nevertheless, some authors still argue that the state where the arbitration proceedings take place should be able to control these proceedings to ensure respect for traditional standards of fairness, as well as the "limits of the arbitral mission" and the rights of

---

① 参见英国《1996 年仲裁法》第 14 条、第 16 条、第 30 条、第 34 条、第 38 条、第 39 条的规定。
② 英国《1996 年仲裁法》在附录 1 中明确列举了属于"强制性规定"的事项,主要涉及法院撤换仲裁员的权力、仲裁员免责、对仲裁庭实体管辖权的异议、保证证人出席、裁决的强制执行、裁决异议等等。当事人的相反约定不影响这些强制性规定的效力。

third parties.①

(二) 当事人没有选择仲裁程序法时由仲裁庭决定

如果当事人没有在仲裁协议中选定仲裁程序法,并且在争议发生后也不能达成一致,此时就需要仲裁员来确定程序法。仲裁员在选择程序法时,首先要考虑的因素是仲裁地法。一般而言,仲裁员倾向于适用仲裁地的仲裁程序法。其次,仲裁庭还要考虑裁决被有关国家承认与执行的问题。在裁决的有效性上,一个无国籍的裁决显然不如一个依据内国程序法作出的裁决。而且在仲裁员有权选择程序法的时候,选择一个成熟的国内法律体系也更加便利。

One of the main characteristics of international arbitration is its multijurisdictional character. An international arbitration usually involves at least two jurisdictions: the forum state and the state in which the award will be enforced. Legal proceedings may be instituted in a third jurisdiction, for example, the home state of one of the parties. It is also possible that a party might seek redress in the courts of the state whose law governs the merits of the dispute.② The legal system of any of these jurisdictions could serve as the lex arbitri. Perhaps the main reason for arbitrators to choose the lex fori more often than the other laws is that the place of arbitration is the most likely forum for court proceedings concerning the arbitration.

因此,一般来说,仲裁庭最经常适用的仲裁程序法是仲裁地的法律。

1. 适用仲裁地法的理论依据与实践

根据国际私法上的"场所支配行为"原则,在某个国家进行的诉讼,必须适用该国的程序法。将这个原则推及国际商事仲裁上,则意味着仲裁的行为必须受仲裁地法律的支配,整个仲裁程序必须完全符合仲裁地法律。③ 根据国家主权中的属地管辖权原则,国家对在其领土内发生的一切活动(当然包括仲裁)都具有属地管辖权,仲裁的合法性和效力来源于仲裁地国的法律。因此,传统理论认为仲裁地法与仲裁程序有不可分割的密切联系,仲裁程序应当受仲裁地国法律的支配。仲裁地是仲裁程序法得以适用的最具决定性意义的连结因素。④ 通常情况下,商事仲裁过程中发生的,如仲裁协议效力的认定、仲裁文书的送达、仲裁员的权利和义务、仲裁员的回避、临时措施的实施、证据的收集和使用等等,都要受到仲裁地法的支配。

Although the scholars recognize the arbitrator's freedom in choosing the

---

① See Vitek Danilowicz, The Choice of Applicable Law in International Arbitration, 9 Hastings Int'l & Comp. L. Rev. (1986), p.235.
② See e.g., Int'l Tank & Pipe S.A.K. v. Kuwait Aviation Fueling Co. K.S.C., 1975 Q.B., p.224.
③ 参见陈治东:《国际商事仲裁法》,法律出版社1998年版,第206页。
④ 参见李双元、谢石松:《国际民事诉讼法概论》,武汉大学出版社1990年版,第538—539页。

applicable law in the case where no expressed choice is made by the parties, the extent of this freedom is only limited to the substantive law of the contract, rather than the procedural law. Therefore, without a procedural law being specified, it would be compulsory for the arbitrators to refer to the law of the place where arbitration is held to decide the appropriate procedures they should follow.[①]

实践中,该原则获得了广泛支持。德国《民事诉讼法》第1025条规定:"根据第1043条第1款的规定,本法适用于位于德国境内的仲裁。"[②]第1042条规定:当事人选择仲裁程序不得违背"本编强制性规定"。我国《仲裁法》第65条规定:"涉外经济、运输和海事中发生的仲裁适用本章的规定。本章没有规定的适用本法其他规定。"瑞典《仲裁法》规定:"依法在瑞典进行的一切仲裁,有关程序方面的问题,均受瑞典仲裁法的约束。"俄罗斯《联邦国际商事仲裁法》第1条规定:"本法适用于仲裁地点位于俄罗斯联邦境内的国际商事仲裁。"第19条规定:无论是当事人自由选择仲裁程序还是仲裁庭决定仲裁程序,都必须"在遵循本法规定的前提下"进行。英国《1996年仲裁法》第2条第1款规定:"本编的规定适用于仲裁地位于英格兰、威尔士和北爱尔兰的仲裁。"第4条规定:"本编之强制性规定列于附录一,当事人之相反约定不影响其效力;本编之其他规定(非强制性规定)允许当事人约定适用,如没有约定,则适用本编规定。"

《纽约公约》第5条第1款(a)项、(d)项从裁决被拒绝执行的角度表明了仲裁地法律的重要地位:

(a) The parties to the agreement referred to in article II were, under the law applicable to them, under some incapacity, or the said agreement is not valid under the law to which the parties have subjected it or, failing any indication thereon, under the law of the country where the award was made;...

(d) The composition of the arbitral authority or the arbitral procedure was not in accordance with the agreement of the parties, or failing such agreement, was not in accordance with the law of the country where the arbitration took place; or...

Whilst parties are free to select an arbitral law of procedure other than the lex loci arbitri, there is some doubt as to whether they may exclude the mandatory procedural law of the forum. Article 1(2) of the UNCITRAL Rules states:

---

① See Hong-Lin Yu, Is the Territorial Link between Arbitration and the Country of Origin Established by Article I and V(1)(E) Being Distorted by the Application of Article VII of the New York Convention, International Arbitration Law Review, Vol. 5, No. 6, 2002.

② Section 1043 Subs. 1 provides that:"The parties are free to agree on the place of arbitration. Failing such agreement, the place of arbitration shall be determined by the arbitral tribunal having regard to the circumstances of the case, including the convenience of the parties."转引自赵秀文编著:《国际商事仲裁法》,中国人民大学出版社2004年版,第264页。

These Rules shall govern the arbitration except that where any of these Rules is in conflict with a provision of the law applicable to the arbitration from which the parties cannot derogate, that provision shall prevail.

This indicates that the Rules are subject to the mandatory law applicable to the parties, which may include any mandatory procedural law of the forum.①

2. 仲裁庭可以选择适用除仲裁地法以外的其他程序法或程序规则

如前所述,在当事人没有选择仲裁程序法的时候,只能说大部分情况下仲裁员将适用仲裁地法的程序规范。仲裁地法究竟在多大程度上影响仲裁程序,还没有统一的意见,一般来说目前并存着四大类观点:

第一类观点认为仲裁地与仲裁密不可分,仲裁地法应当绝对地控制仲裁活动,在仲裁条款中应当明确规定仲裁员要适用仲裁地的程序法。

第二类看法是允许仲裁员和当事人选择除了仲裁地以外的其他程序法,但是,仲裁地的强行法必须强制适用。

The third theory maintains that the parties and the arbitrators are the masters of the arbitral procedure without being bound by provisions of domestic procedural laws. Article 11 of the I. C. C. Arbitration Rules②has clearly been influenced by this theory.

Fourthly, a different perspective is present in some recent arbitration laws which depart from the conflict of laws analysis regarding the arbitral procedure. Rather than trying to localize the arbitral procedure, these laws unilaterally provide for rules regarding the procedure. Irrespective of the applicable law, these statutes have transnational procedural rules applicable to arbitral procedures taking place under the regime of those statutes. These rules deregulate arbitral proceedings from the procedural law of the arbitral place and give parties or arbitrators large freedom to determine the applicable rules of procedure.③

一般认为,除非与仲裁地强制性规定相违背,仲裁庭没有义务一定要适用仲裁地的法律。法国《民事诉讼法》第1494条规定:"仲裁协议可以通过直接规定或援引一套仲裁规则来明确仲裁应遵循的程序;它也可以选择特定的程序法作为准据法。如果协议没有规定,仲裁员应通过直接适用或援引法律或一套仲裁

---

① See Pippa Read, Delocalization of International Commercial Arbitration: Its Relevance in the New Millennium, American Review of International Arbitration, 1999.

② Article 11 states that gaps in the Arbitration Rules might be filled by the parties or the arbitrators whether or not reference is thereby made to a municipal procedural law to be applied to the arbitration.

③ See Filip De Ly, The Place of Arbitration in the Conflict of Laws of International Commercial Arbitration: An Exercise in Arbitration Planning, 12 Nw. J. Int'l L. & Bus. (1991), p.48.

规则来确立所需的程序规则。"瑞士《联邦国际私法法典》第182条规定:"(1)当事人可以直接地或按照仲裁规则确定仲裁程序,他们也可以按其选择的程序法进行仲裁程序;(2)当事人没有确定程序的,仲裁庭应当根据需要,直接或者按照法律或仲裁规则,确定仲裁程序。"①1998年德国《民事诉讼法》第1042条"一般程序规则"第4项规定:"当事人没有约定,且本编也没有规定,则仲裁庭应以其认为适当的方式进行仲裁。"1998年比利时《司法法典》第1693条规定,如果当事人没有就仲裁程序规则达成协议,"应由仲裁员确定"。1997年《美国仲裁协会国际仲裁规则》第16条规定:"除非本规则另有规定,只要当事人得到平等对待,每一方有权被听取意见并得到公平的陈述案件的机会,仲裁庭得按其认为适当的任何方式进行仲裁。"1998年《伦敦国际仲裁院仲裁规则》第14条"仲裁程序的进行"规定:"除非当事人另有协议,仲裁庭在其可决定适用的法律或法律规范的范围内享有最充分的履行职责的自由裁量权。"1985年《示范法》第19条"仲裁规则的确定"规定:"当事人如果未达成协议,仲裁庭可以在本法规定的限制下,按照它认为适当的方式进行仲裁。"

(三) 非内国化理论(Delocalization Theory)及其影响

1. 非内国化理论产生的背景

传统观点认为,所有仲裁都要服从仲裁地法。当事人在多大程度上能自行决定其仲裁活动完全取决于仲裁地法的规定。但是随着现代国际商事仲裁的发展,商事争议与仲裁地间的联系越来越具有偶然性。在许多情况下,当事人对仲裁地的选择不是因为看重当地的仲裁程序法而是其便利性和中立性。实际上可能双方都不是仲裁地的公民,也没有任何财产在仲裁地。强制性地将仲裁地法适用于争议是与当事人的意思自治相违背的。

ICC的一位仲裁员在裁决书中说:"The rules determining the applicable law vary from one country to the next. State judges derive them from their own national legislation, the lex fori. But an arbitral tribunal has no lex fori in the strictest sense of the word, particularly when the arbitration case is of an international nature."②

2. 非内国化理论的内容

在此背景下,非内国化理论产生了。它的支持者认为国际仲裁不应当受到仲裁地法包括仲裁地的强制性程序法的限制,在理论上可以是"浮动"(float)的,即完全与仲裁地国分离。

---

① 郑远民、吕国民编著:《国际私法——国际民事诉讼法与国际商事仲裁法》,中信出版社2002年版,第319页。

② ICC Case No. 1689. See Hong-Lin Yu, Is the Territorial Link between Arbitration and the Country of Origin Established by Article I and V(1)(E) Being Distorted by the Application of Article VII of the New York Convention, International Arbitration Law Review, Vol.5, No.6, 2002.

非内国化主要表现在两个方面：一是仲裁过程的非内国化（delocalization of the arbitration process），指的是仲裁地国（主要是其司法系统）不应当干预仲裁庭发挥仲裁功能。二是仲裁裁决的非内国化（delocalization of award）。这是指一项裁决如果因为违反了仲裁地法而被宣告无效或被撤销（be annulled or set aside）时，它仍然可以得到其他国家的承认和执行。

20世纪80年代以来，该理论的影响日益扩大。比较著名的案例有 SEEE v. 南斯拉夫案、戈特韦肯案（Gotaverken）、克罗玛罗案（Chromalloy）。这些案例都涉及一项裁决即使在一国被撤销，仍然得到了他国法院的承认与执行。与此同时，一些国内立法也出现了承认非内国理论的倾向。例如，1985年比利时立法规定："只有当仲裁裁决的争端当事人一方是具有比利时国籍或居所的自然人，或者在比利时设立或具有分支机构或其他营业地的法人时，比利时法院才受理该裁决的撤销请求。"这意味着如果仲裁当事人双方都是外国人，即使仲裁是在比利时境内作出的，比利时法院也不会撤销该仲裁裁决。1987年瑞士《联邦国际私法法典》第192条规定，如果当事人都不是瑞士人并已经达成明确协议排除法院对仲裁裁决的审查，那么仲裁就是完全自治的。

It states：

"1. Where none of the parties has its domicile, its habitual residence, or a business establishment in Switzerland, they may, by an express statement in the arbitration agreement or by a subsequent agreement in writing, exclude all setting aside proceedings, or they may limit such proceedings to one or several of the grounds [for annulment] listed in Art. 190 (2).

2. Where the parties have excluded all setting aside proceedings and where the awards are to be enforced in Switzerland, the New York Convention of 10 June 1958 on the recognition and enforcement of Foreign Arbitral Awards shall apply by analogy."①

1981年法国《民事诉讼法》第1502条拒绝承认与执行仲裁裁决的理由中没有包括《纽约公约》第5条第1款（e）项的规定，这表明如果一项裁决已经被他国撤销，该裁决在法国仍然可以得到执行。②

3. 对非内国化理论的评价

我们认为，非内国化理论还停留于理论探索阶段，没有受到实践的广泛接

---

① William W. Park, National Law and Commercial Justice: Safeguarding Procedural Integrity in International Arbitration, Tulane Law Review, Vol. 63, 1989, p. 647.

② See Hong-Lin Yu, Is the Territorial Link between Arbitration and the Country of Origin Established by Article I and V (1) (E) Being Distorted by the Application of Article VII of the New York Convention, International Arbitration Law Review, Vol. 5, No. 6, 2002.

受。该理论的产生主要是为了反对仲裁地法院对国际商事仲裁的过分干预。它根源于仲裁的契约性和意思自治原则。但是,真理再迈出一步就会成为谬误。非内国化裁决理论的支持者看到了法院对仲裁干预、阻碍的一面,却忽略了仲裁地法支持仲裁裁决、实现仲裁裁决、保证仲裁公正性的积极作用。

首先,仲裁机构的权限来自于当事人的授权,除此以外它没有强制力。因此,仲裁过程的进行常常需要仲裁地法院的协助。Courts become actors in arbitration when business managers ask that arbitration agreements be enforced against recalcitrant parties, that assets be attached, that the scope of the arbitration clause be determined, or that poorly drafted (sometimes pathological) arbitration clauses be made workable.① Assistance may take the form of enforcing the agreement to arbitrate, compelling production of documents, or granting attachment of assets ultimately used to secure payment of the award.②

其次,仲裁地法有力地保护了仲裁的公正性。国际商事仲裁中,仲裁员的裁决虽然是在一国内作出的,但是其裁决将影响到多个国家,特别是当裁决被其他国家承认和执行的时候。因此,如果出现仲裁员不公正、仲裁员超裁、仲裁协议无效等重大瑕疵时,仲裁地法就应该发挥作用,即使当事人并没有选择适用仲裁地法律。在程序上受到不公正对待的一方有权依据仲裁地法请求法院撤销该裁决,保护自己的正当利益。该制度在实践中有重要的意义。如果仲裁裁决在程序上显失公正(如败诉方被剥夺了陈述的机会),坚持仲裁裁决非内国化的结果将是败诉方无法向仲裁地法院起诉仲裁员的不公正行为。如果他不能在仲裁地法院撤销仲裁裁决,胜诉方就可以在败诉方有财产的任何国家请求当地法院的承认与执行,败诉方不得不在这些国家不断地应付类似的请求承认与执行的诉讼,一次又一次地证明存在程序违法的情况。更糟糕的情况是,如果败诉方恰好是仲裁申请人,此时他不但不能在仲裁地法院请求撤销裁决,同时对于他来说又不存在裁决的承认与执行地——申请人不存在财产被执行的问题。于是他面临着无计可施的尴尬局面。

最后,非内国裁决能否得到有关国家的承认和执行还是存在疑问的。

The arbitral seat gives the award an international currency merely by letting the award be rendered within its territory. The place of the proceedings provides support to the arbitral process by allowing an award to take on a presumptive validity under the New York Convention. That validity facilitates enforcement against assets found in

---

① For example, the arbitration clause may not provide for the way arbitrators will be appointed, or may be ambiguous on the question of whether the parties have actually renounced recourse to courts.

② See William W. Park, National Law and Commercial Justice: Safeguarding Procedural Integrity in International Arbitration, Tulane Law Review, Vol.63, 1989, p.647.

jurisdictions that adhere to the Convention.

反之,如果裁决的相关事项违反仲裁地法,可能就面临无法得到承认和执行的危险。例如,前文所述的《纽约公约》第5条第1款(a)项、(d)项,以及(e)项规定:

Recognition and enforcement of the award may be refused, at the request of the party against whom it is invoked, only if that party furnishes to the competent authority where the recognition and enforcement is sought, proof that:

(a) The parties to the agreement referred to in article II were, under the law applicable to them, under some incapacity, or the said agreement is not valid under the law to which the parties have subjected it or, failing any indication thereon, under the law of the country where the award was made;...

(d) The composition of the arbitral authority or the arbitral procedure was not in accordance with the agreement of the parties, or failing such agreement, was not in accordance with the law of the country where the arbitration took place; or...

(e) The award has not yet become binding, on the parties, or has been set aside or suspended by a competent authority of the country in which, or under the law of which, that award was made.

三、我国法律对仲裁程序法的规定

我国《仲裁法》第65条规定:"涉外经济贸易、运输和海事中发生的纠纷的仲裁,适用本章规定。本章没有规定的,适用本法其他有关规定。"第73条规定:"涉外仲裁规则可以由中国国际商会依照本法和民事诉讼法的有关规定制定。"CIETAC 2005年《仲裁规则》第4条第2款规定:"凡当事人同意将争议提交仲裁委员会仲裁的,均视为同意按照本规则进行仲裁。当事人约定适用其他仲裁规则,或约定对本规则有关内容进行变更的,从其约定,但其约定无法实施或与仲裁地强制性法律规定相抵触者除外。"

这意味着,在我国进行的仲裁,其程序必须适用中国法。当事人不得选择其他国家的法律作为仲裁程序法。但是,依据上述仲裁规则,当事人可以选择仲裁规则,或对该仲裁规则有关内容进行变更。但需要注意的是,选择仲裁规则不等于有权选择仲裁程序法。当事人约定的仲裁规则不得违反我国的仲裁法规定,并且仲裁规则未涉及的程序性事项仍然必须适用我国法律。由此可见,我国法律更倾向于仲裁地法的适用,对当事人意思自治是有所限制的,对所谓的非内国化仲裁是不予承认的。

第二节　国际商事仲裁实体问题的法律适用

在程序法确定之后,仲裁就进入了实质性审理阶段。此时,选择恰当的法律来解决实体争议是十分重要的,它直接关系到当事人的权利义务关系和仲裁的结果。鉴于国际商事交易涉及不同国家的法律,而不同国家可能就相同的事项作出不同的规定,如何决定解决争议实体问题的法律适用和该适用法律的主要内容是通过仲裁方式解决国际交易不可避免的问题。

在国际商事仲裁实践中,解决国际商事争议可适用的法律是广泛的,从争议所依据的合同本身,到有关国家的法律,再到有关的国际公约和国际惯例,以及商人习惯法等,都可能成为适用于解决争议的法律。

在选择可适用的实体法时,我们要考虑的是如何选择解决争议的准据法,以及由谁来选择。[①] 一般而言,解决国际商事争议的适用法律方法主要分为两种:一是争议当事人共同选择实体争议的法律;二是当事人无明确选择的,由仲裁庭确定。

一、当事人选择实体法

（一）当事人意思自治原则

国际商事仲裁具有跨国性,在实体问题上必然要考虑由何种法律来解决争议。此时,首先应当尊重的是当事人所选择的法律,这已经是国际私法普遍承认的一项原则。仲裁机构审理商事争议的权力来源于当事人的授权,仲裁员有义务尊重当事人作出的法律选择。

Compared with proceedings conducted in the national courts, the most significant feature of international commercial arbitration is that the parties enjoy a great deal of autonomy. In accordance with such autonomy, the parties are free to have their disputes governed by any law they desire. In respect of the choice of law rules, the Rome Convention provides new rules to be followed by the judges and the arbitrators sitting in the United Kingdom. Article 3(1) confirms the principle of party autonomy and stipulates: "A contract shall be governed by the law chosen by the parties."[②]

除非法律另有规定,各国法律一般都允许当事人对他们之间进行的国际商事交易应适用的法律作出约定。这也就是各国国际私法上普遍适用的"当事人

---

① 参见赵秀文编著:《国际商事仲裁法》,中国人民大学出版社 2004 年版,第 353 页。
② Vitek Danilowicz, The Choice of Applicable Law in International Arbitration, 9 Hastings Int'l & Comp. L. Rev. (1986), p.235.

意思自治原则"在通过仲裁的方法解决国际商事争议中的体现。在实践中,仲裁本身就是当事人之间自愿达成的解决争议的方法。而在解决争议的过程中,如果当事人就他们之间的争议应当适用的法律规则达成一致,仲裁庭一般都应当尊重当事人的选择,除非此项法律规则违反相关国家法律的禁止性规定。例如,1998 年《国际商会仲裁规则》第 17 条第 1 款规定:"The parties shall be free to agree upon the rules of law to be applied by the Arbitral Tribunal to the merits of the dispute. In the absence of any such agreement, the Arbitral Tribunal shall apply the rules of law which it determines to be appropriate."1998 年《伦敦国际仲裁院仲裁规则》第 22 条第 3 款也有类似规定:"The Arbitral Tribunal shall decide the parties' dispute in accordance with the law(s) or rules of law chosen by the parties as applicable to the merits of their dispute. If to the extent that the Arbitral Tribunal determines that the parties have made no such choice, the Arbitral Tribunal shall apply the law(s) or rules of law which it considers appropriate."

可见,如果当事人就他们之间的争议应适用的法律或者法律规则作出约定,按照上述仲裁机构的仲裁规则,此项约定均可以得以适用。在国际商事仲裁中,当事人约定的法律或者法律规则通常情况下均指实体法规则,而不是冲突法规则。对此,世界知识产权组织仲裁与调解中心 2002 年起实施的《仲裁规则》第 59 条第 1 款作出了专门规定:"The Tribunal shall decide the substance of the dispute in accordance with the law or rules law chosen by the parties. Any designation of the law of a given State shall be construed, unless otherwise expressed, as directly referring to the substantive law of that State and not to its conflict of laws rules. Failing a choice by the parties, the Tribunal shall apply the law or rules of law that it determines to be appropriate. In all cases, the Tribunal shall decide having due regard to the terms of any relevant contract and taking into account applicable trade usages. The Tribunal may decide as amiable compositeur or ex aequo et bono only if the parties have expressly authorized it to do so."[1]

(二)当事人选择实体法受到的限制

许多学者认为,由于国际商事仲裁的自治性和国际性,当事人对法律的选择应该是自由的、不受限制的。但是,也有人认为,如果当事人可以通过自由选择实体法来规避国家的强行法,或者法院无权审查仲裁裁决是否符合公共政策,就可能导致仲裁背离基本的公平正义原则。虽然许多国家已经通过法律承认了意思自治原则,但同时也对意思自治施加了各种限制。仲裁的自治性不是绝对的,因为任何裁决的撤销、承认和执行最终都要归结到法院的司法权。因此,尽管在

---

[1] 转引自赵秀文编著:《国际商事仲裁法》,中国人民大学出版社 2004 年版,第 349 页。

学术上可以探讨,但是在实践中,当事人必须考虑到裁决的执行问题,在法律选择问题上应当注意到相关国内法的限制。

第一,当事人不得通过选择实体法来规避法律。

Courts generally do not uphold a party's choice of law if the purpose of the choice is to avoid provisions of the law. For example, suppose X & Co., an English firm having chartered an Estonian ship, issues through its agents, a Palestinian company, bills of lading for the carriage of oranges from Jaffa to England. The bills of lading, which are issued at Jaffa contain a provision requiring that the bill of lading be construed in accordance with English law. However, according to the Palestine Carriage of Goods by Sea Ordinance of 1926, every bill of lading issued in Palestine must contain a statement that it takes effect subject to the Hague rules and is deemed subject to those rules notwithstanding the omission of such a statement. An exceptions clause contained in the bill of lading, which would have been valid in accordance with English domestic law but which is void under the Ordinance, is considered void as being contrary to the law of the place where the bills of lading were issued.

第二,国内公共政策可能会限制当事人的法律选择。在英美法系国家,如英国,法院虽然支持选择法律的意思自治,但是要求这种选择必须是"诚信的、合法的"(bona fide and legal),如果当事人选择的法律明显不合理或者反复无常,这种选择就是无效的。法官在 Vita Food Products Inc. v. Unus Shipping Co. Ltd.案①中指出,如果当事人有明确的意图选择了合同准据法,很难认为应该对他们施加限制,但是他们的意图应该是诚信的和合法的并且不违反公共政策。

二、当事人无明确选择时由仲裁庭确定实体法

如果当事人没有约定解决争议应适用的法律或者法律规则,根据国际商会国际仲裁院、伦敦国际仲裁院和世界知识产权组织仲裁与调解中心的仲裁规则的规定,应当由仲裁庭决定争议实体问题应适用的法律或者法律规则。而仲裁庭决定应适用的此项法律并非特指某一特定国家的法律,它可以是一个国家的法律也可以是几个国家的法律,还可以是某些仲裁庭认定为"适当的"的法律规则(rules of law)。②

In international commercial arbitration, the choice of law issue can be more complicated than the parties might have expected, especially when no expressed

---

① Vita Food Products Inc. v. Unus Shipping Co. Ltd., [1939] A.C. 277 (P.C.).
② 参见赵秀文编著:《国际商事仲裁法》,中国人民大学出版社2004年版,第349页。

choice of law is found in the arbitration agreement, or the arbitrators experience difficulties in inferring the implied choice of law.①

If the parties do not choose the law, how is it decided? There is no strict approach because an international arbitrator has no lex fori providing a fixed conflict of laws system. In addition, arbitration procedural laws and private rules leave arbitrators enormous flexibility regarding the substantive law. The possible solutions will be discussed from a mainly theoretical perspective. The solutions vary in degrees of flexibility for the arbitrator. Of course, whether each of these solutions is available depends on whether the lex arbitri and/or the procedural rules and/or the arbitration agreement imposes any restrictions. Consequently, within the theoretical discussion examples of current positive law solutions used by domestic legal systems and institutional rules will be given where appropriate.②

仲裁庭决定实体法的适用,或者依据某一冲突规则来选择;或者不依据任何冲突规则,直接确定实体法。

(一) 依冲突规则确定仲裁实体法

1. 仲裁地国家的冲突规则

在当事人未作法律选择的场合,仲裁员一般依据仲裁地的冲突规则选择准据法。传统上认为,当事人的任何行为都必须得到法律的许可;而只有行为地法,才能赋予当事人行为以法律效力。当事人有权指定仲裁员作出裁决所依据的法律,但这一权利只能在仲裁庭所在国法律许可的范围内行使。这一观点被国际法学会所通过的《关于私法仲裁的决议》所采纳。该决议第11条规定:"关于适用于争议实质的法律,须依仲裁庭所在地国现行选择规则确定。"适用仲裁地法的优点,是具有统一性和可预见性。在当事人未作法律选择时,可以适用统一的程序和规则决定适用的法律,当事人也可预见仲裁员将依什么冲突规则确定可适用的法律。

在国际商事仲裁实践中,仲裁地国冲突规则曾得到广泛适用。国际商会仲裁庭曾多次援用仲裁地国冲突规则决定仲裁适用的实体法。

The method using the conflict of laws rules of the place of arbitration has traditionally been one of the most commonly used approaches to resolving choice of law problems in arbitration. It was the solution recommended by the Institute of International Law as early as 1957 and was used in the U. K. prior to the introduction

---

① See Vitek Danilowicz, The Choice of Applicable Law in International Arbitration, 9 Hastings Int'l & Comp. L. Rev. (1986), p.235.

② See Simon Greenberg, The Law Applicable to the Merits in International Arbitration, 8 V.J. (2004), p.315.

of the International Arbitration Act 1996 (U. K.). Theoretical support for this method comes from the juridical conception of international arbitration. According to this theory, the arbitrator is acting within a certain State and under the legal auspices of that State. As an arbitrator's power to decide which law applies derives from the arbitral procedural law, and ultimately from the lex arbitri, the local conflict of laws rules must be applied. This argument implies that international arbitration has a lex fori at the place of arbitration.

From a practical perspective, using local conflict rules has many advantages being simple, predictable and avoiding time wasted on choice of law disputes. It's also the advantage that it provides not only the substantive law to govern the contract ("lex contractus") but a complete set of conflict rules for resolving any choice of law issues that arise. However, the choice of seat remains insufficiently proximate to the dispute to justify using its conflict of laws rules. Domestic conflict rules are developed to promote national sovereignty interests and are thus connected to the local jurisdiction. Moreover, if an arbitrator uses the place of arbitration's conflict rules, she or he is acting as would a judge in that jurisdiction. This confuses the respective roles of judges and arbitrators in light of the fundamental differences discussed above. As a result of the increasing internationalisation of arbitration, and the needs of international business, arbitrators should be free from any lex fori that might unduly limit their determination of the applicable law.[①]

2. 仲裁员认为适当的冲突规则

基于仲裁的契约性质以及仲裁员的特殊地位,大多数学者主张,在当事人未作出法律选择的情况下,应当赋予仲裁员广泛的自由裁量权,允许仲裁员依据其认为适当的或可以适用的冲突规则决定仲裁实体法。这表明仲裁员可以依据非仲裁地的冲突规则来选择实体法。仲裁员享有广泛的自由裁量权,可以在不同国家的国际私法体系、国际条约、国际惯例、仲裁与司法判例等相当大的范围内寻找适当的可适用的冲突规则。

This solution is called "Choosing an Appropriate Set of Conflict of Laws Rules", which may be chosen ad hoc by arbitrators with freedom to choose their method. It has also been adopted in the UNCITRAL Model Law on International Commercial Arbitration. Article 28(2) says:

[①] See Simon Greenberg, The Law Applicable to the Merits in International Arbitration, 8 V. J. (2004), p. 315.

Failing any designation by the parties, the arbitral tribunal shall apply the law determined by the conflict of laws rules which it considers applicable.

It is debatable whether the phrase "the conflict of laws rules" in Art. 28(2) requires the arbitrator to choose an established system of conflict rules or whether she or he can simply choose an appropriate rule from her/his general knowledge of private international law. The arbitration experts seem divided but do not explain why. Mark Blessing says expressly that the Model Law does not require a state conflict system and that a conflict rule is satisfactory. Some commentators suggest that there is little practical difference between the Model Law and the direct approach because under the Model Law an arbitrator can still directly choose the law. Yves Derains implies the opposite. It is submitted that the plurality of "rules" suggests a set of rules and thus a system, such as a domestic system or a system of international conflict of laws rules. However, an unduly technical reading of the legislation is unlikely. Further, model laws should be interpreted consistently across the adopting States. It is interesting that the French version of Art. 28(2) refers to "la règle de conflit", which is singular, suggesting that the arbitrator needs only to choose a conflict rule rather than a set of rules.①

既然各国大多允许仲裁员适用其认为可以适用的或适当的冲突规则决定实体法的适用,这就意味着不会仅限于特定国家的冲突法规则。从仲裁实践看,除了仲裁地的冲突规则,仲裁员一般适用的冲突规则的范围是:

第一,仲裁员本国的冲突规则。一般而言,仲裁员都对其本国法较为熟悉,因此,有人主张可以适用仲裁员本国的冲突规则。事实上,仲裁员本身也确实不可避免地有这种倾向,来自不同法律体系的仲裁员,其所作出的裁决无不反映出其本国的法律观念和法律文化,但是这种观点受到许多学者的批评,尤其是在仲裁员分属不同国家时,其缺点显而易见。

First, if the arbitrator's familiarity with a legal system plays a role in choosing the applicable law, it should influence the choice of substantive rather than conflict law, because the substantive law determines the rights and obligations of the parties. Second, the proposition that the conflict rules of the arbitrator's home state should apply underestimates the arbitrator's intellectual capacities. Third, this approach runs into the practical problem of determining the arbitrator's home state, namely whether it is the place of the arbitrator's nationality, citizenship, domicile, or residence.

---

① See Simon Greenberg, The Law Applicable to the Merits in International Arbitration, 8 V. J. (2004), p. 315.

Finally, application of the conflict rules of the arbitrator's home state implies a nexus between that state and the dispute. In most cases, however, such a nexus does not exist.①

第二,裁决执行地国家的冲突规则。有学者基于仲裁裁决有效性的考虑,主张适用裁决承认和执行地国的冲突规则。

However, practical considerations reinforce the conclusion that application of the conflict rules of a state where the award will be enforced is not a viable alternative. In most cases, when the arbitrator makes a decision concerning the applicable conflict rules, the state where execution of the award will be sought is unknown. Moreover, enforcement of the award might be sought in more than one jurisdiction.②

第三,国际私法公约中的冲突规则。1961 年《欧洲公约》未限定仲裁员必须选择适用一个特定国家的国际私法体系,这使得仲裁员援用国际条约中的冲突规则成为可能。在国际商事仲裁中,就曾经有过此类案例,即仲裁员援引 1955 年《关于国际货物买卖法律适用的海牙公约》的规定,而与该争议有关的国家均未参加该公约。③

第四,国际私法一般原则(General Principles of Private International Law)。在仲裁实践中,有些仲裁员并不援引任何特定国家的冲突规则,而是援引国际私法一般原则作为可适用的冲突规则。This is a vague concept. Despite calls for a "supranational" system, there is no universally accepted codification. An arbitrator using this method has several options. She or he might perform a comparative law analysis on the conflict of laws rules of the domestic legal systems connected to the dispute to establish common threads. Alternatively, an arbitrator inclined towards public international law principles might look for an appropriate choice of law principle in customary international law.④

第五,与争议有最密切联系国家的冲突规则。⑤ 最密切联系原则是当代各国国际私法立法和实践普遍接受和采纳的一项基本原则。最初只是适用于合同领域,现在已经扩展到了侵权、亲子关系等领域。在这种新的法律选择模式下,最密切联系至多属于仲裁员考察、寻求可适用的仲裁规则的一种方法或者因素。

---

① See Vitek Danilowicz, The Choice of Applicable Law in International Arbitration, 9 Hastings Int'l & Comp. L. Rev. (1986), p.235.
② Id.
③ See ICC Case 1717/1972. Cf. O. Lando, The Law Applicable to the Merits of the Dispute, P. Sarcevic ed., Essays on International Commercial Arbitration, 1989, p.139.
④ See Simon Greenberg, The Law Applicable to the Merits in International Arbitration, 8 V. J. (2004), p.315.
⑤ 参见朱克鹏:《国际商事仲裁的法律适用》,法律出版社 1999 年版,第 150 页。

仲裁员如果一定要依照最密切联系原则来选择法律的话,实际上是局限了仲裁实体法选择的灵活性,这就意味着仲裁员只能依据"最密切联系"这一连结因素来确定仲裁适用的实体法,缩小了仲裁员自由裁量的范围,这也是该原则目前只处于仲裁员参考因素的地位的原因。

(二) 直接确定仲裁实体法

在当事人未作法律选择的场合,传统的方法是依有关冲突规则确定仲裁实体法。但是,依据冲突规则选择实体法存在着一些弊端,如程序上比较复杂,缺乏灵活性,可选择的实体法范围相对狭窄等。随着实践的发展,仲裁员开始抛开冲突规则直接选择实体法。

Some modern laws and rules provide broad freedom for the arbitrator directly to choose the law without passing through a conflict of laws system. Article 1496 of the French New Code of Civil Procedure says that failing a choice of law by the parties, the arbitrator "shall decide according to the rules he deems appropriate".

这种方法的优势在于:

首先,法律适用的简易性。直接适用方法使仲裁员摆脱了依据仲裁规则确定实体法这一困难的任务。依此方法,仲裁员不必花费大量时间和精力去确定适当的冲突规则,而可以直接根据公正解决争议的需要决定应当适用的实体法,由此避免了繁琐的确定实体法适用的过程。

其次,法律适用结果的合理性。通过这个方法,仲裁员可考虑到案件的多种情况,运用多种方法考察与案件有关的因素,其最终确定的实体法律规则一般是比较适当的。由此确定当事人实体权利义务较易获得合理的处理结果。

再次,确定适当实体法规则方法的多样性。通过直接适用方法确定实体法的适用,仲裁员不必固守僵化的某一种方法,他可以同时或分别采用多种理论和方法,如实体规则适用结果比较的方法、利益分析的方法、特征履行的方法、最密切联系的方法等。

最后,实体法律适用规则的灵活性。因为冲突规则多是以地域为连结因素,它往往指向某一国家的国内法,所以适用冲突规则容易把仲裁实体法的选择限制在国内法规则的范围之内。直接适用方法则使仲裁员有可能适用非国内法规则,如适用国际法、国际合同法、贸易习惯或惯例、商事习惯法、一般法律原则等。

仲裁庭采用直接适用方法,一般会适用的实体法包括:

1. 仲裁地国家的实体法

The traditional approach in the U. S. was that if the parties had not chosen the applicable law, they were assumed to have intended application of the substantive laws of the place of arbitration. This solution is simple, predictable and saves resources otherwise wasted on conflict of laws analyses early in the dispute resolution process. However, this approach is now well out of favour. The place of arbitration is chosen for its qualities of neutrality and procedural efficiency; that is its qualities as a venue to regulate the dispute itself, and not to regulate the parties' substantive rights and obligations. The place of arbitration may have no further connection with the dispute. Applying the place of arbitration's substantive laws would not only come as a shock to some disputants but could mean that the choice of place of arbitration would be complicated by the need to ensure an acceptable substantive law. Finally this method is even less relevant when an arbitral institution, or the tribunal, has fixed the place of arbitration rather than the parties.①

2. 统一商事法

统一商事法是指由世界各国缔结或共同参与的调整国际经济贸易活动的国际条约构成的统一实体规范体系,目的在于避免因各国法律互异而产生的法律冲突,以及因国内法的变动带来的法律规则的不确定性。典型的统一商事法包括:《联合国国际货物销售合同公约》(CISG)、《统一提单若干法律规则的公约》、《统一国际航空运输某些规则的公约》、《关于汇票、本票的日内瓦公约》等等。以CISG为例,当事人可以选择适用该公约来解决争议,也可以选择公约的部分条文,甚至修改公约的部分条款。这体现了很大的灵活性,表现了对意思自治的尊重。

3. 一般法律原则

《联合国国际法院规约》第38条规定,可以将一般法律原则作为裁判的依据。国际商事仲裁法中所说的一般法律原则与国际公法中的一般法律原则没有本质的不同。② 我国学者一般认为,一般法律原则是基于国际社会中各民族的一致法律意识,各国法律所共同具有的指导思想和原则。例如,合同必须遵守、公平善意、禁止反言等均属于一般法律原则。不过,我国大部分学者认为一般法律原则的内容过于抽象和空泛,在商事仲裁领域适用难以保证裁决的确定性和准确性。

哈佛法律评论协会曾经总结了7项国际商事仲裁的可适用的法律原则,可供大家参考:

(1) A sovereign government may make and be bound by contractual agreements with foreign private parties.

(2) The corporate veil may be pierced to prevent a beneficial owner from

---

① See Simon Greenberg, The Law Applicable to the Merits in International Arbitration, 8 V. J. (2004), p.315.

② 参见朱克鹏:《国际商事仲裁的法律适用》,法律出版社1999年版,第177页。

escaping contractual liability.

(3) Force majeure justifies nonperformance of a contract such that the loss is borne fairly by the parties.

(4) Contracts that seriously violate bonos mores or international public policy are invalid.

(5) Equitable compensation constitutes the primary remedy for damages.

(6) The right of property and of acquired vested rights is generally inviolable——a state may not effect a taking without equitable compensation.

(7) A party may not receive unjust enrichment.[①]

4. 友好仲裁

友好仲裁(amiable arbitration)是指在国际商事仲裁中,仲裁庭基于当事人的授权,基于公平善意原则(ex aequo et bono)对实体争议作出裁决。仲裁当事人通过协议授权仲裁庭依"公平善意"对争议作出裁决,意味着当事人要承受仲裁庭不按照任何法律规则作出裁决的后果。友好仲裁为一些国际条约和仲裁规则所确认,如《欧洲公约》、《国际商会仲裁规则》、《美国仲裁协会国际商事仲裁规则》。由于基于"公平善意"原则作出裁决给了仲裁庭很广泛的自由裁量权,所以,为了防止其滥用权力和专断裁决以保证裁决的有效性,许多国家又同时在其商事仲裁立法中,对仲裁庭行使这一权力施加了必要的限制。

5. 商事习惯法[②]

商事习惯法来源于拉丁文 lex marcatoria,也翻译为商人习惯法、商业习惯法等,英文的对应词为 Law Merchant。它主要表现为:

第一,国际贸易惯例,包括在国际上反复适用的贸易惯例和做法,以及长期贸易活动而形成的成文统一惯例。当事人可自由协商是否适用,如已经明示采用还可以协商变动其中内容。如国际商会 1936 年制定并多次修订的《国际贸易术语解释通则》(International Rules for the Interpretation of Trade Terms, INCOTERMS)、《跟单信用证统一惯例》(Uniform Customs and Practice for Documentary Credits, UCP)等。

第二,标准格式合同,这是国际组织或者专业公司或协会为供当事人签订合同而预先准备的。只有双方当事人自愿采用时,标准格式合同或标准条款才能约束当事人。当事人在缔约时也享有修改和补充的权利,并把格式合同的内容确定为双方权利义务关系的依据。[③]

[①] See Harvard Law Review Association, General Principles of Law in International Commercial Arbitration, 101 Harv. L. Rev. (1988), p.1816.
[②] 参见赵秀文编著:《国际商事仲裁法》,中国人民大学出版社 2004 年版,第 381 页。
[③] 参见杨树明主编:《国际商事仲裁法》,重庆大学出版社 2002 年版,第 164 页。

从我国国内立法上看,现行许多法律上的具体规定都体现了商人习惯法的基本原则。如我国《民法通则》中体现的当事人法律地位平等、公平竞争与交易、权利与义务对等等商人习惯法中的原则;《合同法》中关于允许涉外合同的当事人选择处理合同争议所适用的法律。此外,我国缔结和参加的双边或多边国际公约和我国在国际商事交往中适用的国际惯例,许多都体现了商人习惯法的原则。同时,依照一些著名学者的观点,国际公约、示范法和国际惯例本身就是商人习惯法的表现形式。可见,我国立法实践中,允许商人习惯法的存在。[①]

三、我国仲裁实体问题的法律适用

目前,我国涉外立法没有专门涉及国际商事仲裁的法律适用,《仲裁法》除第7条极为原则性地规定"仲裁应当根据事实,符合法律规定,公平合理地解决纠纷"之外,也没有作出任何具体规定。在我国提起的国际商事仲裁,关于实体法的选择主要依据的是《合同法》第126条的规定:"涉外合同的当事人可以选择处理合同争议所适用的法律,但法律另有规定的除外。涉外合同的当事人没有选择的,适用与合同有最密切联系的国家的法律。在中华人民共和国境内履行的中外合资经营企业合同、中外合作经营企业合同、中外合作勘探开发自然资源合同,适用中华人民共和国法律。"2007年8月起施行的《最高人民法院关于审理涉外民事或商事合同纠纷案件法律适用若干问题的决定》将要求适用中国法律的上述三类合同补充为八类合同,[②]另外五类适用中国法律的合同为:中外合资经营企业、中外合作经营企业、外商独资企业股份转让合同;外国自然人、法人或者其他组织承包经营在中华人民共和国领域内设立的中外合资、合作经营企业的合同;外国自然人、法人或者其他组织购买中华人民共和国领域内的非外商投资企业股权的合同;外国自然人、法人或者其他组织认购中华人民共和国领域内的非外商投资有限责任公司或者股份有限公司增资的合同;外国自然人、法人或者其他组织购买中华人民共和国领域内的非外商投资企业资产的合同。

从我国涉外仲裁机构的仲裁规则看,2005年的《中国国际经济贸易仲裁委员会仲裁规则》仅第43条涉及法律适用,该条规定:"仲裁庭应当根据事实,依照法律和合同规定,参考国际惯例,并遵循公平合理原则,独立公正地作出裁决。"该条规定抽象笼统,在赋予仲裁庭充分自由裁量权的同时,没有提供必要的规则或指引,甚至在依法仲裁和友好仲裁上含混其辞。依据该规定,仲裁庭有权直接适用其认为适当的法律,而无须借助于冲突规范的指引——至少遵守仲

---

① 参见赵秀文:《国际商事仲裁及其适用法律研究》,北京大学出版社2002年版,第293页。
② 参见该决定的第8条。第8条第9项为"兜底"条款,即"中华人民共和国法律、行政法规规定应适用中华人民共和国法律的其他合同"。

裁地(如中国)的冲突规范已不再是一项法律义务。2004年的《中国海事仲裁委员会仲裁规则》第60条作出了相同的规定。相比之下,2005年的《中国国际经济贸易仲裁委员会金融争议仲裁规则》中的规定比较完备,体现了国际商事仲裁领域实体法律适用的潮流。该仲裁规则第21条规定:"除非法律另有强制性规定,涉外案件的当事人可以约定适用于案件实体问题的法律。当事人未作约定的,仲裁庭可以适用其认为适当的法律。无论在何种情形下,仲裁庭均应考虑合同条款、相关行业惯例和行业标准实务,并遵循公平合理原则。"

我国学者一般认为,商人习惯法可以在我国得到适用。其法律渊源体现在《民法通则》、《合同法》及《仲裁法》中。《合同法》第125条规定:"中华人民共和国法律未作规定的,可以适用国际惯例。"《中国国际经济贸易仲裁委员会仲裁规则》第53条规定:"仲裁庭应当根据事实,依照法律和合同规定,参照国际惯例,并遵循公平合理原则,独立公正地作出裁决。"

但是,不论是当事人意思自治还是仲裁庭选择适用法律或商事习惯,都不得违背我国的公共利益。《民法通则》第150条对此有明确规定:"依照本章规定适用外国法律或者国际惯例的,不得违背中华人民共和国的社会公共利益。"

第三节 国际商事仲裁裁决撤销与执行中的法律适用

仲裁裁决作出以后,对当事人而言,争议还没有完全结束。仲裁庭的权力只限于作出裁决,而执行裁决还有赖于司法权的作用。胜诉方希望裁决能够迅速执行,败诉方则有可能对裁决不服。此时,有关国家的法院就要发挥重要的作用。一方面,法院可能撤销仲裁裁决;另一方面,法院也可能承认并执行仲裁裁决。这两个方面,都涉及法律适用的问题。

一、撤销裁决的法律适用

(一) 撤销裁决的请求应当向仲裁地法院提出

裁决的撤销,一般是向裁决作出地(即仲裁地)的法院提出。这是因为,仲裁地法院对裁决有监督权。例如,我国《仲裁法》第58、70条分别规定了国内仲裁裁决和涉外仲裁裁决的撤销,而对于有瑕疵的外国仲裁裁决只能拒绝承认与执行。《示范法》第1条第2款规定:"本法之规定,除第8、9、35及36条外,只适用于仲裁地点在本国领土内的情况。"关于仲裁裁决的撤销规定在《示范法》第34条,不是第1条第2款里列举的例外,这意味着撤销仲裁裁决的前提是裁决是在本国领土内作出的。撤销裁决的管辖权属于仲裁地法院。

The fact that the place of arbitration in general has nothing to do with the place where the hearings take place can already be derived from Art. 20(2) of the Model Law.① It is even possible that the whole proceedings are conducted at a different place without that place becoming the place of arbitration. This is well evidenced by the decision of Singapore Court of Appeal in PT Garuda Indonesia v. Birgen Air. The Belgian defendant had agreed to lease a DC 10 airplane to the Indonesian plaintiff. The dispute resolution clause inserted into the contract provided for arbitration in Jakarta. So did the terms of reference signed by both parties after a dispute had arisen and had been referred to arbitration. Owing to the political turmoil in Jakarta the chairmen of the tribunal first suggested having a hearing in Zurich. Finally with the consent of both parties a three-day hearing was held in Singapore. The final award was rendered thereafter and stated that it was rendered in Jakarta, though the tribunal never met there. The award further stated that it "had not been suggested by either of the parties, nor is it the view of the tribunal, that the use of Singapore as a convenient place for the hearing had any substantive or procedural impact on the proceedings".

Irrespective of this clear indication that according to the tribunal's view the place of arbitration was in Jakarta, Garuda on January 3, 2001 started setting aside proceedings in Singapore. Garuda's position was that the parties had, by consenting to hold the complete hearing in Singapore, subsequently changed the arbitration agreement. The court rejected that view and held that no subsequent change of the place of arbitration had taken place. Unlike the cases relied upon by Garuda, no express agreement to that effect existed. While Garuda tried to rely on the fact that the arbitration was held in its entirety in Singapore the court made clear that an arbitration was not only made up of a hearing but consisted of a number of facts commencing with the appointment of arbitrators and going to render the final award.②

裁决的撤销是仲裁地对仲裁裁决的司法监督,各仲裁地国的国内法一般都对其作出了明确规范。1989年瑞士《联邦国际私法法典》第190条规定:"遇有

---

① Art. 20(2) of the UNCITRAL Model Law provides: "the arbitral tribunal may, unless otherwise agreed by the parties, meet at any place it considers appropriate for consultation among its members, for hearing witnesses, experts or the parties, or for inspection of goods, other property or documents."

② See Stefan Kroll, Setting Aside Proceedings in Model Law Jurisdictions—Selected Procedural and Substantive Questions from the Case Law, Int. A. L. R., Vol.8, No.5, 2005. pp.170—178.

下述情况,当事人可以提出异议:1.仲裁员的指定或仲裁庭的组成不合乎规则的;2.仲裁员声明对该案无管辖权的;3.仲裁庭所选定的仲裁员超出当事人指定的范围的;4.仲裁中没有体现平等原则,当事人的合法权益没有得到合法维护的;5.仲裁裁决违背公共秩序的。"1994年意大利《民事诉讼法典》第829条、英国《1996年仲裁法》第68条、1999年瑞典《仲裁法》第34条都分别对仲裁裁决的撤销作了规定。

In most countries, the grounds for vacating arbitral awards are mandatory: the parties cannot contract around them. In the United States, some courts have found the grounds for vacating an award to provide a mandatory minimum but not a mandatory maximum: in other words, parties cannot contract for less court supervision than provided in the statute but can contract for more supervision. In some countries, however, the grounds for vacating international arbitration awards are default rules, at least for arbitrations involving foreign parties. For example, the Swiss international arbitration law provides:

Where none of the parties has its domicile, its habitual residence, or a business establishment in Switzerland, they may, by an express statement in the arbitration agreement or by a subsequent agreement in writing, exclude all setting aside proceedings, or they may limit such proceedings to one or several of the grounds listed in Art. 190, para. 2.

In 1998, Belgium amended its arbitration law to follow the Swiss model, repealing a prior version that precluded actions to vacate awards unless one of the parties to the proceeding was Belgian.[①]

(二) 某些事项上允许适用其他国家法律

根据某些国家的国内法,撤销裁决的事由不同,将会导致适用不同国家的法律。例如,比较典型的1985年《示范法》是这样规定的:

Article 34 Application for setting aside as exclusive recourse against arbitral award

(1) Recourse to a court against an arbitral award may be made only by an application for setting aside in accordance with paragraphs (2) and (3) of this article.

(2) An arbitral award may be set aside by the court specified in article 6 only if:

[①] See Christopher R. Drahozal, Enforcing Vacated International Arbitration Awards: An Economic Approach, 11 Am. Rev. Int'l Arb. (2000), p.451.

(a) the party making the application furnishes proof that:

(i) a party to the arbitration agreement referred to in article 7 was under some incapacity; or the said agreement is not valid under the law to which the parties have subjected it or, failing any indication thereon, under the law of this Sate; or

(ii) the party making the application was not given proper notice of the appointment of an arbitrator or of the arbitral proceedings or was otherwise unable to present his case; or

(iii) the award deals with a dispute not contemplated by or not falling within the terms of the submission to arbitration, or contains decision on matters beyond the scope of the submission to arbitration, provided that, if the decisions on matters submitted to arbitration can be separated from those not so submitted, only that part of the award which contains decisions on matters not submitted to arbitration may be set aside; or

(iv) the composition of the arbitral tribunal or the arbitral procedure was not in accordance with the agreement of the parties, unless such agreement was in conflict with a provision of this Law from which the parties cannot derogate, or, failing such agreement, was not in accordance with this Law; or

(b) the court finds that:

(i) the subject-matter of the dispute is not capable of settlement by arbitration under the law of this State; or

(ii) the award is in conflict with the public policy of this State.

从《示范法》的条文看,仲裁地法适用于裁决的撤销不是绝对的。在某些事项上,仲裁地的法院需要适用非仲裁地的法律。归纳起来:

1. 对于仲裁协议当事人的行为能力,一般适用行为地法和属人法。

2. 对于仲裁协议的效力,适用当事人选择的法律;如果没有选择,适用仲裁地法律。

3. 对于仲裁庭的组成和仲裁程序的合法性,适用当事人选择的法律;如果没有选择,适用仲裁地法律。

4. 对于当事人是否获得表达意见的机会、仲裁裁决是否超越仲裁范围、仲裁事项是否具有可仲裁性以及裁决是否违反公共政策等事项,适用仲裁地法。

许多国家的仲裁法都受到了《示范法》的影响。1993年俄罗斯《联邦国际商事仲裁法》第34条("申请撤销作为对仲裁裁决异议的唯一手段")第2款规定:"仲裁裁决只有在下列情况下才可以被第6条第2款规定的法院撤销:A. a. 第7条所指的仲裁协议的一方当事人在任何程度上无行为能力,或者根据当事人约定的适用于仲裁协议的法律,如双方未约定则根据俄罗斯联邦的法律仲裁协议无效;b. 仲裁庭的组成或仲裁程序与当事人协议不一致,除非这种协议与本法中当事人不能背离的任何规定相抵触,或者在当事人无此种协议的情况下与本法不符;或 B. 法院认定:a. 根据俄罗斯联邦的法律,争议不能成为仲裁解决的对象;或 b. 仲裁裁决与俄罗斯联邦的公共政策相抵触。"

1998 年德国《民事诉讼法》第 1059 条("申请撤销仲裁裁决")也有类似规定:"A. 申请方有充分理由表明:a. 第 1029 条和第 1031 条所指的仲裁协议的当事人根据适用于其的法律系无行为能力,或者所述仲裁协议根据当事人约定的法律或无此约定时根据德国法是无效的;或 b. 仲裁庭的组成或仲裁程序不符合本编规定或与当事人的协议不符,并且确有可能影响此项裁决;或者 B. 法院认为 a. 争议事项根据德国法不能以仲裁方式解决;或者 b. 裁决的承认或执行之结果有悖公共秩序。"

总之,从国际社会的普遍实践看,在仲裁裁决的撤销问题上,仲裁地法占据着中心地位。在某些事项上虽然可能导致适用非仲裁地的法律,但是这还是仲裁地冲突规范指引的结果。仲裁地法在撤销问题上的突出地位是由仲裁地对于仲裁的直接的监督权决定的。可以说,撤销裁决的法律适用最终可以归结为仲裁地法。

二、承认与执行外国仲裁裁决的法律适用

谈到承认与执行外国仲裁裁决的法律适用,首先要澄清什么是"外国裁决"?《纽约公约》第 1 条对外国裁决作出了定义:

Article I of the New York Convention provides that the Convention applies to two types of arbitral awards in recognition and enforcement proceedings: (1) those awards made in a state other than the one where the recognition and enforcement of such awards are sought, or so-called "foreign awards"; and (2) those awards that are not considered domestic in the state where their recognition and enforcement are sought, or so-called "non-domestic awards." The first category is easily understood as it is defined by a clear criterion: the location of the arbitral award. The second, more controversial category refers to awards entered locally but for some reason considered "international" by the contracting state.

根据公约的规定,所有在被请求国境外作出的仲裁裁决都属于外国裁决,从而适用公约。而当被请求国国内法不认为某一裁决是内国裁决时,该裁决也适用公约。"非内国裁决"标准的目的是扩大公约的适用范围。

例如,在 Bergesen v. Joseph Muller A. G. 案中,美国法院认为裁决虽然在美国境内作出,但是由于其适用的法律是外国法,或者当事人双方的住所地和主要

营业地在国外,该裁决就是非内国裁决,应当适用《纽约公约》。①

Therefore, to properly determine whether an award is non-domestic, one must look to the municipal law of the state where recognition and enforcement are sought. The language plainly implies that the Convention allows variations in the non-domestic definition across different countries. As a result of this flexibility in interpretation, controversies have broken out in courtrooms around the world. ②

(一) 直接适用《纽约公约》

目前全球已经有 144 个国家加入了《纽约公约》。因此,大部分国家在承认与执行外国仲裁裁决时适用该公约的规定。例如:

Article 194 of Switzerland's Federal Code on Private International Law, 1987 stipulates that "the recognition and enforcement of foreign arbitral awards shall be governed by the New York Convention of June 10, 1958 on the Recognition and Enforcement of Foreign Arbitral Awards."

1998 年德国《民事诉讼法》第 1061 条("外国裁决")第 1 款规定:"外国裁决的承认与执行应根据 1958 年 6 月 10 日的《承认与执行外国仲裁裁决公约》进行。其他有关承认与执行仲裁裁决的条约将不受影响。"

具体而言,《纽约公约》的第 3 条和第 4 条集中规定了承认与执行外国裁决的法律适用问题。

Article III

Each Contracting State shall recognize arbitral awards as binding and enforce them in accordance with the rules of procedure of the territory where the award is relied upon, under the conditions laid down in the following articles.

Article V

1. Recognition and enforcement of the award may be refused, at the request of the party against whom it is invoked, only if that party furnishes to the competent authority where the recognition and enforcement is sought, proof that:

(a) The parties to the agreement referred to in article II were, under the law applicable to them, under some incapacity, or the said agreement is not valid under the law to which the parties have subjected it or, failing any indication thereon, under the law of the country where the award was made; or

(b) The party against whom the award is invoked was not given proper notice of

---

① See Jean-Francois Poudret, Sebastien Besson, Comparative Law of International Arbitration, Sweet & Maxwell Ltd., 2007, p.819.

② See Jian Zhou, Judicial Intervention in International Arbitration: A Comparative Study of the Scope of the New York Convention in U.S. and Chinese Courts, 15 Pac. Rim L. & Pol'y J. (2006), p.403.

the appointment of the arbitrator or of the arbitration proceedings or was otherwise unable to present his case; or

(c) The award deals with a difference not contemplated by or not falling within the terms of the submission to arbitration, or it contains decisions on matters beyond the scope of the submission to arbitration, provided that, if the decisions on matters submitted to arbitration can be separated from those not so submitted, that part of the award which contains decisions on matters submitted to arbitration may be recognized and enforced; or

(d) The composition of the arbitral authority or the arbitral procedure was not in accordance with the agreement of the parties, or, failing such agreement, was not in accordance with the law of the country where the arbitration took place; or

(e) The award has not yet become binding, on the parties, or has been set aside or suspended by a competent authority of the country in which, or under the law of which, that award was made.

2. Recognition and enforcement of an arbitral award may also be refused if the competent authority in the country where recognition and enforcement is sought finds that:

(a) The subject matter of the difference is not capable of settlement by arbitration under the law of that country; or

(b) The recognition or enforcement of the award would be contrary to the public policy of that country.

The New York Convention, by referring explicitly to the law under which the award was made, stresses that the law of the arbitral situs is not necessarily applicable in determining whether an award should be recognized and enforced. Indeed, the reference to the law under which the award was made was inserted because of two realizations: That the arbitral situs is often selected for reasons other than the parties' intention to have the law of the situs govern the arbitration and that the properly applicable law is frequently that of another country. In a real sense, therefore, the Convention provides potent support for the view that the applicable law is not necessarily the lex loci arbitri. ①

由此看来,承认与执行外国仲裁裁决可能适用的法律可以分为几种情况:

1. 承认外国仲裁裁决所依据的程序规则——适用被请求国法律。

---

① See Hans Smit, Eason-Weinmann Center for Comparative Law Colloquium: The Internationalization of Law and Legal Practice, 63 Tul. L. Rev. (1989), p.439.

2. 仲裁协议当事人的行为能力,一般适用行为地法和属人法。It is not clear what law is here being referred to, although it would seem that an English court, applying English common law conflict rules, would look to the domicile of the parties.①

3. 仲裁协议的效力,适用当事人选择适用于仲裁协议的法律;如果没有选择,适用仲裁地法律。有学者认为, the proper law of the arbitration agreement is normally the same as the proper law of the contract of which it forms a part. If there is an express choice of the proper law of the contract as a whole, the arbitration agreement will usually be governed by that law. The validity of the arbitration agreement must be determined with respect to the law governing the contract, which is usually either the law chosen by the parties, the law of the country where the award was made, or the law of the country where the contract was executed.②也有学者认为,仲裁协议独立于主合同,因此适用于仲裁协议的法律也独立于适用于主合同的法律。③ 如果当事人没有专门就仲裁协议适用的法律作出选择,应当适用与仲裁协议有最密切联系国家的法律,一般是仲裁地法律。从《纽约公约》和各国国内法的内容上看,后者的观点比较合理。

The common law approach to the ascertainment of the applicable law is a three-stage process. The court will first look to see whether there is express agreement on the applicable law. In the absence of express agreement the courts will consider whether there is an implied choice based on the remaining terms of the agreement. Finally, in the absence of any express or implied choice, it will be necessary for the courts to ascertain the intention of the parties from all the surrounding circumstances. If the parties have not expressly or impliedly nominated a law to govern the arbitration agreement, the law of the seat of the arbitration determines the validity of the arbitration agreement.④

4. 仲裁庭的组成和仲裁程序是否合法,适用当事人选择的法律;如果没有选择,适用仲裁地法律。⑤

5. 当事人是否获得表达意见的机会、仲裁裁决是否超越仲裁范围、仲裁事项是否具有可仲裁性以及是否违反公共政策,适用被请求国法律。这些内容都

---

① See Robert Merkin, Arbitration Law, Informa Legal Publishing, 2004, p.821.
② See Robert B. von Mehren, Enforcement of Foreign Arbitral Awards in the United States, Int. A. L. R., Vol.1, No.6, 1998, pp.198—204.
③ 参见赵秀文:《论法院对涉外仲裁协议有效性及其适用法律的认定》,载《杭州师范学院学报》(社会科学版)2003 年第 5 期。
④ See Robert Merkin, Arbitration Law, Informa Legal Publishing, 2004, pp.190,197.
⑤ 关于仲裁程序的法律适用,详见本章第一节的内容。

与被请求国的公共政策密切相关,所以受到被请求国法律的密切监督。

(二)适用被请求国法律

《纽约公约》的缔约国包括了世界上多数国家,它们或者直接适用该公约,或者把公约的条文转化为国内法,间接适用《纽约公约》。因此,其适用的结果与直接适用《纽约公约》差异不大。例如,1993 年俄罗斯《联邦国际商事仲裁法》第 36 条("拒绝承认或执行的理由")规定:"不论裁决是在哪一个国家作出的,只有在下列情况下才能拒绝承认或执行:A. 经申请承认和执行人的请求,如果该方当事人向被要求承认或执行的有管辖权的法院举证证明:a. 第 7 条所指的仲裁协议的一方当事人在任何程度上无行为能力,或者根据当事人约定的适用于仲裁协议的法律,如双方未约定则根据俄罗斯联邦的法律仲裁协议无效;……d. 仲裁庭的组成或仲裁程序与当事人协议不一致,或如无这种协议则与仲裁地国家的法律不符;e. 裁决尚未对当事人产生约束力,或作出裁决的国家的法院,或据其法律作出裁决的国家的法院已撤销或终止执行裁决,或 B. 如法院认定:a. 根据俄罗斯联邦的法律,争议不能成为仲裁解决的对象;或 b. 承认和执行该仲裁裁决与俄罗斯联邦的公共政策相抵触。"

1999 年瑞典《仲裁法》第 54 条规定:"如被申请执行人证明外国裁决有如下情形,则该裁决在瑞典将不能得到承认和执行:1. 仲裁协议的当事人根据应适用的法律缺乏签订仲裁协议的能力且未被有效的代理,或根据当事人选择的法律,如无此约定时根据裁决作出国的法律,仲裁协议是无效的;……4. 仲裁庭的组成或仲裁程序违反当事人的约定,或无此约定时仲裁地国的法律;5. 裁决尚未对当事人产生约束力或已经为裁决作出国或裁决所依据的法律的国家的有关权力机关撤销或中止。"

类似的规定还有 1982 年土耳其《国际私法和国际诉讼程序法》第 45 条("拒绝承认与执行")[①]、1982 年南斯拉夫《国际冲突法》第 99 条[②]、英国《1996

[①] 土耳其《国际私法和国际诉讼程序法》第 45 条规定:"遇有下述情况,法院有权驳回请求执行外国仲裁裁决的申请:1. 没有仲裁协议或主要合同中没有仲裁条款的;2. 外国仲裁裁决违反社会道德和公共秩序的;3. 根据土耳其法律仲裁协议无效的;4. 在仲裁过程中,仲裁庭没有通知一方当事人出庭,即作出仲裁裁决的;5. 请求执行外国仲裁裁决时双方当事人没有被通知选择仲裁员,或没有能够为自己提出辩护的;6. 根据当事人选择的法律,或根据仲裁地国家的法律,仲裁协议或仲裁条款无效的;7. 仲裁员的选择或仲裁程序的适用与当事人缔结的合同规定或仲裁地国家的法律规定不符的;8. 仲裁裁决所涉及的事项,在仲裁协议或仲裁条款中未作规定的,或超出仲裁协议或仲裁条款规定的范围的;9. 根据仲裁所适用的法律,或根据仲裁地国家的法律,仲裁裁决没有生效或不能执行的,或被仲裁机构裁定为无效的。"

[②] 南斯拉夫《国际冲突法》第 99 条规定:"如果查明有下列情况,则拒绝承认和执行外国仲裁裁决:1. 按照南斯拉夫社会主义联邦共和国法律,争议的问题不应通过仲裁解决;……8. 仲裁庭成员或仲裁程序不符合仲裁协议的规定;……10. 仲裁裁决不是终局的和可对当事人执行的,或已经被作出裁决那国的主管机关,或被按其法律作出裁决那国的主管机关所撤销或停止执行……"

年仲裁法》第 103 条①和 1994 年意大利《民事诉讼法典》第 840 条。

对于少数非《纽约公约》缔约国而言,它们适用其本国法或有关仲裁的双边条约来处理外国裁决的承认与执行问题。

三、我国撤销与执行仲裁裁决的法律适用

(一) 我国撤销涉外仲裁裁决的法律适用

1. 我国法律对仲裁裁决的分类

我国主要是依仲裁机构的所在地和裁决的性质来区分裁决的种类。对于我国境内仲裁机构作出的不具有涉外因素的裁决,视为国内裁决;对于我国境内仲裁机构作出的有涉外因素的裁决,视为涉外裁决;对于我国领土以外的仲裁机构的裁决,视为外国裁决。

There are three main types of arbitral awards: foreign, foreign-related, and domestic. Foreign arbitral awards refer to any awards made outside of China. Foreign awards include both Conventional and non-Conventional awards. Conventional awards are enforceable under the Convention on the Recognition and Enforcement of Foreign Arbitral Awards ("New York Convention"), whereas non-Conventional awards refer to foreign awards that are not enforceable under the New York Convention.

Foreign-related awards are awards by CIETAC, CMAC, or local arbitration commissions that involve a foreign element. Domestic awards are awards by local arbitration commissions that do not involve foreign elements. According to a Supreme People's Court (SPC) interpretation, a "foreign element" refers to civil cases in which: one party or both parties are foreigners, stateless persons, foreign enterprises, or foreign organizations; or the legal fact of establishment, modification, or termination of the civil legal relationship between the parties occurred in a foreign country; or the object of the action is located in a foreign country.②

2. 撤销涉外仲裁裁决适用中国法律

撤销涉外仲裁裁决适用我国的《仲裁法》和《民事诉讼法》的有关规定。

---

① 英国《1996 年仲裁法》第 103 条规定:"a. 仲裁协议的一方当事人(根据适用于他的法律)无行为能力;b. 根据当事人选择适用于仲裁协议的法律,或未指明适用的法律时根据裁决作出地国法律规定,仲裁协议是无效的;c. 一方当事人未给予指定仲裁员或仲裁程序的通知,或无法为代表自己的利益参与仲裁程序的;d. 裁决所涉及的并不是当事人所预期的争议,或者不是提交仲裁条款中的内容,也不是基于仲裁条款而由法院作出决定的事项;e. 仲裁庭组成或仲裁程序未依当事人的约定,或无约定而未依仲裁发生地国家的法律;f. 仲裁裁决尚未对当事人产生约束力,或已被裁决作出地国或裁决所依法律之国家有权机构撤销或中止。"

② See Randall Peerenboom, The Evolving Regulatory Framework for Enforcement of Arbitral Awards in the People's Republic of China, 1 Asian-Pac. L. & Pol'y J. 12 (2000).

As far as the setting aside of the award is concerned, a two-pronged regime exists: one for domestic awards and one for foreign-related awards. Specifically, the setting aside of domestic awards is governed by Article 58 of the Arbitration Law. The setting aside of foreign-related awards is regulated by Article 70 of the Arbitration Law and Article 260 of the Civil Procedure Law 1991(CPL).①

由上文分析可见,我国法院可以撤销的是国内仲裁裁决和涉外仲裁裁决,而无权撤销外国仲裁裁决。本书所要讨论的特指涉外仲裁裁决的撤销。

《仲裁法》第65条规定:"涉外经济贸易、运输和海事中发生的纠纷的仲裁,适用本章规定。本章没有规定的,适用本法其他有关规定。"可见,涉外仲裁的相关法律问题原则上都适用我国国内法。

3. 撤销涉外仲裁裁决的理由仍然指向中国法

我国《仲裁法》第58、70条分别规定了国内仲裁裁决和涉外仲裁裁决的撤销。第70条规定:"当事人提出证据证明涉外仲裁裁决有民事诉讼法第二百六十条②第一款规定的情形之一的,经人民法院组成合议庭审查核实,裁定撤销。"

Article 258 of Civil Procedure Law

If a defendant provides evidence to prove that the arbitration award made by a foreign-affair arbitration institution of the People's Republic of China involves any of the following circumstances, the people's court shall, after examination and verification by a collegial bench, rule to disallow the enforcement of the award:

(1) The parties have not stipulated any clause regarding arbitration in their contract or have not subsequently reached a written agreement on arbitration;

(2) The defendant is not duly notified of the appointment of the arbitrators or the arbitration proceeding, or the defendant fails to express his defense due to the reasons for which he is not held responsible;

(3) The formation of the arbitration panel or the arbitration procedure is not in conformity with rules of arbitration; or

(4) The matters decided by arbitration exceed the scope of the arbitration agreement or the authority of the arbitration institution.

If a people's court determines that the enforcement of an award will violate the social and public interest, the court shall make a ruling to disallow the enforcement of the arbitration award.

---

① See Li Hu, Setting Aside an Arbitral Award in the People's Republic of China, 12 Am. Rev. Int'l Arb. 1 (2001).
② 这里指的是1991年《民事诉讼法》,2007年修改后的《民事诉讼法》的对应条文应当是第258条。

(二) 承认和执行外国仲裁裁决的法律适用

1. 对于在《纽约公约》缔约国国内所作的裁决，适用《纽约公约》

《最高人民法院关于执行我国加入的〈承认及执行外国仲裁裁决公约〉的通知》第1条第1款规定："根据我国加入该公约时所作的互惠保留声明，我国对在另一缔约国领土内作出的仲裁裁决的承认和执行适用该公约。该公约与我国民事诉讼法（试行）有不同规定的，按该公约的规定办理。"

我国与外国签订的一系列双边司法协助条约也重申了该规则。例如，1987年《中华人民共和国和波兰人民共和国关于民事和刑事司法协助的协定》第21条"仲裁庭裁决的承认与执行"规定："缔约双方应根据1958年6月10日在纽约签订的关于承认和执行外国仲裁裁决的公约，相互承认与执行在对方境内作出的裁决。"与之类似的规定还有：1991年《中华人民共和国和意大利共和国关于民事司法协助的条约》第28条[①]、1992年《中华人民共和国和俄罗斯联邦关于民事和刑事司法协助的条约》第21条[②]、1992年《中华人民共和国和古巴共和国关于民事和刑事司法协助的协定》第26条[③]等等。

2. 对于在非《纽约公约》缔约国国内所作的裁决，适用《民事诉讼法》

《最高人民法院关于执行我国加入的〈承认及执行外国仲裁裁决公约〉的通知》第1条第2款规定："对于在非缔约国领土内作出的仲裁裁决，需要我国法院承认和执行的，应按民事诉讼法（试行）第二百零四条[④]的规定办理。"

《民事诉讼法》第267条规定："国外仲裁机构的裁决，需要中华人民共和国人民法院承认和执行的，应当由当事人直接向被执行人住所地或者其财产所在地的中级人民法院申请，人民法院应当依照中华人民共和国缔结或者参加的国际条约，或者按照互惠原则办理。"

Although Article 267 of the Civil Procedure Law provides a possible legal basis for the enforcement of foreign awards that are not New York Convention awards, in practice it would be difficult to obtain enforcement. A PRC court would only enforce the award pursuant to a treaty or in accordance with the principle of reciprocity. To enforce under the principle of reciprocity would require that the award be rendered in

---

[①] 《中华人民共和国和意大利共和国关于民事司法协助的条约》第28条规定："在缔约一方境内作出的仲裁裁决，应根据1958年6月10日订于纽约的关于承认和执行外国仲裁裁决的公约，在缔约另一方境内得到承认并被宣告可予执行。"

[②] 《中华人民共和国和俄罗斯联邦关于民事和刑事司法协助的条约》第21条规定："缔约双方应根据1958年6月10日在纽约签订的关于承认与执行外国仲裁裁决的公约，相互承认与执行在对方境内作出的仲裁裁决。"

[③] 《中华人民共和国和古巴共和国关于民事和刑事司法协助的协定》第26条规定："缔约双方应根据1958年6月10日在纽约签订的关于承认和执行外国仲裁裁决的公约，相互承认与执行在对方境内作出的仲裁裁决。"

[④] 这里指的是1991年《民事诉讼法》，2007年修改后的《民事诉讼法》的对应条文应当是第267条。

a nation that was not a party to the New York Convention but had previously recognized and enforced arbitral awards or judicial judgments issued in the PRC. More than 100 countries are now parties to the New York Convention, including most of China's major trading partners. Thus, the likelihood of such situations arising is extremely small. China has entered into bilateral judicial assistance treaties and investment protection agreements with several countries, some of which contain provisions relating to arbitration. For the reasons already noted, however, enforcement under such agreements would be cumbersome.[①]

（三）承认与执行我国涉外仲裁裁决的法律适用

涉外仲裁裁决是我国仲裁机构作出的，它本质上仍然是一种国内仲裁裁决。因此，它当然适用我国的国内法。

《民事诉讼法》第258条规定，对中华人民共和国涉外仲裁机构作出的裁决，被申请人提出证据证明仲裁裁决有下列情形之一的，经人民法院组成合议庭审查核实，裁定不予执行：

（1）当事人在合同中没有订有仲裁条款或者事后没有达成书面仲裁协议的；

（2）被申请人没有得到指定仲裁员或者进行仲裁程序的通知，或者由于其他不属于被申请人负责的原因未能陈述意见的；

（3）仲裁庭的组成或者仲裁的程序与仲裁规则不符的；

（4）裁决的事项不属于仲裁协议的范围或者仲裁机构无权仲裁的。

人民法院认定执行该裁决违背社会公共利益的，裁定不予执行。

案例

1. Pabalk v. Norsolar[②]

仲裁员不适用特定国家的国内法，而是适用商事习惯法所作出的裁决能否得到有关国家的承认与执行？对此，不同法院和仲裁机构有其自己的理解。

Issue

Whether the arbitrators, who were not granted the powers to rule in equity as amiable compositeurs, could disregard all national legal systems and rely on lex

---

[①] See Randall Peerenboom, The Evolving Regulatory Framework for Enforcement of Arbitral Awards in the People's Republic of China, 1 Asian-Pac. L. & Pol'y J. 12 (2000).

[②] See Cour de Cassation Decision, 24 I. L. M. 360 (1985).

mercatoria only?

Facts & Reasoning

Whereas Pabalk Ticaret Limited Sirketi (Pabalk), a Turkish company incorporated in Turkey, and Ugilor, a company incorporated in France, which has since become Norsolor, were parties to an agency agreement which contained an arbitration clause referring to the Rules for the International Chamber of Commerce (ICC) Court of Arbitration and in particular to Article 13 of these Rules prescribing that in the absence of any indication by the parties as to the applicable law, the arbitrators should apply the law designated as the proper law by the rule of conflict which they deem appropriate, it being specified that they shall take account of the provisions of the contract and the relevant trade usages;

Whereas in their award rendered on October 26, 1979, the arbitrators stated that, faced with the difficulty of choosing a national law the application of which is sufficiently compelling, it was appropriate, given the international nature of the agreement, to leave aside any compelling reference to a specific legal system, be it Turkish or French, and to apply the international lex mercatoria, of which one of the fundamental principles is that of good faith which must govern the formation and performance of contracts;

Whereas the arbitral tribunal found that the termination of the agreement was attributable to Ugilor and that Ugilor's conduct caused unjustified damages to Pabalk, which equity required to be compensated;

Whereas this award, in its four-point decree, ordered Norsolor to pay various sums to Pabalk.

We reverse and set aside the decision rendered November 19, 1982, by the Court of Appeals of Paris and send the case to the Court of Appeals of Amiens ...

Comment

Pursuant to Article 595(5) and (6) of the Austrian Code of Civil Procedure (ZPO), an award rendered in Austria could be set aside, inter alia, "if the Arbitral Tribunal dealt with matters beyond those referred to it" and "if the award violated mandatory provisions of law". Later on, the Federal Law of February 2, 1983, which came into effect on May 1, 1983, limited the latter provision to cases in which "the award is incompatible with the basic principles of the Austrian legal system or infringes mandatory provisions of the law, the application of which cannot be derogated by a choice of law of the parties even in a case where a foreign contract according to paragraph 35 of the International Private Law Act is involved".

Contrary to the decision of the Tribunal of Commerce of Vienna, which dismissed Pabalk's claim on June 29, 1981, the Vienna Court of Appeals partially set aside the award in its decision of June 29, 1982, on the ground that the Arbitral Tribunal, which had to determine the applicable law pursuant to Article 13, paragraph 3 of the ICC Rules, exceeded its powers in referring to lex mercatoria, which was described by the Court as a "world law of questionable validity" instead of grounding its decision in a particular national legal order.

On November 18, 1982, the Austrian Supreme Court reversed this decision on the ground that (1) in relying on the principle of good faith to determine the principal's liability for the damage caused by the termination of the agency agreement, it did not infringe any mandatory rule in force in any of the two concerned jurisdictions within the meaning of Article 595(6) ZPO and that (2) in determining the amount of damages on the basis of equity without special authorization from the parties, the Arbitral Tribunal did not transgress the limits of its competence within the meaning of Article 595(5) ZPO.

Similarly, in the enforcement proceeding, the Tribunal de Grande Instance of Paris held on March 4, 1981, that in applying the principle of good faith as one of the "general principles of obligations applicable to international trade," the arbitrators did not rule as amiables compositeurs and, therefore, did not exceed their powers under the terms of the arbitral agreement.

On appeal, the Paris Court of Appeals did not address this issue because of the answer it gave to the second question raised in this case. However, the Cour de Cassation followed the Tribunal de Grande Instance solution in deciding the SNCT Fougerolle v. Banque du Proche Orient case on December 9, 1981.

Only the possible conflict between lex mercatoria and mandatory rules of a legal order with a close connection with the case remains undecided. If such a situation arose, recognition and enforcement would not be carried out in France if they were held "contrary to international public policy (ordre public)" within the meaning of Article 1502(5) of the New Code of Civil Procedure and would not be carried out in Austria if they were held contrary to the mandatory rules "applicable even to foreign contracts" within the meaning of the new Article 595(6) ZPO.

2. Vita Food Products Inc. v. Unus Shipping Co. Ltd.[①]

在本案中,英国法官详细阐明了当事人意思自治在合同实体法律适用中应当受到高度尊重的观点;同时他也强调了意思自治应当符合诚信原则,并且不违反有关国家的公共政策。

Facts

Vita Food Products Inc. v. Unus Shipping Co. Ltd. was an appeal to the Privy Council from Nova Scotia. Newfoundland was not part of Canada. Herrings were shipped in Newfoundland under bills of lading which did not contain the statement required by section 3 of the Newfoundland Carriage of Goods by Sea Act 1932 that every bill of lading "shall contain an express statement that it is to have effect subject to the provisions of the Hague Rules as expressed in this Act." The bills of lading by their terms provided for exemption from liability for master's negligence in navigation which exemption was also part of the Hague Rules. The Hague Rules further provided that any clause or agreement in the bills of lading relieving the carrier from liability for negligence imposed by the Rules was void. There was a further provision in the bills of lading that, in the case of shipment from the United States, the Harter Act 1893, should apply and that, save as so provided, the bill of lading was subject to the terms of the Canadian Water Carriage of Goods Act 1910. Finally the bills of lading contained the following clause: "This contract shall be governed by English law." On the voyage the ship ran ashore in Nova Scotia, admittedly through the negligence of the master in navigation. The herrings suffered damage.

Dispute & Issue

It was contended by the cargo interests before the Nova Scotia courts that, as there was no paramount clause including the Hague Rules in the bills of lading as required by the Act of 1932, the bills of lading contracts were illegal and accordingly the exceptions did not avail the shipowners and they were subject to the liabilities of common carriers. The provisions of section 3 were imperative and not merely directory and failure to comply with them rendered the bills of lading void.

The shipowners, on the other hand, submitted that the Hague Rules applied even though the paramount clause was not expressly incorporated. They further submitted that the rights of the parties under the bills of lading must be worked out

---

① [1939] A.C. 277 (P.C.).

under English law. The Hague Rules, they said, were imported by the clause that the contract shall be governed by English law with the result that the English Carriage of Goods by Sea Act applied.

Reasoning

The courts in Nova Scotia held that the Rules applied even though there was no paramount clause as required by the Act. The shipowners were accordingly exempted from liability under the Rules.

The Privy Council, with Lord Atkin as a member of the Board, affirmed the decision in favour of the shipowners but on a different logical basis. The Privy Council gave effect to the express words of the bill of lading that the contract was governed by English law and gave effect to the bill of lading exemption and not the exemption under the Newfoundland Carriage of Goods by Sea Act 1932 or the British Carriage of Goods by Sea Act 1924. The latter Act applied only to cargo carried from Britain. Lord Wright speaking for the Council said:

It is now well settled that by English law (and the law of Nova Scotia is the same) the proper law of the contract is the law which the parties intended to apply. That intention is objectively ascertained, and, if not expressed, will be presumed from the terms of the contract and the relevant surrounding circumstances.

He then cited the statement of Lord Atkin in the *International Trustee case* and added that some qualifications were necessary. He said that:

> ... in questions relating to the conflict of laws rules cannot generally be stated in absolute terms but rather as prima facie presumptions. But where the English rule that intention is the test applies, and where there is an express statement by the parties of their intention to select the law of the contract, it is difficult to see what qualifications are possible, provided the intention expressed is bona fide and legal, and provided there is no reason for avoiding the choice on the ground of public policy. Connection with English law, is not as a matter of principle essential.

Lord Wright went on to say that the bills of lading could not be regarded as illegal by reason of non-inclusion of the Rules. The Act did not in terms provide that a bill of lading was to be deemed illegal and void merely because it contravened section 3, nor did it in terms expressly prohibit the non-inclusion. The inconveniences that would follow from holding bills of lading illegal in such cases as that in question were very serious. A foreign merchant or banker could not be assumed to know or to inquire what the Newfoundland law was, at any rate when the bill of lading was not expressed to be governed by Newfoundland law and still less when it provided that it was governed by English law, and it would seriously impair business dealings with bills of lading if they could not be taken at their face value and as expressing all the relevant conditions of the contract. Section 3 accordingly was directory and not obligatory. This was the true construction of the statute, having regard to its scope and its purpose and to the inconvenience which would follow from any other conclusion.

Lord Wright disagreed with the reasoning of the Court of Appeal in "*The Torni*". According to him a provision in bills of lading providing that they were "to be construed in accordance with English law" meant that they "shall be governed by English law". The Privy Council dissented from "*The Torni*" for it contravened the fundamental principle of the English rule of conflict of laws that intention as to what law should apply was the paramount test.

Comment

The true principle was established by the Privy Council in the following statement: *English law will recognize and give effect to an express choice of law by the parties to the contract provided the choice is bona fide and legal and provided there is no reason for avoiding the choice on the ground of public policy.*

The principle stated above has received adverse comments. But the Conflict of Laws by Dicey and Morris (10th ed.), at p. 755 says that: "There appears to be no reported case in which an English court refused to give effect to an express selection by the parties, merely because the other facts of the case showed no connection between the contract and the chosen law." Indeed an immeasurable volume of international business is transacted on the assumption that the choice of law by parties is supreme.

3. Chromalloy Aeroservices v. Arab Republic of Egypt ("Chromalloy" case)[①]

美国法官认为,仲裁裁决虽然已经被仲裁地法院撤销,但是美国的国内法不认可埃及法律的撤销理由。这个已经被撤销的仲裁裁决获得了美国的承认与执行。

---

① See Pippa Read, Delocalization of International Commercial Arbitration: Its Relevence in the New Millennium, 10 Am. Rev. Int'l Arb. (1999), p. 177.

Facts

The 1996 case of Chromalloy Aeroservices v. Arab Republic of Egypt ("Chromalloy") concerned an arbitration between Chromalloy Aeroservices, a U.S. company, and the Arab Republic of Egypt ("Egypt"), which took place in Cairo. An award was issued in 1994 against Egypt, which subsequently applied to the Court of Appeal of Cairo for annulment of the award under the grounds in the (new) Egyptian Law of Arbitration (1994). Whilst the new arbitration law was closely modelled upon the UNCITRAL Model Law on arbitration, it contained two grounds which were peculiar to Egypt. One of these grounds, which states that an action for annulment is permissible "if the arbitral award excluded the application of the Law agreed upon by the parties to govern the subject matter of the dispute," provided the basis for Egypt's challenge of the award. Egypt claimed that the "arbitral tribunal had wrongly failed to apply Egyptian administrative law, which the Court considered to be the law agreed upon by the parties when providing in their arbitration clause for the application of 'Egypt laws.'" As the Court characterized the contract as "administrative," the application of the Egyptian Civil Code rather than "administrative law" was seen as an exclusion of the law as chosen by the parties. Accordingly, the Court concluded that the award was null. Despite this decision, the U.S. District Court enforced the award in 1996.

Issue

Whether a court can enforce a foreign arbitral award that has been set aside by the country of origin?

Analysis of the U.S. Court

The U.S. court, in coming to this decision, relied (amongst other things) upon two provisions of the New York Convention: Article V(1)(e) and Article VII. As discussed previously, Article V(1)(e) contains the discretionary provision which permits nonrecognition in cases where an award has been set aside or annulled in the country in which the arbitration took place. Article VII(1) provides:

> The provisions of the present Convention shall not affect the validity of multilateral or bilateral agreements concerning the recognition and enforcement of arbitral awards entered into by the Contracting State nor deprive any interested party of any right he may have to avail himself of an arbitral award in the manner and to the extent allowed by the law or the treaties of the country where such award is sought to be relied upon.

The Court in Chromalloy found that under Article VII, enforcing courts must provide the full protection of domestic laws to the winning party seeking enforcement of an award. Under U. S. law, an award will be enforced unless there is evidence of fraud, corruption, bias, procedural misconduct or where an arbitrator has exceeded his or her other powers, including a manifest disregard of the law. Accordingly, the Court found that, as the ground for nullification applied by the Cairo Court of Appeal did not exist under U. S. law (the selection of incorrect law could not be seen as a "manifest disregard" of the law), the Egyptian decision nullifying the award would not be recognized in the United States as a valid foreign judgment. The U. S. judge found:

> While Article V provides a discretionary standard, Article VII of the Convention requires that, "the provisions of the present Convention shall not ... deprive any interested party of any right he may have to avail himself of an arbitral award in the manner and to the extent allowed by the law ... of the country where such award is sought to be relied upon." In other words, under the Convention, CAS [Chromalloy] maintains all rights to enforcement of this Arbitral Award that it would have had in the absence of the Convention.

This conclusion, paired with the "unmistakable U. S. public policy" in favor of enforcing the parties' intention to make their award final and binding, led to the decision to enforce the award in the U. S., notwithstanding the fact that it had been annulled in Egypt.

Comment

It appears from this decision that the application of Article VII could justify enforcing an award annulled in its country of origin, if it were done on a ground not recognized under the law of the enforcing country. Thus, even if a breach of mandatory lex loci arbitri resulted in an award being annulled or set aside in the country of origin, this would have little bearing upon the winning party if the arbitration laws of the place of enforcement were more favorable. In Paulsson's view, the use of Article VII to justify enforcing an annulled award is a much more preferable approach to simply exercising the discretionary power given under Article V(1)(e), the mandatory requirement to enforce the award under the domestic law of the place of enforcement being less of an affront to judicial comity.

It would follow that the most practical way to ensure that international arbitrations are subject only to the lex loci arbitri which accord with minimum international standards, would be to include only those standards as grounds for refusal in domestic arbitration laws. This is currently the case, not only in the European Convention, as mentioned above, but also in Belgium, France and now, it appears, the United States. The Chromalloy award was in fact taken to France, where it was also enforced by the Paris Court of Appeal, as the award had been set aside on a ground not contained in French law (Article 1502 of the New Code of Civil Procedure). Using reasoning similar to that in the U. S. Chromalloy case, the winning party was held to be entitled to avail itself of the more favorable provisions for enforcement in the domestic law, according to Article VII of the New York Convention.

The Chromalloy decision has not escaped criticism, however, with one commentator Thomas Carbonneau, arguing that the "exercise of would-be discretion under article V could destabilize the transborder framework for enforcement established by the Convention. Moreover, the meaning and effect that the court affixes to the language of article VII could not have been part of the intent of the drafters of the Convention and has not been part of the contemporary decisional practice under the Convention ... Evaluated from the standard point of the orderliness and stability of governing norms, the court's tendencious interpretative pragmatism renders the Convention framework chaotic."

阅读材料

1. 强行法对当事人法律选择的限制

Mandatory national laws are particularly controversial because their application seems to contradict the very nature of arbitration. Arbitration, as a private means of settling disputes, is often considered transnational or outside the jurisdiction of any one country. Thus, the idea that one country's laws can upset the parties' choice of law governing a private contractual relationship is problematic.

A primary example of when a mandatory national law trumped the parties' choice of governing law arose in a recent arbitration between an American construction company and a Turkish construction company. The contract provided for Swiss law to govern the joint venture between the two companies. When a dispute arose, the Turkish construction company argued that a mandatory Turkish law, regarding tax benefits and export incentives, settled the dispute. The arbitral tribunal looked to Swiss Private International Law (PILA), international conventions, publications of legal scholars, and Swiss case law, to determine if a mandatory national law had to be followed. Relying on language in article 19 of PILA, the tribunal concluded "it is the arbitrator's duty to see how to harmonize the agreement, lex causae and the Turkish law." Thus, the arbitrators could not rely solely on the parties' choice of Swiss law and neglect to consult mandatory rules of Turkey in order to "find a reasonable solution." Consequently, the arbitral tribunal conducted an analysis of the Turkish contacts with the dispute, because a "sufficient and close connection, genuine and not merely vague, must exist with the system of law from which the mandatory provision originated." Here, there was a clear connection with Turkey and a compelling interest for the Turkish Construction Company who could be subject to fines if it failed to follow the mandatory law. Finally, the "quality of the mandatory rules has to be determined according to the law containing such rules and without any regard to the proper law of the contract." The arbitral tribunal ultimately concluded the Turkish law was mandatory and should be accounted for.

The decision of this arbitral tribunal to consider a mandatory Turkish law, even when the parties' choice of law clause designated Swiss law as controlling the contract, is significant because it suggests that, in some situations, arbitrators feel compelled to follow a law contrary to the parties' express agreement. This presents a danger for those engaged in private contractual arrangements. Parties to a contract specifying arbitration need to have some certainty to the effect that their agreement will be followed, particularly in light of the difficulty in knowing every aspect of the laws for every country. Consider the case of a multinational corporation who contracts with corporations in many different countries. The multinational corporation may seek arbitration as a means of avoiding the other country's legal system, but also, it may seek arbitration in order to avoid being subject to provisions of unknown foreign law. Ultimately, however, the fact that arbitrators have discretion to determine the applicable law, and may feel compelled to consider public policy and mandatory national laws, in derogation of parties' express choice of law provision, instills both instability and uncertainty in international arbitration. ①

2. 仲裁与诉讼在法律适用问题上的区别

There are important differences between conflict of laws issues before a domestic court and before an international arbitral tribunal. Judges operate within a defined

---

① See Rachel Engle, Party Autonomy in International Arbitration: Where Uniformity Gives Way to Predictability, 15 Transnat'l Law (2002), p.323.

legal forum created by their national jurisdiction (the "lex fori"). They apply local law unless there is a foreign element in the case and the conflict of laws rules of the lex fori, which are simply domestic laws, direct the judge otherwise. In international arbitration, it is widely accepted that there is no lex fori. The place of arbitration provides no further connection to the dispute than being the State jurisdiction where the award is made, and whose courts are competent to supervise the arbitration and set aside the award. There is thus no domestic jurisdiction providing a background legal system. Consequently, there is no fallback system of conflict of laws rules.

Courts and arbitral tribunals also differ according to the source of their authority. The authority of judges results from State sovereignty and from their national legislatures. An international arbitrator's authority derives from the will of the parties to the dispute. That authority is supported by the States connected to the international arbitration. That is the place of arbitration, the parties' nationalities and the States that have ratified the relevant international conventions enabling the enforcement of international awards. Arbitrators and judges are thus the servants of different masters. Judges are bound by the will and authority of their sovereign appointer and are limited by broad public policy issues. Arbitrators are bound by the will of the parties to the dispute and are mainly concerned with the interests of those parties.

Finally, it should be noted that even if applied by an arbitrator, State conflict of laws rules are made with juridical and politically nationalistic considerations. This means they may not be well suited to international disputes where there is no lex fori.[①]

思考题

1. What's the role of party autonomy in the choice of the law governing an international commercial arbitration?

2. Discuss the steps to determine the applicable substantive law.

3. What's your comment on the delocalization theory? Is there any reasonable element in it?

4. What's the legal status of the lex fori in an international commercial arbitration?

[①] See Simon Greenberg, The Law Applicable to the Merits in International Arbitration, 8 V. J. (2004), p.315.

5. Should an annulled arbitral award be enforced in another country?

推荐阅读

1. 朱克鹏:《国际商事仲裁的法律适用》,法律出版社 1999 年版,第二、三、四章。

2. 谢石松主编:《商事仲裁法学》,高等教育出版社 2003 年版,第七章第一节、第九章第六节。

3. 赵秀文:《国际商事仲裁及其适用法律研究》,北京大学出版社 2002 年版,第四、八章。

4. Simon Greenberg, The Law Applicable to the Merits in International Arbitration, 8 V. J. (2004).

5. Robert Merkin, Arbitration Law, Informal Legal Publishing, 2004.

6. Christopher R. Drahozal, Richard W. Naimark, Towards a Science of International Arbitration, Kluwer Law International, 2005, pp.195—252.

第四章　国际商事仲裁协议

第一节　国际商事仲裁协议概述

一、国际商事仲裁协议的基本概念

西方私法有一个重要特色就是意思自治,意思自治原则奠定了西方私法的基调,而仲裁制度也是这一原则的直接表现。要仲裁,首先就必须要有仲裁协议,仲裁协议是仲裁的前提。争议双方当事人达成的仲裁协议是通过仲裁方式解决争议的前提和基础,这种协议是通过仲裁方式解决争议的法定依据和先决条件。仲裁协议的订立必须谨慎,因为一旦双方当事人发生争议只能申请仲裁,这是一种权利也是一项义务。因此在签订仲裁协议之前必须充分考虑清楚,是不是确定要通过仲裁来解决争端。

何谓仲裁协议?各国的仲裁立法和各仲裁机构的仲裁规则对仲裁协议概念的规定不尽相同,但是它们对于仲裁协议的理解却是一样的。简单地说,仲裁协议就是当事人对于已经发生或未来有可能发生的争议提交仲裁解决的一种合意(mutual consent)。这样的理解简明扼要,而且充分体现了仲裁协议的核心内容,包含了仲裁协议最基本的要素,即当事人将争议提交仲裁的"合意"。

由于仲裁协议本身是一种合意,那么,仲裁协议就其性质而言其实就是一个特殊的合同。其特殊之处在于,通过这个合同,当事人确立的是一种争端的解决方式,而不是买卖某种商品或服务。虽然它们就外表而言差异很大,但这并不能妨碍我们看到它们内在本质的一致性,因为无论是仲裁协议还是普通合同,它们都是双方当事人意思的一致。由此我们可以这样认为:仲裁协议本身就是一个契约。

An agreement to arbitrate by its nature possesses certain characteristics, namely:

(a) the results (decision or award) are to be binding on the parties;

(b) the substantive rights are to be determined by the person to whom disputes are referred;

(c) the Tribunal's jurisdiction is determinable from what the parties have agreed;

(d) the parties to the agreement must either agree upon an arbitrator or a method by which he or she may be appointed;

(e) impartiality must be explicit or implicit; and

(f) the parties must intend that the decision or award will be enforceable.①

二、仲裁协议的独立性

多数情况下,仲裁协议以合同条款的形式存在于当事人的商业合同之中。仲裁条款是合同中重要的组成部分,合同有效,仲裁协议当然有效。但是,当主合同不存在、无效、解除、终止或不可执行时,是否会导致仲裁条款无效呢?这是一个值得思考的重要问题。

传统的合同法理论认为,仲裁条款是主合同中的一部分,所以当主合同无效或不存在时,仲裁条款应当无效。但是我们应当看到,仲裁条款的性质与合同中的其他条款的性质完全不同。因为合同中的其他条款规定的都是当事人应承担的义务,而仲裁条款规定的不是一方当事人对另一方当事人的义务。仲裁条款是当事人双方的协议,即如果产生了有关一方当事人对另一方当事人承担的义务的争议,则这些争议将由他们自己成立的机构解决。② 这使得仲裁协议有其更特殊的性质。这也就引出了一个重要理论:仲裁协议的独立性理论,也可称之为自治权理论、可分离性理论或可分割性理论。

It is a generally recognized principle of the law of international arbitration that arbitration clauses continue to be operative, even though an objection is raised by one of the parties that the contract containing the arbitration clause is null and void. The jurisdiction of an arbitrator or arbitration board designated in accordance with an arbitration clause is unimpaired, even though the contract containing the arbitration clause is alleged to be null and void.

由此,我们可以把仲裁协议的独立性理论表述为:仲裁协议的效力不因合同不存在、无效、失效或不可执行而受影响,合同中的仲裁条款是与合同相分离的、独立存在的条款。仲裁庭依据有效的仲裁协议或仲裁条款对争议案件享有管辖权,排除法院的管辖权。

仲裁协议是不是绝对独立的呢?从字面意思上看,仲裁协议排除了法院对案件争议的管辖权,但是这种"排除"不是绝对的排除。法院是保障社会公平正义的最后一道屏障,司法机关当然保留对仲裁的监督,也就是说仲裁绝对不能游离于国家司法体制之外,这从各国的仲裁法中都可以得到体现。所以说,仲裁协议的独立不是绝对的独立,而是相对的独立。我们可以认为仲裁协议排除法院

---

① See David Joseph, Q. C., Jurisdiction and Arbitration Agreements and their Enforcement, 1st ed., Sweet & Maxwell Press, 2005, pp.95—96.

② 参见赵秀文编著:《国际商事仲裁法》,中国人民大学出版社 2004 年版,第 67 页。

对于案件的管辖权是法院对于案件管辖权的一种让渡。

仲裁协议的独立性理论最早在法国的司法判例中得到肯定,随着该理论在法国法院得到适用以后,便迅速得到了世界各国和国际社会的广泛认同,并发展成为仲裁法律制度中的一项基本原则。①

三、国际商事仲裁协议的效力

如果双方当事人达成合意,就未来可能发生以及已经发生的争议签订了一份有效的仲裁协议,那么将带来一些不可回避的法律效果。作为一份有效的仲裁协议,它究竟会产生什么样的法律效果呢?经过学者们的多年研究,理论界基本上已经形成了共识,仲裁协议的效力主要表现在对当事人、仲裁机构和仲裁庭以及法院三个方面。

(一) 对当事人的效力

仲裁协议既然是由双方当事人合意将其现存的或未来的有关争议提交仲裁而不提交法院解决的一种协议,它自然直接对当事人发生效力。这里我们必须首先将当事人的概念界定清楚。这里的当事人仅仅是指签订仲裁协议的当事人,范围限定得非常小。一份有效的仲裁协议当然不仅仅对签订协议的当事人产生法律效力,同时也对虽然不是仲裁协议的签字方,但与该争议有利益关系的人产生影响,我们称之为争议纠纷的当事人,也就是仲裁协议的第三方。关于仲裁协议第三方的问题,我们在下文会有详细介绍。

Where the parties have agreed to submit to arbitration under the Rules, they shall be deemed to have submitted ipso facto to the Rules in effect on the date of commencement of the arbitration proceedings, unless they have agreed to submit to the Rules in effect on the date of their arbitration agreement.②

仲裁协议对当事人最主要的法律效力表现在,当争议发生后,当事人任何一方都有义务将争议提交仲裁解决。仲裁协议一旦有效订立,双方当事人都要受其约束,都要履行协议规定的义务,任何一方都应当将他们之间的特定争议提交仲裁解决,而不得提交法院解决。也就是说,它在一定程度上限制了法院对于该争议的管辖权。这是因为,一项有效的仲裁协议排除了当事人将争议提交法院解决的权利,使当事人承担了将争议提交仲裁解决的义务。如果一方当事人违反了仲裁协议规定的这一义务而向法院起诉,另一方当事人就有权依据仲裁协议要求法院终止司法诉讼程序,并将争议提交给仲裁机构解决。③

---

① 参见谢石松主编:《商事仲裁法学》,高等教育出版社 2003 年版,第 157 页。
② See Michael W. Bühler & Thomas H. Webster, Handbook of ICC Arbitration: Commentary, Precedents, Materials, Sweet & Maxwell, 2005, p.79.
③ 参见谢石松主编:《商事仲裁法学》,高等教育出版社 2003 年版,第 149—150 页。

(二) 对仲裁机构和仲裁庭的效力

仲裁协议决定了仲裁机构、仲裁庭与当事人之间的关系,以及仲裁员和仲裁庭的权利义务。一旦选定了仲裁机构,该仲裁机构就不得不受理该案,因为仲裁机构在设立之初便已默认对任何提交到本机构的案件必须受理,受理成了一种义务。与此不同的是,如果仲裁协议指明了某人担任仲裁员,一旦发生争议,该人则可以拒绝担任仲裁员。仲裁协议并不对该名仲裁员产生约束力。[①]

仲裁协议对仲裁机构和仲裁庭的法律效力主要表现在以下两个方面:

1. 决定仲裁管辖权的范围

仲裁协议决定仲裁管辖权的范围。具体言之:(1)它赋予仲裁庭审理当事人提交仲裁的争议,并作出裁决的权力。(2)决定仲裁庭可以审理和裁决何项争议或何种问题。例如,仲裁协议只规定了一项争议或者几项争议,在仲裁程序的进行过程中,如果无进一步的仲裁协议,仲裁庭就无权审理新出现的其他争议。如果仲裁庭审理其他的争议,就会出现超越管辖权范围的问题,当事人完全可以就仲裁庭对该新的争议缺乏管辖权提出异议。

这里有一个问题值得注意,即仲裁协议生效后,如果选定了仲裁机构,一旦争议发生,当事人只能向选定的仲裁机构提起仲裁。这时,仲裁机构对于案件享有的管辖权是"潜在的"。只有当事人提起仲裁后,仲裁机构才享有"实际的"管辖权。[②]

2. 确定仲裁庭具有决定自身管辖权的权力

仲裁协议可以确定仲裁庭是否具有决定自身管辖权的权力。如果仲裁协议合法有效,即使没有明确规定,根据有关国家的商事仲裁立法和司法实践及相关的商事仲裁规则,也可以基于仲裁协议的存在来确定仲裁庭具有该项权力。这就是著名的管辖权/管辖权原则。

If the Respondent does not file an Answer, as provided by Article 5, or if any party raises one or more pleas concerning the existence, validity or scope of the arbitration agreement, the court may decide, without prejudice to admissibility or merits of the plea or pleas, that the arbitration shall proceed if it is prima facie satisfied that an arbitration agreement under the Rules may exist. In such a case, any decision as to the jurisdiction of the Arbitral Tribunal shall be taken by the Arbitral Tribunal itself. If the court is not so satisfied, the parties shall be notified that the arbitration can not proceed. In such a case, any party retains the right to ask any

---

① 参见林一飞:《国际商事仲裁法律与实务》,中信出版社 2005 年版,第 68 页。
② 同上。

court having jurisdiction whether or not there is a binding arbitration agreement.[①]

商事仲裁庭所拥有的决定自身管辖权的权力这一规则,最先起源于德国,后被法国和其他欧洲大陆法系国家的理论界与司法实践所采用。联合国国际贸易法委员会在制定《示范法》时的工作文件和评述中也提到了这一规则。目前它已经得到了各主要的国际商事仲裁条约、各主要国家的商事立法和司法实践以及各主要仲裁机构的仲裁规则普遍承认。

(三) 对法院的效力

仲裁协议以当事人的自由意志排除了法院的司法管辖权,这是仲裁协议的法律效力所产生的主要的、也是最直接的效果之一。这种效果不仅能够排除法院一般的司法管辖权,而且能排除其专属管辖权。

Exclusion of the courts. One of the main effects aimed at and produced by, the arbitration agreement is to exclude the jurisdiction of the courts. This effect of the arbitration agreement is universally admitted when the agreement refers to an existing dispute. It is open to doubt in a number of countries when the agreement refers to a future dispute.[②]

If any of the parties refuses or fails to take part in the arbitration or any stage thereof, the arbitration shall proceed notwithstanding such refusal or failure.[③]

仲裁协议作为当事人之间的合意,是基于意思自治而排除法院对纠纷的管辖权,因而具备合同的效力。如果一方当事人在争议发生后不按仲裁协议将争议提交仲裁解决,而是将该项争议向法院提起诉讼,法院完全可以因其无管辖权而要求当事人交由仲裁加以解决。如果法院已经受理了有关当事人所提起的诉讼,另一方当事人有权以他们之间存在仲裁协议,法院无管辖权为由,要求法院终止有关的诉讼程序,驳回该当事人的起诉。

仲裁协议排除法院的司法管辖权,已经得到了世界各国仲裁立法和司法实践以及国际商事仲裁立法的普遍认可,并已经成为仲裁法律制度中的一项基本原则。1998年德国《仲裁法》第1032(1)条规定,就仲裁协议的标的向法院提起诉讼,如被告在对争议实体予以聆讯前提出异议,则法院应以不可受理为由驳回起诉,除非法院认定仲裁协议是绝对或相对无效或者不可执行的。我国《仲裁法》也规定,当事人达成仲裁协议,一方向人民法院起诉的,人民法院不予受理,但仲裁协议无效的除外。

---

① See Michael W. Bühler & Thomas H. Webster, Handbook of ICC Arbitration: Commentary, Precedents, Materials, Sweet & Maxwell, 2005, p.79.
② See Katherine V. W. Stone, Arbitration Law, Foundation Press, 2003, p.210.
③ See Michael W. Bühler & Thomas H. Webster, Handbook of ICC Arbitration: Commentary, Precedents, Materials, Sweet & Maxwell, 2005, p.79.

当然,排除法院就案件实体进行审理的管辖权不等于排除法院具有的其他程序管辖权。例如,当事人可能请求法院采取临时措施、请求法院委任仲裁员、主持作证等,此类程序事项仍应由法院进行。而此时法院的管辖权与仲裁协议并不冲突。例如,1998 年德国《仲裁法》第 1033 条规定,在仲裁程序开始或进行之中,法院应当事人请求就仲裁标的采取临时保全措施,与仲裁协议并不冲突。①

What's more, the validity of an arbitration clause determines whether the court or the arbitration tribunal has the jurisdictional authority to rule on the parties' disputes. Where the arbitration clause is invalid, the dispute shall be within the jurisdiction of the people's court; if the arbitration clause is valid, the dispute shall be subject to the jurisdiction of an arbitration tribunal and settled there accordingly. Article 20 of the Arbitration Law of the People's Republic of China provides that "where the parties believe the validity of an arbitration clause is disputed, such parties shall file a petition at an arbitration commission or at a people's court. Where one party files a petition at an arbitration commission and the other party initiates an act at a people's court, the case shall be adjudicated by the people's court." The said provision indicates that both the people's court and the arbitration institution are empowered to examine and establish the validity of an arbitration clause, and the court's power prevails that of the arbitration tribunal.

此外,仲裁协议是仲裁裁决得以向法院申请强制执行的依据。在通常情况下,仲裁败诉的一方当事人会以种种理由为借口,不会主动、自觉地履行仲裁裁决所确定的实体义务。此时,胜诉的一方当事人只有依据有效的仲裁协议和仲裁裁决书依法请求法院强制执行,迫使败诉方履行义务,以实现自己的权利。Article 62 of Arbitration Law of the People's Republic of China provides that: The parties shall execute an arbitration award. If one party fails to execute the award, the other party may apply to a people's court for enforcement in accordance with the relevant provisions of the Civil Procedure Law, and the court shall enforce the award.

《示范法》第 35 条第 1 款也明确规定:

An arbitral award, irrespective of the country in which it was made, shall be recognized as binding and, upon application of the country in which it was made, shall be recognized as binding and, upon application in writing to the competent court, shall be enforced subject to the provisions of this article and of article 36.

由此可以看到,仲裁协议虽然排除了法院对纠纷的管辖权,但这种排除不是

---

① 参见林一飞:《国际商事仲裁法律与实务》,中信出版社 2005 年版,第 63—64 页。

绝对的排除,法院对案件仍然起着不可忽视的监督作用。不妨做这样的理解:仲裁协议排除法院的管辖权,与其说是绝对的排除,还不如说是司法管辖权对意思自治作出的一定程度的让步。

第二节 国际商事仲裁协议的表现形式

仲裁协议对于仲裁而言,其重要性不容置疑,它是仲裁的前提和基础。纵观各国立法及实践,仲裁协议有两种形式:一种是在争议发生之前订立的,通常作为合同中的一项仲裁条款出现;另一种是在争议发生之后订立的,旨在把已经发生的争议提交仲裁。前者称之为仲裁条款(the arbitration clause),后者称之为交付仲裁的协议(the submission agreement)。这两种形式的仲裁协议的法律效力是相同的。

一、仲裁条款

仲裁条款一般出现在合同之中,是合同的重要组成部分且具备独立的地位。仲裁条款规定将来可能遇到的任何与合同有关的纠纷应当通过仲裁的形式来加以解决。仲裁条款是仲裁协议最重要的表现形式。

Once any dispute arises actually, the arbitration tribunal may be promptly built up according to the arbitration clause of the contract. But most arbitration clauses are very simple. They only provide that once disputes arise when performing the contracts, they shall be settled by some arbitral institutions or provisional arbitral institutions, the awards of which are final.

以下列举了几个仲裁机构的示范仲裁条款:

北京仲裁委示范仲裁条款规定:因本合同引起的或与本合同有关的任何争议,均提请北京仲裁委员会按照该会仲裁规则进行仲裁。仲裁裁决是终局的,对双方均有约束力。

上海仲裁委的示范仲裁条款表述为:

The disputes, arising between the parties of the contract, shall be settled by consultation; the disputes, if may not be settled by consultation, shall be submitted to Shanghai Arbitration Commission for arbitration according to the arbitration rules of the Arbitration Commission.

中国国际经济贸易委员会(CIETAC)示范仲裁条款为:

Any disputes arising out of or in connection with this contract shall be submitted to the CIETAC for arbitration in accordance with the arbitration rules in effect at the time when the arbitration is applied. The arbitration award is final, and is of binding on both parties.

国际商会(ICC)示范仲裁条款为：

All disputes arising out of or in connection with the present contract shall be finally settled under the Rules of Arbitration of the International Chamber of Commerce by one or more arbitrators appointed in accordance with the said Rules.

美国仲裁协会(AAA)示范仲裁条款为：

Any controversy or claim arising out of or relating to this contract shall be determined by arbitration in accordance with the International Arbitration Rules of the American Arbitration Association.

The parties may wish to consider adding：

A：The number of arbitrators shall be (one or three)；

B：The place of arbitration shall be (city and/or country)，or

C：The language(s) of the arbitration shall be [   ].

仲裁条款的内容并非千篇一律,各种类型的合同中的仲裁条款详略不等。有的仲裁条款(通常在大型成套设备买卖合同、贷款合同、工程承包合同等中)详细规定了可以提交仲裁的事项、仲裁地点、仲裁机构、仲裁庭的组成方式和程序、仲裁裁决的效力及仲裁所应适用的法律、仲裁所使用的语言等内容。而关于仲裁庭的组成方式,一般则由仲裁机构按其仲裁规则来加以解决。其中的法律适用问题,是一个十分敏感的问题,对当事人权利义务关系重大。但是在一般贸易过程中,当事人为了实现利益的最大化,往往更加注重签订合同的效率及效益,当事人不可能在商务条款均达成一致的情况下仅因为法律适用问题而使得整个交易搁浅。再者,对于一般的国际货物买卖来说,当前国际上存在若干调整国际货物买卖关系的国际公约或国际惯例,如《联合国国际货物销售合同公约》、《国际贸易术语解释通则》等,它们为大多数国家的商人们所接受。所以,载于小额国际货物买卖合同中的仲裁条款通常均不涉及法律适用等方面的内容。[①]

二、交付仲裁的协议

交付仲裁的协议是在争议发生之后由当事人签订的、表示愿意把已经发生的争议交付仲裁解决的协议,它是独立于商业合同的一项专门协议。因为交付仲裁的协议是在争议发生后单独签订的,所以它对当事人的效力、独立性等问题,各界均有不同意见。[②]

[①] 参见陈治东：《国际商事仲裁法》,法律出版社1998年版,第102页。
[②] 同上书,第103页。

一般来说,当事人及其法律顾问在处理提交仲裁协议上的立场,与仲裁条款已经被写进合同时存在的立场有很大的区别。首先,争议已经在事实上发生,而这通常意味着当事人双方处于某种敌对状态。其次,从专业化角度看,法律顾问知道其所面临的是何种类型的争议,他们会希望构造整个仲裁,以有效适当地处理此种争议。再次,当事人的利益可能存在冲突,因为申请人通常希望争议得到快速解决,而被申请人一般会认为拖延对其有利。不过,应当记住,申请人可以通过利息裁决而就延迟得到赔偿,并且延迟通常通过成本花费而达到。最终,被申请人可能被要求支付仲裁费用。基于所有这些理由,提交协议的协商过程可能冗长。①

三、对仲裁条款以及交付仲裁的协议的分析比较

An arbitration clause looks to the future, whereas a submission agreement looks to the past. The first, which is most common, is usually contained in the principal agreement between the parties and is an agreement to submit *future* disputes to arbitration. The second is an agreement to submit *existing* disputes to arbitration.

另外,就上述两类不同的仲裁协议的效力而言,世界上绝大多数国家的法律均承认它们具有同等的效力。只要双方当事人在合同中订有仲裁条款,在争议发生后,任何一方都可以依据仲裁条款提起仲裁,而毋需另行签订专门的协议。再者在实践中,一旦发生争议,当事人之间的关系紧张,很难就仲裁协议的内容(尤其是仲裁地点)达成一致意见。因此,国际上都倾向于在国际商业合同中订立仲裁条款,以便在实际发生争议时避免重新谈判仲裁协议的麻烦,尽快将争议交付仲裁。②

第三节 国际商事仲裁协议的法律要件

仲裁协议必须满足一定的要件才能称之为有效的仲裁协议。一般而言,仲裁协议必须同时满足形式要件与实质要件才能具备法律效力。

一、仲裁协议的形式要件

仲裁协议的形式要件,指的是法律对于有效的仲裁协议在形式方面的要求。按照现在大多数国家及国际的做法,一份有效的仲裁协议必须是书面的,并且要

---

① 参见〔英〕艾伦·雷德芬、马丁·亨特等:《国际商事仲裁法律与实践》,林一飞、宋连斌等译,北京大学出版社2005年版,第171—172页。
② 参见陈治东:《国际商事仲裁法》,法律出版社1998年版,第106—107页。

经过当事人的签署或在当事人之间实现了交换。书面和签署、交换是分开的两要件。书面表明仲裁协议存在的形式,签署、交换则表明双方的合意。①

（一）书面要求

尽管到目前为止,世界各国和国际社会对仲裁协议的形式要件并没有一个统一的标准,但是通常仲裁协议应该具备书面形式。大多数国家和一些重要的国际条约都对仲裁协议的书面形式作了规定。由于书面形式本身没有一个统一的定义,因此关于书面形式的解释容易发生争议,但是对于书面形式的解释有了日趋宽泛的趋势。

1. 各国国内立法和国际条约对于仲裁协议书面形式的规定

（1）各国国内立法对于仲裁协议书面形式的规定

纵观世界各国的国内立法,对于仲裁协议书面要求的做法,大致有三种。第一种立法明确规定要求仲裁协议应当具备书面形式;第二种立法不但要求仲裁协议具备书面形式,还要求其必须经过特殊程序;第三种立法为不排斥非书面形式的仲裁协议。

采取第一种做法的国家和地区最为普遍,包括英国、瑞士、法国以及我国的大陆及港、澳、台地区。如英国《1996 年仲裁法》强调了仲裁协议的书面形式要求。② 瑞士《联邦国际私法法典》规定,关于仲裁协议的形式,如果以电报、电传、传真或任何其他通讯方式,其内容可作为证据的书面形式做成,仲裁协议应为有效。③ 法国 1997 年新的《民事诉讼法》也规定了仲裁条款和交付协议书必须采用书面形式。④ 我国《仲裁法》也规定仲裁协议必须采用书面形式。⑤

France—Code of Civil Procedure

Article 1443

To be valid, an arbitration clause shall be in writing and included in the contract or in a document to which it refers.

To be valid, an arbitration clause shall furthermore appoint the arbitrator or arbitrators, or provide for the method of their appointment.

Article 1449

A submission agreement shall be in writing. It may be contained in the minutes of a meeting of the arbitrators and the parties, signed by them.

---

① 参见林一飞:《国际商事仲裁法律与实务》,中信出版社 2005 年版,第 84 页。
② 参见英国《1996 年仲裁法》第 5 条第 1 款。
③ 参见瑞士《联邦国际私法法典》第 178 条。
④ 参见法国 1997 年《民事诉讼法》第 1443 条和 1449 条。
⑤ 参见《仲裁法》第 16 条。另外,我国澳门地区 1996 年《仲裁法》第 6 条、我国香港地区 2000 年《仲裁(修订)条例》第 2AC 条、我国台湾地区 1998 年"仲裁法"第 1 条第 3 款等都有类似规定。

采取第二类做法的国家有数个,较为典型的为西班牙、葡萄牙以及委内瑞拉等。这些国家对仲裁协议的形式进行更加严格的限制,甚至要求仲裁协议必须经以公证文书的形式做出,或需要经过法院的批准。①

另外,还有一些国家采取第三类做法,如德国、荷兰、希腊、瑞典、丹麦以及日本等。这些国家的国内法上虽然规定了仲裁协议的书面形式,但也不排斥非书面形式的仲裁协议,主要是允许口头的或默示的仲裁协议。如德国《民事诉讼法》规定,仲裁协议首先要求"必须书面形式做成",其次"参与案件的实质问题的讨论即弥补了仲裁协议形式上的缺陷"。该法还明确规定了仲裁协议可以其他形式做成:"如仲裁协议系双方当事人的一项业务事项,并双方当事人均非商事法典第四项所述之贸易职业者",则仲裁协议可以以非书面形式做成。② 又如瑞典,其对于仲裁协议的形式,一贯以来就没有什么特别的要求,对于处理未来的争议,协商的协定或更加例外一些的统一意见,在瑞典都视为有效,③甚至承认仲裁协议以口头形式达成,是世界上为数不多的几个承认口头仲裁协议的国家之一。瑞典新的仲裁法律中,仍然坚持对仲裁协议的形式不作强制性要求,即只要当事人将他们之间产生的纠纷提交仲裁解决并被仲裁院接受即可,口头合同和书面合同一样得到法律的承认。

Greek courts will give effect to a valid arbitration agreement in both domestic and international cases. Under Greek law, to be legally binding, an arbitration agreement must be in writing and signed by the parties. If the agreement is not in writing, it will only be enforceable if all the parties appear before the arbitrator(s) and enter into the arbitral process without reservation (Article 869, Greek Code of Civil Procedure).

(2) 国际条约对于仲裁协议书面形式的规定

1923年《日内瓦议定书》和1927年《日内瓦公约》仅仅要求各缔约国根据其国内法确定仲裁协议在形式上的有效性,并未规定仲裁协议一定要采用书面的形式。但是,二战以后的条约更多的是统一要求仲裁协议应当具备书面形式。如1958年《纽约公约》要求仲裁协议必须是书面的,并以此作为承认及执行仲裁裁决的条件之一。《纽约公约》要求各缔约国应对当事人以书面形式订立的,约定将协议下已产生的,或将来产生的,可以仲裁方式解决的契约性或非契约性争议提交仲裁的协议予以承认。1985年《示范法》和1975年《美洲国家间国际商事仲裁公约》也对仲裁协议的书面形式要求作了规定。当然,也有条约并没有强制要求仲裁协议的书面形式。如《欧洲国家商事仲裁公约》规定,在法律不

---

① 参见韩健:《现代国际商事仲裁法的理论与实践》,法律出版社2000年版,第51页。
② 参见德国1998年《民事诉讼法》第1027条第1款、第2款以及第3款。
③ 参见丁建中:《外国仲裁法与实践》,中国对外经济贸易出版社1992年版,第312页。

要求仲裁协议必须以书面形式签订的国家,仲裁协议可依该国法律许可的形式订立。

Convention on the Recognition and Enforcement of Foreign Arbitral Awards (New York Convention):

Each Contracting State shall recognize an agreement in writing under which the parties undertake to submit to arbitration all or any differences which have arisen or which may arise between them in respect of a defined legal relationship, whether contractual or not, concerning a subject matter capable of settlement by arbitration. The term "agreement in writing" shall include an arbitral clause in a contract or an arbitration agreement, signed by the parties or contained in an exchange of letters or telegrams.

Inter-American Convention on International Commercial Arbitration:

An agreement in which the parties undertake to submit to arbitral decision any differences that may arise or have arisen between them with respect to a commercial transaction is valid. The agreement shall be set forth in an instrument signed by the parties, or in the form of an exchange of letters, telegrams, or telex communications.

2. 书面形式的扩张解释

无论是国内立法还是国际公约,对于仲裁协议的书面要求已经达成了共识,但是随着国际商事贸易实践及仲裁制度的进一步发展,仲裁协议书面要求的绝对化受到了挑战。

There has been a revolution in communications since the New York Convention was drawn up in 1958. Telegrams, which were a frequent method of communicating an urgent message in writing, were largely replaced by telex, and later by fax and now email. This change in methods of communication is reflected in the Model Law, which goes much further than the New York Convention in its definition of "writing".

The Model Law provides that the arbitration agreement shall be in writing. An agreement is in writing if it is contained in a document signed by the parties or in an exchange of letters, telex, telegrams or other means of telecommunication which provides a record of the agreement, or in an exchange of statements of claim and defense in which the existence of an agreement is alleged by one party and not denied by another. The reference in a contract to a document containing an arbitration clause constitutes an arbitration agreement provided that the contract is in writing and the reference is such as to make that clause part of the contract.

从国际条约和各国立法的趋势看,解释书面形式的趋势是扩张性解释。《纽约公约》作为一个具有典型意义的关于仲裁的国际条约,将"书面协议"定义为应包括当事人签订的或在互换函电中达成的合同中的仲裁条款或仲裁协议。① 但是这种规定显然落后于国际商事活动的发展和变化,事实上,电传和传真等先进的通讯方式在现代社会已经非常普遍,因此《纽约公约》的这一条款遭遇诟病,要求修改这一条款的呼声也较为高涨。鉴于此,之后的《示范法》在书面形式的规定上走出了一步:"协议如载于当事各方签字的文件中,或载于往来的书信、电传、电报或提供协议记录的其他电讯手段中,或在申诉书和答辩书的交换中当事一方声称有协议而当事他方不否认即为书面协议。在合同中提出参照载有仲裁条款的一项文件即构成仲裁协议,如果该合同是书面的而且这种参照足以使该仲裁条款构成该合同的一部分的话。"②

相比之下,一些国家在国内立法上对于仲裁协议书面形式作了更宽泛的规定。如英国《1996年仲裁法》规定,以下任何一种协议都为书面仲裁协议:以书面形式达成的协议,无论当事人签字与否;以书面通讯交换方式达成的协议;有书面证明的协议,如一项由一位当事人或经所有当事人委托授权的第三人记录下来的口头协议,甚至可以包括仲裁员记录下来的协议;当事人以非书面方式约定援引某些条款,只要该条款是书面的,当事人之间的协议即是书面的,通常可以援引包括仲裁条款的书面合同,也可以援引一套书面仲裁规则(如 LMAA 条款);当事人在仲裁或司法程序中进行书面文件交换时,一方当事人书面主张他们之间存在一项非书面的仲裁协议,另一方当事人在书面答复中未作否认表示的,即在他们之间构成一项书面仲裁协议。③ 这表明英国《1996年仲裁法》并没有全盘接受《示范法》,其认为《示范法》主要是为了帮助那些在仲裁立法方面不成熟的国家制定本国的仲裁法,而英国在这方面已有丰富的经验,因此其新仲裁法在吸收《示范法》有利方面,反映《示范法》主导精神的同时,继续保留并发展了英国已成熟和更先进的内容。④

English: Arbitration Act 1996

5 Agreements to be in writing

(1) The provisions of this Part apply only where the arbitration agreement is in writing, and any other agreement between the parties as to any matter is effective for the purposes of this Part only if in writing.

The expressions "agreement", "agree" and "agreed" shall be construed accordingly.

---

① 参见1958年《纽约公约》第2条第1款、第2款。
② 《示范法》第7条第2款。
③ 参见英国《1996年仲裁法》第5条第1款。
④ 参见梁慧星主编:《民商法论丛》第19卷,金桥文化出版(香港)有限公司2001年版,第468页。

(2) There is an agreement in writing—

(a) if the agreement is made in writing (whether or not it is signed by the parties),

(b) if the agreement is made by exchange of communications in writing, or

(c) if the agreement is evidenced in writing.

(3) Where parties agree otherwise than in writing by reference to terms which are in writing, they make an agreement in writing.

(4) An agreement is evidenced in writing if an agreement made otherwise than in writing is recorded by one of the parties, or by a third party, with the authority of the parties to the agreement.

(5) An exchange of written submissions in arbitral or legal proceedings in which the existence of an agreement otherwise than in writing is alleged by one party against another party and not denied by the other party in his response constitutes as between those parties an agreement in writing to the effect alleged.

(6) References in this Part to anything being written or in writing include its being recorded by any means.

(二) 签署、交换

1.《纽约公约》对签署和交换的要求

由于《纽约公约》将"书面协议"定义为应包括当事人签订的或在互换函电中达成的合同中的仲裁条款或仲裁协议,这似乎包含了对仲裁协议"签署"和"交换"的要求。

按照《纽约公约》的规定,书面的仲裁协议有两类,一类是经当事人签署的仲裁协议,包括仲裁议定书或仲裁条款;另一类是经过当事人往来的电报、书信中所包含的合同中的仲裁条款或仲裁议定书。也就是说,如果书面仲裁协议是仲裁议定书或合同中的仲裁条款,就需要经过当事人"签署"。如果书面仲裁协议是包含在电报、书信当中的合同中的仲裁条款或仲裁议定书,则需要经过当事人的交换。但是,对于"签署"和"交换"的具体定义,公约并没有提供统一的标准。

2. 签署、交换的关键在于体现当事人的意思自治

由于《纽约公约》在国际商事仲裁领域不言而喻的重要性,又由于其并没有进一步解释签署和交换的具体含义,那么实践当中如何对这两者进行把握就比较重要。对于"签署",就合同中的仲裁条款来说,当事人对合同的签署是否可视为对其中所包含的仲裁条款的签署,公约对该问题的字面解释是不明确的。[①]

---

① 参见刘晓红:《国际商事仲裁协议的法理与实证研究》,商务印书馆2005年版,第35页。

另外,单方的传送或单方的确认是否可以认为构成了"互换"的条件呢?

应当认为,《纽约公约》对签署和互换的要求实际上是为了证明当事人之间的合意,从而保障当事人的意思自治性。签署也好、互换也好,实际上都是表明当事人自愿仲裁的合意的表达形式,因此关键在于判断是否体现了当事人的合意。从各国法院的实践看,互换规则的具体要求是指:当记载有仲裁协议或仲裁条款的文件以电报或信函方式发出后,收到该文件的一方须将该文件以电报或信函方式发回至发出该文件的一方且未表示反对;或者收到该文件的一方虽未将文件发回,但在以后回传的其他函电或其他文件(如发票、信用证、仲裁或诉讼文书)中认可收到了该文件。凡未将该文件发回,也未在以后回传的函电或其他文件中对已收到的文件表示认可的情况下,不构成《纽约公约》所称的"互换"(往来),因而也不能认定书面仲裁协议的存在。

从这个目的出发,实践当中对于签署和互换的理解不应太过于僵化,应当主要考虑当事人的合意。① 因此,法院在实践当中通常认为未经另一方书面接受或双方互相交换,不足以构成《纽约公约》规定的书面仲裁协议,故仲裁裁决不予执行。②

既然签署的要求只是为了证明当事人之间的合意,那么只要表明仲裁条款是由当事人自愿达成的,签署的解释就可以灵活一些。在 Compagnie de Navigation et Transports SA (France) v. MSC-Mediterranean Shipping Company SA (Switzerland)一案中,瑞士法院指出,由于现代通讯方式的发展,签署和未签署文件的区别不应以过于严格的方式处理。③ 另外,由于国际社会对仲裁协议书面形式的扩张解释,函件的形式应不限于《纽约公约》所述及的书信、电报两种形式,更多的现代通讯工具应被用于达成书面仲裁协议,故而互换的对象也不能局限于书信和电报两种形式,更多的如传真、电传甚至电子邮件的互换同样应视为满足《纽约公约》关于互换的要求。

(三)对于仲裁协议书面要求的评述

仲裁协议其实是一种特殊的合同,其本质是一种契约。作为合同,各国国内法明确规定合同可以是书面的也可以是口头的,那么仲裁协议为何必须采取书面形式呢?这是由仲裁在实践操作中的必然要求所决定的。就仲裁而言,仲裁地和执行地往往不同,有的甚至是两个不同的国家(如国际货物买卖),为了确保仲裁协议的有效以及避免可能产生的不必要的麻烦,国内法和国际公约均要求仲裁协议必须书面为之。

---

① 参见杨弘磊:《中国内地司法实践视角下的〈纽约公约〉问题研究》,法律出版社 2006 年版,第 104—105 页。
② 参见黄亚英:《论〈纽约公约〉与仲裁协议的形式》,载《法学杂志》2004 年第 2 期。
③ See ICCA Yearbook, Vol. XXI, 1996, pp.690—698.

二、仲裁协议的实质要件

仲裁协议的实质要件是指使仲裁协议有效的基本构成要素。一项有效的仲裁协议应当包括哪些基本内容,各国仲裁立法的规定不尽相同。综合多数国家的仲裁立法和司法实践及商事仲裁实务,一般认为,一项有效并具有可执行性的仲裁协议一般应当包括:签订仲裁协议的当事方具备缔约能力、请求仲裁的意思表示、提交仲裁的事项。另外,有些国家和国际仲裁庭的仲裁立法同时也认为仲裁机构、仲裁地点、仲裁规则及仲裁裁决的效力等也是一项仲裁协议的基本构成要件。

(一) 签订仲裁协议的当事方具备缔约能力

签订仲裁协议的当事人必须具备完全的民事行为能力,这是最基本的要求,限制民事行为能力人、无民事行为能力人签订的仲裁协议无效。

Parties to a contract must have legal capacity to enter into that contract, otherwise it is invalid. The position is no different if the contract in question happens to be an arbitration agreement. The general rule is that any natural or legal person who has the capacity to enter into a valid contract has the capacity to enter into an arbitration agreement. Accordingly, the parties to such agreements include individuals, as well as partnerships, corporations, states and state agencies.

If an arbitration agreement is entered into by a party who does not have the capacity to do so, the provisions of the New York Convention (or the Model Law, where applicable) may be brought into operation, either at the beginning or at the end of the arbitral process. At the beginning, the requesting party asks the competent court to stop the arbitration, on the basis that the arbitration agreement is void, inoperative or incapable of being performed. At the end of the arbitral process, the requesting party asks the competent court to refuse recognition and enforcement of the award, on the basis that one of the parties to the arbitration agreement is "under some incapacity" under the applicable law.

(二) 请求仲裁的意思表示

请求仲裁的意思表示被普遍认为是仲裁协议最根本的要素。一项符合要求的请求仲裁协议的意思表示,包含以下几个要素:

1. 请求仲裁的意思表示是真实的。仲裁协议体现的是当事人的意思自治,请求仲裁的意思表示必须是体现当事人的真实意愿。有关仲裁的国际仲裁庭规则及国内立法都普遍规定,一方以欺诈、胁迫等手段或迫使另一方当事人同其订立的仲裁协议无效。

2. 请求仲裁的意思表示是明确的。一项仲裁协议不仅仅需要体现当事人真实的意思表示,而且这种意思表示必须是明确的。通常情况下,有关仲裁的国际仲裁庭规则及国内立法都普遍要求仲裁协议必须采用书面的形式。否则,当事人请求仲裁协议的意思表示就可能因为模糊不清而被认定为无效。

It is important to ensure that the wording adopted in an arbitration agreement is adequate to fulfill the intentions of the parties. Usually, when parties agree to resolve any disputes between them by arbitration, they intend to resolve *all* disputes between them by this method (unless a specific exception is made). Accordingly, the arbitration agreement should be drafted in broad, inclusionary terms, rather than referring only certain categories of dispute to arbitration and leaving others to the jurisdiction of national courts.

(三) 提交仲裁的事项

提交仲裁的事项指当事人提交仲裁解决的争议内容,也可以理解为争议的范围。① 提交仲裁的事项同样也是仲裁协议最根本的要素。

一方面,提交仲裁的事项决定了仲裁范围。如果当事人在仲裁协议中未约定仲裁事项,仲裁庭就无权审理案件和作出裁决;而当事人对仲裁事项的约定也决定了仲裁庭的管辖权范围,仲裁庭审理和裁决的事项只能限于仲裁协议所规定的仲裁事项。

另一方面,并非所有的事项都可以提交仲裁。提交仲裁的事项,必须符合一个法律要求,即事项的可仲裁性。对于哪些争议是属于可仲裁的,不同国家的法律规定不尽相同,但通常认为,与合同有关的争议大部分都是可仲裁的。而对于其他事项,特别是侵权争议是否可仲裁则存在不同的看法。不过总体来讲,争议的可仲裁性范围是逐渐在扩大的,越来越多的国家都开始赋予侵权争议可仲裁性。如我国最高人民法院就在相关的司法解释中指出:合同、侵权或者根据有关法律而产生的经济上的权利义务关系是可以仲裁的。②

(四) 约定明确的仲裁机构

我国《仲裁法》明确规定,仲裁机构是仲裁协议的最根本要素之一。仲裁协议如果没有明确约定仲裁机构,则无效。仲裁协议约定的仲裁机构,严格地讲,必须是准确无误地指出这个仲裁机构的名称。但是,基于种种原因,对仲裁机构的约定这一仲裁协议实质要件,在仲裁实践中总是遭遇诸多问题。这些问题包括没有约定仲裁机构、约定了两家以上仲裁机构、约定的仲裁机构的名称不准确等等。例如,当事人约定由中国国际经济贸易仲裁委员会仲裁的时候,可能会使用该仲裁机构的旧称"中国对外贸易仲裁委员会"。对于约定不准确的仲裁机

---

① 参见陈治东:《国际商事仲裁法》,法律出版社1998年版,第108页。
② 参见《最高人民法院关于执行我国加入的〈承认及执行外国仲裁裁决公约〉的通知》。

构名称是否会导致仲裁协议的无效,实践中往往会采取较为宽容的态度,只要从这个不甚准确的名称可以推断出它实际所指的仲裁机构,一般都认为这样的仲裁协议是有效的。

三、有瑕疵的仲裁条款

有瑕疵的仲裁条款是指不能完全满足有效要件的仲裁条款。有瑕疵的仲裁条款和无效的仲裁条款是不一样的,有瑕疵的仲裁条款通常被视为是有效的,或者是可以补救的;而无效的仲裁条款则是没有办法补救的。所以,有瑕疵的仲裁条款在实质上是有效的,但又不是完全有效的,因为它并不完全满足法律的规定。当然,由于各国仲裁立法中对有效仲裁协议设定的标准各异,对于那些有瑕疵的仲裁协议,在一国可能是被认为有效或至少是可以补救的,而在另一国就可能被确定为是无效的。仲裁条款是有瑕疵的还是无效的,最终取决于一国仲裁法的具体规定。

由于请求仲裁的意思表示和仲裁事项一般在仲裁条款中都会比较明确,因此,有瑕疵的仲裁条款主要体现在以下方面:

(一)仲裁机构规定上的瑕疵

我国《仲裁法》规定,一项有效的仲裁条款必须包括仲裁机构。但是,仲裁协议当事人对仲裁机构的约定,却经常会存在以下问题,从而导致产生有瑕疵的仲裁条款:

1. 同时约定两个以上仲裁机构

当事人在仲裁协议中约定既可以由甲仲裁机构仲裁,又可以由乙仲裁机构仲裁。对这种有瑕疵的仲裁条款,理论界和大多数国家和地区的仲裁立法和司法实践均采取了肯定态度,因为尽管当事人在仲裁协议中选择了两个甚至多个仲裁机构,使得仲裁协议存在了不确定因素,但只要在提起仲裁时选择其中之一的仲裁机构,该协议就可得到执行。《最高人民法院关于适用〈中华人民共和国仲裁法〉若干问题的解释》第6条规定:"仲裁协议约定由某地的仲裁机构仲裁且该地仅有一个仲裁机构的,该仲裁机构视为约定的仲裁机构。该地有两个以上仲裁机构的,当事人可以协议选择其中的一个仲裁机构申请仲裁;当事人不能就仲裁机构选择达成一致的,仲裁协议无效。"

2. 选择的仲裁机构不存在

这种情况下,尽管在表面上看,仲裁协议具备了各项要素而有效,但由于所选择的仲裁机构不存在,所以仲裁协议是无法执行的。这就导致了该仲裁协议实际上是无效的。

3. 选择的仲裁机构名称不准确

当事人在仲裁协议中对仲裁机构名称称谓不准确的情况是国际商事仲裁中

常见的现象。对于这种有瑕疵的仲裁协议,理论界和司法实践通常也会采取比较宽容的态度,只要能根据仲裁协议中的名称合理推断出当事人实际所指的仲裁机构,这样的仲裁协议就是有效的。

4. 既选择仲裁机构又选择法院

当事人在仲裁协议中约定以仲裁方式解决纠纷或者向人民法院起诉。对于这种有瑕疵的仲裁协议,主流的观点认为仲裁协议无效,因为这种约定违反了"或裁或审"制度。当然,也有一部分人认为约定"仲裁解决纠纷或者向人民法院起诉"的表达之中已经肯定了接受仲裁的意思表示,根据"利于有效性"的解释原则,应当确认仲裁协议有效。[①] 对于这种有瑕疵的仲裁协议,如果一方当事人申请仲裁,而另一方当事人不对仲裁机构受理该案提出异议,则更适合认定为该仲裁协议有效。《最高人民法院关于适用〈中华人民共和国仲裁法〉若干问题的解释》第7条规定:"当事人约定争议可以向仲裁机构申请仲裁也可以向人民法院起诉的,仲裁协议无效。但一方向仲裁机构申请仲裁,另一方未在仲裁法第二十条第二款规定期间内提出异议的除外。"

(二)仲裁地点规定上的瑕疵

在实践中,很多仲裁协议都只规定了仲裁机构而没有规定仲裁地点,对于这种有瑕疵的仲裁协议,应当分以下两种情形区别对待:

1. 规定的仲裁机构所在地是明确的。大部分仲裁机构的所在地是明确的,规定了仲裁机构,一般都可以视为在仲裁机构所在地进行仲裁,即这种情况下仲裁地点可以默视为是仲裁机构所在地。因此,没有规定仲裁地的有瑕疵仲裁协议在大部分情况下都应该被视为是有效的仲裁协议。

2. 规定的仲裁机构所在地不明确,有些仲裁机构在两个以上地点都有分支机构,这种情况下,仅仅规定仲裁机构就无法判断究竟在哪个地方的该仲裁机构进行仲裁。例如,中国国际经济贸易委员会在北京、上海和深圳都有分会。在这种情况下,如果仅规定仲裁机构就能够合理推定是某个明确地点的该仲裁机构,则仲裁协议还可以是有效的;如果无法明确作上述推定,则该仲裁协议就得不到实际的执行。

(三)仲裁规则上的瑕疵

仲裁规则上的瑕疵分成以下两种情况:

1. 没有约定仲裁规则。如果在仲裁协议中仅约定了仲裁机构,但没有约定仲裁规则,这类有瑕疵的仲裁协议一般被视为有效及可执行的仲裁协议。通常情况下,如果当事人选择了特定的仲裁机构仲裁,就视为当事人选择了该

---

① 参见王元歌:《无效还是有效——既选择仲裁又选择诉讼之仲裁协议的认定》,载《中国对外贸易》2002年第2期。

仲裁机构的仲裁规则。如《国际商会商事仲裁规则》第 6 条规定,双方当事人按国际商会仲裁规则仲裁的,除双方已经约定适用订立仲裁协议时有效的仲裁规则外,应当视为事实上接受本规则。当然,也不排除仲裁机构没有自己的仲裁规则。这种情形下,该缺陷可由当事人在仲裁机构或法院的协助下加以补充和完善。

2. 约定了仲裁规则,但和所选择的仲裁机构的规定相矛盾。有些仲裁机构的仲裁规则规定:当事人选择该仲裁机构仲裁,就必须按照它的仲裁规则进行仲裁。而这个时候如果当事人选择了其他仲裁规则,那么这些仲裁机构就可能不予接受。这时候,就有可能产生两种结局:一是仲裁机构强制使用其自身的仲裁规则,这种情况下,仲裁协议还是部分有效的;另一种情况就是仲裁机构不予接受该仲裁,这时候就意味着仲裁协议无法得到执行。

(四) 仲裁裁决效力上的瑕疵

当事人约定了仲裁,同时约定对仲裁不服,可以向人民法院起诉,或者约定对仲裁不服,可以向其他仲裁机构提起仲裁。这种约定,违背了仲裁一裁终局原则,因此对于仲裁不服可向人民法院起诉或其他仲裁机构仲裁的约定是无效的、不可执行的。但是,这并不意味着当事人一开始就不能提交仲裁。因此,这种仲裁协议应该是部分有效的。

第四节 国际商事仲裁协议的继受

一、仲裁协议继受的概念和特征

仲裁协议的继受又被称为仲裁协议第三人责任,这是近年来理论界讨论非常热烈的一个话题。仲裁协议的第三方指的是虽未在仲裁协议上签字但是与纠纷有利益关系的第三方当事人。

An arbitration agreement may not validly confer any powers on an arbitral tribunal that directly affect persons who are not parties to that agreement unless a special provision of the applicable law enables them to do so; and this is rare. The principle applies to matters of substance as well as of procedure. For example, the award of an arbitral tribunal cannot properly direct a person who is not a party to the arbitration agreement to pay a sum of money or to perform a particular act. As regards procedural matters, the most common examples arise in relation to the production of documents and evidence.

20 世纪 80 年代以来,伴随着社会经济和法律环境的不断变化发展,各种新型争议大量出现,仲裁的作用也越来越大。在这种背景下,仲裁制度也必须根据案件解决的需要而不断地更新和发展。这种需求,在仲裁协议效力方面的表现之一就是仲裁协议效力范围不断扩大和延伸,即在特定情况下,不再固守传统的仲裁理论,仅使仲裁协议的效力及于书面协议的签字方,而是将其扩大到未签字方。我国有学者将这种仲裁协议的效力适用于未签字的第三方的现象称为"长臂仲裁协议"。[①]

仲裁协议继受的概念,简单地讲,是指非仲裁条款的第三方,因基于某种法律事由,而继受了仲裁条款所附之合同的权利义务,从而一并继受了仲裁条款,成为仲裁协议的当事人。

仲裁协议的继受主要有以下几个特征:

1. 仲裁协议的继受,一般是指仲裁条款的继受。仲裁协议主要包括两种形式,即仲裁协议书和仲裁条款。由于仲裁协议书一般是争议后产生的,且又是独立于合同的协议,因此,仲裁协议书一般不会出现继受的问题,仲裁协议的签订双方就是仲裁法律关系的直接当事人,不会涉及其他第三方。而仲裁条款则是在争议发生前签订的,且仅仅是主合同的一个条款,所以会因为合同的继受而发生仲裁协议的继受。

2. 仲裁协议的继受,是基于法律规定的事由发生,而不是基于当事人的约定。仲裁协议继受的原因,主要包括因母子公司之间的特定关系而使得一方签订的仲裁协议对另一方产生约束力,代理人订立的仲裁协议对委托人产生约束力,代位求偿情形下仲裁协议对代位求偿权人的约束力,合同一方当事人被合并、分立或终止情况下仲裁协议的约束力,以及提单转让中仲裁条款的约束力等几种情况。这些情况都是仲裁协议继受的法定事由,当事人并没有就仲裁协议是否转让明确地达成一致,而仲裁协议在发生上述情况下,被默认为是发生了继受。如果是当事人明确约定的,那么实际上就产生了新的仲裁协议,而不再是仲裁协议的继受。

3. 仲裁协议的继受,是一种附属性质的继受,它必定附随于主合同的权利义务的继受。仲裁协议继受发生的原因,必定是主合同的权利义务发生了转移,而不存只有仲裁条款发生转移的情况。如因母子公司之间的特定关系而发生的仲裁协议的继受,必定附属于子公司的权利义务转移给母公司或母公司的权利义务转移给子公司的情况;又如因代位求偿权而发生的仲裁协议的继受,必定附属于代位求偿权人取得原权利人的权利这样一种权利的转让。因此,仲裁协议的继受是附属性的,仲裁协议和仲裁协议所涉及的可能发生的争议是一起转移给第三方的。

4. 仲裁协议的继受产生了主体地位的变化。随着仲裁协议的继受,原来仲

---

① 参见赵键:《长臂的仲裁协议:论仲裁协议对未签字人的效力》,载《仲裁与法律》2000年第1期。

裁协议的第三方变成了仲裁协议的当事人,而原来仲裁协议的当事人则可能会成为仲裁协议的第三人。仲裁协议的第三方和仲裁第三人是不同的,仲裁第三人是指在仲裁程序开始以后,和仲裁当事人之间就系争案件无直接的仲裁协议但案件的处理与其有着法律上的利害关系,经仲裁当事人一致要求或经仲裁庭要求并得到当事人的一致同意,经其本人同意而加入到已经开始的仲裁程序当中的人;或者是由其本人提出要求,并获得仲裁当事人的一致同意而加入到已经开始的仲裁程序当中的人。仲裁协议的第三方则是指特定第三方并非仲裁条款的签字一方,但却因法律的规定及运行所产生的特定事实,如代理、代位求偿、合同主体变更、合同项下的权利义务转让等成为原合同一方当事人(仲裁条款签字方)的权利义务承继者。仲裁协议的继受,是仲裁协议的第三方变成了仲裁协议的当事人,而不是仲裁第三人变成仲裁协议的当事人。

二、关于仲裁协议继受的主张

仲裁协议只对签字方生效,体现了仲裁协议的意思自治原则。对于仲裁协议是否能够继受的问题,目前并没有统一的定论,也存在很多反对的声音,认为仲裁协议的继受有违仲裁的意思自治原则。但是,仲裁协议的继受也受到了学者的支持。支持仲裁协议继受的理由,主要是基于以下原则:

(一)"禁止反言"原则

禁止反言是指一个人对他人所作出的陈述,已被他人合理的相信,之后再允许这个人推翻过去所作出的陈述,对他人将会是不公正的。所以不允许这个人推翻自己已经作出的陈述。

禁止反言原则在仲裁条款的继受方面,主要有以下几种情形:

1. 当附属仲裁条款的合同发生转移后,仲裁条款的签字方可以利用合同中的实体条款对仲裁条款的非签字方主张自己的权利,并且签字方的主张完全来源于合同或者与合同的内容相关。这种情况下,签字方事实上确认了他和非签字方之间合同的存在,这意味着他对非签字方作出了一种陈述,包括对将与合同有关的争议提交仲裁的承诺。此时,如果他否认非签字方的仲裁权利,是不被允许的。这种情况适用于合同一方当事人被合并、分立或终止情况下仲裁协议的继受,提单转让中仲裁条款的继受,以及代理人订立的仲裁协议对委托人的继受等各种情况。

2. 当附属仲裁条款的合同发生转移后,仲裁协议的非签字方获得合同的权利义务,并利用合同中的实体条款对仲裁条款的签字方主张自己的权利,且非签字方的主张完全来源于合同或者与合同的内容相关。这种情况下,同样意味着非签字方事实上确认了他和签字方之间合同的存在,是他对遵守包括仲裁条款在内的合同规定的一种承诺。此时,如果他否认自己的仲裁权利,是不被允许的。这种情况适用于代位求偿情形下仲裁协议对代位求偿权人的继受。

3. 仲裁条款的签字方主张的权利是针对其他签字方和未签字方在本质上相互依存、不可分割的行为而提出的,签字方可以对未签字方援引仲裁条款。特别是当仲裁条款的其他签字方和未签字方在本质上人格混同,其他签字方履行仲裁条款所附之合同义务的行为实质上就是未签字方的行为的时候,意味着未签字方事实上确认了他和签字方之间合同的存在,并对合同的权利义务以及仲裁条款的遵守作出了承诺,因此,他同样也不能对此反言。这种情况适用于母子公司之间的特定关系而使得一方签订的仲裁协议对另一方的继受。

(二)"揭开公司面纱"原则

"揭开公司面纱"又称公司法人人格否定,是指当公司的独立人格和股东的有限责任被公司背后的股东滥用时,就具体法律关系中的特定事实,否定公司的独立法人机能,将公司与其背后的股东视为一体并追究其共同的连带法律责任,以保护公司债权人或其他相关利害关系群体的利益及社会共同利益,实现公平、正义的一种法律措施。[①]

在"揭开公司面纱"理论下,仲裁协议可以约束未签字的母公司。"揭开公司面纱"原则在仲裁条款的继受方面,主要有以下情形:

1. 母公司利用子公司的独立人格这一"面纱"进行欺诈,谋取不正当利益,损害债权人的利益。在这种情况下,债权人可以主张"揭开公司面纱",对母公司直接追究责任。而如果债权人和子公司之间存在仲裁协议,则债权人也可以依据"揭开公司面纱"原则,要求未在该仲裁协议上签字的母公司亦受该协议约束,从而由仲裁庭就债权人向子公司和母公司的追偿一并进行裁决。就"揭开公司面纱"原则在仲裁协议继受方面的应用而言,债权人必须有证据表明,母公司对子公司存在着足够的控制,并将子公司作为傀儡、工具从事欺诈行为,且对债权人造成不公正的损失。

2. 在仲裁协议上未签字的母公司主动要求"揭开公司面纱",从而参与到仲裁程序中来。这又分成两种情况:一是子公司和其他仲裁协议签字方的行为可能会损害到母公司的利益,如子公司怠于行使它对其他仲裁协议签字方的权利,从而损害到母公司的利益,因此母公司主动"揭开法人面纱",要求参与仲裁,这种情形类似于司法程序中股东的派生诉讼请求权。但这种情形发生的几率比较小,因为在子公司被母公司控制而丧失法人人格的前提下,通常不会发生子公司的行为可能会损害到母公司的利益的情况。二是母公司和子公司虽然自身存在欺诈或其他不法行为,但还是"主动"要求"揭开公司面纱",参与仲裁程序。这

[①] 参见梁建平:《"揭开公司面纱"——西方法人资格否认制度探讨》,载《税收与企业》1996年第8期。

种情形通常不会被当地的司法机关所接受,因为这种情形下母公司"揭开公司面纱"的目的通常是逃避法院的审理,而"揭开公司面纱"原则则是为了保护善意当事人的利益,如果允许这种情形下母公司对仲裁协议的继受,无疑是和"揭开公司面纱"原则的出发点相违背的。

除了以上原则外,支持仲裁协议转让的理论还包括:"合同相对性原则的例外",是指特定的第三人(不是指合同继受关系中的第三人)依据合同或法律上的规定向有关的合同当事人主张权利时,也可以适用合同中的仲裁条款;"公平合理的期待"原则,是指在特定的情况下,让第三方成为仲裁的当事人符合各方当事人的合理的利益和意图。

三、仲裁协议继受的具体情形

仲裁协议继受的具体情形,主要包括:委托人对代理人订立的仲裁协议的继受;代位求偿权人对仲裁协议的继受;合同一方当事人被合并、分立情况下仲裁协议的继受;合同转让情形下仲裁协议的继受;鉴于子、母公司之间特定关系而产生的仲裁协议的继受;提单转让中仲裁条款的继受等等。本书仅就其中比较常见的继受情形加以讨论。

(一)代理情况下的仲裁协议的继受

代理可以分成直接代理和间接代理。直接代理是代理人在代理权限内,以被代理人的名义实施民事法律行为。被代理人对代理人的代理行为,承担民事责任。[①] 直接代理在英美法系又被称为显名代理。相应的,间接代理可以理解为是代理人在代理权限内,以自己的名义实施民事法律行为,并承担民事责任。间接代理在英美法系又被称为隐名代理。

不同类型的代理,对仲裁协议的继受不一样。

1. 在直接代理的情形下,由于代理行为是代理人以被代理人的名义进行的,其法律后果直接由被代理人承担,若代理人与第三人签订的合同中存在仲裁条款,则该仲裁条款的签字方实际上是被代理人,因此仲裁条款直接对被代理人和第三人产生法律效力。所以,直接代理的情形下不发生仲裁协议的继受。

2. 在间接代理的情形下,由于代理行为是代理人以自己的名义进行的,若代理人与第三人签订的合同中存在仲裁条款,则该仲裁条款的签字方是代理人,这样就可能会发生仲裁协议的继受。在这种情况下,被代理人或者和代理人签订仲裁条款的第三人都可以使附属仲裁条款的合同在被代理人和第三人之间发生效力。我国《合同法》第403条规定:"受托人以自己的名义与第三人订立合同时,第三人不知道受托人与委托人之间的代理关系的,受托人因第三人的原因

---

① 参见《民法通则》第63条。

对委托人不履行义务,受托人应当向委托人披露第三人,委托人因此可以行使受托人对第三人的权利……受托人因委托人的原因对第三人不履行义务,受托人应当向第三人披露委托人,第三人因此可以选择受托人或者委托人作为相对人主张其权利,但第三人不得变更选定的相对人。……"这就是委托人和第三人分别被赋予的"介入权"和"选择权"。而此时,仲裁条款也应当随之发生继受。

(二) 代为求偿下的仲裁协议的继受

代位求偿,是指与债的履行有利害关系的第三人,在为债务人向债权人作出清偿以后,取得代位权,可以在其清偿的范围内,以自己的名义代位行使债权人的权利。例如,保险公司在向投保人作出赔付之后,在赔偿范围内取得了投保人的地位,可以"代替"投保人向相对人进行追偿。如果债务人和债权人之间存在仲裁协议,那么,代位求偿权人在取得债权人的地位时,同时也成为仲裁协议的当事人,也就发生了仲裁协议的继受。

这里应当注意和代位求偿概念类似的代位权。我国《合同法》第73条规定:"因债务人怠于行使其到期债权,对债权人造成损害的,债权人可以向人民法院请求以自己的名义代为行使债务人的债权,但该债权专属于债务人自身的除外。"此条款规定的便是一种代位权。假设债务人与次债务人之间的合同中订有仲裁条款,这种代位权是否可以发生仲裁协议的继受则比较复杂。因为这种代位权的实现形式是应当向人民法院提出,而没有准予债权人通过其他途径行使该权利。在实践中,法院是否还允许债权人通过仲裁来实现权利是存在疑问的。

(三) 合同一方当事人被合并、分立情况下仲裁协议的继受

公司的合并是指两个或两个以上的法人根据法律的规定或合同的约定变为一个法人的现象,包括新设合并和吸收合并两类。公司的分立是指一个法人分为两个或两个以上法人的现象。法人分立也可分为创设式分立和存续式分立两种。公司合并和分立的情况不同,对仲裁协议的继受结果也不同。

1. 公司的新设合并。新设合并是指两个以上的法人合并为一个新的法人,而原法人人格全部消失。此时,原法人的权利义务全部由新法人承受。这种情况下,原仲裁协议的一方当事人也发生人格消失,新设的公司继受仲裁协议,成为仲裁协议新的当事人。

2. 公司的吸收合并。吸收合并是指一个或多个法人归入到一个现存的法人之中,被合并的法人主体资格消灭,存续的法人主体资格依然存在,存续的法人承受被吸收的法人的权利义务。这种情况下,如果被吸收的法人和第三人之间存在仲裁协议,则该仲裁协议被继受给继存的企业。

3. 公司的创设分立。创设分立是指原法人分成两个或两个以上的新法人,原法人消灭。因分立而消灭的法人的权利义务由分立后的法人承受。这种情况

下,仲裁协议由两个新法人中的一个继受还是两个都继受,应当视附属该仲裁协议的合同权利义务是由谁来承受而定。如果两个法人共同承受了合同的权利义务,则两个新法人都应当继受该仲裁协议。

4. 公司的存续分立。存续分立是指原法人存续,并从其中分出一部分财产设立新法人。各国在立法及实践中普遍接受了这样的观点:因分立而消灭的法人的权利义务由分立后的法人承受。存续分立的情况下,仲裁协议对继存的公司继续有效,但是,如果分立出来的新公司也继承了附属仲裁协议的合同的权利义务,则该新公司也应当成为仲裁协议的继受者。

(四)合同转让情形下仲裁协议的继受

合同转让情形下仲裁协议的继受,分成以下几种情况:

1. 合同的概括转让。合同概括转让是指合同的整体权利义务全部转让给受让人。在合同承受的情形下,各国普遍适用的是仲裁条款"自动移转规则"。[1] 根据该规则,如果原合同中订有仲裁条款,该仲裁条款对合同的受让人与合同的其他当事人具有约束力。

2. 合同债权的转让。合同债权的转让,不需要经过债务人的同意。基于仲裁协议意思自治原则,且仲裁协议独立于主合同,债务人虽无法阻止合同债权的转让,但并不代表其同意仲裁条款也在新的债权人和他之间生效,仲裁条款不应随主合同债权的转让而转让,这样就不发生仲裁协议的继受问题。

3. 合同债务的转让。合同债务的转让,需要经过债权人的同意。债权人如果不同意仲裁协议在他和新的债务人之间生效,则可以明确地提出反对意见。如果债权人在同意合同债务转让的过程中,没有对仲裁协议提出明确反对意见,那么应当默示其同意仲裁协议的继受。

(五)鉴于子、母公司之间特定关系而产生的仲裁协议的继受

该种情形主要出现在集团公司,尤其是跨国公司内部控制公司与受控公司之间存在特定关系的情况下。一般情况下,母公司和子公司都是依据有限责任原则组成的各自独立的法人实体,各自以自身的财产对外独立承担责任。但是,如果由于集团公司内部控制因素的存在,或由于其他原因,致使子公司丧失了自己独立的意志,为母公司所控制,成为母公司的傀儡公司,那么,债权人可根据法律规定直接追究母公司的责任。

A number of arbitral tribunals and national courts have been called upon to consider whether an arbitration agreement concluded by a company may be binding on

---

[1] See Sigvard Jarvin, Assignment of Rights under a Contract Containing an Arbitration Clause: Assignee Bounded to Arbitrate, Decision by Sweden's Court in the "EMJA" Case, Swedish and International Arbitration 1997 Yearbook of the Arbitration Institute of Stockholm Chamber of Commerce, p.65. 转引自刘晓红:《国际商事仲裁协议的法理与实证》,商务印书馆2005年版,第219页。

its group affiliates or even a natural person who is the group's ultimate controlling shareholder. Such attempts to pierce the corporate veil are often motivated by the stated aim to find the "true" party in interest; and, of greater practical importance, to target a more creditworthy member of the relevant group of companies.

这便是上文所述及的"揭开法人面纱"原则的基本内容。而这种情况下如果子公司和第三方之间存在仲裁协议,则亦会发生仲裁协议的继受。目前,国际上已不乏适用"揭开公司面纱"原则确定子公司签订的仲裁条款效力可以扩展到未签约的母公司的案例。

关于仲裁协议的继受在理论和实践上尚未形成统一,争论依旧很大。但我们认为,仲裁协议的继受是顺应经济贸易发展的潮流的。

阅读材料

1. Separability of Arbitration clause

The concept of the separability of the arbitration clause, is both interesting in theory and useful in practice. It means that the arbitration clause in a contract is considered to be separate from the main contract of which it forms part and, as such, survives the termination of that contract. Indeed, it would be entirely self-defeating if a breach of contract or a claim that the contract was voidable was sufficient to terminate the arbitration clause as well; this is one of the situations in which the arbitration clause is most needed.

As those who drafted the Model Law observed in relation to the principle of separability:

"The main practical advantage of this principle is that it constitutes a serious bar, for a party who desires delay or wishes to repudiate his arbitration agreement, to subvert the arbitration clause by questioning in court the existence or validity of the arbitration agreement [by questioning the validity of the main contract]."

Separability thus ensures that if, for example, one party claims that there has been a total breach of contract by the other, the contract is not destroyed for all purposes. Instead, "It survives for the purpose of measuring the claims arising out of the breach, and the arbitration clause survives for determining the mode of their settlement. The purposes of the contract have failed, but the arbitration clause is not one of the purposes of the contract."

Another method of analysing this position is that there are in fact two separate contracts. The primary or main contract concerns the commercial obligations of the parties; the secondary or collateral contract contains the obligation to resolve any disputes arising from the commercial relationship by arbitration. This secondary contract may never come into operation; but if it does, it will form the basis for the appointment of an arbitral tribunal and for the resolution of any dispute arising out of the main contract.

The doctrine of separability is endorsed by institutional and international rules of arbitration, such as those of UNCITRAL, which state in the context of pleas as to the jurisdiction of an arbitral tribunal:

"... an *arbitration clause* which forms part of a contract and which provides for arbitration under the Rules shall be treated as an *agreement independent of the other terms of the contract.*"

Following the provisions of the UNCITRAL Rules, the Model Law provides that: "The arbitral tribunal may rule on its own jurisdiction, including any objections with respect to the existence or validity of the arbitration agreement. For that purpose, an arbitration clause which forms part of a contract shall be treated as an agreement independent of the other terms of the contract. A decision by the arbitral tribunal that the contract is null and void shall not entail *ipso jure* the invalidity of the arbitration clause."

2. Forms of wording of arbitration agreement

It is important to ensure that the wording adopted in an arbitration agreement is adequate to fulfil the intentions of the parties. Usually, when parties agree to resolve any disputes between them by arbitration, they intend to resolve *all* disputes between them by this method (unless a specific exception is made). Accordingly, the arbitration agreement should be drafted in broad, inclusionary terms, rather than referring only certain categories of dispute to arbitration and leaving others to the jurisdiction of national courts.

Fortunately, most national courts now regard arbitration as an appropriate way of resolving international commercial disputes and accordingly seek to give effect to arbitration agreements wherever possible, rather than seeking to narrow the scope of the agreement so as to preserve the court's jurisdiction. Thus, an English court held that a provision for the arbitration of disputes arising "in connection with" the contract was sufficient to give the arbitral tribunal the power to rectify the contract so as to achieve its true meaning. Similarly, a US court interpreted the same words as giving arbitrators broad powers to rule on disputes, thus enabling the court to stay litigation in favour of a referral to arbitration, even though the claim had been framed in terms of tort (libel, conspiracy and violation of legislation concerning unfair trading practices). The court held:

"The International Chamber of Commerce recommended clause which provides for arbitration of 'all disputes arising in connection with the present contract' must be construed to encompass a broad scope of arbitrable issues. The recommended clause does not limit arbitration to the literal interpretation or performance of the contract. It embraces every dispute between the parties having a significant relationship to the contract regardless of the label attached to the dispute."

Where an issue *does* arise as to the scope of an arbitrator's jurisdiction the issue may fall to be determined by the arbitrator (possibly at the outset of the arbitration) or by a competent court (for instance, where enforcement of the award is sought). There is a chance that the answer will differ, according to the tribunal before which it is raised. In general, arbitrators are likely to take a less restrictive approach than the courts. This is understandable. An arbitrator is likely to consider that as there *are* disputes between the parties, it would be sensible to try, so far as possible, to resolve them all in the same set of proceedings. A national court would no doubt be sympathetic to this approach; but it would nevertheless have it in mind that, unlike an arbitral award, its judgment might set a precedent for the future. Whatever the tribunal, its decision will depend upon its interpretation of the words of the arbitration agreement and the intention of the parties, in the light of the law that governs that agreement.

It has been suggested that the precise wording used in an arbitration agreement is likely to be subjected to closer analysis by common law jurisdictions than by civil law jurisdictions. Be that as it may, the case law raises a number of issues. First, general words such as "claims", "differences", and "disputes" have been held by the English courts to encompass a wide jurisdiction in the context of the particular agreement in question. Similarly, the term "controversies or claims" has been held to have a wide meaning in the US. If other words are used, it may be considered that the parties have intended some limitation on the kind of disputes referred to arbitration.

Linking words such as "in connection with", "in relation to", "in respect of", "with regard to", "under" and "arising out of" are also important in any dispute as to the scope of an arbitration agreement. For example, English courts have given a wide meaning to the phrase "arising out of", and this form of words will usually embrace all disputes capable of being submitted to arbitration. By contrast, the use of the words "under this contract" may be interpreted as excluding any claims other than those when the cause of action is contractual.

案例

中国人民保险公司广东省分公司与广东广合电力有限公司等保险合同纠纷案

一、事实部分

1999年12月30日,中国人民保险公司广东省分公司向广东广合电力有限公司签发了五份财产保险单,在该五份保险单中,都约定以中华人民共和国法律进行解释,并约定有关保险单的一切争议应提交仲裁解决。广东广合电力有限公司向中国人民保险公司广东省分公司支付了相应的保险费。后由于有关事项的变更,经双方协商,又形成了一系列批单。变更后的被保险人为广东广合电力有限公司和广东省沙角发电(C厂)公司等其他三家公司。2000年10月15日,被承保的沙角发电C厂发生爆炸事故,造成重大经济损失。广东广合电力有限公司经向中国人民保险公司广东省分公司索赔未果,遂以中国人民保险公司广东省分公司为被告、广东省沙角(C厂)发电公司等其他被保险人为第三人,向广东省高级人民法院提起诉讼,请求判令被告依据保险单赔偿损失。

二、争议点

本案所涉保险单中有仲裁条款,但仲裁条款中没有约定明确的仲裁机构。法院是否对本案有管辖权?

三、判决

本案一审在广东省高院进行,一审判决后,被告中国人民保险公司广东省分公司不服判决提起上诉。最高人民法院审理后认为:保险单中虽然约定了仲裁条款,但对于仲裁条款的效力,应当根据当事人选择的准据法作出认定,即应根据中华人民共和国法律认定本案仲裁条款的效力。根据《仲裁法》的规定,仲裁协议应当具有选定的仲裁委员会。而保单中的仲裁条款则没有约定仲裁委员会,事后双方当事人也未能就此达成一致,因此,本案中仲裁条款无效,法院对本案有管辖权,并判决被告应当承担赔偿义务。

四、分析

本案是关于仲裁条款有效性的一个判决,根据我国《仲裁法》的规定,仲裁协议应当具有下列内容:(1)请求仲裁的意思表示;(2)仲裁事项;(3)选定的仲裁委员会。从本案所涉仲裁条款的内容看,其中并没有关于仲裁委员会的选定。在仲裁条款对仲裁委员会没有约定、当事人亦未就此达成补充协议的情况下,该仲裁条款应认定为无效。因此,本案的判决是正确的。仲裁委员会作为仲裁条款的必要条件之一,合同的当事人在约定将争议交由仲裁解决的时候,必须注意在仲裁条款中确定一个明确的仲裁机构,否则就会导致仲裁协议的无效。

五、思考

如果中国只有一个仲裁机构,则本案是否要通过仲裁来解决纠纷?

铁行渣华有限公司与华兴海运(中国)有限公司申请确认提单仲裁条款无效纠纷案

一、事实部分

1998年5月,铁行渣华有限公司向华兴海运(中国)有限公司托运10个集装箱的货物,装于"Guang Bin Ji74"轮由香港运到广东云浮六都。华兴海运(中国)有限公司于1998年5月16日签发提单,提单号为74/9805LD02。该提单背面条款第2条规定:"所有因此提单产生的争议应按照中国法律在中国法院审理或在中国仲裁。"本案当事人事后没有关于仲裁的补充协议,本案当事人对上述事实均确认无异。此后,因货物没有能够及时运输而给铁行渣华有限公司造成了一定的损失。铁行渣华有限公司依据仲裁条款向中国的仲裁机构申请仲裁,而华兴海运(中国)有限公司则向法院申请确认该仲裁协议无效。

二、争议点

本案所涉的仲裁条款中既规定了仲裁,又规定了提交法院管辖,这种双重选择的仲裁条款是否有效?

三、判决

本案法院认为,对仲裁协议的效力作出认定,应适用当事人约定的准据法即中华人民共和国法律。根据仲裁法,司法程序与仲裁程序是两个相互排斥不能并存的程序,当事人如果同时选择了该两个程序,则整个选择无效。因此,本案的仲裁协议是无效的。

四、分析部分

74/9805LD02号提单背面条款第2条是一个管辖权条款,旨在确定解决该提单项下争议的途径和方法。根据我国加入的《承认及执行外国仲裁裁决公约》第2条规定的原则,当事人就诉讼事项订有仲裁协议者,缔约国法院受理诉讼时应依当事人一造之请求,命当事人提交仲裁。由此可见,一项争议的解决如果约定了提交仲裁,那么它本身应排斥诉讼,仲裁和诉讼不能同时进行,否则就违背了仲裁制度的根本原则。在本案所涉管辖权条款中,当事人既约定了进行仲裁又约定了进行诉讼,是一个管辖权选择条款,该条款实际上包括了上述两个选择管辖权的协议。根据一般法理,司法程序与仲裁程序是两个相互排斥不能并存的程序,当事人如果同时选择了该两个程序,则整个选择无效。在这里,整个选择无效是建立在每个选择都有效的基础之上的,正是因为每个选择都属有效,才会达到相互排斥相互否定而导致整个选择无效的后果。也就是说,既选择仲裁又选择法院管辖的仲裁条款是无效的。

五、思考

该案中仲裁协议既约定进行仲裁又约定诉讼,这种有瑕疵的仲裁条款可否加以补救?如果可以补救,应如何补救?

Court of Appeal, Fourth District, Division 1, California
Sherry L. Weeks and Larry D. Weeks, Plaintiffs and Respondents, v. Lawrence J. Crow et al., Defendants and Appellants

Civ. 22357.

113 Cal. App. 3d 350

Dec. 16, 1980.

*352 GERALD BROWN, Presiding Justice.

Facts

Defendants in a medical malpractice action petitioned the court to order arbitration (Code Civ. Proc., section 1281.2). The superior court found the arbitration agreement did not apply to plaintiffs' action for the wrongful death of their newborn baby and denied the petition. Defendants appeal.

On January 20, 1978, plaintiff Sherry L. Weeks entered Mt. Helix General Hospital for childbirth. She and her husband, plaintiff Larry D. Weeks, signed an agreement providing for arbitration of "any dispute as to medical malpractice, that is as to whether any medical services rendered under this contract were unnecessary or unauthorized or were improperly, negligently or incompetently rendered, ..." FN1 As required by section 1295(b) of the Code of Civil Procedure, the agreement also contains the following notice: "By signing this contract you are agreeing to have any issue of medical malpractice decided by neutral arbitration and you are giving up your right to a jury or court trial." The contract defines "patient" as "the undersigned patient or dependent of patient (whether or not a minor), or the heirs-at-law or personal representative of patient..." Only Mrs. Weeks is named as the patient. Mrs. Weeks gave birth to a daughter, Summer Tawny Weeks, later that same day. During delivery, the complaint alleges, the umbilical cord was improperly cut and tied off, causing the baby to develop an abdominal infection which resulted in her death on February 4, 1978.

FN1. Section 1295(a) of the Code of Civil Procedure requires this specific language.

Issue

Does the agreement of January 20 require the parents to accept arbitration of their claim for wrongful death which alleges malpractice in the care and treatment of the baby?

Analysis

Section 1281.2 of the Code of Civil Procedure empowers the court to order arbitration of a controversy if it finds the parties have agreed to arbitrate that particular dispute. Because the obligation to arbitrate arises from contract, the court may compel arbitration only if the dispute in question is one which the parties have agreed to arbitrate. Since arbitration is a favored method of dispute resolution, arbitration agreements should be liberally interpreted, and arbitration should be ordered unless the agreement clearly does not apply to the dispute in question. However, "there is no policy compelling persons to accept arbitration of controversies which they have not agreed to arbitrate..." In determining whether an arbitration agreement applies to a specific dispute, the court may examine only the agreement itself and the complaint filed by the party refusing arbitration. The court should attempt to give effect to the parties' intentions, in light of the usual and ordinary meaning of the contractual language and the circumstances under which the agreement was made. Here an examination of the parties' agreement shows they did not agree to arbitrate claims of malpractice in the care and treatment of the baby. Even though Mrs. Weeks was entering the hospital to give birth, the agreement contains no reference at all to the expected child; only the expectant mother is named as the patient. If the parties had intended to agree to arbitration of claims of negligence in treating the child, they could easily have done so by also naming the expected child as a patient. The omission of any reference to the child expresses an intention not to apply the agreement to malpractice claims arising out of medical services rendered to the child.

In asserting arbitration is required, defendants rely in part on the agreement's definition of "patient." Since the definition includes dependents of the named patient, they argue, the agreement requires arbitration of claims of malpractice in treating dependents, even if they are not named as patients. Defendants' argument assumes the definition is intended to describe the individuals to whom treatment is to be rendered. This is not the case. Rather, the definition includes those individuals who may have a cause of action if negligent medical treatment of the named patient results in his injury or death, and the provision is intended as an enumeration of the parties to be bound by the agreement to arbitrate claims arising out of the treatment of the named patient. The definition does not extend the scope of the arbitration agreement to cover disputes arising out of the treatment of persons other than the named patient.

The order is affirmed.

Question

Despite of the exclusion by the arbitration agreement of the court's jurisdiction, the court involved in this case dealt with the case. What kind of rule had the court played in this case?

Court of Appeals of Texas,

Houston (14th Dist.)

In re Choice Homes, Inc.,

Micky May, and James B. White

174 S. W. 3d 408

No. 14-04-01008-CV.

Sept. 30, 2005.

KEM THOMPSON FROST, Justice.

Facts

The real parties in interest, Carl M. Bright and Dennis J. Czajka, are former employees of relator, Choice Homes, Inc., and are the plaintiffs in the underlying case. They brought suit against Choice Homes, its current employee, Micky May, and two of the company's former employees, James B. White and David A. Roskos. The plaintiffs contend that they were wrongfully terminated or constructively terminated from their employment at Choice Homes. They assert claims based on alleged statutory and common law wrongful termination, fraud, negligent misrepresentation, breach of contract, unconscionability, promissory estoppel, reformation/quantum meruit, unjust enrichment, tortious interference, negligence, defamation, invasion of privacy by disclosure of private facts, intentional infliction of emotional distress, and civil conspiracy. All four defendants filed a motion to compel arbitration, arguing that all of the claims asserted are subject to arbitration under two identical written arbitration agreements the plaintiffs signed upon their employment with Choice Homes. Under these contracts, entitled "Election and Arbitration Agreement" (hereinafter, "Arbitration Agreement"), each of the plaintiffs agreed to resolve through binding arbitration certain disputes with Choice Homes that might arise during or after their employment. The scope and enforceability of this arbitration agreement is at the heart of this mandamus proceeding.

Following a hearing, the trial court signed an order on October 21, 2004, in which it granted the motion to compel arbitration as to all claims asserted against Choice Homes and Roskos and as to some of the claims asserted against May and White. The trial court declined to compel arbitration of two groups of claims: (1) the claims against May and White in their individual capacities based on alleged defamation, invasion of privacy, and civil conspiracy alleged to have occurred outside the scope of May's and White's employment with Choice Homes and after the plaintiff's separation from employment with Choice Homes, and (2) the claim brought by Czajka against White in his individual capacity, alleging breach of promise relating to an alleged loan of money.

The relators filed their petition for writ of mandamus, asserting the trial court misapplied the law and abused its discretion in refusing to compel arbitration of these claims. They ask this court to issue a writ of mandamus ordering the trial judge to withdraw the October 21, 2004 order and to issue a new order compelling all claims asserted by the plaintiffs to arbitration.

Issue and Analysis

Does Choice Homes have standing to seek mandamus relief?

We must determine if Choice Homes has standing to seek mandamus relief in this proceeding. The trial court's order unambiguously states that all claims against Choice Homes, including all claims for vicarious liability, are ordered to arbitration. There is nothing in the record that would show Choice Homes has any interest in whether the claims at issue against White and May are compelled to arbitration. To have standing a party must be affected by the controversy at hand. Because Choice Homes has been granted all the relief sought and will not be adversely affected if Bright's and Czajka's claims against White and May are not ordered to arbitration, Choice Homes lacks standing to challenge the trial court's refusal to order these claims to arbitration. Accordingly, we dismiss the petition for writ of mandamus as to relator Choice Homes for lack of jurisdiction.

Conclusion

Because Choice Homes received all relief requested in the trial court, and will not be adversely affected if Bright's and Czajka's claims are not ordered to arbitration, we conclude that Choice Homes lacks standing to seek mandamus relief. Accordingly, we dismiss the petition for writ of mandamus as to relator Choice Homes for lack of jurisdiction.

Question

If in this case, the dispute would have got beyond the arbitration agreement, had the court issued an order for enforcement?

思考题

1. 如何理解仲裁协议的独立性？
2. 仲裁条款与交付仲裁的协议相比有何优势？
3. 关于有瑕疵的仲裁协议，我国法律是如何具体规定的？
4. 仲裁协议可否继受现在还是个争论比较大的问题，你认为仲裁协议能否继受？

推荐阅读

1. 林一飞:《国际商事仲裁法律与实务》,中信出版社 2005 年版。
2. Mark Huleatt-James & Nicholas Gould, International Commercial Arbitration: A Handbook, 2nd ed., LLP, 1999.

3. 韩健:《现代国际商事仲裁的理论与实践》,法律出版社 2000 年版。

4. 刘晓红:《国际商事仲裁协议的法理与实证》,商务印书馆 2005 年版。

5. The Denning Lecture 1995(Arbitration and the Court)by Lord Justice Saville,(1995)61 Arbitration 157 at 161,以及 DAC 报告第 44 节。

第五章 仲裁员与仲裁庭

仲裁庭基于当事人的授权获得管辖权,控制仲裁的审理程序,决定案件的最后裁决。仲裁庭独立裁决,不受任何机构和个人的干预和控制,其裁决的公正性是国际商事仲裁制度赖以存在的基础。同时,仲裁庭只是一个拟制的实体,真正发挥作用的是组成仲裁庭的仲裁员,仲裁员作为整个仲裁制度的灵魂,影响着每一个争议的解决,也从根本上影响着仲裁的发展。选择符合法律资格要求、德才兼备的人担任仲裁员是维护当事人正当权益的需要,也是实现仲裁公正与效率价值的关键。

第一节 仲裁员的资格与选任

仲裁员对仲裁裁决掌握着最后的话语权,当事人选择什么样的仲裁员直接影响着仲裁程序的进行和最后的裁决结果。只有具备一定条件的人才有资格担任仲裁员,这是各国法律和各常设仲裁机构的仲裁规则的一致要求,因此当事人选择仲裁员时首先要遵守法律规定。由于仲裁活动很大程度上依赖于仲裁员的个人素质,仲裁员选择还应充分考虑其道德和专业素养,并且尽量选择符合当事人利益的仲裁员。

一、仲裁员资格

当事人在选任仲裁员时,仲裁员是否符合法律或仲裁机构要求是其首要考虑的因素,只有选择有资格的仲裁员,仲裁裁决最终才能不受妨碍地执行。

(一)法律要求

法律对仲裁员资格有最基本的要求,只有满足这些条件的仲裁员所作的仲裁裁决才能得到法律的承认,否则仲裁裁决会因违反仲裁程序而被撤销或宣告无效。法律对仲裁员资格的要求包括一般要求和特殊限制。

1. 一般要求

一般来说,完全的民事权利能力和行为能力是法律完全承认行为人的法律行为有效性的前提,仲裁作为专业行为,其后果对当事人产生约束力,仲裁员对相关行为还要承担一定法律责任,因此各国法律一致规定,仲裁员依法应具有完全的民事权利能力和行为能力,未成年人、禁治产人皆不具有一般仲裁员的资格。

大部分国家都主张只有自然人才能担任仲裁员,因为当事人选择仲裁的一个原因是出于对仲裁员个人的人身信赖。即使允许法人担任仲裁员,其活动仍是通过自然人来进行的,法人本身不能对当事人之间的纠纷作出判断和裁决,因此,法人本身不能承担仲裁员审理和裁决的任务。

But it is possible to provide for arbitration by a legal person in France. Art. 1451 of the Code of Civil Procedure in France provides that, "the function of arbitrator may be given to a physical person only", but a second paragraph in the same article brings a precision as to the meaning of this provision by saying: "If a legal person has been designated in the agreement, such legal person is only invested with the power of organizing the arbitration."

世界上大多数国家和地区都对仲裁员的资格作尽可能少的限制。如我国香港地区的《仲裁条例》就未对仲裁员资格作出限制:任何人,包括商人、律师、工程师、会计师、审计师、教授以及其他一切有行为能力的人,不管是否在香港拥有住所,无论国籍,均可被指定为仲裁员。某人一旦接受指定,即取得对某一案件进行审理的授权。

但是,有一些国家对仲裁员一般的任职条件要求非常严格。如在我国,根据《仲裁法》第13条规定,只有从事仲裁工作满八年的;从事律师工作满八年的;曾任审判员满八年的;从事法律研究、教学工作并具有高级职称的;具有法律知识、从事经济贸易等专业工作并具有高级职称或者具有同等专业水平的自然人,才有资格担任仲裁员。如此严格的立法要求在世界上是比较罕见的。作为我国首部商业仲裁立法,谨慎的立法态度可以理解,这是为了保障高质量的仲裁员队伍,但它在实践中大大缩小了当事人自由选择仲裁员的范围,在商事仲裁日益发达的今天,这种严格的规定显然已经不合时宜。

In Spain and Portugal, and in some counties in Latin America only a qualified lawyer can be appointed when parties have agreed on an arbitration in which the arbitrator is bound to decide in accordance with the law. In Iran there exists a "list of candidates for the function of arbitrator"; the arbitrator is necessarily chosen from this list when he has to be designated by a court. In Mexico a list of candidates for function of arbitrator is likewise drawn up every year by the Supreme Court and also different States of the Federation; the arbitrator must be chosen from this list when his designation has to be made by a court. ①

2. 特殊限制

很多国家限制受过刑事处罚的人担任仲裁员,因为仲裁员需要有极高的个

---

① See René David, Arbitration in International Trade, Kluwer Law and Taxation Publishers, 1985, p.250.

人声誉,受过刑事处罚的人往往很难得到当事人的认同。德国《民事诉讼法》第1032条第3款还同时规定:"经法院宣告剥夺其担任公职资格的人不具有仲裁员资格。"在瑞士,犯了不名誉的轻重罪行而受到自由刑的处分者无仲裁员资格。① 比利时、瑞典等国的法律亦有上述类似规定。另外,由于聋哑人等生理缺陷的存在可能会影响仲裁的进行,所以一些国家也明确禁止此类人员担任仲裁员。如德国法律明文规定,聋人、哑人不具有仲裁员资格。② 其他国家大多无德国法中这样的明文规定,但在这些国家的实践中,聋哑人实际上是成不了仲裁员的。

Besides, Judges are forbidden to act as arbitrators in a number of countries. Different reasons are adduced in support of this rule. Complaints are frequently made that justice is too slow, and one reason for this is that the burden on the courts is excessive: judges should not be distracted from their duties in the courts to administer arbitration. The rules governing the administration of justice in the State courts must not be jeopardized either; a judge ought not to administer arbitration in a case which might be brought before him in his capacity as judge. There are on the other hand good reasons for allowing judge to act as arbitrators. They are well prepared for it by reason of their education, their experience and their psychology. Nor are judges, as was thought in former times, the interpreters of a law which is always of utmost clarity; judges are in many cases recognized as having broad powers nowadays, and they are perhaps the best qualified persons to operate the synthesis of law and equity which is often looked for by parties when they resort to arbitration.

(二) 仲裁机构要求

常设仲裁机构一般都设有仲裁员名册,名册内的仲裁员必须满足仲裁机构的特殊要求。机构仲裁时,虽然大部分国家都没有强行要求当事人选择名册内的仲裁员,但仲裁机构一般都推荐当事人选择这些经过其特别资格审查和专业仲裁培训的仲裁员。

Unqualified arbitrator will affect the arbitral award and also will hurt the institution's reputation. This is the reason why numerous institutions have drawn up list, general or specialized, in which parties are invited, sometimes bound, to select their arbitrators if they wish as arbitration to be placed under the guidance of the institution. AAA has an important activity in this respect in the United States. In England it is necessary, to become a member of the Institute of Arbitrator, to pass an

---

① 参见瑞士《联邦仲裁协约》第18条第1款。
② 参见德国《民事诉讼法》第1032条第3款。

examination under the control of the Institute; and a person cannot be included in a special list a drawn up for international cases unless he has already been an arbitrator at least in ten cases concerned with domestic litigation.[①] Provisions are frequently made in Arbitration Rules requiring the arbitrators either to be selected from some list.

仲裁机构制作仲裁员名册,既是国外仲裁机构的惯常做法,也见之于我国《仲裁法》的有关规定。在我国,仲裁委员会按不同专业设仲裁员名册。在受理仲裁申请后,仲裁委员会有义务将名册送达申请人和被申请人。仲裁员名册的最大意义在于方便当事人了解仲裁机构中仲裁员的构成,以便在仲裁程序中选择仲裁员。我国《仲裁法》未明确各个仲裁委员会的仲裁员名册是当事人必须采纳的,但从我国一些地方仲裁机构的规则和以往实践看,当事人只能在仲裁委送达的仲裁员名册中选定仲裁员,但北京仲裁委员会2008年仲裁规则和CIETAC 2005年仲裁规则对此有所突破,允许当事人在仲裁员名册之外选择仲裁员。

另外,一些专业的仲裁机构还建议或要求当事人选择的仲裁员必须具备相关的行业背景。CIETAC已设立专门的金融专业仲裁员名册,这将有助于仲裁员发挥金融行业专业知识,提高仲裁的效率和质量。此外,在2004年10月1日起实施的《中国海事仲裁委员会仲裁规则》第10条的规定中,要求"仲裁委员会设立仲裁员名册,仲裁员由仲裁委员会从对海事、海商、物流以及法律等方面具有专门知识和实际经验的中外人士中聘任。仲裁委员会根据需要,可以设立特定的专业仲裁员名册"。

二、仲裁员素质

由于仲裁是一项专业性极强的工作,裁决的质量很大程度上取决于仲裁员的素质,因此,当事人除了要选任符合法律和仲裁规则规定的有资格的仲裁员外,还应当选任具有较高道德素质和专业素质的仲裁员。

(一)道德素质

公正与独立是仲裁员最基本的道德素质,缺少了公正与独立,无法树立仲裁员的权威与公信力,也无法取得当事人的信任,仲裁制度也就丧失其存在的基础。因此,各国法律及各仲裁机构都将保证仲裁员独立与公正作为着力的重点,当事人在选任时应尤其注意从这两个方面考察仲裁员。

---

① See René David, Arbitration in International Trade, Kluwer Law and Taxation Publishers, 1985, p. 250.

1. 公正

仲裁员作为争议的裁决者,与法官一样,公正地裁判案件是当事人对其最基本的期待,选任不偏不倚的仲裁员是实现仲裁公正这一价值取向的关键因素。然而,公正是对仲裁员的主观要求,当事人很难在选任时判断该仲裁员是否公正,实践中也往往无法获得仲裁员是否存在偏见的证据。

An arbitrator is partial towards one party if he displays preference for, or partiality towards one party or against another, or whether a third person reasonably apprehends such partiality. Such partiality goes to whether it is reasonable to believe that the arbitrator will favor one party over the other for reasons that are unrelated to a reasoned decision on the merits of the case. These unrelated factors could include a relationship, such as the influence that a professional, business, or personal relationship might give rise to the reasonable belief that the arbitrator is partial. It could also relate to the arbitrator's conduct in the absence of such a relationship, such as a statement during the course of an arbitration proceeding that persons of a particular nationality are liars, or that a member of an ethnic minority is in some way inferior. The test applicable to impartiality is subjective in the sense that it goes to the actual state of mind and where applicable, ensuing conducts of the arbitrator. Partiality is sometimes associated with bias, while the reasonable anticipation of partiality by an arbitrator is identified with the reasonable apprehension of bias. [①]

2. 独立

判断仲裁员的独立性,通常看其与他人的关系如何。比如说,仲裁员是否与一方当事人有业务关系,或者是否与一方当事人有私交,是不是与其熟识或者存在生意上的往来。业务关系可能包括仲裁员或其搭档曾经或正在担任一方当事人的顾问、雇员、律师等;生意上的往来关系则包括仲裁员或其搭档担任了一个商业实体的管理职务,或者他自身就是该实体的投资一方,无论他是以实物还是以股权形式进行出资,而与此同时,他所仲裁案件的一方当事人也参与了这个商业实体。如果仲裁员或其搭档或其商业伙伴是一方当事人的配偶、子女或堂、表亲关系,那么从亲属关系上看,该仲裁员也不具备独立性。仲裁员有可能和当事人是很好的朋友,或者其他社会关系,在判断仲裁员是否具备独立性上,还要看这些关系的亲疏程度。总体说来,关联程度应因时因地而进行个案判断。

The measure of an arbitrator's independence is sometimes conceived objectively: would a reasonable person conclude, in light of the relationship in issue, that the

---

① See Leon Trakman, The Impartiality and Independence of Arbitrators Reconsidered, Int. A. L. R., Vol. 10, No. 4, 2007, pp. 124—135.

arbitrator is independent?① The nature of that objective test, including the extent to which a reasonable person is informed about the arbitration, and whether someone called upon to reach such a determination might superimpose his or her sense of reasonableness for that of the reasonable person. However, the "reasonable person" is amorphous, not a fixed and constant being.

3. 公正与独立的关系

公正与独立作为仲裁员的两种基本素质要求,既相互区别又相互联系。公正是仲裁员针对当事人或判决本身的内心主观意见,通过其仲裁行为而表现出来;独立是仲裁员自身不受其他人或事的影响,是对仲裁员与外界客观联系的判断。要求仲裁员独立即是为保持仲裁员的内心公正,独立与公正都旨在实现裁决公平。因此,它们被认为是一个硬币的两面,经常是合起来作为一个术语运用,将其作为评估实际或表面偏见的可能性的并行方式。②

There is clearly an overlap between arbitral independence and impartiality. For example, a great deal of debate takes place in the United States as to whether and when a party appointed arbitrator lacks independence on account of a relationship between the arbitrator and the party making the appointment, and being partial on account of that relationship. However, the relationship associated with arbitral independence may be immaterial, while a lack of partiality may be material. For example, a party appointed arbitrator may be unrelated to the appointee, such as when the appointee chooses him because he works in the same industry but for a different company to the appointee; but the arbitrator may still display conduct that demonstrates bias or a reasonable apprehension of bias in favor of the appointing party. The prevailing issue in determining partiality is to establish the extent to which the arbitrator acts as an advocate for the party appointing him, whether he purports to negotiate on behalf of that party, or whether there is a reasonable apprehension that he may do so.③

4. 公正与独立的判断

如前所述,公正与独立的判断和证明很有难度,但根据一些学者和律师的总结,还是有一些经验可以参考。

---

① See Leon Trakman, The Impartiality and Independence of Arbitrators Reconsidered, Int. A. L. R., Vol.10, No.4, 2007, pp.124—135.
② 参见〔英〕艾伦·雷德芬、马丁·亨特等:《国际商事仲裁法律与实践》,林一飞、宋连斌译,北京大学出版社 2005 年版,第 215 页。
③ See Leon Trakman, The Impartiality and Independence of Arbitrators Reconsidered, Int. A. L. R., Vol.10, No.4, 2007, pp.124—135.

Six factors are proposed as so indicative of partiality that they can reasonably be treated as generally disqualifying for a party-appointed arbitrator:

A. an arbitrator has a significant financial interest in the relevant project or dispute, or in a party or its counsel;

B. an arbitrator has a close family relationship with a party or its counsel;

C. an arbitrator has a non-financial involvement in the relevant project, dispute or the subject matter of the dispute;

D. an arbitrator has taken a public position on the specific matter in dispute;

E. an arbitrator is involved in the settlement discussions of the parties; and

F. an arbitrator has an adversarial relationship with a party.

Three factors which sometimes raise questions are proposed as to the appropriateness of an appointment but which should not be considered to be disqualifying factors:

A. professional writings and lectures;

B. professional associations; and

C. relationship with the arbitral institution.

Finally, we come to what might be called a "grey area", and these include a potential arbitrator's:

A. past business relationship with a party or its counsel;

B. friendship with a party or its counsel; and

C. service in other arbitrations.[①]

(二) 专业素质

只有具备一定专门知识和资历的人才有能力合理、公正和有效地处理当事人之间的纠纷。尽管基于私法意思自治原则，多数国家的法律并不要求商事纠纷的当事人只能选择有专门知识和资历的人作仲裁员，但当事人一般只相信具有专门知识和资历人士的能力，因此，很多常设仲裁机构的仲裁规则或推荐名单中列举的仲裁员一般都是具有一定专门知识和资历的知名人士。如《维也纳联邦经济联合会仲裁中心仲裁与调解规则》第7条第1款规定：在法律和经济方面具有专门知识和经验的人可被任命为仲裁员。其他仲裁机构及其仲裁规则对仲裁员的知识和资历要求一般也是体现在法律和经济这两个方面，只是有些仲裁机构的仲裁规则规定得更为具体一些。在某些特殊领域，如英国著名的谷物及饲料贸易协会(GAFTA)仲裁中，所有的仲裁员都需符合高标准的专业要求，他

---

① See Constantine Partasides, The Selection, Appointment and Challenge of Arbitrators, 5 V. J. (2001), p. 217.

们必须对于贸易所面临的复杂情况和问题有深刻的了解,必须参加训练课程并符合专业持续发展项目规定的标准。

(三) 仲裁员培训

仲裁员要公正合理地解决现实经济活动中各种类型的纠纷,就必须不断提高自身的知识水平及专业修养。因此,很多仲裁机构均对仲裁员提出了培训要求,并把培训作为获取仲裁员资格或保有仲裁员资格的条件之一。也有国家或地区通过立法对仲裁员培训作出规定,如我国台湾地区"仲裁法"第 8 条规定:"仲裁人应经训练或讲习。仲裁人之训练讲习办法,由行政院会同司法院定之。"

我国法律并没有关于仲裁员培训的内容,国内立法与理论研究尚不成熟。美国全国证券交易商协会(NASD)培训证券仲裁员的一整套成熟的方法,可以供国内参考。

The interactive nature of the live training session helps establish a sense of the trainees' receptivity to the following important principles of a fair and impartial arbitration proceeding.

1. Full Disclosure of Potential Conflicts of Interest at the Outset.

2. The Structure of an Arbitration Proceeding from Start to Finish is Thoroughly Discussed.

3. Motions. Trainees learn that certain pre-hearing motions may be in their purview. They may be required to rule on the severance and/or joiner motions relating to parties or claims which may be asserted in the same arbitration.

4. Hearing. Trainees are taught to expect a short meeting among the arbitrators prior to commencing the hearing. Trainees learn that at the commencement of the hearing all previously disclosed potential conflict information is restated for the record. Trainees are also taught how to manage the behavior of the participants when the participants fail to control themselves. Trainees learn of the importance of hearing all relevant evidence; but they are also taught that it is not necessary to hear irrelevant evidence. Trainees are taught to follow the law and/or established principles of equity in coming to arbitral decisions. Trainees learn that it is the parties' case, and that the arbitration panel must accept the evidence and the law as tendered by the parties. Trainees are cautioned from attempting to rely on their own expertise in any of the matters brought by the parties, and to rely upon presented arguments and authority in the same fashion that a judge might. Finally, trainees hear (over and over) a warning to minimize ex parte contact throughout the hearing and thereafter.

5. Post-Hearing Deliberations and Activity. Trainees learn that a decision need not be made immediately upon closing the hearing. In fact, when issues and/or facts and law are, or may be, complex, arbitrators are told to take enough time in order to make a good decision. Arbitrators are trained not to "split the baby" simply because it appears to be the easiest thing to do.

6. Confidentiality. Finally, the arbitrators learn that confidentiality relating to the circumstances of the hearing, deliberations, and the final rulings is an absolute requirement.①

三、当事人要求

在法院诉讼中当事人无权选择法官,而在国际商事仲裁中当事人可以选择任何其认为合适的人担任仲裁员。只要不违反法律,当事人可以对仲裁员设定任何积极或消极的条件,这些条件对仲裁员而言往往是最主要的限制。如果个案中仲裁员任职的依据不符合当事人的仲裁协议,有关当事人就可以仲裁员的资格不合约定(或称仲裁程序不当)为由要求有管辖权的法院或仲裁庭发布禁令,终止该仲裁程序,或者撤销已作出的裁决。

Commercial contracts frequently provide that the arbitrator shall possess certain stipulated qualification. These may be expressed in a positive or negative form. Where the appointed arbitrator does not possess the required qualifications, his appointment is nugatory and any award which he may make is void. By their agreement to arbitrate, the parties contracted to honor an award made by a duly qualified arbitrator; but they promised nothing with regard to the award of anyone else.

在实践中,比较常见的主要有当事人对仲裁员有关行业要求和国籍要求的约定:

(一) 行业要求

在某些特定的国际格式合同条款中,当事人会约定只有从事特定行业的人才能担任仲裁员。因为在如证券交易、石油交易、工程回购等某些特别专业的领域中,在解决纠纷时只具备法律知识是远远不够的,当事人经常会对这类仲裁员有特别严格的要求,以保证纠纷的顺利解决。

In some instances, the contract sates positive qualification, for example, the arbitrator may have to be member of a specified trade association. On other

---

① See John A. Bender, NASDR Securities Arbitrators: Trainning + Practice = Quality Decisions, 1061 PLI/Corp., p.283.

occasions, the qualifications are less specific: for example, the arbitrator may have to be chosen from person engaged in a particular trade. Sometimes again, it is expressed in very general terms: for example, the arbitrator is to be a "merchant" or a "commercial man". But the meaning of "merchant" is not difficult to express, and the "commercial man" presents more problems. The general purpose of such a stipulation is plainly to ensure that the tribunal shall consist of men with a "feel" for trade, rather than professional people, who are assumed to have a less informed and practical approach to business matters.① But it is not easy to say where the line should be drawn. In Pando Compania v. Filmo SAS②, it was held that a full-time arbitrator who had retired many years earlier from practice as a solicitor was a "commercial man" under a charter party arbitration clause.

（二）国籍要求

对仲裁员的国籍，大部分国家已经不再作出强行规定，即使外国人也可以担任本国仲裁机构的仲裁员，如 CIETAC 的仲裁员名册中就有多位外籍仲裁专业人士。虽然无法确定国籍是否能实质影响仲裁裁决，但是对当事人信心却有一定的影响，因此很多仲裁机构还是建议当事人不要选择与其具有同国籍的人担任仲裁员，特别是首席仲裁员。如《联合国国际贸易法委员会仲裁规则》第 6 条第 4 款规定："在做出任命时，有任命权的机构应尽可能地考虑到确保任命一名独立和公正的仲裁员，并应同时考虑，最好任命一名与双方当事人国籍不同的仲裁员。"实践中，很多当事人也经常对仲裁员的国籍作出一定的限制，特别是对独任仲裁员或者是三人仲裁庭中的首席仲裁员的国籍要求更为严格。仲裁员不具备约定的国籍或有被限制的国籍，无权担任该案的仲裁员。对国籍的认定一般不存在困难，但假设甲同时具备 A、B 两国国籍，而当事人又通过消极条款约定具有 A 国国籍的不得担任仲裁员或者约定由 B 国国籍的人担任仲裁员，在这两种情况下，甲能否担任本案仲裁员？实践中可能会引发争议。

此外，当事人选任仲裁员还应当从仲裁员的教育背景、受训情况、研究领域、社会职务等入手，对仲裁员能否尽职勤勉，是否有强烈的道德操守，是否有丰富的经验，在其专业领域有怎样的声望等诸多方面综合评判。另外，身体和年龄因素在选任仲裁员时也必须考虑，以避免因仲裁员身体状况欠佳而导致仲裁程序的迟延。

---

① See Sir Michael J. Mustill & Stewart C. Boyd, Q. C., Commercial Arbitration, 2nd ed., Butterworths, 1989, p. 248.

② 1 Lloyd's Rep. 560, [1975] QB, p. 742.

第二节 仲裁庭组成

仲裁庭作为争议的最终决断者,掌控着整个仲裁程序的进行和实质问题的判断,对当事人影响重大。一旦完成组庭,对仲裁庭的质疑往往十分困难,因此当事人一般都对仲裁庭的组庭人数、方式等予以明确约定,各仲裁机构也着力在其规则中完善组庭程序。同时,为保证程序公正,法律给予当事人在组庭阶段的救济权利。

一、仲裁庭的组建时间

组庭阶段诸多事项均需要当事人合意,特别是在仲裁协议中约定不明的情况下。实践中被申请方往往不愿与申请人事后达成协议,导致仲裁程序迟延甚至无法启动。仲裁员确定程序是最容易被恶意拖延方利用的组庭环节。为防止过分迟延影响仲裁的效率,法律或仲裁规则都对协议确定仲裁员的最长期限予以限定,该期限一般不超过30天。如根据英国《1996年仲裁法》第16条,独任仲裁员的委任应当事人向对方送达委任仲裁员的书面请求之日起28日内作出;两人仲裁庭应当在14日内各自委任;三人仲裁庭应当在14日内分别委任一名仲裁员。1998年《国际商会仲裁规则》第8条也规定,三人仲裁庭的仲裁员委任,申请人应在收到仲裁院审理决定通知后15日内提名一位仲裁员,被申请人应在收到申请人已指定仲裁员的通知后15日内提名另一名仲裁员;独任仲裁员的委任,应在收到申请书之日起30日内共同提名。我国《仲裁法》并没有关于确定仲裁员期限的法律强制性规定,但各仲裁机构一般都有限定。如根据《北京仲裁委仲裁规则(2004)》第18条,双方当事人应当自收到仲裁通知之日起15日内或者在仲裁协议确定的期限内,指定一名仲裁员或共同选定第三名仲裁员。如果当事人未能在约定或规定的期限内确定仲裁员人选,多数情况下,将由仲裁机构负责指定。

Time limits for appointing arbitrators in arbitration may take two forms:①

(a) Contractual—Being limits contained in the parties' agreement. The relevant period should easily be established from any properly drafted agreement. A very short contractual period which has been overlooked need not always be fatal. The law of some countries (like England) may permit the time limits to be extended where undue hardship would otherwise be caused.

---

① See Mark Huleatt-James & Nicholas Gould, International Commercial Arbitration: A Handbook, 2nd ed., LLP, 1999, p.131.

(b) Statutory—Being limits established in relevant legislation. Many countries (notably those from the civil law tradition) treat time limits as matters of substance which will therefore be governed by the lex cause(the country whose law is applicable to the dispute). Other, often common law, countries tend to regard time limits as procedural in nature. Accordingly, when an arbitration takes place in such a country, and the lex cause views time limits as substantive, a conflict may arise where the lex arbitri (the country in which the arbitration takes place) only permits a shorter period than that available under the lex cause. This will usually be resolved in favor of the lex arbitri. (Where the shorter period is that of the lex cause, the claim will in any event be barred, and the limitation provision of the lex arbitri will cease to be relevant.)

二、仲裁庭人员的委任

在仲裁庭组成阶段,组成仲裁庭的人数以及如何组成仲裁庭是当事人最需要关心的问题,它们与仲裁费用和仲裁公正及效率问题休戚相关。另外,在不同的法律条件下,组庭人数和方式可能也各有不同,当事人应避免因组庭而违反强行性法规所带来的风险。

(一) 组庭人数

1. 独任仲裁庭

独任仲裁庭是指对当事人的争议进行审理的仲裁庭由一名仲裁员组成,它目前已经为大部分国家的仲裁立法认可。如我国《仲裁法》第 30 条规定:"仲裁庭可以由三名仲裁员或者一名仲裁员组成。"在商事仲裁机构中,独任仲裁庭极为常见,特别是采用简易程序的案件,基本都采用独任仲裁庭。

According to the rules/laws, parties have to pay fee to the arbitrator, and the fee is very expensive nowadays. The tribunal with a single arbitrator may have the advantage in this respect. Another argument in favor of a single arbitrator is that this system may speed up the procedure and the settlement of the dispute. In the case of a State court, all judges have their residence in a same town and devote all their time to their profession as judges; to sit together is for them no problem. Arbitrators, on the other hand, live in different places and will have, as a rule, some other activities. To determine dates acceptable to the arbitrators and also to the parties and their counsel is frequently difficult in international arbitrations.[①] The single tribunal can make it

---

[①] See René David, Arbitration in International Trade, Kluwer Law and Taxation Publishers, 1985, p. 224.

easier.

2. 两人仲裁庭

只有英国等少数国家允许两人仲裁庭的存在,并且在制度设计上还辅之以公断人制度,即当两人仲裁庭不能形成一致意见时,需要选择仲裁庭外的第三人作出最终判断,这样并不利于保证仲裁的效率,所以很多国家都不认可这种制度。大部分国家都规定仲裁庭组成人数应为奇数,以确保裁决能以多数意见作出。

印度最高法院在 MMTC v. Sterlite Industries (India) Ltd. 案中指出:"The aforementioned provision in the Act states that parties are free to determine the number of arbitrators, provided that such number shall not be an even number."[①]

It is a peculiarity of English arbitration procedure that an agreement to arbitrate is not always construed literally. This is so particularly where the agreement is for a reference to two arbitrators.[②] If the parties agree for a tribunal of two arbitrators, unless the agreement otherwise provides (which in practice it rarely does) the two-man panel is reinforced by a secondary tribunal, consisting of an umpire appointed by the two arbitrators, who replaces the arbitrators if and when they disagree. A reference to two arbitrators and an umpire never involves a tribunal consisting of three members. The dispute is decided either by the two arbitrators or by the umpire, depending upon whether or not the arbitrators have disagreed.

3. 三人或三人以上仲裁庭

除了一些简单案件,或者当事人为快速低廉地结案,实践中大部分仲裁庭由三人仲裁庭组成,在个别较复杂的案件中,当事人也可能选定五人组成仲裁庭。个别仲裁机构的仲裁规则对仲裁员的人数作了硬性规定,如维也纳商品交易仲裁院规则要求仲裁庭只能由三人组成。在当事人无协议规定仲裁庭人数时,各国法律或仲裁规则或国际公约一般皆规定:仲裁庭应由三名仲裁员组成。根据瑞士法律,如果双方当事人没有同意一个其他单数,特别是没有同意只设独任仲裁员,仲裁庭应该由三名仲裁员组成。[③]

The main reason for preferring a tribunal of three arbitrators is the concern about relying on the judgment of one person who the counsel or the parties may or may not

---

① [1996] 10 S.C. 390.
② See Sir Michael J. Mustill & Stewart C. Boyd, Q.C., Commercial Arbitration, 2nd ed., Butterworths, 1989, p.173.
③ 参见瑞士《联邦仲裁协约》第10条第1款。

be familiar with.① The question of one versus three arbitrators is less difficult. The accepted practice is that, unless a dispute is relatively straightforward and involves a reasonably small sum, three arbitrators are preferable to one. Although the relevant institutional rules do not necessarily favor three arbitrators over one (and in many cases state the opposite), in practice in complex international arbitrations three-member tribunals are preferable to sole arbitrator.② The UNCITRAL Arbitration Rules, Article 5, provides that: If the parties have not previously agreed on the number of arbitrators (i.e., one or three), and the parties have not agreed that there shall be only one arbitrator, three arbitrators shall be appointed.

(二) 组庭方式

1. 当事人约定

意思自治是仲裁的本质属性,因此当事人约定是仲裁庭组庭的最主要方式,也是最根本途径。允许当事人将争议交给由其自己选择的仲裁员解决是仲裁区别于诉讼程序的重要特征,对当事人而言也是最为理想的组庭方式。但是,这种方式必须同时满足:(1) 当事人合意选择;(2) 被选人接受选任。这就大大限制了该种方式在实践中的运用。因为如果没有事先约定,当事人很难就独任仲裁员或首席仲裁员的选任达成一致,恶意拖延方甚至会故意提名一些因身体、住址等各种原因很难接受当事人选任的人作为仲裁员。因此,只有在当事人约定的基础上结合其他方式,才能有效地组成仲裁庭。

The constitution of the arbitral panel and the number in which it is to be appointed depends upon the type of substantive agreement, as most classes of contract have developed established structures and procedures, and upon any individual variations which have been settled by the parties to suit the circumstances of their particular agreement. The most common forms of arbitral tribunal, and appointment mechanisms, are the following:③

(a) Arbitration is to be before a single arbitrator whose identity is to be agreed upon by the parties after a dispute has arisen.

(b) Arbitration is to be before a single arbitrator to be nominated by the chairman of a trade or professional association.

(c) Arbitration is to be before two arbitrators, generally one to be appointed by each of the parties.

---

① See Michael W. Bühler and Thomas H. Webster, Handbook of ICC Arbitration: Commentary, Precedents, Materials, Sweet & Maxwell, 2005, p.129.

② See Wendy Miles, International Arbitrator Appointment, Dispute Resolution Journal, August 2002.

③ See Robert Merkin, Arbitration Law, LLP, 2004, p.422.

(d) Arbitration is to be before three arbitrators, one to be appointed by each of the parties and a third to be appointed either by the arbitrators or by some third party. Where a third is appointed, he is, subject to contrary agreement, to be the chairman.

(e) Arbitration is to be before two or three arbitrators appointed by the parties and approved by a trade or professional body.

(f) Arbitration is to be before a single arbitrator who is named in the arbitration agreement, although in practice this rarely encountered.

2. 仲裁机构负责人指定

为避免因当事人不能达成组庭的一致意见而使仲裁陷入困境,大多数商事仲裁机构在仲裁规则中规定,仲裁机构的最高权力机构(如主席/主任、主席团/委员会)有权指定仲裁员。但这种权力的行使受到一定限制,只有在当事人无协议时,或一方当事人不履行协议时,或已选定的两名仲裁员无一致意见时,一方当事人可提请依仲裁协议中选定的仲裁规则而享有任命权的机构或个人任命仲裁员。瑞典《斯德哥尔摩商会仲裁院规则》和《伦敦国际仲裁院规则》还明确规定,如果当事人选择它们的仲裁规则,则当事人各自只能任命数目相等的仲裁员,至于仲裁庭的主席或独任仲裁员则必须由制定了该仲裁规则的仲裁院任命。

Take the ICC for example. Under Article 7.4 of the ICC Rules, decisions of the Court as to the appointment, confirmation, challenge or replacement of an arbitrator shall be final and the reasons for such decisions shall not be communicated. In general, the provision that decisions of the Court "shall be final" only means that the decisions shall not be the subject of further recourse before the ICC Court. It does not deprive a party of recourse to a national court which it may enjoy as a matter of law, either against the decision itself or the arbitral award ultimately rendered. There are considerable differences among the laws of different jurisdictions in this regard, and it is therefore a matter that should be considered when choosing a venue for an arbitration proceeding.①

仲裁规则由当事人约定,所以从这个意义上说这种方式也属于当事人的约定范畴,但是有一些国家在立法中明确赋予了仲裁机构这一权力,意味着仲裁机构指定仲裁员不再需要当事人的特别授权。如我国《仲裁法》第32条规定:"当事人没有在仲裁规则规定的限期内约定仲裁庭的组成的方式或者选定仲裁员的,由仲裁委员会主任指定。"

在当事人没有约定仲裁庭人数或者组庭人选无法达成一致时,在具体做法

---

① See Jose Rosell, The Challenge of Arbitrators, p.553.

上各个仲裁机构还存在差别。这里以国际商会仲裁院为例:

Both the Rules and the standard ICC arbitration clause leave open the number of arbitrators. At first sight, this may seem odd; however, the overall objective is to permit the ICC Court and the parties to adapt the ICC arbitration procedure not just to the parties and the contract but also to the dispute itself.

A contract in a relatively small amount may give rise to a substantial and complex claim for damages. Large contracts may give rise to apparently intractable disputes as to smaller amounts that the parties to the contract may wish to have adjudicated especially if they have an ongoing relationship.

This flexibility sometimes results in the first dispute between the parties with respect to the arbitral procedure. One party may see an advantage in having a sole arbitrator. In case of dispute as to the number of arbitrators, the ICC Court will decide the issue in accordance with Article 8.[①]

8.1　The disputes shall be decided by a sole arbitrator or by three arbitrators.

8.2　Where the parties have not agreed upon the number of arbitrators, the court shall appoint a sole arbitrator, save where it appears to the Court that the dispute is such as to warrant the appointment of three arbitrators. In such case, the Claimant shall nominate an arbitrator within a period of 15 days from the receipt of the notification of the nomination made by the Claimant.

8.3　Where the parties have agreed that the dispute shall be settled by a sole arbitrator, they may, by agreement, nominate the sole arbitrator for confirmation. If the parties fail to nominate a sole arbitrator within 30 days from the date when the Claimant's Request for Arbitration has been received by the other party, or within such additional time as may be allowed by the Secretariat, the sole arbitrator shall be appointed by the Court.

8.4　Where the dispute is to be referred to three arbitrators, each party shall nominate in the Request and the Answer, respectively, one arbitrator for confirmation. If a party fails to nominate an arbitrator, the appointment shall be made by the Court. The third arbitrator, who will act as chairman of the Arbitral Tribunal, shall be appointed by the Court, unless the parties have agreed upon another procedure for such appointment, in which case the nomination will be subject to confirmation pursuant to Article 9. Should such procedure not result in a nomination

---

[①] See Michael W. Bühler and Thomas H. Webster, Handbook of ICC Arbitration: Commentary, Precedents, Materials, Sweet & Maxwell, 2005, pp. 128—129.

within the time limit fixed by the parties or the Court, the third arbitrator shall be appointed by the Court.

3. 法院指定

在机构仲裁中,即使当事人不能就仲裁庭的组成达成一致意见,仲裁机构也能予以补救,因此一般不会涉及法院指定仲裁员的问题。但是在临时仲裁中,仲裁庭的组成并不涉及任何仲裁机构,一旦当事人无法对组庭达成协议,并且没有明示授权某机构或某人任命,当事人只能申请法院指定仲裁员。法院的指定权力来自于法律的明确授权,一般在承认临时仲裁的国家都有这样的规定。如瑞士《联邦仲裁协约》规定,如果当事人无法就独任仲裁员和/或首席仲裁员的选任达成一致,并且仲裁协议又不规定仲裁机构,则由州高级普通民事法庭依一方当事人的请求指派仲裁员。日本、英国、德国、比利时、美国等大部分国家都有类似规定,授予法院在必要时任命仲裁员的权力。中国法律只认可机构仲裁,因此并没有在法律中对法院指定仲裁员的权力作出明确规定。一旦一项符合《纽约公约》的外国裁决在仲裁程序中涉及法院指定仲裁员,如果该裁决申请在中国承认和执行,法院能否因仲裁程序不符合中国法律而拒绝承认和执行则是个问题。

If one of the parties refuses to assist in making the necessary appointment, or for some other reason an appointment cannot be made, the court will have jurisdiction, or make an appointment so that the arbitration can go ahead. The statutory power to make an appointment is the only possible power available to it, for even though a failure by one of the parties to make an appointment may be a breach of contract which gives rise to an action for damage, the court will not grant specific performance.① The most thorough guidance is given by the Model Law, art. 11(5) of which provides as follows:

"The court... in appointing an arbitrator, shall have due regard to any qualifications required of the arbitrator by the agreement of the parties and to such considerations as are likely to secure the appointment of an independent and impartial arbitrator and, in the case of a sole or third arbitrator, shall take into account as well the advisability of appointing an arbitrator of a nationality other than those of the parties."

三、当事人的救济手段

在仲裁员的选任过程中,由于当事人对仲裁员的了解一般基于仲裁员主动

---

① See Robert Merkin, Arbitration Law, LLP, 2004, pp. 425—428.

披露,一旦仲裁员信息披露不全或有误,可能存在对当事人不公正的风险。尽管在完成组庭之后当事人对仲裁庭的质疑并不受仲裁机构的欢迎,但只要满足一定的条件,当事人能够举证证明相关事实,法律仍然赋予当事人一定的救济权利——申请仲裁员回避并重新组庭。

(一) 申请仲裁员回避

商事仲裁中的仲裁员回避既可以是主动的,也可以是被动的。前者是指仲裁员在组庭之后发现自己与案件有利害关系而主动要求回避。基于对仲裁员较高的道德要求,各国法律、各常设仲裁机构规则及有关的国际公约也都施以仲裁员主动回避义务,但该义务的履行更多取决于仲裁员的意愿,且少有监督措施,一旦仲裁员不完整地披露信息及相关行为是故意时,主动申请回避事实上是不可能发生的。因此,各法律、仲裁规则同时赋予当事人申请仲裁员回避的权利,只要仲裁庭成员不具备一般仲裁员及本案仲裁员资格,或仲裁员在仲裁程序中作出不当行为,无论其是否主动申请回避,当事人都可对该仲裁庭成员甚至整个仲裁庭提出异议,请求该仲裁员回避。申请仲裁员回避是当事人应对仲裁员不公正行为最为直接的救济手段。

申请仲裁员回避主要是基于可能减损当事人对仲裁员公正性信任的事由。如荷兰《民事诉讼法》规定,如果存在对仲裁员的公正和独立产生合理疑问的情况,可对仲裁员提出异议。德国、瑞士、英国、日本等国也都有类似规定。至于具体何种事由属于可能影响仲裁员公正和独立的,各国法律规定有所区别。根据瑞典《仲裁法》,这类事由通常包括:仲裁员或与其密切联系者是一方当事人,或争议的结果可能对其产生一定的利益或损失;仲裁员或与其密切联系者是作为一方当事人的公司或其他组织的负责人,或代表一方当事人,或争议的结果可能对其产生约定的利益或损失;仲裁员曾经在争议中担任专家或者其他身份,或曾经协助一方当事人在争议案件中作准备或指导案件的工作;仲裁员违反规定接受报酬或者要求报酬。根据我国《仲裁法》的规定,当事人在四种情况下能够申请仲裁员回避:(1) 仲裁员是案件当事人或者是当事人、代理人的近亲属;(2) 仲裁员与案件有利害关系;(3) 仲裁员与案件有其他关系,并且可能影响公正仲裁的;(4) 仲裁员私自会见当事人、代理人,或者接受当事人、代理人请客送礼。此外,当事人还可以基于仲裁员主体资格或相关能力不合法申请回避,如英国《1996年仲裁法》就规定,当仲裁员不具备仲裁协议所要求的资格或者仲裁员在体力上或精神上无力进行仲裁程序时,当事人可申请撤换仲裁员。

An arbitrator may be removed for the following reasons:

(a) Where there are justifiable doubts as to the arbitrator's impartiality or independence.

(b) Where the arbitrator lacks qualifications agreed on by the parties.

(c) Where the arbitrator is prevented from fulfilling his functions (such as by illness), or is not fulfilling them with reasonable diligence and in accordance with the rules governing the arbitration.

Depending on the type of arbitration, an application for removal is dealt with as follows:

(a) Institutional arbitrations. Applications are usually dealt with by the ICC (International Court of Arbitration or the LCIA Court). The application may be made by one of the parties (or, in the case of the LCIA, by the remaining arbitrators) and must be made within the prescribed time limit, or else the party will be deemed to have waived its right to object. Time limits for many institutions are short—typically 15 days from the date the party became aware of the circumstances upon which the application is based.

A number of institutions provide that their decisions on such applications are to be regarded as final. This should nevertheless be viewed as subject to any mandatory provisions of the law applicable to the arbitration proceedings, which may permit a further application to be made to the courts.

(b) Ad hoc arbitrations. Applications for removal of an arbitrator are usually made in the first instance to the tribunal itself. If unsuccessful, a further application can generally be made to the courts of the county where the arbitration is being conducted.

为避免仲裁程序迟延,当事人申请仲裁员回避应当在一定的期限内提出,否则将被视为放弃申请回避的权利,无正当理由逾期申请,不会被有关决定机关接受。关于异议提出的期限,大部分国家的仲裁法律或仲裁规则都有明确的规定。如瑞士《联邦仲裁协约》第20条规定:要求回避,应该在仲裁开始时提出,或者申请人在知悉回避原因后立即提出。瑞典《仲裁法》规定,一方当事人要求仲裁员回避的,应当在其知晓相关回避事由后15日内提出。《联合国国际贸易法委员会仲裁规则》对当事人提出异议的时间也作出了明确规定。该规则第11条第1款规定,对仲裁员准备提出异议的一方当事人,应在该仲裁员的任命已通知提出异议的一方当事人后15日内或该方当事人知悉存在异议理由后15日内,发出异议通知书。还有一些国家的仲裁法并无明确时间限定,仅规定当事人在知悉有可提出异议的理由时即应立即提出,否则事后即可能被有关机关视做放弃提出异议的权利。如在美国,如果披露后双方或一方当事人并未提出异议而开始了仲裁程序,美国仲裁协会即认为双方当事人都放弃了提出异议的权利。但对仲裁员行为不当提出的异议却可以在仲裁审理过程中提出,也可在仲裁裁决后以仲裁员的行为不当请求法院对仲裁裁决审查时提出。根据我国《仲裁法》,

当事人提出回避申请,应在首次开庭前提出;回避事由在首次开庭后知道的,可以在最后一次开庭终结前提出。国内仲裁机构针对法律这种模糊的时间规定,在仲裁规则中进一步增强其操作性。如果选择 CIETAC 2005 年《仲裁规则》,当事人如果以仲裁员披露的事实或情况为理由要求该仲裁员回避,则应于收到仲裁员的书面披露后 10 天内向仲裁委员会书面提出。在其他情况下,对仲裁员的回避请求应在收到组庭通知之日起 15 天内以书面形式提出。如果要求回避事由的得知是在此之后,则可以在得知回避事由后 15 天内提出,但不应迟于最后一次开庭终结。

一般而言,当事人对仲裁员的回避申请形式上都要求是书面的,口头申请往往不被认可,大部分仲裁机构的仲裁规则对此都有明确的要求。如 1998 年《国际商会仲裁规则》第 11 条第 1 款规定,申请仲裁员回避的,应向秘书处书面陈述要求回避的事实和依据。2007 年新加坡《国际仲裁中心仲裁规则》第 11 条第 2 款也有类似规定,即提出异议的一方当事人必须向主簿官抄送异议通知书,同时向另一方当事人、被异议的仲裁员和仲裁庭其他仲裁员发送。异议通知必须采用书面形式,并说明理由。对仲裁庭成员的异议可以向仲裁员资格确认的机构提起,即有管辖权的法院或者受理仲裁案件的仲裁机构或有任命仲裁员之权的机构。对仲裁庭成员的异议一旦为有权机构确认成立,被异议的仲裁员不得再担任该案件的仲裁员。根据目前大部分国家的立法和仲裁机构的规则,关于仲裁员回避的决定:(1)可由仲裁庭或仲裁机构决定;(2)仲裁庭或仲裁机构否决当事人申请后,交由法院作出最后裁决。这一决定程序事实上也有一个发展演变的过程。早期,仲裁机构试图独立于法院,排除法院对仲裁庭的干涉,所以在仲裁规则中确定其对此享有唯一的决定权。但这种做法过于理想,如果得不到仲裁地法律的支持,这种规定徒然无用。如在 ICC 仲裁,根据原来的仲裁规则,仲裁院是唯一有权对仲裁员回避申请作出决定的机构,并且其决定是最终的,但最新版本的仲裁规则改变了这一做法,仲裁院不再有绝对的最后决定权。《联合国国际贸易法委员会仲裁规则》第 12 条作了更为合理的规定,即由仲裁员的任命机构对回避申请作出决定。在我国,根据《仲裁法》的规定,由仲裁委员会主任决定仲裁员回避,且如果异议是针对仲裁委主任时,则由仲裁委员会集体决定。

(二) 重新组庭

对仲裁员异议成立、仲裁员主动申请回避、仲裁员死亡或健康原因不能履行仲裁职责等都可能会导致仲裁庭重组。重新组庭的程序与首次组庭在组庭人数、方式等方面并无很大区别。

1. 重新组庭的方式

在组庭方式上,由于要求当事人重新达成协议会十分困难,因此大部分仲裁法律和规则都要求重新组庭应按照首次组庭约定或规定的方式进行。《联合国国际贸易法委员会仲裁规则》第 13 条规定,任命或选择一名替代的仲裁员,应适用任命或选择原仲裁员的程序。CIETAC 对替代仲裁员的确定也采用了相同的做法,即仲裁员因回避或者由于死亡、除名等其他原因不能履行职责时,应按照原选定或者指定该仲裁员的程序,选定或者指定替代的仲裁员。①《解决投资争议国际中心仲裁程序规则》第 11 条规定:"由于资格不符合、死亡、无行为能力或辞职而产生的空缺应通过其被任命时相同方法及时填补之。"

When an arbitrator is removed, a vacancy is created which must normally be filled before the arbitration proceedings can continue. A vacancy may also be created when an arbitrator dies or, in effect, removes himself from the appointment by resigning or refusing to participate further in the arbitration proceedings. The vacancy will usually be filled by an appointment made in the same manner as that in which the original appointment was made. When that is no longer possible (for example, when arbitrators have agreed on a chairman, but cannot agree on who is to fill the vacancy left on the chairman's removal), the procedure set out in any relevant rules must be followed. In ad hoc arbitrations the courts of the country where the arbitration is being conducted may, provided that they have power under their law to do so, act on an application made by one of the parties and fill the vacancy.

在临时仲裁中,双方当事人有时并未约定仲裁员空缺时应采用的补缺方法。当仲裁员出现空缺时,如果双方当事人仍不能达成一致意见,一般都由法院来决定有关仲裁员的选择或选择方法。这时因为已经组建过仲裁庭,仲裁地也多半已经确定,关于应由哪个国家或哪个地方的法院来处理仲裁员补缺的问题,也一般不会有什么问题。重新任命或选择仲裁员的申请,可以直接向仲裁地法院提出。在大多数商事仲裁立法比较完备的国家,对此都有非常明确的规定。

2. 重新组庭对仲裁程序的影响

仲裁庭的重组属于仲裁程序中的特殊变化,这一变化通常会对仲裁审理产生一定的影响。其中最主要的问题在于:仲裁庭重组后,以前已经进行的全部或部分审理程序是否需要重新进行。

如果仲裁庭的重组发生于首次开庭审理之前,就案件审理而言,因为现在还没有进行过任何的庭审程序,所有的仲裁员,包括新更替的仲裁员都有参加所有庭审程序的机会,仲裁庭的裁决是在全体仲裁员听取了当事人的陈述和辩论之后作出的,因而通常不会涉及重复已经进行的仲裁程序的问题。

Any incoming arbitrator must have an opportunity to become acquainted with the

---

① 参见 CIETAC 2005 年《仲裁规则》第 37 条第 2 款。

pleadings and documents. If a replacement takes place after a hearing has commenced, the hearing will usually have to be halted to enable the arbitrator to read the relevant papers. The parties may agree that the hearing need not be repeated, particularly where a transcript of the hearing has been made and which can be read by the incoming arbitrator. Where hearings are likely to be lengthy, and an arbitrator is elderly, it is common to insure the life of the arbitrator so that if he dies before signature of the award, the additional costs in the arbitration arising out of his death may be recovered.

考虑到仲裁程序的正当要求，当事人有权在仲裁庭的庭审时进行充分的陈述和辩论，也有权使其陈述和辩论意见被全体仲裁员知悉。如果仲裁庭中一位仲裁员没有参加先前进行的审理程序，没有听取当事人的陈述和辩论，没有听取有关证人的证词，当事人就可能基于程序不当而对裁决提出异议。因此，重新组成的仲裁庭通常应该重复以前进行过的审理程序，尤其是在独任仲裁员或首席仲裁员被更替时，以前已经进行的庭审程序更应该重新进行。例如，《联合国国际贸易法委员会仲裁规则》第14条就作了这样的规定："独任仲裁员或首席仲裁员被替换时，以前举行过的任何庭审均应重新进行。倘其他仲裁员被替换时，仲裁庭得自行决定是否重新进行开庭审理。"在我国，已经进行的仲裁程序是否重新进行由仲裁庭决定[1]，不过对于独任仲裁员或首席仲裁员被更替的特殊情况发生时如何处理的问题，法律没有作出特别的规定[2]。

第三节 仲裁庭的管辖权

仲裁管辖权是仲裁庭审理案件并作出裁决的前提，也是一项仲裁裁决得到法院承认和执行的根据。管辖权是仲裁庭最为重要的一项权力，它来自于仲裁协议，同时得到了法律的支持。目前，管辖权/管辖权原则已经成为国际商事仲裁法律制度中一项非常重要的原则，得到了实践的支持与推动。在理论上，管辖权问题一直被作为仲裁核心问题之一予以研究；在仲裁庭审中，管辖权问题也是律师和仲裁员在仲裁过程中关注的焦点。

一、仲裁管辖权

仲裁管辖权作为仲裁庭的最基本权力，对它的性质、内涵等认识目前还存在很大争议，但对仲裁庭取得管辖权的条件，认识上还是比较一致的。

---

[1] 参见《仲裁法》第37条。
[2] 参见谢石松主编：《商事仲裁法学》，高等教育出版社2003年版，第214—215页。

（一）仲裁管辖权的概念

仲裁管辖权（jurisdiction of arbitration）是指仲裁庭对某一商事争议从事仲裁审理活动，对该案进行整体仲裁的法律权限。① 关于仲裁管辖权的理解在学界有诸多争议，有学者认为仲裁管辖权直接来自于仲裁协议，因此将仲裁管辖权视为仲裁协议赋予仲裁庭对有关商事仲裁案件进行审理并作出裁决的权限。② 也有学者认为仲裁管辖权是仲裁庭依据当事人的授权和法律的授权所享有的，可以对当事人之间的争议进行审理并作出有约束力裁决的权力。③ 这种争议的背后实质是对仲裁本质的不同理解，前一种观点将仲裁视为当事人意思自治的结果，仲裁协议是仲裁庭权限的唯一来源；后者除了认同仲裁是当事人授权之外，还强调仲裁是国家立法支持的结果，仲裁权还来自于国家立法的授权。我们认为，法律并没有直接授予仲裁庭管辖案件的权力，只是确定了仲裁庭可以获得管辖权的条件，同时给予一定范围限制，仲裁庭只有在当事人约定的基础上才存在，因此其管辖权是基于仲裁协议而非法律规定，只有诉讼管辖权才直接源于国家法律的强制性规定。

（二）仲裁管辖权的取得

1．核心——有效的仲裁协议

仲裁庭获得管辖权虽然需要有法律的支持，但是最根本的还是来自于当事人的合意授权，因此一个有效的仲裁协议是仲裁管辖权取得的基础。管辖权的范围也以仲裁协议约定为限，未经当事人附加同意，仲裁庭无权管辖仲裁协议以外的事项。

The jurisdiction of a tribunal is usually considered from two viewpoints: (a) Whether the tribunal has any jurisdiction at all. A tribunal will lack jurisdiction altogether if no enforceable arbitration agreement has been created. A tribunal will also lack jurisdiction where the only matter in dispute between the parties does not fall within the scope of the arbitration agreement, or where some condition precedent to arbitration (such as obtaining a decision from the engineer in the scope of certain construction disputes) has not been fulfilled at the time of the commencement of the arbitration. (b) Whether the tribunal has jurisdiction over all of the disputes submitted to it, or only some of them. The answer to this question will be found by construing the arbitration agreement to determine what disputes the parties have

---

① 参见刘晓红：《国际商事仲裁协议的法理与实证》，商务印书馆2005年版，第92页。
② 参见谢石松主编：《商事仲裁法学》，高等教育出版社2003年版，第204页。
③ 参见乔欣：《仲裁权研究》，法律出版社2001年版，第143页。

agreed should be submitted to arbitration.①

2. 前提——当事人申请

一份有效的仲裁协议并不能使仲裁庭立即获得管辖权,仲裁庭只有在当事人申请组庭后才能享有。一般而言,当事人需首先向仲裁机构提交仲裁申请,由仲裁机构对争议的管辖权作初步的形式审查,然后经当事人选任仲裁员之后,组成仲裁庭。只有满足这些程序要件之后,仲裁管辖权才能被仲裁庭真正享有。

3. 仲裁管辖权的范围

仲裁庭的管辖范围不可能像法院那样无所不包,绝大部分国家多通过法律或积极或消极地限制仲裁管辖权。法律对仲裁管辖权的限制主要体现在,法律禁止仲裁庭对某些特定事项具有管辖权,将对这些事项进行仲裁的仲裁协议视为无效,从根本上使仲裁庭获得管辖权失去依据。我国《仲裁法》明确规定下列纠纷不得仲裁:(1)婚姻、收养、监护、抚养、继承纠纷;(2)依法应当由行政机关处理的行政纠纷。此外,劳动争议、农村土地承包争议等也不得提交商事仲裁。

What matters may be arbitrated? In practice therefore, the question has not been whether a particular dispute is capable of settlement by arbitration, but whether it ought to be referred to arbitration or whether it has given rise to an enforceable award. The general principle is, we submit, that any dispute or claim concerning legal rights which can be the subject of an enforceable award, is capable of being settled by arbitration. This principle must be understood, however, subject to certain reservation. First, certain types of dispute are resolved by methods which are not properly called arbitration. Second, the types of remedies which the arbitrator can award are limited by considerations of public policy and by the fact that he is appointed by the parties and not by the state. For example, he cannot impose a fine or a term of imprisonment, commit a person for contempt or issue a writ of subpoena; nor can he make an award which is binding on third parties or affects the public at large, such as a judgment in rem against a ship, an assessment of the rateable value of land, a divorce decree.②

二、仲裁管辖权的异议

主张仲裁庭对争议案件无管辖权是被申请人对仲裁申请的一项重要抗辩。特别在国际商事仲裁中,由于需要花费申请人大量的时间和金钱以及暴露大量的

---

① See Mark Huleatt-James & Nicholas Gould, International Commercial Arbitration: A Handbook, 2nd ed., LLP, 1999, p.62.
② See Sir Michael J. Mustill & Stewart C. Boyd, Q.C., Commercial Arbitration, 2nd ed., Butterworths, 1989, p.149.

证据材料,一旦被申请人无管辖权的抗辩成功,申请人就会处于十分被动的地位。

(一)管辖权异议的理由

对仲裁庭管辖权异议的理由主要集中于仲裁协议的有效性问题,前面章节讨论的影响仲裁协议有效性的因素都可以成为当事人异议的理由。不论书面问题还是实质条件,包括争议的可仲裁性等都可以为当事人利用。

The most common ground for a challenge to the entire jurisdiction of the arbitral tribunal is the absence of a valid and enforceable arbitration agreement. Other grounds include the following: (a) The subject matter of the dispute is not arbitral under the law of the place of arbitration; (b) The conditions precedent agreed upon by the parties for arbitration have not been fulfilled: for example, in certain construction disputes, the engineer's decision may not have been obtained; (c) Absence of a dispute; (d) The entire dispute between the parties is not one which they have agreed should be submitted to arbitration.①

在国际社会普遍支持仲裁的情况下,仲裁庭的管辖权原则上都能得到立法和司法实践的承认,仲裁庭的决定也是在其拥有管辖权基础上作出的,因此在实践中,主张管辖权异议一方往往要承担很重的举证责任来证明存在上述情形,而且还很难得到支持。基于仲裁条款独立性理论,仲裁条款不因主合同无效而无效,因此以主合同存在无效或可撤销的理由来主张仲裁庭无管辖权不能得到支持。In a recent ICC case, the Tribunal dealt with this pointing a rather "classic" fashion:"The Tribunal also considered [Respondent's] argument, apparently raised in the Guatemalan proceedings that the arbitration clauses did not survive [Claimant's] termination of the Agreements. We cannot accept that argument, however, because it contradicts the well-established doctrine of severability, which provides that an arbitration agreement forming part of another agreement (as in this case) should not be regarded as invalid, nonexistent or ineffective because the other agreement has been terminated; rather the arbitration clause is to be treated as a distinct and independent agreement for that purpose. This doctrine is embodied in the ICC Rules of Arbitration, article 6(4), which provides expressly that the Tribunal shall continue to have jurisdiction to determine the respective rights of the parties and to adjudicate on their claims and pleas even though the contract itself may be non-existent or null and valid."②

---

① See Mark Huleatt-James & Nicholas Gould, International Commercial Arbitration: A Handbook, 2nd ed., LLP, 1999, p.66.

② Michael W. Bühler & Thomas H. Webster, Handbook of ICC Arbitration: Commentary, Precedents, Materials, Sweet & Maxwell, 2005, p.101.

主张仲裁庭对部分争议没有管辖权是更为常见的做法,因为仲裁协议一旦订立,各国法律都倾向于使之有效,部分无管辖权是在承认仲裁协议有效的前提下对仲裁庭管辖权的有力抗辩。这里有个国际商会关于管辖权部分异议的实例:承包商的仲裁申请包含了为更改或增加的工作提出的23项个别的请求,以及基于迟延提出的总的赔偿请求。承包商在仲裁申请中提出的有些个别请求,没有取得或等待工程师的决定。被申请人为政府,其抗辩认为,由于未遵守合同规定程序,相关请求未能适当地提交仲裁,因此不属于仲裁庭的管辖权范围。仲裁庭在三项个别请求上,支持了对管辖权提出的抗辩;承包商承认另外两项缺乏管辖权,撤回了该两项请求。[①]

(二) 管辖权异议的程序

异议申请由当事人向法院或仲裁庭提出,申请应满足法律或仲裁规则对异议时间、方式等程序上的要求。法院或仲裁庭有权接受或不接受这种异议申请,对于应在多长时间内作出裁定,很少有法律或仲裁规则对此作出专门规定。一般的,只要在法定或约定的仲裁时间内作出裁决即可。法院或仲裁庭接受当事人申请之后是否应当中止原先已经开始的仲裁程序,各国规定有所区别,大部分国家都认为仲裁程序不受当事人异议的影响,仲裁庭可以继续对案件进行实体审查。在我国,如果当事人异议申请被仲裁机构接受,根据仲裁规则,仲裁庭可以继续审理案件[②];但若法院受理异议申请,法院有权通知仲裁庭中止案件审理,仲裁庭只有在法院确认异议不成立之后才能继续仲裁程序。

在该问题上,瑞士的做法是,原则上,仲裁庭应该将管辖权的异议作为先决问题作出裁定。但仲裁庭也可以继续进行仲裁审理程序而在最终裁决中对该异议作出裁定。在德国,由于法院对仲裁管辖权具有最后决定权,如果仲裁庭认为其有管辖权,应以初步裁定的形式作出,当事人可以在收到书面裁定通知后一个月内请求法院决定该事项。即使法院裁决未作出,仲裁庭仍然可以继续仲裁程序并作出裁决。[③] 仲裁庭对案件管辖权之决定,也可以中间裁决或临时裁决方式作出。[④] 如 CIETAC 2005 年《仲裁规则》第44条规定,如果仲裁庭认为必要或者当事人提出请求经仲裁庭同意时,仲裁庭可以在作出最终仲裁裁决之前的任何时候,就案件的任何问题作出中间裁决或部分裁决。任何一方当事人不履行中间裁决,不影响仲裁程序的继续进行,也不影响仲裁庭作出最终裁决。

An arbitrator is under no legal duty to raise questions of jurisdiction on his own

---

① 参见〔英〕艾伦·雷德芬、马丁·亨特等:《国际商事仲裁法律与实践》,林一飞、宋连斌译,北京大学出版社 2005 年版,第 267 页。
② 参见 CIETAC 2005 年《仲裁规则》第 6 条。
③ 参见林一飞:《国际商事仲裁法律与实务》,中信出版社 2005 年版,第 200 页。
④ 参见陈治东:《国际商事仲裁法》,法律出版社 1998 年版,第 172 页。

initiative. Unlike objections on the ground of illegality, which the arbitrator is bound to investigate irrespective of what the parties desire, jurisdiction involves no considerations of public policy. On the other hand, common sense demands that any obvious objection to the jurisdiction should be dealt with at an early stage, in order to spare both the arbitrator and the parties the waste of time and money involved in conducting a reference which ultimately proves to be a nullity. Thus, before accepting an invitation to act, or at the latest before making any substantial progress with the reference, the arbitrator should study the arbitration agreement to see whether, for example, it prescribes any qualification or disqualifications which might affect the validity of his appointment.[①]

（三）异议决定机关

1. 仲裁庭

由仲裁庭决定其是否对争议具有管辖权被称为管辖权/管辖权原则（后文将重点论述），它避免了繁琐拖沓的法院决定程序，能很好地满足当事人对仲裁效率的要求。很多国家的法律都赋予仲裁庭可以自己决定其管辖权的权力。然而，我国的仲裁庭并不享有这一权力。

If a question is raised on the jurisdiction of the arbitrator and if the objection is pressed, the arbitrator should see whether the parties themselves take steps to obtain a final ruling on the question of jurisdiction—by seeking declaratory relief, or by empowering him to decide the matter himself, or to start a case upon it.

If the parties remain inactive, the arbitrator can choose between two procedures—

(1) to decide the question of jurisdiction himself, subsequently continuing or abandoning the arbitration according to what he decides; or

(2) to set the question of jurisdiction on one side, leaving the parties to raise it in Court, either before or after the award has been published.[②]

2. 仲裁机构

一般认为，仲裁机构是服务行业性质的法人实体，绝大部分国家都不认为仲裁机构具有决定仲裁管辖权的权力。国际商会仲裁院承认仲裁院具有初步决定权是一种比较特殊的做法。由于国际商会仲裁院有较高的国际声誉，仲裁机构行使决定权能提高仲裁的效率，同时也不至于招致机构干预的非议，这是一般的

---

① See Sir Michael J. Mustill & Stewart C. Boyd, Q.C., Commercial Arbitration, 2nd ed., Butterworths, 1989, pp.574—575.

② Ibid., p.575.

仲裁机构很难做到的。同时,国际商会仲裁院的决定权也不是完全的,仲裁院有权否定仲裁管辖权,但是如果初步决定是肯定的,仲裁庭享有最终的决定权。

Contrary to common belief, the decision of the ICC Court is not binding upon the Tribunal and is not to be seen as prejudging the Tribunal's decision on jurisdiction. The decision of the ICC Court is administrative and only means that the ICC Court believes that "an arbitration agreement ... may exist". It is for the Tribunal to decide if the arbitration agreement does exist. In deciding whether an ICC arbitration agreement does exist, Tribunals are conscious of the fact that the ultimate decision on jurisdiction belongs to the national courts.[①]

根据我国《仲裁法》第 20 条的规定,仲裁机构对仲裁庭管辖权具有决定权,而且这种决定权完全取代了仲裁庭。由于我国仲裁机构浓厚的行政色彩,很难保证其独立地位,这一"家长式"的规定招来多方批评,严重影响了我国仲裁的声誉,国内一些重要的仲裁机构已经开始尝试在法律规定的范围内对此有所突破。

In 2005, the CIETAC officially introduced the jurisdictional autonomy of the arbitral tribunals through Art. 6 of the amendment to its Rules, "The CIETAC shall have the power to determine the existence and validity of an arbitration agreement and its jurisdiction over an arbitration case. The CIETAC may, if necessary, delegate such power to the arbitral tribunal. Where the CIETAC is satisfied by prima facie evidence that an arbitration agreement providing for arbitration by the CIETAC exists, it may make a decision based on such evidence that it has jurisdiction over the arbitration case. Such a decision shall not prevent the CIETAC from making a new decision on jurisdiction based on facts and/or evidence found by the tribunal during the proceedings that are inconsistent with the prima facie evidence." To begin with, the commission may now delegate the jurisdictional power to the individual tribunal. This is evidence of the encouraging efforts by the CIETAC in advancing the tribunal's competence-competence. In addition, the new Rules officially affirm the long-established "underground" practice of "joint" ruling on arbitral jurisdiction. Thus the commission may make a decision allowing the tribunal to assume jurisdiction if the prima facie evidence so suggests; and may ultimately make a new decision should

---

① See Michael W. Bühler & Thomas H. Webster, Handbook of ICC Arbitration: Commentary, Precedents, Materials, Sweet & Maxwell, 2005, p. 99.

later evidence suggest inconsistency based on the tribunal's findings. ①

3. 法院

绝大多数国家都赋予法院决定仲裁庭管辖权的绝对权力,而且在与仲裁庭异议程序相冲突时,法院的决定权具有优先性。但法院是否有对仲裁管辖权的最终决定权,各国实践有所不同。荷兰和瑞士的仲裁法以及德国 1998 年《仲裁法》修改以前的实践,都认为仲裁庭有最终决定自己管辖权的权力。但大部分国家或组织,包括 UNCITRAL《示范法》,认为仲裁庭可以在仲裁过程中确定自己的管辖权,但无最终确定自己管辖权的权力,最终确定管辖权的权力应当由法院享有。从近十年的立法看(参见附表 1),该理论的发展趋势是从绝对的管辖权/管辖权理论发展到相对的管辖权/管辖权理论,法院对仲裁庭的管辖权具有最终的决定权。

Whilst a tribunal generally has the power to decide on its own jurisdiction, that decision will seldom be final, in that:

(1) the courts of the place if arbitration may set the decision aside; and

(2) the courts of the place where enforcement of an award is sought may refuse enforcement of an award if they are of the view that the tribunal did not have jurisdiction.

(四)异议的限制

为保证仲裁的效率,防止当事人恶意拖延仲裁程序,法律或仲裁规则限制仲裁管辖权异议主要体现在时间限定方面,即要求异议方应当在一定的时间内提出异议,否则将被视为放弃该权利,即使仲裁庭根据仲裁协议无法获得管辖权也被视为当事人一致同意仲裁。如英国《1996 年仲裁法》第 31 条规定,当事人关于仲裁庭缺乏实体管辖权的异议,必须不迟于其在程序中就与所异议之仲裁庭管辖权有关的任何事项予以抗辩之前提出。根据我国澳门地区的仲裁专门制度,对仲裁庭无管辖权之抗辩仅得在作出答辩之前提出。

The rules and laws frequently impose time limits on the making of a challenge to the tribunal's jurisdiction. Article 16(2) of the UNCITRAL Model Law provides that a challenge shall be made not later than the submission of the defense. The existence of such time limit may, however, not be effective in preventing a party from raising lack of jurisdiction as a defense to recognition or enforcement of the award, except, in the case of a partial challenge, where the court comes to view that the party has

---

① See Weixia Gu, Xianchu Zhang, The China-Style "Commission-Oriented" Competence on Arbitral Jurisdiction: An Analysis of Chinese Adaptation into Globalization, Int. A. L. R., Vol. 9, No. 6, 2006, pp. 185—200.

waived the lack of jurisdiction.①

在仲裁中时间要求很严格,当事人一旦没有在规定的时间内提出异议申请,就会丧失异议权利,甚至面临败诉的风险。In People's Insurance Co. of China (Hebei Branch) v. Vysanthi Shipping Co. Ltd.,②P, the insurer of a receiver in a salvage claim over V's vessel, J., sought to challenge the jurisdiction of a sole London based arbitrator under the Arbitration Act 1996 s. 67. The application was brought outside the 28 day time limit stipulated in s. 70 of the Act. Prior to the London arbitration, P had commenced an action in the Chinese court claiming a contribution for the salvage costs. V however disputed the jurisdiction of the Chinese court on the basis that the bill of lading provided for London arbitration under a jurisdiction and choice of law clause. The Chinese court held that it had jurisdiction as the claim did not arise in the course of a contract for affreightment and was not brought under the bill of lading. V applied to enforce the London arbitration award and for the striking out of P's claim on the ground that it was an abuse of process. Judge Thomas, J. held, refusing P's application and granting summary judgment for V, that there was no basis upon which the power to extend time could be granted under either s. 79 or s. 80 of the Act. P's application was brought nearly a year after the award was made. Both the failure to identify the nature of the claim brought in the Chinese court and the delay were prejudicial to V, applied. Leave was therefore granted to enforce the award given that there was no valid basis on which it could be impugned with summary judgment in V's favor as P's claim had no possibility of success.

我国 2006 年施行的《最高人民法院关于适用〈中华人民共和国仲裁法〉若干问题的解释》第 13 条第 1 款明确规定,当事人在仲裁庭首次开庭之前没有对仲裁协议的效力提出异议,而后向人民法院申请确认仲裁协议无效的,人民法院不予受理。CIETAC 2005 年《仲裁规则》中也规定,"当事人对仲裁协议及/或仲裁案件管辖权的异议,应当在仲裁庭首次开庭前书面提出;书面审理的案件,应当在第一次实体答辩前提出",并且"一方当事人知道或者理应知道本规则或仲裁协议中规定的任何条款或情事未被遵守,但仍参加仲裁程序或继续进行仲裁程序而且不对此不遵守情况及时地、明示地提出书面异议的,视为放弃其提出异议的权利"。因此,对于开庭审理的案件,在我国进行仲裁的当事人管辖权异议

---

① See Mark Huleatt-James & Nicholas Gould, International Commercial Arbitration: A Handbook, 2nd ed., LLP, 1999, p. 64.
② [2003] 2 Lloyd's Rep. 617.

的申请必须是在仲裁庭首次开庭之前提出。由于法律规定仍存在空缺,对书面审理的案件当事人在开庭之后向人民法院提出异议能否被受理仍不明确。

三、管辖权/管辖权原则

(一)概述

管辖权/管辖权原则(Competence-Competence)的核心内容是:仲裁庭享有对其自身的管辖权包括对仲裁协议的存在或效力等问题作出裁定的权力,而不需要事先的司法决定。[①] 该学说解决的是对管辖权的管辖权问题,就实质而言,它讨论的是在仲裁庭及内国法院之间分配对于仲裁协议的解释和执行的管辖权。仲裁庭的此项权力来自于当事人的仲裁协议,是目前对此问题比较一致的看法。

(二)理论争鸣

仲裁立法和实践中的管辖权/管辖权原则最早源于20世纪50年代的德国。1955年德国高等法院认定,仲裁员对作为其权限基础的仲裁协议的范围有作出最终决定的权力。这一判决引起很大争议。1977年德国高等法院又作出了完全不同的判决,认为当事人只能另行签订独立的协议赋予仲裁员自裁管辖权的权力,且该协议还需要法院审查。在英国法院实践中,20世纪50年代法官 P. Devlin 认为,仲裁员有权对自己审理的案件有无管辖权的问题进行调查,这样做不是为了能够得出对双方当事人产生约束力的任何结论,因为他们并没有此项权限,而是为了解决他们是否应该把仲裁继续下去的先决问题。[②] 但在后来的一个案子中,法官 Roskill 指出:One thing is clear in this branch of the law. It has been clear since the decision of the House of Lords in Heyman v. Darwins(1942). An arbitrator cannot decide his own jurisdiction. Therefore whenever a question arises whether or not there has been a submission to arbitration, an arbitrator cannot in English law decide that issue. The only tribunal to decide it is the court, and that is one of the issues the plaintiff wants the court to decide.[③]

管辖权/管辖权原则赋予了仲裁庭决定其自身管辖权的权力,在当事人对仲裁管辖权提出异议时,仲裁庭有权自己进行调查并作出决定,而没有必要等法院作出决定之后再进行仲裁程序,充分保证了仲裁的效率。它增强并完善了仲裁庭的权力,一定程度上避免了当事人恶意拖延时间和减少了法院对仲裁的干预,使得仲裁程序不受干扰地快捷、连续进行,这是该原则常为人称道的价值所在。

---

① 参见刘晓红:《国际商事仲裁协议的法理与实证》,商务印书馆2005年版,第98页。
② 参见〔英〕施米托夫:《国际贸易法文选》,赵秀文译,中国大百科全书出版社1993年版,第646—647页。
③ See Willcock v. Pickfords Removals Ltd., [1979] 1 Lloyd'd Rep. 244, CA, p.245.

But asking the tribunal to deal with questions of jurisdiction would have prompted the objection that the tribunal had no authority to decide on jurisdiction, because the challenge was based on the fact that there was no valid arbitration agreement at all. Moreover, in the absence of an agreement, the tribunal itself had no legal standing, and there was nothing to delineate its jurisdiction.①

针对这些批评,有学者认为对该原则的设立要在理论上作出合理的解释,应从仲裁制度的本质出发,同时结合国际商事仲裁的实际需要。② 有观点更直接指出,仲裁庭决定其管辖权大部分理由是基于实用主义,另一部分理由是基于支持仲裁的公共政策,而不应着重其逻辑性。从合理利益进行分析,这应当是国际上采用该种理论的出发点。③ 近来的立法实践倾向于法院的最终控制权,从这种意义上说也走出了"自己决定自己权力"的逻辑怪圈。

(三) 各国实践

随着仲裁实践的不断发展,仲裁作为一种高度自治的商事争议解决机制被国际社会广泛接受,国际商事立法和实践开始逐步肯定和接受管辖权/管辖权原则。如1961年《欧洲国际商事仲裁公约》第5条第3款就规定,仲裁庭能够决定仲裁协议是否存在,有权对自己的管辖权作出决定。1966年《欧洲统一仲裁法》更是完全采纳了这一原则,并规定仲裁庭可以决定仲裁审理中的任何法律问题。

"Competence-Competence" has been accepted by the UNCITRAL Model Law. Article 16(1) of the Model Law provides: "The arbitral tribunal may rule its own jurisdiction, including any objections with respect to the existence or validity of the arbitration agreement. For that purpose, an arbitration clause, which forms part of a contract, shall be treated as an agreement independent of the other terms of the contract. A decision by the arbitral tribunal that the contract is null and void shall not entail ipso jure the invalidity of the arbitration clause." This principle also can be found in: Article 15(1) of the AAA International Arbitration Rules; Article 6(2) of the ICC Arbitration Rules; Article 23(1) of the LCIA Arbitration Rules; and Article 21(2) of the UNCITRAL Arbitration Rules.

法国属于较早在国内立法上接受该原则的国家之一,其1983年《民事诉讼法》第1458条规定,在仲裁庭根据仲裁协议而受理的异议被提交到法院时,法院应当宣告无管辖权。同时该法典第1466条进一步规定,如果当事人在仲裁中对仲裁员的管辖权的成立或范围提出异议,仲裁员应当就该问题作出决定。此

---

① See Mark Huleatt-James & Nicholas Gould, International Commercial Arbitration: A Handbook, 2nd ed., LLP, 1999, p.66.
② 参见刘晓红:《国际商事仲裁协议的法理与实证》,商务印书馆2005年版,第101页。
③ 参见林一飞:《国际商事仲裁法律与实务》,中信出版社2005年版,第201页。

外,立法上接受管辖权/管辖权原则的还包括比利时、瑞士、荷兰、保加利亚、埃及、西班牙、瑞典、印度、肯尼亚、新加坡等。①

Usually, one would expect to have jurisdictional issues dealt with by the Tribunal and then by the national court. There has been suggestion by one author that this should be part of the negative rule of the Competence-Competence. That is the national courts should generally refrain from deciding jurisdictional issues until the arbitral tribunal has rendered its decision on the point. The French Courts refuse to take jurisdiction in a dispute involving an arbitration agreement so as to allow the Tribunal to proceed with the case unless the arbitration agreement is manifestly null and void. In some instances, a party may seek to cut short the proceedings by obtaining a court ruling as to jurisdiction. The German Supreme Court has confirmed that under the 1998 German Arbitration Act, a Tribunal had the power to decide upon its own jurisdiction. However, the court held that the ultimate power to decide the Tribunal's jurisdiction was for the courts. The German Supreme Court further held that, if a party challenges the validity of the arbitration agreement, the Courts did not have to wait for a determination by the Tribunal, but could decide immediately upon the validity of the arbitration agreement. In other countries, the Respondent in the arbitral proceedings may seek a stay or injunction to prevent the arbitration from proceeding or the Claimant may seek an injunction to enforce the arbitration clause and to enjoin parallel national proceedings.

If a party applies to a national court for a ruling on a jurisdictional issue, the general rule is that the Tribunal will continue to have jurisdiction to proceed with the arbitration notwithstanding the national proceedings. This is reflected, for example in the UNCITRAL Model Law. The English Arbitration Act of 1996 adopts this approach with a twist. In Article 31 of the Act, the law expressly permits (but does not require) a Tribunal to stay proceedings pending jurisdictional proceedings under Article 32 of the Act. That section limits jurisdictional applications to the court without either the consent of the parties or of the Tribunal. Therefore, in England, it is the Tribunal that decides whether the court should hear the matter at the outset. The Swiss arbitration law appears to also take the approach that it should be the Tribunal in the first instance that decides jurisdictional issues. Only then can a party

---

① 参见王瀚、李广辉:《论仲裁庭自裁管辖权原则》,载《中国法学》2004年第2期。

bring annulment proceedings with respect to the Award on jurisdiction.①

尽管管辖权/管辖权原则已经成为国际商事仲裁管辖权方面的重要原则,但是在我国并没有得到法律的认可。我国《仲裁法》规定仲裁庭并没有对其自身管辖权的决定权,而是赋予仲裁机构决定仲裁庭管辖权以及法院决定权的优先性,这种做法带有鲜明的"中国特色",与管辖权/管辖权原则的内涵相差甚远。

首先,仲裁委员会对仲裁庭管辖权有决定权是我国独有的方式。它最早出现在中国国际经济贸易仲裁委员会和中国海事仲裁委员会1988年版的两个仲裁规则中:"仲裁委员会有权就仲裁协议的有效性和仲裁案件的管辖权作出决定",两机构在后来的规则中又进一步扩大了权力范围,对仲裁协议的有效与否也有权作出决定②,该规定最终被《仲裁法》认可。在国际商事仲裁领域,仲裁机构一般被视为服务性机构,其作用在于管理日常仲裁事务,为当事人进行仲裁提供便利。而我国仲裁法赋予仲裁委员会决定权,将本属于仲裁庭的裁决权部分分割给仲裁机构,这一做法极具行政色彩,有深刻的计划经济时代的痕迹。同时,它分割实体问题和管辖权问题的审理,增加了仲裁的成本,减损了仲裁的效率价值,也影响到我国仲裁机构在国际上的声誉,近年来受到学界越来越多的批判。

其次,法院对仲裁管辖权具有决定权与国际立法一致,但法院决定权具有优先性则是又一中国特色。法院对仲裁管辖权的优先性主要体现在,一方当事人请求仲裁委员会作出决定,而另一方请求法院作出裁定时,由人民法院裁定。1998年最高人民法院发布的《关于确认仲裁协议效力问题的批复》中对该问题作了进一步的解释:首先,当事人对仲裁协议的效力存有异议,一方当事人申请仲裁机构确认仲裁协议的效力,另一方当事人请求人民法院确认仲裁协议无效,如果仲裁机构先于人民法院接受申请并已作出决定,人民法院不予受理;如果仲裁机构接受申请后尚未作出决定,人民法院应予受理,同时通知仲裁机构中止仲裁。其次,一方当事人就合同纠纷或者其他财产纠纷申请仲裁,另一方当事人对仲裁协议的效力有异议,请求人民法院确认仲裁协议无效并就合同纠纷或者其他财产权益纠纷起诉的,人民法院受理后应当通知仲裁机构中止仲裁。人民法院依法作出仲裁协议有效或者无效的裁定后,应当将裁定书副本送达仲裁机构,由仲裁机构根据人民法院的裁定恢复仲裁或者撤销仲裁案件。人民法院依法对仲裁协议作出无效的裁定后,另一方当事人拒不应诉的,人民法院可以缺席判决;原受理仲裁申请的仲裁机构在人民法院确认仲裁协议无效后仍不撤销其仲

---

① See Michael W. Bühler & Thomas H. Webster, Handbook of ICC Arbitration: Commentary, Precedents, Materials, Sweet & Maxwell, 2005, p.101.
② 参见谢石松主编:《商事仲裁法学》,高等教育出版社2003年版,第211—212页。

裁案件的,不影响人民法院对案件的审理。根据上述决定,当事人只要在仲裁机构作出正式决定之前,不论是否已对该异议提出申请,人民法院都可以受理并作出裁决,这就容易给有意回避仲裁、拖延争议解决时间的一方当事人提供可乘之机,会严重影响仲裁程序的进行。当然,对于已经作出的关于管辖权的决定,不论是法院还是仲裁机构作出,都具有最终的效力。2006年施行的《最高人民法院关于适用〈中华人民共和国仲裁法〉若干问题的解释》首次明确规定,仲裁机构对仲裁协议的效力作出决定后,当事人向人民法院申请确认仲裁协议的效力或申请撤销仲裁机构的决定的,人民法院不予受理。

In the Chinese arbitration system, the principle of Competence-Competence has been "painted with Chinese characteristics"—the arbitral tribunal is denied ruling on its own jurisdiction; rather, it is determined by the arbitration commission and subject to judicial review by the people's court. There are three aspects on how to determine the arbitral jurisdiction in China. Firstly, either the arbitration commission or the people's court has the power to rule on the validity of the arbitration agreement. Secondly, the arbitral tribunal is not entitled to rule on such issues. Thirdly, if there exists a jurisdictional conflict between the arbitration commission and the people's court, the court prevails over the commission on determining the jurisdictional matter.

The law leaves other ambiguities. To begin with, it only considers the challenge to the validity of the arbitration agreement, but fails to mention the jurisdictional disputes arising from the existence of the agreement. The Chinese legislature used to share a similar ignorance on the issue of separability where the separable effect under a non-existent main contract is excluded. By analogy, it might be argued that the drafters had not thought carefully about the scope of the jurisdictional issue. Moreover, it fails to explain the jurisdictional challenge in cases of document-only arbitration. Pursuant to Art. 39, arbitration cases could be processed on the basis of the written submissions by the parties without the hearing held. The silence of the law leaves jurisdictional practice defective, until it was recently remedied by the CIETAC Rules that "where a case is to be decided on the basis of document only, such an objection shall be raised before the submission of the first substantive defense". [1]

由此可见,除了于1992年批准加入的《关于解决国家和他国国民民间投资争议的公约》和一些双边投资条约中有管辖权/管辖权原则的规定外,我国仲裁法实际上并没有承认仲裁庭有权决定自身的管辖权,而是将这一权力交给了法

---

[1] See Weixia Gu, Xianchu Zhang, The China-Style "Commission-Oriented" Competence on Arbitral Jurisdiction: Analysis of Chinese Adaptation into Globalization, Int. A. L. R., Vol. 9, No. 6, 2006, pp. 185—200.

院和仲裁机构。

附表1[①]

国家	决定权主体	仲裁过程中最终决定权主体	决定期间程序可否进行	撤销和不予执行程序是否仍审查管辖权问题(均为《纽约公约》缔约国)
荷兰	仲裁庭		可以	是
瑞士	仲裁庭		可以	是
德国	仲裁庭	法院	可以	是
瑞典	仲裁庭	法院	可以	是
日本	仲裁庭	法院	可以	是
英国	仲裁庭	法院	行使裁量权中止或应当事人要求中止	是
	符合一定条件,法院		可以	是
中国	仲裁机构		(CIETAC)不影响程序进行	是
	法院(如机构未作出决定)		通知中止	是

第四节 仲裁庭的权力(利)和义务

赋予仲裁庭一定的权力(利)是仲裁程序顺利进行的必要条件,同时为保证裁决的公正和效率,法律和仲裁规则还赋予仲裁庭相应的义务,并要求仲裁庭和仲裁员在违反义务时应承担相应的法律责任。

一、仲裁庭的权力(利)

仲裁庭区别于法院,其权力(利)和义务来源于当事人约定、法律规定和仲裁机构规定等多方面,而且各个方面的约定或规定具有重合性,下文三种区分并不具有严格的界限。

(一) 当事人授予的权力(利)——对特定事项进行审理并作出裁决

对特定事项进行审理既是仲裁庭应严格遵循的一项义务,同时也是当事人赋予仲裁庭的一项最主要的权力。作为一项权力,任何人或机关不得随意干涉,特别是法院和仲裁机构不得进行不适当的干预。由于该权力是当事人合意的结果,除非双方协商一致否定,否则任何一方不能主张否定仲裁庭享有该权力。

---

① 参见林一飞:《国际商事仲裁法律与实务》,中信出版社2005年版,第201页。

(二) 法律授予的权力(利)

1. 拒绝委任

仲裁员区别于法官,虽然很少有法律直接规定仲裁员有权拒绝委任,但法律也从来没有将接受委任作为仲裁员的一种强制义务,因此根据现代法律的一般原则,仲裁员有权拒绝委任是法律的应有之义。如果将仲裁员与当事人之间的关系视为合同关系,作为合同的一方当事人,仲裁员自然有权拒绝签订合同;如果将仲裁员与当事人之间的关系视为一种特定身份关系,这种特定身份是仲裁员在接受委任之后才具备的,所以仲裁员有权为这种特定身份作出选择。从实践的角度看,被选定的仲裁员很可能因为身体、家庭、工作等原因无法在规定的时间内完成仲裁审理,拒绝委任也是为了防止日后给仲裁造成不必要的麻烦。一般而言,仲裁员拒绝委任时并无义务向当事人或仲裁机构说明理由。

2. 确定仲裁管辖权

确定仲裁管辖权是现代商事仲裁中仲裁庭的一项重要权力,本章第三节已详细论述。

3. 发表异议

仲裁员有权在裁决中发表异议是法律赋予仲裁员为履行独立裁决义务的一项重要权利。我国《仲裁法》第54条规定:"裁决书应当写明仲裁请求、争议事实、裁决理由、裁决结果、仲裁费用的负担和裁决日期。当事人协议不愿写明争议事实和裁决理由的,可以不写。裁决书由仲裁员签名,加盖仲裁委员会印章。对裁决持不同意见的仲裁员,可以签名,也可不签名。"仲裁裁决是根据仲裁员个人意见作出的,而并非以仲裁庭整体的名义,所以持有异议的仲裁员有权保留其对案件的判断。虽然这种异议不影响裁决的效力,但是如果事后被查明生效裁决是由仲裁员故意或重大过失造成的,发表异议的仲裁员可能会因此而免责。

The process of decision leads to further questions when the award is written. In the view of some, an arbitrator has no right to prepare a written dissent from an award made by the majority. The ICC Commission studied this subject and issued a report in 1988. Although no nation's law was said to forbid arbitrator dissents, there was nevertheless a view that they should be discouraged. The rationale is threefold: A dissenting opinion would be contrary to the integrity of the arbitral process because it would (1) disclose something of the deliberative process of the tribunal; (2) tend to emphasize identification of a dissenter with the view of an appointing party; and (3) provide a basis for challenge to the award.[①]

---

① See James H. Carter, Rights & Obligations of the Arbitrator, Disp. Resol. J., pp.52—56.

4. 进行调解

仲裁庭的调解权是指在仲裁过程中,在双方当事人请求或同意下,仲裁庭具有主持双方当事人自愿协商、相互谅解,并达成协议的权利,这是我国仲裁庭特有的一项权利,国内主流观点对此基本持支持态度①。很多仲裁机构都将调解作为一个独立的程序,调解由专门组成的调解庭组成,与仲裁程序不存在交叉。如《瑞士联邦苏黎世商会调解与仲裁规则》第 3 条规定:"调解与仲裁基本是两种各自独立的程序。"第 14 条还规定:"在调解程序以后的仲裁程序中,只有经双方当事人和调解员本人同意,才得任命调解员为独任仲裁员、首席仲裁员或仲裁员。"有些仲裁专家对我国仲裁庭在调解中向当事人交换仲裁员对案件的看法持否定态度,认为这违反自然公正。②

(三) 仲裁规则授予的权力(利)

由于仲裁规则本身就是当事人选定的,所以仲裁规则授予的权力(利)实质上也属于当事人约定的权力(利),这里特别将其归为一类主要因为仲裁规则授予的权力(利)大部分属于仲裁程序中的权力(利)。

1. 决定程序事项

只要当事人没有相反的约定和不违反相关义务,仲裁庭有权采取任何合适的方式进行仲裁审理。仲裁庭有权决定开庭审理的程序,有权决定当事人陈述、辩论的顺序以及当事人举证质证的具体程序,以保证仲裁的顺利进行。另外,针对有些特殊情形,仲裁庭还有权对当事人撤回申请进行处理,有权责令当事人对某些费用提供担保,有权作出缺席裁决等。

There is no document proclaiming all these procedure rights, and some of them can be found in institution's rules. They are, nevertheless, inherent in the arbitrator's role. They arise from the interplay between some of the major factors that shape that role:(ⅰ) the arbitrator's quasi-judicial responsibilities, (ⅱ) the autonomy of the parties to agree on how their dispute is to be handled, and (ⅲ) the arbitrator's responsibility to the parties and to the process of arbitration for efficient results. They are all aspects of the arbitrator's inherent right to ask that those who review his or her conduct incorporate in the ethical standards a "rule of reasonableness" permitting the arbitrator to exercise responsible, sound judgment.③

2. 证据的获取和认定

仲裁庭对证据的获取和认定直接决定着案件的审理,关系到仲裁庭对当事

---

① 参见王生长:《仲裁与调解相结合的理论与实务》,法律出版社 2001 年版,第 1 页。
② 参见杨良宜:《国际商务和海事仲裁》,大连海运学院出版社 1994 年版,第 8—9 页。
③ See James H. Carter, Rights & Obligations of the Arbitrator, Disp. Resol. J., pp.52—56.

人权利义务关系的认定。仲裁庭的该项权力主要包括三个方面:一是有权要求当事人在规定期限内提供证据;二是仲裁庭有权指定专家,获取专家证据;三是仲裁庭在特定情况下有权自行收集证据,有权确定证据的可采性、相关性、实质性和重要性。

3. 获得报酬

就仲裁员个人而言,获得仲裁报酬是其最主要的权利。

The idea that an arbitrator should be entitled to a fee would have been a shocking one for our ancestors; it would have been contrary to the very spirit of arbitration, as this institution was thought of before the end of the 19th century. The arbitrator, a friend of the parties or a person of quality, would have felt offended if he had been offered a fee. Now, the arbitration, on this point as on many others, differs profoundly from the traditional institution whose name it perpetuates. The same kind of relation does not exist anymore; the arbitrator is now in general a person alien to the parties and the same disinterestedness cannot be expected of him as in the past. Is an arbitrator entitled to claim a fee? This question is to be answered in the affirmative by a number of laws, where due account has been taken of the transformation undergone by arbitration in modern times. Such is the case for example in Italy, Japan, the Netherlands, and also in Germany.[①]

In the vast majority of cases, the amount to be paid the arbitrators, or at least the machinery for establishing this amount, will be agreed in advance between the parties and the arbitrators. Four broad approaches to the fixing of fees and expenses may be adopted:[②]

(1) The parties may agree a fixed fee with the arbitrators. This method is comparatively uncommon where complex issues are at stake, as it may be difficult at the outset to determine how long the arbitration is to last, although in small arbitrations the sum is agreed on the basis that resolution will be completed within a specific time. If a fixed fee is agreed upon, and the arbitrators have underestimated the time which the arbitration actually takes, they cannot subsequently insist upon a new fixed fee.

(2) The fee may be based on an hourly or daily rate. This would seem to be the most common method of determining the sums involved.

---

① See René David, Arbitration in International Trade, Kluwer Law and Taxation Publishers, 1985, p. 271.
② See Robert Merkin, Arbitration Law, LLP, 2004, p.399.

(3) The fee may be based on a proportion of the amount awarded.

(4) The parties may agree that the fee is to be determined by an arbitral institution or body.

二、仲裁庭的义务

(一) 当事人设定的义务

1. 对特定事项进行审理并作出裁决

如前所述,这是当事人授予仲裁庭最基本的权力,也是对仲裁庭设定的最根本的义务,通常是当事人在仲裁协议中对仲裁庭设定的最明确的义务。该义务要求仲裁庭做到:首先,必须对当事人约定的特定争议事项进行审理并作出仲裁裁决,这是当事人将争议提交仲裁的根本目的,同时也是仲裁庭组庭的根本目的;其次,不得对当事人约定以外的争议事项进行仲裁,这是由仲裁的本质决定的。仲裁庭在审理案件之前,首先必须确定其审理范围,大部分机构仲裁中,都要求仲裁庭书面列出具体的审理事项,并允许当事人提出异议。

2. 在约定的仲裁地点进行仲裁

当事人可以选择任何地点进行仲裁是仲裁的一大特点,仲裁庭有义务在当事人约定的地点进行仲裁程序。在仲裁协议中,一般对仲裁地有明确约定(因为仲裁地往往决定了仲裁裁决的国籍),但这并不意味着仲裁员只要在仲裁地进行仲裁即可。仲裁审理地区别于仲裁地,其范围远比仲裁地宽泛。如当事人约定 A 地为仲裁地,根据实际情况,仲裁可以在 B 地或多个地点甚至公海等进行。仲裁庭有义务根据当事人的临时指示,在任何地点审理争议事项。

3. 在约定时间内进行仲裁

当事人通过约定仲裁的审理时间以满足其对争议解决效率的要求是选择仲裁的一个重要因素,仲裁庭有义务严格遵守并采取措施确保仲裁程序在约定时间内进行。

The parties are free to impose upon the arbitrators whatever time limits the parties think appropriate for the completion of the arbitration proceedings and the making of an award. Express provisions are of three types. First, the arbitrators may be under duty to adhere to an agreed timetable. The second type of provision imposes a fixed period on the arbitrators within which they must make their award. The third type of provision is more general, and simply requires the arbitrators to proceed with the reference as speedily as they can, failing which the agreed procedure may provide an appropriate remedy.①

---

① See Robert Merkin, Arbitration Law, LLP, 2004, p.395.

(二) 法律规定的义务

1. 中立

仲裁界有句名言:"The arbitration is only as good as its arbitrators",因此仲裁员素质关系着价值目标的实现。仲裁员的中立义务是法律对仲裁员素质的最基本要求,只有在解决纠纷过程中保持中立地位,仲裁才能取信于当事人,裁决才能得到法院的支持。不论国籍、种族、背景等,仲裁员都应该平等公允地对待当事人。菲律宾的仲裁法明确规定,禁止有偏袒的仲裁员进行仲裁。中立义务是一个十分原则的规定,对中立义务的履行内容、方式等各国的规定往往不同,而且多将这些具体规定交给仲裁机构和当事人来设置。如在开庭审理时,仲裁员不得出现倾向性,应注意提问的方式,并给予当事人平等的提供材料和发表意见的机会。

There is no doubt that an arbitrator owes a duty to act impartially, and that this duty is to some degree legally enforceable. If the arbitrator has shown partially in making his award, this is a ground for setting it aside. If the lack of fairness is displayed in the course of the reference itself, the arbitrator's connection with the reference can be severed. The court would have little difficulty in ensuring that the arbitrator receives no further remuneration, and is required to hand back whatever he had already been paid. Furthermore, if the party goes so far as to complain that the partiality results from corruption or improper collusion with his opponent, he should join the arbitrator as respondent to any application to set aside the award.[①]

2. 不得利用优势地位谋私

仲裁员对仲裁的审理和裁决具有决定作用,拥有裁判者的强势地位,具备以权谋私的条件。为保持仲裁员的廉洁,增强公众对仲裁制度的信心,各国强行法都严令禁止仲裁员利用其仲裁的优势地位为自己谋取不正当利益,对这种行为的处罚也最为严重,甚至会处以刑罚。

3. 谨慎注意

国际商事仲裁界有观点认为,仲裁员是专业人员,与医生、审计员、建筑师和工程师一样,应当对其所从事的专业工作尽格外谨慎的义务,符合职业上的专业注意标准,如果他没有用适当的技术和谨慎完成专业工作而对当事人造成损害的,可能被认定承担损害赔偿责任。[②] 仲裁员谨慎从事仲裁工作是一种道德义务自不必说,但它是否同时也是一种法律义务则存在争议,这个问题涉及仲裁员

---

① See Sir Michael J. Mustill & Stewart C. Boyd, Q. C., Commercial Arbitration, 2nd ed., Butterworths, 1989, pp.231—232.

② 参见〔英〕艾伦·雷德芬、马丁·亨特等:《国际商事仲裁法律与实践》,林一飞、宋连斌译,北京大学出版社2005年版,第256页。

与当事人关系的核心。主张责任豁免的,注意义务则被认为是道德义务,而主张责任承担的,该义务则是一种法律义务。

There are three situations in which a party may be entitled to limited redress from an arbitrator who has acted carelessly.

(1) The award may be set aside if the arbitrator admits a mistake. The setting aside of the award destroys both the award of fees which it contains and the right to remuneration, and hence enables the party to recover any sums which he has paid taking up the award.

(2) A series of glaring errors committed by the arbitrator in the course of the reference might perhaps be regarded as a reason for granting leave to revoke the authority of the arbitrator since it might justify the inference that he is liable to make further mistakes during the remainder of the reference.

(3) There may just be room for an argument that even in cases where the consideration cannot be said to have totally failed, the mishandling of the reference may form a partial defense to an arbitrator's claim for fees, and a ground for recovering at least part of any that have been paid.[①]

(三) 仲裁规则规定的义务

1. 信息披露

披露信息是仲裁员履行法律规定的中立义务中的一个重要的程序义务。虽然很多国家也在立法中将信息披露义务作为一种强行法规范,法国法院甚至在判决中创造性地将披露义务作为国际仲裁中直接使用的规则[②],但是披露信息的具体行为方式更多地体现在各个仲裁机构的仲裁规则中,如《联合国国际贸易法委员会仲裁规则》第 9 条、《WIPO 快速仲裁规则》第 22 条第 2 款、《美国仲裁协会国际仲裁规则》第 19 条等。

仲裁员信息披露义务在时间上具有持续性的特点,仲裁员在接受任命前直至作出仲裁裁决的整个仲裁过程中,都有义务披露所发现的任何应予披露的信息。在披露方式上,很多仲裁规则都明确规定仲裁员应采用书面方式向所有当事人和仲裁庭披露有关信息。

The IBA (the International Bar Association) adopts a subjective test ("in the eyes of the parties") with respect to disclosure, provides as follows:

"(a) If facts or circumstances exist that may, in the eyes of the parties, give

---

① See Sir Michael J. Mustill & Stewart C. Boyd, Q. C., Commercial Arbitration, 2nd ed., Butterworths, 1989, pp. 229—230.

② 参见张圣翠:《论国际商事仲裁员披露义务规则》,载《上海财经大学学报》2007 年第 3 期。

rise to doubts as to the arbitrator's impartiality or independence, the arbitrator shall disclose such facts or circumstances to the parties, the arbitration institution or other appointing authority (if any, and if so required by the applicable institutional rules) and to the co-arbitrators, if any, prior to accepting his or her appointment or, if thereafter, as soon as he or she learns about them.

(b) It follows from General Standards 1 and 2 (a) that an arbitrator who has made a disclosure considers himself or herself to be impartial and independent of the parties despite the disclosed facts and therefore capable of performing his or her duties as arbitrator. Otherwise, he or she would have declined the nomination or appointment at the outset or resigned.

(c) Any doubt as to whether an arbitrator should disclose certain facts or circumstances should be resolved in favor of disclosure."

2. 关联关系人不得担任仲裁员

仲裁员如果与所审理的案件有利害关系,很可能会影响到仲裁的公正裁决,即使仲裁员保持公正中立,仍然会受到当事人对裁决的质疑,影响仲裁的公信力。因此,几乎所有的仲裁机构都要求与案件有利害关系的人不得担任该案件的仲裁员。该义务与当事人申请仲裁员回避的权利相对。但何谓有"利害关系",在实践中有不同的认定,也给当事人和仲裁员造成一定的困惑。

With respect to the best practices, the International Bar Association has published the IBA Guideline on Conflict of Interest in International Arbitration in 2004. It gives the practical examples of the types of relationships. The Red List is a checklist of examples where the relationship in general does give rise to issues as to the arbitrator's impartiality and independence. It is divided into two parts. The Non-Waivable Red List, where the relationship should preclude the person from acting as an arbitrator, and the Waivable Red List, where there is generally an issue as to the arbitrator's impartiality and independence, but where the parties may waive the objection.

The Non-Waivable Red List is as follows:

"1.1 There is an identity between a party and the arbitrator, or the arbitrator is a legal representative of an entity that is a party in the arbitration.

1.2 The arbitrator is manager, director or member of the supervisory board, or has a similar controlling influence on one of the parties.

1.3 The arbitrator has a significant financial interest in one of the parties or the outcome of the case.

1.4 the arbitrator regularly advises the appointing party or an affiliate of the appointing party, and the arbitrator or his /her firm derives a significant financial income therefrom."

The Waivable Red List is as follows:

"2.1 Relationship of the arbitrator to the dispute...

2.2 Arbitrator's direct or indirect interest in the dispute...

2.3 Arbitrator's relationship with the parties or counsel..."

3. 独立裁决

仲裁员依据法律、合同,根据自己的良心独立裁决是仲裁公正的最重要保证,仲裁员在裁决案件时不应受到仲裁机关、其他仲裁庭成员及其他任何人的影响。仲裁员绝对不能将裁决委托他人代为完成,也不得因为压力、威慑等原因影响裁决制作。独立是仲裁员应具备的最基本的素质,独立作出裁决则是这种素质的主要表现之一。

4. 保密

仲裁的不公开进行是当事人选择仲裁的一个重要原因,仲裁员应当对整个仲裁过程与裁决结果承担保密义务,具体包括仲裁程序不公开、评议不公开、仲裁裁决不公开、仲裁程序获得的或由当事人提供的涉及当事人营业秘密或其他秘密资讯的文件或证据不公开。仲裁员不得向外界透露上述不得公开的信息、文件等,并且对裁决内容在正式送达当事人之前亦应保守秘密。

三、仲裁员责任

(一) 仲裁员与当事人的关系

仲裁员与当事人之间的关系是仲裁员责任理论,特别是民事责任理论的前提。关于仲裁员责任理论的争论,本质上就是由对仲裁员和当事人关系认识的分歧造成的。

1. 合同说

合同说是一种比较传统的学说,它认为仲裁员与当事人之间存在着合同关系,仲裁员接受当事人的指定,提供专业知识解决争议,并在作出仲裁裁决后接受报酬,双方有着对价支付关系,所以是一种合同。至于属何种性质的合同还存在着委托合同说、雇佣合同说、承揽合同说和特殊合同说等观点。

Under the contract theory, arbitrators are experts whose liability should be based upon the terms of their appointment agreement with the parties. The precise nature of the contract between the parties and the arbitrators is not yet settled. Arbitrators are free to create their own express contract with the parties setting out their rights, responsibilities, and liabilities regarding the arbitration. In some countries, primarily Islamic, arbitrators must accept their appointment in writing; but it is unclear whether this "acceptance" creates a distinct contract between the parties and the arbitrators. Unfortunately, as arbitrators do not regularly enter into a separate contract with the parties for the provision of arbitral services, a different method is necessary to determine the terms and conditions.

Under a second approach, by consenting to act as an arbitrator, an individual impliedly becomes a third party to the parties' original arbitration agreement. For example, the Norjarl v. Hyundai court explained that the "arbitration agreement is a bilateral contract between the parties to the main contract. On appointment the arbitrator becomes a third party to the arbitration agreement which becomes a trilateral contract."① At least one South African court holds that when two persons ask a third to arbitrate a dispute between them, a contractual mandate exists between the disputants and the arbitrator. This perspective is also accepted in some Islamic law countries. For example, in Lebanon and Yemen, an arbitrator becomes a party to the agreement to arbitrate and has a contractual relationship with the parties that may result in contractual liability.

当然合同说也有一些无法解决的问题,实践中,在组成仲裁庭时,仲裁员与当事人之间不一定有明确的意思表示过程,仲裁员的很多义务由国家强行法规定,很难说是他们合意的结果。因此也有观点认为仲裁庭与当事人是准合同关系,虽然当事人不具备合同成立的条件,不是严格意义上的合同关系,但是仲裁员在提供专业服务的时候预期因此会获得报酬,而当事人也知道其应当支付报酬,符合英美合同法上的偿还请求权的构成要件。但这种学说只解决了仲裁员对当事人的费用请求权问题,对其他问题并没有提出解决方案,因此,其影响也远没有合同说大。

2. 特定身份说

特定身份说主张仲裁员一旦接受指定,即以准司法官的身份执行职务,对当事人有巨大的影响力,除了双方当事人同意或法院命令外,仲裁员的职权将持续到仲裁终了之时。该职权是基于当事人对特定仲裁员人格的信任,具有严格的人身性。仲裁员的权力(利)义务均来自其特定身份,而非当事人约定。仲裁员作为特殊的专业人员,履行着依法裁判的职责,与法官的作用相似。唐纳森法官甚至对仲裁员与法官的职能不作区分,他说:"法院(法官)与仲裁员的业务相同,他们都是在执行法律。二者之间的唯一区别是:法院在公共领域执法,而仲裁员在私营工业领域执法。"②

---

① Norjarl v. Hyundai, [1991] 1 Lloyd's Rep., p.536.
② 转引自〔英〕施米托夫:《国际贸易法文选》,赵秀文译,中国大百科全书出版社 1993 年版,第 667 页。

(二) 仲裁员的民事责任

仲裁员的民事责任是仲裁员责任制度的核心,由于仲裁理论和实践对仲裁员法律地位认识的分歧,各国仲裁法在仲裁员是否要承担民事责任及如何承担等方面的规定差异较大,围绕仲裁员能否享受责任豁免问题形成了责任豁免理论、责任承担理论和有限豁免理论三大观点。

1. 责任豁免理论

责任豁免理论的起点来自于特定身份说,它将法官的司法豁免理论扩大至仲裁员,将仲裁程序视为一种"准司法"程序。该理论主要被英美普通法国家所接受,因此当事人不能根据普通法对仲裁员给当事人造成损害的不适当行为提起诉讼,要求其承担民事责任。由于根据该理论,仲裁员承担的责任为侵权责任,即只有在故意或重大过失情况下才承担责任,而且当事人对此要承担相当的举证责任,因此胜诉的可能性很小,特别在美国,仲裁员免受当事人追诉几乎是绝对的。[1]

Arbitral immunity stems from judicial immunity. In brief, the rule is that judges of courts of record are not liable for damages for their decisions. The rule's purposes are to ensure finality of judicial decisions, preserve judicial independence, and maintain confidence in the judicial system. An arbitrator's decision-making in a contract dispute is, without doubt, functionally comparable to that of a judge. Like a judge, an arbitrator must render an impartial decision based on evidence and applicable interpretive principles. Arbitral immunity cases follow two policy strands, one common to both judges and arbitrators (finality and independence), the other peculiar to arbitrators (which for lack of a better term we call "recruitment"). Typical of the first strand is Fong v. American Airlines, "the integrity of the arbitral process is best preserved by recognizing the arbitrators as independent decision-makers who have no obligation to defend themselves in a reviewing court."[2] The second strand reflects significant distinctions between arbitrators and judges. A risk of liability in extreme circumstances would not deter many applicants for the judiciary, but it might well limit the number of those willing to serve as arbitrators.

Arbitral immunity thus rests on the following bases: (1) Some quasi-judicial immunity for arbitrators is essential to guarantee finality to their awards, to protect their independence and impartiality, and to encourage their recruitment. (2) This

---

[1] See Alan Redfern & Martin Hunter, Law and Practice of International Commercial Arbitration, 2nd ed., Sweet & Maxwell, 1991, p.266.

[2] 431 F. Supp. 1340, 1343—1344 (N.D. Cal. 1977).

immunity applies only to an arbitrator's quasi-judicial, or "arbitral" acts. (3) Arbitral immunity extends only to acts performed in the course of a dispute over which the arbitrator arguably has jurisdiction. (4) The arbitrator's immunity varies with the nature of the case.①

2. 责任承担理论

责任承担理论的起点来自于合同说,即仲裁员与当事人之间是一种契约关系,仲裁员主要是根据与当事人的约定履行契约上的义务,如果由于其自身的故意或过失给当事人造成损害,则要对当事人承担违约责任。这种契约性责任主要包括专业小心责任和公正责任。持该理论的学者还提出一些反对责任豁免的理由:第一,商事仲裁程序毕竟是不同于诉讼的"准司法"程序,仲裁员与法官存在本质区别;第二,为当事人在仲裁中设立的权利救济程序只是对损害未实际发生时的补救措施,一旦仲裁员的行为造成实际的损害发生,这些措施不能补偿当事人的损失;第三,那种认为确立仲裁员责任制度会妨碍商事仲裁发展的想法只是一种主观推断。②

The contractual approach to liability is usually associated with civil law countries, and some Islamic countries. In many civil law jurisdictions, arbitrators are merely professionals whose liability is determined by the general principles of contractual liability contained within the civil code. This approach usually bases liability on the terms of appointment rather than the functions an arbitrator performs. Countries such as Italy, Austria, and Spain have express provisions for liability, while the Netherlands, France, Poland, and Germany have implied ones. In general, however, the contract between the parties and the arbitrator is subject to private law and can be characterized as a mandate with service elements or a quasi mandate in exchange for the remuneration of the arbitrator. Although German law contains no express statute creating liability, it bases arbitrator liability on contract. German law implies general terms of liability. However, different types of contracts create different obligations, so proper categorization of the receptum arbitri is crucial. In particular, if an arbitrator's appointment contract is a mandate with service elements, the arbitrator "is bound to perform the service promised" and is subject to personal obligations. If the receptum arbitri is a "contract for works," an arbitrator would have different obligations. It is probably not a "works" contract, as these usually involve parties who wish to obtain a specific result, whereas the results of a

---

① See Dennis R. Nolan & Roger I. Abrams, Arbitral Immunity, 11 Indus. Rel. L. J., p.228.
② 参见谢石松主编:《商事仲裁法学》,高等教育出版社2003年版,第192—193页。

service contract are not precisely known before but result from the obligor's personal effort and skills. The receptum arbitri is probably a mandatory service contract, and even German arbitration law discusses arbitral responsibilities in terms of a "mandate." For Islamic countries, arbitrators also may be bound by the terms of the parties' arbitration agreement. Particularly because of the influence of the civil law tradition on Islamic law, it is likely that liability can be based upon contract. However, because of the strong religious tradition, it is also necessary to consider the Qur'an and the Shari'a to determine liability. Although there is no general theory of contract law, the Qur'anic saying, "Fulfill your Obligations," is the fundamental principle that governs contracts and could create a basis for arbitrator liability. At the same time, "service contracts [are] of a dubious nature, [and] are also outlawed on the basis of illegal Mahall [subject matter] and Sabab [motivating cause]." Ultimately, however, it is necessary to consult the Qur'an, the Shari'a, and the Code of the relevant country before making a final determination.①

3. 有限豁免理论

面对普通法系与大陆法系关于仲裁员责任豁免的重大分歧,有学者为缓和此种矛盾,提出了"有限的仲裁员责任豁免理论"。其基本观点是:仲裁员仅在一定的范围内享有责任豁免,如果仲裁员故意或重大过失导致未能履行其接受指定时当事人所赋予的职责,则必须为其不当行为给当事人造成的损失承担法律责任。② 这种观点也慢慢地被一些国家接受。如奥地利《民事诉讼法典》第584条规定,如果仲裁员未履行其在接受任命时所承担的职责或未在适当的时间里履行其职责,则要为由此给当事人造成的损失承担责任。一向坚持"豁免理论"的英国在《1996年仲裁法》中也作了变动,规定在一些情况下仲裁员不能享受豁免。有限豁免理论融合了前面两种理论的特点,其优越性自不必说,但该理论也存在缺陷,主要在于仲裁员豁免的范围不够明确,由于界限的模糊性导致理论的真正作用十分有限,两大法系的博弈仍在继续。

The issue of an arbitrator's immunity has received increased attention, and the scope of arbitrator immunity is currently a controversial issue. Because an arbitrator's potential liability plays a key role in the effective use of arbitration, commentators have suggested addressing this issue, but have not yet proposed specific statutory or regulatory solutions. Instead, different countries and arbitral institutions deal with this

---

① See Susan D. Franck, The Liablity of International Arbitrators: A Comparative Analysis and Proposal for Qualified Immunity, 20 N. Y. L. Sch. J. Int'l & Comp. L. 1.
② 参见谢石松主编:《商事仲裁法学》,高等教育出版社2003年版,第193页。

issue in a myriad of ways, and even the watershed UNCITRAL Model Law on International Arbitration does not contain any provision regarding the immunity of arbitrators. Ultimately, there is a startling lack of international harmonization regarding the scope of liability for international arbitrators.①

4. 中国实践

我国《仲裁法》对仲裁员民事责任的规定不够明确,只在第38条笼统规定:"仲裁员有本法第三十四条第四项规定的情形(私自会见当事人、代理人,或者接受当事人、代理人的请客送礼的——引者注),情节严重的,或者有本法第五十八条第六项规定的情形的(仲裁员在仲裁该案时有索贿受贿,徇私舞弊,枉法裁决行为的——引者注),应当依法承担法律责任,……"至于是何种责任,《仲裁法》并没有明说,学界对此争议也较大。仲裁员民事责任制度在我国基本属于空白,对于仲裁员要不要承担民事责任问题,存在两种对立观点:有人认为应在一定程度上、一定范围内承认仲裁员的民事责任,这种观点与有限豁免理论比较接近②;还有人认为,就目前我国的现状而言,不宜要求仲裁员承担民事责任③。我国主流观点认为,一方面为了保证仲裁员的独立性,可以对仲裁员在执行准司法职务过程中的行为予以豁免;另一方面,为了保证仲裁员的公正性,这种豁免只限于仲裁员的一般过失行为。④

(三) 仲裁员的刑事责任

与仲裁员在民事责任承担上的巨大争议不同,世界上各主要国家对仲裁员的严重违法行为都课以刑事责任。比如《德国刑法典》第331—340条就将仲裁员置于与法官相同的地位,规制其滥用职权、枉法裁判行为;《瑞士联邦刑法》(2003年修订)第322条和《法国刑法典》第439-9条等都有严格的刑事责任规定。美国法学会在其起草的《示范刑法典》中将仲裁员的此类行为归在商业贿赂中,规定仲裁员明知违反或者同意违反因其身份而负有的忠实职责,索要、收受或者同意收受任何利益的,成立轻罪。⑤

仲裁员枉法裁决行为所侵犯的客体已经不再单纯是当事人的利益,最主要是危害了整个仲裁制度的公正性,影响了人们对仲裁制度的信心,而作为民间的争端解决机制,当事人的信任是仲裁存在的唯一基础。所以,建立严格的刑事责任制度来规制仲裁员的枉法裁决行为是必要且必需的。与民事责任制度相同,

---

① See Susan D. Franck, The Liablity of International Arbitrators: A Comparative Analysis and Proposal for Qualified Immunity, 20 N. Y. L. Sch. J. Int'l & Comp. L. 1.
② 参见黄进主编:《国际私法与国际商事仲裁》,武汉大学出版社1994年版,第114页。
③ 参见陈敏:《仲裁员的行为规范》,载《仲裁与法律通讯》1994年第3期。
④ 参见谢石松主编:《商事仲裁法学》,高等教育出版社2003年版,第195页。
⑤ 参见该法第224.8条(1)(e)。转引自美国法学会编:《美国模范刑法典及其评注》,刘仁文、王祎等译,法律出版社2005年版,第171页。

我国《仲裁法》和其他相关法律对仲裁员的刑事责任保持了沉默,直到2006年《刑法修正案(六)》的出台。《刑法修正案(六)》在第20条中规定:"依法承担仲裁职责的人员,在仲裁活动中故意违背事实和法律作枉法裁决,情节严重的,处三年以下有期徒刑或者拘役;情节特别严重的,处三年以上七年以下有期徒刑。"

案例

1. MBNA America Bank N. A. v. Credit, 281 Kan. 655, 132 P.3d 898 (2006)

Facts

MBNA initiated an arbitration proceeding under the Code of Procedure of the National Arbitration Forum (NAF) against Loretta K. Credit, in which it sought to recover an alleged credit card debt of more than $21,000. Credit did not participate in the arbitration proceeding, other than to write a letter to the arbitrator objecting that she had not agreed to arbitrate. Nor did she seek to enjoin the arbitration proceeding. Likewise, MBNA did not petition a court to compel Credit to arbitrate. Instead, it proceeded with the arbitration in Credit's absence—i. e., on an ex parte basis.

On Sept. 7, 2004, the arbitrator ruled in favor of MBNA and awarded it $21,094.74. In the award, the arbitrator found that "the Parties entered into an agreement providing that this matter shall be resolved through binding arbitration." The award included a certificate of service, signed by the director of arbitration for the NAF, which provided as follows:

This award was duly entered and the Forum hereby certifies that a copy of this Award was sent by first class mail postage prepaid to the parties at the above referenced addresses on this date.

The record contained no evidence that Credit actually received the award. At oral argument, she stated that the address listed on the award was her correct address but that she did not know if she had ever received the award.

MBNA moved to confirm the award at the end of December 2004. It did not file a copy of the arbitration agreement with its motion. In response, Credit filed a pro se motion to vacate the award, arguing that she had never agreed to arbitrate the dispute. MBNA challenged the motion as untimely because it was filed more than 90 days after the date shown on the certificate of service. The district court nonetheless vacated the award, finding that "there is no existing agreement between the parties to arbitrate and therefore the award entered against Defendant is null and void."

The Kansas Supreme Court Decision:

The Kansas Supreme Court affirmed. It identified one controlling question: "Did Credit's effort to thwart confirmation of the award come too late? If so, the district court did not have authority to vacate the award. If not, the district court had the authority it needed to enter its rulings." In answering that question, the Court indicated that it "evaluated both federal and state law as well as National Arbitration Forum rules when relevant."

The Court's analysis proceeded in four steps. The first two steps addressed the timeliness issue, and the last two steps addressed the correctness of the district court's rulings on MBNA's motion to confirm and Credit's motion to vacate.

The Court stated that MBNA could not "rely on Credit's tardiness in challenging the award" because she denied that she had agreed to arbitrate. There is authority supporting that proposition, although the Court does not cite it.

Because the arbitration award was not served on Credit as required by the Kansas Uniform Arbitration Act (KUAA), the Court held that the time for filing a motion to vacate the award never began to run. As a result, Credit's motion to vacate was not untimely. The Court found service flawed in two respects under the KUAA.

First, the certificate of service recited that the NAF (rather than the arbitrator) had served the award. Second, the award was served by regular mail rather than by certified mail or personal service. Of course, service of the award appears to comply with the NAF Code of Procedure, which provides that the "Forum shall serve a copy of the Award upon all Parties or their Representatives or as directed by any Party" using "the postal service of the United States or any country, or ... a reliable private service, or ... facsimile, e-mail, electronic, or computer transmission." Because the KUAA requirements for service apply only when the parties have not agreed otherwise, service appeared improper to the Court only because of the dispute over the existence of an arbitration agreement (compounded by MBNA's inexplicable failure to attach the arbitration agreement to its motion to confirm the award).

Third, the Court concluded that the district court properly denied MBNA's motion to confirm. According to the Court, MBNA's failure to attach a copy of the arbitration agreement to its motion "violated the Federal Arbitration Act" and "alone would have justified the district court in its decision to deny MBNA's motion to confirm the award." The Court does not suggest, however, that the KUAA contains such a requirement.

Fourth, the Court held that the district court properly vacated the award. The fact that a party did not agree to arbitrate is a ground for vacating an award under both the KUAA (because "[t]here was no arbitration agreement") and the FAA (because "the arbitrators exceeded their powers"). The Court emphasized that "MBNA made no legally sufficient response" to Credit's contention that she had not agreed to arbitrate.

Questions

What's the problem with the court's decision? What rule did the court violate in international arbitration?

2. Oberlandesgericht (Bremen) (2 Sch 2/2006) (Unreported, May 24, 2006) (Germany)

Facts

The contract provided for dispute settlement by arbitration under the Arbitration Rules of the Construction Industry ("SGO Bau"). In accordance with those Rules the claimant initiated arbitration proceedings in September 2005 and nominated arbitrator X. After the respondent nominated arbitrator Y from Munich, the claimant referred to information taken from the JUVE handbook on German business law firms and reminded Y that in accordance with applicable Arbitration Rules he was obliged to disclose that he or his law firm had served as counsel to the respondent on several occasions. The claimant further stated that since the respondent was an important client with a considerable turnover it raised doubts as to the neutrality and objectivity of Y.

Y replied that he also represented other major construction companies against the respondent in other cases as counsel. He added that he did not know the project in dispute and the people involved. In his view it was normal that well-known attorneys specialising in construction law dealt regularly with major construction companies.

The claimant then challenged Y in a written statement. Y wrote back to the claimant:"Certainly I respect your dedicated but also somewhat passionate approach which, however, will not be helpful in this case". Y then wrote to X, the arbitrator appointed by the claimant, stating inter alia: "I am somewhat surprised by the approach adopted by the claimant and believe that we are dealing with a young colleague who does not have a long experience with arbitration ... Maybe you will succeed to convince him that such an overeager approach will not be helpful."

After the constitution of the arbitral tribunal the claimant submitted a written challenge mentioning that Y represented the respondent in three pending and finalised cases. He also stressed the fact that Y did not disclose his working relationship with the respondent on his own initiative, as required by a respective section of the applicable arbitration rules. Y replied that he had not represented the Bremen branch of the respondent which was party to the dispute. He mentioned that his law firm worked as counsel for several well-known construction companies and also represented, especially from its offices in Düsseldorf, Berlin and Hamburg, other companies against the respondent. He further added that he had no connection to the people involved in the dispute.

The Decision of the Arbitral Tribunal:

The arbitral tribunal rejected the challenge as unfounded. It held that the mere existence of a relationship between the respondent and its arbitrator was not sufficient for a challenge. The latter may only succeed if the relationship is in its kind, scope and content of such a nature that it raises doubts as to the arbitrator's independence and impartiality. In the tribunal's view a different standard had to be applied in this respect to arbitrators on the one hand and court judges on the other hand, so that the case law dealing with challenges of judges was of limited relevance. The tribunal considered it to be in the nature of arbitration that the parties appoint someone as arbitrator whom they already know from professional activities. Therefore only a very intensive connection of Y with "his" party could qualify for a successful challenge. According to the tribunal there was not such an intensive connection in this case as the respondent was a company of such size operating internationally, that it used the services of various law firms. Y was not a "regular counsel" for the respondent and in particular had no connection to the Bremen branch of respondent involved in the dispute.

Questions

(1) If the challenges to arbitrations have been dismissed, how should the claimant do?

(2) Do you agree with the arbitral awards renderred by the arbitral tribunal and why?

阅读材料

Practising Law Institute Corporate Law and Practice Course Handbook Series
PLI Order No. B4-7147 July-August, 1996
How to Select Arbitrators in Securities Arbitration
Theodore G. Eppenstein, Madelaine Eppenstein

...

Investigation of Arbitrators:

... Counsel should pose additional questions to the panelists concerning many different types of information, and should consider requesting information such as:

1) gaps in the employment history of the arbitrator;

2) specific information about the arbitrator's duties at various jobs;

3) specific questions about whether the arbitrator has any affiliation with the respondent broker/dealer, or its counsel. If the arbitrator is an attorney, he must be asked whether or not the arbitrator or the law firm who employs the arbitrator has represented the respondent broker/dealer before, and if so, identification of all the matters represented should be disclosed;

4) a list of potential witnesses within the broker/dealer, especially all those who have knowledge of the facts, should be disclosed by counsel and the arbitrator should be requested to disclose any knowledge or association with those individuals;

5) the names of the attorneys for the parties and their law firms should be included in this list. Counsel should ask whether the respondent's attorney has appeared before the arbitrator, information about the case including the identification of the opposing party, and how the arbitrator ruled in that case;

6) the arbitrator training and experience of each nominee;

7) other related information based on the disclosures of the panelist...

Check the Arbitrator's Decisional Records:

Obtaining the prior decisions of the proposed arbitrators is useful in determining whether a challenge for cause or a peremptory challenge is warranted... The award summary sheet for the arbitrator provides a synopsis of all the cases which went to award and includes the forum, case number, type of case (customer vs. broker/dealer as opposed to employee vs. broker/dealer), the names of the parties, the three arbitrators involved, the amount of both the compensatory demand and the award, and SAC's remarks on particular decisions. With summaries in hand, you will have an overview of the types of cases heard by the arbitrators and the frequency of when and where the arbitrator has sat through award. Settled cases are not reported...

Claimant's Counsel Can Be a Valuable Resource:

You may find you are familiar with counsel who has represented claimants in prior cases in which a proposed panelist rendered an award. This presents a great appeared before the same arbitrator who is up for nomination. Among the issues that you want to discuss are:

1) the attorney's overall impression of the arbitrator;

2) the arbitrator's demeanor during the case;

3) the arbitrator's attentiveness;

4) whether the arbitrator interrupted opening statements;

5) whether the arbitrator was overly friendly towards the respondents during the hearings;

6) whether the arbitrator conducted his own cross-examination of the claimant, claimant's expert or the broker;

7) whether the rulings at the preliminary hearing on discovery matters were fair to both parties;

8) whether the arbitrator appeared evenhanded in the way discovery decisions were rendered;

9) whether the arbitrator challenged the claimant's attorney to make an "offer of proof" in order to hear testimony; and

10) whether the arbitrator was faced with pre-hearing motion and how the arbitrator dealt with them.

...

The selection of a panel is an adventure which begins with little information to inform your choice. Accumulate as much knowledge as you can and then make your best educated guess.

Columbia Journal of Transnational Law (2001)

An Efficient Method for Determining Jurisdiction in International Arbitrations

John Yukio Gotanda

Many complain that arbitration is often expensive and rarely results in a quick decision. These problems are exacerbated when a party challenges the jurisdiction of the tribunal. In this article, I offer a new approach for determining the proper method to resolve questions of arbitral jurisdiction, which would make the arbitration process more efficient, both in monetary and temporal terms.

Today, parties commonly challenge a tribunal's jurisdiction to hear all or part of the dispute even when they previously signed a written agreement to arbitrate. Resolving these claims is often crucial to the arbitration because an award made without jurisdiction may be unenforceable. In addition, the method for resolving jurisdictional challenges is important because it affects the cost of arbitration as well as the length of time it will take to resolve the dispute.

In general, an arbitral tribunal has two options when faced with a jurisdictional challenge at the outset of the dispute. It can either hold separate hearings on the merits and the issues relating to jurisdiction and issue separate awards resolving these claims or it can resolve all of the issues in a single proceeding and award. Bifurcating the proceedings may result in savings to the parties if the tribunal rules that there is no jurisdiction to hear the dispute and, therefore, need not consider the merits. However, a single unitary proceeding may be more efficient when the jurisdiction of the tribunal is clear and the facts needed to decide the jurisdictional issue are also needed to resolve the merits.

Currently, there exists no consensus as to whether the jurisdictional challenges should be separated from the merits. Some commentators have argued that, in principle, all issues should be decided in a single proceeding. In contrast, others have advocated that, as a general rule, jurisdictional issues should be decided separately from the merits. Furthermore, there is no agreement on the factors that a tribunal should consider when resolving this question, or on the weight to give those factors. Some advocate resolving this question by determining how closely the jurisdictional issues are intertwined with the merits; that is, the tribunal should use a unitary proceeding if jurisdictional questions are intimately linked to the merits. Others argue that the arbitrator must take into account the delay that will ensue from bifurcating the issues. However, commentators only rarely give any consideration to the likelihood that the respondent will succeed on the jurisdictional challenge.

The lack of uniformity in approaches for resolving jurisdictional objections results in the inability of the parties to predict, with any degree of certainty, the procedure that tribunals will use to resolve jurisdictional issues and, therefore, the resolution of those issues. Moreover, because tribunals do not consider the likelihood of success of the jurisdictional challenge, they resolve jurisdictional challenges without using the most efficient method. This increases the cost of the arbitration and unduly delays the resolution of the dispute.

To remedy these problems, I propose that tribunals employ a new model, which seeks to use the procedure that will result in the most efficient method for resolving the dispute. The model includes three steps. The first step calls for the tribunal to determine whether the parties have agreed to let it resolve the jurisdictional issues and the merits in a unitary or in bifurcated proceedings. If they have, then the tribunal should honor their request, unless there exists a mandatory rule of law that overrides their private contractual arrangement. However, if the parties do not agree on a procedure, then the arbitrators would proceed to the second step. This step directs the tribunal to examine the relevant arbitral rules and national laws to see if they set forth a procedure for handling jurisdictional objections. If they do, then the tribunal should employ that approach. In the event that neither step provides sufficient guidance, then the tribunal would proceed to step three. Here, the tribunal compares the cost of a unitary proceeding to the cost of bifurcated proceedings, after having computed various factors and having weighed them by the tribunal's preliminary assessment of the likelihood of the claimant's success on the jurisdictional issue(s). The tribunal then selects the procedure that results in the lowest transactional cost to resolve the dispute.

This model provides a clear method for resolving jurisdictional challenges. It respects the parties' freedom to determine the procedures that they would prefer be used to resolve the dispute and conforms to applicable arbitral rules and national arbitration laws. As a default, it uses an approach that focuses on efficiency to determine whether the jurisdictional issues should be decided either as a preliminary matter or together with the merits. This approach ultimately should result in temporal and monetary savings to the parties...

思考题

1. 当事人对仲裁员提出异议,获得成功的因素有哪些?
2. Whether a standard of "independent/impartiality" exists? If not, why? And if does, what is it?
3. What kind of obstacle will the parties meet during the constitution of arbitral tribunal? How to deal with it?
4. 管辖权/管辖权原则的矛盾在哪里? Is there any theory to solve this problem? How does the claimant challenge the jurisdiction of the arbitral tribunal?
5. Some argue that the disclosure of information is the most significant obligation

of the arbitrator, do you agree? Why?

6. Why arbitrators have the arbitral immunity? What are the criteria for distinguishing between those who are and those who are not entitled to the immunity?

推荐阅读

1. Constantine Partasides, The Selection, Appointment and Challenge of Arbitrators, 5 V. J. (2001).

2. 乔欣:《仲裁权研究》,法律出版社 2001 年版。

3. Michael W. Bühler & Thomas H. Webster, Handbook of ICC Arbitration: Commentary, Precedents, Materials, Sweet & Maxwell, 2005.

4. John Yukio Gotanda, An Efficient Method for Determing Jurisdiction in International Arbitrators, Columbia Journal of Transnational Law, 2001.

5. Susan D. Franck, The Liability of International Arbitrators: A Comparative Analysis and Proposal for Qualified Immunity, N. Y. L. Sch. J. Int'l & Comp. L., 2000.

6. 王瀚、李广辉:《论仲裁庭自裁管辖权原则》,载《中国法学》2004 年第 2 期。

第六章 国际商事仲裁程序

第一节 国际商事仲裁程序概述

国际商事仲裁程序是仲裁制度的重要组成部分,通常意义上的仲裁程序是指从国际民商事案件一方当事人提请仲裁直至仲裁裁决得到执行的整个过程,包括仲裁机构、仲裁员、申请人、被申请人、证人、代理人、鉴定人等参与仲裁活动所必须遵守的程序和规则,是仲裁制度的动态组成部分。

与诉讼程序相比,仲裁程序有其自身的特点。首先,仲裁实行的是一审终审制,当事人不得就同一事实再次申请仲裁,也不能向人民法院再行起诉、上诉;而民事诉讼可经过一审、二审和再审三个阶段。当事人采用仲裁程序解决纠纷,除了期待获得公正的审理以外,更注重的是争议的解决是否快捷、便利,这也是许多当事人放弃诉讼选择仲裁的一项重要考虑。其次,仲裁一般不公开审理,而民事诉讼无特殊情况必须公开审理。这是由商事仲裁的本质属性——契约性决定的,它不仅有利于尊重当事人对仅在他们之间开展的私人性的商事仲裁这种争议解决方式的选择,更有利于体现和发挥商事仲裁的优势。在保密的状态下,当事人不必担心自己的有关信息被公之于众,有效地保护了商业秘密和声誉,使当事人有可能放下戒备,减少甚至消除对立情绪,从而在一种轻松平和的气氛中解决争议。最后,意思自治原则在仲裁程序中的应用,这构成了国际商事仲裁与诉讼程序的主要区别之一。在国际商事诉讼中,不论受诉法院在哪一国,诉讼程序必须受该国诉讼程序法管辖,即该国的诉讼法基于公法性质而具有了天生的管辖权。国际商事仲裁正好与之相反。当事人有权约定仲裁过程中所使用的程序,而不必然使用仲裁地的诉讼法,也不必然使用仲裁地的仲裁法。

当事人在仲裁程序中的意思自治得到大多数国家国内仲裁法的支持,国际商事仲裁界亦普遍接受此观点,各大国际仲裁机构也明确采用此方法。例如,《示范法》第19条规定:"(1)在不违背本法规定的情况下,当事各方可以自由地就仲裁庭进行仲裁所应遵循的程序达成协议。(2)如未达成此种协议,仲裁庭可以在本法规定的限制下,按照它认为适当的方式进行仲裁。授予仲裁庭的权力包括确定任何证据的可采性、相关性、实质性和重要性的权力。"仲裁程序中的意思自治首先表现为当事人在仲裁协议或仲裁条款中就仲裁程序作出约定,许多国家都支持这种选择应当超过任何其他关于法律适用的理由。如果当事人未选择仲裁程序,而只是选定了仲裁机构,这仍然是意思自治的表现。当事人还可以在选择了 A 仲裁机构的同时选择 B 机构的仲裁规则。

如前所述,仲裁程序研究的是从申请到裁决作出所应遵循的规则,本章讨论的内容有的在其他章节中已有提及,在此不详述,以下结合我国法律和实践,就仲裁程序作"流水线"式的描述。

1. 申请

国际商事仲裁申请,是指国际商事仲裁协议中所约定的争议事项发生以后,仲裁协议一方当事人依据协议将有关争议交给选定的仲裁机构或仲裁庭,请求以仲裁方式解决争议的行为,是启动仲裁程序的必要环节。

2. 受理

当事人仅仅向仲裁机构提出仲裁申请还不能进行仲裁,只有申请被仲裁机构受理后,仲裁程序才实质性地开始。有关仲裁机构在收到仲裁申请书后应进行初步审查,确定仲裁协议是否有效,争议事项是否属于仲裁协议的范围,从而确定其是否有合法有效的仲裁管辖权。一旦决定受理,仲裁机构便按仲裁规则的规定及时通知全体当事人,并开始准备下一步的仲裁程序。

3. 答辩

商事仲裁案件中的被申请人为了维护自己的权益,需要对申请人在商事仲裁申请书中所提出的商事仲裁请求和该项请求所依据的事实和理由作出回应,并提出自己的立场。

被申请人收到仲裁申请书后,应在一定期限内提出答辩书,对仲裁答辩书的要求与仲裁申请书相似,但强调答辩书的内容应当针对申请书的内容。在仲裁实务中,被申请人还常常需要在答辩期内选定仲裁员或委托指定仲裁员,申请仲裁员的回避,提出反请求,对仲裁庭管辖权进行抗辩等。被申请人既可以在仲裁庭开庭审理案件前通过书面形式进行答辩,也可以在开庭审理案件的当时以书面或口头的形式提出。一般地,如果被申请人不按期提交答辩书进行答辩,即可推定其自愿放弃答辩的权利,不影响仲裁程序的继续进行,仲裁庭可以根据已有证据作出裁决。

4. 反请求

针对已经提出的仲裁请求,申请人可以放弃或变更,被申请人可以承认或反驳。由被申请人提出的,且与申请人的仲裁请求有直接联系的独立仲裁请求即为反请求。

被申请人提出反请求时,应在答辩书中附有关证明文件,在反请求中附有关事实和证据,此外,反请求人还要预交一定的仲裁费用。仲裁庭受理反请求后,通常将原请求和反请求合并审理,但由于反请求的独立性特征,合并审理后的裁决还是应当分别作出,因此即使提出仲裁申请的申请人在审理过程中撤回申请,也不影响反请求审理的继续进行。

5. 保全措施

仲裁程序中的保全措施包括财产保全和证据保全两方面。在仲裁庭作出最后裁决前,为了防止有关当事人的财产被隐匿、转移、变卖,保证将来发生效力的仲裁裁决被执行,从而确保胜诉方及时获得损害赔偿,有必要对当事人有关财产采取临时强制措施。我国《仲裁法》未规定诉前财产保全,只规定了提起仲裁或进入仲裁后的财产保全。但是为了避免当事人的损失难以挽回,民事诉讼中的诉前保全制度也应当适用于仲裁。证据保全,则是在仲裁庭审理程序终结前对于那些可能灭失或以后难以取得的证据所采取的一种临时强制措施。我国《仲裁法》第68条对此作出了规定。

6. 组成仲裁庭

组成仲裁庭的仲裁员应当规定在仲裁员名册中,仲裁庭可由三名仲裁员或一名仲裁员组成。由三名仲裁员组成的,应由当事人各自选定或委托仲裁委员会主任指定一名仲裁员,第三名由当事人共同选定或共同委托仲裁委员会主任指定,第三名是首席仲裁员。由一名仲裁员组成的,应由当事人共同选定或共同委托仲裁委员会主任指定仲裁员。当事人没有在仲裁规则规定的期限内约定仲裁庭的组成方式或者选定仲裁员的,由仲裁委员会主任指定。

7. 开庭审理

商事仲裁的审理方式有需要开庭听审的口头审理方式,以及无须开庭仅依当事人提交的文件进行的书面审理方式两种。开庭审理是主要的案件审理方式。仲裁委员会应当在仲裁规则规定的期限内将开庭日期通知双方当事人。当事人有正当事由的可以在仲裁规则规定的期限内请求延期开庭,是否延期由仲裁庭决定。申请人经书面通知,无正当理由不到庭或未经仲裁庭许可中途退庭的,可以缺席判决。开庭审理过程中,当事人可以当庭出示证据、质证和口头辩论。辩论终结时,由首席仲裁员或独任仲裁员征询当事人的最后意见。国内仲裁中,仲裁庭应当将开庭情况记入笔录,当事人和其他仲裁参与人认为对自己陈述的记录有遗漏或差错的,有权申请补正。如果不予补正,应当记录该申请。

第二节 国际商事仲裁程序启动

一、申请

从广义上讲,仲裁程序正式启动以一方提交仲裁申请,仲裁机构决定受理该仲裁案件为标志。在机构仲裁中,商事仲裁申请通常是向仲裁协议中约定的仲裁机构提出并由该机构将有关申请书送达对方当事人;而在临时仲裁中,申请通常向当事人依仲裁协议组成的仲裁庭或能为临时仲裁提供服务的有关仲裁机构提出,有关申请书通常也可由申请人自己送达对方当事人。

一般来说,申请需要满足这样几个条件:一是当事人首先应当提交仲裁协议。这是申请仲裁的必备条件。某些条件下仲裁委员会可能会对无仲裁协议的申请进行立案,如果当事人对此表示同意并签订书面仲裁协议,则仲裁程序得以进行;如果不同意或不答复,则程序不继续进行。二是当事人要向仲裁协议中选定的仲裁委员会提出仲裁申请。三是仲裁请求应当明确,并且提交该请求赖以提出的事实、理由。四是仲裁申请的事项必须在仲裁委员会受理的范围内,依据我国《仲裁法》第2、3条,即为属于平等主体的公民、法人和其他组织之间发生的合同纠纷和其他财产权益纠纷,而不是婚姻、收养、监护、扶养、继承纠纷,也不是依法应当由行政机关处理的争议。五是提交仲裁申请书及其副本。

国际商事仲裁申请书类似于诉讼中的起诉状,提出申请一方称为"申请人"(claimant),另一方称为"被申请人(respondent)"。申请人提交的申请中应当包含事实(facts)、争议事项(points at issue)以及仲裁请求(relief or remedy)。各国际仲裁机构的仲裁规则对应当提交的文件有具体规定。① 如果仲裁是以临时仲裁方式进行,则应在申请书中指明临时仲裁机构的组成方式。

依据我国《仲裁法》第23条,仲裁申请书应载明的事项有:(1) 当事人的姓名、性别、年龄、职业、工作单位和住所,法人或者其他组织的名称、住所和法定代表人或者主要负责人的姓名、职务;(2) 仲裁请求和所根据的事实、理由;(3) 证据和证据来源、证人姓名和住所。

Under the Model Law, the claimant is to submit to the arbitrators and respondent a statement of the facts supporting his claim, the points at issue and relief or remedy sought, and the respondent is to submit a statement of his defense. It is open to the parties to submit with their statement, or to refer to, all documents they consider to be relevant. This is more or less the position under the UNCITRAL Rules: the LCIA rules provide for initial exchanges of documents leading to the appointment of the arbitrators, and thereafter the parties are to submit formal written statements to the arbitrators within the time limits allowed. Under the ICC Rules, the arbitration is initiated by formal pleadings: the file is transmitted to the arbitrators on the basis of

---

① For example, CIETAC Arbitration Rules 2005, Article 10: "A party applying for arbitration under these Rules shall: 1. Submit a Request for Arbitration in writing signed by and/or affixed with the seal of the Claimant and/or its authorized representative(s), which shall, inter alia, include: (a) the names and addresses of the Claimant and the Respondent, including the zip code, telephone, telex, fax and telegraph numbers, Email addresses or any other means of electronic telecommunications; (b) a reference to the arbitration agreement that is invoked; (c) a statement of the facts of the case and the main issues in dispute; (d) the claim of the Claimant; and (e) the facts and grounds on which the claim is based. 2. Attach to the Request for Arbitration the relevant evidence supporting the facts on which the Claimant's claim is based..."

which the arbitrators draw up their terms of reference.

申请人提出仲裁申请书时,应当依照仲裁机构的规定,预付仲裁费用。① 如果仲裁是以临时仲裁方式进行,则应当按照当事人在仲裁协议中所作的约定,预付一笔仲裁费用。仲裁申请书应有申请人或其授权的代理人的签名或盖章。

与诉讼类似,仲裁申请具有中断诉讼时效的效力。在某些国家,仲裁申请的提出,意味着仲裁程序的开始(如 ICC 和 CIETAC,申请开始是 date of receipt by secretariat),也就对以后的仲裁中的每一步所规定的时限产生影响。在另外一些国家,被申请人收到商事仲裁通知时,商事仲裁程序才被视为开始(如 SIAC 和 AAA,申请开始是 date of receipt of notice by the other party)。先前的申请书有瑕疵,并不必然导致申请书无效。

The omission of a claim from the points of claim was mere oversight or error, and did not mean that the claim had been abandoned.

Art. 23(2) of the Model Law lays down a presumption in favor of the validity of amendments, and provides that either party may amend or supplement his claim or defence during the proceedings, unless the arbitral tribunal considers it inappropriate to allow such amendment having regard to the delay in making it. The UNCITRAL Rules are similarly drafted. The ICC Rules allow the parties to make new claims or counterclaims, and the arbitrators may admit them even if they do not fall within the arbitrators' term of reference as set out in the formal documentation signed by both parties. The LCIA Rules confer upon the arbitrators the power to allow the amendment of claims and counterclaims, but conditions (including terms as to the payment of costs) may be imposed.

二、受理

商事仲裁的申请、受理是两个内容不同但紧密联系的行为。申请是受理的前提,受理是申请的进一步发展。一般来说,仲裁程序在当事人提出商事仲裁申请之时就已经启动,但作为实质仲裁程序的审理程序则通常要在商事仲裁申请被受理之后才能开始。

仲裁机构在收到申请人提交的仲裁申请书及有关材料后,应立即进行初步审查以决定立案与否。各机构确定的审查条件不尽相同,但是各机构的仲裁规则一般都规定,如果确定仲裁机构对案件缺乏管辖权,或者当事人未及时缴清立

---

① For instance, CIETAC Arbitration Rules 2005, Article 10.3: "Make payment of the arbitration fee in advance to the CIETAC according to its Arbitration Fee Schedule."

案费等,该商事仲裁申请便不被受理。①

我国《仲裁法》第 21 条规定,申请商事仲裁必须具备三个条件:(1) 有仲裁协议;(2) 有具体的仲裁请求和事实、理由;(3) 属于仲裁委员会的受理范围。除此之外,仲裁委员会通常还会对当事人申请商事仲裁手续是否完备,是否已经依照仲裁委员会的缴费通知预缴仲裁费用等问题进行审查。只有满足了其预设的条件,仲裁委员会才最终决定受理其申请,予以立案,否则将仲裁申请书及有关材料退回申请人,并说明不予受理的理由。如果仅仅是某些形式要件不符合规定,仲裁机构将要求申请人予以补正。以下就仲裁协议和时效具体进行解释。

(一) 仲裁协议

仲裁案件的受理主要是针对机构仲裁而言的,有关的仲裁机构在收到仲裁申请人提交的仲裁申请书以后,应立即进行初步审查。仲裁机构仅对当事人的仲裁协议作表面审查,被申请人对申请人提起仲裁或仲裁委员会的管辖权有异议的,可提出管辖权异议。但仲裁协议是否有效,应当由仲裁庭决定,即"管辖权的管辖权"。② 应注意的是,该异议的提出必须符合一定的时间限制,这与国内诉讼上的管辖权异议时限类似。③

仲裁庭对管辖权问题的裁定,可以作为先决问题先行作出,也可以在最终仲裁裁决书中与其他事实、法律问题一并作出。虽然如上文所说,仲裁庭拥有"管辖权的管辖权",但并不意味着法院对仲裁庭的管辖权问题没有决定权。④

---

① 参见 1997 年《日本商事仲裁协会商事仲裁规则》第 12.4 条和第 13.1 条;1998 年《国际商会仲裁规则》第 4.5 条;1998 年《斯德哥尔摩商会仲裁院仲裁规则》第 7 条;1998 年《斯德哥尔摩商会快速仲裁规则》第 6 条;1998 年《德国仲裁协会仲裁规则》第 8 条;1998 年《印度仲裁委员会仲裁规则》第 16.2 条。

② For instance, UNCITRAL Model Law on International Commercial Arbitration, Article 16.1: "The arbitral tribunal may rule on its own jurisdiction, including any objections with respect to the existence or validity of the arbitration agreement. For that purpose, an arbitration clause which forms part of a contract shall be treated as an agreement independent of the other terms of the contract. A decision by the arbitral tribunal that the contract is null and void shall not entail ipso jure the invalidity of the arbitration clause."

③ For instance, UNCITRAL Model Law on International Commercial Arbitration, Article 16.2: "A plea that the arbitral tribunal does not have jurisdiction shall be raised not later than the submission of the statement of defence. A party is not precluded from raising such a plea by the fact that he has appointed, or participated in the appointment of, an arbitrator. A plea that the arbitral tribunal is exceeding the scope of its authority shall be raised as soon as the matter alleged to be beyond the scope of its authority is raised during the arbitral proceedings. The arbitral tribunal may, in either case, admit a later plea if it considers the delay justified."

For instance, UNCITRAL Model Law on International Commercial Arbitration, Article 16.3: "If the arbitral tribunal rules as a preliminary question that it has jurisdiction, any party may request, within thirty days after having received notice of that ruling, the court specified in Article 6 to decide the matter, which decision shall be subject to no appeal; while such a request is pending, the arbitral tribunal may continue the arbitral proceedings and make an award."

④ For instance, Arbitration Act of Singapore, Chapter 10 Application of Limitation Act 11: (1) The Limitation Act (Cap. 163) shall apply to arbitration proceedings as it applies to proceedings before any court and a reference in that Act to the commencement of any action shall be construed as a reference to the commencement of arbitration proceedings.

（二）时效

仲裁时效通常从两个方面考虑：一为法律中对时效问题（statutory time bar）的规定；一为当事人具体合同中对提起仲裁的时间限制（contractual limitation）。

Statutory Time Bar

法律中的时效问题，涉及对"时效"问题到底属于实体法还是程序法的争论。对此各个国家有不同规定。一个仲裁案件，通常可能会面临两个时效法律的规制，即合同实体法中的时效规定（substantive law of the contract）和仲裁所在地的法律关于时效的规定（law of situs）。在将仲裁时效识别为程序法的国家，将仲裁地的仲裁时效规定适用于仲裁案件；在将仲裁时效识别为实体法的国家，仲裁过程中则应适用合同实体法中的仲裁时效规定。一旦时效问题得到仲裁庭的支持，申请人的申请就将被驳回。被申请人向仲裁庭提交答辩并不代表其放弃时效抗辩，这与诉讼中的做法相同。实践中，为防止仲裁裁决承认与执行中出现争议，当事人可在此两个时效中的任何一个届满之前提起仲裁，以保证对方无法以时效抗辩。

我国《仲裁法》规定，我国法律的仲裁时效应当优先适用。《仲裁法》第74条规定："法律对仲裁时效有规定的，适用该规定。法律对仲裁时效没有规定的，适用诉讼时效的规定。"

However, the statutory time bar issue will not affect the jurisdiction of the arbitrator. The World Era [1992] 1 LLR 45. Oppositely, Issue of whether claim is time-barred falls within the jurisdiction of the tribunal. Grimaldi Compagna Di Navigazione SpA v. Sekihyo Lines [1999] 1 LLR 708.

Contractual Time Limitation

Contractual limitation periods are found in many arbitration agreements particularly chose incorporating trade association rules and other standard wordings. The wording of the clause often requires fine distinctions to be drawn by the courts. Five particular problems have emerged. Firstly, is the effect of the expiry of the time limit in the clause to prevent the claim being pursued at all, or does it merely bar the remedy? A number of issues consequent upon this distinction also arise. The second problem is that of isolating the event which triggers the running of time, as there is no necessary consistency on this matter as between clauses. Thirdly, it is necessary to decide exactly what conduct by the applicant amounts to a commencement of arbitration proceedings in compliance with the provision. Fourthly, there is the question of the scope of the barring clause, as it may not be applicable to all of the matters in dispute between the parties. Finally, difficult questions of construction arise where the applicant seeks to raise additional matters after the time limits have expired. The issues are discussed in the following paragraphs.

某些重要的合同范本中对"contractual time limitation"作出了明确规定。

For instance, United Nations Convention on Contracts for the International Sale of Goods (1980) [CISG] Article 39:

(1) The buyer loses the right to rely on a lack of conformity of the goods if he does not give notice to the seller specifying the nature of the lack of conformity within a reasonable time after he has discovered it or ought to have discovered it.

(2) In any event, the buyer loses the right to rely on a lack of conformity of the goods if he does not give the seller notice thereof at the latest within a period of two years from the date on which the goods were actually handed over to the buyer, unless this time-limit is inconsistent with a contractual period of guarantee.

The arbitrators have jurisdiction to determine whether a clause bars the claim or bars the remedy. This was first decided in Aktiebolaget v. Berg Sons, in which the umpire made an award to the effect that the buyers had failed to appoint their arbitrator in time and that as a result the claim was barred.

If the clause is construed as barring the claim and not the right to present the claim to arbitrators, it would seem that, subject to contrary wording, the arbitrators retain jurisdiction to determine whether or not the claim is indeed out of time....

If the clause bars the right of the applicant to seek arbitration, he remains entitled, on the expiry of the time specified, to pursue his claim in the High Court and any other conditions applicable to the commencement of the arbitration proceedings cease to apply.

三、答辩

商事仲裁答辩,是指商事仲裁案件中的被申请人为了维护自己的权益,对申请人在商事仲裁申请书中所提出的商事仲裁请求和该项请求所依据的事实及理由,进行答复和辩解。被申请人对申请人在仲裁申请书中提出的仲裁请求和事实及理由,有合理机会提出充分答辩,这是被申请人享有的一项程序性权利。该项程序性权利直接关系到实体性权利的实现。

被申请人在进行答辩时,应当依照申请人的申请书进行反驳。简单地说,可以从管辖权和事实两部分进行反驳。一般而言,被申请人在答辩书中应当针对申请人的商事仲裁请求作出回应,或反驳或承认,答辩书应当陈述事实,列举证据或证据线索,具体应当附哪些材料,要视所适用的仲裁程序而定。① 一般来说,各国的仲裁立法和仲裁规则既允许被申请人在仲裁庭开庭之前以书面形式进行答辩,②同时也允许仲裁庭开庭审理时以书面形式或口头形式进行答辩。

在提交仲裁答辩书的过程中,要特别注意"时限"问题。有些仲裁规则并没有明确规定具体天数。③ 如果被申请人不按期进行答辩,即可推定其已经自愿放弃进行答辩的权利,此时仲裁程序继续进行,仲裁庭可以依据已有的证据作出裁决。因此,针对这项维护自己合法权益的重要权利和必要手段,被申请人应当特别重视,认真准备答辩书并及时提交,放弃或怠于行使都是极不可取的。

另外,在国际商事仲裁中,有时被申请人还需要在答辩期内完成与仲裁庭组成相关的事宜,如指定仲裁员、申请仲裁员回避等,有时还涉及反请求问题,要视具体仲裁规则而定。这些事项虽然要求在答辩期内作出,但通常可以单独文件的方式提交。

四、反请求

商事仲裁反请求,是指在商事仲裁程序进行过程中,被申请人为了维护自己的权益,针对申请人提出的且与申请人的仲裁请求有直接联系的、独立的仲裁请求。与诉讼中的反诉类似,反请求也是为了达到抵消或者吞并申请人的仲裁申请的目的,因而是被申请人用以维护自身利益的又一重要手段。

商事仲裁反请求是特定形式下的仲裁申请的做法,有其自身特点:(1) 对象的特定性。反请求只能针对申请人提出。(2) 独立性。反请求实质上是一种特殊的申请,只不过是以对方已经提出请求为前提。反请求也应当具有请求所要

---

① For instance, CIETAC Arbitration Rules 2005, Article 12: The Statement of Defense shall be signed by and/or affixed with the seal of the Respondent and/or its authorized representative(s), and shall, inter alia, include: (a) the names and addresses of the Respondent, including the zip code, telephone, telex, fax and telegraph numbers, Email addresses or any other means of electronic telecommunications; (b) the defense to the Request for Arbitration setting forth the facts and grounds on which the defense is based; and (c) the relevant evidence supporting the defense.

② 如1994年《意大利仲裁协会国际仲裁规则》第7.1条;1997年《日本商事仲裁协会商事仲裁规则》第15.1条;1998年《国际商会仲裁规则》第5.1条;1998年《伦敦国际仲裁院仲裁规则》第2.1条;1998年《印度仲裁委员会仲裁规则》第17.1条。

③ For instance, UNCITRAL Model Law on International Commercial Arbitration, Article 23:"(1) Within the period of time agreed by the parties or determined by the arbitral tribunal, the claimant shall state the facts supporting his claim, the points at issue and the relief or remedy sought, and the respondent shall state his defence in respect of these particulars, unless the parties have otherwise agreed as to the required elements of such statements. The parties may submit with their statements all documents they consider to be relevant or may add a reference to the documents or other evidence they will submit..." However, CIETAC Arbitration Rules 2005 rules clearly that the time limitation is 45 days. Article 12.1 provides:"Within forty-five (45) days from the date of receipt of the Notice of Arbitration, the Respondent shall file a Statement of Defense in writing with the Secretariat of the CIETAC or its Sub-Commission. The arbitral tribunal may extend that time period if it believes that there are justified reasons."

求的所有内容,符合相应的方式和时限。与反诉相似,反请求一经受理,不因对方当事人撤回仲裁申请而终结,也不因申请人放弃仲裁请求而失效。(3)目的的对抗性。反请求的目的是抵消或吞并申请人的请求,使请求人的请求部分或全部被抵消,甚至有可能最终导致申请人向被申请人赔偿。(4)理由的关联性。反请求是针对先前对方的请求而提出的。反请求也必须属于仲裁范围,符合仲裁协议。

反请求与请求是基于同一个仲裁协议提出的,所以反请求的审理也应当由原仲裁庭进行,其依据的仲裁规则也与原请求所适用的相同。被申请人应当在答辩书上附上相关证明文件。[1]

由于反请求具有独立性,因此当被申请人提出反请求而申请人却撤回了商事仲裁申请时,仲裁程序并不必然停止或结束,仲裁庭继续对反请求进行审理。当然,如果申请人没有撤回仲裁申请,仲裁庭可将申请人的仲裁申请和被申请人的反请求合并审理并分别作出裁决。

与被申请人一样,申请人对于反请求所提事项,应当在规定时间内进行答辩,如拒绝答辩,只能表示其放弃答辩,不影响仲裁程序的进行。[2]

There is also time limitation in counterclaim. CIETAC Arbitration Rules 2005, Article 13.1: Within forty-five (45) days from the date of receipt of the Notice of Arbitration, the Respondent shall file with the CIETAC its counterclaim in writing, if any. The arbitral tribunal may extend that time period if it believes that there are justified reasons.

For instance, CIETAC Arbiration Rules 2005, Article 13.4: Where the formalities required for filing a counterclaim are found to be complete, the CIETAC shall send the Statement of Counterclaim and its attachments to the Claimant. The Claimant shall, within thirty (30) days from the date of receipt of the Statement of Counterclaim and the attachment, submit in writing its Statement of Defense to the Respondent's counterclaim.

我国《仲裁法》第 27 条规定:"申请人可以放弃或者变更仲裁请求。被申请人可以承认或者反驳仲裁请求,有权提出反请求。"CIETAC 2005 年《仲裁规则》第 13.1 条规定:"被诉方当事人如有反请求应当自收到仲裁通知之日起 45 天内以书面形式提交仲裁委员会;仲裁委员会认为有正当理由的,可以适当延长此期

---

[1] For instance, CIETAC Arbitration Rules 2005, Article 13.2: "When filing a counterclaim, the Respondent shall specify its counterclaim in its written Statement of Counterclaim and state the facts and grounds upon which its counterclaim is based with relevant evidence attached thereto."

[2] For instance, CIETAC Arbitration Rules 2005, Article 13.6: "Failure of the Claimant to file a Statement of Defense to the Respondent's counterclaim shall not operate to affect the arbitral proceedings."

限。"2004年《中国海事仲裁委员会仲裁规则》则将提交反请求申请书的时限缩短为30天。

第三节 国际商事仲裁审理过程

一、仲裁地法律

在仲裁特别是国际商事仲裁中,仲裁地选择是一个至关重要的因素,对仲裁的整体运作具有广泛的影响。

(一)仲裁地点影响仲裁协议的效力

由于各国对商事仲裁协议有效成立的条件规定不一,因而在国际商事仲裁中,对于仲裁协议效力的确定往往存在法律冲突。在确定仲裁协议效力时,除当事人另有约定外,一般都是以仲裁地的法律作为准据法。例如,我国《仲裁法》规定,选定仲裁委员会是仲裁协议应当具备的基本内容之一,因而是仲裁协议生效条件之一,但如果仲裁地在英国,依英国法律,没有选定仲裁委员会的仲裁协议因没有违反英国法而有效。

(二)仲裁地点影响仲裁程序的进行

当事人没有明确约定仲裁程序法时,一般适用仲裁地的法律。即使当事人选择了仲裁程序法,审理案件的程序也不能违背仲裁地程序法的规定。此外,如果当事人在仲裁协议中没有约定解决争议所适用的仲裁规则,或约定不明确,有关仲裁机构更有可能直接适用仲裁地的仲裁程序法来进行相关的仲裁程序。适用仲裁地法会对仲裁案件产生实质性的影响。同时,仲裁地的民事诉讼程序也不同程度地控制着仲裁程序。

The different concepts of procedural and substantive law in different countries may cause some surprise to the unwary when choosing the place of arbitration. This is what the parties learnt in one case, concerning the question of the stature of limitation. The claimant asserted that Finnish substantive law applied and that there is no statute of limitation in Finnish law. The arbitrator applied the rules of lex fori, which stipulated that limitation is a matter of procedure and not of substance. Since he was witting in England, the application of lex fori on the issue was mandatory and the arbitrator came to the conclusion that the claim was statute barred under English law and dismissed the case. The choice of place of arbitration decided the outcome of the case.

(三)仲裁地点影响争议解决所适用的实体法

当事人在国际商事仲裁中一般会就解决争议所适用的实体法作出选择,如果没有明确选择,仲裁庭可以按仲裁地的冲突规范确定所应适用的实体法,或直接适用仲裁地的实体法。即使当事人明确选择了实体法作为解决争议所适用的法律,也有可能发生仲裁地不允许当事人选择,仲裁庭最终适用了仲裁地法律的情况。

(四)仲裁地点影响仲裁裁决的承认与执行

仲裁地点决定了国际商事仲裁裁决的国籍。在仲裁地国作出的裁决如果在他国请求承认和执行,就会产生外国仲裁裁决的承认与执行问题。如果仲裁裁决作出国与承认和执行国都是《纽约公约》的成员国,那么该仲裁地国的裁决,就可以按照该公约的规定在该有关外国得到承认和执行。因为在《纽约公约》一百四十多个成员中,有五十多个国家按公约的规定作了如下保留:本国只对在另一缔约国领土内所作的仲裁裁决的承认与执行适用本公约。如果在仲裁作出地国与承认和执行国之中,任何一国不是该公约的成员国,甚至不是其他有关国际条约的缔约国,则只能按互惠原则予以承认和执行。如果不存在互惠,在仲裁地国所有的裁决有可能得不到有关国家的承认和执行。

对于仲裁地,国际商事仲裁的当事人通常可以自由作出选择。如果没有约定,在当事人选择常设仲裁机构仲裁时,通常以该被选定的常设仲裁机构所在地为仲裁地点。但是,一些常设仲裁机构在不同地方设立分支机构,而且大多数常设仲裁机构并不禁止当事人选择其他地方作为仲裁地。在临时仲裁的情况下,由于没有机构所在地,当事人在仲裁协议中必须明确约定仲裁地点。

二、预备会议

"preliminary meeting"(预备会议)这一术语也被英国律师称为"preliminary hearing"(预备庭审),21世纪初产生并使用的一个词是"case management meeting"(案件管理会议)。不可否认,预备会议具有诸多优势。在国内仲裁中,特别是在仲裁庭由一名独任仲裁员组成的时候,涉及程序的预备事项通常在仲裁庭和当事人未召开会议的情况下即得到确定,这降低了成本。在国际商事仲裁中,无论仲裁庭由一名还是三名仲裁员组成,预备会议均有助于确定程序进行的框架。特别是,在当事人及其代理人来自不同的文化背景,或者来自不同的法律体系时,仲裁庭最好在程序尽可能早的阶段与当事人举行一次会议。这可以确保仲裁庭和当事人对于仲裁如何进行达成共识,并有利于仲裁进行框架的设计和确定。

As with most commercial activities, arbitration proceedings will be conducted more effectively and efficiently if adequate plans have been made for their conduct. Some of the planning can take place at the time that the arbitration agreement is being prepared. But many arbitration agreements are not carefully thought out and even when they are, circumstances may have changed by the time a dispute arises. It is therefore the invariable practice for a tribunal to hold, at an early stage in the proceedings, a preliminary meeting (or preliminary conference, as it is referred to in some countries) to discuss and, if possible, agree on the procedure and timetable for the arbitration. In large and complex arbitrations there may be a second or third preliminary meeting convened, as time goes on, to take account of changing circumstances or, where insufficient information has been made available to the tribunal at the time of its appointment, to deal with matters arising later on in the arbitration as and when that information becomes available.

Certain international arbitration rules omit the stage of preliminary meeting, and simply require the parties to prepare their respective cases in documentary form and to submit their claims to the arbitrators and to the other side. The substantive arbitration proceedings then take place after the exchange of documents. The Rules of the London Court of International Arbitration, for example, do not provide for the preliminary hearing. This is also the position under the Model Law and under the UNCITRAL Rules, although it is anticipated that the parties may between themselves agree on the matter to be decided by the arbitrators prior to the exchange of documents. The ICC Rules, by contrast, require the parties to submit to the ICC Secretariat a description of the dispute and of the relief sought, including if possible an indication of the amount claimed, at the first stage. After this, the arbitrators are to draw up a document, which may be done in the presence of the parties at a preliminary meeting, which sets out the parties' respective cases and the procedural rules governing the arbitration. This document must be dinged by both parties.

CIETAC 2005年《仲裁规则》与2000年的相比的一个不同之处在于,前者在第三节第29条第5款中规定:"除非当事人另有约定,仲裁庭认为必要时可以发布程序指令、发出问题单、举行庭前会议、召开预备庭、制作审理范围书等。"在此确认了仲裁庭在必要时可以举行庭前会议,但是对于该庭前会议的程序问题和需要决定的事项并未作进一步的详细规定。

实践中,预备会议在各个阶段都可进行。在与当事人见面前,仲裁庭的成员通常不公开地举行会议。在会议上,一方面可以对案件作出初步介绍,另一方面可以讨论有关组织仲裁的临时想法。在临时仲裁中,各方当事人的代理人在预备会议前见面,可以向仲裁庭提交就仲裁员的报酬和费用达成一致的意见,从而避免了不必要的尴尬。

为了使预备会议富有成效,各方当事人应该派出有权当场作出决定的高层代表,否则就会出现一种情况,即一方律师提出需要取得客户的命令或指示后才能去回应或同意,导致在预备会议上能够定下来的程序很少,使得预备会议形同虚设。在当事人与仲裁庭之间的主会议召开之前可能先行举行仲裁庭的不公开会议及当事人之间的不公开会议。仲裁庭成员不公开协商会导致主会议延期或几次短暂延期。在仲裁庭的指引下,当事人的代理人可利用此机会进一步私下讨论,并就程序的基本框架和组织达成一致。

The agenda for such a meeting will typically include determinations on the place and the language of the proceedings as well as the form, length, and time limits for the written submissions that will be presented before the main oral hearing. The preliminary meeting will usually be the moment to raise objections against the tribunal's jurisdiction or to discuss challenges against arbitrators. Also, a first discussion of the merits of the dispute will be attempted with a view towards defining and perhaps limiting the issues, or even achieving a settlement.

The preliminary hearing will usually be held early on, as soon as practicable after the exchange of the initial statement between the parties. In ICC arbitration, the timing is influenced by the requirement the Terms of Reference be submitted to the ICC Court for confirmation within two months after the transaction of the file to the arbitral tribunal which, in turn, is supposed to happen immediately after receipt by the ICC Secretariat of the defendant's answer. The terms of the Reference are of great practical importance because they define the mandate, the "mission" of the arbitrators (the French terms is "acte de mission") and may later be used as the bench-mark in determining whether the arbitral tribunal exceeded the scope of its authority. Art. 18.1 of the ICC Rules lists the particulars to be included in the terms of Reference:"As soon as it has received the file from the Secretariat, the Arbitral Tribunal shall draw up, on the basis of documents or in the presence of the parties and in the light of their most recent submissions, a document defining its Terms of Reference. This document shall include the following particulars: a) the full names and descriptions of the parties; b) the addresses of the parties to which notifications and communications arising in the course of the arbitration may be made; c) a summary of the parties' respective claims and of the relief sought by each party, with an indication to the extent possible of the amounts claimed or counterclaimed; d) unless the Arbitral Tribunal considers it inappropriate, a list of issues to be determined; e) the full names, descriptions and addresses of the arbitrators; f) the place of the arbitration; and g) particulars of the applicable procedural rules and, if such is the case, reference to the power conferred upon the Arbitral Tribunal to act as amiable compositeur or to decide ex aequo et bono."

These are issues that set the parameters for the entire procedure and therefore have to be decided by the tribunal before entering into a discussion of the merits...

联合国国际贸易法委员会1996年通过的《关于安排仲裁程序的说明》所附"清单"中提供了仲裁庭在组织仲裁程序时可能需要谨记的事项,这些事项不具有穷尽性或确定性,仅对仲裁庭可能希望考虑的问题点作出了有用的指示。

三、书面审理和口头审理

仲裁审理是指仲裁庭以一定的方式和程序征集、审查证据,询问证人、鉴定人,并对整个争议事项的实质性问题进行全面审查的仲裁活动。仲裁审理在整个仲裁程序中占有重要地位。仲裁审理往往是影响案件裁决结果的关键因素,因为有时双方当事人提供了大量材料,仲裁员不一定详细了解每一材料的来龙去脉,特别是对一些复杂的案件。双方当事人陈述的事实与提供的证据不一致时,往往只有通过开庭审理才能查清和确定。

从世界范围看各国立法和仲裁实践,仲裁审理的方式是多种多样的。在大多数国家,仲裁审理的方式由当事人通过协议方式确定,在缺乏此种约定时,有关仲裁庭可依授权在授权范围内决定审理方式。当然,少数国家(如英国)不允许当事人协议确定审理方式。

仲裁审理方式主要有两种:开庭审理(口头审理)和书面审理。为了保证当事人各方享有充分表达各自意见的机会,一些国家(如英国、德国等)的仲裁立法和仲裁规则规定,仲裁必须采用开庭审理的方式,以此保证各方意见得以充分陈述;而另外一些国家(如中国、美国、俄罗斯和日本等)的仲裁立法和规则规定,在缺乏当事人约定时,仲裁方式必须以开庭审理的方式进行,但若当事人有约定,则从其约定,可以书面审理的方式进行。

(一)口头审理

仲裁中的口头审理,与诉讼中的口头审理概念类似,指仲裁当事人和/或其代理人出席仲裁,以口头答辩方式,接受仲裁庭对仲裁案件的审理。仲裁中的口头审理的过程与诉讼中的口头审理过程也很相似。某一案件若被确定采用口头审理,仲裁机构的相关工作人员(一般是秘书处)应首先依据适用的法律或规则,确定开庭审理的具体时间(精确到日期)和地点,之后在规定时间内送达开庭通知。若当事人没有申请延期开庭,则口头审理在此前确定的时间举行。开庭审理时,先由仲裁庭首席仲裁员宣布仲裁庭组成人员,若当事人对人员组成有任何异议,可以提出,若无异议,则由首席仲裁员宣布仲裁审理开始。口头审理可大致分为三部分:事实调查、当事人辩论和仲裁庭总结。事实调查部分先由申请人陈述案情事实,被申请人答辩,再由仲裁庭提问;事实调查结束后进入当事人辩论阶段;最后由仲裁庭总结审理情况。如果口头审理已经将案情查实,仲裁庭可以在闭庭前宣布终结审理,并在一定期限内作出仲裁裁决;若案情尚未查清楚,需要当事人进一步提交相关材料和证据,仲裁庭应在闭庭前向当事人提出,并规定提交补充材料和证据的期限;如果认为需要再次开庭审理的,可告知当事人。在整个开庭审理过程中,仲裁机构应当做好庭审记录工作(笔录或录音等)。

仲裁审理中对仲裁地点的认定也很重要,各仲裁机构的仲裁规则对此都有详细规定。

For instance, Article 16 of UNCITRAL Arbitration Rules provides that, "1. Unless the parties have agreed upon the place where the arbitration is to be held, such place shall be determined by the arbitral tribunal, having regard to the circumstances of the arbitration. 2. The arbitral tribunal may determine the locale of the arbitration within the country agreed upon by the parties. It may hear witnesses and hold meeting for consultation among its members at any place it deems appropriate, having regard to the circumstances of the arbitration. 3. The arbitral tribunal may meet at any place it deems appropriate for the inspection of goods, other property or documents. The parties shall be given sufficient notice to enable them to be present at such inspection. 4. The award shall be made at the place of arbitration."

《美国仲裁协会国际仲裁规则》第13条也作了大致相同的规定。

基于仲裁特点之一"保密性"的要求,除各方当事人同意外,仲裁审理一般不公开。但是,《美国仲裁协会国际仲裁规则》和《日本商事仲裁协会商事仲裁规则》规定,与案件有利害关系的人有出庭听审的权利。

(二) 书面审理

书面审理,顾名思义,指仲裁庭仅根据当事人提供的书面材料,如仲裁申请书、答辩书、证人证言、各方往来信函、合同等书面材料审理案件,而当事人和/或其代理人无须亲自到庭。正如上文所说,采用书面审理的方式必须是经该国法律允许且经当事人事前同意。大多数仲裁规则对书面审理都有规定,如CIETAC《仲裁规则》第22条规定:"仲裁庭应当开庭审理案件。但经双方当事人申请或者征得双方当事人同意,也可以不开庭审理,只依据书面文件进行审理,作出裁决。"审理过程中,仲裁庭仅依据当事人向仲裁机构有效提供的材料进行审理,并可要求当事人按仲裁规则提供补充材料。在书面材料充足的情况下,仲裁庭可以结束书面审理并通知当事人,在此之后,当事人提供的材料均不被接受也无法影响仲裁裁决。但在仲裁裁决作出前,仲裁庭会给当事人限定一个最终期限作为其提供材料的最后机会。

Article 15 of UNCITRAL Arbitration Rules provides that, "1. Subject to these Rules, the arbitral tribunal may conduct the arbitration in such manner as it considers appropriate, provided that the parties are treated with equality and that at any stage of the proceedings each party is given a full opportunity of presenting his case. 2. If either party so requests at any stage of the proceedings, the arbitral tribunal shall hold hearings for the presentation of evidence by witnesses, including expert witnesses, or for oral argument. In the absence of such a request, the arbirtral tribunal shall decide whether to hold such hearings or whether the proceedings shall be conducted on the basis of documents and other materials."

四、证据

在仲裁过程中,各方当事人为了证明各自的主张和要求,一般都在其提交的仲裁申请书、答辩书及其他有关文件中,提供各种各样的证据材料,仲裁庭应对这些证据材料进行分析和审查,找出能证明案件事实的证据。仲裁庭为了公正、恰当地裁决有关仲裁案件,可以基于一方当事人的请求,或者在它认为必要时依职权传讯证人或鉴定人,或者通过主动调查收集其他与案件有关的证据材料。在采取书面审理方式时,可以要求有关当事人提取证据材料。

(一) 当事人提供的证据

在基本证据规则方面,国际商事仲裁采用各国诉讼中普遍适用的"谁主张谁举证"的基本证据规则。当事人可以主动提供证据,也可以是基于仲裁庭的要求而提供。在仲裁程序中,一方当事人向仲裁庭提交的证据,也必须同时向另一方当事人提供。CIETAC、伦敦国际仲裁院和美国仲裁协会的仲裁规则对此均有明确规定。

(二) 证人证言

国际商事仲裁中的证人证言,既可以是书面形式,也可以是口头形式,这与大多数国家诉讼中的证人证言形式相同。但是,与诉讼不同的是,国际商事仲裁中的证人作证必须出于自愿,仲裁庭无权强迫证人作证。仅在相关法律允许的情况下,仲裁庭可基于一方当事人请求或其职权向有管辖权的法院提出申请,要求法院协助强制该证人作证。

在国际商事仲裁实践中,仲裁庭不强求证人实际出庭口头作证,而是通常让证人以书面方式作证。这主要是因为国际商事仲裁中当事人及仲裁员背景的国际化,无法保证证人能悉数出庭。

The right to take oral evidence: If the parties have agreed upon a documents-only arbitration, the arbitrators have no power to require them to provide oral evidence, and the ultimate decision of the arbitrators can not be attacked simply on the ground that their failure to demand oral evidence contravenes the fair hearing principle in s. 33 of the Arbitration Act 1996. The same principle applies where the arbitrators have a discretion to call oral evidence but choose not to do so.

...Dalmia Dairy Industries Ltd. v. National Bank of Pakistan Ltd. [1978] 2 Lloyd's Rep. 223, which involved an ICC arbitration. The ICC Rules empower, but do not require, the arbitrators to summon the parties to a hearing. ICC Rules, art. 21.1.

Art. 20.3 of the Rules of the London Court of International Arbitration allows a witness to present evidence by way of affidavit or signed statement, but either party can request his attendance. Art. 20.4 provides that if he fails to attend, the arbitrators are empowered to put such weight on the written evidence as they think fit. For a comparative study on the obtaining of evidence in international arbitrations, see Webster, (1991) 17 Arb. Int'l. 143.

Under s. 44(1)(a) of the 1996 Act, the English court may lend its assistance to an arbitration with a foreign seat by directing the taking of evidence from a witness who is within the jurisdiction of the court. It was held by Moore-Bick J. in Commerce and Industry Insurance Co. of Canada v. Lloyd's Underwriters that the court may exercise its powers even though the curial law of the arbitration is not English law.

Documentary evidence

Disclosure

In High court actions, Standard disclosure—the exchange by the parties of lists of documents in their possession, custody or power and which affect the case of either side—takes place as a matter of routine. ... in international arbitrations, particular those under the auspices of the ICC or LCIA, there is unlikely ever to be formal disclosure by lists of documents on which it intends to rely in its written submissions. However, the arbitrators have the power to order a party to disclose any document that the arbitrators deem to be relevant. The ICC Rules, by contrast, are silent as to disclosure of documents, though the arbitrators may at any time summon a party "to provide additional evidence". Nevertheless, it is regarded as unusual in ICC arbitrations for formal disclosure by list of documents and inspection. Instead, while the normal practice is for each party, in its written submissions, to include documents on which it seeks to rely, ICC tribunals have the power to employ the disclosure process, though orders for document disclosure are generally limited in scope.

Inspection of documents

Of the institutional rules, only the LCIA Rules specifically mention "inspection", in that arbitrators are given the power to produce the any documents in their possession, custody or control to the arbitrators, and to the other parties "for inspection". In practice, however, such orders are only likely to be upon receipt of a reasoned request by the other party, e. g. where there is a justifiable doubt as to a document's authenticity. In ICC arbitrations, copies of documents are presumed authentic unless challenged which then requires a determination by the arbitrators.

Inspection of property

Orders by the arbitrators

Many forms of arbitration agreement expressly empower the arbitrators to inspect property for the purposes of their award. The most obvious example is a commodity arbitration in which the only issue is the quality of the goods supplied. In the absence of any express power to order inspection, the arbitrators have an implied power to do so, under s. 38 (4)(b) of the Arbitration Act 1996.

It is noteworthy that art. 24(2) of the Model Law provides that the parties are to be given sufficient advance notice of any meeting of that arbitral tribunal for the purpose of inspection of goods and other property or documents.

Rules of evidence: England—before the Arbitration Act 1996—was said to apply the same strict rules of evidence on arbitrators sitting in England as those applying to English courts. The rules regarding the admissibility of evidence were part of the law to which arbitrators—including foreign arbitrators ruling on a dispute between non-English parties—were bound. . . . The 1996 Arbitration Act leaves to the parties and the arbitrators to decide whether to apply strict rules of evidence (or any other rules) as to the admissibility, relevance or weight of any material (oral, written or other), s. 34(2)(f). This new provision, based on the UNCITRAL Model Law, seems to be a complete change from the previous situation, although one commentator has said that it remains to be seen whether s. 34(2)(f) amounts to a substantial change in the law. . .

Meanwhile, most of the international arbitration institutions adopt evidence rules with more flexibility. For instance, China International Economic and Trade Arbitration Commission (CIETAC) Arbitration Rules 2005, Article 36. 2: The arbitral tribunal may specify a time period for the parties to produce evidence and the parties shall produce evidence within the specified time period. The arbitral tribunal may refuse to admit any evidence produced beyond the period. If a party has difficulties to produce evidence within the specified time period, it may apply for an extension before the expiration of the period. The arbitral tribunal shall decide whether or not to extend the time period.

上述规则并没有明确规定仲裁案件的举证期间,而由个案中的仲裁员自行决定。

虽然没有统一的国际证据规则,但一些国际专业性组织,如国际律师协会,起草了可供参考的证据规则范本,可供当事人选择。

International Bar Association Supplementary Rules Governing the Presentation and Reception of Evidence in International Commercial Arbitration (adopted May 28, 1983 and reproduced with acknowledgement), Introduction: These Supplementary Rules are the product of a working party of Committee D (Procedures for Settling Disputes) of the Section on Business Law of the International Bar Association (IBA). They are solely concerned with the presentation and reception of evidence in arbitrations and are recommended by the International Bar Association for incorporation in, or adoption together with, institutional and other general rules or procedures governing international commercial arbitrations. Even if not specifically adopted by agreement between the parties, they can serve as a guide to arbitrators conducting such arbitrations when the parties in contention come from law areas having rules of procedures derived from different systems. They may be referred to as the IBA Rules of Evidence. It is recommended that when the parties desire to adopt the IBA Rules of Evidence as supplementary to the general rules applicable to a particular arbitration, the following additional clause be adopted: "The IBA Rules of Evidence shall apply together with the General Rules governing any submission to arbitration incorporated in this Contract. Where they are inconsistent with the aforesaid General Rules, these IBA Rules of Evidence shall prevail but solely as regards the presentation and reception of evidence."

(三) 专家证人

由于国际商事争议中经常会涉及专业问题,而且这些专业问题可能已经超出了当事人和仲裁庭的判断能力,大多数仲裁机构的仲裁规则允许仲裁庭在其认为有必要的情况下指定专家证人。专家证人就专业问题所作认定即为专家证据,包括检验报告、鉴定报告等。专家证据必须送交给双方当事人以便其就该专家报告阐述意见。若一方当事人要求且经仲裁庭同意,专家可以参与庭审回答当事人提问并阐述所涉及的专业问题。

The manner in which expert evidence is to be dealt with lies at the heart of many heated debates in international arbitration. In common law countries it is customary for each of the parties to appoint its own expert witness (or witnesses, where more than one discipline is involved) to provide an opinion for the tribunal...

In civil law countries it is common to find an expert (often selected from a court-approved panel) appointed to prepare a report for the tribunal and the parties...

Again a convergence of the system is noticeable in international arbitration.

Common features of the AAA International Arbitration Rules (Article 22), the LCIA Arbitration Rules (Article 21), the UNCITRAL Arbitration Rules (Article 27) and the UNCITRAL Model Law (Article 26) are that:

(a) the tribunal may appoint experts to report to it and to the parties;

(b) the parties may question the experts at a hearing; and

(c) the parties may present their own expert witnesses at the hearing.

The ICC Arbitration Rules only refer to tribunal appointed experts (Article 20 (4)), but it is not uncommon to come across party-appointed experts in ICC arbitrations.

Pursuant to the broad procedural discretion enjoyed by the tribunal it has developed its own procedural framework for receiving evidence from parties and from experts. The complexity of this framework has varied from case to case and from chamber to chamber. Thus, claimants have been allowed to give oral testimony as to the factual bases of their claims, for example, for purpose of establishing nationality, breach of contract, expropriation etc., without formal classification as to their status as "witness" or "claimants" or any other category of persons.

In other more complex cases one of the chambers has adopted the civil law practice of receiving "information" from person classified as "representatives" rather than "witnesses". Such representatives, for purpose of receiving testimony, are persons other than those giving legal advice or assistance under art. 4 of the rules, and would include the parties themselves or current employees of corporate parties.

All testimony allowed by the tribunal must be subject to challenge or cross-examination at the option of either party. Thus, both art. 25(2) of the tribunal rules and art. 27(4) require adequate prior notice so that an opposing party can prepare for rebuttal testimony cross-examination. Acceptance by the tribunal of informational statements without prior notice could be prejudicial to a party and be a violation of the spirit of arts. 25 and 27.

Another aspect of the tribunal's procedural discretion in the gathering of testimony that enables it to make decisions is the power to appoint one or more experts under art. 27. The tribunal can appoint experts, and establish their terms of reference. It may also do so in consultation with the parties, or hear expert witness, called by the parties "at any stage of the proceedings".

(四)仲裁庭自行调查证据

虽然国际商事仲裁的基本证据规则是"谁主张谁举证",但这并不排除仲裁庭在必要时有自行调查取证的权力(如美国仲裁协会、伦敦国际仲裁院的仲裁规则对此有明确规定)。一些仲裁规则(如联合国国际贸易法委员会仲裁规则)虽然没有明确规定仲裁庭的自行调查取证权力,但规定仲裁庭指定的专家有权接触到与案件相关的任何信息,这也被视为仲裁庭的自行调查取证权力。

国际商事仲裁中,在满足一定的条件下,有管辖权法院可基于仲裁庭或当事人的申请协助取证。

For instance, UNCITRAL Model Law on International Commercial Arbitration, Article 27 Court Assistance in Taking Evidence: The arbitral tribunal or a party with the approval of the arbitral tribunal may request from a competent court of this State assistance in taking evidence. The court may execute the request within its competence and according to its rules on taking evidence.

仲裁庭自行调查证据,依赖于仲裁规则的"授权"。

For instance, CIETAC Arbitration Rules 2005, Article 37 Investigation by the Arbitral Tribunal: (1) The arbitral tribunal may, on its own initiative, undertake investigations and collect evidence as it considers necessary. (2) When investigating and collecting evidence by itself, the arbitral tribunal shall promptly notify the parties to be present at such investigation if it considers it necessary. In the event that one or both parties fail to be present, the investigation and collection shall proceed without being affected.

与2000年的《仲裁规则》相比,2005年CIETAC《仲裁规则》在仲裁庭自行调查取证上更注重了公平公正,在第37条增加了第3款:The arbitral tribunal shall, through the Secretariat of the CIETAC, transmit the evidence collected by itself to the parties and afford them an opportunity to comment.

五、小额案件索赔程序

从整个国际商事仲裁看,仲裁是一种法律商品,而且价格不菲。从高昂的律师费,到不菲的仲裁费用和其他开庭费用,当事人将在经济上付出不小的代价。同时,国际商事仲裁所需时间也不短,对时间就是金钱的商人来说,是必须考虑的问题。很多时候,出于对仲裁所花费的金钱和时间的考虑,当事人会放弃仲裁。故此,某些机构发展出一套小额索赔程序,即由独任仲裁员审理,主要是以文书控辩,附以双方提供的文件以支持,没有正式的披露程序,也不用开庭,一般是由索赔的一方在期限内先提供索赔文书请求及有关文件证据,抗辩的一方在指定的时间内提供抗辩及反索赔(如果有),也包括提供相关的文件证据。

这些小额索赔程序,以伦敦海事仲裁员协会(LMAA)的小额索赔程序(The LMAA Small Claims Procedures)在国际仲裁上最为普遍适用,主要用于海事仲裁,尤其涉及租约的争议。根据LMAA 2002年规则,"小额"为标的额5万美金以下的案件。仲裁员收取的费用是固定的,称为"局限仲裁费用"(capping cost)。仲裁庭的审理程序非常灵活,仲裁庭对所有程序事项有自由裁量权,甚至可以背离小额案件的审理程序。此外,该程序有严格的时间限制,对于超过时限而提交的文件,仲裁员可不予考虑,这主要是出于达到快速解决小额案件的矛盾的目的。在律师费用上,仲裁庭有权对一方补偿给另一方的律师费用进行限额。

我国在这方面也正在学习国际上的先进经验。CIETAC 2005 年《仲裁规则》中,Chapter IV Summary Procedure 是对简易程序的规定。这些规定与 LMAA 的 Small Claims Procedure 有相似之处,但 CIETAC 的规定很简单笼统,当事人无法根据实际需要作出灵活选择。CIETAC 的规则,应当进一步细化,才能让我国的仲裁机构在国际商事仲裁市场上获得竞争力。

六、缺席庭审

一方当事人(几乎总是被申请人)拒绝或未出席,则仲裁庭可以,并且事实上也应当进行缺席审理。此时,仲裁庭应继续其庭审,作出裁决,并确定进行程序的确切情形已经写明于裁决之中。

这是必要的,因为通常的推定是,抵制国际商事仲裁的一方当事人打算拒绝执行最终作出的任何裁决。由于一方当事人未有充分机会陈述其案件是拒绝承认或执行裁决的合法理由,因此,裁决本身在文字上表明被申请人没有出席的情况是很有必要的。缺席审理通常涉及两个主要问题:第一个是何谓"拒绝"参与;第二个是此时仲裁庭应如何进行审理。

(一)拒绝参与

这时有种情形很明显。如有关利比亚石油国有化的三个案件。在这些案件中,利比亚政府一开始即明确表明,拒绝参与任何仲裁程序,理由是各个案件中仲裁庭均无管辖权。如果被告明确拒绝回复仲裁庭的函件,或者遵守仲裁庭有关提交书面申辩等的程序性指令,则拒绝的情形很明显。

还有两种情形仲裁庭应当缺席审理,但这两种情形更加难以确认。第一种是,一方当事人未告知他不愿意参与仲裁,而是制造某些不合理的延迟,以至于仲裁庭有理由认为该不出席的一方已经放弃了陈述的权利。在任何特定的程序中,准确说明何时发生这种情况不太可能。仲裁庭必须使用最好的判断力,权衡所涉及的各种因素。不过仲裁庭如果太早同意缺席审理的申请,可能并不是在帮申请人,因为申请人在申请执行仲裁裁决时,该裁决可能因此被成功地提出异议。

第二种情况是指一方当事人中断了程序,以至于无法有序进行程序。此类情况现实中并不多见,但理论上可能发生,此时仲裁庭就需要将缺席方当事人的行为视为等同于拒绝参加仲裁。

(二) 缺席庭审的程序

仲裁庭不是法院,无权作出类似缺席判决的裁决。仲裁庭的任务是对向其提交的争议作出决定。因此,即使一方当事人未能陈述,仲裁庭也必须考虑争议的是非,并对争议实体作出决定。如果一开始一方当事人就明显不打算参与仲裁,则仲裁庭通常确保所有参与方的意见和证据都以书面形式向其提交。这样它就有正当理由仅在缺席基础上举行简单的庭审,审查仲裁请求并提出任何问题。

关于此类程序应当如何进行的最好指南是,参与仲裁的一方当事人必须拿出实足的证据,使仲裁庭确信可以支持其请求。仲裁庭没有义务选择不出席一方的辩护人,但它必须审查参与方当事人提出的法律和事实观点,以认定这些观点具有充分的理由。然后由仲裁庭对争议问题作附具理由的决定。

关于此种情况下的庭审,不同仲裁庭实践各不相同。这主要取决于仲裁庭进行书面程序所采取的形式。如果书面程序非常全面,仲裁庭可能会感到,在发出裁决前,进行一次简单和纯形式性的庭审有正当的理由。如果书面申辩非常简单、不正式,仅仅是界定争议点的文件,并且没有提交任何书面的证明文件或证人证据,则仲裁庭可能认为,在认定参与方当事人已经履行有关其请求(或答辩)的举证义务前,有必要听取口头证据。

《示范法》包含了一个条款,授权仲裁庭在一方当事人未作出符合当事人约定或仲裁庭确定的需要的行为时,继续进行仲裁程序,作出裁决。类似的条款可见于各国的仲裁法,即使它们并非直接以《示范法》为依据。

如被申请人未能进行抗辩,特别是如果其未能依据《示范法》第 23 条的规定提交答辩陈述,仲裁庭仍然可以进行程序,但是不得将此类行为视为对申请人主张的承认。因此,仲裁庭没有法院作出有利申请人缺席判决的同等权力。它必须对提交仲裁的请求作出决定,并且将此类决定纳入裁决。ICSID 规则对缺席程序进行了类似的、详细的规定。

七、庭审后提出的证据

理论上,庭审完结意味着当事人参与仲裁程序的终结。事实上,当事人庭审后提交新材料一般不被允许,这些新材料会要求仲裁庭发出进一步的程序命令以使另一方当事人可以作出回应。

庭审结束后,仲裁庭作出裁决前可能会发现新证据。此时经希望提交新证据的一方当事人请求,仲裁庭有权重开程序。如果新证据对于合议并无必要,或者新证据看起来是为拖延程序而伪造的,则仲裁庭应当拒绝该请求。但是通常而言,仲裁庭倾向于考虑其所拥有的所有相关证据后对争议作出决定。如果新证据此后证明是没有价值或没有益处的,则提交该证据的一方当事人,可就额外增加的费用受到仲裁庭的处罚,此种处罚在适当情况下通过利息裁决的形式进行。

仲裁庭应当采取的做法,依赖于个案的情况以及必须作出回应的资料的性质。不过仲裁庭通常试图确保不延期庭审,除非确有必要。如果一方当事人在庭审时提交了新的材料,则仲裁庭一般会允许另一方当事人提交进一步的书面证据和意见。另一方当事人有时候会提出异议,但是如果所涉情形是由该方当事人自己通过在后一阶段提交新资料造成的,则这种异议不具有正当理由。任何进一步的书面意见或证据均应转交对方当事人和仲裁庭;仲裁庭必须决定何时中止进一步的答辩、反驳和再答辩。

阅读材料

1. Do the Differences between Cultures Still Influence International Commercial Arbitration Despite Harmonization?

Lara M. Pair J. D.

Copyright © 2002 International Law Students Association; Lara M. Pair J. D.

I. Introduction

Imagine an International Commercial Arbitration hearing. Imagine how the procedure of your International Commercial Arbitration works. Maybe you are already savvy and know of some international rules or you have looked up the UNCITRAL Model Law on International Commercial Arbitration to get a picture. You are, for example, an Anglo-American plaintiff's lawyer. Now imagine the other party to this International Commercial Arbitration. Where are they from? Let us say they are East Asian. So you assume the other party has read the same rules since you have agreed to the use of the UNCITRAL Model Law on International Commercial Arbitration. The arbitrator is French and knows the rules quite well, mainly because she is the arbitrator. Now, as a plaintiff's lawyer you want to "start the show", when the French arbitrator tells you to limit your witness examination to 20 minutes each. Perplexed you protest, because this is not what you are used to, but the arbitrator will hear nothing.

What has happened? Differing expectations. In International Commercial Arbitration more than just the legal issues are issues. Whether procedure is agreed upon ad hoc, or institutional rules are used, expectations of the process may well differ from participant to participant. Why? Divergence in cultural backgrounds. This paper argues that despite harmonization of procedural rules in International Commercial Arbitration, expectations of the process differ based on cultural background of parties or arbitrators. In order to overcome cultural barriers of this and other sorts, one should understand the differences and use them creatively. This paper is intended to shed light on some of the differences and thereby advocate understanding.

There are two caveats for this text. First, it must be clarified that the lawyers may well be better informed than the parties and the expectations may differ with increased experience and knowledge of background of other participants. Second, my analysis applies to both ad hoc and institutional arbitrations. The extent of the cultural influence on the process may differ. Institutional arbitrations usually have more clearly defined rules of procedure and tend to adopt a common approach for arbitrations, instead of a case-by-case determination.

...

II. What is Culture Anyway?

...

While the substantive outcome in International Commercial Arbitration is not usually based on cultural expectation, procedure is. Substantive law and even basic norms will differ not only from culture to culture but also from country to country. Laws are specific and while the expectation is that the decision is at least based on some legal principle, there is no expectation of one concrete and certain outcome. Procedure however, in its most basic form is expected to be the same based on continuous, substantially identical reoccurrence in one's own culture. Participants expect procedure as a part of the formal aspect of culture. A common law, Anglo-American Lawyer will most likely expect a highly adversarial approach, while a civil law East Asian will expect that an inquisitorial and conciliatory approach be taken by the arbitral panel and all parties involved. This basic difference plays out in the timing and ease of introduction of evidence, record keeping, and other examples further discussed below. Expectancy of a certain procedure is worth analyzing in light of the predominant legal systems. The arbitrator may be of a culture that expects the proceeding to be conducted in one way, while the parties may be prepared for another, their own way. What the main differences are and how exactly they can play out will be discussed below.

III. Differences in Legal Culture

...

Recent doctrinal writings indicate an increasing trend toward harmonization of international arbitral procedure. For example, it is generally accepted that a person who has served as mediator or conciliator between the parties to the current dispute shall not serve as umpire. Domestic legislation and procedures of international organizations concerning International Commercial Arbitration evidence this assessment further. This text will focus on the remaining differences. Nevertheless, cultural differences are far from irrelevant today, because neither ad hoc nor institutional rules adopted by the parties answer all procedural questions.

A. Common Law & Civil Law

While rules, which have been agreed upon by the parties, give some guidelines for the procedure, the individual preference of the participants plays an important role. This preference relates to the cultural background of each participant and influences all aspects of the International Commercial Arbitration, for example, choice of International Commercial Arbitration rules, arbitrators, location for the International Commercial Arbitration, and expectations in process and outcome.

...

Most commonly cited differences that influence the expectations are:

a) Whether the proceedings are oral or in writing;

b) Discovery and pre-hearing procedure;

c) Treatment of other witnesses, specifically parties and cross-examination; and

d) Record keeping.

1. Oral or Written Proceedings

The UNCITRAL rule 24(1) leaves the decision whether to hold a hearing to the arbitral tribunal, unless parties agree otherwise. A hearing shall be held if a party so requests. It is not stated which weight will be given to such pleadings and how much detail will be good practice depends on any given arbitrator's preference.

Under the Common Law, pleadings have little value, because the oral hearing is of most importance. The fact finder has to be convinced during the "show", the proceeding of whatever nature. This can largely be explained by the need for persuasion of a jury of laypersons. Paper tends to be less persuasive than emotions and live testimony. In Civil Law all information has to be identified and provided in writing and often in excessive detail as soon as possible. This is evidenced by e. g. , the German Code of Civil Procedure § 296. A judge is not (should not be as easily) moved by emotion and a judge could extract the relevant facts more quickly from paper than from lengthy witness testimony and cross-examination. The Civil Law lawyer expects the documents provided to amply support the point of view, and the Common Law lawyer is perplexed because of the lack of weight given to his advocacy by the Civil Law arbitrator.

2. Discovery and Pre-Hearing Procedures

The secondly impacted area of arbitral procedure is the pre-hearing stage, including discovery. The UNCITRAL rules provide in article 23 (1) that parties should support their claims and defenses with all relevant documents, but are also allowed to use references to evidence to be submitted later only, unless otherwise agreed. In other words, information must be provided, but the point in time is up to the party, so long as a reference to this evidence exists. In article 24 (3), UNCITRAL requires all material submitted to the panel to be submitted to the other party as well. This is the extent to which pre-hearing procedure is discussed in the Model Law.

Due to this freedom of procedure, culture has room to create expectations. In Common Law, discovery and pre-hearing procedure are considered one of the most important tools in dispute resolution (either judicial or through ADR). Pre-hearing discovery is necessary in Common Law. The evidence needs to be neatly presented for the reasons discussed supra, which is impossible if the hearing is the first time the evidence is encountered by the parties. Thus, while attempting to receive as much information as possible before the hearing, the Common Law advocate will seek to delay rendering information to obtain a strategic benefit. With these considerations in mind, the advocate will submit evidence late and potentially upset the Civil Law arbitrator, who seeks prompt disclosure of all relevant information.

In Civil Law the obligation to disclose every relevant piece of information as soon as possible renders extensive Common Law discovery (partially) unnecessary. For many Civil Law jurisdictions, such as Germany, discovery is also connected with privacy concerns. In Civil Law there is no need to present the evidence the neat Common Law way. Evidence is presented over time and is reviewed by the judge regardless of when it becomes known. If any information appears to be missing, the arbitrator or judge will request it. Also depositions take on varying degrees of importance for Common Lawyer and Civil Lawyer. If the hearing is approached with the expectation of a deposition not being primary evidence, the conduct at the deposition (if they take place at all) is going to be different from the expectation of it being equivalent to a witness statement on the stand. Preparation needs to be adapted, the lawyer has to take into account that the entire material will be reviewed and that withholding of information harms the case rather than helping it. In addition, a Civil Law arbitrator may even prefer a written statement to an oral one for reasons of efficiency, as mentioned above.

3. Treatment of Witnesses

Treatment of witnesses is another area where cultural difference is most visible. The UNCITRAL is silent on the matter. Several issues are implicated in the treatment of witnesses:

1) Whether a party can be a witness;

2) Whether the statements can be written;

3) Whether written statements are preferable over directly examined witnesses; and

4) Whether cross-examination should take place.

In Common Law a party may be called as witness, while the Civil Law does generally not allow parties to be witnesses. In Civil Law, the expectation is that the position of parties will be amply reproduced through other documents. In Civil Law, managers of a company are considered parties. Although the question whether a party can be a witness remains a distinction between Common and Civil Law, in International Commercial Arbitration it is a distinction without a difference. Practice has settled toward the Common Law approach.

Whether written witness statements are admissible depends on the procedure chosen, but largely, as in the UNCITRAL. The inference drawn from a written statement depends on the legal culture of the arbitrator. In Common Law countries, due to the importance of the actual hearing and the separation of information gained before the hearing from information presented at the hearing, cross-examination remains the best tool to test witness credibility and to bring out facts not otherwise presentable. In Civil Law countries, the judge examines witnesses as to contentious issues. He, as the fact-finder and a professional, is deemed to assess the witness credibility by himself and only with reference to statements he deems important. Although a difference between the two traditions, this point adds little to the point made supra concerning pretrial procedure.

The distinction in treatment for unwilling witnesses depends less on culture and more on country, the procedure what one needs to compel the witness differs. These issues are related much more to substantive law and not relate as strongly to culture. Hence, it exceeds the scope of this paper and will not be treated in more detail.

4. Record Keeping

The UNCITRAL does not mention record keeping. In the Common Law tradition, a reporter records the proceeding verbatim. In the Civil Law system, the chairman usually takes notes of the witness statement in the manner in which he sees fit. The parties discuss these notes and supplement them to prepare a written summary. A summary makes sense where the evidence is mostly documentary and witnesses are heard for specific information only. This method obviously reduces the impact of cross-examination in case it is conducted and can be the source of great dismay on Common Law lawyers, who rely on every word that the witness utters.

Although the above-mentioned differences in legal cultures factor into the proceedings, they are not the only issues to be considered. Within the predominant legal systems, further subdivisions exist.

The Common Law and Civil Law concepts and the respective conceptions of International Commercial Arbitration and legal culture have radiated throughout the world. The concepts are largely colonial remainders and can be traced in individual tradition to the respective colonial powers and their legal systems.

2. International Commercial Arbitration: Americanized, "Civilized," or Harmonized?

Elena V. Helmer

Copyright © 2003 Ohio State Journal on Dispute Resolution; Elena V. Helmer

I. Has International Commercial Arbitration Become "Americanized"?

...

The whole debate of Americanization of international commercial arbitration springs from what has been called the "Common Law-Civil Law Divide." The differences between the two legal systems are most visible in the area of procedure, and, not surprisingly, the majority of publications discussing the Americanization of international commercial arbitration concentrate on procedural issues. However, the concept of the "Great Divide" is not fully accepted in either legal tradition, and a "clash of legal cultures" is at most a questionable proposition. For the purpose of this discussion, we will simply accept the existence of numerous differences between the

Anglo-Saxon and Continental legal systems without going into this issue any further.

Do the procedural tactics and techniques of U. S. litigators in international commercial arbitration mean that arbitration has become "Americanized"? And if American influence on international commercial arbitration is broader than the procedural element alone, does it amount to Americanization of arbitration?

...

The author believes that American influence on international arbitration is significant, but falls short of Americanization. Rather, the current trends and developments in international commercial arbitration demonstrate an ongoing process of harmonization in many areas of international arbitration. This includes national arbitration laws, rules of major arbitration institutions, and arbitration practices, as demonstrated by the United Nations Commission on International Trade Law (UNCITRAL) and International Bar Association (IBA) documents as well as procedures adopted by international arbitral tribunals.

II. Procedure

...

International commercial arbitration began experiencing strong American influence in the 1970s when the first teams of U. S. lawyers arrived in Europe to represent their clients in the large petroleum arbitrations. Almost immediately, the American litigation style and trial techniques, which the U. S. lawyers brought with them, began changing the way international commercial arbitrations were conducted in that they started looking "more like litigation." Not surprisingly, arbitral procedure is the single element of international arbitration that is said to be most "Americanized."

...

During the last quarter of a century, major U. S. law firms active in the international arbitration arena have become quite sophisticated in the arbitration game, be it Continental or Anglo-American style. However, the continuing flow of American newcomers into international arbitration necessarily means that they keep bringing with them the familiar procedural techniques, court standards of minimum contacts between the arbitrators and the parties (and their counsel), and other practices foreign to traditional international arbitration.

The Anglo-American litigation tradition has a number of useful features, and lawyers trained in the United States do possess some unique skills-procedural management being just one of them. In the words of a Swiss practitioner, "Common law lawyers have ... often-demonstrated greater energy and training in obtaining, analyzing and arguing the facts on which most arbitrations are won or lost." The strength of American attorneys in procedural management and litigation tactics may not be liked on the Continent, but it is well recognized there.

It is natural for lawyers to use the skills and methods they are trained in and accustomed to whenever they are called on to provide their professional services. There is no problem if it happens within the context of domestic arbitration as usually both parties come with the same expectations as to the procedure to be followed. However, in international arbitration, parties usually come from different countries and, not infrequently, from countries that belong to different legal traditions. In such a setting, imposition of procedural rules and methods of one of the parties may denounce the sense of fairness of the entire proceeding and leave the other party (and possibly at least one arbitrator) feeling disadvantaged and disappointed.

Not surprisingly, international arbitration has rapidly begun to develop ways to deal with the "Great Divide" in arbitration procedure through the evolving practice of arbitral tribunals; changes in institutional and other arbitration rules; numerous initiatives of various arbitration institutions; and the efforts of UNCITRAL, the International Bar Association, and other organizations. As a result, the "invasion," which has brought "more rigor and increased competition into the European arbitral system,... has strengthened arbitration generally and resulted in better awards." We will discuss some of these improvements later.

...

思考题

1. 如何理解仲裁程序中的意思自治原则？
2. 列举各不同仲裁机构对"仲裁受理"的不同标准，并阐述"仲裁受理"的确认在仲裁程序中的意义。
3. 仲裁申请书中必须包含哪些内容？仲裁申请书有固定格式吗？
4. 被申请人提交答辩状时应注意哪些问题？
5. 讨论"the seat of arbitration"和"place of arbitration"的区别。
6. 比较 CIETAC 仲裁规则和其他仲裁机构仲裁规则的主要不同点，并试对 CIETAC 仲裁规则的改进提出建议。

推荐阅读

1. 谢石松主编:《商事仲裁法学》,高等教育出版社 2003 年版,第 217—218 页。

2. 杜新丽:《国际民事诉讼和商事仲裁》,中国政法大学出版社 2005 年版,第 277—282 页。

3. 杨良宜:《仲裁法:从 1996 年英国仲裁法到国际商务仲裁》,法律出版社 2006 年版,第 967—979 页。

4. 〔英〕艾伦·雷德芬、马丁·亨特等:《国际商事仲裁法律与实践》,林一飞、宋连斌译,北京大学出版社 2005 年版,第 284—289 页。

5. 杨树明主编:《国际商事仲裁法》,重庆大学出版社 2002 年版,第 168—170 页。

6. Mark Huleatt-James & Nicholas Gould, International Commercial Arbitration: A Handbook, 2nd ed., LLP, 1999, pp.75—93.

7. Christian Buhring-Uhle, Lars Kirchhoff, Gabriele Scherer, Arbitration and Mediation in International Business, 2nd ed., Kluwer Law International, 2006, pp.69—88.

8. Robert Merkin, Arbitration Law, Informa Legal Publishing, 2004.

9. Stefan N. Frommel and Barry A. K. Rider, Conflicting Legal Cultures in Commercial Arbitration, Old Issues and New Trends, Kluwer Law International, pp.39—40.

第七章 国际商事仲裁裁决

裁决是国际商事仲裁中的一个核心内容。在确认当事人的仲裁协议有效后,有管辖权的仲裁庭可以对有关争议事项进行审理,在该过程中往往能产生具有法律效力的仲裁裁决。国际商事仲裁中的裁决类型具有多样性,这使得不同类型的裁决对当事人的权利义务产生的影响存在着差异。此外,仲裁庭作出的终局裁决虽然具有终局性的法律效力,但是并非说就不存在相应的法律救济措施。

第一节 国际商事仲裁裁决概述

一、裁决的定义

目前,各国对于裁决的定义并没有统一的结论。因为各国间不可避免地存在法律文化的差异,这使得各国在解释仲裁裁决的定义时存在较大的差异。

我国有学者认为,就裁决本身而言,国际商事仲裁裁决是指国际商事仲裁庭就双方当事人提交仲裁的争议事项所作出的对双方当事人均具有约束力的终局性的决定。① 但是实践中常常存在仲裁庭发布临时裁决、部分裁决和仲裁中出现临时性保全措施的情况,暴露了这种观点存在片面性的缺陷。

There is no internationally accepted definition of the term "award". Indeed, none is to be found in the international conventions dealing with arbitration, including the Geneva treaties, the New York Convention or the Model Law. Even though the New York Convention is directed to the recognition and enforcement of awards, the nearest it comes to a definition is:

"The term 'arbitral awards' shall include not only awards made by arbitrators appointed for each case but also those made by permanent arbitral bodies to which the parties have submitted."

This is helpful, but incomplete. At one stage it was proposed that there should be a definition of the term "award" in the Model Law, but ultimately none was adopted.

---

① 参见杨树明主编:《国际商事仲裁法》,重庆大学出版社2002年版,第222—223页。

有学者建议"裁决"意指对所有提交仲裁庭解决的事项作出的最终裁决以及仲裁庭对所有实体问题作出的最后决定,或者是仲裁庭对于本身的管辖问题或其他任何程序问题所作出的决定。但是仅在仲裁庭将其决定称为裁决时方如此。① 这种建议虽强调了在仲裁过程中区分多种裁决的必要性,但其表述无疑使裁决的定义变得更为复杂。这是不利于其在国际商事仲裁领域中被采纳和运用的。

In practice, "award" should be reserved for decisions that finally determine the substantive issues. This involves distinguishing between awards and procedural orders and directions. Procedural orders and directions help to move the arbitration forward; they deal with such matters as the exchange of written evidence, the production of documents and the arrangements for the conduct of the hearing. They do not have the status of awards; and they may perhaps be called into question after the final award has been made (for instance, as evidence of bias on the part of the arbitral tribunal).

通过勉强创造出一些定义来限定裁决,反而使得这样的定义很难经得起推敲。况且,裁决定义设立的目的,归根究底是要准确地把握裁决的内涵。对于如何理解裁决的内涵,我们是可以通过分析和掌握裁决的特性和种类来进行把握的。因此,在各国协调确立统一的裁决定义前,我们大可不必深究这个问题。

二、裁决的形式与内容

裁决的形式关系到一个裁决是否能成为有效的裁决。因此,大多数国家对裁决的形式都有立法上的明文规定。一般来说,绝大多数国家都将书面形式作为有效裁决的载体。但是,也有极个别国家存在例外的规定。英国在这方面就是个典型的例子。例如,英国《1996年仲裁法》第52条规定:"(1)当事人可以自由约定裁决书的形式;(2)如无此约定,则适用以下规定;(3)裁决应当以书面形式作出,并由所有仲裁员或者所有同意该裁决的仲裁员在仲裁书上签名。"1998年《伦敦国际仲裁院仲裁规则》第26条第1款规定:"除非当事人各方另有书面约定,仲裁裁决应当以书面形式作出,并应说明裁决所依据的理由。还应当述明作出裁决的时间和仲裁地,并应由仲裁庭或者同意此裁决的成员签署。"②

此外,根据世界各国商事仲裁立法和司法实践的一致要求,裁决中还应当有

---

① 参见〔英〕艾伦·雷德芬、马丁·亨特等:《国际商事仲裁法律与实践》,林一飞、宋连斌译,北京大学出版社2005年版,第378页。
② 转引自汪祖兴:《国际商会仲裁研究》,法律出版社2005年版,第333页。

仲裁员的签名。对于如何签名,则因各国规定的不同而有所区别。一般来说,以全体仲裁员签名为原则,以多数仲裁员签名为例外。① 还有极少数国家或仲裁机构有更特别的规定,例如:

Article 32.3 of Arbitration Rules of the Arbitration Institute of the Stockholm Chamber of Commerce:

"The parties may agree that the Chairman alone shall sign the Award."

由于仲裁员签名并非强制性的,所以对于上文提到的一般原则,实践中常遇到某些仲裁员不愿签名的情况。此时,仲裁庭就必须在裁决书上作必要的说明。

The award should be signed by all arbitrators or, where one of the arbitrators refuses to sign the award, by the majority of the members of the arbitral tribunal, provided that the reasons why an arbitrator's signature is omitted are stated in the award.

Article 48 of Netherlands Arbitration Institute:

"1. If the arbitral tribunal is composed of more than one arbitrator, it shall decide by a majority of votes.

2. If a minority of the arbitrators refuses to sign, the other arbitrators shall make mention thereof beneath the award signed by them. This statement shall also be signed by them."

仲裁员不签署通常都是因为不同意裁决意见。当仲裁员意见不一致时,少数意见是否可写在仲裁裁决中呢?各仲裁机构或仲裁法的做法也不尽相同。当前主要有两种做法:

一种意见是,裁决中不得提到少数仲裁员的意见。但是不得提到少数仲裁员意见,并不表示少数仲裁员就不能发表自己的意见了。在国际仲裁中,少数仲裁员是可以以单独文件的形式向其他仲裁员或当事人发表其意见的。不过需要特别注意的是,此类文件不应视为裁决的一部分。

另一种意见是,可以在裁决中提到少数意见。我国就是该做法的典型例子。我国目前的涉外仲裁实践中,通常将少数仲裁员的意见做成记录附卷。

裁决的内容是指商事仲裁裁决书中所必须载明的事项。包括有关当事人的情况、仲裁程序事项、案情和裁决事项、裁决所依据的理由以及裁决结果等。世界各国和仲裁机构对此都有各自规定,因此内容要求上并不统一。② 例如,我国《仲裁法》第54条规定,裁决书应当写明仲裁请求、争议事项、裁决理由、裁决结果、仲裁费用的负担和裁决日期。当事人协议不愿写明争议事项和裁决理由的,

---

① 参见谢石松主编:《商事仲裁法学》,高等教育出版社2003年版,第268页。
② 同上书,第269页。

可以不写。

三、裁决的种类

在国际商事仲裁中,不仅仅存在仲裁庭审理案件所作的终局裁决,还包括其他裁决,如中间裁决和部分裁决等。根据各国和国际商事仲裁机构的仲裁实践,商事仲裁裁决可以根据不同标准划分出不同的种类。为了便于掌握,我们将对从不同角度分类的裁决分别介绍。

(一)中间裁决(interim or interlocutory award)、部分裁决(partial award)和终局裁决(final award)

中间裁决、部分裁决和终局裁决是以裁决的内容和作出裁决的时间为标准进行划分的。这种划分方式也是仲裁实践中最重要的划分方式之一。

1. 中间裁决,又称临时裁决,是在仲裁过程中作出的未解决当事人之间所有争议的裁决。中间裁决主要针对程序问题。例如,《日本商事仲裁协会仲裁规则》中就规定,仲裁庭如认为适当,可就仲裁程序中发生的争议作出中间裁决。由于中间裁决针对的是程序问题,因而临时保全措施可能采用中间裁决的形式发布。这在《美国仲裁协会国际仲裁规则》中有所体现。

Article 21. 2 of International Arbitration Rules of the American Arbitration Association:

"Such interim measures may be taken in the form of an interim award and the tribunal may require security for the costs of such measures."

虽然中间裁决针对的主要是程序问题,但也可能涉及实体问题。例如,仲裁庭可能作出中间裁决,确定哪一方当事人应当承担责任,而在最终裁决中决定责任的大小问题。由于中间仲裁并不具有终局性,因此,中间裁决确定的责任义务还要受到终局裁决的影响。中间裁决作出后,仲裁程序结束时,仲裁庭会作出确定当事人最终权利义务关系的终局裁定。

2. 部分裁决,仅处理当事人提交争议的一部分,是在仲裁庭认为争议的某一部分已经审理清楚且有必要先行作出裁决,或者经当事人请求或当事人承认对方当事人的请求时,采取的一种裁决方式。

A partial award is an effective way of determining matters that are susceptible to determination during the course of the proceedings and which, once determined, may save considerable time and money for all involved. One obvious example is where an issue of jurisdiction is involved. An arbitral tribunal that spent months hearing a dispute only to rule in its final award that it had no jurisdiction would, to put it mildly, look foolish (unless the issue of jurisdiction was inseparably bound up with the merits of the case).

3. 终局裁决,又称最终裁决或最后裁决,是指仲裁庭在案件审理终结后就提交仲裁的争议的全部问题所作的最后裁决。终局裁决最重要的特性就是终局性,如同民事诉讼中的终局判决一样,一旦作出,即发生法律约束力,整个案件也随即终结。裁决的这种终局性也排除了当事人上诉的可能。

The term "final award" is customarily reserved for an award that completes the mission of the arbitral tribunal. Subject to certain exceptions, the delivery of a final award renders the arbitral tribunal functus officio. It ceases to have any further jurisdiction over the dispute, and the special relationship that exists between the arbitral tribunal and the parties ends. This has significant consequences. An arbitral tribunal should not issue a final award until it is satisfied that its mission has actually been completed. If there are outstanding matters to be determined, such as questions relating to costs (including the arbitral tribunal's own costs) or interest, or further directions to be given relating to the disposal of property, the arbitral tribunal should issue an award that is expressly designated as a partial or interim award.

(二) 合意裁决(consensual award)和非合意裁决(non-consensual award)

合意裁决和非合意裁决是从裁决是否反映了双方当事人的合意的角度来划分的。

1. 合意裁决,是指仲裁庭依据仲裁双方当事人所达成的和解协议或者仲裁调解协议所作出的裁决。

As in litigation, parties often arrive at a settlement of their dispute during the proceedings. If this occurs the parties may simply implement the settlement agreement and in effect revoke the man date of the arbitral tribunal. This means that the jurisdiction and powers previously given to the arbitral tribunal by the parties are terminated.

合意裁决的方式是非常可取的,它能激励当事人双方通过协商来解决争议,同时又赋予当事人和解协议强制执行的效力。这种建立在双方自愿基础上的裁决方式,对国际民商事行为是非常有利的。基于双方和解或调解产生的合意裁决,如果彼此能按协议履行各自义务,那么就达到了解决争议的目的。

2. 非合意裁决,是指凡是仲裁庭不依当事人达成的和解协议或者在仲裁中达成的调解协议作出的裁决。在国际商事仲裁实践中,非合意裁决是主要的裁决方式。

(三) 缺席裁决(default award)和对席裁决

从仲裁当事人及其代理人是否出席商事仲裁庭的仲裁审理程序和行使了辩护权的角度,可以将裁决划分为缺席裁决和对席裁决两类。

1. 缺席裁决,是指商事仲裁庭在被申请人(包括反请求中的被申请人)及其代理人都没有依法出席庭审程序或者没有出席整个庭审程序,没有行使辩论权的基础上所作出的仲裁裁决。① 缺席裁决在各仲裁机构规则中都有体现。例如,《斯德哥尔摩商会仲裁院仲裁规则》第28条规定,任何一方当事人无正当理由而未能出席庭审或未能遵守仲裁庭的决定,不影响仲裁庭继续进行程序直至作出仲裁。《印度仲裁委员会仲裁规则》规定,如被申请人在规定的时间内因疏忽未出席或拒绝出席进行答辩或提交材料,或者因为疏忽未缴付或拒绝缴付仲裁庭或登记员命其缴付之费用或保证金,则仲裁庭可以作出缺席裁决。

缺席裁决也是有约束力的裁决,但应当注意下列事项:

The default of the respondent does not affect the burden of proof.

The Appearing Party and the Arbitral Tribunal must ensure that the Defaulting Party is constantly given Proper Notice of the ongoing Arbitration Proceedings.

The defaulting party has been duly notified of the arbitration.

All correspondence between the arbitral tribunal and the diligent party is sent to the defaulting defendant at a valid address.

Since a party which boycotts arbitration proceedings is likely to resist enforcement of the award, it is important that the award itself enunciates the circumstances of the default by the respondent as well as the opportunities given to that party to state its case.

The Arbitral Tribunal shall accept the subsequent Intervention of a Defaulting Respondent, but it is not bound to repeat Procedural Steps missed by the absent Respondent. As a consequence of each party's right to present its case, a respondent shall not be barred from appearing at a subsequent stage of the proceedings where it failed to participate in the earlier stages. Accordingly, the respondent which has not filed its statement of defense within the prescribed time-limit is still authorized to appear at the hearing and present witnesses. However, the right of a party to be heard does not go as far as to entitle the defaulting party to request the arbitral tribunal to resume all procedural stages ab initio. ②

2. 对席裁决,即指商事仲裁庭在仲裁双方当事人或其代理人都依法出席了整个庭审程序,行使了辩论权的基础上所作出的仲裁裁决。

(四) 补充裁决(additional award)和被补充裁决

补充裁决与被补充裁决的划分是基于仲裁裁决之间的补充与被补充关系。

---

① 参见谢石松主编:《商事仲裁法学》,高等教育出版社2003年版,第262页。

② See Daniel E. Tunik, Default Proceedings in International Commercial Arbitration, International Arbitration Law Review, 1998.

1. 补充裁决,是指对当事人提出但仲裁庭在仲裁裁决中未作出决定的请求作出的裁决。补充裁决通常可由当事人提出申请或仲裁庭主动进行,并且需要在规定的时间内作出。许多国际商事仲裁规则基于弥补商事仲裁中出现的缺漏的目的,也纷纷引入了补充裁决制度。

《伦敦国际仲裁院仲裁规则》第 17 条第 3 款规定:"除非当事人另有约定,一方当事人于收到裁决起 30 日内,经通知另一方或另几方当事人,要求仲裁庭就其在仲裁程序中提出的、裁决中未加处理的请求作出附加裁决。如果仲裁庭认为该要求理由正当,它应在 60 日内作出附加裁决。"

Article 33.3 of Model Law:

"Unless otherwise agreed by the parties, a party, with notice to the other party, may request, within thirty days of receipt of the award, the arbitral tribunal to make an additional award as to claims presented in the arbitral proceedings but omitted from the award. If the arbitral tribunal considers the request to be justified, it shall make the additional award within sixty days."

2. 被补充裁决,即指补充裁决所弥补的存在缺漏的裁决。

四、裁决的作出

一份有效裁决的作出,除了应具备前述的形式要件以外,还要涉及以下几方面的问题:

(一) 缺员裁决

前文中介绍的"缺席裁决"是一方当事人或其代理人缺席的情况,在仲裁实践中不仅存在此类缺席,还有仲裁员缺席的情况。对于仲裁员缺席情况下作出的裁决,我们称之为缺员裁决。如果出现仲裁员缺席的情况,仲裁庭是否需要中止审理,重新确认仲裁员呢?依某些国家的法律和仲裁机构的规定,其他仲裁员在该名仲裁员缺席的情况下,可继续进行仲裁程序,作出相关决定和终局裁决。

Article 26.2 of the London Court of International Arbitration (LCIA) Arbitration Rules:

"If any arbitrator fails to comply with the mandatory provisions of any applicable law relating to the making of the award, having been given a reasonable opportunity to do so, the remaining arbitrators may proceed in his absence and state in their award the circumstances of the other arbitrator's failure to participate in the making of the award."

另外,要求仲裁员作出缺员裁决应提前进行通知的做法也为一些国家所采纳。如德国在 1998 年《仲裁法》第 1052 条规定,如某仲裁员拒绝参加对裁决的表决,除非当事人另有约定,其他仲裁员可以在其缺席的情况下作出裁决。当事人应得到提前通知。

因此,在仲裁员缺席情况下,不论是仲裁庭可继续审理的规定,还是作出裁决前需提前通知的做法,都表明了仲裁员缺席并不一定导致仲裁程序的中止。

(二) 裁决的作出期限

在民事审判中,不管是一审、二审,还是再审,都对审判期限有具体的规定。这样做是为了防止法院久审不决所导致的当事人合法利益的损害。在仲裁过程中,为避免仲裁庭拖延裁决,也确立了裁决作出期限的规定来规制仲裁庭。

世界各国的商事仲裁法律制度对于商事仲裁庭作出仲裁裁决的期限的长短、计算该期限的方式和起点等方面的规定都有所不同。一般来说,各国对裁决作出期限的规定可以分为以下几种做法:

1. 约定期限

约定期限,即允许当事人通过仲裁协议具体约定作出商事仲裁裁决的时间,仲裁庭应当在当事人约定的期限内作出裁决。这种做法体现了当事人意思自治的精神。

Article 8.2 of the Uniform Arbitration Act:

"An award shall be made within the time fixed therefore by the agreement or, if not so fixed, within such time as the court orders on application of a party. The parties may extend the time in writing either before or after the expiration thereof. A party waives the objection that an award was not made within the time required unless he notifies the arbitrators of his objection prior to the delivery of the award to him."

如果商事仲裁裁决书没有在规定的期限内做成,则任何一方当事人都可以在该项裁决书送达前通知有关仲裁庭,对该项裁决的期限表示异议。当事人对裁决期限的异议对仲裁庭的裁决效力具有巨大的影响力。一旦异议被确认有效,当事人就可以否决仲裁庭所作裁决的效力。但当事人依法表示异议时,必须意思明确,只有这样才可以认定他已否认这一裁决的效力,否则该裁决仍应视为有效裁决。

2. 法定期限

法定期限,是指由仲裁法直接规定的仲裁庭应该作出仲裁裁决的期限。世界上许多国家的商事仲裁立法都明确规定了商事仲裁庭应该作出裁决的时间,以及该时间计算的起点和方法。仲裁庭只能在规定期限内作出裁决,否则仲裁当事人可以对有关的仲裁裁决的效力提出异议。如瑞典、泰国、日本等。

Article 37 of Arbitration Rules of the Arbitration Institute of the Stockholm Chamber of Commerce:

"The final award shall be made not later than six months from the date upon which the arbitration was referred to the Arbitral Tribunal pursuant to Article 18. The

Board may extend this time limit upon a reasoned request from the Arbitral Tribunal, or if otherwise deemed necessary."

3. 将约定期限和法定期限相结合

一些国家也采用将约定期限和法定期限相结合的方式,即规定首先由当事人约定仲裁裁决的期限,仲裁裁决在此约定期限内作出;如当事人没有此项约定的,则在仲裁法或仲裁规则规定的期限内作出。如葡萄牙、埃及。①

(三) 形式审查

仲裁裁决如果是仲裁机构仲裁,根据一些仲裁规则的规定,可以由机构最后对裁决作形式审查,只有经过机构的审查,仲裁庭才可能发出裁决书。形式审查的目的是预防有瑕疵的仲裁裁决的形成。由于仲裁的最后裁决具有终局性,一旦裁决发布,即具有约束力。所以在其发布之前,通过形式审查可以为有瑕疵的仲裁裁决再设一道防护屏障。如 CIETAC《仲裁规则》第 56 条第 2 款规定,仲裁员应在签署裁决前将裁决书草案送交仲裁委员会;在不影响仲裁员独立仲裁的情况下,仲裁委员会可以就裁决书的形式问题提请仲裁员注意。CIETAC《仲裁规则》只涉及形式审查,而未提及实体问题。但有些机构仲裁规则还规定仲裁机构可以提请仲裁庭注意实体问题。

Article 27 of the Rules of Arbitration of the International Chamber of Commerce:

"Before signing any Award, the Arbitral Tribunal shall submit it in draft form to the Court. The Court may lay down modifications as to the form of the Award and, without affecting the Arbitral Tribunal's liberty of decision, may also draw its attention to points of substance. No Award shall be rendered by the Arbitral Tribunal until it has been approved by the Court as to its form".

(四) 裁决的公布

仲裁程序具有保密性。一般来说,仲裁程序以不公开为原则,公开为例外。我们在此主要介绍一下作为例外情况的仲裁程序公开问题。一般在两种情况下,裁决可以公开:一是所有当事人均同意,这种情况也符合当事人意思自治的要求;二是法律要求公开,这种情况属于强行性规定,当事人无权拒绝。对于仲裁程序公开的情况,并不难找到相应的例子。例如,CIETAC《仲裁规则》规定,裁决仅在双方当事人同意的情况下方得公开。《美国仲裁协会仲裁规则》第 27 条第 4 款规定,裁决仅在各方当事人同意或法律根据本规则有此要求时方可公布。《伦敦国际仲裁院仲裁规则》第 30 条第 3 款还规定,仲裁员公布裁决时需要得到所有当事人和仲裁庭事前的书面同意。大多数仲裁机构均规定了裁决不公开原则。

---

① 参见谢石松主编:《商事仲裁法学》,高等教育出版社 2003 年版,第 271 页。

不过,少数仲裁机构也规定以裁决公开作为原则。但是这种规定在国际商事仲裁领域是比较鲜见的。印度是比较典型的例子。《印度仲裁委员会仲裁规则》第 68 条 d 款规定,为发展仲裁法或创立仲裁先例以对将来之仲裁有所裨益并起到指引作用,印度仲裁委员会可以在任何仲裁杂志、期刊、报告中印刷、出版或以其他方式传播由其管理或作出的裁决。任何一方当事人均不得对上述之裁决公布提出异议,但是在公布裁决时争议双方当事人的名称和地址应予省略,且如当事人希望,其身份应予适当地保密。

第二节　国际商事仲裁中的临时性保全措施

在民事诉讼中,为了保证最终裁决能得以顺利实施或保护当事人的利益,法院可以主动或依据当事人申请采取民事保全措施。这类措施的存在能有效阻止恶意当事人故意转移财产或破坏证据的行为。同样地,在仲裁领域中也存在类似的措施来保护仲裁当事人的利益,我们称之为仲裁中的临时性保全措施。

一、临时性保全措施概述

虽然仲裁中的临时性保全措施在目的和形式方面与民诉中的民事保全措施有相似的地方,但是两者并非等同,仲裁中的临时性保全措施自身仍具有比较明显的特征。

(一) 临时性保全措施的概念和特征

If arbitration is to remain an effective means to resolve commercial disputes, it must accommodate the practical requirements of those who resort to it. Interim measures of protection, sometimes known as conservatory and protective measures, are a feature of domestic litigation in most countries. Interim measures permit domestic courts to guard against the eventuality that the subject-matter of the dispute will vanish, or be passed into the hands of a third party or that the object of the proceedings will be defeated.[①]

国际商事仲裁中的临时性保全措施,是指在国际商事仲裁程序开始前或进行中,一方认为对方出现转移财产、抽逃资金等可能危及最终仲裁裁决执行的行为,而提出申请,由仲裁庭或有管辖权的法院所采取的诸如扣押、查封财产、责令保管或出售争议标的物,保全证据以及维持某种状态等具有强制性的临时措施。

According to the definition given by the European Court of Justice, provisional

---

① See Jason Fry, Interim Measures of Protection: Recent Developments and the Way Ahead, International Arbitration Law Review, 2003.

measures are "intend to preserve a factual or legal situation so as to safeguard rights the recognition of which is sought elsewhere from the court having jurisdiction as to the substance of the matter". They aim to protect the parties' rights for the duration of the proceeding.① The terminology varies and the following expressions are also found.

在国际商会规则的英文版中,临时性保全措施被称为"interim or conservatory measures";在法文版中,被称为"measures provisoires ou conservatoires"。在瑞士适用于国际仲裁的法律中,它们被称为"provisional or conservatory measures"②。英国将此类措施称为玛瑞瓦禁令"Mareva Injunction"③。我国《民事诉讼法》、《仲裁法》中一般称为财产保全或证据保全措施。

本书所称的"临时性保全措施"是指联合国国际贸易法委员会《示范法》第17条中规定的"临时性保全措施"。

The Model Law Art. 17 states simply:

"Unless otherwise agreed by the parties, the arbitral tribunal may, at the request of a party, order any party to take such interim measure of protection as the arbitral tribunal may consider necessary in respect of the subject-matter of the dispute..."

尽管这些措施在各国的名称各异,其本质特征是相同的,主要表现在以下三个方面:第一,这些措施都是在争议解决之前,即在仲裁裁决作出之前采取的,包括在仲裁程序开始之前或者在仲裁程序的进行之中采取的。第二,这些措施都是临时性的,其特点是暂时性和临时性的应急措施。第三,采取这些措施的要求通常是紧急的,如果不采取这些措施,则存在着可能给一方当事人造成伤害的威胁。④ 由于临时性保全措施自身所具备的这些特点,法律规定在采取该类措施前,通常需要具备一方当事人的请求。也就是说,若缺少当事人的请求,仲裁庭或法院是无权启动临时性保全措施的。而且这些措施的实施也有比较严格的限制,一般只有法院有权执行临时性保全措施。仲裁庭即使按照一国的立法或仲

---

① See Jean-Francios, Sebastien Besson, Comparative Law of International Arbitration, Sweet & Maxwell Ltd., 2007, p.604.

② 〔英〕艾伦·雷德芬、马丁·亨特等:《国际商事仲裁法律与实践》,林一飞、宋连斌译,北京大学出版社2005年版,第354页。

③ Mareva Injunction 的名称出自于英国法院在20世纪70年代所审理的两个案件:Nippon Yusen Kaisha v. Karageorfis, (1975) 1 W.L.R. 1093 (C.A.); Mareva v. International Bulkcarriers, (1975) 2 Lloyd's Rep. 509 (C.A.)。此项禁令的内容是禁止一方当事人转移法院管辖范围内的财产,有时也包括从外国转移财产,或者对这些财产进行处分,致使法院的最终判决不能执行。See D. Alan Bedfern, Arbitration and the Courts: Interim Measures of Protection—Is the Tide about to Turn? Taxas International Law Journal, No.1, 1995 Winter, p.77, Note 35. 也可参见杨良宜、杨大明:《禁令》,中国政法大学出版社2000年版,第274—408页。

④ 参见赵秀文主编:《国际商事仲裁法》,中国人民大学出版社2004年版,第211页。

裁机构的仲裁规则有权采取该类措施,也无权自行将该类措施付诸实施。

The interim measures have the affect of compelling parties to behave in a way that is conductive to the success of the proceedings, preserving the rights of the parties, preventing self-help, keeping peace among the parties, and ensuring that an eventual final award can be implemented. The concern many practitioners have is that if interim measures of protection are not made, or are made but are unenforceable, a favorable final award may become meaningless. For example, without interim measures of protection, a party could remove goods or assets from a jurisdiction, hide or destroy evidence, or sell assets. The possibility of a party taking these precautions to protect themselves from an unfavorable arbitral award is a threat to the attractiveness of arbitral proceedings. The importance of interim measures of protection has increased in recent years as more parties are seeking interim relief. It is very likely that requests for interim measures of protection will continue to increase in future years as more parties select arbitration over civil litigation to resolve their disputes.①

(二) 临时性保全措施的形式

在民事诉讼法中,较为常见的民事保全措施主要是财产保全和证据保全。而在仲裁中,临时性保全措施的形式要丰富得多。这样的立法设计,使得临时性保全措施在仲裁程序中的使用更为灵活,当事人对临时性保全措施也有了更大的选择余地。

In all civilized countries, courts have developed detailed procedures under which parties to their proceedings may apply for, and in appropriate circumstances, obtain a variety of interim measures. For example, in England, a party to an action in the courts may obtain interim measures, including orders to freeze assets, require interim payments, search and seize property in the hands of a party, preserve documents and other forms of evidence, restrain or compel particular acts or conduct by a party, or provide security for costs. Such orders may be enforced against persons within the territorial jurisdiction of the court, by proceedings for attachment or contempt.②

The following measures have been ordered by arbitrators or suggested by legal scholars:

---

① See Stephen M. Ferguson, Interim Measures of Protection in International Commercial Arbitration: Problems, Proposed Solutions and Anticipated Results, Currents: International Trade Law Journal, 2003, p. 1.

② See Raymond J. Werbicki, Arbitral Interim Measures: Fact or Fiction? Dispute Resolution Journal, 2003, p. 1.

(1) measures aimed at clarifying or continuing a contractual relationship for the duration of the proceedings:

—an order to the constructor to continue construction works and/or an injunction to the owner to continue paying instalments, if necessary into an escrow account controlled by the arbitral tribunal;

—an authorisation to suspend work or the performance of other contractual obligations;

—a prohibition to call upon a bank guarantee or an order to return to the bank a guarantee called upon in an unjustified manner;

—a prohibition to one of the parties to continue to sell the other party's products.

(2) measures aimed at ensuring the effective enforcement of the final award:

—an order freezing assets;

—an order to provide the applicant with a bank guarantee.

(3) an order to make a provisional payment ("provision").

(4) an order for security for costs.

(5) reimbursement of half of the arbitration costs paid by one party on the behalf of the other.

(6) measures relating to the preservation of evidence:

—an authorisation to inspect the site or have the site inspected in the event of foreseeable changes;

—access to machines;

—expert report.

(7) anti-suit injunctions? This question is controversial. ①

一般来说,可以按照临时性保全措施的功能和性质来划分其形式,归纳起来可以分成以下几类:

1. 与取证或保护证据有关的措施

与取证或保护证据有关的措施是最主要的临时性保全措施之一。各国法律几乎都有规定这种类型的临时性保全措施。因为证据是描绘当事人间争议事实状况最有效的依据,所以证据是否被及时收集或保全对于案件的最终裁决往往具有决定性影响。

《示范法》第 27 条规定:"仲裁庭或一方当事人经仲裁庭批准,可以请求有

---

① See Jean-Francios, Sebastien Besson, Comparative Law of International Arbitration, Sweet & Maxwell Ltd., 2007, p. 628.

管辖权的国家法院协助取证,法院可在其管辖权限内,根据当地的取证规则,协助当事人取证。"该规定对当事人和仲裁庭自行调查取证进行了限制,也是当前为许多国家采用的一个做法。因为考虑到如果赋予当事人和仲裁庭自行调查取证可能引发的一系列利益冲突,许多国家的法律都不允许当事人或仲裁庭自行调查取证,除非得到法院的许可。在国际商事仲裁中,一些关键性的证据的调取,如果没有有关法院的协助,是很难成功的。

2. 维持现状的措施

所谓维持现状(preserving the status quo),是指在争议得到解决之前,按原来的合同规定或双方当事人的最初约定继续履行合同中的规定或双方当事人的最初约定。无论是对仲裁庭还是对法院来说,作出这类临时性措施的决定,妥善地处理这些问题,都是很棘手的。特别是在涉及一些大宗复杂交易的争议中,因无法预料的原因可能导致合同履行成本的增加,从而牵涉到双方当事人如何协调这额外费用的支付。在这种情形下,法院或仲裁庭可能因为当事人内容大相径庭的请求而陷入两难的境地。

3. 防止转移财产的措施

这类措施通常限于对与仲裁案件有关的财产所实施的查封、扣押等措施,或者是发布禁止当事人转移财产的禁令,或者将这些财产交由第三者保管等。特别是针对一些在当地没有住所的当事人,如果不及时对其财产采取相应的措施,就会导致财产被转移后,当事人没有可供履行的财产的尴尬处境。在国际商事仲裁实践中,无论此类措施是由法院发布,还是由仲裁庭发布,最终执行的只有法院一家,仲裁庭并无此类强制性措施的执行权。[①]

4. 费用担保

The legal nature of security for cost is controversial. Security for cost is a provisional measure since its aim is to guarantee the future enforcement of that part of the award which deals with the costs of the arbitral proceedings, and thus with one of the respondent's claims. It is nonetheless subject to specific rules in most national laws of civil procedure.[②]

虽然同属于临时保全,费用担保不同于财产保全。费用担保由仲裁庭直接执行,无须执行地国法院的协助,它的典型执行手段就是中止仲裁甚至驳回申请,而财产保全往往需要法院的协助。

---

① 参见赵秀文主编:《国际商事仲裁法》,中国人民大学出版社2004年版,第212—213页。
② See Jean-Francios, Sebastien Besson, Comparative Law of International Arbitration, Sweet & Maxwell Ltd., 2007, p.605.

二、临时性保全措施的发布

正如合同的成立需要满足法律规定的成立要件一样,临时性保全措施也有自己的成立要件。在发布临时性保全措施之前,我们必须保证该临时性保全措施具备法律所要求的成立要件,而非随意为之。不同的国家和仲裁机构对采取临时性保全措施的先决条件的规定也各不相同。

The most frequently required prerequisites for obtaining provisional measures from an arbitral tribunal are the following:

a request from a party;

prima facie jurisdiction of the arbitral tribunal to rule on the merits of the case;

reasonable chance of success on the merits (prima facie case);

urgency or impending injury to the rights of the applicant;

risk of substantial harm in the absence of protection;

the forthcoming decision on the merits must not be prejudiced;

the providing of security.

These prerequisites are not always mentioned and analysed by arbitrators when making their decision. They are not exhaustive and it is conceivable that other procedural considerations be invoked to justify the refusal of the order (e.g. the request is too late, an award on the merits is imminent or it is impossible to ensure that the measure, if ordered, will be effective) or, on the contrary, the granting of the order (e.g. repeatedly abusive behaviour of the respondent or a balance of interests in favour of the applicant).[①]

当临时性保全措施的成立要件得以满足后,就涉及由谁发布临时性保全措施的问题。由于仲裁保全措施的实施在法律上是一种强制性措施,因此,在任何国家实施仲裁保全措施的权力都专属于法院。但是作出仲裁保全措施裁定的权力则不同,除极个别国家将该权力排他地赋予仲裁庭外,大多数国家或者排他地赋予法院行使,或者赋予法院与仲裁庭共同行使。以下我们将对这几种情况分别进行研究:

(一)由法院作出

Some early arbitration laws gave the courts exclusive jurisdiction to order provisional measures. Italian law is even more restrictive, for it contains a mandatory

---

① See Jean-Francios, Sebastien Besson, Comparative Law of International Arbitration, Sweet & Maxwell Ltd., 2007, p.626.

provision prohibiting arbitrators from attachment or other provisional measures.①

希腊《民事诉讼法典》第889条规定:"仲裁员不得命令、修改或废除临时保全措施。"奥地利、瑞士等国都有类似规定。

然而,单纯由法院发布临时性保全措施的做法在世界各国立法上是很鲜见的。在实践过程中,仲裁庭往往比法院更了解由其审理的案件,赋予其发布临时性保全措施的权力有利于案件审理。如果立法强制性地剥夺仲裁庭的这种权力,很可能会伤及当事人的利益。因为法院发布决定前,往往需要一段时间了解案情,这很可能延误发布临时性保全措施的最有利时机。

(二) 由仲裁庭或仲裁机构作出

Several arbitration laws presume that arbitrators have jurisdiction to order provisional measures. This is the solution under German law (ZPO, § 1041(1)), Swedish law (Su, Art. 25(4)) and Swiss law (PILS, Art. 183(1)), as well as under UNCITRAL Model Law, Art. 17.

一些国家从仲裁协议具有排除法院管辖的效力角度,主张将采取财产保全措施的权力赋予仲裁庭,②但将这种权力排他性地赋予仲裁庭或仲裁机构的国家是极少数的。1974年美国第三巡回区上诉法院在McCreary案的判决中主张,依《纽约公约》,凡是存在有效的仲裁协议,美国的法院就不得作出采取临时措施的裁定;仲裁当事人向法院申请临时措施,是试图逃避约定的以仲裁解决争议的方法。对这个判决,美国学理界是存在很大异议的。纵观众多仲裁机构的规则,都未能接受这种过于极端的做法。况且仲裁庭审理当事人争议的基础是法院对其司法权力的让渡,并非是法院无权管辖。

The fact that provisional or protective measures are compatible with the arbitration agreement is set forth in the ICC Rules of Arbitration (Art. 23(2) of the 1998 Rules)③, the UNCITRAL Arbitration Rules (Art. 26 (3))④, the AAA International Arbitration Rules (Art. 21(3) of the 1997 Rules) and the Rules of the

---

① See Jean-Francios, Sebastien Besson, Comparative Law of International Arbitration, Sweet & Maxwell Ltd., 2007, p.606.

② 参见笪恺:《论国家商事仲裁中的财产保全——兼论我国的立法和司法实践》,载《法学评论》1995年第4期,第55页。

③ Article 23(2):"Before the file is transmitted to the Arbitral Tribunal, and in appropriate circumstances even thereafter, the parties may apply to any competent judicial authority for interim or conservatory measures. The application of a party to a judicial authority for such measures or for the implementation of any such measures ordered by an Arbitral Tribunal shall not be deemed to be an infringement of a waiver of the arbitration agreement and shall not affect the relevant powers reserved to the Arbitral Tribunal. Any such application and any measures taken by the judicial authority must be notified without delay to the Secretariat. The Secretariat shall inform the Arbitral Tribunal thereof."

④ Article 26(3): A request for interim measures addressed by any party to a judicial authority shall not be deemed incompatible with the agreement to arbitrate, or as a waiver of that agreement.

Arbitration Institute of the Stockholm Chamber of Commerce (Art. 31(2) of the 1999 Rules). The UNCITRAL Model Law expressly provides so in its Article 9. Arbitral case law likewise recognizes that by applying for such measures before a court, a party hasn't necessarily waived its rights under the arbitration agreement.①

（三）法院和仲裁庭均有权作出采取财产保全的决定

The jurisdiction of arbitrators recognized by various statutory provisions is therefore not exclusive and does not prevent that of the courts. Even where the arbitration law provides for a support mechanism allowing requests to the courts to enforce a measure ordered by an arbitral tribunal, it is recognized that the latter does not have exclusive jurisdiction to order provisional measures and that the parties retain the possibility of directly applying to the courts without a detour via the arbitral tribunal.② The various sources of arbitration law—statutes, institutional rules, international conventions and arbitral awards—reveal a growing acceptance of the principle that courts and arbitral tribunals have concurrent powers to order provisional or protective measures.③

根据这种原则,仲裁庭和法院在一定条件下都有权决定仲裁保全措施。之所以采取这种做法,正是由于仲裁庭和法院在发布临时性保全措施时都存在着一定的不足之处。

While the courts are less well placed to implement a provisional regime which is often closely linked with the proceedings and the merits of the case, the arbitrators cannot ensure alone an effective protection, notably when the measures require powers of coercion (imperium) or are addressed to third parties and are thus not within the arbitrators' jurisdiction.④

同时赋予仲裁庭和法院发布该类措施的权力能促使两者相互协调,弥补彼此不足,最大程度上保护当事人的利益。这一做法也在众多著名的国际仲裁机构的仲裁规则中得到体现,如 ICC、AAA、LCIA 和 UNCITRAL。为了进一步了解这种做法是如何被各仲裁规则和仲裁法所接受的,我们可以参考 UNCITRAL《仲裁规则》和《示范法》对此的有关规定。

---

① 参见〔法〕菲利普·福盖德、伊曼纽尔·盖拉德、贝托尔德·戈德曼:《国际商事仲裁》,中信出版社 2004 年版,第 715 页。
② See Jean-Francios, Sebastien Besson, Comparative Law of International Arbitration, Sweet & Maxwell Ltd., 2007, p.611.
③ 参见〔法〕菲利普·福盖德、伊曼纽尔·盖拉德、贝托尔德·戈德曼:《国际商事仲裁》,中信出版社 2004 年版,第 711 页。
④ See Jean-Francios, Sebastien Besson, Comparative Law of International Arbitration, Sweet & Maxwell Ltd., 2007, p.605.

UNCITRAL Arbitration Rules (UNCITRAL Rules)

Article 26

"1. At the request of either party, the arbitral tribunal may take any interim measures it deems necessary in respect of the subject-matter of the dispute, including measures for the conservation of the goods forming the subject-matter in dispute, such as ordering their deposit with a third person or the sale of perishable goods.

2. Such interim measures may be established in the form of an interim award. The arbitral tribunal shall be entitled to require security for the costs of such measures.

3. A request for interim measures addressed by any party to a judicial authority shall not be deemed incompatible with the agreement to arbitrate, or as a waiver of that agreement."

UNCITRAL Model Law on International Commercial Arbitration (UNCITRAL Model Law)

Article 9 Arbitration Agreement and Interim Measures by Court

"It is not incompatible with an arbitration agreement for a party to request, before or during arbitral proceedings, from a court an interim measure of protection and for a court to grant such measure."

Article 17 Power of Arbitral Tribunal to Order Interim Measures

"Unless otherwise agreed by the parties, the arbitral tribunal may, at the request of a party, order any party to take such interim measures of protection as the arbitral tribunal may consider necessary in respect of the subject-matter of the dispute. The arbitral tribunal may require any party to provide appropriate security in connection with such measure."

The above articles empower courts and arbitral tribunals to make interim measures of protection in the form of any measure they think is appropriate or necessary upon the request of a party.[①]

虽然到目前为止,关于临时性保全措施的问题还没有统一的解决办法,《示范法》第17条也并非尽善尽美,但不可否认,《示范法》在大多数情况下还是在有效地运作,大多数国家和仲裁机构都接受了临时性保全措施。各个国际仲裁机构根据《示范法》及各国的国内立法,也形成了一套惯性做法。申请临时性措施的条件必须是情况十分紧急,所造成的损害以后难以弥补。大部分国家赋

---

① See Stephen M. Ferguson, Interim Measures of Protection in International Commercial Arbitration: Problems, Proposed Solutions and Anticipated Results, Currents: International Trade Law Journal, 2003.

予了仲裁机构作出临时性保全措施命令的权力。此外,仲裁机构是没有强制执行临时性措施的权力的,尽管仲裁庭对不履行措施的一方可以作出否定性的推论,但在某些情况下也不足以防止当事人转移财产。一些强制措施的施行还主要依靠法院的支持。

值得提及的是,2006年《示范法》在修订后增设了有关法院下令采取临时性措施的条款,以期对各国的立法有所启示。《示范法》第17条之十一规定:"无论仲裁进行地是否在法院所在国,法院采取与仲裁程序有关的临时措施的权力应等同于其在诉讼程序方面的权力。法院应按其程序行使这种权力,同时考虑到国际仲裁的特点。"该条款明确了法院在协助仲裁庭发布临时性措施时的权力,但其规定较为原则,没有明确规定法院在何种情况下可以发布临时性措施,而留给国内立法具体规定。临时性措施的修改是UNCITRAL七年来努力的成果,是国际社会在临时性措施问题上取得高度一致意见的表现,反映了仲裁立法的国际趋势。目前越来越多的国家根据《示范法》的规定修订了自己的仲裁立法,根据UNCITRAL公布的数据,截至目前,有63个国家或独立法域(包括中国香港和澳门、美国的6个州等)已根据《示范法》颁布仲裁立法,同时有4个国家已经根据2006年修改后的《示范法》颁布法令。我们有理由相信,随着《示范法》被更多的国家所借鉴,国际商事仲裁中的临时性措施制度必将能够得到协调统一。

第三节 国际商事仲裁裁决的效力与撤销

一个仲裁裁决形成后,就会涉及该裁决的效力问题。仲裁裁决的效力跟民事判决的效力是有明显区别的。在民事诉讼一审判决形成后,是允许当事人就该判决上诉的。在上诉期间,该民事判决暂不生效。而仲裁裁决一旦形成,就发生效力,具有既判力。同时该裁决又是终局性的,当事人无权向法院或仲裁庭要求上诉。由于仲裁裁决效力的特殊性,使得对裁决的救济方式也与民事诉讼的判决有较大的区别。本节将围绕裁决的效力和救济两方面内容进一步为大家介绍仲裁裁决。

一、裁决的效力

仲裁裁决的效力包括既判力和执行力两方面内容。仲裁裁决的既判力指裁决具有的终局性。仲裁裁决一旦作出,就发生法律效力,无论仲裁庭还是法院都不应再受理该裁决事项。仲裁裁决的既判力保证了仲裁裁决较民事审判所具有的高效和快捷,这也是当事人愿意将争议事项提交仲裁的主要原因之一。仲裁裁决的执行力是指仲裁裁决内容能得以实施的效力。既判力无法解决仲裁裁决法律效力得以实现的问题,所以执行力对于仲裁裁决的最终实现是不可或缺的。

(一) 既判力

既判力是仲裁裁决效力最重要的体现。既判力原本是西方国家民事诉讼法理论中的一个概念。从西方国家的法律看,既判力是指形成确定的终局判决内容的判断的通用力,也称为实质性(或内部的)确定力。具有既判力的判决无论是对当事人还是法院,都产生强制性的法律约束力。对当事人来讲,当终局判决作出后,就不得以同一诉讼请求重新提起诉讼。对法院来说,终局判决作出后,亦不得再就已裁判的法律关系作出相反的判决。如果当事人再就已裁判的法律关系提出诉讼,则法院应以其诉讼违背一事不再理原则为由,裁定驳回诉讼。①

尽管仲裁与诉讼之间存在多方面的差异,但是生效的仲裁裁决和生效的诉讼判决在确定争议法律关系上是一致的。承认生效仲裁裁决的既判力,也是对仲裁裁决的权威性认同的表现。仲裁裁决的既判力体现在,仲裁裁决一经作出,任何一方当事人都无权向法院起诉或请求其他机构变更裁决;法院和任何其他机构都必须承认该项裁决是对本案中已决事项所作的正确的理解;而且除非双方当事人一致同意,任何一方都无权不理会或否定该项裁决。②

许多著名的仲裁规则,如《国际商会仲裁规则》、《伦敦国际仲裁院仲裁规则》和《美国仲裁协会国际仲裁规则》等,都对仲裁裁决的既判力给予了肯定。

Rules of Arbitration of ICC

Article 28 (6):"Every Award shall be binding on the parties. By submitting the dispute to arbitration under these rules, the parties undertake to carry out any Award without delay and shall be deemed to have waived their right to any form of recourse insofar as such waiver can validly be made."③

American Arbitration Association (AAA)

Article 27 (1):"Awards shall be made in writing, promptly by the tribunal, and shall be final and binding on the parties. The parties undertake to carry out any such award without delay."

Arbitration Rules of LCIA

Article 26 (9):"All awards shall be final and binding on the parties. By agreeing to arbitration under these Rules, the parties undertake to carry out any award

---

① 参见谢石松主编:《商事仲裁法学》,高等教育出版社2003年版,第276页。
② 同上。
③ 转引自刘颖、吕国民编:《国际私法资料选编》,中信出版社2004年版,第490页。

immediately and without any delay (subject only to Article 27); and the parties also waive irrevocably their right to any form of appeal, review or recourse to any state court or other judicial authority, insofar as much waiver may be validly made."

既判力这种效力本身包括了以下几个不同方面:

1. 裁决对于当事人之间现存争议的效力

裁决一旦作出,对于当事人即具有约束力。当事人不得以相同的诉讼理由再次提起仲裁申请或直接向法院起诉。如果当事人以作出裁决的仲裁标的提起诉讼,并且基于相同的诉讼理由,那么法院将基于仲裁裁决的既判力,驳回起诉。这种效力表现也是一事不再理原则的体现。我国《仲裁法》第9条规定:

"A system of a single and final award shall be practised for arbitration. If a party applies for arbitration to an arbitration commission or institutes an action in a people's court regarding the same dispute after an arbitration award has been made, the arbitration commission or the people's court shall not accept the case."

根据法国新《民事诉讼法》第1476、1500条的规定,仲裁裁决对其所确定的争议具有既判力。另外,比利时、德国、奥地利和瑞士等国也存在类似的规定。

2. 裁决对于当事人之间此后争议的效力

Where there are subsequent disputes between the same parties, more difficult questions arise. Since there is no doctrine of stare decisis in arbitration, the previous decision of an arbitral tribunal will not be binding on any subsequent disputes that arise between the same parties. However, this does not mean that a previous decision will necessarily be irrelevant to the resolution of a subsequent dispute between the same parties, particularly for the purposes of establishing an issue estoppel. In the US, courts have often applied res judicata (also referred to as "claim preclusion") to bar claims that could have been, but were not, asserted in a prior arbitral proceeding.

3. 裁决对第三人的效力

仲裁庭无权针对非仲裁协议的第三人发出命令或指令,除非该第三人明确表达或以某种方式默许自己愿意接受裁决约束。因此,仲裁裁决不能擅自决定赋予第三人权利,或为第三人设定义务。我国目前对有关仲裁第三人的立法还比较滞后,并没有确立相应的规定。

(二) 执行力

由于本书第八章将重点讨论仲裁裁决的执行力问题,本章在此简要介绍仲裁裁决执行力为何产生的原因。当事人选择仲裁来解决彼此间的争议,是以仲裁裁决能够被执行为前提的。如果仲裁裁决不具有执行效力,那么设定仲裁制度的意义也就丧失了。因此,无论是否存在法律义务,仲裁庭都会尽力确保裁决是可执行的;既然接受当事人的委托解决争议,仲裁庭自然也希望能有效和妥当地履行自身的义务。UNCITRAL《示范法》第 35 条第 1 款就强调仲裁裁决应当被确保执行。

Article 35 (1) of Model Law:

"An arbitral award, irrespective of the country in which it was made, shall be recognized as binding and, upon application in writing to the competent court, shall be enforced subject to the provisions of this article and of the article 36."

二、裁决的撤销

前文提到仲裁裁决具有一裁终局的效力,那么可能有人会有这样的疑问:是否对于明显不公乃至错误的裁决就没有相应的救济措施了? 对于这种顾虑,在仲裁实践中我们可以求助某种程度的司法审查来解决。法院的司法监督职能在这方面的作用尤为突出,裁决的撤销就是法院监督职能的一种体现。但是,为了发挥仲裁的最大效益,法院的这种监督职能也是有一定的限度的。

(一) 概述

裁决的撤销,是指国际商事仲裁裁决存在法律规定的撤销情形时,由当事人申请并经法院审查核实,判定或裁定予以撤销,使之归于无效的一种特殊程序。

Arbitration is a widely used alternative to litigation for resolving international commercial disputes. By choosing an arbitral forum, parties agree not to have their disputes resolved in national courts. But in most cases national courts retain some supervisory authority over the arbitral award. A court in the arbitral situs (the "vacating court") has the authority to vacate the award under standards set out in its national arbitration law. In addition, when the prevailing party seeks to enforce the award in another jurisdiction, the court in which enforcement is sought (the "enforcement court") may decline enforcement under standards set out in its national arbitration law, as constrained by international treaty.[①]

By revocation (application to reopen the case or to reconsider the award), it is understood an extraordinary means of setting aside a final award because of serious vices which affect it, of new facts or arguments so far unknown to a party and leading to the case being reopened. Revocation results in the reopening of the initial instance and not the filing of a new procedure. It is named "revocazione" in Italy, "requite

---

① See Christopher R. Drahozal, Enforcing Vacated International Arbitration Awards: An Economic Approach, American Review of International Arbitration, 2000.

civile" in Belgium and in France, "revision" or "Revisionsgesuch" in Switzerland, "Restitutionsgrund" in Germany. Even if provided by most legislations with respect to judgments, it is rarely provided for with regard to arbitral awards. This silence can be the result either of a gap or of a deliberate omission in order not to question an award after the time-limit for challenging it has expired, whatever the defects which may appear afterwards. In other words, the final character of the award and the certainty that it is attached thereto would prevail over all other legal considerations. The opponents of the revocation in arbitration matters point out that these defects would constitute violations of public policy which could be objected to when the award is enforced. This is true only if they are discovered before the recognition. Furthermore, the refusal to recognize does not set aside the award which remains in force and is an obstacle to a new arbitration. In such case, the claimant is practically helpless. The needs and the inconveniences do not differ fundamentally whether it is an award or a court judgment, reason why certain legislatures have provided for revocation in both cases.①

裁决的撤销对仲裁裁决的公正性也有重要的影响。公正性是仲裁所追求的基本价值之一，而不公正或错误的裁决将使得仲裁背离其本身的价值追求。撤销是一国法院对国际商事仲裁裁决进行监督的重要方式，同时也是当事人寻求司法救济的重要手段。裁决撤销程序设立的主要原因之一就是认为裁决损害了当事人的利益，导致了不公正。因此，裁决撤销程序对于裁决公正性的实质监督，在一定程度上能推动裁决的公正化。

从仲裁撤销的概念看，仲裁裁决的撤销有以下几个特征：第一，撤销程序是仲裁结束后一种特殊的司法程序，是对仲裁的一种监督程序；第二，裁决撤销的理由是由各国法律直接规定的，只有在仲裁裁决具备了申请撤销受理国法律或接受的条约规定的撤销事由时，才可启动撤销程序；第三，撤销程序可由当事人申请提起；第四，裁决一经撤销即归于无效，裁决对双方当事人不再具有约束力，当事人可自行决定是选择重新仲裁还是向法院提起诉讼。

（二）国际商事仲裁裁决撤销权的归属

撤销程序的开始，首先应确定谁享有撤销权。"一项国际商事仲裁裁决往往涉及当事人的国籍国、住所地国、仲裁地国、财产所在地等两个或多个国家，如果当事人对仲裁裁决有异议，要求撤销该仲裁裁决，由哪一个国家的法院管

---

① See Jean-Francios, Sebastien Besson, Comparative Law of International Arbitration, Sweet & Maxwell Ltd., 2007, p.843.

辖?"①这就涉及仲裁裁决撤销权的归属问题了。

撤销权为一国司法机构对存有瑕疵的仲裁裁决所行使的撤销的权力,司法机构根据当事人的申请对仲裁裁决进行审查,根据一定的程序规则最终作出撤销或者驳回当事人撤销之诉的裁定,即撤销仲裁裁决是一种特殊的司法程序。撤销权的这种特殊性,是司法机构对仲裁的监督的表现,其实际上是司法机构的一种管辖权。这种管辖权来自于国家的管辖权,但与对国际民商事争议的管辖权并非同一性质。

各国根据属人、属地等标准通过立法行使对具有国际因素的民商事案件的管辖权,与之相同,各国立法也设定了一定的连结因素,行使对仲裁程序等事项的管辖权。由于各国法律制度和法律历史的不同,造成各国司法机构对仲裁程序行使管辖权的条件和依据都有所不同。

国际和各国立法关于仲裁裁决撤销权归属的立法和实践主要有以下两种:

1. 仲裁地法院对在该国境内作出的仲裁裁决行使撤销权

在一国进行的仲裁,该国法院对其享有撤销的权力。英国《1996年仲裁法》规定,对仲裁地在英格兰、威尔士和北爱尔兰的仲裁,仲裁程序的一方当事人可在仲裁程序中以存在影响仲裁庭、仲裁程序或裁决的严重不当行为为由就裁决向法院提出异议,如果存在严重不当行为,法院则可全部或部分地撤销裁决。②

"The Arbitration Act 1996, s. 68(2) sets out a series of grounds upon which an application may be made to court for an award to be set aside or remitted on the basis that the proceedings or the award itself have been tainted by a serious irregularity."③

1998年德国《民事诉讼法》也有相同的规定,即对于仲裁地位于德国境内的仲裁,法院根据当事人的申请对仲裁进行审查,如果具有第1059条第2款第1项的情形,则可撤销该裁决。④《示范法》中也有关于法院对在其国家境内作出的仲裁裁决行使撤销的权力的规定。仲裁地国对仲裁裁决享有专属的撤销权是国际社会普遍接受的做法。

2. 仲裁程序准据法国家的法院行使对裁决的撤销权

法国和德国曾经主张仲裁程序准据法国家对仲裁裁决有撤销权。在Gotaverken案中,巴黎上诉法院认为非依据法国法律作出的裁决,由于与法国没有任何的联系,因此不能被认为是法国的裁决,法国法院不受理当事人对裁决提

---

① 赵健:《国际商事仲裁的司法监督》,法律出版社2000年版,第237页。
② 参见宋连斌、林一飞译编:《国际商事仲裁新资料选编》,武汉出版社2001年版,第3—33页。
③ Robert Merkin, Arbitration Law, Informa Legal Publishing, 2004, p. 207.
④ 参见杨良宜:《国际商务仲裁》,中国政法大学出版社1997年版,第55—56页。

出的异议。① 联邦德国在加入《纽约公约》后,在其颁布的《关于实施〈纽约公约〉的法律》第 2 条规定:"如果《纽约公约》项下的仲裁裁决在另一缔约国境内作出时所适用的是德国的程序法,当事人就可以在联邦德国申请撤销此项仲裁裁决。撤销的程序适用《民事诉讼法》第 1041、1043、1045(1)和 1046 条的规定。"②

此外,还有其他一些不同的立法模式,比如一些国家规定当事人可以明示协议的方式排除撤销程序或将其限定在特定的理由上。1989 年瑞士《联邦国际私法法典》第 192 条的规定就是采取这种做法。

(三) 国际商事仲裁裁决撤销的理由

所谓仲裁裁决的撤销理由,是指当事人申请撤销裁决及法院接受申请并处理撤销裁决事宜的条件和根据。撤销裁决的理由以及理由成立与否,直接关系到裁决有效与否,进而影响到当事人的实体权益能否实现。虽然各国撤销仲裁裁决的理由五花八门,但作为一项基本原则,多数国家的法院均对仲裁裁决所涉及的实体问题不予审查。③

National arbitration laws prescribe varying grounds on which arbitration awards can be vacated. Many national laws follow the UNCITRAL Model Law on International Commercial Arbitration, which tracks the list of grounds for nonenforcement of awards contained in the New York Convention. Other national arbitration laws contain grounds for vacating awards in addition to those in the UNCITRAL Model Law. One example is Egypt, which has adopted the UNCITRAL Model Law but with two additional grounds on which awards can be vacated. Other examples are England and the United States, each of which engages in some degree of court oversight of arbitral rulings on legal issues. On the other hand, some national laws contain fewer grounds for vacating arbitral awards than the UNCITRAL Model Law.

In most countries, the grounds for vacating arbitral awards are mandatory: the parties cannot contract around them. In the United States, some courts have found the grounds for vacating an award to provide a mandatory minimum but not a mandatory maximum: in other words, parties cannot contract for less court

---

① See Mauro Rubino-Sammartano, International Arbitration Law and Practice, Kluwer Law International, p. 878.
② A. J. van den Berg, The New York Arbitration Convention of 1958, Kluwer Law and Taxation Publishers,1981, p. 27. 转引自宋航:《国际商事仲裁裁决的承认和执行》,法律出版社 2000 年版,第 76 页。
③ See A. J. van den Berg, The New York Arbitration Convention of 1958, Kluwer Law and Taxation publishers, 1981, p.135. 转引自赵秀文主编:《国际商事仲裁法》,中国人民大学出版社 2004 年版,第 432 页。

supervision than provided in the statute but can contract for more supervision.①

裁决的撤销是对商事仲裁裁决的司法监督,其本身对商事仲裁裁决起的是一种限制作用。这种限制的大小跟裁决的撤销理由有着密切的联系。裁决撤销的理由对撤销权的行使范围起着决定性作用。如果撤销理由涉及范围太广,势必会降低仲裁的效能,这样产生的直接后果就是当事人不愿仲裁。如果撤销理由涉及范围太窄,则会使得某些不公正裁决难以得到救济,也会间接影响当事人对仲裁的选择。因此,撤销理由内容的设定意义不亚于撤销权的设立。我们可以了解一些欧洲国家和著名的国际公约是如何谨慎设定撤销理由的。

This is first of all the case of the Belgian legislature. CJB, Art. 1704(3) provides that the award can be set aside in three cases: if it has been obtained through fraud, if it is based on evidence that is found to be false by a final court decision or acknowledged as false by the party who benefited therefrom, and finally, if decisive evidence which was not disclosed by the other party is discovered subsequently. Contrary to the ordinary application to setting aside which must be filed within three months from notification of the award, these grounds can be raised within a time-limit of three months starting from their discovery and within an absolute time-limit of five years (CJB, Art. 1707(3)).

Article 1068 of the Dutch code also provides that the revocation of an award can be requested in three similar cases, fraud, forged documentary evidence or the discovery of a decisive document. In these last two cases, Dutch law is however more restrictive than Belgian law since it only covers documents and not all evidence, in particular witness evidence.②

UNCITRAL《示范法》第34条规定了可以撤销裁决的理由。类似理由在《纽约公约》中是作为可以拒绝承认和执行国际裁决的理由。《示范法》该条规定的内容是被各国所能普遍接受的。通过确定适当的撤销裁决的理由,能有效防止撤销权的滥用,有利于建立良好的国际商事仲裁环境。本书也将围绕《示范法》该条的规定探讨仲裁裁决的撤销理由。

Article 34(2): An arbitral award may be set aside by the court specified in article 6 only if:

(a) the party making the application furnishes proof that:

(ⅰ) a party to the arbitration agreement referred to in article 7 was under some

---

① See Christopher R. Drahozal, Enforing Vacated International Arbitration Awards: An Economic Approach, American Review of International Arbitration, 2000.

② See Jean-Francois Poundert, Sebatien Besson, Comparative Law of International Arbitration, Sweet & Maxwell Ltd., 2007, p.844.

incapacity; or the said agreement is not valid under the law to which the parties have subjected it or, failing any indication thereof, under the law of this State; or

(ii) the party making the application was not given proper notice of the appointment of an arbitrator or of the arbitral proceedings or was otherwise unable to present his case; or

(iii) the award deals with a dispute not contemplated by or not falling within the terms of the submission to arbitration, or contains decisions on matters beyond the scope of the submission to arbitration, provided that, if the decisions on matters submitted to arbitration can be separated from those not so submitted, only that part of the award which contains decisions on matters not submitted to arbitration may be set aside; or

(iv) the composition of the arbitral tribunal or the arbitral procedure was not in accordance with the agreement of the parties, unless such agreement was in conflict with a provision of this Law from which the parties cannot derogate, or, failing such agreement, was not in accordance with this Law; or

(b) the court finds that:

(i) the subject-matter of the dispute is not capable of settlement by arbitration under the law of this State; or

(ii) the award is in conflict with the public policy of this State.[①]

归纳起来,这些理由如下:

没有订立仲裁协议的能力,或者不存在有效的仲裁协议;

对裁决不满的一方当事人未得到选定仲裁庭或仲裁程序的适当通知,或者因其他原因未能陈述案件的;

裁决所处理的事项非为仲裁条款或交付仲裁之协议所指事项,或者不在其范围之内,或者是超出了仲裁申请的范围;

仲裁庭的组成或仲裁程序与当事人之间的协议或与《示范法》本身的强制性规定不符;

依据仲裁地的法律,争议事项不能通过仲裁方式解决;

裁决(或其任何决定)与仲裁地的公共政策相冲突。

综上所述,结合国际商事仲裁裁决撤销的实际,我们将进一步分析仲裁裁决撤销的理由:

---

① 资料来源:联合国国际贸易法委员会网站,http://www.uncitral.org/uncitral/en/uncitral_texts/arbitration/1985Model_arbitration.html,2009年7月10日访问。

1. 仲裁协议的效力瑕疵

在协议仲裁制度下,仲裁协议是整个仲裁的基础,仲裁协议存在效力瑕疵,当然可以作为撤销仲裁裁决的理由。这在众多国家的国内立法中均有体现,我国《仲裁法》第58条第1款第1项就将"没有仲裁协议"作为裁决撤销情形之一。国际仲裁协议的效力取决于该仲裁协议应当适用的法律。有权撤销裁决的法院如果认定裁决所依据的仲裁协议无效,即可撤销此项裁决。①

2. 缺乏正当程序

"正当程序"是程序法上的一个重要概念,仲裁必须遵循正当程序的基本理念是,如果国际商事仲裁要公正适当地进行,必须遵守某些最低的程序标准。这最低的程序标准主要用以确保仲裁庭适当组成、仲裁程序符合当事人的协议(受限于可适用的法律中的强制性规定),以及在程序、聆讯等方面给予当事人适当的通知。"正当程序"的目的就在于使当事人在仲裁程序上能得到公平的对待,确保其能享有并能行使程序上的权利。② 该标准在《示范法》中主要体现在第34条第2款(a)(ii)项。

3. 仲裁庭越权

《示范法》对仲裁裁决撤销的第三项理由,是管辖权问题。根据该法第34条第2款(a)(iii)项的规定,仲裁庭对仲裁案件的管辖权来源于当事人双方在仲裁协议中的约定,对于约定之外的事项,仲裁庭无权管辖。

4. 仲裁庭组成不当

仲裁庭的组成或仲裁员的指定存在不当,法院也可以撤销仲裁裁决。例如,当事人在仲裁协议中约定仲裁庭成员都是由律师组成,而不能是其他行业从业者。如果仲裁庭组成中违反了这个约定,吸收了其他人员来担任仲裁员,该仲裁庭的组成就是不当的。对于由此产生的仲裁裁决,当事人可以仲裁庭组成不当为由,请求法院撤销该裁决。

5. 可仲裁性和公共政策

之所以将这两项理由放在一起介绍,是因为它们都可由国内法院自行提出,不同于以上四类理由。上述四类理由根据《示范法》的规定必须由申请人证明。

可仲裁性涉及确定何种类型的争议可以通过仲裁解决,何种类型的争议专属于法院的范围。《纽约公约》第5条第2款(a)项规定了仲裁裁决被拒绝承认和执行的一种情况:

"The subject matter of the difference is not capable of settlement by arbitration

---

① 参见赵秀文主编:《国际商事仲裁法》,中国人民大学出版社2004年版,第432页。
② 参见〔英〕艾伦·雷德芬、马丁·亨特等:《国际商事仲裁法律与实践》,林一飞、宋连斌译,北京大学出版社2005年版,第442页。

under the law of that country."

除《示范法》第 34 条第 2 款(b)(i)项规定了"可仲裁性"要求外,《示范法》第 36 条第 1 款(b)(i)项也在拒绝承认和执行仲裁裁决中作了同样的要求:

"the subject-matter of the dispute is not capable of settlement by arbitration under the law of this State."

公共政策在英美法中被称为公共政策(public policy),法语中被称为公共秩序(order public),而德语中被称为保留条款(Vorbehaltsklausel)。尽管各国对公共政策并没有统一的定义,但一般认为它包含了各国的重大利益、基本政策、道德的基本观念或法律的基本原则等方面的内容。例如,可以设想一个博彩公司的利润分割争议。该争议提交仲裁并作出了裁决。在许多国家只要提交裁决的交易是正常交易,那么所作出的裁决也是有效的。然而在禁止博彩的国家,裁决很可能以违反公共政策因而是非法的为由被撤销。

但公共政策这一原则被成功援引的案例在国际商事仲裁实践中并不常见,一般只有在违反了国家最起码的道德标准或对公平的看法时,才能撤销或拒绝承认与执行业已作出的仲裁裁决。各国法院在运用这一原则时,都非常谨慎,一般都不会轻易地以仲裁裁决违反公共政策为由撤销或拒绝执行已经作出的仲裁裁决。

(四) 裁决撤销的后果

仲裁裁决被撤销以后,当事人之间的争议并未解决。如果撤销仲裁裁决的原因是争议事项不可仲裁或者仲裁协议本身不存在或无效,当然不存在通过另外一个仲裁程序解决争议的问题,争议只能通过法院解决。但是,如果是因为仲裁庭组成不当、仲裁程序不当等原因被撤销,那么,原来的仲裁协议是否继续有效成为一个问题。根据各国的立法,对这个问题主要有以下几类做法:

做法一:裁决一经撤销,除非当事人之间另有约定,法院将对争议取得管辖权。荷兰《民事诉讼法》第 1067 条规定:"除非当事人另有约定,已经撤销裁决的决定成为终局,法院的管辖权即应恢复。"有类似国内立法的国家和地区还有法国、我国台湾地区、意大利等。

做法二:裁决一经撤销,争议实体问题仍应通过仲裁解决。1998 年德国《民事诉讼法》第 1059 条第 5 款规定:如无任何相反的因素,裁决的撤销应导致仲裁协议就争议事项而言重新有效。在此,"如无任何相反因素"是指仲裁裁决的撤销非因争议事项不可仲裁或仲裁协议本身无效等原因而作出的。另外,1969 年瑞士《联邦仲裁协约》第 40 条第 4 款规定:"如仲裁员并未因其参加前次仲裁程序或其他原因而回避时,仲裁裁决经撤销后,应由原仲裁员作出新的裁决。"

做法三:美国法律将裁决撤销后争议实体问题是否可通过仲裁解决的问题交由法院决定。

Article 10 (a)(5) of Federal Arbitration Act:

"Where an award is vacated and the time within which the agreement required the award to be made has not expired the court may, in its discretion, direct a rehearing by the arbitrators."

做法四:英国采取的是一种特殊的制度。依据英国《1996 年仲裁法》,仲裁裁决遭到司法追诉后,法院对争议的处理方式有修改裁决和发回重裁。另外,《1996 年仲裁法》在法院不采取上述方式而单纯撤销裁决时,在第 71 条第 4 款又规定:"在仲裁协议适用上,法院可以裁定任何关于仲裁裁决是提起诉讼的前提条件的规定都是无效的。"

应予注意的是,《示范法》虽未规定撤销裁决的后果,但却将重新仲裁作为裁决撤销程序的非强制性前置程序。

Article 34 (4) of Model Law:

"The court, when asked to set aside an award, may, where appropriate and so requested by a party, suspend the setting aside proceedings for a period of time determined by it in order to give the arbitral tribunal an opportunity to resume the arbitral proceedings or to take such other action as in the arbitral tribunals opinion will eliminate the grounds for setting aside."

(五)我国有关仲裁裁决撤销的法律和实践

1. 裁决撤销的双轨制

我国法律对我国仲裁机构所作的裁决的撤销,按国内仲裁和涉外仲裁分别作了不同的规定。对于国内仲裁,我国《仲裁法》第 58 条对申请主体、举证责任、管辖法院以及可撤销情形作了规定。关于涉外仲裁,我国《仲裁法》第 70 条规定,当事人提出证据证明涉外仲裁裁决有《民事诉讼法》第 258 条第 1 款规定的情形之一的,经人民法院组成合议庭审查核实,裁定撤销。《民事诉讼法》第 258 条第 1 款规定的情形如下:

(1) the parties have not had an arbitration clause in the contract or have not subsequently reached a written arbitration agreement;

(2) the party against whom the application for enforcement is made was not given notice for the appointment of an arbitrator or for the inception of the arbitration proceedings or was unable to present his case due to causes for which he is not responsible;

(3) the composition of the arbitration tribunal or the procedure for arbitration was not in conformity with the rules of arbitration; or

(4) the matters dealt with by the award fall outside the scope of the arbitration agreement or which the arbitral organ was not empowered to arbitrate.①

以上四点理由涉及的均为程序事项。

2. 报告制度(The Prior Reporting System)

报告制度是最高人民法院通过司法解释确定的旨在处理与涉外仲裁及外国仲裁事项有关问题的一项制度。其目的是通过设立法院系统的内部监控程序，以遏制涉外仲裁监督方面不严肃执法的现象。这里的司法解释是指最高人民法院《关于人民法院处理与涉外仲裁及外国仲裁事项有关问题的通知》和《关于人民法院撤销涉外仲裁裁决有关事项的通知》。

The Prior Reporting System—Revocation. Subsequently, in April 1998, the Supreme People's Court issued a notice② establishing a Prior Reporting System specifically applicable to any decision of the Intermediate or Higher People's Court to revoke a foreign-related arbitral award rendered by a PRC based arbitral institution. It provides that if, in considering an application for the revocation of an arbitral award rendered by a PRC based foreign-related arbitration institution, the People's Court determines that the arbitral award was rendered in any one or more of the circumstances set forth in Article 260 of the Civil Procedure Law, then, prior to rendering its decision to revoke the award or to direct a re-arbitration of the dispute, the court must, within 30 days from the date of acceptance of the relevant application, refer the matter to the Higher People's Court for a determination. Should the latter concur with the decision of the lower level court, then it must, within 15 days from the date of receipt of the report from the Intermediate People's Court, submit an *Approval Advice* to Supreme People's Court and may not render any decision until the Supreme People's Court has replied to the *Approval Advice*. This mechanism effectively serves to ensure that the revocation of a foreign-related arbitral award, or the issuing of an order to an arbitration commission to re-arbitrate the dispute, may not occur without the prior examination and confirmation of the Supreme People's Court.③

3. 裁决撤销后的重新仲裁

申请撤销可能产生三个后果：一是裁决被撤销；二是申请被驳回；三是法院将案件发回仲裁庭重审。我国《仲裁法》第61条规定：

---

① 资料来源：中国人大网，http://www.npc.gov.cn/englishnpc/Law/2007-12/12/content_1383880.htm，2009年7月10日访问。

② Notice of the Supreme People's Court on Relevant Issues Relating to the Revocation by the People's Court's of Foreign-Related Arbitration Awards, issued by the Supreme People's Court on and effective from April 23, 1998.

③ See Jingzhou Tao, Arbitration Law and Practice in China, Kluwer Law International, 2004, p.445.

"If, after accepting an application for setting aside an arbitration award, the people's court considers that the case may be re-arbitrated by the arbitration tribunal, it shall notify the tribunal that it shall re-arbitrate the case within a certain time limit and shall rule to stay the setting-aside procedure. If the arbitration tribunal refuses to re-arbitrate the case, the people's court shall rule to resume the setting-aside procedure."①

2006年施行的最高人民法院《关于适用〈中华人民共和国仲裁法〉若干问题的解释》第21条进一步规定了裁决撤销后可以重新仲裁的具体情形:(1)仲裁裁决所根据的证据是伪造的;(2)对方当事人隐瞒了足以影响公正裁决的证据的。实践中,大部分向法院申请撤销的案件均没有可予撤销的正当理由,但仍有一部分案件,由于存在或此或彼的情形,而被法院撤销或发回重新仲裁。这里的重新仲裁与裁决被撤销后的重新仲裁相比,有着自身显著的特点。根据《仲裁法》有关规定的精神,重新仲裁无须另组仲裁庭,因为仲裁庭的组成方式和仲裁员本身就是由当事人直接或间接地选定的,体现了当事人的自由意愿。由原仲裁庭重新仲裁,既尊重了当事人的意愿,也给仲裁庭一个自我纠正错误的机会,从而有利于仲裁庭作出公正裁决。② 另外,在重新仲裁中,仲裁庭对于当事人新提出的实体请求是不应审理的。因为重新仲裁的目的是弥补影响公正裁决的程序问题,除非当事人因自身以外的原因而没有得到进行仲裁程序的通知,造成其无法提出相应请求。

案例

1. United States District Court, S.D. New York
Shanghai Foodstuffs Import & Export Corporation, Petitioner, v. International Chemical, Inc., Respondent

No. 99 CV 3320 RCC.

Feb. 4, 2004.

Facts

Chinese seller of goods sued United States buyer, seeking enforcement of American Arbitration Association (AAA) arbitral award. The controversy between

---

① 资料来源:中国人大网,http://www.npc.gov.cn/englishnpc/Law/2007-12/12/content_1383756.htm,2009年7月10日访问。

② 参见林一飞:《国际商事仲裁法律与实务》,中信出版社2005年版,第252页。

the parties arose out of a series of agreements to buy and sell foodstuffs. The agreements each contained identical arbitration clauses requiring arbitration of "any controversy of claim relating to the interpretation, performance, or enforcement of the contract [s] ... in the country of the defendant in accordance with the country's arbitration rules governing international commercial transactions." Petitioner commenced arbitration, alleging that Respondent failed to pay for eight shipments.

A three-member arbitral panel, appointed under the Rules of the American Arbitration Association ("AAA"), rendered an award for Petitioner for \$647,244.00, plus interest at the rate of 6% per year from September 1996 through the date of payment. Petitioner then filed this petition for confirmation of the award, and for costs and attorney's fees. Respondent filed a cross-petition to vacate the award due to the arbitrators' manifest disregard of the law. In addition, Respondent asserts that this Court lacks subject matter jurisdiction over the case.

Issues

Whether the arbitrators' manifest is disregard of the law? Whether this Court lacks subject matter jurisdiction over the case?

Reasoning

A. Subject Matter Jurisdiction

As an initial matter, the Court possesses subject matter jurisdiction over the suit pursuant to 9 U.S.C. § 203. Chapter 2 of the Federal Arbitration Act ("FAA") incorporates the United Nations Convention on the Recognition and Enforcement of Foreign Arbitral Awards, 330 U.N.T.S. 3, which was signed in New York. See 9 U.S.C. § 201. Section 203 provides, "An action or proceeding falling under the Convention shall be deemed to arise under the laws and treaties of the United States. The district courts ... shall have original jurisdiction over such an action or proceeding, regardless of the amount in controversy." 9 U.S.C. § 203. Thus, the Court has subject matter jurisdiction if the award falls under the New York Convention.

Here, Petitioner is a corporation organized under the laws of the People's Republic of China, with its principal place of business in Shanghai, China. The relationship between the parties involved the international shipment of goods, and a significant part of the relationship occurred abroad. Therefore, the award falls under the New York Convention. The Court has subject matter jurisdiction pursuant to 9 U.S.C. § 203.

B. Manifest Disregard of the Law

Respondent contends that the arbitral tribunal manifestly disregarded provisions of the Uniform Commercial Code ("UCC"), which, according to Respondent, governed the parties' dispute. Respondent identifies four specific examples of manifest disregard: (1) The arbitrators incorrectly placed the burden of proof on Respondent, the buyer, to establish nonconformance of the goods with contract specifications; (2) the arbitrators failed to find that Respondent did not timely reject the goods; (3) the arbitrators did not apply the UCC provisions requiring that goods conform to contract specifications before payment is due; and (4) the arbitrators failed to credit Respondent's evidence showing that the goods did not conform to contract specifications. None of these arbitrator errors, even if they actually occurred, demonstrate that the award was rendered in manifest disregard of the law.

To qualify as manifest disregard of the law:

The error must have been obvious and capable of being readily and instantly perceived by the average person qualified to serve as an arbitrator. Moreover, the term "disregard" implies that the arbitrator appreciates the existence of a clearly governing legal principle but decides to ignore or pay no attention to it.

Factual findings and conclusions of law are not reviewable. Respondent's second and fourth challenges cannot meet this stringent standard because they focus on the arbitrators' factual findings and not on their application of the law. Respondent's third challenge also fails because it suggests—and examination of the award confirms—that the arbitral tribunal never discussed the applicability of the UCC provisions to which Respondent alludes. There is nothing to suggest that the tribunal determined that the UCC applied, or, more importantly, that it acknowledged its application but consciously decided to ignore the provisions. There can be no *manifest* disregard if there is no acknowledgment by the arbitrators that the UCC applied. In any event, the tribunal did seek to determine if the shipments conformed to contract specifications and reduced the contract price for the goods according to its determination that six of the eight shipments were nonconforming.

Finally, Respondent's argument that the tribunal manifestly disregarded the law by placing the burden of persuasion on it to prove nonconformance of the goods also is without merit. Respondent does not identify what provision of law clearly places the burden of persuasion on the Petitioner to prove nonconformance, nor is there anything in the arbitral award that suggests the arbitrators (1) determined that the law required Petitioner to prove nonconformance, but (2) decided to disregard that law.

Therefore, Respondent's petition to vacate the award is denied.

Conclusion

For the foregoing reasons, the petition to confirm the arbitral award is GRANTED and the cross-petition to vacate the award is DENIED. Petitioner is granted judgment in the amount of $647,244.00, plus interest of 6% per year from March 2, 1999 through February 2, 2004, for a total of $215,051.45 in interest, and a total sum of $862,295.45. Petitioner shall also receive post-judgment interest from February 2, 2004 through the date of payment at a rate of 1.25%. The Clerk of the Court is directed to close this case and remove it from the Court's active docket.

2. United States District Court, S.D. New York
Architectural and Ornamental Iron Workers Local Union No. 580 of the International Association of Bridge, Structural and Ornamental Iron Workers, Petitioner, v. JMB Corporation, Respondent

Facts

This dispute arises out of respondent's obligation, pursuant to a collective bargaining agreement, to make payments to various employee benefit and welfare funds. The Abitrator awarded petitioner $14,274 for outstanding fund contributions, $1,603 for audit costs, $3,568.50 for attorney's fees, $2,854 for liquidated damages, $1,600 for arbitration costs, and $3,211.65 for simple interest on the underpayments.

Issues

Petitioner moves to confirm an arbitration award dated January 24, 1986 (the "Award"). Respondent moves to vacate the Award.

Respondent's motion to vacate the Award is based on only two grounds. Respondent contends that the Arbitrator exceeded his authority by: 1) awarding punitive damages in the guise of liquidated damages; and 2) ordering payment of benefits on behalf of an individual who was allegedly never employed by respondent.

Discussion

Respondent claims that the award of liquidated damages was punitive because the other components of damages will fully compensate petitioner for its losses. This argument ignores 29 U. S. C. § § 1132 & 1145, which govern the enforcement of employer contributions to employee pension and welfare trust funds. Section 1132(g)(2) provides that an award shall include the unpaid contributions, attorney's fees, costs and, in addition, double interest or interest plus liquidated damages provided for by contract, whichever is greater. Congress was concerned that the "[f]ailure of employers to make promised contributions in a timely fashion imposes a variety of costs" on the funds, including the loss of "the benefit of investment income that could have been received and invested on time." Walker and Laberge Co., (quoting legislative history.) Thus, " § 1132(g)(2) was enacted to provide stiffer sanctions against employers..." Accordingly, respondent's assertion that the award of liquidated damages is "contrary to public policy," Respondent's Memorandum of Law at 3, is without merit.

Respondent also contends that the Arbitrator erred by awarding 440 hours worth of benefits on behalf of Erby McCall, despite respondent's evidence that he "did not work for [respondent] but rather worked for Gichner Iron Works, a totally separate corporation..." Respondent's Memorandum of Law at 13. "It is well-recognized that it is not within the province of the federal courts to review the merits of an arbitration award." "[A]n arbitration award will not be vacated when the arbitrator explains his decision 'in terms that offer even a barely colorable justification for the outcome reached...'". In this case, the Arbitrator specifically treated the issue of contributions on behalf of McCall, and offered a colorable justification for his conclusion.

The Arbitrator stated, "[A]ny payments that may have been made to McCall through Gichner [Iron Works, Inc.] for work within Local 580's jurisdiction [are] also properly subject to contributions to the Funds. By [respondent J. M. B.'s] refusal to provide the auditor with Gichner pay and related records, the audit covered only J. M. B. data containing payments to McCall. These dat[a] were in large part the basis for the auditor's underpayment findings."

Conclusion

Accordingly, petitioner's motion to confirm the Award is hereby granted. Petitioner's motion, pursuant to Fed. R. Civ. P. 11 and the Court's inherent authority, for attorney's fees and costs incurred herein is denied. Petitioner is hereby directed to submit a judgment in conformity with this opinion within seven days from the date hereof.

阅读材料

1. Discussion on Interim Measures

At first sight, the ability of parties to a commercial arbitration to obtain interim measures from the arbitral tribunal might not appear to pose any particular problem. For example, parties who agree to arbitrate under the International Arbitration Rules of the American Arbitration Association (AAA international rules) have the benefit of Article 21, which authorizes the tribunal, at a party's request, to "take whatever interim measures it deems necessary, including injunctive relief and measures for the protection or conservation of property." Article 21 also states that a request for interim measures from a court "shall not be deemed incompatible with the agreement to arbitrate or a waiver of the right to arbitrate." On the face of it, this would seem to provide the best of both worlds: an option to obtain virtually any interim remedy from either an arbitral tribunal or a court.

International arbitration practitioners are all too aware that the availability of arbitral interim measures is not nearly so simple. The conundrum is this: in certain circumstances, an arbitral tribunal's ability to grant interim measures may be limited. If that is the case, a party to an international arbitration will have to seek interim measures in a national court that it may have wished to avoid when it agreed to arbitration. Further, if that happens, the court may decline to grant the measure requested, either because it concludes that seeking judicial interim relief is incompatible with the arbitration agreement or that it is undesirable for the court to interfere in the arbitration process.

The problem is not merely academic. In a recent survey of international arbitrators by the Global Center for Dispute Resolution Research, 64 respondents identified 50 separate arbitration cases in which interim relief was sought either to restrain or stay an activity, order specific performance, or provide security for costs. These figures are consistent with earlier reports to the United Nations Commission on International Trade Law (UNCITRAL), which indicated that parties are seeking interim measures in an increasing number of cases. The availability of arbitral interim measures is not a subject that can safely be ignored.

Limitations

What may limit or prevent an arbitral tribunal from granting interim measures? The answers most frequently given to this question are:

- Interim measures may be urgently needed before the tribunal has been formed.

- Although the arbitrators may have the knowledge and expertise required to decide the substantive issues in dispute, they may not consider it part of their function or within their area of competence to issue emergency or provisional orders.

- Arbitral orders granting interim measures may be difficult to enforce.

- To be effective, interim measures may require the involvement of third parties over whom the arbitrators do not have jurisdiction.

- The tribunal's jurisdiction to grant interim measures may be limited by the governing law of the arbitration.

Formation of the Tribunal

Under Article 6 of the AAA international rules, the parties have 45 days from the commencement of the arbitration to designate arbitrators or a procedure for appointing them, failing which they may be appointed by the AAA case administrator. As noted above, in some cases, interim measures may be needed before the arbitrators are appointed. However, the AAA has addressed this need by making available Optional Rules for Emergency Measures of Protection. Under these rules, a special arbitrator can be quickly appointed by the administrator for the purpose of hearing a request for interim relief before the tribunal is formed. It is important to note that to take advantage of these rules the parties must specifically incorporate them into their agreement to arbitrate. It is not enough simply to agree to the AAA international rules because the AAA Optional Rules are entirely separate.

If included in the parties' agreement to arbitrate, the AAA Optional Rules will cover a number of situations in which interim relief may be required, but not all. They will not help in cases in which the need for interim relief is absolutely immediate, as at least a few days will be required to appoint an arbitrator, establish a schedule and obtain submissions from the parties. Nor will they be of assistance when the application is made without notice to the other party, as the Optional Rules require that notice be given to all parties.

The Arbitrator's Function

Whether or not it is an arbitrator's function to issue interim measures was addressed in the Kostas Melas. Mr. Justice Goff stated that arbitrators did not have power to order one party to pay a sum to another in an interim award that does not decide any matters in dispute. This statement has been interpreted as a finding that under earlier English Arbitration Acts, it was not an arbitrator's function to make temporary or provisional financial arrangements between the parties to an arbitration. Critics of this view ask: If an arbitrator has jurisdiction to issue a final award affecting the financial arrangements between the parties, why should the arbitrator's function not include the ability to make interim arrangements designed to ensure that the final award is just and effective? Surely the parties and arbitral institutions can choose arbitrators who have the necessary expertise to make appropriate interim orders, whether by adopting procedures like the AAA Optional Rules or by agreeing to appoint arbitrators with particular qualifications.

Enforceability Issues

Whether enforceability is a limitation on the effectiveness of an interim measure ordered by an arbitral tribunal depends mainly on the mechanisms for enforcement available (1) in the arbitration process itself, (2) under the procedural law of the arbitration, and (3) in national courts having jurisdiction over the party against whom the interim measure is to be enforced or that party's assets.

The enforceability of arbitral interim measures was considered by UNCITRAL to be of sufficient importance to justify consideration by a Working Group on Arbitration composed of all 39 state members. The Working Group initially identified three types of interim measures: (a) measures aimed at facilitating the conduct of arbitral proceedings, (b) measures to avoid loss or damage and preserve the status quo until the dispute is resolved, and (c) measures to facilitate later enforcement of the award.

The Working Group considered that the need for an enforcement mechanism is greatest for measures to facilitate later enforcement of the award, such as orders freezing or attaching assets or orders to provide security. It considered that a mechanism to enforce interim measures to preserve the status quo (including orders regulating contractual performance during the arbitration) was needed to lesser extent. There was even less of a need for enforcement support for measures aimed at facilitating the arbitration, since the tribunal normally has the ability to regulate compliance with such measures by means of its final decision on arbitration costs.

The UNCITRAL Working Group has prepared draft revisions and additions to Article 17 of the UNCITRAL Model Law on International Commercial Arbitration which, in its unrevised form, is very similar to Article 21 of the AAA international rules referred to above. The draft additions, which are still under discussion, would require in courts in countries that adopt the Model Law to enforce interim measures of protection ordered by arbitral tribunals, except in specified circumstances, such as where the arbitration agreement is invalid or the measure is contrary to public policy.

The English Arbitration Act 1996 provides mechanisms supporting enforcement of orders, directions and awards of the arbitral tribunal. For example, if a party fails to comply with a directive from the tribunal, where the seat of the arbitration is in England, the Act authorizes the tribunal to issue a peremptory order to the same effect prescribing the time for compliance. If the party fails to comply with the peremptory order, the Act gives the tribunal broad powers to issue further directions, draw adverse inferences, proceed to an award, or make an appropriate order as to costs of the arbitration. Ultimately, unless otherwise agreed by the parties, the court may issue an order requiring a party to comply with a peremptory order of the tribunal.

Thus, when English law is the procedural law of the arbitration, there should be few, if any, difficulties in enforcing arbitral interim measures against a party in England. When the party against whom enforcement is sought is elsewhere, the enforceability of an arbitral interim measure will depend on the law of the place where enforcement is sought. If the measure is in the form of an interim award, there is at least an argument that the award can be enforced under the 1958 United Nations Convention on the Recognition and Enforcement of Foreign Arbitral Awards (New York Convention) where the requirements of the Convention are otherwise met. This position is not, however, free from doubt.

The English Act also provides the English Court with powers to support arbitral proceedings where the seat of the arbitration is elsewhere. In this case, however, the Court may refuse to act if, in its opinion, the fact that the arbitration is abroad makes it inappropriate to do so.

Involvement of Third Parties

Subject to certain narrow exceptions, an arbitral tribunal does not have authority to make any orders affecting persons who are not parties to the arbitration. This follows from the fundamental principle that the jurisdiction of an arbitral tribunal is based on the consent of the parties. Accordingly, a tribunal may not grant a request for interim measures when a third party is involved, such as an application to freeze monies in a party's bank account. Similarly, the tribunal may not grant a request to compel a third party to produce documents.

In some cases this limitation on the tribunal's authority can be circumvented by dealing with the request in another way. For example, instead of a "freezing" order, the tribunal could order the arbitrating party to pay monies into an escrow account. If documents from a third party are sought, the tribunal may be able to order an arbitrating party to request them from the third party.

Ultimately, however, only a court will be in a position to grant an order requiring a third party to act in a certain way.

Governing Law

International arbitration practitioners are aware of the significance of the place of arbitration. Where the parties locate the arbitration ought not to be merely a matter of neutrality or amenities.

Under the New York Convention, the UNCITRAL Model Law, and the conflict-of-law rules of most countries, the governing law of the arbitration—the lex arbitri—will normally be the law of the country in which the arbitration takes place. The governing law of the arbitration is of immense importance since it defines the legal requirements according to which the arbitration is to be conducted, including the division between arbitral tribunals and courts of powers to grant interim measures. As a result, the power of arbitrators to order interim measures can vary substantially from one country to another.

Italy and the Canadian province of Quebec, for example, are at one extreme. They subscribe to the view that interim measures ought to be granted only by courts, which are in a position to enforce them, and not by arbitral tribunals. Article 818 of the Italian Code of Civil Procedure expressly provides, "The arbitrator may not grant attachment or other interim measures of protection."

The Italian approach to interim measures may have the advantage of clarity. However, the approach is criticized by those who believe that the parties should be able to choose the rules and procedures under which their arbitration will be conducted (including rules giving the tribunal full authority to grant interim measures, as in Article 21 of the AAA international rules), and that the parties' chosen rules and procedures should be given effect whenever possible.

Switzerland is at the other extreme. Under Swiss law, in the absence of an agreement to the contrary, the parties are to apply initially to the arbitral tribunal, rather than to the courts, for "provisional or protective measures." If the tribunal grants an interim measure, and the party against whom it is directed fails to comply, the tribunal may seek assistance from a competent court.

In England and in several other "pro-arbitration" countries, such as France, Germany and the United States, the power of an arbitral tribunal to grant interim measures lies between these two extremes.

Under the English Arbitration Act 1996, where England is the seat of the arbitration:

- Unless otherwise agreed by the parties, the arbitral tribunal has the power to make certain interim orders specified in the Act, including orders to provide security for costs or to inspect or preserve property or evidence. [Sections 38, 39]

- Parties are free to agree to the powers exercisable by an arbitral tribunal, including the power "to order on a provisional basis any relief which it would have power to grant in a final award." [Sections 38, 39]

- Interim measures ordered by an arbitral tribunal are enforceable as peremptory orders, by the tribunal or, after available arbitral enforcement procedures have been exhausted, by the court. [Sections 41, 42]

- Where the arbitral tribunal has no power or is unable for the time being to act effectively, the court may grant interim measures largely on the same basis as in court proceedings. Where the matter is urgent, a party may apply directly to the court; where not urgent, the court will act only with the permission of the arbitral tribunal or the agreement of all parties. [Section 44]

Therefore, the English Arbitration Act 1996 gives the tribunal only limited authority, in the absence of the parties' agreement, to make interim orders, for example, to order security for costs or require the inspection or preservation of property. If the parties wish the tribunal to have broader power to grant "provisional" measures, they must provide for such powers in their arbitration agreement.

Channel Tunnel Case

In a case where there is an arbitration clause, the practical difficulty is to establish the division of powers with respect to interim measures. When does one apply to the arbitral tribunal and when does one apply to the court?

This difficulty is illustrated by Channel Tunnel Group v. Balfour Beatty, a now famous English case involving Trans-Manche Link (TML), the consortium building the Channel Tunnel, and Eurotunnel, the owner. TML threatened to suspend work on the cooling system after a dispute arose with Eurotunnel over the sufficiency of payments under a change order. Under a two-tier dispute resolution clause in the main contract, disputes between the parties were to be decided by a dispute resolution board (DRB) within 90 days, following which either side could refer the matter to arbitration in Belgium under ICC Rules. Article 8.5 of the ICC Rules (which was very similar to Article 21(3) of the AAA international rules) provided:

> Before the file is transmitted to the arbitrator ... the parties shall be at liberty to apply to any competent judicial authority for interim or conservatory measures, and they shall not by so doing be held to infringe the agreement to arbitrate or to affect the relevant powers reserved to the arbitrator. ①

2. American Review of International Arbitration

By choosing to resolve their disputes in arbitration, parties to international contracts opt out of national court systems. But in most cases, national courts retain some supervisory authority over the arbitration award. First, courts in the arbitral situs can vacate the award and declare it a nullity. The grounds on which an award can be vacated, which define the degree of court supervision, are set out in the national arbitration law of the situs. Second, courts elsewhere (wherever the party that lost in the arbitration has assets) also may supervise the arbitration by deciding whether to enforce the award—turn it into a court judgment that can be collected on in the jurisdiction. The grounds on which an enforcement court can refuse to enforce an award likewise are set out in national arbitration laws, as constrained by international treaty. Differences between the grounds for vacating awards and the grounds for enforcing awards (or the application of those grounds) give rise to the possibility that an award that has been vacated in the arbitral situs may nonetheless be enforceable elsewhere.

A. Actions to Enforce Arbitral Awards

The enforcement of international arbitration awards is governed by the Convention on the Recognition and Enforcement of Foreign Arbitral Awards (the "New York Convention"), to which over 120 nations are party. The New York Convention requires contracting states to "recognize arbitral awards as binding and enforce them in accordance with the rules of procedure of the territory where the award is relied upon." Article V sets out limited grounds on which "[r]ecognition and enforcement of the award may be refused." Included among those grounds is that the award "has been set aside or suspended by a competent authority of the country in

---

① See Raymond J. Werbicki, Arbitral Interim Measures: Fact or Fiction? Dispute Resolution Journal, 2003.

which, or under the law of which, that award was made." In other words, an enforcement court may refuse to enforce a vacated award without violating the Convention. Article VII of the Convention, however, makes clear that the Convention "shall not . . . deprive any interested party of any right he may have to avail himself of an arbitral award in the manner and to the extent allowed by the law or the treaties of the country where such award is sought to be relied upon."

The New York Convention addresses only the grounds on which a contracting state may decline to enforce an award; it does not limit the grounds on which a court in the arbitral situs may vacate an award. Instead, that is left to the national law of the situs, where the award is made. Indeed, unless the parties provide for a different arbitration law to govern the proceeding, the arbitral situs is the exclusive jurisdiction that can consider an action to vacate the arbitration award.

B. Actions to Vacate Arbitral Awards

National arbitration laws prescribe varying grounds on which arbitration awards can be vacated. Many national laws follow the UNCITRAL Model Law on International Commercial Arbitration, which tracks the list of grounds for nonenforcement of awards contained in the New York Convention. Other national arbitration laws contain grounds for vacating awards in addition to those in the UNCITRAL Model Law. One example is Egypt, which has adopted the UNCITRAL Model Law but with two additional grounds on which awards can be vacated. Other examples are England and the United States, each of which engages in some degree of court oversight of arbitral rulings on legal issues. On the other hand, some national laws contain fewer grounds for vacating arbitral awards than the UNCITRAL Model Law.

In most countries, the grounds for vacating arbitral awards are mandatory: the parties cannot contract around them. In the United States, some courts have found the grounds for vacating an award to provide a mandatory minimum but not a mandatory maximum: in other words, parties cannot contract for less court supervision than provided in the statute but can contract for more supervision. In some countries, however, the grounds for vacating international arbitration awards are default rules, at least for arbitrations involving foreign parties. For example, the Swiss international arbitration law provides:

Where none of the parties has its domicile, its habitual residence, or a business establishment in Switzerland, they may, by an express statement in the arbitration agreement or by a subsequent agreement in writing, exclude all setting aside proceedings, or they may limit such proceedings to one or several of the grounds listed in Art. 190, para. 2.

In 1998, Belgium amended its arbitration law to follow the Swiss model, repealing a prior version that precluded actions to vacate awards unless one of the parties to the proceeding was Belgian.

As noted above, the New York Convention does not regulate the grounds on which an arbitration award can be vacated. But competition among jurisdictions for international arbitration business may influence the standards for vacating awards set out in national arbitration laws. Serving as a situs for international arbitration proceedings can be lucrative. As a result, jurisdictions compete to provide favorable settings in which to hold arbitrations—including providing a favorable legal environment. International arbitration proceedings are sufficiently mobile that if a national arbitration law is seen as unfavorable, parties can choose a different situs in future agreements to arbitrate. Or arbitration institutions may avoid locating arbitrations in a jurisdiction with legal provisions they find objectionable. Although some have decried interjurisdictional competition among arbitral sites as a " race to the bottom," in other areas such competition has been beneficial in improving the quality of regulation. Indeed, as discussed in more detail below, in the case of the Belgian arbitration law, competition has resulted in more oversight of arbitration at the arbitral situs, rather than less.

C. Enforcement of Vacated Awards

Because of differences between the grounds for vacating awards and the grounds for nonenforcement of awards (or perhaps the interpretation of those grounds), an award may be vacated by a court in the arbitral situs, yet nonetheless be enforceable under the national arbitration law of the enforcement court. In such a case, there may be no ground—other than that the award was vacated in the situs—for declining to enforce an award. Should the enforcement court decline to enforce the vacated award? This section first describes the facts of in re Chromalloy Aeroservices, the leading American case on point, which illustrate the problem. The section then discusses the varying approaches taken by courts and suggested by commentators for its resolution.

思考题

1. What is your opinion on the standard of the nationality of an arbitral award?
2. Can arbitrators adopt the interim measures of protection directly in China?
3. Why are courts prohibited to modify the arbitration award?
4. What are the grounds of setting aside an arbitration award?
5. What is the difference between vacation of award and refusal of recognition and enforcement of award?

推荐阅读

1. 〔英〕艾伦·雷德芬、马丁·亨特等:《国际商事仲裁法律与实践》,林一飞、宋连斌译,北京大学出版社 2005 年版,第七、八、九章。
2. 林一飞:《国际商事仲裁法律与实务》,中信出版社 2005 年版,第五章第四节、第六章第四节。
3. Katherine V. W. Stone, Arbitration Law, Foudation Press, 2003.
4. Jean-Francois Poudret, Sebastien Besson, Comparative Law of International Arbitration, Sweet & Maxwell Ltd., 2007, Chapter 6, Chapter 8.
5. Jingzhou Tao, Arbitration Law and Practice in China, Kluwer Law International, 2004, Chapter V.
6. Raymond J. Werbicki, Arbitral Interim Mesures: Fact or Fiction? Dispute Resolution Journal, 2003.
7. Jason Fry, Interim Measures of Protection: Recent Developments and the Way ahead, International Arbitration Law Review, 2003.

第八章 国际商事仲裁裁决的执行

第一节 概　　述

一、仲裁裁决的"命运"

作为争端解决方式之一,国际商事仲裁最终必须达成一份仲裁裁决对当事人之间的是非做个了断。商事仲裁裁决的作出标志着仲裁程序的终止,仲裁庭或仲裁机构的使命也就完成了。裁决一旦作出,无论争端当事方是否满意,都必须按照裁决规定的内容履行裁决义务,除非存在一些法定的事由可以使得这份裁决被有管辖权的法院裁定撤销或不予执行。

仲裁裁决的效力,如前所述具有终局性和执行力两大效力。① 终局性避免了重复仲裁或仲裁裁决与法院判决间的相互矛盾,以此确保仲裁裁决的法律效力,但终局性不能解决如何使仲裁裁决法律效力得以实现的问题,于是各国仲裁法纷纷赋予仲裁裁决以执行力。仲裁裁决的执行力从广义上理解有两个方面的含义:一是指作为当事人自觉履行仲裁裁决的根据的效力;二是指作为法院强制执行该仲裁裁决依据的效力,即在当事人不自愿履行仲裁裁决的情况下,另一方当事人有权向法院申请强制执行,在法院作出予以强制执行的裁定后,当事人即可通过法院采取的强制措施,使得仲裁裁决的内容得到实现。如果从狭义上理解,仲裁裁决的执行力就是指仲裁裁决作为强制执行依据的效力,一般意义上所谓的"执行力"就是这个含义。下文涉及的"执行"和"执行力"都是在这个狭义理解上使用的。

Most arbitral awards are voluntarily complied with and do not require judicial enforcement. It is only if an arbitral award can be adequately enforced, however, a successful claimant can ensure that it will actually recover the damages awarded it.② In its normal sense, an action for enforcement denotes an action before the competent authority or court of law against an award debtor resisting enforcement of the award. As a matter of fact, it is quite often that an enforcement is required because of the

---

① 所谓"一裁终裁"便是指仲裁裁决的"终局性"。
② See Gary B. Born, International Commercial Arbitration in the United States, Kluwer Law and Taxation Publishers, 1994, p.460.

losing party's noncompliance with the arbitral award. ①

由于在执行和强制执行的表述方面不够严谨,可能会使有些初学者对于执行的理解有扩大的倾向,即把所有实现仲裁裁决内容的行为都理解为裁决的执行,所以,这里需提醒读者注意,所谓仲裁裁决的执行是指仲裁裁决的强制执行,即在裁决义务人不自愿履行裁决义务的情况下,裁决权利人根据一国国内法律或者条约的规定向当地相应级别的法院申请,由法院通过采取法定的措施强制裁决义务人履行裁决义务。

二、国际商事仲裁裁决的执行主体

对于法院作出的民商事判决的执行来说,其强制执行机关也是法院(当然执行法院并不一定就是作出判决的法院),这是因为法院有法律所赋予的执行职权。但是仲裁裁决的强制执行则不一样,仲裁庭或者仲裁机构是没有权力作出强制执行的裁定并采取强制执行措施的。这是因为仲裁裁决的作出机关从性质上看通常是社会团体或者公民个人,各国法律赋予了仲裁机构或者临时仲裁的个人通过仲裁庭等形式对商事争议进行裁判的权力,但是并没有也不可能赋予它们以强制执行的权力。同时也是基于司法对于仲裁活动的审查和监督的理念,绝大多数国家都规定仲裁裁决的强制执行必须由法院来进行,也即仲裁庭、仲裁机构或者仲裁员对于自己作出的裁决的强制执行没有管辖权。

A meaningful arbitral award is conditional on an effective and reliable enforcement mechanism. In China, as elsewhere, this task lies beyond the remit of the arbitration tribunal. The tribunal is invariably disbanded once the arbitral award is rendered except in a few special cases where an additional award or re-arbitration is required. Should one party to the arbitration fail to honor the tribunal award, the other party will have no alternative but to seed enforcement thereof via a competent court. ②

三、仲裁裁决的承认与执行的关系

在很多著述中,"承认"与"执行"会作为双生子一起出现,如1958年《纽约公约》在涉及这个问题时采用的就是外国仲裁裁决的"承认与执行",但是有些地方又会采取其他的表述,比如1927年《日内瓦公约》中使用的就是"承认或执行",所以无论从名词本身还是从各种规定看,两者在含义和具体操作上都是存

---

① 参见 Wang Sheng Chang:《Resolving Disputes through Arbitration in Mainland China》,法律出版社2003年版,第322页。

② See Jingzhou Tao, Arbitration Law and Practice in China, Kluwer Law International, 2004, p.131.

在差异的。"承认",被认为是一种防御程序①,仲裁裁决的胜诉方或债权方可以以裁决为依据,反对法院受理诉讼,这意味着仲裁裁决具有既判力,即当地法院承认一份仲裁裁决有效力。而"执行"则是法院在"承认"的基础上,进一步采取法律所允许的手段使得裁决的内容得以实现。简言之,"承认"是"执行"的前提和必经阶段,一份被执行的仲裁裁决必然是获得法院承认的,但有时候只需"承认"而无须"执行",通常认为只有含有给付内容且败诉方不自动履行的仲裁裁决才需要强制执行。《示范法》对商事仲裁裁决的承认与执行的概念也有明确的区分,该法第 35 条第 1 款规定:"仲裁裁决不论在何国境内作出,均应承认具有约束力,而且经向主管法院提出书面申请,即应予以执行,但须服从本条和第 36 条的规定。"而在其后的第 36 条又提及"承认或执行",表明裁决的约束力并不依赖于裁决的实际履行,裁决的承认与执行是不同的两个阶段,需要给予一定的区分。②

然而,从实践操作上看,强调承认与执行的不同阶段意义不大,因为一份"不予执行"的仲裁裁决通常也意味着不被"承认"。另外,绝大多数的商事仲裁裁决特别是那些败诉方拒绝自动履行的商事仲裁裁决一般都含有给付内容,从而总是需要进入执行程序。所以本书舍弃"仲裁裁决的承认与执行"的说法,直接冠以本章为"仲裁裁决的执行"。

四、国内仲裁裁决的执行

对于一国法院而言,仲裁裁决的作出机构从地域的角度看,就是两种:在法院所在地国成立的仲裁机构(通常被称为内国)和在法院所在地国之外成立的仲裁机构。③ 一般而言,一国法院要审查执行的仲裁裁决有两类:国内仲裁机构在国内所作的裁决和国外仲裁机构在国外所作的仲裁裁决。④ 大多数国家的仲裁法都会作这样的区分,因为基于管辖权的考虑,一国主管机关对于国内仲裁机构所作的仲裁裁决的监督力度肯定要大于其对外国仲裁机构所作的裁决。而我国,因为历史的原因,在此基础上又进行了一个层次的区分,即又把国内仲裁机构所作的仲裁裁决分为纯粹国内仲裁裁决和涉外仲裁裁决。

---

① See A. Redfern & M. Hunter, Law and Practice in International Commercial Arbitration, 2nd ed., 1991, p.448.
② 一些著作在标题中使用"承认与执行",但实际上只讲到"执行"并不涉及"承认"。
③ 因为我国目前不承认临时仲裁,所以本书在介绍仲裁裁决主体时使用仲裁机构及仲裁庭。
④ 在表述上,有学者习惯使用内国裁决和非内国裁决,在采用仲裁裁决国籍认定的"领域标准"情况下,这种表述是清楚的。但按照仲裁裁决作出主体来划分裁决种类则无法涵盖所有仲裁裁决的情况,比如说在国内仲裁机构在国外所作的仲裁裁决和国外仲裁机构在国内所作的仲裁裁决的认定问题上,就是存在争议的,特别是目前 ICC 在中国国内进行仲裁,ICC 认为其裁决属于中国国内仲裁,但是中国实务界则更多是从仲裁机构的国籍来判断是否为外国仲裁裁决。

这样,在我国,国际商事仲裁裁决的执行包括外国仲裁裁决的执行和涉外仲裁裁决的执行。

In China the manner of enforcement depends on the type of the award: domestic, foreign-related or international. This is an important distinction, as Chinese law treats each differently. Actually there is no explicit standard by law for distinguishing among them. Moreover, arbitral awards rendered in the Hong Kong SAR, Macao SAR and Taiwan are also effectively treated as foreign-related awards. The difference in the treatment of these awards and their respective enforcement in China are explained below.

本书旨在介绍国际商事仲裁裁决的执行问题,但是为了使读者能够对仲裁裁决的执行的全貌有所了解,也为了使读者能够明白三种仲裁执行时的具体差异,下面将简要介绍一下我国法院关于国内仲裁裁决的执行规则。

Prior to the present Arbitration Law, most domestic arbitral institutions fell under the remit of administrative organs and did not exercise jurisdiction based on the agreement of disputing parties. Awards rendered by domestic arbitration commissions were not final. A party against whom an award was made could effectively block enforcement proceedings by filling a lawsuit with the People's Court within a specific time period.

In September 1995, the Arbitration Law provided the legislative basis for establishing the system of single and final award, which prohibits a party that objects to a domestic arbitration award from subsequently instituting civil proceedings in respect of the same dispute, thereby ensuring that the enforcement mechanism assumes greater importance. However, the losing party, bearing the burden of proof, still enjoys the right to challenge an arbitral award and may apply to the People's Court for an order setting aside the award or an order denying enforcement.

(一)国内仲裁裁决的执行主体

根据法律明文规定,当事人有义务履行仲裁裁决,如果一方当事人不履行仲裁裁决,另一方当事人可以向有管辖权的人民法院申请强制执行。根据我国《民事诉讼法》及其司法解释,国内仲裁裁决的管辖法院是被执行人住所地或者被执行的财产所在地人民法院。

(二)申请执行的期限

根据我国2007年修订的新《民事诉讼法》,申请仲裁强制执行的期间为两年,并且申请执行时效的中止、中断,适用法律有关诉讼时效中止、中断的规定。①

(三) 不予执行的事由

不是所有的仲裁裁决都能得到执行,所以一国法律必须明确什么样的仲裁裁决可以获得法院的认可并予以执行。大多数国家在涉及对于仲裁裁决是否予以执行的法律规定方面,都采取了"否定清单"式的立法方式,我国亦如此,即明确列明若干仲裁裁决不能被执行的情形,如果一份裁决符合其中的任何一种情形,该仲裁裁决就会被法院裁定不予执行。

In determining non-enforcement of domestic arbitral awards, the People's Court is empowered to review both procedural and substantive matters. Specifically, Article 63 of the PRC Arbitration Law and Article 217 of the PRC Civil Procedure Law provides that the respondent (party against whom execution is filed) may apply to the Intermediate People's Court in the place where the arbitration commission is located for non-enforcement of a domestic arbitration award. The respondent will be required to produce evidence providing that the arbitration award was rendered in one or more of the following circumstances, viz., where:②

(1) There is no arbitration agreement between the parties;

(2) The matters determined in the award exceed the scope of the arbitration agreement or are beyond the arbitral authority of the arbitration commission;

(3) The formation of the arbitration tribunal of the arbitration procedures was not in conformity with statutory procedures;

(4) The evidence on which the arbitral award is based was forged;

(5) The other party withheld evidence sufficient to affect the impartiality of the arbitrations;

(6) While arbitrating the case, the arbitrator commits embezzlement, accepts bribes, resorts to deception for personal gain or renders an award that perverts the law;

If the court finds the award be contrary to the social and public interest, it shall rule not to enforce an award.

在上述数种情形中,前六种不予执行的情形要求被申请执行人提出证据证明,如果被申请执行人不能证明,则法院不会给予不予执行的裁定;而对于"违背社会公共利益"的事由,被申请执行人没有举证责任,法院可以自行查明。

---

① 而在此之前,仲裁裁决执行期间根据当事人的身份有一年和六个月之分,而且法律也没有明确说明这个期间是否适用中止、中断的规定。

② See Jingzhou Tao, Arbitration Law and Practice in China, Kluwer Law International, 2004, p.132.

第二节 涉外仲裁裁决的执行

一、涉外仲裁裁决的定义

我国《仲裁法》第七章为"涉外仲裁的特别规定",其在一定程度上吸取了我国涉外仲裁的理论成果和实践的经验,也借鉴了外国立法和国际组织立法的经验,参考了《示范法》的有关规定,是我国涉外仲裁发展过程中的里程碑。我国法律中的"涉外仲裁"的概念并不是独有的,其他如法国的《民事诉讼法》中也有这样一个概念,但是含义并不相同。大多数国家在仲裁裁决的执行问题上,对国内仲裁机构所作的裁决不再加以区分,即一般对于国内仲裁机构所作的仲裁裁决的执行标准是一致的,而不像我国这样把国内仲裁机构的裁决区分为两个方面,采取不同的执行标准。涉外仲裁裁决被区分出来,是出于一定的历史原因和人们对于国际商事仲裁裁决的认识不断发展的结果。

从"涉外"一词的语义看,一般可以认为它是"国际"的同义词,但是我国法上的涉外仲裁一词是具有特定含义的。从《仲裁法》、《民事诉讼法》以及配套的解释、规定看,所谓"涉外仲裁裁决"主要是指我国国内的仲裁机构也即通常所谓的涉外仲裁机构所处理的具有"涉外因素"的商事案件的裁决,而不能被理解成还包含外国仲裁机构所作的外国仲裁裁决。换言之,我国法律区分国内仲裁裁决(包括纯粹的国内仲裁裁决和涉外仲裁裁决)和外国仲裁裁决的首要标准就是仲裁机构的所在地。[①]

就我国法律而言,仲裁机构从国籍上看包括两类:一是国内的仲裁机构,比如中国国际经济贸易仲裁委员会、中国海事仲裁委员会、各地的仲裁委员会,它们所作的裁决往往被称为"内国裁决"。二是位于外国的仲裁委员会和国际组织的仲裁委员会,其所作出的仲裁裁决在我国法上一般被视为"外国仲裁裁决",由国际公约及双边协议或者互惠关系来调整。根据《纽约公约》的规定,所谓外国仲裁裁决,是指"因自然人或法人间之争议而产生且在申请执行国以外的国家领土内做成的仲裁裁决"。《纽约公约》区分内外国裁决的标准有两个:仲裁地标准和非内国仲裁标准。在我国,国内的仲裁机构所作出的裁决分两种,

---

[①] 学界在关于区分国内仲裁和外国仲裁的标准方面有很多学说,比如仲裁地标准(领域标准)、仲裁员国际标准等学说。另外,关于这个区分标准问题,有学者指出,从我国《民事诉讼法》、《仲裁法》的有关措辞看,以涉外仲裁机构或涉外委员会作出的裁决为涉外仲裁裁决,而《关于适用〈中华人民共和国民事诉讼法〉若干问题的意见》却以"法律关系的主体、客体和内容"为标准来界定涉外民事案件,从而推导出我国立法在涉外仲裁概念界定上的冲突与矛盾。事实上,在实践中这两种标准是可以同时参照适用的。例如,中国国际经济贸易仲裁委员会毫无争议地可以成为法条里的"涉外仲裁机构",但是很显然,它所作的裁决不全是涉外仲裁裁决,这点从它自身的规则里也有所反映。

一是"涉外仲裁",另一种就是纯粹的国内仲裁裁决。那么该如何区分这两类裁决呢?

《仲裁法》以"纯粹的国内仲裁裁决"为基准进行规定,以"涉外仲裁"为特别规定。但法律对于什么是"涉外仲裁"并没有明确的界定,通常涉外仲裁产生的原因是国内仲裁机构拟裁决的法律关系具有"涉外因素",那么所谓的"涉外因素"究竟是指哪些呢?参考《关于适用〈中华人民共和国民事诉讼法〉若干问题的意见》关于"涉外民事案件"的界定,可以得出这样几个标准:(1)争端当事人的一方或双方(自然人、法人或非法人组织)为非内国人。这里要注意一点,因为历史的特殊性,我国对于涉港、涉澳的仲裁裁决目前有两个安排可以参照,后文将专门述及;对于涉台的仲裁裁决,还是要按照涉外的规则来进行;另外,对于涉及华侨的仲裁裁决在某些情况下也是按照涉外仲裁裁决来处理的。(2)当事人之间的商事关系的设立、变更或者消灭发生在外国或具有其他涉外因素。(3)当事人之间争议的标的物在外国或跨国界。只要具有这三种情况下的任何一种就可称为涉外商事仲裁。

因此,涉外仲裁裁决的界定标准应是"国内仲裁机构"加"仲裁事项的涉外性"。

二、涉外仲裁裁决执行的实体问题

所谓涉外仲裁裁决的实体问题,是指法院在仲裁裁决满足什么样的条件下会执行仲裁裁决。在上文我们已经讲到,在决定是否执行仲裁裁决的时候,法律采取的是"否定清单"式的立法方式,我国涉外仲裁裁决执行的法律规定亦是如此。我国对于涉外仲裁裁决的执行不适用1958年《纽约公约》,但通过下文的分析可以看出,事实上我国的《民事诉讼法》、《仲裁法》在裁决的执行方面在一定程度上借鉴了该公约的规定。

Prior to the Arbitration Law, foreign-related awards merely referred to awards rendered by the two foreign-related arbitration institutions, CIETAC and CMAC. The legal basis for the enforcement of foreign-related awards in China dates back to the Decision.① Article 11 of the Decision provided as follows, "The award of the Arbitration Commission shall be executed by the parties themselves within the time fixed by the award. In case an award is not executed after the expiration of the fixed time, a People's Court of the People's Republic of China shall, upon the request of

---

① 即1954年5月6日政务院第215次政务会议通过的《中央人民政府政务院关于在中国国际贸易促进委员会内设立对外贸易仲裁委员会的决定》(Decision of the Government Administration Council of the Central People's Government Concerning the Establishment of a Foreign Trade Arbitration Commission within the China Council for the Promotion of International Trade)。

one of the parties, enforce it in accordance with the law."

This position remained unaltered until the Trial Civil Procedure Law took effect. On the issue of enforcement of arbitral awards rendered by foreign-related arbitration commissions, Article 195 of the Trial Civil Procedure Law provided as follows:

"When one of the parties concerned fails to comply with an award made by a foreign-related arbitration institution of the People's Republic of China, the other party may request that the award be executed in accordance with the provisions of this article by the Intermediate People's Court at the place where the arbitration institution is located or where the property is located."

In 1991, the Civil Procedure Law substantially amended the Trial Civil Procedure Law. The new law contains new provisions treating the enforcement of foreign-related awards in China. In 2007, the 1991 Civil Procedure Law got some amendment, but the provisions on enforcement of arbitral awards were unaltered.[①]

Article 257 provides that after a PRC arbitration organ for foreign-related disputes has rendered an award, no party may institute an action in a People's Court. If a Party fails to perform the arbitral award, the other party may apply for enforcement to the Intermediate People's Court of the place where the domicile of the person against whom an application is made is located or where the property is located.

Article 258 of the CPL enumerates the circumstances to be proved by the respondent for refusing the enforcement of foreign-related arbitration awards as follows:[②]

(1) the parties have neither included an arbitration clause in their contract nor subsequently concluded a written arbitration agreement;

(2) the party against whom the enforcement is sought was not notified to appoint an arbitrator or to take part in the arbitration proceedings or the party against whom the enforcement is sought was unable to state his opinion due to reasons for which he is not responsible;

(3) the formation of the arbitration tribunal or the arbitration procedure was not in conformity with the rules of arbitration; or

(4) the matters decided in the award exceed the scope of the arbitration agreement or are beyond the authority of the arbitration institution.

---

① 下文中,法条在该法律中的位置以新《民事诉讼法》为准。
② 《仲裁法》第71条的规定与该法条内容完全相同。

The grounds enumerated above are restricted to procedural irregularities and not touch on the merits of an award, which is so different from enforcement of domestic one.

The people's court may rule ex officio to deny enforcement of a foreign-related or international award if it finds that enforcement of the award will be contrary to the social and public interest.

从这里可以看出,对于涉外仲裁裁决来说,人民法院决定不予执行的情形有五类;从举证责任的角度看则可以分为两类:第一款的四种情况举证责任明确在于被申请人,且不涉及裁决的事实问题;第二款中的"公共利益"的违反与否则属于法院自裁事项,这就有可能从事实本身出发全盘考虑该裁决了。

下面具体解释每一类"不予执行"情形的含义:

（1）没有仲裁协议。一项争议在提交仲裁委员会仲裁时,必须要有表明双方当事人仲裁意思表示的书面文件,这可以是一份纯粹的仲裁协议,也可以是双方民商事合同或者其他来往书信、电报等法律认可的书面材料里所含有的仲裁条款。如果法院在一份仲裁裁决的申请书中看不到这样的证据,就很难甚至根本不会相信这个仲裁裁决的自治性和合法性,所以说缺乏仲裁协议或仲裁条款的裁决不会被执行。

（2）申请人没有被通知前去参与仲裁程序,或者虽然参与但却因为非自身的原因没有阐述自己观点的机会。这也是一个合情合理的理由,如果一份仲裁裁决是基于这样的前提制定出来的,那么无论最终裁决是否合情合理,这样的仲裁都是不能得到提倡的。

（3）仲裁庭的组成和仲裁程序不合法。我国《仲裁法》第四章对于仲裁程序有比较细致的规定,各地仲裁委员会也有一套依据《仲裁法》制定的细则。以仲裁庭的组成为例,我国《仲裁法》目前只承认机构仲裁,那么临时仲裁肯定是得不到法律保护的。又如,仲裁庭如果是三名仲裁员组成的话,那么其中首席仲裁员必须是由双方共同选定出来或者由仲裁委员会主任指定的,其他两名仲裁员则各由一方当事人指定一名,因此如果仲裁庭的仲裁员都是一方当事人指定的或者另一方当事人指定仲裁员的要求不被认可的话,都属于本项情形。

（4）超裁。这里有两种情形,一种是超出仲裁协议可仲裁范围的事项,另一种是超出法定范围。就前者而言,如果双方当事人对于买卖合同的可仲裁范围只约定了"迟延履行合同义务",那么就"产品瑕疵"问题产生的争议就不属于可以仲裁的范围,基于此产生的裁决就是不予执行的。超出法定范围主要是指《仲裁法》第 3 条所规定的几种情形:"下列纠纷不能仲裁:（一）婚姻、收养、监护、扶养、继承纠纷;（二）依法应当由行政机关处理的行政争议。"所以,一份涉及"婚姻是否有效"的仲裁裁决是不可能得到法院支持的。

比较涉外仲裁裁决不予执行和国内仲裁裁决不予执行的"清单",可以发现,人民法院对于国内仲裁的执行的监督力度要大于涉外仲裁裁决,这主要表现在对于国内仲裁裁决的执行方面,法院可以审查案件的事实、适用法律以及仲裁员的行为,即其不仅可以审查案件的程序方面是否合法,对于实体方面的问题也可以审查,但是对于涉外仲裁裁决的执行,法院的审查只能止步于程序,而不涉及案件在事实、法律等实体方面的错误。

三、涉外仲裁裁决执行的程序问题

所谓涉外仲裁裁决执行的程序问题,主要包括仲裁裁决执行的管辖法院、申请文件以及申请期限的问题。

(一)涉外仲裁裁决执行的管辖法院

涉外仲裁裁决执行的管辖法院与纯粹国内仲裁裁决的规则是一样的。

In proceedings for the enforcement of foreign-related arbitral awards, Article 257 of the Civil Procedure Law provides that if, following the rendering of an arbitral award by a foreign-related arbitral institution, a party fails to comply with the terms of that arbitral award, the other party may institute enforcement proceedings with the Intermediate People's Court. It further provides that the Intermediate People's Court empowered to exercise such jurisdiction shall be the Intermediate People's Court located in:

(1) Where the person subjects to the enforcement proceedings is a natural person, the place where he has applied for household registration or his place of residence;

(2) Where the person subjects to the enforcement proceedings is a legal person, the location of its principal place of business;

(3) Where the person subjects to the enforcement proceedings has no place of domicile, place of residence or principal place of business but has property within the territory of China, the location of the said property.

The basic-level People's Court is excluded from exercising jurisdiction over the enforcement of foreign-related awards.

(二)执行申请文件

申请执行人往往都是仲裁裁决中的债权人,其在提出执行申请时,必须提交一套完整的文件。

According to the Regulations of the Supreme People's Court for Certain Issues Concerning Enforcement by the People's Court (for Trial Implementation) (the "Enforcement Regulations"), in making an application for enforcement, the applicant must present the following documents to the court, viz.:

(1) The enforcement application: This must specify the grounds upon which the application is grounded, the subject matter of enforcement, and such details as are known to the applicant regarding the property an assets status of the party against whom enforcement is sought. Notably, a foreign party applies for enforcement with application in Chinese unless there is some treaty or convention as an exception.

(2) A copy of the arbitration award together with a copy of the arbitration agreement or a copy of the contract containing the arbitration clause that provided the basis for the arbitration.

(3) The applicant's identity certificate, meaning identity card of a natural person, or the business license of a corporation or other such legal person.

(4) Other documents or certificates contingent on the specific situation.

(三) 申请期限

申请执行必须要及时提出,所以法律对于当事人提出申请有期限上的限制,超出法律所规定的最大期限,法院根本不会去理会是否存在上述执行与否的事由而完全不予受理。对于仲裁裁决的执行,我国法律并没有专门的规定,而是由《民事诉讼法》及其相关司法解释或意见对于执行的期限进行了统一的规定。同时,在执行的期限上不区分国内仲裁裁决还是涉外仲裁裁决,这两类裁决的申请期限是一致的。1991年《民事诉讼法》对于执行的申请期限的规定比较短,从实际操作上看也是问题重重,有时候显得极不合理,2007年修订的《民事诉讼法》对于申请期限作了很大的改动。

Article 219 of the Civil Procedure Law 1991 set forth a unified time limit for the initiation of enforcement proceedings, not taking into account the nature of the award for which enforcement is sought. Where one of the parties is a Chinese natural person, the application for the enforcement of domestic, foreign-related and international arbitral awards must be made within one year, and six months where both parties are legal persons. After April 1, 2008, when the amended Civil Procedure Law 2007 is executed, the time limit for the initiation of enforcement proceedings is two years, no matter the parties are natural persons or legal persons.

四、我国涉外仲裁裁决在国外的执行

我国涉外仲裁机构作出的发生法律效力的仲裁裁决,如果败诉一方当事人是外国公司且仅在境外有财产的,外方当事人又不予自动履行的,就需要到境外申请强制执行。这里就涉及有关国家执行我国涉外仲裁裁决的问题。

我国《仲裁法》第72条规定:"涉外仲裁机构作出的发生法律效力的仲裁裁

决,当事人请求执行的,如果被执行人或者其财产不在中华人民共和国领域内,应当由当事人直接向有管辖权的外国法院申请承认和执行。"我国自1987年加入《纽约公约》之后,涉外仲裁裁决在外国的执行开始具备了条约基础,由于目前加入《纽约公约》的国家和地区已达144个,这就意味着我国涉外仲裁裁决可以在这144个缔约国和地区内得到相应的执行。

如果被申请执行人所属的国家不是1958年《纽约公约》的成员国,如双方存在双边条约或协定,则可根据双边条约或协定中的有关相互执行仲裁裁决的内容予以执行。我国已经同世界上一百多个国家和地区订有双边贸易协定,在这些协定中,一般都含有关于通过仲裁方式解决贸易争议的规定,并且大多约定缔约双方应设法保证被申请执行仲裁裁决的国家主管当局根据适用的法律规定,执行仲裁裁决。此外,在投资领域,我国也与六十多个国家和地区签订了双边投资保护协定,在这些双边协定中大多都规定了相互执行仲裁裁决。另外,我国还与许多国家签订了有关民商事司法互助的协定。上述的公约、条约、协定构成了我国涉外仲裁裁决在有关国家得到执行的依据。

如果我国与某一国家签订的双边贸易协定或者双边投资保护协议或者司法互助协定中有关裁决执行的条件比1958年《纽约公约》规定的条件更为优惠,即使双方均是《纽约公约》的缔约国,裁决的执行仍可以依据上述有关协定以更便利的方式进行。如果该外国与我国既无《纽约公约》缔约国关系,又无双边条约关系,则应当通过外交途径,向对方多家的主管机关申请执行。①

第三节　外国商事仲裁裁决的执行

对于一个国际商事仲裁裁决来说,需要识别其属于内国裁决还是外国裁决。从裁决执行角度而言,这种识别的意义在于,如果属于内国裁决,则依照执行地国关于裁决执行程序的规定予以执行;如果属于外国裁决,通常还要进一步识别属于哪一个国家的裁决,执行问题则颇为复杂。

在未形成统一的多边国际条约之前,各国对于裁决执行的态度和做法往往有很大的不同,这一点阻碍了国际商事仲裁制度的发展和国际经济贸易纠纷的有效解决。但在1927年《日内瓦公约》和1958年《纽约公约》这两个专门针对外国仲裁裁决的执行问题而订立的国际公约诞生之后,各国在仲裁裁决执行方面最大程度地达成了共识。特别是《纽约公约》具有非常大的影响,其对外国仲裁裁决的定义、执行外国仲裁的条件与程序问题等等都予以了明确,而本节对于执行外国仲裁裁决有关的国际公约,也将主要介绍《纽约公约》。

---

① 参见宋航:《国际商事仲裁裁决的承认与执行》,法律出版社2000年版,第227—228页。

一、有关执行外国仲裁裁决的国际公约——《纽约公约》

(一)《纽约公约》概述

在国际商事仲裁领域,最主要的国际公约之一就是 1958 年《纽约公约》。《纽约公约》的订立可以说是树立了国际统一立法的典范,现在世界上大多数国家都已经加入了该公约,有关外国仲裁裁决的执行,各国大都依据《纽约公约》来进行,各国关于外国仲裁裁决执行的立法也或多或少地体现了公约的精神。[①]

The increase and reliance on international arbitration to resolve trans-border commercial disputes has been more remarkable. While speed, confidentiality and efficiency are mentioned reasons to arbitrate, the indisputable advantage is the enforceability of the award, under the Convention on the Recognition and Enforcement of Foreign Arbitral Awards (Hereinafter referred to as the New York Convention, or the Convention). The New York Convention is such an international agreement as creates a dependable system of laws in trading nations under which enforcement of awards is obtained. The goal of the New York Convention is to encourage the enforcement of commercial arbitration agreements in international contracts and to unify the standards by which agreements to arbitrate are observed and arbitral awards are enforced in the signatory countries.[②]

(二)外国仲裁裁决的定义——《纽约公约》第 1 条

《纽约公约》第 1 条规定:"仲裁裁决,因自然人或法人间之争议而产生且在申请承认及执行地所在国以外至国家领土内做成者,其承认及执行适用本公约。本公约对于仲裁裁决经申请承认及执行地所在国认为非内国裁决者,亦适用之。"根据公约的规定,若一裁决是在执行地国以外的国家做成,即为外国仲裁裁决。同时,若裁决在执行地国作出,但该国不认为其是本国裁决,也属于公约上的外国裁决。

Article I of the New York Convention: "This Convention shall apply to the enforcement of arbitral awards made in the territory of a State other than the State where the enforcement of such awards are sought, and arising out of differences between persons, whether physical or legal. It shall also apply to arbitral awards not considered as domestic awards in the State where their recognition and enforcement are sought."

---

① 参见宋航:《国际商事仲裁裁决的承认与执行》,法律出版社 2000 年版,第 94 页。
② Cf. Scherk v. Alberto-Culver Co., 417 U.S. 506, 520 n. 15 (1974).

（三）关于执行外国仲裁裁决的程序——《纽约公约》第3条

对于外国仲裁裁决的执行，需要当事人向有管辖权的法院提出申请，法院按照规定的程序审查当事人的申请是否符合法定的条件，以决定是否予以执行。

对此，《纽约公约》第3条规定："各缔约国应承认仲裁裁决具有拘束力，并依援引裁决地之程序规则及下列各条所载条件执行之。承认或执行适用本公约之仲裁裁决时，不得较承认或执行本国仲裁裁决附加之过苛之条件或征收过多之费用。"

Article Ⅲ of the New York Convention: "Each Contracting State shall recognize arbitral awards as binding and enforce them in accordance with the rules of procedure of the territory where the award is relied upon, under the conditions laid down in the following articles. There shall not be imposed substantially more onerous conditions or higher fees or charges on the enforcement of arbitral awards to which this Convention applies than are imposed on the enforcement of domestic arbitral awards."

这一规定确立了外国仲裁裁决执行程序的两个基本原则：一是执行外国仲裁裁决的程序规则，适用被申请执行地国的法律。这是因为各国国内法对于执行程序的规定各不相同，使用法院地的程序规则是较好的选择。二是在具体实施上，只要求各缔约国在执行公约裁决时不应较执行国内裁决以更苛刻的条件和过高的费用。

Contracting states are required to enforce arbitral awards in accordance with their own procedural rules, which cannot be more onerous than those applicable to domestic awards. Thus, the New York Convention remits the parties to domestic laws with respect to enforcing awards. Also, if domestic awards are difficult to enforce, the New York Convention does not make the enforcement of foreign awards any easier.①

（四）关于执行外国仲裁裁决的条件——《纽约公约》第4条

执行外国仲裁裁决的条件应包括形式要件和实质要件两个方面，各国法院在审查裁决是否可以执行时，要从形式和内容两方面着手，因此广义的裁决执行条件应包括申请人申请执行的条件和审查被申请人举证要求拒绝执行裁决的理由，即执行的积极要件和消极要件。② 这里要讨论的问题是执行裁决的积极要件，有关消极要件在拒绝执行外国裁决内容中讨论。

Article IV of the New York Convention: "1. To obtain the recognition and

---

① See Ramona Martinez, Recognition and Enforcement of International Arbitral Awards under the United Nations Convention of 1958: The "Refusal" Provisions, 24 the International Lawyer (1990), pp.487—496.

② 参见宋航：《国际商事仲裁裁决的承认与执行》，法律出版社2000年版，第102页。

enforcement mentioned in the preceding article, the party applying for recognition and enforcement shall, at the time of the application, supply: (a) The duly authenticated original award or a duly certified copy thereof; (b) The original agreement referred to in article II or a duly certified copy thereof.

2. If the said award or agreement is not made in an official language of the country in which the award is relied upon, the party applying for recognition and enforcement of the award shall produce a translation of these documents into such language. The translation shall be certified by an official or sworn translator or by a diplomatic or consular agent."

《纽约公约》第 4 条规定了申请执行的当事人获取裁决执行必备的条件,包括两个方面:一是文件的认证或证明,二是文件的翻译问题。规定申请人提交裁决书和仲裁协议的正本或者经过认证的副本,便可依此向有管辖权的法院申请执行裁决,从而开始裁决的执行程序。

《纽约公约》规定的执行显示出简单化的趋势,公约只要求当事人提供经正式认证的裁决正本或其经正式证明的副本,以及仲裁协议或其经正式证明的副本等,这些简单的要求,对于当事人来说是很容易做到的。申请执行人不需要提供证据证明裁决在原作出国已经终局,也不需要为裁决是否存在不予执行的事由承担举证责任。而被申请人如要反对执行裁决,则必须证明存在公约中规定的据以拒绝执行公约裁决的理由之一,因而公约是把主要的举证责任施加给被申请人,这也体现出了公约的"执行倾向",其宗旨是为执行裁决提供更为便利的条件,推进仲裁裁决在全球范围内的执行,实践的结果也表明公约第 4 条在使用时并未遇到多大困难,已为各国所接受。①

(五) 关于拒绝执行外国仲裁裁决的理由——《纽约公约》第 5 条

1. 概述

上文提到申请执行仲裁裁决的当事人只要提交符合条件的有关文件,受理案件的法院便可以开始执行程序。但存在两种例外,一种是被申请人可能因反对该裁决而不愿自动履行裁决中确定的义务,可以提出证据并请求法院拒绝执行仲裁裁决;另一种就是作为被申请执行裁决的法院,可以通过对裁决的审查拒绝执行仲裁裁决。②

Article V of the New York Convention exhaustively lists the grounds for refusal of recognition or enforcement:

(1) Recognition and enforcement of the award may be refused, at the request of

---

① See Commentaries to Art. IV, YCA I (1997), p.260; YCA IV (1979), p.245.
② 参见宋航:《国际商事仲裁裁决的承认与执行》,法律出版社 2000 年版,第 112 页。

the party against whom it is invoked, only if that party furnishes to the competent authority where the enforcement and recognition is sought, proof that:

(a) the parties to the agreement referred to in Article II were, under the law applicable to them, under some incapacity, or the said agreement is not valid under the law to which the parties has subjected it or, failing any indication thereon, under the law of the country where the award was made; or

(b) the party against whom the award is invoked was not given proper notice of the appointment of the arbitrator or the arbitration proceedings or was otherwise unable to present its case; or

(c) the award deals with a difference not contemplated by or not falling within the terms of the submission to arbitration, or it contains decisions on matters beyond the scope of submission to arbitration, provided that, if the decisions on matters submitted to arbitration can be separated from those not so submitted, that part of the award which contains decisions on matters submitted to arbitration may be recognized and enforced; or

(d) the composition of the arbitral authority or the arbitral procedure was not in accordance with the agreement of the parties, or, failing such agreement, was not in accordance with the law of the country where the arbitration took place; or

(e) the award was not yet become binding on the parties, or has been set aside or suspended by a competent authority of the country in which, or under the law of which, that award was made.

(2) Recognition and enforcement of an arbitral award may also be refused if the competent authority in the country where recognition and enforcement is sought finds that:

(a) the subject matter of the difference is not capable of settlement by arbitration under the law of that country; or

(b) the recognition or enforcement of the award would be contrary to the public policy of that country.

《纽约公约》第5条规定了拒绝执行外国仲裁裁决的理由。被请求执行裁决的法院只有在作为裁决执行对象的当事人提出下列情况的证明的时候,才可以根据该当事人的请求,拒绝执行该项裁决:仲裁协议无效、违反正当程序、仲裁员超越职权、仲裁庭的组成或仲裁程序不当、裁决不具约束力、争议不具有可仲裁性、违反公共政策。其中前五项理由必须由当事人提供证据证明,而最后两个理由,法院可自行拒绝执行裁决。

The list of the grounds on which enforcement may be refused is meant to be exhaustive. The grounds listed can be grouped into two distinct categories. The first category consists of grounds for refusal with respect to which the resisting party has the burden of proof. The second category is made up of grounds that the court may apply on its own initiative.

这些拒绝执行的理由之间有一定的关联性:仲裁协议的效力与可仲裁性问题紧密相关,争议事项的不可仲裁性足以导致仲裁协议无效。因此,不可仲裁性问题应由法院主动查明和援引,而当事人可以以不可仲裁性为由主张仲裁协议无效。另外,正当程序与公共政策也是紧密相关的,由于正当程序原则反映了程序正义的要求,因此构成公共政策的一部分。虽然公约规定不可仲裁性问题和公共政策问题可以由法院主动援引和查明,但可以肯定的是,若当事人主动提出这方面的理由,法院当然也应予以审查。[1]

2. 拒绝执行外国仲裁裁决的具体理由

下面具体解释每一种"拒绝执行"的理由。[2]

(1) 仲裁协议无效(Invalidity of the Arbitration Agreement)

《纽约公约》从拒绝执行裁决的角度要求被诉人证明仲裁协议是无效的,实际上是要求仲裁协议在实质上有效才能执行。这涉及当事人的能力问题、可适用仲裁协议的法律问题以及仲裁协议的形式问题,这些问题是确定仲裁协议是否有效的根据,同时也是反对裁决执行的一方当事人可以推翻裁决的理由。Under the New York Convention, a valid arbitration agreement is treated as a cornerstone of arbitration, as is also the case for the enforcement of awards.

(2) 违反正当程序(Violation of Due Process)

根据《纽约公约》的规定,违反正当程序包括未给予适当的通知、拒绝给予当事人听审机会以及仲裁程序中的其他不正当行为,后两个方面实际上是公约所指的未给予当事人申辩的机会。The New York Convention stresses that in case the party against whom enforcement is sought can prove that he was not properly notified or was otherwise unable to present his case, enforcement may be refused. However, this perception should be construed narrowly. [3]

(3) 仲裁员超越权限(Excess by Arbitrator of His Authority)

以仲裁员超越权限为由直接提出的抗辩,在实际案例中比较少见。在法国

---

[1] 参见于喜富:《国际商事仲裁的司法监督与协助——兼论中国的立法与司法实践》,知识产权出版社2006年版,第441页。

[2] 参见宋航:《国际商事仲裁裁决的承认与执行》,法律出版社2000年版,第120—178页;Wang Sheng Chang:《Resolving Disputes through Arbitration in Mainland China》,法律出版社2003年版,第353—365页。

[3] See A. J. van den Berg, The New York Convention: Summary of Court Decisions, ASA Special Series No.9, p.84.

的一个案例中,当事人认为仲裁员超越权限仲裁,因为仲裁是在约定的仲裁请求期限届满以后才开始的,法院据此否定了仲裁庭的管辖权,这实际上是因仲裁协议无效的问题,并不属于仲裁员超越权限的范围。

另外,如果仲裁庭在仲裁协议范围内作出的决定可以与超越仲裁协议范围所作的决定分开,则未超出部分的决定仍可以执行。Excess of authority may result in the denial of enforcement as far as the excessive part of decision is concerned. The court cannot deny the enforcement of an award as a whole if only part of the decisions in the award was decided ultra vires.

(4) 仲裁庭的组成或仲裁程序不当(Irregularities in the Composition of the Arbitral Tribunal or Arbitral Procedure)

如果仲裁庭的组成或仲裁程序同当事人之间的协议不符,或者当事人之间未订有此种协议,则可以拒绝执行裁决。例如,在一起涉及货物品质的仲裁案中,仲裁的进行分为两个步骤,先是由两名专家组成品质仲裁庭,确认货物的品质问题;其后则由三名仲裁员进行审理,解决赔偿问题。法院拒绝执行裁决,认为这一仲裁程序即使符合仲裁地的习惯,也明显违反了当事人之间的明示协议,因为协议中指明:"以一个或同一仲裁程序解决所有争议"。

(5) 裁决不具约束力(Award Not Binding)

《纽约公约》未对裁决有约束力作进一步解释,从公约的立法史和条文本身看,裁决有约束力应指大多数裁决一经作出,只要遵守了有关法律,就具有了公约范围的"约束力"而可以得到执行。The article of the New York Convention is obviously relaxed and liberal. It states that the court has discretionary power to adjourn its decision on enforcement of the award and to order the respondent to provide security, pending the setting aside or suspension proceedings in the country of origin.①

(6) 不可仲裁性(Non-Arbitrability)

争议事项的可仲裁性问题,是指哪些争议事项可以交付仲裁,哪些争议不能提交仲裁,也就是仲裁的范围问题。归纳起来,只有当事人能自由处分或通过和解解决的争议才允许交付仲裁;有关民事身份、父母和子女之间的关系、离婚、劳资争议等事项不能提交仲裁。

(7) 违反公共政策(Contrary to the Public Policy)

公共政策,是英美法系通用的概念,而大陆法系常用公共秩序(Public Order)一词来表达。《纽约公约》未对公共政策的含义、范围以及具体内容作出

---

① See A. J. van den Berg, The New York Convention: Summary of Court Decisions, ASA Special Series No. 9, p. 95.

统一解释,实际上也不可能达成统一解释,这是因为各国在政治、经济、法律、道德、文化、宗教等方面存在很大差异,认定公共政策的标准不可能达成一致,在具体案件中,法院地国在这方面均有各自的自由裁量权。Courts across the world may refuse to enforce arbitral awards if such enforcement would be contrary to the public policy of their countries. The public policy exception to the enforcement of arbitral awards is one of the most controversial exceptions to the enforcement of arbitral awards, causing judicial inconsistency and unpredictability in application.

各国法院以公共政策为由拒绝执行裁决发生在少数案件中,且往往是在当事人用尽其他抗辩理由后法院才考虑是否援用公共政策的理由,限于对有关国家法律程序根本观念的违反。同时,对公共政策原则的解释也日趋严格,只有在执行裁决会导致危害执行国利益的实质性后果情况下,才能运用公共政策原则拒绝执行。公共政策的内容也趋向具体化,许多国家或对公共政策的主要内容作了规定,或从反面限制了其范围,譬如法国《民事诉讼法》第1502条规定:仲裁员的不公正可导致裁决执行的拒绝;美国通过司法判例指出,外交政策不是公共政策。

应该说,《纽约公约》被全世界广泛地接受,促成了外国裁决执行在一定程度上的统一。但是,公约将执行程序及判定可仲裁性和公共政策等问题留给执行地国法解决,而内国法对此规定又各有不同,会以自己的方式适用《纽约公约》的规定。因此,对于仲裁裁决的执行而言,形式上的统一与实质上的不统一并存。当然,反过来说,也正是因为公约在具体规则上的"放手"才促成了全世界最大范围的"一致",这种模式应值得关注,对于一些约束力日渐减少的国际法制度框架是可以借鉴的。

二、外国仲裁裁决在我国的执行

在我国执行外国仲裁裁决的依据是我国《民事诉讼法》和《仲裁法》中的有关规定以及我国缔结或参加的双边或多边国际公约。在我国执行的外国仲裁裁决,可以分为《纽约公约》项下的裁决(简称公约裁决)和非公约裁决,公约裁决为在我国境外的《纽约公约》缔约国领土内作出的仲裁裁决,这些裁决执行的条件只能依照公约规定的条件执行。对于非公约裁决,按照我国《民事诉讼法》第267条的规定,根据互惠原则予以执行。

The New York Convention became effective in China on April 22, 1987. Where a country is a contracting party to the New York Convention, the issue of enforcement in China of an international arbitral award rendered in such circumstance shall be dealt with according to the New York Convention. Where a country is not a contracting party to the New York Convention but has entered into a bilateral judicial assistance treaty or protocol with China, the issue of enforcement in China of an international arbitral award rendered within such state shall be dealt with in accordance with the provisions set forth (if any) in the applicable treaty or protocol.①

(一) 依据《纽约公约》执行外国仲裁裁决

1. 我国执行公约裁决的范围

我国在加入《纽约公约》时作了互惠保留声明和商事保留声明。根据我国加入该公约时所作的互惠保留声明,在另一缔约国领土内作出的仲裁裁决的执行适用该公约。根据我国加入该公约时所作的商事保留声明,我国仅对按照我国法律属于契约和非契约性商事法律关系所引起的争议适用该公约。所谓"契约性和非契约性商事法律关系",具体是指由于合同、侵权或者根据有关法律规定而产生的经济上的权利义务关系,如货物买卖、财产租赁、工程承包、加工承揽、技术转让、合资经营、合作经营、勘探开发自然资源、保险、信贷、劳务、代理、咨询服务和海上、民用航空、铁路、公路的客货运输以及产品责任、环境污染、海上事故和所有权争议等,但不包括外国投资者与东道国政府之间的争端。②

When ratifying the New York Convention, China made two reservations, namely the reciprocity reservation and the commercial reservation. In the Decision of the Standing Committee of the National People's Congress on China Joining the Convention on the Recognition and Enforcement of the Foreign Arbitral Awards within which it was decided that China shall join the 1958 New York Convention, two reservations were declared as follows:

(1) The People's Republic of China will apply the Convention to the recognition and enforcement of arbitral awards rendered in the territory of another Contracting State only on the basis of reciprocity (the "reciprocity" reservation).

(2) The People's Republic of China will apply the Convention only to disputes which have, according to the laws of the People's Republic of China, been determined as arising out of contractual relationship or non-contractual commercial legal relationships (the "commercial" reservation).

2. 我国执行公约裁决的管辖法院

申请我国法院执行在另一缔约国领土内作出的仲裁裁决,是由仲裁裁决的一方当事人提出的。对于当事人的申请,应由我国下列地点的中级人民法院受理:被执行人为自然人的,为其户籍所在地或者居所地;被执行人为法人的,为其

---

① See Jingzhou Tao, Arbitration Law and Practice in China, Kluwer Law International, 2004, p.136.
② 参见宋航:《国际商事仲裁裁决的承认与执行》,法律出版社 2000 年版,第 243 页。

主要办事机构所在地;被执行人在我国无住所、居所或者主要办事机构,但其财产在我国境内的,为其财产所在地。

3. 我国执行公约裁决的执行

根据《民事诉讼法》第二十一章的规定,法院强制执行的措施主要包括以下几种:(1)冻结、划拨被执行人的存款;(2)扣留、提存被执行人应当履行义务的部分收入;(3)查封、扣押、冻结、拍卖、变卖被执行人应当履行义务的部分财产;(4)传唤双方当事人当面交付法律文书指定交付的财物或者票证,或者由执行员转交;(5)强制被执行人迁出房屋或者强制退出土地等。

以上各项强制性措施的采取,均应由人民法院作出裁定,并向有关人员发出协助执行的通知,有关人员或单位必须执行。法院查封、扣押财产时通知被执行人到场的,拒不到场者不影响法院的执行。例如,在锐夫动力公司(香港)诉上海远东航空技术进出口公司一案中,上海市第二中级人民法院1996年3月裁定承认瑞典斯德哥尔摩商会仲裁院作出的仲裁裁决的效力,由于被告未能在规定的期限内履行该裁决,法院于1996年4月2日再次裁定,根据我国1991年《民事诉讼法》第221条和第223条的规定,决定冻结和查封被告的银行存款账户中的款项,如果此款不足以支付,余款将从拍卖和变卖被告的财产所得款项中予以清除。①

4. 法院拒绝执行国际商事仲裁裁决的报告制度

我国法院在裁定不予执行我国涉外仲裁机构和拒绝执行外国仲裁裁决时,必须严格依照《民事诉讼法》及我国缔结或参加的有关国际公约中的规定行事,并且自1995年8月28日起,执行最高人民法院规定的报告制度。

我国有管辖权的人民法院接到反对执行的当事人的申请后,应对仲裁裁决进行审查,如果认为不具有1958年《纽约公约》第5条第1、2两项所列的情形,应当裁定承认其效力,并且依照我国的民事诉讼法律规定的程序执行;如果认定具有第5条第2项所列的情形之一,或者根据被执行人提供的证据证明具有第5条第1项所列的情形之一,应当裁定驳回申请,拒绝执行。

根据最高人民法院规定的报告制度的规定,凡一方当事人向人民法院申请执行的外国仲裁裁决不符合我国参加的国际公约的规定或者不符合互惠原则的,在裁定拒绝执行之前,必须报请所属高级人民法院进行审查;如果高级人民法院同意拒绝执行,应将其审查意见报最高人民法院,待最高人民法院答复后,方可拒绝执行。这一规定实际上取消了地方法院对拒绝执行外国裁决的决定

---

① 关于该案的案情及其评析,参见赵秀文主编:《国际商事仲裁案例评析》,中国法制出版社1999年版,第1—34页。另参见王生长:《外国仲裁裁决在中国的承认与执行》,载陈安主编:《国际经济法论丛》第2卷,法律出版社1999年版,第516—519页。

权,赋予了最高人民法院对这一问题的最终决定权,无疑为执行外国裁决提供了便利条件,使得地方法院不能随意作出拒绝执行的决定。如果违反报告制度作出拒绝执行的裁定,最高人民法院将依职权撤销该裁定,并指定重审或提审,从而保护当事人的权益,加强了我国对《纽约公约》的执行。①

On 28 August 1995, the Supreme People's Court issued the *Notice on People's Courts' Handling of Issues in Relation to Matters of Foreign-Related Arbitration and Foreign Arbitration*, within which it was decided to establish a pre-reporting mechanism in relation to issues where the people's courts accept foreign-related arbitral awards and refuse enforcement of foreign arbitral awards.

Paragraph 2 of the Notice stipulates: "Where one party files an application to the People's Court for enforcement of the arbitral award made by the foreign-related arbitral institution of our country, or files an application for enforcement of awards made by foreign arbitral body, and if the People's Court contemplate that the award made by a foreign-related arbitral institution of our country bears one of the circumstances enumerated by Art. 260 of the Civil Procedure Law, or a foreign arbitral award sought for enforcement is not in compliance with the provisions of international convention acceded to by China or is not in conformity with the principle of reciprocity, the contemplating court, before deciding to refuse enforcement or refuse enforcement, must report its findings to the Higher People's Court in the same jurisdiction for review; if the Higher People's Court also agrees with the findings that enforcement should be refused, it should report its findings to the Supreme People's Court. Only after the Supreme People's Court confirms the findings then the Intermediate People's Court may rule to refuse enforcement."

(二) 依据我国国内法或双边条约执行外国裁决

《民事诉讼法》第267条明确规定了外国仲裁裁决可以在我国直接申请承认和执行。根据该条规定,当事人可以直接向被执行人财产所在地或法定住所地的中级人民法院申请执行外国仲裁机构作出的裁决,人民法院依照我国缔结或者参加的国际条约或协议办理;在没有可适用的国际条约或协议的情况下,人民法院也可根据互惠原则决定执行申请。因此,外国仲裁裁决在我国的执行已具备充分的法律基础。

Enforcement of foreign arbitration awards that are made in the territory of a foreign country other than China may be pursued according to Art. 267 of the Civil Procedure Law of the PRC which permits the applicant to apply for enforcement of

---

① 参见宋航:《国际商事仲裁裁决的承认与执行》,法律出版社2000年版,第246—247页。

foreign arbitral awards either by invoking relevant international treaties, or, in the absence of international treaties, by relying on the principle of reciprocity.①

Article 267: If an award made by a foreign arbitral organ requires the recognition and enforcement by a People's Court of the People's Republic of China, the party concerned shall directly apply to the Intermediate People's Court of the place where the party subjected to enforcement has his domicile or where his property is located. The People's Court shall deal with the matter in accordance with the international treaties concluded or acceded to by the People's Republic of China or with the principle of reciprocity.

The bilateral treaties in force, or those contemplated, should not be permitted to interfere with the goals of the 1958 U. N. Convention or other multilateral conventions, which is to create one system for the effective implementation of a harmonized, if not uniform, process for arbitration in international transactions and other relations of a transactional nature.②

我国在加入《纽约公约》时对公约的适用作了互惠保留,对公约裁决和非公约裁决作了区别对待,问题是,法律和司法解释对于非公约裁决仅规定了按互惠原则办理,这方面的研究和实践较少,虽然公约裁决随着《纽约公约》缔约国的增加占到了大部分,但对非公约裁决的执行制度也应该予以完善。

第四节 我国区际仲裁裁决的执行

因为"一国两制"的原因,我国成为一个多法域的国家,内地、香港、澳门和台湾各自实行着不同的法律制度,各自的仲裁制度自然也有所不同。在"一国两制"的前提下且基于台湾问题的特殊性,两岸之间也有着相互承认和执行仲裁裁决的需要。以下将分别从内地与香港、内地与澳门、大陆与台湾之间相互执行仲裁裁决三个方面来阐述。

一、内地与香港特别行政区仲裁裁决的相互执行

(一)香港仲裁制度概况及内地与香港特区相互执行仲裁裁决的历史沿革

1963年,港督第22号令发布了香港《仲裁条例》,并将该条例列入香港法律第341章,从而实现了香港仲裁法律制度的成文法化。1979年4月21日,英国

---

① 参见 Wang Sheng Chang:《Resolving Disputes through Arbitration in Mainland China》,法律出版社2003年版,第337页。
② See Domke on Commercial Arbitration, rev. ed. by Gabriel M. Wilner, p.604.

根据《纽约公约》及英国《1975年仲裁法》的规定,将《纽约公约》扩大适用于香港地区,《仲裁条例》据此增订了第四部分"公约裁决的执行"。此外,该条例在1982、1989、1990、1996及2000年作了多次修正。特别是在1989年《仲裁条例》采取了港内仲裁和国际仲裁分立规范的模式,为次年香港将《示范法》纳入《仲裁条例》提供了基础,并使香港成为世界上为数不多的采取《示范法》的地区之一。

内地与香港特区相互执行仲裁裁决可以分为三个阶段:第一个阶段,自我国参加1958年《纽约公约》时起至香港回归祖国之前,香港法院承担《纽约公约》项下的执行内地仲裁裁决的义务是基于英国参加1958年《纽约公约》并将其效力扩张适用于香港地区的结果。据不完全统计,自从1989年香港最高法院首次执行了CIETAC在内地作出的仲裁裁决以来到1997年6月30日,香港法院执行了CIETAC在内地作出的一百六十余份涉港仲裁裁决。[①] 内地法院也基于《纽约公约》成功地执行了多份在香港地区作出的仲裁裁决。

第二个阶段,是自香港回归之日到《关于内地与香港特别行政区相互执行仲裁裁决的安排》(以下简称《99安排》)实施之前。在香港回归之后,内地与香港特区之间继续适用《纽约公约》存在两个难以逾越的障碍:第一,香港特区是中国的一部分,不能根据英国所承担的义务将《纽约公约》继续扩展适用于香港地区;第二,中国政府在加入《纽约公约》时所作的"互惠保留"表明,香港特区不能被视为《纽约公约》的"其他缔约国",这样《纽约公约》不再适用于内地和香港之间的仲裁裁决。另外,因为香港特区的特殊地位,也不能总是简单地比照涉外仲裁裁决的规则,于是便产生了一个真空地带。

第三个阶段,自《99安排》实施以来,内地与香港特区之间相互执行仲裁裁决便有了法律依据。在香港回归祖国以后,为排除两地仲裁裁决相互执行上的法律障碍,1999年6月21日,我国最高人民法院与香港特别行政区政府在深圳签署了《99安排》。香港《仲裁条例》就是在这样的背景下于2000年完成修订的。这次修订集中体现了"一国两制"框架下仲裁制度的协调和合作,既保留了香港作为独立司法领域的特点,又保持了《纽约公约》这一国际条约在我国的继续适用,进而开创了"一国两制"下区际法律协助的先河。[②]

(二)在《99安排》项下,内地与香港地区仲裁裁决的相互执行

1. 管辖法院

内地有执行管辖权的法院为被申请人住所地或者财产所在地的中级人民法院,这一点与涉外仲裁裁决的执行是一致的。如果被申请人住所地或者财产所

---

① 参见张赋生主编:《仲裁法新论》,厦门大学出版社2004年版,第548页。
② 同上书,第529页。

在地在内地不同的中级人民法院辖区内的,申请人可以选择其中一个人民法院申请执行裁决,不得分别向两个或者两个以上人民法院提出申请。

香港有执行管辖权的法院为香港特区高等法院。如果被申请人的住所地或者财产所在地,既在内地又在香港特区的,申请人不得同时分别向两地有关法院提出申请。只有一地法院执行不足以偿还其债务时,才可就不足部分向另一地法院申请执行。两地法院先后执行仲裁裁决的总额,不得超过裁决数额。

2. 申请文件

申请人向有关法院申请执行在内地或者香港特区作出的仲裁裁决的,应当提交以下文书:(1)执行申请书;(2)仲裁裁决书;(3)仲裁协议。执行申请书的内容必须包括:(1)申请人为自然人的情况下,该人的姓名、地址;申请人为法人或者其他组织的情况下,该法人或其他组织的名称、地址及法定代表人姓名;(2)被申请人为自然人的情况下,该人的姓名、地址;被申请人为法人或者其他组织的情况下,该法人或其他组织的名称、地址及法定代表人姓名;(3)申请人为法人或者其他组织的,应当提交企业注册登记的副本;申请人是外国籍法人或者其他组织的,应当提交相应的公证和认证材料;(4)申请执行的理由与请求的内容,被申请人的财产所在地及财产状况。执行申请书应当以中文文本提出,裁决书或者仲裁协议没有中文文本的,申请人应当提交正式证明的中文译本。

3. 申请期限

申请人向有关法院申请执行内地或者香港特区仲裁裁决的期限依据执行地法律有关时限的规定。比如向内地人民法院申请执行香港仲裁裁决的期限即为两年。

4. 受理

有关法院接到申请人申请后,应当按执行地法律程序处理及执行。即人民法院按照《仲裁法》、《民事诉讼法》进行,香港法院按照《仲裁条例》等法律规定进行。

5. 不予执行

在内地或者香港特区申请执行的仲裁裁决,被申请人接到通知后,提出证据证明有下列情形之一的,经审查核实,有关法院可裁定不予执行:

(1)仲裁协议当事人依对其适用的法律属于某种无行为能力的情形;或者该项仲裁协议依约定的准据法无效,或者未指明以何种法律为准时,依仲裁裁决地的法律是无效的;(2)被申请人未接到指派仲裁员的适当通知,或者因他故未能陈述意见的;(3)裁决所处理的争议不是交付仲裁的标的或者不在仲裁协议条款之内,或者裁决载有关于交付仲裁范围以外事项的决定的;但交付仲裁事项的决定可与未交付仲裁的事项划分时,裁决中关于交付仲裁事项的决定部分应当予以执行;(4)仲裁庭的组成或者仲裁庭程序与当事人之间的协议不符,或者在有关当事人没有这种协议时与仲裁地的法律不符的;(5)裁决对当事人尚无约束力,或者业经仲裁地的法院或者按仲裁地的法律撤销或者停止执行的。

有关法院认定依执行地法律,争议事项不能以仲裁解决的,则可不予执行该裁决。

内地法院认定在内地执行该仲裁裁决违反内地社会公共利益,或者香港特区法院决定在香港特区执行该仲裁裁决违反香港特区的公共政策,则可不予执行该裁决。

The Major Provisions of the Agreement on Mutual Recognition and Enforcement of Judgments in Civil and Commercial Matters between Hong Kong and Mainland China are:①

As far as the procedure is concerned, the Intermediate People's Court of the Mainland (where the party subject to the enforcement has their domicile, ordinary residence, or assets) and the High Court of the Hong Kong SAR shall be the competent courts to receive applications for enforcement.

Under Article 6 of the Arrangement, an applicant shall provide the court concerned with the application for enforcement with details of the parties' identity, enforcement request, the condition of the assets of the party subject to the enforcement and the extent of the enforcement that has been carried out in the place of the originating judgment; the copy of the judgment to be enforced with the seal of the final trial court; the certificate issued by the final trial court certifying that the judgment concerned is a final one as defined by the Arrangement and can be enforced at the place where the judgment was rendered; and the proof of the party's identification.

According to Article 7 of the Arrangement, an application for enforcement of a cross-border judgment may be refused if: (1) the jurisdiction agreement is invalid, except where the chosen court has held the agreement is valid; (2) the judgment concerned has been fully performed; (3) under the law of the place of enforcement, the court shall have exclusive jurisdiction over the dispute; (4) according to the law of the originating court, a default judgment is rendered without due service on the defeating party, or despite the due service the party was not allowed sufficient time to defend themselves as stipulated by the law. However, public notice as a means of

---

① See Xianchu Zhang, Philip Smart, Development of Regional Conflict of Laws: On the Arrangement of Mutual Recognition and Enforcement of Judgments in Civil and Commercial Matters between Mainland China and Hong Kong SAR, 36 Hong Kong L. J. (2006), p.553.

service made in accordance with the law or provisions by the originating court shall not be included in this category; (5) the judgment concerned is obtained through fraudulent means; (6) the enforcing court already has enforced an award made by a foreign or overseas court, or an arbitral tribunal, on the same matter; and (7) finally, the recognition and enforcement would violate the public policy of Hong Kong or the social public interest of the Mainland.

二、内地与澳门特别行政区仲裁裁决的相互执行

（一）澳门仲裁制度概况及内地与澳门特区相互执行仲裁裁决的历史沿革

1962 年,《葡萄牙民事诉讼法典》中仲裁制度的规定已经延伸适用于澳门,但是此制度随着葡萄牙民事诉讼改革而在 1986 年被废止。直到 1991 年 8 月 29 日通过的《澳门司法组织纲要法》第 5 条第 2 款才规定:"得设立仲裁庭,并得设非司法性质之方法及方式,以排除冲突。"然而,上述规定仅仅是纲要性质,不能算是有了一套完整的仲裁法律制度,到 1996 年,立法会在此基础上制定了《仲裁法律制度》。该法规规范了仲裁的标的、适用的法律、仲裁协议的形式、仲裁庭的组成、仲裁员的指定、仲裁员与参与人的报酬、仲裁程序、裁决及上诉等内容。澳门政府又于同年 7 月制定了法令,确立了机构自愿仲裁的法律制度。这两部法规虽然设定了澳门仲裁制度的基本框架,但没有处理有关涉外仲裁的问题。而事实上,大部分的仲裁解决因国际或者涉外商事关系产生之争议,为此,立法会于 1998 年 11 月核准了《涉外商事仲裁专门制度》,该法规几乎完全参照联合国《示范法》。澳门立法者对《示范法》所作的修改仅仅包括第 7 条第 1 款、第 36 条第 1 款涉及仲裁标的及拒绝执行仲裁裁决之依据部分。①

在澳门回归之前,尽管葡萄牙是《纽约公约》的缔约国,但是却没有将《纽约公约》延伸适用于澳门,所以内地与澳门之间并没有如同与香港那样以《纽约公约》为基础的相互执行。所以澳门回归后的一段时间内,我国将《纽约公约》在互惠保留前提下扩展适用于澳门特区,这样,外国商事仲裁裁决在澳门的执行,以及澳门的商事仲裁裁决在外国的执行,在一段时间内是可以依照《纽约公约》进行的。②

2007 年 12 月 12 日,最高人民法院发布了《关于内地与澳门特别行政区相互认可和执行仲裁裁决的安排》(以下简称《07 安排》),从 2008 年 1 月 1 日起,该《安排》就是内地与澳门之间相互执行仲裁裁决的主要法律依据。

---

① 参见唐晓晴:《澳门仲裁的现状与机遇》,http://www.wtc-macau.com/arbitration/cht/forms/txq.pdf,2009 年 7 月 10 日访问。

② 参见谢石松主编:《商事仲裁法学》,高等教育出版社 2003 年版,第 327 页。

（二）在《07安排》规定下两地法院相互执行商事仲裁裁决

1. 管辖法院

（1）地域管辖

无论是在澳门还是在内地申请执行，受理法院均为被申请人住所地、经常居住地或者财产所在地的法院。

如果被申请人的住所地、经常居住地或者财产所在地分别在内地和澳门特别行政区的，申请人可以向一地法院提出认可和执行申请，也可以分别向两地法院提出申请。当事人分别向两地法院提出申请的，两地法院都应当依法进行审查。予以认可的，采取查封、扣押或者冻结被执行人财产等执行措施。仲裁地法院应当先进行执行清偿；另一地法院在收到仲裁地法院关于经执行债权未获清偿情况的证明后，可以对申请人未获清偿的部分进行执行清偿。两地法院执行财产的总额，不得超过依据裁决和法律规定所确定的数额。

（2）级别管辖

在内地，不区分仲裁裁决的认可和执行，受理认可和执行仲裁裁决申请的法院均为中级人民法院；如果两个或者两个以上中级人民法院均有管辖权的，当事人应当选择向其中一个中级人民法院提出申请。

在澳门，区分仲裁裁决的认可和执行，有权受理认可仲裁裁决申请的法院为中级法院，有权执行的法院为初级法院。

2. 申请文件

申请人向有关法院申请认可和执行仲裁裁决的，应当提交以下文件或者经公证的副本：(1) 申请书；(2) 申请人身份证明；(3) 仲裁协议；(4) 仲裁裁决书或者仲裁调解书。上述文件没有中文文本的，申请人应当提交经正式证明的中文译本。

3. 申请期限

《07安排》规定，申请期限按照受理申请的法院地的法律来确定，这样如果向内地法院申请执行，则须在仲裁裁决作出之日起两年内提出，并且该期限可以中止、中断。

4. 仲裁裁决不予认可和执行的情形

在内地或者澳门特区申请执行的仲裁裁决，被申请人接到通知后，提出证据证明有下列情形之一的，经审查核实，有关法院可裁定不予执行：

（1）仲裁协议一方当事人依对其适用的法律在订立仲裁协议时属于无行为能力的；或者依当事人约定的准据法，或当事人没有约定适用的准据法而依仲裁地法律，该仲裁协议无效的；

（2）被申请人未接到选任仲裁员或者进行仲裁程序的适当通知，或者因他故未能陈述意见的；

（3）裁决所处理的争议不是提交仲裁的争议，或者不在仲裁协议范围之内；

或者裁决载有超出当事人提交仲裁范围的事项的决定,但裁决中超出提交仲裁范围的事项的决定与提交仲裁事项的决定可以分开的,裁决中关于提交仲裁事项的决定部分可以予以认可;

(4)仲裁庭的组成或者仲裁程序违反了当事人的约定,或者在当事人没有约定时与仲裁地的法律不符的;

(5)裁决对当事人尚无约束力,或者业经仲裁地的法院撤销或者拒绝执行的;

(6)依执行地法律,争议事项不能以仲裁解决的,不予认可和执行该裁决。

内地法院认定在内地认可和执行该仲裁裁决违反内地法律的基本原则或者社会公共利益,或澳门特别行政区法院认定在澳门特别行政区认可和执行该仲裁裁决违反澳门特别行政区法律的基本原则或者公共秩序的,不予认可和执行该裁决。

三、大陆与台湾地区仲裁裁决的相互执行

(一)大陆执行台湾地区仲裁裁决

大陆执行台湾地区裁决,大致可以分为三个阶段:第一阶段,在大陆实行改革开放之前,两岸关系处于极度对立状态,根本不产生执行裁决的问题。第二阶段,我国加入《纽约公约》之后,特别是1991年《民事诉讼法》颁布后,理论上台湾地区裁决可以向大陆法院申请执行,但执行政策性较强。当时最高人民法院院长在1991年《最高人民法院工作报告》中明确:"台湾居民在台湾地区的民事行为和依据台湾地区法规所取得的民事权利,如果不违反中华人民共和国法律的基本原则,不损害社会公共利益,可以承认其效力。"这表明当时已经有条件地承认台湾地区的民事法规。第三阶段,1998年1月15日最高人民法院发布《关于人民法院认可台湾地区有关法院民事判决的规定》(以下称"98规定"),按照该规定第18、19条,台湾地区裁决可以向大陆法院申请认可,并依《民事诉讼法》规定的程序办理。在认可和执行方面,台湾地区的仲裁裁决是比照台湾地区法院的民事判决来处理的。至此,大陆地区执行台湾地区仲裁裁决有了明确的法律依据。[1] 令人高兴的是,最高人民法院《关于人民法院认可台湾地区有关法院民事判决的补充规定》已于2009年3月30日由最高人民法院审判委员会通过,自2009年5月14日起施行。根据该补充规定第2条,申请认可台湾地区有关法院民事裁定、调解书、支付令,以及台湾地区仲裁机构裁决的,适用"98规定"和本补充规定。

---

[1] 参见宋连斌:《我国内地与港澳台地区相互执行仲裁裁决若干问题探讨》,http://www.ccmt.org.cn/ss/explore/exploreDetail.php? sld=826,2009年7月10日访问。

While governments in Beijing and Taipei left contacts and exchanges to the private sector, both sides made their own revisions to statutes and administrative regulations permitting enforcement of each other's arbitral awards. Neither side classified the other side's arbitral awards as "international", but both sides realized the need to differentiate cross-strait arbitral rulings from ordinary "domestic rulings." In China, arbitral rulings from Taiwan are officially viewed as "domestic arbitral rulings, but with special characteristics," means that they are not covered under China's obligations as a party to the 1958 New York Convention.①

On 15 January 1998, the Judicial Committee of the Supreme People's Court approved the Provisions for Recognition by People's Courts of Civil Verdicts Rendered by Courts in the Taiwan Area ("the Provisions"). The Provisions were primarily designed for enforcement of civil verdicts.

"98规定"的主要内容包括管辖法院、申请书及注意事项，以及大陆地区法院对申请的处理、拒绝认可的理由等。其中申请书及注意事项规定：申请认可台湾地区有关法院民事判决的，应在该判决生效后一年内提出。申请人申请认可时应提交申请书，并须附有不违反"一个中国"原则的台湾地区有关法院民事判决书正本或经证明无误的副本、证明文件。而拒绝认可的理由则包括：申请认可的民事判决的效力未确定、程序不当、案件系专属管辖，以及申请认可的民事判决具有违反国家法律的基本原则，或者损害社会公共利益情形等等。"98规定"施行后，当年6月9日，浙江省台州市人民法院就裁定认可了台湾地区南投地方法院作出的一份民事裁定，这是大陆法院首次认可台湾地区法院的民事裁定的法律效力。2004年7月23日，大陆出现了第一个认可和执行台湾地区仲裁裁决的案例。厦门市中级人民法院根据申请人的申请，依据"98规定"第9条和第19条，认为台湾地区的中华仲裁协会就申请人和华（海外）置地有限公司与被申请人凯歌（厦门）高尔夫球俱乐部有限公司之间因投资高尔夫球俱乐部发生的债权债务纠纷作出仲裁裁决的内容没有违反大陆地区的法律规定，于2004年7月23日裁定予以认可。7月28日，厦门市中级人民法院根据申请人的申请裁定予以执行。② 上述规定确立了大陆执行外法域仲裁裁决的新做法，即和执行外法域法院判决的制度相同，既不同于对大陆裁决的执行，也不同于对香港、澳门仲裁裁决的执行，更不依据《纽约公约》对外国仲裁裁决的执行。同时，上述规定还有一个特点，即裁决须先认可而后执行，认可是独立而明确的程序。

---

① See Jason Blatt, Mutual Recognition and Enforcement of Arbitral Awards in Mainland China and Taiwan: A Breakthrough in Cross-Strait Relations, 36 Hong Kong L. J. (2006), p.585.
② 参见宋连斌：《试论我国大陆与台湾地区相互认可和执行仲裁裁决》，载《时代法学》2006年第6期。

（二）台湾地区执行大陆仲裁裁决

在台湾当局结束所谓"戡乱"时期前，大陆裁决不可能在台湾地区发生法律效力。台湾地区在 1982 年以前，没有执行外国仲裁裁决的立法，对于在台湾只是非本土的国内裁决的大陆裁决也没有规定。20 世纪 80 年代两岸关系相对缓和，从理论上讲，大陆裁决参照执行外国裁决的规定在台湾地区予以执行。

台湾地区在 1992 年 7 月 31 日颁布的"台湾地区与大陆地区人民关系条例"（以下简称"两岸关系条例"）第 74 条中规定："在大陆地区做成之民事确定裁判、民事仲裁判断，不违背台湾地区公共秩序及善良风俗者，得声请法院裁定认可。""前项经法院裁定认可之裁判或判断，以给付内容为者，得为执行名义。"这条规定首先对大陆作出之民事裁决在台湾地区执行的可能性予以了肯定，对两岸仲裁的执行是一个突破。之后，该条例历经八次修正。其中，1997 年的修正涉及第 74 条，在保持原有规定的基础上增加了第 3 款："前二项规定，以在台湾地区做成之民事确定裁判、民事仲裁判断，得声请大陆地区法院裁定认可或为执行名义者，始适用之。"

实际上，现在台湾地区法院认可、执行大陆地区的仲裁裁决，唯一的条件就是该裁决不违背台湾地区的公共秩序或善良风俗。在台湾地区，首例认可和执行大陆地区仲裁裁决的案件为 2003 年 6 月 24 日，申请人国腾电子（江苏）有限公司与相对人坤福营造股份有限公司因违反工程合约事件，经中国国际经济贸易仲裁委员会作出裁决，申请人在申请认可时，分别援引了"98 规定"、"两岸关系条例"及相关规定的内容，同时简述了仲裁的根据及仲裁裁决作出的依据。台中地方法院经审查认为，申请人主张的事实及其所依据的证物，应可信为真实。且核诸本件仲裁判断，仲裁程序既合法，且判断并无违背台湾地区公共秩序或善良风俗之情事，则申请人请求予以认可，自应准许。[①]

In 1992, Taiwan's Legislative Yuan passed landmark legislation scrapping the island's policy of eschewing all contacts with the mainland. Passed on 31 July 1992, the Act Governing Relations between Peoples of the Taiwan Area and the Mainland Area, commonly known as the "Cross-Strait Relations Act," established a legal framework for contacts and exchanges between the two sides. Specifically, the Cross-Strait Relations Act divided the Chinese nation into two legally distinct "areas," namely the "Taiwan Area" and the "Mainland Area".

Most importantly, Article 74 of the Cross-Strait Relations Act specifically authorized Taiwan's courts to enforce civil judgments and arbitral awards rendered in

---

[①] 参见宋连斌：《我国内地与港澳台地区相互执行仲裁裁决若干问题探讨》，http://www.ccmt.org.cn/ss/explore/exploreDetail.php? sld = 826，2009 年 7 月 10 日访问。

the Mainland Area: "To the extent that an irrevocable civil ruling, judgment or arbitral award rendered in the Mainland Area is not contrary to the public order or good morals of the Taiwan Area, an application may be filed with a court for a ruling to recognize it. Where any ruling or judgment, or award recognized by a court's ruling as referred to in the preceding paragraph requires performance, it may serve as a writ of execution."①

"98 规定"和"两岸关系条例"是两岸认可、执行彼此仲裁裁决的法律基础,其内容或许仍有不足之处,但其实施有利于两岸在相互执行仲裁裁决方面积累经验。另外,现阶段两岸执行对方的仲裁裁决,主要的依据是单方法规和政策,极易受制于两岸关系的状况,这不利于仲裁在调整两岸经济关系上发挥更大作用,随着两岸关系日趋紧密,这一现状需要改进。内地与香港、内地与澳门经过协商,在参照《纽约公约》实体内容的基础上,已对相互执行仲裁裁决的问题作出安排,这对于两岸也很有启示。大陆地区与台湾地区即使目前不能协商并达成协议,至少也应有意识地采用《纽约公约》或《关于内地与香港特别行政区相互执行仲裁裁决的安排》、《关于内地与澳门特别行政区相互认可和执行仲裁裁决的安排》的内容,使认可、执行对方仲裁裁决的制度趋于一致。只有这样,仲裁在两岸经贸关系中才能发挥出更大的作用。

The growing importance of economic relations between both sides of the Taiwan Strait has compelled both sides to amend relevant laws and regulations so that courts may enforce arbitral awards rendered by each other's arbitral organizations. However, more experience must be accumulated on both sides before the emerging system of cross-taiwan strait arbitral award enforcement can be declared a success.

案例

1. Vysanthi Shipping Company Limited v. China Grains, Oils and Feedstuffs Co., Ltd., etc.②

Facts

Applicant: Vysanthi Shipping Company Limited

Defendants: China Grains, Oils and Feedstuffs Co., Ltd. (GOFCO); PICC

---

① Jason Blatt, Mutual Recognition and Enforcement of Arbitral Awards in Mainland China and Taiwan: A Breakthrough in Cross-Strait Relations, 36 Hong Kong L. J. (2006), p.585.

② See Tianjin Maritime Court of PRC (TMC), Civil order in Writing(2004) TMC (Que) No.1, Date: 29 October 2004, http://www.blawgdog.com/article.asp?id=195, 2009 年 7 月 10 日访问。

Property and Casualty Company Limited Hebei Province Branch (PICC Hebei); PICC Holding Co.

The dispute between the applicant and the first defendant on the B/L of Joanna V Ship issued on 28 June 1996 had been heard by the London Court of International Arbitration (LCIA) and an award was issued on 14 March 2001. According to the award, the applicant should obtain USD 367,136.86 in general average contribution (G. A. C.) and USD 28,500 in damages of resorting. The applicant should also obtain the interest on 7% per year of the above amount. The interest of damages of resorting (USD 28,500) will be calculated from 1 August 1996. The commencement time for calculating the G. A. C interest, however, would depend on the negotiation result between the applicant and the first defendant. If their negotiation failed, the arbitration court would decide the date. The end dates of both damages' interest are the day when the first defendant made the de facto payment to the applicant. On 20 June 2001, LCIA made the second award in that the commencing date of calculating the interest of resorting damages should be 12 July 1996. In the same award, the arbitration fees in two arbitration procedure were decided to be paid by the first defendant. On 13 February 2002, the third award was made to confirm that the cost of the whole dispute should be paid by the first defendant.

On 28 March 2002, the first defendant and the second defendant brought an action to Commercial Court of Queen's Bench Division, applying for setting aside the above first awards. On 10 July 2002, the court ruled that the defendants should perform as the award decided. On 17 January 2004, the Tianjin Maritime Court received the applicant's application of recognizing and enforcing the above three awards.

Issue

When shall be the commencing time of calculating the time limit of enforcing foreign arbitration awards?

Reasoning

Both China and British are members of the Convention on the Enforcement of Foreign Arbitral Awards 1958. So when the cases are in accordance with the regulations of the convention and China legislation, the court should recognize and enforce the awards made by LCIA. The Civil Procedure Law of People's Republic of China rules in Article 219 as follows:

The time limit for the submission of an application for execution shall be one year, if both or one of the parties are citizens; it shall be six months if both parties are legal persons or other organizations.

The three awards are issued on 14 March 2001, 20 June 2001 and 13 February 2002 respectively. The Tianjin Maritime Court received the written application on 17 January 2004. Although the date when the awards was received by the parties of the dispute is not clear, and the performance time period of the awards are also not clear, the fact that the defendants brought the action to British court on 28 March 2002 has clearly proven that the first and second defendants, as well as the applicant, have received the awards before that day. The application of enforcement has been overdue.

Rule

The trails and judgments of British high court do not consist of a reasonable excuse for extending and/or breaking off the calculation of the six-month time limit during which one can successfully apply for enforcement the foreign arbitral awards.

Award

Do not enforce the three awards brought forward by the applicant. These awards were made by London Court of Arbitration on 14 March 2001, 20 June 2001 and 13 February 2002 respectively.

The applicant shall pay the litigation fee (RMB 500).

2. 香港华兴发展公司申请执行中国国际经济贸易仲裁委员会的裁决被裁定部分不予执行案

案情

申请执行人:香港华兴发展公司。

被申请人:厦门东风橡胶制品厂。

1985年6月19日,以香港华兴发展公司为乙方,厦门东风橡胶制品厂、厦门轴承厂、厦门经济特区建设发展公司为甲方,在厦门签订"合资经营厦门橡塑制品有限公司合同"。1985年10月12日,厦门市政府经济贸易委员会批准该合营合同。同年12月24日领取合营企业营业执照。经营中,因合作不协调,合营各方均表示要终止合同。因对终止合同后的清盘方案达不成协议,最终未形成终止合同的董事会决定。申请执行人遂于1991年3月27日按合同约定提交中国国际经济贸易仲裁委员会(下称"仲裁委员会")仲裁。仲裁委员会经审理认为,其中被申请人厦门东风橡胶制品厂是以厂房实物投资,须办理厂房过户手续,以便对合资企业进行清算,并在其1992年12月20日的终局裁决中,以第二项裁决被申请人应于 1993 年 1 月 30 日前将构成其出资的厂房的过户手续办理完毕。

因被申请人未履行裁决,1993 年 6 月 5 日,申请执行人向厦门市中级人民法院申请执行仲裁委员会发生法律效力的〈92〉贸仲字第 2051 号裁定书。

争议点

被申请执行物不属于被申请人所有是否使得裁决不予执行。

法院判决

厦门市中级人民法院受理申请后,在执行仲裁委员会〈92〉贸仲字第 2051 号裁决第二项时,被申请人提出异议,并提供证据证明执行标的物不归其所有。厦门市中级人民法院组成合议庭审查查明,被申请人作为出资的厂房,是其在"文革"期间在他人菜地上所盖的违章建筑,始终未能办理产权登记。据此,厦门市中级人民法院认为,被申请人对裁决中所指的构成其出资的厂房不拥有产权,不可能办理过户手续,该项裁决不能成立。依照《民事诉讼法》第 237 条、第 217 条第 2 款第 4 项的规定,厦门市中级人民法院于 1994 年 5 月 3 日裁定:

申请执行人香港华兴发展公司申请执行的中国国际经济贸易仲裁委员会〈92〉贸仲字第 2051 号第二项裁决不予执行。

评价

本案系人民法院执行的涉外仲裁案。当事人依照 1991 年《民事诉讼法》第 259 条规定,向有管辖权的人民法院申请执行我国涉外仲裁机构发生法律效力的裁决,人民法院受理后,在执行中,被申请人提出执行异议,并提出证据证明裁决事项不能执行,受理申请的人民法院应予审查。本案中中国国际经济贸易仲裁委员会裁决书第二项裁决被申请人厦门东风橡胶制品厂以厂房作实物投资必须办理过户手续。对此,被申请人认为其所投资的厂房虽已投入合营体使用,但未向房管部门进行产权登记。经受理申请的人民法院审查核实,该厂房是被申请人在"文革"期间在他人菜地上违章建成的,始终未办理产权登记,被申请人不拥有合法产权。仲裁委员会没有查明这一事实即裁决被申请人办理厂房过户手续,显系错误。对于这一错误,作为涉外仲裁申请执行案,受理申请的人民法院本应适用《民事诉讼法》有关涉外仲裁的第 260 条规定予以处理。但该条规定的四种不予执行的情形,不包括本案裁决的情形。而本案裁决符合该法第 217 条第 2 款第 4 项仲裁裁决"认定事实主要证据不足"不予执行的规定。厦门市中级人民法院即按《民事诉讼法》第 237 条的规定,即"在中华人民共和国领域内进行涉外民事诉讼,适用本编规定。本编没有规定的,适用本法其他有关规定",适用该法第 217 条第 2 款第 4 项的规定,裁定仲裁裁决部分不予执行是正确的。

阅读材料

1. 我国执行仲裁裁决中的难点—Difficulties in Enforcement of Arbitral Awards in China[①]

(1) Background

When enforcing awards in China, parties encounter excessive local protectionism, undue governmental interference and denial of or delay in enforcement by local courts if the execution hampers significant local interests. Even though the Supreme Court's attitude toward enforcement of foreign arbitral awards and the enforcement of foreign-related domestic awards is favorable, the attitude of substantial numbers of lower courts, in reality, is not. Local protectionism was detrimental to fundamental Chinese interests and proposed a major challenge to the development of China's legal system. Some expert proposed "five prohibitions" for the removal of local protectionism. Those proposals were: local CPC cadres should be prohibited from interfering with the judicial process in an attempt to protect local interests; governmental officials should be prohibited from making threats or leading campaigns against judges carrying out enforcement of court orders; judicial organs should be prohibited from making unfair rulings in favor of local parties; officials of the public security and procurator organs should be prohibited from interfering with the adjudication of commercial cases; and any organ or individual should be prohibited from hindering enforcement of orders of courts in any other way. China has suffered from poor enforcement of civil judgments (zhixing nan). Enforcement of arbitral awards have encountered the same problems as civil judgments when sought in the courts.

Difficulties in enforcement are rooted in Chinese culture and politics. Chinese culture discourages direct conflict. Under Confucian LiZhi, laws are designed to protect the minimum interests of member of a society but are rarely means for attaining social order. These notions of law have survived social and political changes. The Chinese consider that law is one of many norms in resolving disputes in society; that using coercive measures against a member of the society should be discouraged, and that even commercial disputes should be settled by means of persuasion.

[①] See Taroh Inoue, Introduction to International Commercial Arbitration in China, 36 Hong Kong L. J. (2006), p.171.

(2) Subordination of local courts and judges to governments

A court does not enjoy financial autonomy since its budget is determined by other organs of the local government. Judges are concerned that, if a judge hampers an important local interest, the court may be financially disadvantaged.

High-ranking judges of a local court are appointed and removed by the local parliament. They are anxious that, if a decision of the court goes against an important local interest, they may be removed or may not be reappointed. Other judges are appointed by chief judges, whose appointment is subject to the final approval of the standing committee of the local parliament. They seek to safeguard their jobs, which makes a local protectionist attitude on their part inevitable.

A judge may also be influenced by other judges who are not in charge of the case. A draft judgment is reviewed by high-ranking judges of the relevant division or, in important cases, by the president and/or vice presidents of the court. A judicial committee of a court, consisting of the president, vice-presidents and divisional chief judges, whose tasks are to discuss important or complex cases and exchange judicial experiences, virtually determines such cases. High-ranking judges always suggest to lower-ranking judges in charge of important cases what has been recommended or suggested by a local government and CPC through a judicial committee. As lower-ranking judges are not granted tenure, and their appointment and removal depend on their higher-ranking colleagues; they rarely resist a judicial committee's determination or recommendation.

(3) Underdeveloped professionalism in the courts

The courts are undergoing reform but have hardly caught up with China's rapid economic development. Professionalism, ethics and the educational level of an average judge are still low.

China has placed less stress on procedural law than on substantive law and, so far as procedural law is concerned, greater stress is placed on adjudication than on execution. Execution is still thought as a clerical matter. Moreover, China has stressed criminal law more than civil law.

Arbitral awards are no easier to enforce than judgments. Many judges and court staff are unfamiliar with the New York Convention or the international consensus in favor of arbitration. Judges may broadly justify a refusal to enforce a foreign arbitral award by interpreting the public policy exception under the Convention expansively and may overly rely on the ground of social and public interests under the CPL to refuse enforcement of foreign-related arbitral awards.

Education for judges and legal professionals about international commercial arbitration should be promoted so that they will be familiar with the procedure and international consensus in favor of arbitration. Education can eliminate unfamiliarity with international commercial arbitration and pro-litigation attitudes.

(4) Proposals for empowering courts

China is still seeking an optimal legal framework for civil enforcement and establishing legal institutions that will operate within it. Local protectionism and governmental interference may be mitigated by the introduction of an independent and integrated judicial system, under which a court should not be an organ of local government but a constituency of such system.

A local court should be financially independent from the local government. Under a new court system, the budgets of each court should be determined by the Supreme Court (or by the higher court) and administered by its fiscal department. A local government should not decide and control the budgets of the courts in its locality; if this were the case, a local government could no longer use its budgetary power to influence decisions of the courts.

Every judge should be appointed by the Supreme Court and, once appointed, should be granted tenure. Local governments should not have power to appoint and dismiss local judges. Judges should be rotated periodically, so that a government's influence on them could be mitigated to a large extent. Since Chinese laws and regulations are complicated and many new legal notions are frequently introduced from foreign countries, such judges cannot handle cases involving complex issues and new notions. In the meantime, educational opportunities in international trade law for judges and legal professionals should be continuously provided.

2. 简析《关于内地与香港特别行政区相互执行仲裁裁决的安排》[①]—— Comments and Further Practical Concerns

The conclusion of the Arrangement should certainly be welcome as the first step towards establishing a broader cross-border judicial cooperative regime on substantive matters. The Arrangement also ends the legal vacuum in relation to mutual enforcement of judgments following the reunification in 1997. The signing of the Arrangement can be seen as a milestone in implementing the Hong Kong Basic Law

---

[①] See Xianchu Zhang, Philip Smart, Development of Regional Conflict of Laws: On the Arrangement of Mutual Recognition and Enforcement of Judgments in Civil and Commercial Matters between Mainland China and Hong Kong SAR, 36 Hong Kong L. J. (2006), p.553.

and advancing judicial assistance under "one country, two systems". The adoption and implementation of the Arrangement, to an extent, will also facilitate commercial transactions by allowing parties who meet the requirements under the Arrangement greater ease when it comes to enforcing a relevant judgment. The Arrangement in this regard may not only help to increase the confidence protecting of business people's legal interests, and the predictability of their dispute resolution, but it has even been suggested it may also help Hong Kong to develop itself into an international centre of dispute resolution. More generally it has been observed that "the process by which sensitive issues have been solved has set a good example for how obstacles that stand in the way of broader legal cooperation should be addressed. The negotiations have also enhanced the two sides' understanding of the operation of each other's system."

Moreover, the signing of the Arrangement has further confirmed the way forward for future development. Since the reunification, the approach taken with reference to cross-border judicial cooperation has been "following in order from easy to difficult matters and advanced step by step." In this context, the conclusion of the agreements between the Mainland and Hong Kong on service of judicial documents and on mutual enforcement of arbitral awards apparently laid a solid foundation of mutual understanding and trust for both sides' further cooperation.

Nevertheless, progress must be assessed with necessary caution and not be overstated. In a sense, the Arrangement looks more like a semi-finished product, rather than a success in ripe conditions. Apparently, in order to avoid further delay, both sides were willing to accept the current version despite substantial limitations on the scope of the agreement. As a result, the practical usefulness of the Arrangement may be affected, particularly from the Mainland's perspective.

In this context some recent developments on both sides should be noted. In the Mainland, the Supreme People's Court has realized some potential problems with the procedure and has been taking measures to reform it. Recently, the reform of the supervision procedure concerning civil cases has been set out as an important item in the Supreme People's Second Five Year Reform Outline (2004 to 2009).

Meanwhile, in Hong Kong both judges and scholars have developed some new thinking on this matter. In comparison the supervision procedure of the Mainland with the relevant rules in Hong Kong, one found there was no substantial difference in terms of the court's intervention if the court is satisfied that the conclusion reached is plainly wrong.

As stated above, the conclusion of the Arrangement is just the beginning of the cross-border assistance on substantive matters between the Hong Kong SAR and Mainland. The way forward may involve a number of challenges.

Regardless of legal terms and technical grounds, the real concern behind all the worries expressed seems to be the concern with the quality and competence of the judiciary of the Mainland. From the Hong Kong side, it might be argued that a more sensible understanding and political willingness is needed, otherwise the considerable differences between the regions will become an insurmountable barrier to cross-border judicial cooperation. In Xingjiang Xingmei Oil-Pipeline Co. Ltd. v. China Petroleum & Chemical Corp., Stone J. rejected challenges to the quality and experience of the judiciary in China and noted that it was candidly recognized by the Supreme People's Court in its recent Annual Working Report to the National People's Congress that "it is an ongoing process to rectify various perceived inadequacies within the PRC legal system, it being stated that 'further measures' will be intensively and progressively instituted in order to solve the problems ... in terms of the overall quality of justice administrated in the Chinese courts." As such, "at the end of the day all that a (Hong Kong) court fairly can do is to act on the quality of the evidence placed before it in any particular case." In building up an unprecedented regime of inter-regional cooperation within a country, this approach is apparently much more constructive than merely criticizing the judiciary in the Mainland in a general and sweeping way.

In this context, effective measures are needed to safeguard the smooth function of the Arrangement. However, the current provisions of the Arrangement seem somewhat insufficient. Among the refusal grounds only public policy is available to challenge local protectionism or other wrongdoings. However, in the past, public policy has been considered by the Hong Kong court as a very rarely exercised ground for refusing to recognize foreign judgments or arbitral awards and the application of the doctrine is restricted to instances where enforcement would violate Hong Kong's most basic notion of morality and justice. Moreover, in order to deploy the public policy defense, the party against whom the enforcement is sought must bear the burden of proof of the wrongdoing in the Mainland. Without any institutional help, such a task may well amount to an almost impossible mission.

In terms of application, the lack of a set of conflict of laws rules on jurisdiction issues significantly limits the usefulness of the Arrangement. Although it has been suggested that the Arrangement may encourage more people to take advantage of the cross-border scheme by litigating their disputes in Hong Kong through choice of jurisdiction, and thus bring in more business for Hong Kong lawyers, those who have reservations about the Mainland judicial system may choose not to enter into the agreement on jurisdiction selection so as to prevent the Arrangement from being applied. Moreover, given the considerable differences between the two legal systems, it may be difficult for parties to reach such an agreement. Unlike an arbitration agreement, where the parties have autonomy to select the arbitrators, the agreement on jurisdiction selection would mean, in addition to the considerable difference in costs and complexity, the complete judicial control over the dispute and the proceedings and the winning party's entitlement to enforce the judgment concerned on the other side. In this circumstance, a prudent party may have to think twice before voluntarily entering into such an agreement.

Furthermore, although the establishment of the cross-border cooperative regime is encouraging, its implementation may not necessarily guarantee the successful enforcement of any judgment. In Hong Kong execution of judicial judgments has not been considered a concern, but enforcement of judgments in mainland China has been a huge problem, even described as "the most difficult thing in the world", for almost two decades.

The Arrangement is a breakthrough in the establishment of a regime of cross-border judicial assistance between the Hong Kong SAR and mainland China under the "one country, two systems" principle. The implementation of the Arrangement will not only end the long period of having no mutual enforcement scheme, and help to promote the development of cross-border economic and trade relations, but may also pave the way for further development towards a more comprehensive system. However, given the Arrangement being a developing product with tough compromises, at the outset its use may be very limited and the operation of its rules needs to be tested in practice. The current legal conditions of the two sides will inevitably raise many more difficult issues in the operation of the Arrangement. Nevertheless, the first step in this very important legal area deserves a cautious welcome, rather than mere nitpicking.

3. 依《纽约公约》执行国际商事调解协议[①]

International lawmakers are showing a growing interest in mediation. Mediation, or conciliation, offers an attractive option of self-determination to parties involved in international business disputes by allowing them to craft and accept their own

---

① See Brette L. Steele, Enforcing International Commercial Mediation Agreements as Arbitral Awards under the New York Convention, 54 UCLA Law Review 1385 (2007), pp. 1386—1412.

agreement. In a perfect world, no enforcement mechanism is required for mediation because a voluntary agreement yields voluntary compliance. In the world of international business, imperfect circumstances affect the performance of mediation agreements. For instance, human rights abuses could make investors balk, the commodity in question could be subject to embargo, or the currency designated for payment could suffer devaluation. Moreover, recent attempts to standardize the international enforcement of mediated agreements have failed, leaving enforcement dependent on varied national policies. As a result, mediating a settlement in good faith does not immunize it from potential future challenges to compliance.

Aware of the potential challenges, parties considering mediation for international disputes must also consider their enforcement options. One option involves grafting mediation agreements onto arbitration—mediation's private-law counterpart. The New York Convention, a widely adopted international arbitration treaty, may provide an enforcement mechanism, but its application to the amicable process of mediation creates an imperfect fit. This Comment considers the potential for and the challenges of enforcing mediation agreements as arbitral awards under the New York Convention.

If courts interpret the New York Convention to cover consent awards, a larger question is how the standards designed for arbitration apply to mediation. Arbitration is a binding process that begins with a valid arbitration agreement. If a contract contains a valid arbitration agreement, either party can invoke that agreement to demand arbitration when a dispute arises. Once an arbitration clause is invoked, the parties begin convening an arbitration tribunal. Proper convening of a tribunal is important because the parties are bound to the decision of the tribunal. Once a tribunal is convened, it may not conduct private communications with the parties, because due process forbids the presentation of evidence without an opportunity to respond. The tribunal is also tightly held to its mandate of which components of disputes are submitted to it. The grounds for nonenforcement under the New York Convention are interpreted with these concerns in mind.

Mediation is a fundamentally different process than arbitration. Mediation is a noncompulsory process, so a mediation clause does not have the same effect as an arbitration clause. The decision of whether to settle and on what terms is left to the parties. Mediation convening and due process standards are unique because the mediator does not bear binding decision authority. Since agreement is made by consent, parties are generally free to create value with their settlement—for example, by developing new business relationships that were not originally contemplated.

Applying arbitration standards to mediation is an imperfect fit, which creates multiple potential challenges under the New York Convention. Although many of the potential challenges may be avoided by modification of the mediation process, these modifications risk jeopardizing party autonomy and diluting the effectiveness of the process.

Enforcement of mediation agreements under the New York Convention results in an imperfect fit that creates challenges. Since the Convention does not recognize agreements with persisting contract remedies, using the Convention limits remedies to those designed for arbitration. Restrictions on contracting, convening, and caucusing stand to strip mediation of some of its benefits. If arbitration clauses are not drafted carefully, parties may lose the option to avoid arbitration if mediation is unsuccessful, the efficiency of mediation convening, the effectiveness of private caucuses, and the freedom to create value in mediation by developing new business relationships.

Some of these procedural challenges could be surmounted by carefully selecting favorable arbitration rules and national laws. Other challenges could be rendered moot by reason of explicit waiver when consent awards are signed. Unfortunately, until these theories are tested, parties desiring to enforce mediations using the New York Convention must be cautious. Parties must design a procedure that comports with the fiction that mediation is secondary to, and located within, arbitration so that the resulting agreement is enforceable as an award and not subject to arbitration-based procedural challenges.

In addition to procedural adjustments to conform with arbitration requirements, public policy concerns may make the application of the New York Convention ill-advised. Enforcing mediation agreements as arbitral awards may foreclose relevant public policy arguments caused by intervening circumstances. The decision to make the Convention applicable must be made long before these public policy concerns arise. Therefore, the decision to record an award so that it will be enforceable under the Convention should be made by carefully weighing the loss in procedural efficiencies and public policy review against the relative certainty of international enforcement under the New York Convention.

思考题

1. 涉外仲裁裁决的认定标准是什么？
2. 涉外仲裁裁决与国内仲裁裁决在执行方面有哪些不同？

3. 为什么仲裁庭没有仲裁裁决的强制执行力？

4. 拒绝执行外国仲裁裁决的理由有哪些？

5. 应该如何评价《关于内地与澳门特别行政区相互认可和执行仲裁裁决的安排》的意义？

推荐阅读

1. 杨弘磊：《中国内地司法实践视角下的〈纽约公约〉问题研究》，法律出版社 2006 年出版，第五、六章，第 202—371 页。

2. 于喜富：《国际商事仲裁的司法监督与协助——兼论中国的立法与司法实践》，知识产权出版社 2006 年出版，第七章，第 419—460 页。

3. 宋航：《国际商事仲裁裁决的承认与执行》，法律出版社 2000 年出版，第二章，第 24—50 页。

4. Jingzhou Tao, Arbitration Law and Practice in China, Kluwer Law International, 2004, Charter Ⅳ, pp.13—179.

附录　仲裁法律与规则

一、国际法制部分

1. 1958 年《关于承认与执行外国仲裁裁决的公约》(《纽约公约》)

Convention on the Recognition and Enforcement of Foreign Arbitral Awards

Article I

1. This Convention shall apply to the recognition and enforcement of arbitral awards made in the territory of a State other than the State where the recognition and enforcement of such awards are sought, and arising out of differences between persons, whether physical or legal. It shall also apply to arbitral awards not considered as domestic awards in the State where their recognition and enforcement are sought.

2. The term "arbitral awards" shall include not only awards made by arbitrators appointed for each case but also those made by permanent arbitral bodies to which the parties have submitted.

3. When signing, ratifying or acceding to this Convention, or notifying extension under article X hereof, any State may on the basis of reciprocity declare that it will apply the Convention to the recognition and enforcement of awards made only in the territory of another Contracting State. It may also declare that it will apply the Convention only to differences arising out of legal relationships, whether contractual or not, which are considered as commercial under the national law of the State making such declaration.

Article II

1. Each Contracting State shall recognize an agreement in writing under which the parties undertake to submit to arbitration all or any differences which have arisen

or which may arise between them in respect of a defined legal relationship, whether contractual or not, concerning a subject matter capable of settlement by arbitration.

2. The term "agreement in writing" shall include an arbitral clause in a contract or an arbitration agreement, signed by the parties or contained in an exchange of letters or telegrams.

3. The court of a Contracting State, when seized of an action in a matter in respect of which the parties have made an agreement within the meaning of this article, shall, at the request of one of the parties, refer the parties to arbitration, unless it finds that the said agreement is null and void, inoperative or incapable of being performed.

Article III

Each Contracting State shall recognize arbitral awards as binding and enforce them in accordance with the rules of procedure of the territory where the award is relied upon, under the conditions laid down in the following articles. There shall not be imposed substantially more onerous conditions or higher fees or charges on the recognition or enforcement of arbitral awards to which this Convention applies than are imposed on the recognition or enforcement of domestic arbitral awards.

Article IV

1. To obtain the recognition and enforcement mentioned in the preceding article, the party applying for recognition and enforcement shall, at the time of the application, supply:

(a) The duly authenticated original award or a duly certified copy thereof;

(b) The original agreement referred to in article II or a duly certified copy thereof.

2. If the said award or agreement is not made in an official language of the country in which the award is relied upon, the party applying for recognition and enforcement of the award shall produce a translation of these documents into such language. The translation shall be certified by an official or sworn translator or by a diplomatic or consular agent.

Article V

1. Recognition and enforcement of the award may be refused, at the request of the party against whom it is invoked, only if that party furnishes to the competent authority where the recognition and enforcement is sought, proof that:

(a) The parties to the agreement referred to in article II were, under the law applicable to them, under some incapacity, or the said agreement is not valid under the law to which the parties have subjected it or, failing any indication thereon, under the law of the country where the award was made; or

(b) The party against whom the award is invoked was not given proper notice of the appointment of the arbitrator or of the arbitration proceedings or was otherwise unable to present his case; or

(c) The award deals with a difference not contemplated by or not falling within the terms of the submission to arbitration, or it contains decisions on matters beyond the scope of the submission to arbitration, provided that, if the decisions on matters submitted to arbitration can be separated from those not so submitted, that part of the award which contains decisions on matters submitted to arbitration may be recognized and enforced; or

(d) The composition of the arbitral authority or the arbitral procedure was not in accordance with the agreement of the parties, or, failing such agreement, was not in accordance with the law of the country where the arbitration took place; or

(e) The award has not yet become binding on the parties, or has been set aside or suspended by a competent authority of the country in which, or under the law of which, that award was made.

2. Recognition and enforcement of an arbitral award may also be refused if the competent authority in the country where recognition and enforcement is sought finds that:

(a) The subject matter of the difference is not capable of settlement by arbitration under the law of that country; or

(b) The recognition or enforcement of the award would be contrary to the public policy of that country.

Article VI

If an application for the setting aside or suspension of the award has been made to a competent authority referred to in article V (1)(e), the authority before which the award is sought to be relied upon may, if it considers it proper, adjourn the decision on the enforcement of the award and may also, on the application of the party claiming enforcement of the award, order the other party to give suitable security.

Article VII

1. The provisions of the present Convention shall not affect the validity of multilateral or bilateral agreements concerning the recognition and enforcement of arbitral awards entered into by the Contracting States nor deprive any interested party

of any right he may have to avail himself of an arbitral award in the manner and to the extent allowed by the law or the treaties of the country where such award is sought to be relied upon.

2. The Geneva Protocol on Arbitration Clauses of 1923 and the Geneva Convention on the Execution of Foreign Arbitral Awards of 1927 shall cease to have effect between Contracting States on their becoming bound and to the extent that they become bound, by this Convention.

Article VIII

1. This Convention shall be open until 31 December 1958 for signature on behalf of any Member of the United Nations and also on behalf of any other State which is or hereafter becomes a member of any specialized agency of the United Nations, or which is or hereafter becomes a party to the Statute of the International Court of Justice, or any other State to which an invitation has been addressed by the General Assembly of the United Nations.

2. This Convention shall be ratified and the instrument of ratification shall be deposited with the Secretary-General of the United Nations.

Article IX

1. This Convention shall be open for accession to all States referred to in article VIII.

2. Accession shall be effected by the deposit of an instrument of accession with the Secretary-General of the United Nations.

Article X

1. Any State may, at the time of signature, ratification or accession, declare that this Convention shall extend to all or any of the territories for the international relations of which it is responsible. Such a declaration shall take effect when the Convention enters into force for the State concerned.

2. At any time thereafter any such extension shall be made by notification addressed to the Secretary-General of the United Nations and shall take effect as from the ninetieth day after the day of receipt by the Secretary-General of the United Nations of this notification, or as from the date of entry into force of the Convention for the State concerned, whichever is the later.

3. With respect to those territories to which this Convention is not extended at the time of signature, ratification or accession, each State concerned shall consider the possibility of taking the necessary steps in order to extend the application of this Convention to such territories, subject, where necessary for constitutional reasons, to

the consent of the Governments of such territories.

Article XI

In the case of a federal or non-unitary State, the following provisions shall apply:

(a) With respect to those articles of this Convention that come within the legislative jurisdiction of the federal authority, the obligations of the federal Government shall to this extent be the same as those of Contracting States which are not federal States;

(b) With respect to those articles of this Convention that come within the legislative jurisdiction of constituent states or provinces which are not, under the constitutional system of the federation, bound to take legislative action, the federal Government shall bring such articles with a favourable recommendation to the notice of the appropriate authorities of constituent states or provinces at the earliest possible moment;

(c) A federal State Party to this Convention shall, at the request of any other Contracting State transmitted through the Secretary-General of the United Nations, supply a statement of the law and practice of the federation and its constituent units in regard to any particular provision of this Convention, showing the extent to which effect has been given to that provision by legislative or other action.

Article XII

1. This Convention shall come into force on the ninetieth day following the date of deposit of the third instrument of ratification or accession.

2. For each State ratifying or acceding to this Convention after the deposit of the third instrument of ratification or accession, this Convention shall enter into force on the ninetieth day after deposit by such State of its instrument of ratification or accession.

Article XIII

1. Any Contracting State may denounce this Convention by a written notification to the Secretary-General of the United Nations. Denunciation shall take effect one year after the date of receipt of the notification by the Secretary-General.

2. Any State which has made a declaration or notification under article X may, at any time thereafter, by notification to the Secretary-General of the United Nations, declare that this Convention shall cease to extend to the territory concerned one year after the date of the receipt of the notification by the Secretary-General.

3. This Convention shall continue to be applicable to arbitral awards in respect

of which recognition or enforcement proceedings have been instituted before the denunciation takes effect.

Article XIV

A Contracting State shall not be entitled to avail itself of the present Convention against other Contracting States except to the extent that it is itself bound to apply the Convention.

Article XV

The Secretary-General of the United Nations shall notify the States contemplated in article VIII of the following:

(a) Signatures and ratifications in accordance with article VIII;

(b) Accessions in accordance with article IX;

(c) Declarations and notifications under articles I, X and XI;

(d) The date upon which this Convention enters into force in accordance with article XII;

(e) Denunciations and notifications in accordance with article XIII.

Article XVI

1. This Convention, of which the Chinese, English, French, Russian and Spanish texts shall be equally authentic, shall be deposited in the archives of the United Nations.

2. The Secretary-General of the United Nations shall transmit a certified copy of this Convention to the States contemplated in article VIII.

2. 1965年《关于解决国家与他国国民之间投资争端的公约》(《华盛顿公约》)

Convention on the Settlement of Investment Disputes between States and Nationals of Other States

PREAMBLE

The Contracting States

Considering the need for international cooperation for economic development, and the role of private international investment therein;

Bearing in mind the possibility that from time to time disputes may arise in connection with such investment between Contracting States and nationals of other Contracting States;

Recognizing that while such disputes would usually be subject to national legal processes, international methods of settlement may be appropriate in certain cases;

Attaching particular importance to the availability of facilities for international conciliation or arbitration to which Contracting States and nationals of other Contracting States may submit such disputes if they so desire;

Desiring to establish such facilities under the auspices of the International Bank for Reconstruction and Development;

Recognizing that mutual consent by the parties to submit such disputes to conciliation or to arbitration through such facilities constitutes a binding agreement which requires in particular that due consideration be given to any recommendation of conciliators, and that any arbitral award be complied with; and

Declaring that no Contracting State shall by the mere fact of its ratification, acceptance or approval of this Convention and without its consent be deemed to be under any obligation to submit any particular dispute to conciliation or arbitration,

Have agreed as follows:

CHAPTER I International Centre for Settlement of Investment Disputes

Section 1 Establishment and Organization

Article 1

(1) There is hereby established the International Centre for Settlement of Investment Disputes (hereinafter called the Centre).

(2) The purpose of the Centre shall be to provide facilities for conciliation and arbitration of investment disputes between Contracting States and nationals of other Contracting States in accordance with the provisions of this Convention.

Article 2

The seat of the Centre shall be at the principal office of the International Bank for Reconstruction and Development (hereinafter called the Bank). The seat may be moved to another place by decision of the Administrative Council adopted by a majority of two-thirds of its members.

Article 3

The Centre shall have an Administrative Council and a Secretariat and shall maintain a Panel of Conciliators and a Panel of Arbitrators.

Section 2 The Administrative Council

Article 4

(1) The Administrative Council shall be composed of one representative of each Contracting State. An alternate may act as representative in case of his principal's absence from a meeting or inability to act.

(2) In the absence of a contrary designation, each governor and alternate governor of the Bank appointed by a Contracting State shall be *ex officio* its representative and its alternate respectively.

Article 5

The President of the Bank shall be *ex officio* Chairman of the Administrative Council (hereinafter called the Chairman) but shall have no vote. During his absence or inability to act and during any vacancy in the office of President of the Bank, the person for the time being acting as President shall act as Chairman of the Administrative Council.

Article 6

(1) Without prejudice to the powers and functions vested in it by other provisions of this Convention, the Administrative Council shall:

(a) adopt the administrative and financial regulations of the Centre;

(b) adopt the rules of procedure for the institution of conciliation and arbitration proceedings;

(c) adopt the rules of procedure for conciliation and arbitration proceedings (hereinafter called the Conciliation Rules and the Arbitration Rules);

(d) approve arrangements with the Bank for the use of the Bank's administrative facilities and services;

(e) determine the conditions of service of the Secretary-General and of any Deputy Secretary-General;

(f) adopt the annual budget of revenues and expenditures of the Centre;

(g) approve the annual report on the operation of the Centre.

The decisions referred to in sub-paragraphs (a), (b), (c) and (f) above shall be adopted by a majority of two-thirds of the members of the Administrative Council.

(2) The Administrative Council may appoint such committees as it considers

necessary.

(3) The Administrative Council shall also exercise such other powers and perform such other functions as it shall determine to be necessary for the implementation of the provisions of this Convention.

Article 7

(1) The Administrative Council shall hold an annual meeting and such other meetings as may be determined by the Council, or convened by the Chairman, or convened by the Secretary-General at the request of not less than five members of the Council.

(2) Each member of the Administrative Council shall have one vote and, except as otherwise herein provided, all matters before the Council shall be decided by a majority of the votes cast.

(3) A quorum for any meeting of the Administrative Council shall be a majority of its members.

(4) The Administrative Council may establish, by a majority of two-thirds of its members, a procedure whereby the Chairman may seek a vote of the Council without convening a meeting of the Council. The vote shall be considered valid only if the majority of the members of the Council cast their votes within the time limit fixed by the said procedure.

Article 8

Members of the Administrative Council and the Chairman shall serve without remuneration from the Centre.

Section 3 The Secretariat

Article 9

The Secretariat shall consist of a Secretary-General, one or more Deputy Secretaries-General and staff.

Article 10

(1) The Secretary-General and any Deputy Secretary-General shall be elected by the Administrative Council by a majority of two-thirds of its members upon the nomination of the Chairman for a term of service not exceeding six years and shall be eligible for re-election. After consulting the members of the Administrative Council, the Chairman shall propose one or more candidates for each such office.

(2) The offices of Secretary-General and Deputy Secretary-General shall be incompatible with the exercise of any political function. Neither the Secretary-General

nor any Deputy Secretary-General may hold any other employment or engage in any other occupation except with the approval of the Administrative Council.

(3) During the Secretary-General's absence or inability to act, and during any vacancy of the office of Secretary-General, the Deputy Secretary-General shall act as Secretary-General. If there shall be more than one Deputy Secretary-General, the Administrative Council shall determine in advance the order in which they shall act as Secretary-General.

Article 11

The Secretary-General shall be the legal representative and the principal officer of the Centre and shall be responsible for its administration, including the appointment of staff, in accordance with the provisions of this Convention and the rules adopted by the Administrative Council. He shall perform the function of registrar and shall have the power to authenticate arbitral awards rendered pursuant to this Convention, and to certify copies thereof.

Section 4 The Panels

Article 12

The Panel of Conciliators and the Panel of Arbitrators shall each consist of qualified persons, designated as hereinafter provided, who are willing to serve thereon.

Article 13

(1) Each Contracting State may designate to each Panel four persons who may but need not be its nationals.

(2) The Chairman may designate ten persons to each Panel. The persons so designated to a Panel shall each have a different nationality.

Article 14

(1) Persons designated to serve on the Panels shall be persons of high moral character and recognized competence in the fields of law, commerce, industry or finance, who may be relied upon to exercise independent judgment. Competence in the field of law shall be of particular importance in the case of persons on the Panel of Arbitrators.

(2) The Chairman, in designating persons to serve on the Panels, shall in addition pay due regard to the importance of assuring representation on the Panels of the principal legal systems of the world and of the main forms of economic activity.

Article 15

(1) Panel members shall serve for renewable periods of six years.

(2) In case of death or resignation of a member of a Panel, the authority which designated the member shall have the right to designate another person to serve for the remainder of that member's term.

(3) Panel members shall continue in office until their successors have been designated.

Article 16

(1) A person may serve on both Panels.

(2) If a person shall have been designated to serve on the same Panel by more than one Contracting State, or by one or more Contracting States and the Chairman, he shall be deemed to have been designated by the authority which first designated him or, if one such authority is the State of which he is a national, by that State.

(3) All designations shall be notified to the Secretary-General and shall take effect from the date on which the notification is received.

Section 5   Financing the Centre

Article 17

If the expenditure of the Centre cannot be met out of charges for the use of its facilities, or out of other receipts, the excess shall be borne by Contracting States which are members of the Bank in proportion to their respective subscriptions to the capital stock of the Bank, and by Contracting States which are not members of the Bank in accordance with rules adopted by the Administrative Council.

Section 6   Status, Immunities and Privileges

Article 18

The Centre shall have full international legal personality. The legal capacity of the Centre shall include the capacity:

(a) to contract;

(b) to acquire and dispose of movable and immovable property;

(c) to institute legal proceedings.

Article 19

To enable the Centre to fulfil its functions, it shall enjoy in the territories of each Contracting State the immunities and privileges set forth in this Section.

Article 20

The Centre, its property and assets shall enjoy immunity from all legal process, except when the Centre waives this immunity.

Article 21

The Chairman, the members of the Administrative Council, persons acting as conciliators or arbitrators or members of a Committee appointed pursuant to paragraph (3) of Article 52, and the officers and employees of the Secretariat

(a) shall enjoy immunity from legal process with respect to acts performed by them in the exercise of their functions, except when the Centre waives this immunity;

(b) not being local nationals, shall enjoy the same immunities from immigration restrictions, alien registration requirements and national service obligations, the same facilities as regards exchange restrictions and the same treatment in respect of travelling facilities as are accorded by Contracting States to the representatives, officials and employees of comparable rank of other Contracting States.

Article 22

The provisions of Article 21 shall apply to persons appearing in proceedings under this Convention as parties, agents, counsel, advocates, witnesses or experts; provided, however, that sub-paragraph (b) thereof shall apply only in connection with their travel to and from, and their stay at, the place where the proceedings are held.

Article 23

(1) The archives of the Centre shall be inviolable, wherever they may be.

(2) With regard to its official communications, the Centre shall be accorded by each Contracting State treatment not less favourable than that accorded to other international organizations.

Article 24

(1) The Centre, its assets, property and income, and its operations and transactions authorized by this Convention shall be exempt from all taxation and customs duties. The Centre shall also be exempt from liability for the collection or payment of any taxes or customs duties.

(2) Except in the case of local nationals, no tax shall be levied on or in respect of expense allowances paid by the Centre to the Chairman or members of the Administrative Council, or on or in respect of salaries, expense allowances or other emoluments paid by the Centre to officials or employees of the Secretariat.

(3) No tax shall be levied on or in respect of fees or expense allowances

received by persons acting as conciliators, or arbitrators, or members of a Committee appointed pursuant to paragraph (3) of Article 52, in proceedings under this Convention, if the sole jurisdictional basis for such tax is the location of the Centre or the place where such proceedings are conducted or the place where such fees or allowances are paid.

CHAPTER II Jurisdiction of the Centre

Article 25

(1) The jurisdiction of the Centre shall extend to any legal dispute arising directly out of an investment, between a Contracting State (or any constituent subdivision or agency of a Contracting State designated to the Centre by that State) and a national of another Contracting State, which the parties to the dispute consent in writing to submit to the Centre. When the parties have given their consent, no party may withdraw its consent unilaterally.

(2) "National of another Contracting State" means:

(a) any natural person who had the nationality of a Contracting State other than the State party to the dispute on the date on which the parties consented to submit such dispute to conciliation or arbitration as well as on the date on which the request was registered pursuant to paragraph (3) of Article 28 or paragraph (3) of Article 36, but does not include any person who on either date also had the nationality of the Contracting State party to the dispute; and

(b) any juridical person which had the nationality of a Contracting State other than the State party to the dispute on the date on which the parties consented to submit such dispute to conciliation or arbitration and any juridical person which had the nationality of the Contracting State party to the dispute on that date and which, because of foreign control, the parties have agreed should be treated as a national of another Contracting State for the purposes of this Convention.

(3) Consent by a constituent subdivision or agency of a Contracting State shall require the approval of that State unless that State notifies the Centre that no such approval is required.

(4) Any Contracting State may, at the time of ratification, acceptance or approval of this Convention or at any time thereafter, notify the Centre of the class or classes of disputes which it would or would not consider submitting to the jurisdiction of the Centre. The Secretary-General shall forthwith transmit such notification to all

Contracting States. Such notification shall not constitute the consent required by paragraph (1).

Article 26

Consent of the parties to arbitration under this Convention shall, unless otherwise stated, be deemed consent to such arbitration to the exclusion of any other remedy. A Contracting State may require the exhaustion of local administrative or judicial remedies as a condition of its consent to arbitration under this Convention.

Article 27

(1) No Contracting State shall give diplomatic protection, or bring an international claim, in respect of a dispute which one of its nationals and another Contracting State shall have consented to submit or shall have submitted to arbitration under this Convention, unless such other Contracting State shall have failed to abide by and comply with the award rendered in such dispute.

(2) Diplomatic protection, for the purposes of paragraph (1), shall not include informal diplomatic exchanges for the sole purpose of facilitating a settlement of the dispute.

CHAPTER III Conciliation

Section 1 Request for Conciliation

Article 28

(1) Any Contracting State or any national of a Contracting State wishing to institute conciliation proceedings shall address a request to that effect in writing to the Secretary-General who shall send a copy of the request to the other party.

(2) The request shall contain information concerning the issues in dispute, the identity of the parties and their consent to conciliation in accordance with the rules of procedure for the institution of conciliation and arbitration proceedings.

(3) The Secretary-General shall register the request unless he finds, on the basis of the information contained in the request, that the dispute is manifestly outside the jurisdiction of the Centre. He shall forthwith notify the parties of registration or refusal to register.

Section 2   Constitution of the Conciliation Commission

Article 29

(1) The Conciliation Commission (hereinafter called the Commission) shall be constituted as soon as possible after registration of a request pursuant to Article 28.

(2) (a) The Commission shall consist of a sole conciliator or any uneven number of conciliators appointed as the parties shall agree.

(b) Where the parties do not agree upon the number of conciliators and the method of their appointment, the Commission shall consist of three conciliators, one conciliator appointed by each party and the third, who shall be the president of the Commission, appointed by agreement of the parties.

Article 30

If the Commission shall not have been constituted within 90 days after notice of registration of the request has been dispatched by the Secretary-General in accordance with paragraph (3) of Article 28, or such other period as the parties may agree, the Chairman shall, at the request of either party and after consulting both parties as far as possible, appoint the conciliator or conciliators not yet appointed.

Article 31

(1) Conciliators may be appointed from outside the Panel of Conciliators, except in the case of appointments by the Chairman pursuant to Article 30.

(2) Conciliators appointed from outside the Panel of Conciliators shall possess the qualities stated in paragraph (1) of Article 14.

Section 3   Conciliation Proceedings

Article 32

(1) The Commission shall be the judge of its own competence.

(2) Any objection by a party to the dispute that that dispute is not within the jurisdiction of the Centre, or for other reasons is not within the competence of the Commission, shall be considered by the Commission which shall determine whether to deal with it as a preliminary question or to join it to the merits of the dispute.

Article 33

Any conciliation proceeding shall be conducted in accordance with the provisions of this Section and, except as the parties otherwise agree, in accordance with the Conciliation Rules in effect on the date on which the parties consented to conciliation. If any question of procedure arises which is not covered by this Section or the

Conciliation Rules or any rules agreed by the parties, the Commission shall decide the question.

Article 34

(1) It shall be the duty of the Commission to clarify the issues in dispute between the parties and to endeavour to bring about agreement between them upon mutually acceptable terms. To that end, the Commission may at any stage of the proceedings and from time to time recommend terms of settlement to the parties. The parties shall cooperate in good faith with the Commission in order to enable the Commission to carry out its functions, and shall give their most serious consideration to its recommendations.

(2) If the parties reach agreement, the Commission shall draw up a report noting the issues in dispute and recording that the parties have reached agreement. If, at any stage of the proceedings, it appears to the Commission that there is no likelihood of agreement between the parties, it shall close the proceedings and shall draw up a report noting the submission of the dispute and recording the failure of the parties to reach agreement. If one party fails to appear or participate in the proceedings, the Commission shall close the proceedings and shall draw up a report noting that party's failure to appear or participate.

Article 35

Except as the parties to the dispute shall otherwise agree, neither party to a conciliation proceeding shall be entitled in any other proceeding, whether before arbitrators or in a court of law or otherwise, to invoke or rely on any views expressed or statements or admissions or offers of settlement made by the other party in the conciliation proceedings, or the report or any recommendations made by the Commission.

CHAPTER IV   Arbitration

Section 1   Request for Arbitration

Article 36

(1) Any Contracting State or any national of a Contracting State wishing to institute arbitration proceedings shall address a request to that effect in writing to the Secretary-General who shall send a copy of the request to the other party.

(2) The request shall contain information concerning the issues in dispute, the

identity of the parties and their consent to arbitration in accordance with the rules of procedure for the institution of conciliation and arbitration proceedings.

(3) The Secretary-General shall register the request unless he finds, on the basis of the information contained in the request, that the dispute is manifestly outside the jurisdiction of the Centre. He shall forthwith notify the parties of registration or refusal to register.

Section 2　Constitution of the Tribunal

Article 37

(1) The Arbitral Tribunal (hereinafter called the Tribunal) shall be constituted as soon as possible after registration of a request pursuant to Article 36.

(2) (a) The Tribunal shall consist of a sole arbitrator or any uneven number of arbitrators appointed as the parties shall agree.

(b) Where the parties do not agree upon the number of arbitrators and the method of their appointment, the Tribunal shall consist of three arbitrators, one arbitrator appointed by each party and the third, who shall be the president of the Tribunal, appointed by agreement of the parties.

Article 38

If the Tribunal shall not have been constituted within 90 days after notice of registration of the request has been dispatched by the Secretary-General in accordance with paragraph (3) of Article 36, or such other period as the parties may agree, the Chairman shall, at the request of either party and after consulting both parties as far as possible, appoint the arbitrator or arbitrators not yet appointed. Arbitrators appointed by the Chairman pursuant to this Article shall not be nationals of the Contracting State party to the dispute or of the Contracting State whose national is a party to the dispute.

Article 39

The majority of the arbitrators shall be nationals of States other than the Contracting State party to the dispute and the Contracting State whose national is a party to the dispute; provided, however, that the foregoing provisions of this Article shall not apply if the sole arbitrator or each individual member of the Tribunal has been appointed by agreement of the parties.

Article 40

(1) Arbitrators may be appointed from outside the Panel of Arbitrators, except in the case of appointments by the Chairman pursuant to Article 38.

(2) Arbitrators appointed from outside the Panel of Arbitrators shall possess the qualities stated in paragraph (1) of Article 14.

Section 3 Powers and Functions of the Tribunal

Article 41

(1) The Tribunal shall be the judge of its own competence.

(2) Any objection by a party to the dispute that that dispute is not within the jurisdiction of the Centre, or for other reasons is not within the competence of the Tribunal, shall be considered by the Tribunal which shall determine whether to deal with it as a preliminary question or to join it to the merits of the dispute.

Article 42

(1) The Tribunal shall decide a dispute in accordance with such rules of law as may be agreed by the parties. In the absence of such agreement, the Tribunal shall apply the law of the Contracting State party to the dispute (including its rules on the conflict of laws) and such rules of international law as may be applicable.

(2) The Tribunal may not bring in a finding of *non liquet* on the ground of silence or obscurity of the law.

(3) The provisions of paragraphs (1) and (2) shall not prejudice the power of the Tribunal to decide a dispute *ex aequo et bono* if the parties so agree.

Article 43

Except as the parties otherwise agree, the Tribunal may, if it deems it necessary at any stage of the proceedings,

(a) call upon the parties to produce documents or other evidence, and

(b) visit the scene connected with the dispute, and conduct such inquiries there as it may deem appropriate.

Article 44

Any arbitration proceeding shall be conducted in accordance with the provisions of this Section and, except as the parties otherwise agree, in accordance with the Arbitration Rules in effect on the date on which the parties consented to arbitration. If any question of procedure arises which is not covered by this Section or the Arbitration Rules or any rules agreed by the parties, the Tribunal shall decide the question.

Article 45

(1) Failure of a party to appear or to present his case shall not be deemed an admission of the other party's assertions.

(2) If a party fails to appear or to present his case at any stage of the proceedings the other party may request the Tribunal to deal with the questions submitted to it and to render an award. Before rendering an award, the Tribunal shall notify, and grant a period of grace to, the party failing to appear or to present its case, unless it is satisfied that that party does not intend to do so.

Article 46

Except as the parties otherwise agree, the Tribunal shall, if requested by a party, determine any incidental or additional claims or counter-claims arising directly out of the subject-matter of the dispute provided that they are within the scope of the consent of the parties and are otherwise within the jurisdiction of the Centre.

Article 47

Except as the parties otherwise agree, the Tribunal may, if it considers that the circumstances so require, recommend any provisional measures which should be taken to preserve the respective rights of either party.

Section 4 The Award

Article 48

(1) The Tribunal shall decide questions by a majority of the votes of all its members.

(2) The award of the Tribunal shall be in writing and shall be signed by the members of the Tribunal who voted for it.

(3) The award shall deal with every question submitted to the Tribunal, and shall state the reasons upon which it is based.

(4) Any member of the Tribunal may attach his individual opinion to the award, whether he dissents from the majority or not, or a statement of his dissent.

(5) The Centre shall not publish the award without the consent of the parties.

Article 49

(1) The Secretary-General shall promptly dispatch certified copies of the award to the parties. The award shall be deemed to have been rendered on the date on which the certified copies were dispatched.

(2) The Tribunal upon the request of a party made within 45 days after the date on which the award was rendered may after notice to the other party decide any question which it had omitted to decide in the award, and shall rectify any clerical, arithmetical or similar error in the award. Its decision shall become part of the award and shall be notified to the parties in the same manner as the award. The periods of

time provided for under paragraph (2) of Article 51 and paragraph (2) of Article 52 shall run from the date on which the decision was rendered.

Section 5　Interpretation, Revision and Annulment of the Award

Article 50

(1) If any dispute shall arise between the parties as to the meaning or scope of an award, either party may request interpretation of the award by an application in writing addressed to the Secretary-General.

(2) The request shall, if possible, be submitted to the Tribunal which rendered the award. If this shall not be possible, a new Tribunal shall be constituted in accordance with Section 2 of this Chapter. The Tribunal may, if it considers that the circumstances so require, stay enforcement of the award pending its decision.

Article 51

(1) Either party may request revision of the award by an application in writing addressed to the Secretary-General on the ground of discovery of some fact of such a nature as decisively to affect the award, provided that when the award was rendered that fact was unknown to the Tribunal and to the applicant and that the applicant's ignorance of that fact was not due to negligence.

(2) The application shall be made within 90 days after the discovery of such fact and in any event within three years after the date on which the award was rendered.

(3) The request shall, if possible, be submitted to the Tribunal which rendered the award. If this shall not be possible, a new Tribunal shall be constituted in accordance with Section 2 of this Chapter.

(4) The Tribunal may, if it considers that the circumstances so require, stay enforcement of the award pending its decision. If the applicant requests a stay of enforcement of the award in his application, enforcement shall be stayed provisionally until the Tribunal rules on such request.

Article 52

(1) Either party may request annulment of the award by an application in writing addressed to the Secretary-General on one or more of the following grounds:

(a) that the Tribunal was not properly constituted;

(b) that the Tribunal has manifestly exceeded its powers;

(c) that there was corruption on the part of a member of the Tribunal;

(d) that there has been a serious departure from a fundamental rule of procedure; or

(e) that the award has failed to state the reasons on which it is based.

(2) The application shall be made within 120 days after the date on which the award was rendered except that when annulment is requested on the ground of corruption such application shall be made within 120 days after discovery of the corruption and in any event within three years after the date on which the award was rendered.

(3) On receipt of the request the Chairman shall forthwith appoint from the Panel of Arbitrators an *ad hoc* Committee of three persons. None of the members of the Committee shall have been a member of the Tribunal which rendered the award, shall be of the same nationality as any such member, shall be a national of the State party to the dispute or of the State whose national is a party to the dispute, shall have been designated to the Panel of Arbitrators by either of those States, or shall have acted as a conciliator in the same dispute. The Committee shall have the authority to annul the award or any part thereof on any of the grounds set forth in paragraph (1).

(4) The provisions of Articles 41—45, 48, 49, 53 and 54, and of Chapters VI and VII shall apply *mutatis mutandis* to proceedings before the Committee.

(5) The Committee may, if it considers that the circumstances so require, stay enforcement of the award pending its decision. If the applicant requests a stay of enforcement of the award in his application, enforcement shall be stayed provisionally until the Committee rules on such request.

(6) If the award is annulled the dispute shall, at the request of either party, be submitted to a new Tribunal constituted in accordance with Section 2 of this Chapter.

Section 6 Recognition and Enforcement of the Award

Article 53

(1) The award shall be binding on the parties and shall not be subject to any appeal or to any other remedy except those provided for in this Convention. Each party shall abide by and comply with the terms of the award except to the extent that enforcement shall have been stayed pursuant to the relevant provisions of this Convention.

(2) For the purposes of this Section, "award" shall include any decision interpreting, revising or annulling such award pursuant to Articles 50, 51 or 52.

Article 54

(1) Each Contracting State shall recognize an award rendered pursuant to this Convention as binding and enforce the pecuniary obligations imposed by that award

within its territories as if it were a final judgment of a court in that State. A Contracting State with a federal constitution may enforce such an award in or through its federal courts and may provide that such courts shall treat the award as if it were a final judgment of the courts of a constituent state.

(2) A party seeking recognition or enforcement in the territories of a Contracting State shall furnish to a competent court or other authority which such State shall have designated for this purpose a copy of the award certified by the Secretary-General. Each Contracting State shall notify the Secretary-General of the designation of the competent court or other authority for this purpose and of any subsequent change in such designation.

(3) Execution of the award shall be governed by the laws concerning the execution of judgments in force in the State in whose territories such execution is sought.

Article 55

Nothing in Article 54 shall be construed as derogating from the law in force in any Contracting State relating to immunity of that State or of any foreign State from execution.

CHAPTER V Replacement and Disqualification of Conciliators and Arbitrators

Article 56

(1) After a Commission or a Tribunal has been constituted and proceedings have begun, its composition shall remain unchanged; provided, however, that if a conciliator or an arbitrator should die, become incapacitated, or resign, the resulting vacancy shall be filled in accordance with the provisions of Section 2 of Chapter III or Section 2 of Chapter IV.

(2) A member of a Commission or Tribunal shall continue to serve in that capacity notwithstanding that he shall have ceased to be a member of the Panel.

(3) If a conciliator or arbitrator appointed by a party shall have resigned without the consent of the Commission or Tribunal of which he was a member, the Chairman shall appoint a person from the appropriate Panel to fill the resulting vacancy.

Article 57

A party may propose to a Commission or Tribunal the disqualification of any of its members on account of any fact indicating a manifest lack of the qualities required by paragraph (1) of Article 14. A party to arbitration proceedings may, in addition, propose the disqualification of an arbitrator on the ground that he was ineligible for appointment to the Tribunal under Section 2 of Chapter IV.

Article 58

The decision on any proposal to disqualify a conciliator or arbitrator shall be taken by the other members of the Commission or Tribunal as the case may be, provided that where those members are equally divided, or in the case of a proposal to disqualify a sole conciliator or arbitrator, or a majority of the conciliators or arbitrators, the Chairman shall take that decision. If it is decided that the proposal is well-founded the conciliator or arbitrator to whom the decision relates shall be replaced in accordance with the provisions of Section 2 of Chapter III or Section 2 of Chapter IV.

CHAPTER VI　Cost of Proceedings

Article 59

The charges payable by the parties for the use of the facilities of the Centre shall be determined by the Secretary-General in accordance with the regulations adopted by the Administrative Council.

Article 60

(1) Each Commission and each Tribunal shall determine the fees and expenses of its members within limits established from time to time by the Administrative Council and after consultation with the Secretary-General.

(2) Nothing in paragraph (1) of this Article shall preclude the parties from agreeing in advance with the Commission or Tribunal concerned upon the fees and expenses of its members.

Article 61

(1) In the case of conciliation proceedings the fees and expenses of members of the Commission as well as the charges for the use of the facilities of the Centre, shall be borne equally by the parties. Each party shall bear any other expenses it incurs in connection with the proceedings.

(2) In the case of arbitration proceedings the Tribunal shall, except as the parties otherwise agree, assess the expenses incurred by the parties in connection with the proceedings, and shall decide how and by whom those expenses, the fees and expenses of the members of the Tribunal and the charges for the use of the facilities of

the Centre shall be paid. Such decision shall form part of the award.

CHAPTER VII Place of Proceedings

Article 62
Conciliation and arbitration proceedings shall be held at the seat of the Centre except as hereinafter provided.

Article 63
Conciliation and arbitration proceedings may be held, if the parties so agree,

(a) at the seat of the Permanent Court of Arbitration or of any other appropriate institution, whether private or public, with which the Centre may make arrangements for that purpose; or

(b) at any other place approved by the Commission or Tribunal after consultation with the Secretary-General.

CHAPTER VIII Disputes Between Contracting States

Article 64
Any dispute arising between Contracting States concerning the interpretation or application of this Convention which is not settled by negotiation shall be referred to the International Court of Justice by the application of any party to such dispute, unless the States concerned agree to another method of settlement.

CHAPTER IX Amendment

Article 65
Any Contracting State may propose amendment of this Convention. The text of a proposed amendment shall be communicated to the Secretary-General not less than 90 days prior to the meeting of the Administrative Council at which such amendment is to be considered and shall forthwith be transmitted by him to all the members of the Administrative Council.

Article 66
(1) If the Administrative Council shall so decide by a majority of two-thirds of its members, the proposed amendment shall be circulated to all Contracting States for

ratification, acceptance or approval. Each amendment shall enter into force 30 days after dispatch by the depositary of this Convention of a notification to Contracting States that all Contracting States have ratified, accepted or approved the amendment.

(2) No amendment shall affect the rights and obligations under this Convention of any Contracting State or of any of its constituent subdivisions or agencies, or of any national of such State arising out of consent to the jurisdiction of the Centre given before the date of entry into force of the amendment.

CHAPTER X   Final Provisions

Article 67

This Convention shall be open for signature on behalf of States members of the Bank. It shall also be open for signature on behalf of any other State which is a party to the Statute of the International Court of Justice and which the Administrative Council, by a vote of two-thirds of its members, shall have invited to sign the Convention.

Article 68

(1) This Convention shall be subject to ratification, acceptance or approval by the signatory States in accordance with their respective constitutional procedures.

(2) This Convention shall enter into force 30 days after the date of deposit of the twentieth instrument of ratification, acceptance or approval. It shall enter into force for each State which subsequently deposits its instrument of ratification, acceptance or approval 30 days after the date of such deposit.

Article 69

Each Contracting State shall take such legislative or other measures as may be necessary for making the provisions of this Convention effective in its territories.

Article 70

This Convention shall apply to all territories for whose international relations a Contracting State is responsible, except those which are excluded by such State by written notice to the depositary of this Convention either at the time of ratification, acceptance or approval or subsequently.

Article 71

Any Contracting State may denounce this Convention by written notice to the depositary of this Convention. The denunciation shall take effect six months after receipt of such notice.

Article 72

Notice by a Contracting State pursuant to Articles 70 or 71 shall not affect the rights or obligations under this Convention of that State or of any of its constituent subdivisions or agencies or of any national of that State arising out of consent to the jurisdiction of the Centre given by one of them before such notice was received by the depositary.

Article 73

Instruments of ratification, acceptance or approval of this Convention and of amendments thereto shall be deposited with the Bank which shall act as the depositary of this Convention. The depositary shall transmit certified copies of this Convention to States members of the Bank and to any other State invited to sign the Convention.

Article 74

The depositary shall register this Convention with the Secretariat of the United Nations in accordance with Article 102 of the Charter of the United Nations and the Regulations there under adopted by the General Assembly.

Article 75

The depositary shall notify all signatory States of the following:

(a) signatures in accordance with Article 67;

(b) deposits of instruments of ratification, acceptance and approval in accordance with Article 73;

(c) the date on which this Convention enters into force in accordance with Article 68;

(d) exclusions from territorial application pursuant to Article 70;

(e) the date on which any amendment of this Convention enters into force in accordance with Article 66; and

(f) denunciations in accordance with Article 71.

DONE at Washington, in the English, French and Spanish languages, all three texts being equally authentic, in a single copy which shall remain deposited in the archives of the International Bank for Reconstruction and Development, which has indicated by its signature below its agreement to fulfill the functions with which it is charged under this Convention.

3. 1985年《联合国国际贸易法委员会示范法》

UNCITRAL Model Law on International Commercial Arbitration

Chapter I—General Provisions

Article 1—[Scope of application]

(1) This Law applies to international commercial arbitration, subject to any agreement in force between this State and any other State or States.

(2) The provisions of this Law, except articles 8, 9, 35 and 36, apply only if the place of arbitration is in the territory of this State.

(3) An arbitration is international if:

(a) the parties to an arbitration agreement have, at the time of the conclusion of that agreement, their places of business in different States; or

(b) one of the following places is situated outside the State in which the parties have their places of business:

(i) the place of arbitration if determined in, or pursuant to, the arbitration agreement;

(ii) any place where a substantial part of the obligations of the commercial relationship is to be performed or the place with which the subject-matter of the dispute is most closely connected; or

(c) the parties have expressly agreed that the subject-matter of the arbitration agreement relates to more than one country.

(4) For the purposes of paragraph (3) of this article:

(a) if a party has more than one place of business, the place of business is that which has the closest relationship to the arbitration agreement;

(b) if a party does not have a place of business, reference is to be made to his habitual residence.

(5) This Law shall not affect any other law of this State by virtue of which certain disputes may not be submitted to arbitration or may be submitted to arbitration only according to provisions other than those of this Law.

Article 2—[Definitions and rules of interpretation]

For the purposes of this Law:

(a) "arbitration" means any arbitration whether or not administered by a permanent arbitral institution;

(b) "arbitral tribunal" means a sole arbitrator or a panel of arbitrators;

(c) "court" means a body or organ of the judicial system of a State;

(d) where a provision of this Law, except article 28, leaves the parties free to determine a certain issue, such freedom includes the right of the parties to authorise a third party, including an institution, to make that determination;

(e) where a provision of this Law refers to the fact that the parties have agreed or that they may agree or in any other way refers to an agreement of the parties, such agreement includes any arbitration rules referred to in that agreement;

(f) where a provision of this Law, other than in articles 25(a) and 32(2)(a), refers to a claim, it also applies to a counter-claim, and where it refers to a defence, it also applies to a defence to such counter-claim.

Article 3—[Receipt of written communications]

(1) Unless otherwise agreed by the parties:

(a) any written communication is deemed to have been received if it is delivered to the addressee personally or if it is delivered at his place of business, habitual residence or mailing address; if none of these can be found after making a reasonable inquiry, a written communication is deemed to have been received if it is sent to the addressee's last-known place of business, habitual residence or mailing address by registered letter or any other means which provides a record of the attempt to deliver it;

(b) the communication is deemed to have been received on the day it is so delivered.

(2) The provisions of this article do not apply to communications in court proceedings.

Article 4—[Waiver of right to object]

A party who knows that any provision of this Law from which the parties may derogate or any requirement under the arbitration agreement has not been complied with and yet proceeds with the arbitration without stating his objection to such non compliance without undue delay or, if a time-limit is provided therefor, within such period of time, shall be deemed to have waived his right to object.

Article 5—[Extent of court intervention]

In matters governed by this Law, no court shall intervene except where so provided in this Law.

Article 6—[Court or other authority for certain functions of arbitration assistance and supervision]

The functions referred to in articles 11(3), 11(4), 13(3), 14, 16(3) and 34(2) shall be performed by... (Each State enacting this model law specifies the court, courts or, where referred to therein, other authority competent to perform these functions.)

Chapter II—Arbitration agreement

Article 7—[Definition and form of arbitration agreement]

(1) "Arbitration agreement" is an agreement by the parties to submit to arbitration all or certain disputes which have arisen or which may arise between them in respect of a defined legal relationship, whether contractual or not. An arbitration agreement may be in the form of an arbitration clause in a contract or in the form of a separate agreement.

(2) The arbitration agreement shall be in writing. An agreement is in writing if it is contained in a document signed by the parties or in an exchange of letters, telex, telegrams or other means of telecommunication which provide a record of the agreement, or in an exchange of statements of claim and defence in which the existence of an agreement is alleged by one party and not denied by another. The reference in a contract to a document containing an arbitration clause constitutes an arbitration agreement provided that the contract is in writing and the reference is such as to make that clause part of the contract.

Article 8—[Arbitration agreement and substantive claim before court]

(1) A court before which an action is brought in a matter which is the subject of an arbitration agreement shall, if a party so requests not later than when submitting his first statement on the substance of the dispute, refer the parties to arbitration unless it finds that the agreement is null and void, inoperative or incapable of being performed.

(2) Where an action referred to in paragraph (1) of this article has been brought, arbitral proceedings may nevertheless be commenced or continued, and an award may be made, while the issue is pending before the court.

Article 9—[Arbitration agreement and interim measures by court]

It is not incompatible with an arbitration agreement for a party to request, before or during arbitral proceedings, from a court an interim measure of protection and for a court to grant such measure.

Chapter III—Composition of arbitral tribunal

Article 10—[Number of arbitrators]

(1) The parties are free to determine the number of arbitrators.

(2) Failing such determination, the number of arbitrators shall be three.

Article 11—[Appointment of arbitrators]

(1) No person shall be precluded by reason of his nationality from acting as an arbitrator, unless otherwise agreed by the parties.

(2) The parties are free to agree on a procedure of appointing the arbitrator or arbitrators, subject to the provisions of paragraphs (4) and (5) of this article.

(3) Failing such agreement,

(a) in an arbitration with three arbitrators, each party shall appoint one arbitrator, and the two arbitrators thus appointed shall appoint the third arbitrator; if a party fails to appoint the arbitrator within thirty days of receipt of a request to do so from the other party, or if the two arbitrators fail to agree on the third arbitrator within thirty days of their appointment, the appointment shall be made, upon request of a party, by the court or other authority specified in article 6;

(b) in an arbitration with a sole arbitrator, if the parties are unable to agree on the arbitrator, he shall be appointed, upon request of a party, by the court or other authority specified in article 6.

(4) Where, under an appointment procedure agreed upon by the parties,

(a) a party fails to act as required under such procedure, or

(b) the parties, or two arbitrators, are unable to reach an agreement expected of them under such procedure, or

(c) a third party, including an institution, fails to perform any function entrusted to it under such procedure, any party may request the court or other authority specified in article 6 to take the necessary measure, unless the agreement on the appointment procedure provides other means for securing the appointment.

(5) A decision on a matter entrusted by paragraph (3) or (4) of this article to the court or other authority specified in article 6 shall be subject to no appeal. The

court or other authority, in appointing an arbitrator, shall have due regard to any qualifications required of the arbitrator by the agreement of the parties and to such considerations as are likely to secure the appointment of an independent and impartial arbitrator and, in the case of sole or third arbitrator, shall take into account as well the advisability of appointing an arbitrator of a nationality other than those of the parties.

Article 12—[Grounds for challenge]

(1) When a person is approached in connection with his possible appointment as an arbitrator, he shall disclose any circumstances likely to give rise to justifiable doubts as to his impartiality or independence. An arbitrator, from the time of his appointment and throughout the arbitral proceedings shall without delay disclose any such circumstances to the parties unless they have already been informed of them by him.

(2) An arbitrator may be challenged only if circumstances exist that give rise to justifiable doubts as to his impartiality or independence, or if he does not possess qualifications agreed to by the parties. A party may challenge an arbitrator appointed by him, or in whose appointment he has participated, only for reasons of which he becomes aware after the appointment has been made.

Article 13—[Challenge procedure]

(1) The parties are free to agree on a procedure for challenging an arbitrator, subject to the provisions of paragraph (3) of this article.

(2) Failing such agreement, a party who intends to challenge an arbitrator shall, within fifteen days after becoming aware of the constitution of the arbitral tribunal or after becoming aware of any circumstance referred to in article 12(2), send a written statement of the reasons for the challenge to the arbitral tribunal. Unless the challenged arbitrator withdraws from his office or the other party agrees to the challenge, the arbitral tribunal shall decide on the challenge.

(3) If a challenge under any procedure agreed upon by the parties or under the procedure of paragraph (2) of this article is not successful, the challenging party may request, within thirty days after having received notice of the decision rejecting the challenge, the court or other authority specified in article 6 to decide on the challenge, which decision shall be subject to no appeal; while such a request is pending, the arbitral tribunal, including the challenged arbitrator, may continue the arbitral proceedings and make an award.

Article 14—[Failure or impossibility to act]

(1) If an arbitrator becomes de jure or de facto unable to perform his functions or for other reasons fails to act without undue delay, his mandate terminates if he withdraws from his office or if the parties agree on the termination. Otherwise, if a controversy remains concerning any of these grounds, any party may request the court or other authority specified in article 6 to decide on the termination of the mandate, which decision shall be subject to no appeal.

(2) If, under this article or article 13(2), an arbitrator withdraws from his office or a party agrees to the termination of the mandate of an arbitrator, this does not imply acceptance of the validity of any ground referred to in this article or article 12(2).

Article 15—[Appointment of substitute arbitrator]

Where the mandate of an arbitrator terminates under article 13 or 14 or because of his withdrawal from office for any other reason or because of the revocation of his mandate by agreement of the parties or in any other case of termination of his mandate, a substitute arbitrator shall be appointed according to the rules that were applicable to the appointment of the arbitrator being replaced.

Chapter IV—Jurisdiction of arbitral tribunal

Article 16—[Competence of arbitral tribunal to rule on its jurisdiction]

(1) The arbitral tribunal may rule on its own jurisdiction, including any objections with respect to the existence or validity of the arbitration agreement. For that purpose, an arbitration clause which forms part of a contract shall be treated as an agreement independent of the other terms of the contract. A decision by the arbitral tribunal that the contract is null and void shall not entail ipso jure the invalidity of the arbitration clause.

(2) A plea that the arbitral tribunal does not have jurisdiction shall be raised not later than the submission of the statement of defence. A party is not precluded from raising such a plea by the fact that he has appointed, or participated in the appointment of, an arbitrator. A plea that the arbitral tribunal is exceeding the scope of its authority shall be raised as soon as the matter alleged to be beyond the scope of its authority is raised during the arbitral proceedings. The arbitral tribunal may, in either case, admit a later plea if it considers the delay justified.

(3) The arbitral tribunal may rule on a plea referred to in paragraph (2) of this article either as a preliminary question or in an award on the merits. If the arbitral

tribunal rules as a preliminary question that it has jurisdiction, any party may request, within thirty days after having received notice of that ruling, the court specified in article 6 to decide the matter, which decision shall be subject to no appeal; while such a request is pending, the arbitral tribunal may continue the arbitral proceedings and make an award.

Article 17—[Power of arbitral tribunal to order interim measures]

Unless otherwise agreed by the parties, the arbitral tribunal may, at the request of a party, order any party to take such interim measure of protection as the arbitral tribunal may consider necessary in respect of the subject-matter of the dispute. The arbitral tribunal may require any party to provide appropriate security in connection with such measure.

Chapter V—Conduct of arbitral proceedings

Article 18—[Equal treatment of parties]

The parties shall be treated with equality and each party shall be given a full opportunity of presenting his case.

Article 19—[Determination of rules of procedure]

(1) Subject to the provisions of this Law, the parties are free to agree on the procedure to be followed by the arbitral tribunal in conducting the proceedings.

(2) Failing such agreement, the arbitral tribunal may, subject to the provisions of this Law, conduct the arbitration in such manner as it considers appropriate. The power conferred upon the arbitral tribunal includes the power to determine the admissibility, relevance, materiality and weight of any evidence.

Article 20—[Place of arbitration]

(1) The parties are free to agree on the place of arbitration. Failing such agreement, the place of arbitration shall be determined by the arbitral tribunal having regard to the circumstances of the case, including the convenience of the parties.

(2) Notwithstanding the provisions of paragraph (1) of this article, the arbitral tribunal may, unless otherwise agreed by the parties, meet at any place it considers appropriate for consultation among its members, for hearing witnesses, experts or the parties, or for inspection of goods, other property or documents.

Article 21—[Commencement of arbitral proceedings]

Unless otherwise agreed by the parties, the arbitral tribunal proceedings in respect of a particular dispute commence on the date on which a request for that dispute to be referred to arbitration is received by the respondent.

Article 22—[Language]

(1) The parties are free to agree on the language or languages to be used in the arbitral proceedings. Failing such agreement, the arbitral tribunal shall determine the language or languages to be used in the proceedings. This agreement or determination, unless otherwise specified therein, shall apply to any written statement by a party, any hearing and any award, decision or other communication by the arbitral tribunal.

(2) The arbitral tribunal may order that any documentary evidence shall be accompanied by a translation into the language or languages agreed upon by the parties or determined by the arbitral tribunal.

Article 23—[Statements of claim and defence]

(1) Within the period of time agreed by the parties or determined by the arbitral tribunal, the claimant shall state the facts supporting his claim, the points at issue and the relief or remedy sought, and the respondent shall state his defence in respect of these particulars, unless the parties have otherwise agreed as to the required elements of such statements. The parties may submit with their statements all documents they consider to be relevant or may add a reference to the documents or other evidence they will submit.

(2) Unless otherwise agreed by the parties, either party may amend or supplement his claim or defence during the course of the arbitral proceedings, unless the arbitral tribunal considers it inappropriate to allow such amendments having regard to the delay in making it.

Article 24—[Hearings and written proceedings]

(1) Subject to any contrary agreement by the parties, the arbitral tribunal shall decide whether to hold oral hearings for the presentation of evidence or for oral argument, or whether the proceedings shall be conducted on the basis of documents and other materials. However, unless the parties have agreed that no hearings shall be held, the arbitral tribunal shall hold such hearings at an appropriate stage of the proceedings, if so requested by a party.

(2) The parties shall be given sufficient advance notice of any hearing and of any meeting of the arbitral tribunal for the purposes of inspection of goods, other property or documents.

(3) All statements, documents or other information supplied to the arbitration tribunal by one party shall be communicated to the other party. Also any expert report

or evidentiary document on which the arbitral tribunal may rely in making its decision shall be communicated to the parties.

Article 25—[Default of a party]

Unless otherwise agreed by the parties, if, without showing sufficient cause,

(a) the claimant fails to communicate his statement of claim in accordance with article 23(1), the arbitral tribunal shall terminate the proceedings;

(b) the respondent fails to communicate his statement of defence in accordance with article 23 (1), the arbitral tribunal shall continue the proceedings without treating such failure in itself as an admission of the claimant's allegations;

(c) any party fails to appear at a hearing or to produce documentary evidence, the arbitral tribunal may continue the proceedings and make the award on the evidence before it.

Article 26—[Expert appointed by arbitral tribunal]

(1) Unless otherwise agreed by the parties, the arbitral tribunal

(a) may appoint one or more experts to report to it on specific issues to be determined by the arbitral tribunal;

(b) may require a party to give the expert any relevant information or to produce, or to provide access to, any relevant documents, goods or other property for his inspection.

(2) Unless otherwise agreed by the parties, if a party so requests or if the arbitral tribunal considers it necessary, the expert shall, after delivery of his written or oral report, participate in a hearing where the parties have the opportunity to put questions to him and to present expert witnesses in order to testify on the points at issue.

Article 27—[Court assistance in taking evidence]

The arbitral tribunal or a party with the approval of the arbitral tribunal may request from a competent court of this State assistance in taking evidence. The court may execute the request within its competence and according to its rules on taking evidence.

Chapter VI—Making of award and termination of proceedings

Article 28—[Rules applicable to substance of dispute]

(1) The arbitral tribunal shall decide the dispute in accordance with such rules of law as are chosen by the parties as applicable to the substance of the dispute. Any designation of the law or legal system of a given State shall be construed, unless

otherwise expressed, as directly referring to the substantive law of that State and not to its conflict of laws rules.

(2) Failing any designation by the parties, the arbitral tribunal shall apply the law determined by the conflict of laws rules which it considers applicable.

(3) The arbitral tribunal shall decide ex aequo et bono or as amiable compositeur only if the parties have expressly authorised it to do so.

(4) In all cases, the arbitral tribunal shall decide in accordance with the terms of the contract and shall take into account the usages of the trade applicable to the transaction.

Article 29—[Decision making by panel of arbitrators]

In arbitral proceedings with more than one arbitrator, any decision of the arbitral tribunal shall be made, unless otherwise agreed by the parties, by a majority of all its members. However, questions of procedure may be decided by a presiding arbitrator, if so authorised by the parties or all members of the arbitral tribunal.

Article 30—[Settlement]

(1) If, during arbitral proceedings, the parties settle the dispute, the arbitral tribunal shall terminate the proceedings and, if requested by the parties and not objected to by the arbitral tribunal, record the settlement in the form of an arbitral award on agreed terms.

(2) An award on agreed terms shall be made in accordance with the provisions of article 31 and shall state that it is an award. Such an award has the same status and effect as any other award on the merits of the case.

Article 31—[Form and contents of award]

(1) The award shall be made in writing and shall be signed by the arbitrator or arbitrators. In arbitral proceedings with more than one arbitrator, the signatures of the majority of all members of the arbitral tribunal shall suffice, provided that the reason for any omitted signature is stated.

(2) The award shall state the reasons upon which it is based, unless the parties have agreed that no reasons are to be given or the award is an award on agreed terms under article 30.

(3) The award shall state its date and the place of arbitration as determined in accordance with article 20(1). The award shall be deemed to have been made at that place.

(4) After the award is made, a copy signed by the arbitrators in accordance with paragraph (1) of this article shall be delivered to each party.

Article 32—[Termination of proceedings]

(1) The arbitral proceedings are terminated by the final award or by an order of the arbitral tribunal in accordance with paragraph (2) of this article.

(2) The arbitral tribunal shall issue an order for the termination of the arbitral proceedings when:

(a) the claimant withdraws his claim, unless the respondent objects thereto and the arbitral tribunal recognises a legitimate interest on his part in obtaining a final settlement of the dispute;

(b) the parties agree on the termination of the proceedings;

(c) the arbitral tribunal finds that the continuation of the proceedings has for any other reason become unnecessary or impossible.

(3) The mandate of the arbitral tribunal terminates with the termination of the arbitral proceedings, subject to the provisions of articles 33 and 34(4).

Article 33—[Correction and interpretation of award; additional award]

(1) Within thirty days of receipt of the award, unless another period of time has been agreed upon by the parties:

(a) a party, with notice to the other party, may request the arbitral tribunal to correct in the award any errors in computation, any clerical or typographical errors or any errors of similar nature;

(b) if so agreed by the parties, a party, with notice to the other party, may request the arbitral tribunal to give an interpretation of a specific point or part of the award.

If the arbitral tribunal considers the request to be justified, it shall make the correction or give the interpretation within thirty days of receipt of the request. The interpretation shall form part of the award.

(2) The arbitral tribunal may correct any error of the type referred to in paragraph (1)(a) of this article on its own initiative within thirty days of the date of the award.

(3) Unless otherwise agreed by the parties, a party, with notice to the other party, may request, within thirty days of receipt of the award, the arbitral tribunal to make an additional award as to claims presented in the arbitral proceedings but omitted from the award. If the arbitral tribunal considers the request to be justified, it shall make the additional award within sixty days.

(4) The arbitral tribunal may extend, if necessary, the period of time within which it shall make a correction, interpretation or an additional award under

paragraph (1) or (3) of this article.

(5) The provisions of article 31 shall apply to a correction or interpretation of the award or to an additional award.

Chapter VII—Recourse against award

Article 34—[Application for setting a side as exclusive recourse against arbitral award]

(1) Recourse to a court against an arbitral award may be made only by an application for setting aside in accordance with paragraphs (2) and (3) of this article.

(2) An arbitral award may be set aside by the court specified in article 6 only if:

(a) the party making the application furnishes proof that:

(i) a party to the arbitration agreement referred to in article 7 was under some incapacity; or the said agreement is not valid under the law to which the parties have subjected it or, failing any indication thereon, under the law of this State; or

(ii) the party making the application was not given proper notice of the appointment of an arbitrator or of the arbitral proceedings or was otherwise unable to present his case; or

(iii) the award deals with a dispute not contemplated by or not falling within the terms of the submission to arbitration, or contains decisions on matters beyond the scope of the submission to arbitration, provided that, if the decisions on matters submitted to arbitration can be separated from those not so submitted, only that part of the award which contains decisions on matters not submitted to arbitration may be set aside; or

(iv) the composition of the arbitral tribunal or the arbitral procedure was not in accordance with the agreement of the parties, unless such agreement was in conflict with a provision of this Law from which the parties cannot derogate, or, failing such agreement, was not in accordance with this Law; or

(b) the court finds that:

(i) the subject-matter of the dispute is not capable of settlement by arbitration under the law of this State; or,

(ii) the award is in conflict with the public policy of this State.

(3) An application for setting aside may not be made after three months have

elapsed from the date on which the party making that application had received the award or, if a request had been made under article 33, from the date on which that request had been disposed of by the arbitral tribunal.

(4) The court, when asked to set aside an award, may, where appropriate and so requested by a party, suspend the setting aside proceedings for a period of time determined by it in order to give the arbitral tribunal an opportunity to resume the arbitral proceedings or to take such other action as in the arbitral tribunal's opinion will eliminate the grounds for setting aside.

Chapter VIII—Recognition and enforcement of awards

Article 35—[Recognition and enforcement]

(1) An arbitral award, irrespective of the country in which it was made, shall be recognised as binding and, upon application in writing to the competent court, shall be enforced subject to the provisions of this article and of article 36.

(2) The party relying on an award or applying for its enforcement shall supply the duly authenticated original award or a duly certified copy thereof, and the original arbitration agreement referred to in article 7 or a duly certified copy thereof. If the award or agreement is not made in an official language of this State, the party shall supply a duly certified translation thereof into such language.

Article 36—[Grounds for refusing recognition or enforcement]

(1) Recognition or enforcement of an arbitral award, irrespective of the country in which it was made, may be refused only:

(a) at the request of the party against whom it is invoked, if that party furnishes to the competent court where recognition or enforcement is sought proof that:

(i) a party to the arbitration agreement referred to in article 7 was under some incapacity; or the said agreement is not valid under the law to which the parties have subjected it or, failing any indication thereon, under the law of the country where the award was made; or

(ii) the party against whom the award is invoked was not given proper notice of the appointment of an arbitrator or of the arbitral proceedings or was otherwise unable to present his case; or

(iii) the award deals with a dispute not contemplated by or not falling within the terms of the submission to arbitration, or it contains decisions on matters beyond the scope of the submission to arbitration, provided that, if the decisions on matters submitted to arbitration can be separated from those not so submitted, that part of the award which contains decisions on matters submitted to arbitration may be recognised and enforced; or

(iv) the composition of the arbitral tribunal or the arbitral procedure was not in accordance with the agreement of the parties or, failing such agreement, was not in accordance with the law of the country where the arbitration took place; or

(v) the award has not yet become binding on the parties or has been set aside or suspended by a court of the country in which, or under the law of which, that award was made; or

(b) if the court finds that:

(i) the subject-matter of the dispute is not capable of settlement by arbitration under the law of this State; or

(ii) the recognition or enforcement of the award would be contrary to the public policy of this State.

(2) If an application for setting aside or suspension of an award has been made to a court referred to in paragraph (1)(a)(v) of this article, the court where recognition or enforcement is sought may, if it considers it proper, adjourn its decision and may also, on the application of the party claiming recognition or enforcement of the award, order the other party to provide appropriate security.

二、国内法制部分

（一）法律部分

1. 1995年《中华人民共和国仲裁法》

中华人民共和国仲裁法

（1994年8月31日第八届全国人民代表大会常务委员会第九次会议通过 1994年8月31日中华人民共和国主席令第三十一号公布 1995年9月1日起施行）

第一章　总　　则

第一条　为保证公正、及时地仲裁经济纠纷，保护当事人的合法权益，保障社会主义市场经济健康发展,制定本法。

第二条 平等主体的公民、法人和其他组织之间发生的合同纠纷和其他财产权益纠纷,可以仲裁。

第三条 下列纠纷不能仲裁:

(一)婚姻、收养、监护、扶养、继承纠纷;

(二)依法应当由行政机关处理的行政争议。

第四条 当事人采用仲裁方式解决纠纷,应当双方自愿,达成仲裁协议。没有仲裁协议,一方申请仲裁的,仲裁委员会不予受理。

第五条 当事人达成仲裁协议,一方向人民法院起诉的,人民法院不予受理,但仲裁协议无效的除外。

第六条 仲裁委员会应当由当事人协议选定。

仲裁不实行级别管辖和地域管辖。

第七条 仲裁应当根据事实,符合法律规定,公平合理地解决纠纷。

第八条 仲裁依法独立进行,不受行政机关、社会团体和个人的干涉。

第九条 仲裁实行一裁终局的制度。裁决作出后,当事人就同一纠纷再申请仲裁或者向人民法院起诉的,仲裁委员会或者人民法院不予受理。

裁决被人民法院依法裁定撤销或者不予执行的,当事人就该纠纷可以根据双方重新达成的仲裁协议申请仲裁,也可以向人民法院起诉。

第二章 仲裁委员会和仲裁协会

第十条 仲裁委员会可以在直辖市和省、自治区人民政府所在地的市设立,也可以根据需要在其他设区的市设立,不按行政区划层层设立。

仲裁委员会由前款规定的市的人民政府组织有关部门和商会统一组建。

设立仲裁委员会,应当经省、自治区、直辖市的司法行政部门登记。

第十一条 仲裁委员会应当具备下列条件:

(一)有自己的名称、住所和章程;

(二)有必要的财产;

(三)有该委员会的组成人员;

(四)有聘任的仲裁员。

仲裁委员会的章程应当依照本法制定。

第十二条 仲裁委员会由主任一人、副主任二至四人和委员七至十一人组成。

仲裁委员会的主任、副主任和委员由法律、经济贸易专家和有实际工作经验的人员担任。仲裁委员会的组成人员中,法律、经济贸易专家不得少于三分之二。

第十三条 仲裁委员会应当从公道正派的人员中聘任仲裁员。

仲裁员应当符合下列条件之一：

（一）已从事仲裁工作满八年的；

（二）从事律师工作满八年的；

（三）曾任审判员满八年的；

（四）从事法律研究、教学工作并具有高级职称的；

（五）具有法律知识、从事经济贸易等专业工作并具有高级职称或者具有同等专业水平的。

仲裁委员会按照不同专业设仲裁员名册。

第十四条 仲裁委员会独立于行政机关，与行政机关没有隶属关系。仲裁委员会之间也没有隶属关系。

第十五条 中国仲裁协会是社会团体法人。仲裁委员会是中国仲裁协会的会员。中国仲裁协会的章程由全国会员大会制定。

中国仲裁协会是仲裁委员会的自律性组织，根据章程对仲裁委员会及其组成人员、仲裁员的违纪行为进行监督。

中国仲裁协会依照本法和民事诉讼法的有关规定制定仲裁规则。

第三章 仲 裁 协 议

第十六条 仲裁协议包括合同中订立的仲裁条款和以其他书面方式在纠纷发生前或者纠纷发生后达成的请求仲裁的协议。

仲裁协议应当具有下列内容：

（一）请求仲裁的意思表示；

（二）仲裁事项；

（三）选定的仲裁委员会。

第十七条 有下列情形之一的，仲裁协议无效：

（一）约定的仲裁事项超出法律规定的仲裁范围的；

（二）无民事行为能力人或者限制民事行为能力人订立的仲裁协议；

（三）一方采取胁迫手段，迫使对方订立仲裁协议的。

第十八条 仲裁协议对仲裁事项或者仲裁委员会没有约定或者约定不明确的，当事人可以补充协议；达不成补充协议的，仲裁协议无效。

第十九条 仲裁协议独立存在，合同的变更、解除、终止或者无效，不影响仲裁协议的效力。

仲裁庭有权确认合同的效力。

第二十条 当事人对仲裁协议的效力有异议的,可以请求仲裁委员会作出决定或者请求人民法院作出裁定。一方请求仲裁委员会作出决定,另一方请求人民法院作出裁定的,由人民法院裁定。

当事人对仲裁协议的效力有异议,应当在仲裁庭首次开庭前提出。

第四章 仲裁程序

第一节 申请和受理

第二十一条 当事人申请仲裁应当符合下列条件:
(一)有仲裁协议;
(二)有具体的仲裁请求和事实、理由;
(三)属于仲裁委员会的受理范围。

第二十二条 当事人申请仲裁,应当向仲裁委员会递交仲裁协议、仲裁申请书及副本。

第二十三条 仲裁申请书应当载明下列事项:
(一)当事人的姓名、性别、年龄、职业、工作单位和住所,法人或者其他组织的名称、住所和法定代表人或者主要负责人的姓名、职务;
(二)仲裁请求和所根据的事实、理由;
(三)证据和证据来源、证人姓名和住所。

第二十四条 仲裁委员会收到仲裁申请书之日起五日内,认为符合受理条件的,应当受理,并通知当事人;认为不符合受理条件的,应当书面通知当事人不予受理,并说明理由。

第二十五条 仲裁委员会受理仲裁申请后,应当在仲裁规则规定的期限内将仲裁规则和仲裁员名册送达申请人,并将仲裁申请书副本和仲裁规则、仲裁员名册送达被申请人。

被申请人收到仲裁申请书副本后,应当在仲裁规则规定的期限内向仲裁委员会提交答辩书。仲裁委员会收到答辩书后,应当在仲裁规则规定的期限内将答辩书副本送达申请人。被申请人未提交答辩书的,不影响仲裁程序的进行。

第二十六条 当事人达成仲裁协议,一方向人民法院起诉未声明有仲裁协议,人民法院受理后,另一方在首次开庭前提交仲裁协议的,人民法院应当驳回起诉,但仲裁协议无效的除外;另一方在首次开庭前未对人民法院受理该案提出异议的,视为放弃仲裁协议,人民法院应当继续审理。

第二十七条 申请人可以放弃或者变更仲裁请求。被申请人可以承认或者反驳仲裁请求,有权提出反请求。

第二十八条 一方当事人因另一方当事人的行为或者其他原因,可能使裁决不能执行或者难以执行的,可以申请财产保全。

当事人申请财产保全的,仲裁委员会应当将当事人的申请依照民事诉讼法的有关规定提交人民法院。

申请有错误的,申请人应当赔偿被申请人因财产保全所遭受的损失。

第二十九条 当事人、法定代理人可以委托律师和其他代理人进行仲裁活动。委托律师和其他代理人进行仲裁活动的,应当向仲裁委员会提交授权委托书。

第二节 仲裁庭的组成

第三十条 仲裁庭可以由三名仲裁员或者一名仲裁员组成。由三名仲裁员组成的,设首席仲裁员。

第三十一条 当事人约定由三名仲裁员组成仲裁庭的,应当各自选定或者各自委托仲裁委员会主任指定一名仲裁员,第三名仲裁员由当事人共同选定或者共同委托仲裁委员会主任指定。第三名仲裁员是首席仲裁员。

当事人约定由一名仲裁员成立仲裁庭的,应当由当事人共同选定或者共同委托仲裁委员会主任指定仲裁员。

第三十二条 当事人没有在仲裁规则规定的期限内约定仲裁庭的组成方式或者选定仲裁员的,由仲裁委员会主任指定。

第三十三条 仲裁庭组成后,仲裁委员会应当将仲裁庭的组成情况书面通知当事人。

第三十四条 仲裁员有下列情形之一的,必须回避,当事人也有权提出回避申请:

(一)是本案当事人或者当事人、代理人的近亲属;

(二)与本案有利害关系;

(三)与本案当事人、代理人有其他关系,可能影响公正仲裁的;

(四)私自会见当事人、代理人,或者接受当事人、代理人的请客送礼的。

第三十五条 当事人提出回避申请,应当说明理由,在首次开庭前提出。回避事由在首次开庭后知道的,可以在最后一次开庭终结前提出。

第三十六条 仲裁员是否回避,由仲裁委员会主任决定;仲裁委员会主任担任仲裁员时,由仲裁委员会集体决定。

第三十七条 仲裁员因回避或者其他原因不能履行职责的,应当依照本法规定重新选定或者指定仲裁员。

因回避而重新选定或者指定仲裁员后,当事人可以请求已进行的仲裁程序重新进行,是否准许,由仲裁庭决定;仲裁庭也可以自行决定已进行的仲裁程序是否重新进行。

第三十八条 仲裁员有本法第三十四条第四项规定的情形,情节严重的,或者有本法第五十八条第八项规定的情形的,应当依法承担法律责任,仲裁委员会应当将其除名。

第三节 开庭和裁决

第三十九条 仲裁应当开庭进行。当事人协议不开庭的,仲裁庭可以根据仲裁申请书、答辩书以及其他材料作出裁决。

第四十条 仲裁不公开进行。当事人协议公开的,可以公开进行,但涉及国家秘密的除外。

第四十一条 仲裁委员会应当在仲裁规则规定的期限内将开庭日期通知双方当事人。当事人有正当理由的,可以在仲裁规则规定的期限内请求延期开庭。是否延期,由仲裁庭决定。

第四十二条 申请人经书面通知,无正当理由不到庭或者未经仲裁庭许可中途退庭的,可以视为撤回仲裁申请。

被申请人经书面通知,无正当理由不到庭或者未经仲裁庭许可中途退庭的,可以缺席裁决。

第四十三条 当事人应当对自己的主张提供证据。

仲裁庭认为有必要收集的证据,可以自行收集。

第四十四条 仲裁庭对专门性问题认为需要鉴定的,可以交由当事人约定的鉴定部门鉴定,也可以由仲裁庭指定的鉴定部门鉴定。

根据当事人的请求或者仲裁庭的要求,鉴定部门应当派鉴定人参加开庭。当事人经仲裁庭许可,可以向鉴定人提问。

第四十五条 证据应当在开庭时出示,当事人可以质证。

第四十六条 在证据可能灭失或者以后难以取得的情况下,当事人可以申请证据保全。当事人申请证据保全的,仲裁委员会应当将当事人的申请提交证据所在地的基层人民法院。

第四十七条 当事人在仲裁过程中有权进行辩论。辩论终结时,首席仲裁员或者独任仲裁员应当征询当事人的最后意见。

第四十八条 仲裁庭应当将开庭情况记入笔录。当事人和其他仲裁参与人认为对自己陈述的记录有遗漏或者差错的,有权申请补正。如果不予补正,应当记录该申请。

笔录由仲裁员、记录人员、当事人和其他仲裁参与人签名或者盖章。

第四十九条 当事人申请仲裁后,可以自行和解。达成和解协议的,可以请求仲裁庭根据和解协议作出裁决书,也可以撤回仲裁申请。

第五十条 当事人达成和解协议,撤回仲裁申请后反悔的,可以根据仲裁协议申请仲裁。

第五十一条 仲裁庭在作出裁决前,可以先行调解。当事人自愿调解的,仲裁庭应当调解。调解不成的,应当及时作出裁决。

调解达成协议的,仲裁庭应当制作调解书或者根据协议的结果制作裁决书。调解书与裁决书具有同等法律效力。

第五十二条 调解书应当写明仲裁请求和当事人协议的结果。调解书由仲裁员签名,加盖仲裁委员会印章,送达双方当事人。

调解书经双方当事人签收后,即发生法律效力。

在调解书签收前当事人反悔的,仲裁庭应当及时作出裁决。

第五十三条 裁决应当按照多数仲裁员的意见作出,少数仲裁员的不同意见可以记入笔录。仲裁庭不能形成多数意见时,裁决应当按照首席仲裁员的意见作出。

第五十四条 裁决书应当写明仲裁请求、争议事实、裁决理由、裁决结果、仲裁费用的负担和裁决日期。当事人协议不愿写明争议事实和裁决理由的,可以不写。裁决书由仲裁员签名,加盖仲裁委员会印章。对裁决持不同意见的仲裁员,可以签名,也可以不签名。

第五十五条 仲裁庭仲裁纠纷时,其中一部分事实已经清楚,可以就该部分先行裁决。

第五十六条 对裁决书中的文字、计算错误或者仲裁庭已经裁决但在裁决书中遗漏的事项,仲裁庭应当补正;当事人自收到裁决书之日起三十日内,可以请求仲裁庭补正。

第五十七条 裁决书自作出之日起发生法律效力。

第五章 申请撤销裁决

第五十八条 当事人提出证据证明裁决有下列情形之一的,可以向仲裁委员会所在地的中级人民法院申请撤销裁决:

(一)没有仲裁协议的;

(二)裁决的事项不属于仲裁协议的范围或者仲裁委员会无权仲裁的;

(三)仲裁庭的组成或者仲裁的程序违反法定程序的;

(四)裁决所根据的证据是伪造的;

(五)对方当事人隐瞒了足以影响公正裁决的证据的;

(六)仲裁员在仲裁该案时有索贿受贿,徇私舞弊,枉法裁决行为的。

人民法院经组成合议庭审查核实裁决有前款规定情形之一的,应当裁定撤销。

人民法院认定该裁决违背社会公共利益的,应当裁定撤销裁决。

第五十九条 当事人申请撤销裁决的,应当自收到裁决书之日起六个月内提出。

第六十条 人民法院应当在受理撤销裁决申请之日起两个月内作出撤销裁决或者驳回申请的裁定。

第六十一条 人民法院受理撤销裁决的申请后,认为可以由仲裁庭重新仲裁的,通知仲裁庭在一定期限内重新仲裁,并裁定中止撤销程序。仲裁庭拒绝重新仲裁的,人民法院应当裁定恢复撤销程序。

第六章 执 行

第六十二条 当事人应当履行裁决。一方当事人不履行的,另一方当事人可以依照民事诉讼法的有关规定向人民法院申请执行。受申请的人民法院应当执行。

第六十三条 被申请人提出证据证明裁决有民事诉讼法第二百一十七条第二款规定的情形之一的,经人民法院组成合议庭审查核实,裁定不予执行。

第六十四条 一方当事人申请执行裁决,另一方当事人申请撤销裁决的,人民法院应当裁定中止执行。

人民法院裁定撤销裁决的,应当裁定终结执行。撤销裁决的申请被裁定驳回的,人民法院应当裁定恢复执行。

第七章 涉外仲裁的特别规定

第六十五条 涉外经济贸易、运输和海事中发生的纠纷的仲裁,适用本章规定。本章没有规定的,适用本法其他有关规定。

第六十六条 涉外仲裁委员会可以由中国国际商会组织设立。

涉外仲裁委员会由主任一人、副主任若干人和委员若干人组成。

涉外仲裁委员会的主任、副主任和委员可以由中国国际商会聘任。

第六十七条 涉外仲裁委员会可以从具有法律、经济贸易、科学技术等专门知识的外籍人士中聘任仲裁员。

第六十八条 涉外仲裁的当事人申请证据保全的,涉外仲裁委员会应当将当事人的申请提交证据所在地的中级人民法院。

第六十九条 涉外仲裁的仲裁庭可以将开庭情况记入笔录,或者作出笔录要点,笔录要点可以由当事人和其他仲裁参与人签字或者盖章。

第七十条 当事人提出证据证明涉外仲裁裁决有民事诉讼法第二百六十条第一款规定的情形之一的,经人民法院组成合议庭审查核实,裁定撤销。

第七十一条 被申请人提出证据证明涉外仲裁裁决有民事诉讼法第二百六十条第一款规定的情形之一的,经人民法院组成合议庭审查核实,裁定不予执行。

第七十二条 涉外仲裁委员会作出的发生法律效力的仲裁裁决,当事人请求执行的,如果被执行人或者其财产不在中华人民共和国领域内,应当由当事人直接向有管辖权的外国法院申请承认和执行。

第七十三条 涉外仲裁规则可以由中国国际商会依照本法和民事诉讼法的有关规定制定。

第八章　附　　则

第七十四条 法律对仲裁时效有规定的,适用该规定。法律对仲裁时效没有规定的,适用诉讼时效的规定。

第七十五条 在中国仲裁协会制定仲裁规则前,仲裁委员会依照本法和民事诉讼法的有关规定可以制定仲裁暂行规则。

第七十六条 当事人应当按照规定交纳仲裁费用。

收取仲裁费用的办法,应当报物价管理部门核准。

第七十七条 劳动争议和农业集体经济组织内部的农业承包合同纠纷的仲裁,另行规定。

第七十八条 本法施行前制定的有关仲裁的规定与本法的规定相抵触的,以本法为准。

第七十九条 本法施行前在直辖市、省、自治区人民政府所在地的市和其他设区的市设立的仲裁机构,应当依照本法的有关规定重新组建;未重新组建的,自本法施行之日起届满一年时终止。

本法施行前设立的不符合本法规定的其他仲裁机构,自本法施行之日起终止。

第八十条 本法自1995年9月1日起施行。

2. 2007 年《中华人民共和国民事诉讼法》相关条款

中华人民共和国民事诉讼法

(1991 年 4 月 9 日第七届全国人民代表大会第四次会议通过 根据 2007 年 10 月 28 日第十届全国人民代表大会常务委员会第三十次会议《关于修改〈中华人民共和国民事诉讼法〉的决定》修正)

第四编 涉外民事诉讼程序的特别规定

第二十七章 仲 裁

第二百五十五条 涉外经济贸易、运输和海事中发生的纠纷,当事人在合同中订有仲裁条款或者事后达成书面仲裁协议,提交中华人民共和国涉外仲裁机构或者其他仲裁机构仲裁的,当事人不得向人民法院起诉。

当事人在合同中没有订有仲裁条款或者事后没有达成书面仲裁协议的,可以向人民法院起诉。

第二百五十六条 当事人申请采取财产保全的,中华人民共和国的涉外仲裁机构应当将当事人的申请,提交被申请人住所地或者财产所在地的中级人民法院裁定。

第二百五十七条 经中华人民共和国涉外仲裁机构裁决的,当事人不得向人民法院起诉。一方当事人不履行仲裁裁决的,对方当事人可以向被申请人住所地或者财产所在地的中级人民法院申请执行。

第二百五十八条 对中华人民共和国涉外仲裁机构作出的裁决,被申请人提出证据证明仲裁裁决有下列情形之一的,经人民法院组成合议庭审查核实,裁定不予执行:

(一)当事人在合同中没有订有仲裁条款或者事后没有达成书面仲裁协议的;

(二)被申请人没有得到指定仲裁员或者进行仲裁程序的通知,或者由于其他不属于被申请人负责的原因未能陈述意见的;

(三)仲裁庭的组成或者仲裁的程序与仲裁规则不符的;

(四)裁决的事项不属于仲裁协议的范围或者仲裁机构无权仲裁的。

人民法院认定执行该裁决违背社会公共利益的,裁定不予执行。

第二百五十九条 仲裁裁决被人民法院裁定不予执行的,当事人可以根据双方达成的书面仲裁协议重新申请仲裁,也可以向人民法院起诉。

(二) 司法解释部分

1.《关于执行我国加入的〈承认及执行外国仲裁裁决公约〉的通知》

关于执行我国加入的
《承认及执行外国仲裁裁决公约》的通知

全国地方各高、中级人民法院,各海事法院、铁路运输中级法院:

第六届全国人民代表大会常务委员会第十八次会议于1986年12月2日决定我国加入1958年在纽约通过的《承认及执行外国仲裁裁决公约》(以下简称《1958年纽约公约》),该公约将于1987年4月22日对我国生效。各高、中级人民法院都应立即组织经济、民事审判人员、执行人员以及其他有关人员认真学习这一重要的国际公约,并且切实依照执行。现就执行该公约的几个问题通知如下:

一、根据我国加入该公约时所作的互惠保留声明,我国对在另一缔约国领土内作出的仲裁裁决的承认和执行适用该公约。该公约与我国民事诉讼法(试行)有不同规定的,按该公约的规定办理。

对于在非缔约国领土内作出的仲裁裁决,需要我国法院承认和执行的,应按民事诉讼法(试行)第二百零四条的规定办理。

二、根据我国加入该公约时所作的商事保留声明,我国仅对按照我国法律属于契约性和非契约性商事法律关系所引起的争议适用该公约。所谓"契约性和非契约性商事法律关系",具体的是指由于合同、侵权或者根据有关法律规定而产生的经济上的权利义务关系,例如货物买卖、财产租赁、工程承包、加工承揽、技术转让、合资经营、合作经营、勘探开发自然资源、保险、信贷、劳务、代理、咨询服务和海上、民用航空、铁路、公路的客货运输以及产品责任、环境污染、海上事故和所有权争议等,但不包括外国投资者与东道国政府之间的争端。

三、根据《1958年纽约公约》第四条的规定,申请我国法院承认和执行在另一缔约国领土内作出的仲裁裁决,是由仲裁裁决的一方当事人提出的。对于当事人的申请应由我国下列地点的中级人民法院受理:

1. 被执行人为自然人的,为其户籍所在地或者居所地;
2. 被执行人为法人的,为其主要办事机构所在地;

3. 被执行人在我国无住所、居所或者主要办事机构,但有财产在我国境内的,为其财产所在地。

四、我国有管辖权的人民法院接到一方当事人的申请后,应对申请承认及执行的仲裁裁决进行审查,如果认为不具有《1958年纽约公约》第五条第一、二两项所列的情形,应当裁定承认其效力,并且依照民事诉讼法(试行)规定的程序执行;如果认定具有第五条第二项所列的情形之一的,或者根据被执行人提供的证据证明具有第五条第一项所列的情形之一的,应当裁定驳回申请,拒绝承认及执行。

五、申请我国法院承认及执行的仲裁裁决,仅限于《1958年纽约公约》对我国生效后在另一缔约国领土内作出的仲裁裁决。该项申请应当在民事诉讼法(试行)第一百六十九条规定的申请执行期限内提出。

特此通知,希遵照执行。

附一:本通知引用的《承认及执行外国仲裁裁决公约》有关条款

第四条 一、声请承认及执行之一造,为取得前条所称之承认及执行,应于声请时提具:

(甲)原裁决之正本或其正式副本;

(乙)第二条所称协定之原本或其正式副本。

二、倘前述裁决或协定所用文字非为援引裁决地所在国之正式文字,声请承认及执行裁决之一造应具备各该文件之此项文字译本。译本应由公设或宣誓之翻译员或外交或领事人员认证之。

第五条 一、裁决唯有受裁决援用之一造向声请承认及执行地之主管机关提具证据证明有下列情形之一时,始得依该造之请求,拒予承认及执行:

(甲)第二条所称协定之当事人依对其适用之法律有某种无行为能力情形者,或该项协定依当事人作为协定准据之法律系属无效,或未指明以何法律为准时,依裁决地所在国法律系属无效者;

(乙)受裁决援用之一造未接获关于指派仲裁员或仲裁程序之适当通知,或因他故,致未能申辩者;

(丙)裁决所处理之争议非为交付仲裁之标的或不在其条款之列,或裁决载有关于交付仲裁范围以外事项之决定者,但交付仲裁事项之决定可与未交付仲裁之事项划分时,裁决中关于交付仲裁事项决定部分得予承认及执行;

(丁)仲裁机关之组成或仲裁程序与各造间之协议不符,或无协议而与仲裁地所在国法律不符者;

(戊)裁决对各造尚无拘束力,或业经裁决地所在国或裁决所依据法律之国家之主管机关撤销或停止执行者。

二、倘声请承认及执行地所在国之主管机关认定有下列情形之一,亦得拒不承认及执行仲裁裁决：

（甲）依该国法律,争议事项系不能以仲裁解决者；

（乙）承认或执行裁决有违该国公共政策者。

附二：本通知引用的《中华人民共和国民事诉讼法（试行）》有关条款

第一百六十九条 申请执行的期限,双方或者一方当事人是个人的为一年；双方是企业事业单位、机关、团体的为六个月。

第二百零四条 中华人民共和国人民法院对外国法院委托执行的已经确定的判决、裁决,应当根据中华人民共和国缔结或者参加的国际条约,或者按照互惠原则进行审查,认为不违反中华人民共和国法律的基本准则或者我国国家、社会利益的,裁定承认其效力,并且依照本法规定的程序执行。否则,应当退回外国法院。

附三：加入《承认及执行外国仲裁裁决公约》的国家

丹麦(1、2) 法国(1、2) 希腊(1、2) 罗马教廷(1、) 美国(1、2) 奥地利(1) 比利时(1) 联邦德国(1) 爱尔兰(1) 日本(1) 卢森堡(1) 荷兰(1) 瑞士(1) 英国(1) 挪威(1) 澳大利亚 芬兰 新西兰(1) 圣马利诺 西班牙 意大利 加拿大 瑞典 民主德国(1、2) 匈牙利(1、2) 波兰(1、2) 罗马尼亚(1、2) 南斯拉夫(1、2、3) 保加利亚(1) 捷克斯洛伐克(1) 苏联(1) 苏联白俄罗斯共和国(1) 苏联乌克兰共和国(1) 博茨瓦纳(1、2) 中非共和国(1、2) 中国(1、2) 古巴(1、2) 塞浦路斯(1、2) 厄瓜多尔(1、2) 印度(1、2) 印度尼西亚(1、2) 马达加斯加(1、2) 尼日利亚(1、2) 菲律宾(1、2) 特立尼达和多巴哥(1、2) 突尼斯(1、2) 危地马拉(1、2) 南朝鲜(1、2) 摩纳哥(1、2) 科威特(1) 摩洛哥(1) 坦桑尼亚(1) 贝宁 智利 哥伦比亚 民主柬埔寨 埃及 加纳 以色列 约旦 墨西哥 尼日尔 南非 斯里兰卡 叙利亚 泰国 乌拉圭 吉布提 海地 巴拿马 马来西亚 新加坡

注：1. 该国声明,只适用本公约于在另一缔约国领土内作出的仲裁裁决,即作互惠保留。

2. 该国声明,只适用本公约于根据其本国的法律认定为属于商事的法律关系(契约性或非契约性的)所引起争议,即作商事保留。

3. 该国声明,只承认和执行该国加入本公约之后在外国作出的仲裁裁决。

2.《关于人民法院撤销涉外仲裁裁决有关事项的通知》

关于人民法院撤销涉外仲裁裁决有关事项的通知

1998年4月23日,最高人民法院

为严格执行《中华人民共和国仲裁法》(以下简称仲裁法)和《中华人民共和国民事诉讼法》(以下简称民事诉讼法),保障诉讼和仲裁活动依法进行,现决定对人民法院撤销我国涉外仲裁裁决建立报告制度,为此,特作如下通知:

一、凡一方当事人按照仲裁法的规定向人民法院申请撤销我国涉外仲裁裁决,如果人民法院经审查认为涉外仲裁裁决具有民事诉讼法第二百六十条第一款规定的情形之一的,在裁定撤销裁决或通知仲裁庭重新仲裁之前,须报请本辖区所属高级人民法院进行审查。如果高级人民法院同意撤销裁决或通知仲裁庭重新仲裁,应将其审查意见报最高人民法院。待最高人民法院答复后,方可裁定撤销裁决或通知仲裁庭重新仲裁。

二、受理申请撤销裁决的人民法院如认为应予撤销裁决或通知仲裁庭重新仲裁的,应在受理申请后三十日内报其所属的高级人民法院,该高级人民法院如同意撤销裁决或通知仲裁庭重新仲裁的,应在十五日内报最高人民法院,以严格执行仲裁法第六十条的规定。

3.《关于内地与香港特别行政区相互执行仲裁裁决的安排》

关于内地与香港特别行政区 相互执行仲裁裁决的安排

(1999年6月18日由最高人民法院审判委员会第1069次会议通过。根据最高人民法院和香港特别行政区代表协商达成的一致意见,本《安排》在内地以最高人民法院发布司法解释的形式予以公布,自2000年2月1日起施行)

2000年1月24日根据《中华人民共和国香港特别行政区基本法》第九十五条的规定,经最高人民法院与香港特别行政区(以下简称香港特区)政府协商,香港特区法院同意执行内地仲裁机构(名单由国务院法制办公室经国务院港澳事务办公室提供)依据《中华人民共和国仲裁法》所作出的裁决,内地人民法院同意执行在香港特区按香港特区《仲裁条例》所作出的裁决。现就内地与香港特区相互执行仲裁裁决的有关事宜作出如下安排：

一、在内地或者香港特区作出的仲裁裁决，一方当事人不履行仲裁裁决的，另一方当事人可以向被申请人住所地或者财产所在地的有关法院申请执行。

二、上条所述的有关法院，在内地指被申请人住所地或者财产所在地的中级人民法院，在香港特区指香港特区高等法院。

被申请人住所地或者财产所在地在内地不同的中级人民法院辖区内的，申请人可以选择其中一个人民法院申请执行裁决，不得分别向两个或者两个以上人民法院提出申请。

被申请人的住所地或者财产所在地，既在内地又在香港特区的，申请人不得同时分别向两地有关法院提出申请。只有一地法院执行不足以偿还其债务时，才可就不足部分向另一地法院申请执行。两地法院先后执行仲裁裁决的总额，不得超过裁决数额。

三、申请人向有关法院申请执行在内地或者香港特区作出的仲裁裁决的，应当提交以下文书：

（一）执行申请书；

（二）仲裁裁决书；

（三）仲裁协议。

四、执行申请书的内容应当载明下列事项：

（一）申请人为自然人的情况下，该人的姓名、地址；申请人为法人或者其他组织的情况下，该法人或其他组织的名称、地址及法定代表人姓名；

（二）被申请人为自然人的情况下，该人的姓名、地址；被申请人为法人或者其他组织的情况下，该法人或其他组织的名称、地址及法定代表人姓名；

（三）申请人为法人或者其他组织的，应当提交企业注册登记的副本。申请人是外国籍法人或者其他组织的，应当提交相应的公证和认证材料；

（四）申请执行的理由与请求的内容，被申请人的财产所在地及财产状况。

执行申请书应当以中文文本提出，裁决书或者仲裁协议没有中文文本的，申请人应当提交正式证明的中文译本。

五、申请人向有关法院申请执行内地或者香港特区仲裁裁决的期限依据执行地法律有关时限的规定。

六、有关法院接到申请人申请后，应当按执行地法律程序处理及执行。

七、在内地或者香港特区申请执行的仲裁裁决，被申请人接到通知后，提出证据证明有下列情形之一的，经审查核实，有关法院可裁定不予执行：

（一）仲裁协议当事人依对其适用的法律属于某种无行为能力的情形；或者该项仲裁协议依约定的准据法无效；或者未指明以何种法律为准时，依仲裁裁决地的法律是无效的；

（二）被申请人未接到指派仲裁员的适当通知，或者因他故未能陈述意见的；

（三）裁决所处理的争议不是交付仲裁的标的或者不在仲裁协议条款之内，或者裁决载有关于交付仲裁范围以外事项的决定的；但交付仲裁事项的决定可与未交付仲裁的事项划分时，裁决中关于交付仲裁事项的决定部分应当予以执行；

（四）仲裁庭的组成或者仲裁庭程序与当事人之间的协议不符，或者在有关当事人没有这种协议时与仲裁地的法律不符的；

（五）裁决对当事人尚无约束力，或者业经仲裁地的法院或者按仲裁地的法律撤销或者停止执行的。

有关法院认定依执行地法律，争议事项不能以仲裁解决的，则可不予执行该裁决。

内地法院认定在内地执行该仲裁裁决违反内地社会公共利益，或者香港特区法院决定在香港特区执行该仲裁裁决违反香港特区的公共政策，则可不予执行该裁决。

八、申请人向有关法院申请执行在内地或者香港特区作出的仲裁裁决，应当根据执行地法院有关诉讼收费的办法交纳执行费用。

九、1997年7月1日以后申请执行在内地或者香港特区作出的仲裁裁决按本安排执行。

十、对1997年7月1日至本安排生效之日的裁决申请问题，双方同意：

1997年7月1日至本安排生效之日因故未能向内地或者香港特区法院申请执行，申请人为法人或者其他组织的，可以在本安排生效后六个月内提出；如申请人为自然人的，可以在本安排生效后一年内提出。

对于内地或香港特区法院在1997年7月1日至本安排生效之日拒绝受理或者拒绝执行仲裁裁决的案件，应允许当事人重新申请。

十一、本安排在执行过程中遇有问题和修改，应当通过最高人民法院和香港特区政府协商解决。

4.《关于适用〈中华人民共和国仲裁法〉若干问题的解释》

关于适用《中华人民共和国仲裁法》若干问题的解释

(2005年12月26日最高人民法院审判委员会第1375次会议通过)

法释〔2006〕7号

《最高人民法院关于适用〈中华人民共和国仲裁法〉若干问题的解释》已于2005年12月26日由最高人民法院审判委员会第1375次会议通过,现予公布,自2006年9月8日起施行。

二○○六年八月二十三日

根据《中华人民共和国仲裁法》和《中华人民共和国民事诉讼法》等法律规定,对人民法院审理涉及仲裁案件适用法律的若干问题作如下解释:

第一条 仲裁法第十六条规定的"其他书面形式"的仲裁协议,包括以合同书、信件和数据电文(包括电报、电传、传真、电子数据交换和电子邮件)等形式达成的请求仲裁的协议。

第二条 当事人概括约定仲裁事项为合同争议的,基于合同成立、效力、变更、转让、履行、违约责任、解释、解除等产生的纠纷都可以认定为仲裁事项。

第三条 仲裁协议约定的仲裁机构名称不准确,但能够确定具体的仲裁机构的,应当认定选定了仲裁机构。

第四条 仲裁协议仅约定纠纷适用的仲裁规则的,视为未约定仲裁机构,但当事人达成补充协议或者按照约定的仲裁规则能够确定仲裁机构的除外。

第五条 仲裁协议约定两个以上仲裁机构的,当事人可以协议选择其中的一个仲裁机构申请仲裁;当事人不能就仲裁机构选择达成一致的,仲裁协议无效。

第六条 仲裁协议约定由某地的仲裁机构仲裁且该地仅有一个仲裁机构的,该仲裁机构视为约定的仲裁机构。该地有两个以上仲裁机构的,当事人可以协议选择其中的一个仲裁机构申请仲裁;当事人不能就仲裁机构选择达成一致的,仲裁协议无效。

第七条 当事人约定争议可以向仲裁机构申请仲裁也可以向人民法院起诉的,仲裁协议无效。但一方向仲裁机构申请仲裁,另一方未在仲裁法第二十条第二款规定期间内提出异议的除外。

第八条 当事人订立仲裁协议后合并、分立的,仲裁协议对其权利义务的继受人有效。

当事人订立仲裁协议后死亡的,仲裁协议对承继其仲裁事项中的权利义务的继承人有效。

前两款规定情形,当事人订立仲裁协议时另有约定的除外。

第九条 债权债务全部或者部分转让的,仲裁协议对受让人有效,但当事人另有约定、在受让债权债务时受让人明确反对或者不知有单独仲裁协议的除外。

第十条 合同成立后未生效或者被撤销的,仲裁协议效力的认定适用仲裁法第十九条第一款的规定。

当事人在订立合同时就争议达成仲裁协议的,合同未成立不影响仲裁协议的效力。

第十一条 合同约定解决争议适用其他合同、文件中的有效仲裁条款的,发生合同争议时,当事人应当按照该仲裁条款提请仲裁。

涉外合同应当适用的有关国际条约中有仲裁规定的,发生合同争议时,当事人应当按照国际条约中的仲裁规定提请仲裁。

第十二条 当事人向人民法院申请确认仲裁协议效力的案件,由仲裁协议约定的仲裁机构所在地的中级人民法院管辖;仲裁协议约定的仲裁机构不明确的,由仲裁协议签订地或者被申请人住所地的中级人民法院管辖。

申请确认涉外仲裁协议效力的案件,由仲裁协议约定的仲裁机构所在地、仲裁协议签订地、申请人或者被申请人住所地的中级人民法院管辖。

涉及海事海商纠纷仲裁协议效力的案件,由仲裁协议约定的仲裁机构所在地、仲裁协议签订地、申请人或者被申请人住所地的海事法院管辖;上述地点没有海事法院的,由就近的海事法院管辖。

第十三条 依照仲裁法第二十条第二款的规定,当事人在仲裁庭首次开庭前没有对仲裁协议的效力提出异议,而后向人民法院申请确认仲裁协议无效的,人民法院不予受理。

仲裁机构对仲裁协议的效力作出决定后,当事人向人民法院申请确认仲裁协议效力或者申请撤销仲裁机构的决定的,人民法院不予受理。

第十四条 仲裁法第二十六条规定的"首次开庭"是指答辩期满后人民法院组织的第一次开庭审理,不包括审前程序中的各项活动。

第十五条 人民法院审理仲裁协议效力确认案件,应当组成合议庭进行审查,并询问当事人。

第十六条 对涉外仲裁协议的效力审查,适用当事人约定的法律;当事人没有约定适用的法律但约定了仲裁地的,适用仲裁地法律;没有约定适用的法律也没有约定仲裁地或者仲裁地约定不明的,适用法院地法律。

第十七条　当事人以不属于仲裁法第五十八条或者民事诉讼法第二百六十条规定的事由申请撤销仲裁裁决的,人民法院不予支持。

第十八条　仲裁法第五十八条第一款第一项规定的"没有仲裁协议"是指当事人没有达成仲裁协议。仲裁协议被认定无效或者被撤销的,视为没有仲裁协议。

第十九条　当事人以仲裁裁决事项超出仲裁协议范围为由申请撤销仲裁裁决,经审查属实的,人民法院应当撤销仲裁裁决中的超裁部分。但超裁部分与其他裁决事项不可分的,人民法院应当撤销仲裁裁决。

第二十条　仲裁法第五十八条规定的"违反法定程序",是指违反仲裁法规定的仲裁程序和当事人选择的仲裁规则可能影响案件正确裁决的情形。

第二十一条　当事人申请撤销国内仲裁裁决的案件属于下列情形之一的,人民法院可以依照仲裁法第六十一条的规定通知仲裁庭在一定期限内重新仲裁:

（一）仲裁裁决所根据的证据是伪造的;

（二）对方当事人隐瞒了足以影响公正裁决的证据的。

人民法院应当在通知中说明要求重新仲裁的具体理由。

第二十二条　仲裁庭在人民法院指定的期限内开始重新仲裁的,人民法院应当裁定终结撤销程序;未开始重新仲裁的,人民法院应当裁定恢复撤销程序。

第二十三条　当事人对重新仲裁裁决不服的,可以在重新仲裁裁决书送达之日起六个月内依据仲裁法第五十八条规定向人民法院申请撤销。

第二十四条　当事人申请撤销仲裁裁决的案件,人民法院应当组成合议庭审理,并询问当事人。

第二十五条　人民法院受理当事人撤销仲裁裁决的申请后,另一方当事人申请执行同一仲裁裁决的,受理执行申请的人民法院应当在受理后裁定中止执行。

第二十六条　当事人向人民法院申请撤销仲裁裁决被驳回后,又在执行程序中以相同理由提出不予执行抗辩的,人民法院不予支持。

第二十七条　当事人在仲裁程序中未对仲裁协议的效力提出异议,在仲裁裁决作出后以仲裁协议无效为由主张撤销仲裁裁决或者提出不予执行抗辩的,人民法院不予支持。

当事人在仲裁程序中对仲裁协议的效力提出异议,在仲裁裁决作出后又以此为由主张撤销仲裁裁决或者提出不予执行抗辩,经审查符合仲裁法第五十八条或者民事诉讼法第二百一十七条、第二百六十条规定的,人民法院应予支持。

第二十八条　当事人请求不予执行仲裁调解书或者根据当事人之间的和解

协议作出的仲裁裁决书的,人民法院不予支持。

第二十九条 当事人申请执行仲裁裁决案件,由被执行人住所地或者被执行的财产所在地的中级人民法院管辖。

第三十条 根据审理撤销、执行仲裁裁决案件的实际需要,人民法院可以要求仲裁机构作出说明或者向相关仲裁机构调阅仲裁案卷。

人民法院在办理涉及仲裁的案件过程中作出的裁定,可以送相关的仲裁机构。

第三十一条 本解释自公布之日起实施。

本院以前发布的司法解释与本解释不一致的,以本解释为准。

5.《关于内地与澳门特别行政区相互认可和执行仲裁裁决的安排》

关于内地与澳门特别行政区相互认可和执行仲裁裁决的安排

根据《中华人民共和国澳门特别行政区基本法》第九十三条的规定,最高人民法院与澳门特别行政区经协商,达成《关于内地与澳门特别行政区相互认可和执行仲裁裁决的安排》(以下简称《安排》),并于2007年10月30日签署。本《安排》已于2007年9月17日由最高人民法院审判委员会第1437次会议通过,现予公布。根据双方一致意见,本《安排》自2008年1月1日起实施。

最高人民法院
二〇〇七年十二月十二日

根据《中华人民共和国澳门特别行政区基本法》第九十三条的规定,经最高人民法院与澳门特别行政区协商,现就内地与澳门特别行政区相互认可和执行仲裁裁决的有关事宜达成如下安排:

第一条 内地人民法院认可和执行澳门特别行政区仲裁机构及仲裁员按照澳门特别行政区仲裁法规在澳门作出的民商事仲裁裁决,澳门特别行政区法院认可和执行内地仲裁机构依据《中华人民共和国仲裁法》在内地作出的民商事仲裁裁决,适用本安排。

本安排没有规定的,适用认可和执行地的程序法律规定。

第二条 在内地或者澳门特别行政区作出的仲裁裁决,一方当事人不履行的,另一方当事人可以向被申请人住所地、经常居住地或者财产所在地的有关法院申请认可和执行。

内地有权受理认可和执行仲裁裁决申请的法院为中级人民法院。两个或者两个以上中级人民法院均有管辖权的,当事人应当选择向其中一个中级人民法院提出申请。

澳门特别行政区有权受理认可仲裁裁决申请的法院为中级法院,有权执行的法院为初级法院。

第三条 被申请人的住所地、经常居住地或者财产所在地分别在内地和澳门特别行政区的,申请人可以向一地法院提出认可和执行申请,也可以分别向两地法院提出申请。

当事人分别向两地法院提出申请的,两地法院都应当依法进行审查。予以认可的,采取查封、扣押或者冻结被执行人财产等执行措施。仲裁地法院应当先进行执行清偿;另一地法院在收到仲裁地法院关于经执行债权未获清偿情况的证明后,可以对申请人未获清偿的部分进行执行清偿。两地法院执行财产的总额,不得超过依据裁决和法律规定所确定的数额。

第四条 申请人向有关法院申请认可和执行仲裁裁决的,应当提交以下文件或者经公证的副本:

(一) 申请书;

(二) 申请人身份证明;

(三) 仲裁协议;

(四) 仲裁裁决书或者仲裁调解书。

上述文件没有中文文本的,申请人应当提交经正式证明的中文译本。

第五条 申请书应当包括下列内容:

(一) 申请人或者被申请人为自然人的,应当载明其姓名及住所;为法人或者其他组织的,应当载明其名称及住所,以及其法定代表人或者主要负责人的姓名、职务和住所;申请人是外国籍法人或者其他组织的,应当提交相应的公证和认证材料;

(二) 请求认可和执行的仲裁裁决书或者仲裁调解书的案号或识别资料和生效日期;

(三) 申请认可和执行仲裁裁决的理由及具体请求,以及被申请人财产所在地、财产状况及该仲裁裁决的执行情况。

第六条 申请人向有关法院申请认可和执行内地或者澳门特别行政区仲裁裁决的期限,依据认可和执行地的法律确定。

第七条 对申请认可和执行的仲裁裁决,被申请人提出证据证明有下列情形之一的,经审查核实,有关法院可以裁定不予认可:

(一) 仲裁协议一方当事人依对其适用的法律在订立仲裁协议时属于无行为能力的;或者依当事人约定的准据法,或当事人没有约定适用的准据法而依仲

裁地法律,该仲裁协议无效的;

(二)被申请人未接到选任仲裁员或者进行仲裁程序的适当通知,或者因他故未能陈述意见的;

(三)裁决所处理的争议不是提交仲裁的争议,或者不在仲裁协议范围之内;或者裁决载有超出当事人提交仲裁范围的事项的决定,但裁决中超出提交仲裁范围的事项的决定与提交仲裁事项的决定可以分开的,裁决中关于提交仲裁事项的决定部分可以予以认可;

(四)仲裁庭的组成或者仲裁程序违反了当事人的约定,或者在当事人没有约定时与仲裁地的法律不符的;

(五)裁决对当事人尚无约束力,或者业经仲裁地的法院撤销或者拒绝执行的。

有关法院认定,依执行地法律,争议事项不能以仲裁解决的,不予认可和执行该裁决。

内地法院认定在内地认可和执行该仲裁裁决违反内地法律的基本原则或者社会公共利益,澳门特别行政区法院认定在澳门特别行政区认可和执行该仲裁裁决违反澳门特别行政区法律的基本原则或者公共秩序,不予认可和执行该裁决。

第八条 申请人依据本安排申请认可和执行仲裁裁决的,应当根据执行地法律的规定,交纳诉讼费用。

第九条 一方当事人向一地法院申请执行仲裁裁决,另一方当事人向另一地法院申请撤销该仲裁裁决,被执行人申请中止执行且提供充分担保的,执行法院应当中止执行。

根据经认可的撤销仲裁裁决的判决、裁定,执行法院应当终结执行程序;撤销仲裁裁决申请被驳回的,执行法院应当恢复执行。

当事人申请中止执行的,应当向执行法院提供其他法院已经受理申请撤销仲裁裁决案件的法律文书。

第十条 受理申请的法院应当尽快审查认可和执行的请求,并作出裁定。

第十一条 法院在受理认可和执行仲裁裁决申请之前或者之后,可以依当事人的申请,按照法院地法律规定,对被申请人的财产采取保全措施。

第十二条 由一方有权限公共机构(包括公证员)作成的文书正本或者经公证的文书副本及译本,在适用本安排时,可以免除认证手续在对方使用。

第十三条 本安排实施前,当事人提出的认可和执行仲裁裁决的请求,不适用本安排。

自1999年12月20日至本安排实施前,澳门特别行政区仲裁机构及仲裁员作出的仲裁裁决,当事人向内地申请认可和执行的期限,自本安排实施之日起算。

第十四条 为执行本安排,最高人民法院和澳门特别行政区终审法院应当相互提供相关法律资料。

最高人民法院和澳门特别行政区终审法院每年相互通报执行本安排的情况。

第十五条 本安排在执行过程中遇有问题或者需要修改的,由最高人民法院和澳门特别行政区协商解决。

第十六条 本安排自 2008 年 1 月 1 日起实施。

三、仲裁规则部分

(一)国外仲裁规则:1998 年《国际商会仲裁规则》

Rules of Arbitration of the International Chamber of Commerce

In force as from 1 January 1998
Costs scales effective as of 1 July 2003

Introductory Provisions

Article 1　International Court of Arbitration

1. The International Court of Arbitration (the "Court") of the International Chamber of Commerce (the "ICC") is the arbitration body attached to the ICC. The statutes of the Court are set forth in Appendix I. Members of the Court are appointed by the World Council of the ICC. The function of the Court is to provide for the settlement by arbitration of business disputes of an international character in accordance with the Rules of Arbitration of the International Chamber of Commerce (the "Rules"). If so empowered by an arbitration agreement, the Court shall also provide for the settlement by arbitration in accordance with these Rules of business disputes not of an international character.

2. The Court does not itself settle disputes. It has the function of ensuring the application of these Rules. It draws up its own Internal Rules (Appendix II).

3. The Chairman of the Court, or, in the Chairman's absence or otherwise at his

request, one of its Vice-Chairmen shall have the power to take urgent decisions on behalf of the Court, provided that any such decision is reported to the Court at its next session.

4. As provided for in its Internal Rules, the Court may delegate to one or more committees composed of its members the power to take certain decisions, provided that any such decision is reported to the Court at its next session.

5. The Secretariat of the Court (the "Secretariat") under the direction of its Secretary General (the "Secretary General") shall have its seat at the headquarters of the ICC.

Article 2 Definitions

In these Rules:

(i) "Arbitral Tribunal" includes one or more arbitrators.

(ii) "Claimant" includes one or more claimants and "Respondent" includes one or more respondents.

(iii) "Award" includes, inter alia, an interim, partial or final Award.

Article 3 Written Notifications or Communications; Time Limits

1. All pleadings and other written communications submitted by any party, as well as all documents annexed thereto, shall be supplied in a number of copies sufficient to provide one copy for each party, plus one for each arbitrator, and one for the Secretariat. A copy of any communication from the Arbitral Tribunal to the parties shall be sent to the Secretariat.

2. All notifications or communications from the Secretariat and the Arbitral Tribunal shall be made to the last address of the party or its representative for whom the same are intended, as notified either by the party in question or by the other party. Such notification or communication may be made by delivery against receipt, registered post, courier, facsimile transmission, telex, telegram or any other means of telecommunication that provides a record of the sending thereof.

3. A notification or communication shall be deemed to have been made on the day it was received by the party itself or by its representative, or would have been received if made in accordance with the preceding paragraph.

4. Periods of time specified in or fixed under the present Rules, shall start to run on the day following the date a notification or communication is deemed to have been made in accordance with the preceding paragraph. When the day next following such date is an official holiday, or a non-business day in the country where the notification or communication is deemed to have been made, the period of time shall

commence on the first following business day. Official holidays and non-business days are included in the calculation of the period of time. If the last day of the relevant period of time granted is an official holiday or a non-business day in the country where the notification or communication is deemed to have been made, the period of time shall expire at the end of the first following business day.

Commencing the Arbitration

Article 4 Request for Arbitration

1. A party wishing to have recourse to arbitration under these Rules shall submit its Request for Arbitration (the "Request") to the Secretariat, which shall notify the Claimant and Respondent of the receipt of the Request and the date of such receipt.

2. The date on which the Request is received by the Secretariat shall, for all purposes, be deemed to be the date of the commencement of the arbitral proceedings.

3. The Request shall, inter alia, contain the following information:

(a) the name in full, description and address of each of the parties;

(b) a description of the nature and circumstances of the dispute giving rise to the claim(s);

(c) a statement of the relief sought, including, to the extent possible, an indication of any amount(s) claimed;

(d) the relevant agreements and, in particular, the arbitration agreement;

(e) all relevant particulars concerning the number of arbitrators and their choice in accordance with the provisions of Articles 8, 9 and 10, and any nomination of an arbitrator required thereby; and

(f) any comments as to the place of arbitration, the applicable rules of law and the language of the arbitration.

4. Together with the Request, the Claimant shall submit the number of copies thereof required by Article 3 (1) and shall make the advance payment on administrative expenses required by Appendix III ("Arbitration Costs and Fees") in force on the date the Request is submitted. In the event that the Claimant fails to comply with either of these requirements, the Secretariat may fix a time limit within which the Claimant must comply, failing which the file shall be closed without prejudice to the right of the Claimant to submit the same claims at a later date in another Request.

5. The Secretariat shall send a copy of the Request and the documents annexed

thereto to the Respondent for its Answer to the Request once the Secretariat has sufficient copies of the Request and the required advance payment.

6. When a party submits a Request in connection with a legal relationship in respect of which arbitration proceedings between the same parties are already pending under these Rules, the Court may, at the request of a party, decide to include the claims contained in the Request in the pending proceedings provided that the Terms of Reference have not been signed or approved by the Court. Once the Terms of Reference have been signed or approved by the Court, claims may only be included in the pending proceedings subject to the provisions of Article 19.

Article 5　Answer to the Request; Counterclaims

1. Within 30 days from the receipt of the Request from the Secretariat, the Respondent shall file an Answer (the "Answer") which shall, inter alia, contain the following information:

(a) its name in full, description and address;

(b) its comments as to the nature and circumstances of the dispute giving rise to the claim(s);

(c) its response to the relief sought;

(d) any comments concerning the number of arbitrators and their choice in light of the Claimant's proposals and in accordance with the provisions of Articles 8, 9 and 10, and any nomination of an arbitrator required thereby; and

(e) any comments as to the place of arbitration, the applicable rules of law and the language of the arbitration.

2. The Secretariat may grant the Respondent an extension of the time for filing the Answer, provided the application for such an extension contains the Respondent's comments concerning the number of arbitrators and their choice and, where required by Articles 8, 9 and 10, the nomination of an arbitrator. If the Respondent fails to do so, the Court shall proceed in accordance with these Rules.

3. The Answer shall be supplied to the Secretariat in the number of copies specified by Article 3(1).

4. A copy of the Answer and the documents annexed thereto shall be communicated by the Secretariat to the Claimant.

5. Any counterclaim(s) made by the Respondent shall be filed with its Answer and shall provide:

(a) a description of the nature and circumstances of the dispute giving rise to the counterclaim(s); and

(b) a statement of the relief sought, including, to the extent possible, an indication of any amount(s) counterclaimed.

6. The Claimant shall file a Reply to any counterclaim within 30 days from the date of receipt of the counterclaim(s) communicated by the Secretariat. The Secretariat may grant the Claimant an extension of time for filing the Reply.

Article 6　Effect of the Arbitration Agreement

1. Where the parties have agreed to submit to arbitration under the Rules, they shall be deemed to have submitted ipso facto to the Rules in effect on the date of commencement of the arbitration proceedings, unless they have agreed to submit to the Rules in effect on the date of their arbitration agreement.

2. If the Respondent does not file an Answer, as provided by Article 5, or if any party raises one or more pleas concerning the existence, validity or scope of the arbitration agreement, the Court may decide, without prejudice to the admissibility or merits of the plea or pleas, that the arbitration shall proceed if it is prima facie satisfied that an arbitration agreement under the Rules may exist. In such a case, any decision as to the jurisdiction of the Arbitral Tribunal shall be taken by the Arbitral Tribunal itself. If the Court is not so satisfied, the parties shall be notified that the arbitration cannot proceed. In such a case, any party retains the right to ask any court having jurisdiction whether or not there is a binding arbitration agreement.

3. If any of the parties refuses or fails to take part in the arbitration or any stage thereof, the arbitration shall proceed notwithstanding such refusal or failure.

4. Unless otherwise agreed, the Arbitral Tribunal shall not cease to have jurisdiction by reason of any claim that the contract is null and void or allegation that it is non-existent, provided that the Arbitral Tribunal upholds the validity of the arbitration agreement. The Arbitral Tribunal shall continue to have jurisdiction to determine the respective rights of the parties and to adjudicate their claims and pleas even though the contract itself may be non-existent or null and void.

The Arbitral Tribunal

Article 7　General Provisions

1. Every arbitrator must be and remain independent of the parties involved in the arbitration.

2. Before appointment or confirmation, a prospective arbitrator shall sign a statement of independence and disclose in writing to the Secretariat any facts or

circumstances which might be of such a nature as to call into question the arbitrator's independence in the eyes of the parties. The Secretariat shall provide such information to the parties in writing and fix a time limit for any comments from them.

3. An arbitrator shall immediately disclose in writing to the Secretariat and to the parties any facts or circumstances of a similar nature which may arise during the arbitration.

4. The decisions of the Court as to the appointment, confirmation, challenge or replacement of an arbitrator shall be final and the reasons for such decisions shall not be communicated.

5. By accepting to serve, every arbitrator undertakes to carry out his responsibilities in accordance with these Rules.

6. Insofar as the parties have not provided otherwise, the Arbitral Tribunal shall be constituted in accordance with the provisions of Articles 8, 9 and 10.

Article 8　Number of Arbitrators

1. The disputes shall be decided by a sole arbitrator or by three arbitrators.

2. Where the parties have not agreed upon the number of arbitrators, the Court shall appoint a sole arbitrator, save where it appears to the Court that the dispute is such as to warrant the appointment of three arbitrators. In such case, the Claimant shall nominate an arbitrator within a period of 15 days from the receipt of the notification of the decision of the Court, and the Respondent shall nominate an arbitrator within a period of 15 days from the receipt of the notification of the nomination made by the Claimant.

3. Where the parties have agreed that the dispute shall be settled by a sole arbitrator, they may, by agreement, nominate the sole arbitrator for confirmation. If the parties fail to nominate a sole arbitrator within 30 days from the date when the Claimant's Request for Arbitration has been received by the other party, or within such additional time as may be allowed by the Secretariat, the sole arbitrator shall be appointed by the Court.

4. Where the dispute is to be referred to three arbitrators, each party shall nominate in the Request and the Answer, respectively, one arbitrator for confirmation. If a party fails to nominate an arbitrator, the appointment shall be made by the Court. The third arbitrator, who will act as chairman of the Arbitral Tribunal, shall be appointed by the Court, unless the parties have agreed upon another procedure for such appointment, in which case the nomination will be subject to confirmation pursuant to Article 9. Should such procedure not result in a nomination

within the time limit fixed by the parties or the Court, the third arbitrator shall be appointed by the Court.

Article 9　Appointment and Confirmation of the Arbitrators

1. In confirming or appointing arbitrators, the Court shall consider the prospective arbitrator's nationality, residence and other relationships with the countries of which the parties or the other arbitrators are nationals and the prospective arbitrator's availability and ability to conduct the arbitration in accordance with these Rules. The same shall apply where the Secretary General confirms arbitrators pursuant to Article 9(2).

2. The Secretary General may confirm as co-arbitrators, sole arbitrators and chairmen of Arbitral Tribunals persons nominated by the parties or pursuant to their particular agreements, provided they have filed a statement of independence without qualification or a qualified statement of independence has not given rise to objections. Such confirmation shall be reported to the Court at its next session. If the Secretary General considers that a co-arbitrator, sole arbitrator or chairman of an Arbitral Tribunal should not be confirmed, the matter shall be submitted to the Court.

3. Where the Court is to appoint a sole arbitrator or the chairman of an Arbitral Tribunal, it shall make the appointment upon a proposal of a National Committee of the ICC that it considers to be appropriate. If the Court does not accept the proposal made, or if the National Committee fails to make the proposal requested within the time limit fixed by the Court, the Court may repeat its request or may request a proposal from another National Committee that it considers to be appropriate.

4. Where the Court considers that the circumstances so demand, it may choose the sole arbitrator or the chairman of the Arbitral Tribunal from a country where there is no National Committee, provided that neither of the parties objects within the time limit fixed by the Court.

5. The sole arbitrator or the chairman of the Arbitral Tribunal shall be of a nationality other than those of the parties. However, in suitable circumstances and provided that neither of the parties objects within the time limit fixed by the Court, the sole arbitrator or the chairman of the Arbitral Tribunal may be chosen from a country of which any of the parties is a national.

6. Where the Court is to appoint an arbitrator on behalf of a party which has failed to nominate one, it shall make the appointment upon a proposal of the National Committee of the country of which that party is a national. If the Court does not accept the proposal made, or if the National Committee fails to make the proposal

requested within the time limit fixed by the Court, or if the country of which the said party is a national has no National Committee, the Court shall be at liberty to choose any person whom it regards as suitable. The Secretariat shall inform the National Committee, if one exists, of the country of which such person is a national.

Article 10 Multiple Parties

1. Where there are multiple parties, whether as Claimant or as Respondent, and where the dispute is to be referred to three arbitrators, the multiple Claimants, jointly, and the multiple Respondents, jointly, shall nominate an arbitrator for confirmation pursuant to Article 9.

2. In the absence of such a joint nomination and where all parties are unable to agree to a method for the constitution of the Arbitral Tribunal, the Court may appoint each member of the Arbitral Tribunal and shall designate one of them to act as chairman. In such case, the Court shall be at liberty to choose any person it regards as suitable to act as arbitrator, applying Article 9 when it considers this appropriate.

Article 11 Challenge of Arbitrators

1. A challenge of an arbitrator, whether for an alleged lack of independence or otherwise, shall be made by the submission to the Secretariat of a written statement specifying the facts and circumstances on which the challenge is based.

2. For a challenge to be admissible, it must be sent by a party either within 30 days from receipt by that party of the notification of the appointment or confirmation of the arbitrator, or within 30 days from the date when the party making the challenge was informed of the facts and circumstances on which the challenge is based if such date is subsequent to the receipt of such notification.

3. The Court shall decide on the admissibility, and, at the same time, if necessary, on the merits of a challenge after the Secretariat has afforded an opportunity for the arbitrator concerned, the other party or parties and any other members of the Arbitral Tribunal to comment in writing within a suitable period of time. Such comments shall be communicated to the parties and to the arbitrators.

Article 12 Replacement of Arbitrators

1. An arbitrator shall be replaced upon his death, upon the acceptance by the Court of the arbitrator's resignation, upon acceptance by the Court of a challenge or, upon the request of all the parties.

2. An arbitrator shall also be replaced on the Court's own initiative when it decides that he is prevented de jure or de facto from fulfilling his functions, or that he is not fulfilling his functions in accordance with the Rules or within the prescribed

time limits.

3. When, on the basis of information that has come to its attention, the Court considers applying Article 12(2), it shall decide on the matter after the arbitrator concerned, the parties and any other members of the Arbitral Tribunal have had an opportunity to comment in writing within a suitable period of time. Such comments shall be communicated to the parties and to the arbitrators.

4. When an arbitrator is to be replaced, the Court has discretion to decide whether or not to follow the original nominating process. Once reconstituted, and after having invited the parties to comment, the Arbitral Tribunal shall determine if and to what extent prior proceedings shall be repeated before the reconstituted Arbitral Tribunal.

5. Subsequent to the closing of the proceedings, instead of replacing an arbitrator who has died or been removed by the Court pursuant to Articles 12(1) and 12(2), the Court may decide, when it considers it appropriate, that the remaining arbitrators shall continue the arbitration. In making such determination, the Court shall take into account the views of the remaining arbitrators and of the parties and such other matters that it considers appropriate in the circumstances.

The Arbitral Proceedings

Article 13 Transmission of the File to the Arbitral Tribunal

The Secretariat shall transmit the file to the Arbitral Tribunal as soon as it has been constituted, provided the advance on costs requested by the Secretariat at this stage has been paid.

Article 14 Place of the Arbitration

1. The place of the arbitration shall be fixed by the Court unless agreed upon by the parties.

2. The Arbitral Tribunal may, after consultation with the parties, conduct hearings and meetings at any location it considers appropriate unless otherwise agreed by the parties.

3. The Arbitral Tribunal may deliberate at any location it considers appropriate.

Article 15 Rules Governing the Proceedings

1. The proceedings before the Arbitral Tribunal shall be governed by these Rules, and, where these Rules are silent by any rules which the parties or, failing them, the Arbitral Tribunal may settle on, whether or not reference is thereby made

to the rules of procedure of a national law to be applied to the arbitration.

2. In all cases, the Arbitral Tribunal shall act fairly and impartially and ensure that each party has a reasonable opportunity to present its case.

Article 16 Language of the Arbitration

In the absence of an agreement by the parties, the Arbitral Tribunal shall determine the language or languages of the arbitration, due regard being given to all relevant circumstances, including the language of the contract.

Article 17 Applicable Rules of Law

1. The parties shall be free to agree upon the rules of law to be applied by the Arbitral Tribunal to the merits of the dispute. In the absence of any such agreement, the Arbitral Tribunal shall apply the rules of law which it determines to be appropriate.

2. In all cases the Arbitral Tribunal shall take account of the provisions of the contract and the relevant trade usages.

3. The Arbitral Tribunal shall assume the powers of an amiable compositeur or decide ex aequo et bono only if the parties have agreed to give it such powers.

Article 18 Terms of Reference; Procedural Timetable

1. As soon as it has received the file from the Secretariat, the Arbitral Tribunal shall draw up, on the basis of documents or in the presence of the parties and in the light of their most recent submissions, a document defining its Terms of Reference. This document shall include the following particulars:

(a) the full names and descriptions of the parties;

(b) the addresses of the parties to which notifications and communications arising in the course of the arbitration may be made;

(c) a summary of the parties' respective claims and of the relief sought by each party, with an indication to the extent possible of the amounts claimed or counterclaimed;

(d) unless the Arbitral Tribunal considers it inappropriate, a list of issues to be determined;

(e) the full names, descriptions and addresses of the arbitrators;

(f) the place of the arbitration; and

(g) particulars of the applicable procedural rules and, if such is the case, reference to the power conferred upon the Arbitral Tribunal to act as amiable compositeur or to decide ex aequo et bono.

2. The Terms of Reference shall be signed by the parties and the Arbitral

Tribunal. Within two months of the date on which the file has been transmitted to it, the Arbitral Tribunal shall transmit to the Court the Terms of Reference signed by it and by the parties. The Court may extend this time limit pursuant to a reasoned request from the Arbitral Tribunal or on its own initiative if it decides it is necessary to do so.

3. If any of the parties refuses to take part in the drawing up of the Terms of Reference or to sign the same, they shall be submitted to the Court for approval. When the Terms of Reference have been signed in accordance with Article 18(2) or approved by the Court, the arbitration shall proceed.

4. When drawing up the Terms of Reference, or as soon as possible thereafter, the Arbitral Tribunal, after having consulted the parties, shall establish in a separate document a provisional timetable that it intends to follow for the conduct of the arbitration and shall communicate it to the Court and the parties. Any subsequent modifications of the provisional timetable shall be communicated to the Court and the parties.

Article 19 New Claims

After the Terms of Reference have been signed or approved by the Court, no party shall make new claims or counterclaims which fall outside the limits of the Terms of Reference unless it has been authorized to do so by the Arbitral Tribunal, which shall consider the nature of such new claims or counterclaims, the stage of the arbitration and other relevant circumstances.

Article 20 Establishing the Facts of the Case

1. The Arbitral Tribunal shall proceed within as short a time as possible to establish the facts of the case by all appropriate means.

2. After studying the written submissions of the parties and all documents relied upon, the Arbitral Tribunal shall hear the parties together in person if any of them so requests or, failing such a request, it may of its own motion decide to hear them.

3. The Arbitral Tribunal may decide to hear witnesses, experts appointed by the parties or any other person, in the presence of the parties, or in their absence provided they have been duly summoned.

4. The Arbitral Tribunal, after having consulted the parties, may appoint one or more experts, define their terms of reference and receive their reports. At the request of a party, the parties shall be given the opportunity to question at a hearing any such expert appointed by the Tribunal.

5. At any time during the proceedings, the Arbitral Tribunal may summon any

party to provide additional evidence.

6. The Arbitral Tribunal may decide the case solely on the documents submitted by the parties unless any of the parties requests a hearing.

7. The Arbitral Tribunal may take measures for protecting trade secrets and confidential information.

Article 21　Hearings

1. When a hearing is to be held, the Arbitral Tribunal, giving reasonable notice, shall summon the parties to appear before it on the day and at the place fixed by it.

2. If any of the parties, although duly summoned, fails to appear without valid excuse, the Arbitral Tribunal shall have the power to proceed with the hearing.

3. The Arbitral Tribunal shall be in full charge of the hearings, at which all the parties shall be entitled to be present. Save with the approval of the Arbitral Tribunal and the parties, persons not involved in the proceedings shall not be admitted.

4. The parties may appear in person or through duly authorized representatives. In addition, they may be assisted by advisers.

Article 22　Closing of the Proceedings

1. When it is satisfied that the parties have had a reasonable opportunity to present their cases, the Arbitral Tribunal shall declare the proceedings closed. Thereafter, no further submission or argument may be made, or evidence produced, unless requested or authorized by the Arbitral Tribunal.

2. When the Arbitral Tribunal has declared the proceedings closed, it shall indicate to the Secretariat an approximate date by which the draft Award will be submitted to the Court for approval pursuant to Article 27. Any postponement of that date shall be communicated to the Secretariat by the Arbitral Tribunal.

Article 23　Conservatory and Interim Measures

1. Unless the parties have otherwise agreed, as soon as the file has been transmitted to it, the Arbitral Tribunal may, at the request of a party, order any interim or conservatory measure it deems appropriate. The Arbitral Tribunal may make the granting of any such measure subject to appropriate security being furnished by the requesting party. Any such measure shall take the form of an order, giving reasons, or of an Award, as the Arbitral Tribunal considers appropriate.

2. Before the file is transmitted to the Arbitral Tribunal, and in appropriate circumstances even thereafter, the parties may apply to any competent judicial authority for interim or conservatory measures. The application of a party to a judicial

authority for such measures or for the implementation of any such measures ordered by an Arbitral Tribunal shall not be deemed to be an infringement or a waiver of the arbitration agreement and shall not affect the relevant powers reserved to the Arbitral Tribunal. Any such application and any measures taken by the judicial authority must be notified without delay to the Secretariat. The Secretariat shall inform the Arbitral Tribunal thereof.

Awards

Article 24 Time Limit for the Award

1. The time limit within which the Arbitral Tribunal must render its final Award is six months. Such time limit shall start to run from the date of the last signature by the Arbitral Tribunal or of the parties of the Terms of Reference, or, in the case of application of Article 18(3), the date of the notification to the Arbitral Tribunal by the Secretariat of the approval of the Terms of Reference by the Court.

2. The Court may extend this time limit pursuant to a reasoned request from the Arbitral Tribunal or on its own initiative if it decides it is necessary to do so.

Article 25 Making of the Award

1. When the Arbitral Tribunal is composed of more than one arbitrator, an Award is given by a majority decision. If there be no majority, the Award shall be made by the chairman of the Arbitral Tribunal alone.

2. The Award shall state the reasons upon which it is based.

3. The Award shall be deemed to be made at the place of the arbitration and on the date stated therein.

Article 26 Award by Consent

If the parties reach a settlement after the file has been transmitted to the Arbitral Tribunal in accordance with Article 13, the settlement shall be recorded in the form of an Award made by consent of the parties if so requested by the parties and if the Arbitral Tribunal agrees to do so.

Article 27 Scrutiny of the Award by the Court

Before signing any Award, the Arbitral Tribunal shall submit it in draft form to the Court. The Court may lay down modifications as to the form of the Award and, without affecting the Arbitral Tribunal's liberty of decision, may also draw its attention to points of substance. No Award shall be rendered by the Arbitral Tribunal until it has been approved by the Court as to its form.

Article 28 Notification, Deposit and Enforceability of the Award

1. Once an Award has been made, the Secretariat shall notify to the parties the text signed by the Arbitral Tribunal, provided always that the costs of the arbitration have been fully paid to the ICC by the parties or by one of them.

2. Additional copies certified true by the Secretary General shall be made available on request and at any time to the parties, but to no one else.

3. By virtue of the notification made in accordance with Paragraph 1 of this Article, the parties waive any other form of notification or deposit on the part of the Arbitral Tribunal.

4. An original of each Award made in accordance with the present Rules shall be deposited with the Secretariat.

5. The Arbitral Tribunal and the Secretariat shall assist the parties in complying with whatever further formalities may be necessary.

6. Every Award shall be binding on the parties. By submitting the dispute to arbitration under these Rules, the parties undertake to carry out any Award without delay and shall be deemed to have waived their right to any form of recourse insofar as such waiver can validly be made.

Article 29 Correction and Interpretation of the Award

1. On its own initiative, the Arbitral Tribunal may correct a clerical, computational or typographical error, or any errors of similar nature contained in an Award, provided such correction is submitted for approval to the Court within 30 days of the date of such Award.

2. Any application of a party for the correction of an error of the kind referred to in Article 29(1), or for the interpretation of an Award, must be made to the Secretariat within 30 days of the receipt of the Award by such party, in a number of copies as stated in Article 3(1). After transmittal of the application to the Arbitral Tribunal, it shall grant the other party a short time limit, normally not exceeding 30 days, from the receipt of the application by that party to submit any comments thereon. If the Arbitral Tribunal decides to correct or interpret the Award, it shall submit its decision in draft form to the Court not later than 30 days following the expiration of the time limit for the receipt of any comments from the other party or within such other period as the Court may decide.

3. The decision to correct or to interpret the Award shall take the form of an addendum and shall constitute part of the Award. The provisions of Articles 25, 27 and 28 shall apply mutatis mutandis.

Costs

Article 30 Advance to Cover the Costs of the Arbitration

1. After receipt of the Request, the Secretary General may request the Claimant to pay a provisional advance in an amount intended to cover the costs of arbitration until the Terms of Reference have been drawn up.

2. As soon as practicable, the Court shall fix the advance on costs in an amount likely to cover the fees and expenses of the arbitrators and the ICC administrative costs for the claims and counterclaims which have been referred to it by the parties. This amount may be subject to readjustment at any time during the arbitration. Where, apart from the claims, counterclaims are submitted, the Court may fix separate advances on costs for the claims and the counterclaims.

3. The advance on costs fixed by the Court shall be payable in equal shares by the Claimant and the Respondent. Any provisional advance paid on the basis of Article 30(1) will be considered as a partial payment thereof. However, any party shall be free to pay the whole of the advance on costs in respect of the principal claim or the counterclaim should the other party fail to pay its share. When the Court has set separate advances on costs in accordance with Article 30(2), each of the parties shall pay the advance on costs corresponding to its claims.

4. When a request for an advance on costs has not been complied with, and after consultation with the Arbitral Tribunal, the Secretary General may direct the Arbitral Tribunal to suspend its work and set a time limit, which must be not less than 15 days, on the expiry of which the relevant claims, or counterclaims, shall be considered as withdrawn. Should the party in question wish to object to this measure, it must make a request within the aforementioned period for the matter to be decided by the Court. Such party shall not be prevented, on the ground of such withdrawal, from reintroducing the same claims or counterclaims at a later date in another proceeding.

5. If one of the parties claims a right to a set-off with regard to either claims or counterclaims, such set-off shall be taken into account in determining the advance to cover the costs of arbitration in the same way as a separate claim insofar as it may require the Arbitral Tribunal to consider additional matters.

Article 31 Decision as to the Costs of the Arbitration

1. The costs of the arbitration shall include the fees and expenses of the arbitrators and the ICC administrative expenses fixed by the Court, in accordance

with the scale in force at the time of the commencement of the arbitral proceedings, as well as the fees and expenses of any experts appointed by the Arbitral Tribunal and the reasonable legal and other costs incurred by the parties for the arbitration.

2. The Court may fix the fees of the arbitrators at a figure higher or lower than that which would result from the application of the relevant scale should this be deemed necessary due to the exceptional circumstances of the case. Decisions on costs other than those fixed by the Court may be taken by the Arbitral Tribunal at any time during the proceedings.

3. The final Award shall fix the costs of the arbitration and decide which of the parties shall bear them or in what proportion they shall be borne by the parties.

Miscellaneous

Article 32 Modified Time Limits

1. The parties may agree to shorten the various time limits set out in these Rules. Any such agreement entered into subsequent to the constitution of an Arbitral Tribunal shall become effective only upon the approval of the Arbitral Tribunal.

2. The Court, on its own initiative, may extend any time limit which has been modified pursuant to Article 32(1) if it decides that it is necessary to do so in order that the Arbitral Tribunal or the Court may fulfil their responsibilities in accordance with these Rules.

Article 33 Waiver

A party which proceeds with the arbitration without raising its objection to a failure to comply with any provision of these Rules, or of any other rules applicable to the proceedings, any direction given by the Arbitral Tribunal, or any requirement under the arbitration agreement relating to the constitution of the Arbitral Tribunal, or to the conduct of the proceedings, shall be deemed to have waived its right to object.

Article 34 Exclusion of Liability

Neither the arbitrators, nor the Court and its members, nor the ICC and its employees, nor the ICC National Committees shall be liable to any person for any act or omission in connection with the arbitration.

Article 35 General Rule

In all matters not expressly provided for in these Rules, the Court and the Arbitral Tribunal shall act in the spirit of these Rules and shall make every effort to make sure that the Award is enforceable at law.

Appendix I Statutes of the International Court of Arbitration of the ICC

Article 1 Function

1. The function of the International Court of Arbitration of the International Chamber of Commerce (the "Court") is to ensure the application of the Rules of Arbitration of the International Chamber of Commerce, and it has all the necessary powers for that purpose.

2. As an autonomous body, it carries out these functions in complete independence from the ICC and its organs.

3. Its members are independent from the ICC National Committees.

Article 2 Composition of the Court

The Court shall consist of a Chairman, Vice-Chairmen, and members and alternate members (collectively designated as members). In its work it is assisted by its Secretariat (Secretariat of the Court).

Article 3 Appointment

1. The Chairman is elected by the ICC World Council upon the recommendation of the Executive Board of the ICC.

2. The ICC World Council appoints the Vice-Chairmen of the Court from among the members of the Court or otherwise.

3. Its members are appointed by the ICC World Council on the proposal of National Committees, one member for each Committee.

4. On the proposal of the Chairman of the Court, the World Council may appoint alternate members.

5. The term of office of all members is three years. If a member is no longer in a position to exercise his functions, his successor is appointed by the World Council for the remainder of the term.

Article 4 Plenary Session of the Court

The Plenary Sessions of the Court are presided over by the Chairman or, in his absence, by one of the Vice-Chairmen designated by him. The deliberations shall be valid when at least six members are present. Decisions are taken by a majority vote, the Chairman having a casting vote in the event of a tie.

Article 5 Committees

The Court may set up one or more Committees and establish the functions and organization of such Committees.

Article 6 Confidentiality

The work of the Court is of a confidential nature which must be respected by everyone who participates in that work in whatever capacity. The Court lays down the rules regarding the persons who can attend the meetings of the Court and its Committees and who are entitled to have access to the materials submitted to the Court and its Secretariat.

Article 7 Modification of the Rules of Arbitration

Any proposal of the Court for a modification of the Rules is laid before the Commission on Arbitration before submission to the Executive Board and the World Council of the ICC for approval.

Appendix II Internal Rules of the International Court of Arbitration of the ICC

Article 1 Confidential Character of the Work of the International Court of Arbitration

1. The sessions of the Court, whether plenary or those of a Committee of the Court, are open only to its members and to the Secretariat.

2. However, in exceptional circumstances, the Chairman of the Court may invite other persons to attend. Such persons must respect the confidential nature of the work of the Court.

3. The documents submitted to the Court, or drawn up by it in the course of its proceedings, are communicated only to the members of the Court and to the Secretariat and to persons authorized by the Chairman to attend Court sessions.

4. The Chairman or the Secretary General of the Court may authorize researchers undertaking work of a scientific nature on international trade law to acquaint themselves with awards and other documents of general interest, with the exception of memoranda, notes, statements and documents remitted by the parties within the framework of arbitration proceedings.

5. Such authorization shall not be given unless the beneficiary has undertaken to respect the confidential character of the documents made available and to refrain from any publication in their respect without having previously submitted the text for approval to the Secretary General of the Court.

6. The Secretariat will in each case submitted to arbitration under the Rules retain in the archives of the Court all Awards, Terms of Reference, and decisions of

the Court, as well as copies of the pertinent correspondence of the Secretariat.

7. Any documents, communications or correspondence submitted by the parties or the arbitrators may be destroyed unless a party or an arbitrator requests in writing within a period fixed by the Secretariat the return of such documents. All related costs and expenses for the return of those documents shall be paid by such party or arbitrator.

Article 2 Participation of Members of the International Court of Arbitration in ICC Arbitration

1. The Chairman and the members of the Secretariat of the Court may not act as arbitrators or as counsel in cases submitted to ICC arbitration.

2. The Court shall not appoint Vice-Chairmen or members of the Court as arbitrators. They may, however, be proposed for such duties by one or more of the parties, or, pursuant to any other procedure agreed upon by the parties, subject to confirmation.

3. When the Chairman, a Vice-Chairman or a member of the Court or of the Secretariat is involved in any capacity whatsoever in proceedings pending before the Court, such person must inform the Secretary General of the Court upon becoming aware of such involvement.

4. Such person must refrain from participating in the discussions or in the decisions of the Court concerning the proceedings and must be absent from the courtroom whenever the matter is considered.

5. Such person will not receive any material documentation or information pertaining to such proceedings.

Article 3 Relations between the Members of the Court and the ICC National Committees

1. By virtue of their capacity, the members of the Court are independent of the ICC National Committees which proposed them for appointment by the ICC World Council.

2. Furthermore, they must regard as confidential, vis-à-vis the said National Committees, any information concerning individual cases with which they have become acquainted in their capacity as members of the Court, except when they have been requested by the Chairman of the Court or by its Secretary General to communicate specific information to their respective National Committee.

Article 4 Committee of the Court

1. In accordance with the provisions of Article 1 (4) of the Rules and Article 5

of its Statutes (Appendix I), the Court hereby establishes a Committee of the Court.

2. The members of the Committee consist of a Chairman and at least two other members. The Chairman of the Court acts as the Chairman of the Committee. If absent, the Chairman may designate a Vice-Chairman of the Court or, in exceptional circumstances, another member of the Court as Chairman of the Committee.

3. The other two members of the Committee are appointed by the Court from among the Vice-Chairmen or the other members of the Court. At each Plenary Session the Court appoints the members who are to attend the meetings of the Committee to be held before the next Plenary Session.

4. The Committee meets when convened by its Chairman. Two members constitute a quorum.

5. (a) The Court shall determine the decisions that may be taken by the Committee.

(b) The decisions of the Committee are taken unanimously.

(c) When the Committee cannot reach a decision or deems it preferable to abstain, it transfers the case to the next Plenary Session, making any suggestions it deems appropriate.

(d) The Committee's decisions are brought to the notice of the Court at its next Plenary Session.

Article 5 Court Secretariat

1. In case of absence, the Secretary General may delegate to the General Counsel and Deputy Secretary General the authority to confirm arbitrators, to certify true copies of Awards and to request the payment of a provisional advance, respectively provided for in Articles 9(2), 28(2) and 30(1) of the Rules.

2. The Secretariat may, with the approval of the Court, issue notes and other documents for the information of the parties and the arbitrators, or as necessary for the proper conduct of the arbitral proceedings.

Article 6 Scrutiny of Arbitral Awards

When the Court scrutinizes draft Awards in accordance with Article 27 of the Rules, it considers, to the extent practicable, the requirements of mandatory law at the place of arbitration.

Appendix III Arbitration Costs and Fees

Article 1 Advance on Costs

1. Each request to commence an arbitration pursuant to the Rules must be accompanied by an advance payment of US $2500 on the administrative expenses. Such payment is nonrefundable, and shall be credited to the Claimant's portion of the advance on costs.

2. The provisional advance fixed by the Secretary General according to Article 30(1) of the Rules shall normally not exceed the amount obtained by adding together the administrative expenses, the minimum of the fees (as set out in the scale hereinafter) based upon the amount of the claim and the expected reimbursable expenses of the Arbitral Tribunal incurred with respect to the drafting of the Terms of Reference. If such amount is not quantified, the provisional advance shall be fixed at the discretion of the Secretary General. Payment by the Claimant shall be credited to its share of the advance on costs fixed by the Court.

3. In general, after the Terms of Reference have been signed or approved by the Court and the provisional timetable has been established, the Arbitral Tribunal shall, in accordance with Article 30(4) of the Rules, proceed only with respect to those claims or counterclaims in regard to which the whole of the advance on costs has been paid.

4. The advance on costs fixed by the Court according to Article 30(2) of the Rules comprises the fees of the arbitrator or arbitrators (hereinafter referred to as "arbitrator"), any arbitration-related expenses of the arbitrator and the administrative expenses.

5. Each party shall pay in cash its share of the total advance on costs. However, if its share exceeds an amount fixed from time to time by the Court, a party may post a bank guarantee for this additional amount.

6. A party that has already paid in full its share of the advance on costs fixed by the Court may, in accordance with Article 30(3) of the Rules, pay the unpaid portion of the advance owed by the defaulting party by posting a bank guarantee.

7. When the Court has fixed separate advances on costs pursuant to Article 30(2) of the Rules, the Secretariat shall invite each party to pay the amount of the advance corresponding to its respective claim(s).

8. When, as a result of the fixing of separate advances on costs, the separate advance fixed for the claim of either party exceeds one half of such global advance as

was previously fixed (in respect of the same claims and counterclaims that are the subject of separate advances), a bank guarantee may be posted to cover any such excess amount. In the event that the amount of the separate advance is subsequently increased, at least one half of the increase shall be paid in cash.

9. The Secretariat shall establish the terms governing all bank guarantees which the parties may post pursuant to the above provisions.

10. As provided in Article 30(2) of the Rules, the advance on costs may be subject to readjustment at any time during the arbitration, in particular to take into account fluctuations in the amount in dispute, changes in the amount of the estimated expenses of the arbitrator, or the evolving difficulty or complexity of arbitration proceedings.

11. Before any expertise ordered by the Arbitral Tribunal can be commenced, the parties, or one of them, shall pay an advance on costs fixed by the Arbitral Tribunal sufficient to cover the expected fees and expenses of the expert as determined by the Arbitral Tribunal. The Arbitral Tribunal shall be responsible for ensuring the payment by the parties of such fees and expenses.

Article 2 Costs and Fees

1. Subject to Article 31(2) of the Rules, the Court shall fix the fees of the arbitrator in accordance with the scale hereinafter set out or, where the sum in dispute is not stated, at its discretion.

2. In setting the arbitrator's fees, the Court shall take into consideration the diligence of the arbitrator, the time spent, the rapidity of the proceedings, and the complexity of the dispute so as to arrive at a figure within the limits specified or, in exceptional circumstances (Article 31(2) of the Rules), at a figure higher or lower than those limits.

3. When a case is submitted to more than one arbitrator, the Court, at its discretion, shall have the right to increase the total fees up to a maximum which shall normally not exceed three times the fees of one arbitrator.

4. The arbitrator's fees and expenses shall be fixed exclusively by the Court as required by the Rules. Separate fee arrangements between the parties and the arbitrator are contrary to the Rules.

5. The Court shall fix the administrative expenses of each arbitration in accordance with the scale hereinafter set out or, where the sum in dispute is not stated, at its discretion. In exceptional circumstances, the Court may fix the administrative expenses at a lower or higher figure than that which would result from

the application of such scale, provided that such expenses shall normally not exceed the maximum amount of the scale. Further, the Court may require the payment of administrative expenses in addition to those provided in the scale of administrative expenses as a condition to holding an arbitration in abeyance at the request of the parties or of one of them with the acquiescence of the other.

6. If an arbitration terminates before the rendering of a final Award, the Court shall fix the costs of the arbitration at its discretion, taking into account the stage attained by the arbitral proceedings and any other relevant circumstances.

7. In the case of an application under Article 29(2) of the Rules, the Court may fix an advance to cover additional fees and expenses of the Arbitral Tribunal and may make the transmission of such application to the Arbitral Tribunal subject to the prior cash payment in full to the ICC of such advance. The Court shall fix at its discretion any possible fees of the arbitrator when approving the decision of the Arbitral Tribunal.

8. When an arbitration is preceded by an attempt at amicable resolution pursuant to the ICC ADR Rules, one half of the administrative expenses paid for such ADR proceedings shall be credited to the administrative expenses of the arbitration.

9. Amounts paid to the arbitrator do not include any possible value added taxes (VAT) or other taxes or charges and imposts applicable to the arbitrator's fees. Parties have a duty to pay any such taxes or charges; however, the recovery of any such charges or taxes is a matter solely between the arbitrator and the parties.

Article 3 Appointments of Arbitrators

1. A registration fee normally not exceeding US $2500 is payable by the requesting party in respect of each request made to the ICC to appoint an arbitrator for any arbitration not conducted under the Rules. No request for appointment of an arbitrator will be considered unless accompanied by the said fee, which is not recoverable and becomes the property of the ICC.

2. The said fee shall cover any additional services rendered by the ICC regarding the appointment, such as decisions on a challenge of an arbitrator and the appointment of a substitute arbitrator.

Article 4 Scales of Administrative Expenses and Arbitrator's Fees

1. The Scales of Administrative Expenses and Arbitrator's Fees set forth below shall be effective as of 1 July 2003 in respect of all arbitrations commenced on or after such date, irrespective of the version of the Rules applying to such arbitrations.

2. To calculate the administrative expenses and the arbitrator's fees, the

amounts calculated for each successive slice of the sum in dispute must be added together, except that where the sum in dispute is over US $80 million, a flat amount of US $88,800 shall constitute the entirety of the administrative expenses.

（二）国内仲裁规则：2005年《中国国际经济贸易仲裁委员会仲裁规则》

中国国际经济贸易仲裁委员会仲裁规则

（中国国际贸易促进委员会/中国国际商会2005年1月11日修订并通过，2005年5月1日起施行）

第一章 总 则

第一条 规则的制定

根据《中华人民共和国仲裁法》和有关法律的规定以及原中央人民政府政务院的《决定》和国务院的《通知》及《批复》，制定本规则。

第二条 名称和组织

（一）中国国际经济贸易仲裁委员会，原名中国国际贸易促进委员会对外贸易仲裁委员会，后名中国国际贸易促进委员会对外经济贸易仲裁委员会，现名中国国际经济贸易仲裁委员会（以下简称仲裁委员会），以仲裁的方式，独立、公正地解决契约性或非契约性的经济贸易等争议。

（二）仲裁委员会同时使用"中国国际商会仲裁院"名称。

（三）仲裁协议或合同中的仲裁条款订明由中国国际经济贸易仲裁委员会或其分会仲裁或使用其旧名称为仲裁机构的，均应视为双方当事人一致同意由仲裁委员会或其分会仲裁。

（四）当事人在仲裁协议或合同中的仲裁条款订明由中国国际贸易促进委员会/中国国际商会仲裁或由中国国际贸易促进委员会/中国国际商会的仲裁委员会或仲裁院仲裁的，均应视为双方当事人一致同意由中国国际经济贸易仲裁委员会仲裁。

（五）仲裁委员会主任履行本规则赋予的职责，副主任根据主任的授权可以履行主任的职责。

（六）仲裁委员会设秘书局，在仲裁委员会秘书长的领导下负责处理仲裁委员会的日常事务。

（七）仲裁委员会设在北京。仲裁委员会在深圳设有仲裁委员会华南分会（原名仲裁委员会深圳分会），在上海设有仲裁委员会上海分会。仲裁委员会分会是仲裁委员会的组成部分。仲裁委员会分会设秘书处，在仲裁委员会分会秘书长的领导下负责处理仲裁委员会分会的日常事务。

（八）双方当事人可以约定将其争议提交仲裁委员会在北京进行仲裁，或者约定将其争议提交仲裁委员会华南分会在深圳进行仲裁，或者约定将其争议提交仲裁委员会上海分会在上海进行仲裁；如无此约定，则由申请人选择，由仲裁委员会在北京进行仲裁，或者由其华南分会在深圳进行仲裁，或者由其上海分会在上海进行仲裁；作此选择时，以首先提出选择的为准；如有争议，应由仲裁委员会作出决定。

（九）仲裁委员会可以视需要和可能，组织设立特定行业仲裁中心，制定行业仲裁规则。

（十）仲裁委员会设立仲裁员名册，并可以视需要和可能设立行业仲裁员名册。

第三条　管辖范围

仲裁委员会受理下列争议案件：

（一）国际的或涉外的争议案件；

（二）涉及香港特别行政区、澳门特别行政区或台湾地区的争议案件；

（三）国内争议案件。

第四条　规则的适用

（一）本规则统一适用于仲裁委员会及其分会。在分会进行仲裁时，本规则规定由仲裁委员会主任和仲裁委员会秘书局或秘书长分别履行的职责，可以由仲裁委员会主任授权的副主任和仲裁委员会分会秘书处或秘书长分别履行，但关于仲裁员是否回避的决定权除外。

（二）凡当事人同意将争议提交仲裁委员会仲裁的，均视为同意按照本规则进行仲裁。当事人约定适用其他仲裁规则，或约定对本规则有关内容进行变更的，从其约定，但其约定无法实施或与仲裁地强制性法律规定相抵触者除外。

（三）凡当事人约定按照本规则进行仲裁但未约定仲裁机构的，均视为同意将争议提交仲裁委员会仲裁。

（四）当事人约定适用仲裁委员会制定的行业仲裁规则或专业仲裁规则且其争议属于该规则适用范围的，从其约定；否则，适用本规则。

第五条　仲裁协议

（一）仲裁委员会根据当事人在争议发生之前或者在争议发生之后达成的将争议提交仲裁委员会仲裁的仲裁协议和一方当事人的书面申请，受理案件。

（二）仲裁协议系指当事人在合同中订明的仲裁条款，或者以其他方式达成的提交仲裁的书面协议。

（三）仲裁协议应当采取书面形式。书面形式包括合同书、信件、电报、电传、传真、电子数据交换和电子邮件等可以有形地表现所载内容的形式。在仲裁申请书和仲裁答辩书的交换中一方当事人声称有仲裁协议而另一方当事人不做否认表示的，视为存在书面仲裁协议。

（四）合同中的仲裁条款应视为与合同其他条款分离地、独立地存在的条款，附属于合同的仲裁协议也应视为与合同其他条款分离地、独立地存在的一个部分；合同的变更、解除、终止、转让、失效、无效、未生效、被撤销以及成立与否，均不影响仲裁条款或仲裁协议的效力。

第六条 对仲裁协议及/或管辖权的异议

（一）仲裁委员会有权对仲裁协议的存在、效力以及仲裁案件的管辖权作出决定。如有必要，仲裁委员会也可以授权仲裁庭作出管辖权决定。

（二）如果仲裁委员会依表面证据认为存在由仲裁委员会进行仲裁的协议，则可根据表面证据作出仲裁委员会有管辖权的决定，仲裁程序继续进行。仲裁委员会依表面证据作出的管辖权决定并不妨碍其根据仲裁庭在审理过程中发现的与表面证据不一致的事实及/或证据重新作出管辖权决定。

（三）当事人对仲裁协议及/或仲裁案件管辖权的异议，应当在仲裁庭首次开庭前书面提出；书面审理的案件，应当在第一次实体答辩前提出。

（四）对仲裁协议及/或仲裁案件管辖权提出异议不影响按仲裁程序进行审理。

（五）上述管辖权异议及/或决定包括仲裁案件主体资格异议及/或决定。

第七条 诚信合作

各方当事人应当诚信合作，进行仲裁程序。

第八条 放弃异议

一方当事人知道或者理应知道本规则或仲裁协议中规定的任何条款或情事未被遵守，但仍参加仲裁程序或继续进行仲裁程序而且不对此不遵守情况及时地、明示地提出书面异议的，视为放弃其提出异议的权利。

第二章 仲 裁 程 序

第一节 仲裁申请、答辩、反请求

第九条 仲裁程序的开始

仲裁程序自仲裁委员会或其分会收到仲裁申请书之日起开始。

第十条 申请仲裁

当事人依据本规则申请仲裁时应：

（一）提交由申请人及/或申请人授权的代理人签名及/或盖章的仲裁申请书。仲裁申请书应写明：

1．申请人和被申请人的名称和住所，包括邮政编码、电话、电传、传真、电报号码、电子邮件或其他电子通讯方式；

2．申请仲裁所依据的仲裁协议；

3．案情和争议要点；

4．申请人的仲裁请求；

5．仲裁请求所依据的事实和理由。

（二）在提交仲裁申请书时，附具申请人请求所依据的事实的证明文件。

（三）按照仲裁委员会制定的仲裁费用表的规定预缴仲裁费。

第十一条 案件的受理

（一）仲裁委员会收到申请人的仲裁申请书及其附件后，经过审查，认为申请仲裁的手续不完备的，可以要求申请人予以完备；认为申请仲裁的手续已完备的，应将仲裁通知连同仲裁委员会的仲裁规则、仲裁员名册和仲裁费用表各一份一并发送给双方当事人；申请人的仲裁申请书及其附件也应同时发送给被申请人。

（二）仲裁委员会或其分会受理案件后，应指定一名秘书局或秘书处的人员协助仲裁庭负责仲裁案件的程序管理工作。

第十二条 答辩

（一）被申请人应在收到仲裁通知之日起45天内向仲裁委员会秘书局或其分会秘书处提交答辩书。仲裁庭认为有正当理由的，可以适当延长此期限。答辩书由被申请人及/或被申请人授权的代理人签名及/或盖章，并应包括下列内容：

1．被申请人的名称和住所，包括邮政编码、电话、电传、传真、电报号码、电子邮件或其他电子通讯方式；

2．对申请人的仲裁申请的答辩及所依据的事实和理由；

3．答辩所依据的证明文件。

（二）仲裁庭有权决定是否接受逾期提交的答辩书。

（三）被申请人未提交答辩书，不影响仲裁程序的进行。

第十三条 反请求

（一）被申请人如有反请求，应当自收到仲裁通知之日起45天内以书面形式提交仲裁委员会。仲裁庭认为有正当理由的，可以适当延长此期限。

（二）被申请人提出反请求时，应在其反请求书中写明具体的反请求及其所依据的事实和理由,并附具有关的证明文件。

(三)被申请人提出反请求,应当按照仲裁委员会制定的仲裁费用表在规定的时间内预缴仲裁费。

(四)仲裁委员会认为被申请人提出反请求的手续已完备的,应将反请求书及其附件发送申请人。申请人应在接到反请求书及其附件后30天内对被申请人的反请求提交答辩。

(五)仲裁庭有权决定是否接受逾期提交的反请求答辩书。

(六)申请人对被申请人的反请求未提出书面答辩的,不影响仲裁程序的进行。

第十四条 变更仲裁请求或反请求

申请人可以对其仲裁请求提出更改,被申请人也可以对其反请求提出更改;但是,仲裁庭认为其提出更改的时间过迟而影响仲裁程序正常进行的,可以拒绝受理其更改请求。

第十五条 提交仲裁文件的份数

当事人提交仲裁申请书、答辩书、反请求书和有关证明材料以及其他文件时,应一式五份;如果当事人人数超过两人,则应增加相应份数;如果仲裁庭组成人数为一人,则可以减少两份;如果当事人提出财产保全申请或证据保全申请,则应相应增加一份。

第十六条 仲裁代理人

(一)当事人可以授权委托仲裁代理人办理有关的仲裁事项。当事人或其仲裁代理人应向仲裁委员会提交授权委托书。

(二)中国公民和外国公民均可以接受委托,担任仲裁代理人。

第十七条 财产保全

当事人申请财产保全的,仲裁委员会应当将当事人的申请转交被申请财产保全的当事人住所地或其财产所在地有管辖权的法院作出裁定。

第十八条 证据保全

当事人申请证据保全的,仲裁委员会应当将当事人的申请转交证据所在地有管辖权的法院作出裁定。

第二节 仲 裁 庭

第十九条 仲裁员的义务

仲裁员不代表任何一方当事人,并应独立于各方当事人且平等地对待各方当事人。

第二十条 仲裁庭的人数

(一)仲裁庭由一名或三名仲裁员组成。

（二）除非当事人另有约定或本规则另有规定，仲裁庭由三名仲裁员组成。

第二十一条　仲裁员名册

（一）当事人从仲裁委员会提供的仲裁员名册中选定仲裁员。

（二）当事人约定在仲裁委员会仲裁员名册之外选定仲裁员的，当事人选定的或根据当事人之间的协议指定的人士经仲裁委员会主任依法确认后可以担任仲裁员、首席仲裁员或独任仲裁员。

第二十二条　三人仲裁庭的组成

（一）申请人和被申请人应当各自在收到仲裁通知之日起15天内选定一名仲裁员或者委托仲裁委员会主任指定。当事人未在上述期限内选定或委托仲裁委员会主任指定的，由仲裁委员会主任指定。

（二）首席仲裁员由双方当事人在被申请人收到仲裁通知之日起15天内共同选定或者共同委托仲裁委员会主任指定。

（三）双方当事人可以各自推荐一至三名仲裁员作为首席仲裁员人选，并将推荐名单在第（二）款规定的期限内提交至仲裁委员会。双方当事人的推荐名单中有一名人选相同的，为双方当事人共同选定的首席仲裁员；有一名以上人选相同的，由仲裁委员会主任根据案件的具体情况在相同人选中确定一名首席仲裁员，该名首席仲裁员仍为双方共同选定的首席仲裁员；推荐名单中没有相同人选时，由仲裁委员会主任在推荐名单之外指定首席仲裁员。

（四）双方当事人未能按照上述规定共同选定首席仲裁员的，由仲裁委员会主任指定。

第二十三条　独任仲裁庭的组成

仲裁庭由一名仲裁员组成的，按照本规则第二十二条第（二）、（三）、（四）款规定的程序，选定或指定该独任仲裁员。

第二十四条　多方当事人对仲裁员的选定

（一）仲裁案件有两个或者两个以上申请人及/或被申请人时，申请人方及/或被申请人方应当各自协商，在仲裁委员会仲裁员名册中各自共同选定或者各自共同委托仲裁委员会主任指定一名仲裁员。

（二）如果申请人方及/或被申请人方未能在收到仲裁通知之日起15天内各自共同选定或者各自共同委托仲裁委员会主任指定一名仲裁员，则由仲裁委员会主任指定。

（三）首席仲裁员或独任仲裁员应按照本规则第二十二条第（二）、（三）、（四）款规定的程序选定或指定。申请人方及/或被申请人方按照本规则第二十二条第（三）款的规定选定首席仲裁员或独任仲裁员时，应各自共同协商，将其各自共同选定的候选人名单提交仲裁委员会。

第二十五条　披露

（一）被选定或者被指定的仲裁员应签署声明书,向仲裁委员会书面披露可能引起对其独立性或公正性产生合理怀疑的任何事实或情况。

（二）在仲裁过程中出现应当披露情形的,仲裁员应当立即书面向仲裁委员会披露。

（三）仲裁委员会将仲裁员的声明书及/或披露的信息转交各方当事人。

第二十六条　仲裁员的回避

（一）当事人收到仲裁委员会转交的仲裁员的声明书及/或书面披露后,如果以仲裁员披露的事实或情况为理由要求该仲裁员回避,则应于收到仲裁员的书面披露后10天内向仲裁委员会书面提出。逾期没有申请回避的,不得以仲裁员曾经披露的事项为由申请该仲裁员回避。

（二）当事人对被选定或者被指定的仲裁员的公正性和独立性产生具有正当理由的怀疑时,可以书面向仲裁委员会提出要求该仲裁员回避的请求,但应说明提出回避请求所依据的具体事实和理由,并举证。

（三）对仲裁员的回避请求应在收到组庭通知之日起15天内以书面形式提出;如果要求回避事由的得知是在此之后,则可以在得知回避事由后15天内提出,但不应迟于最后一次开庭终结。

（四）仲裁委员会应当立即将当事人的回避申请转交另一方当事人、被提请回避的仲裁员及仲裁庭其他成员。

（五）如果一方当事人申请回避,另一方当事人同意回避申请,或者被申请回避的仲裁员主动提出不再担任该仲裁案件的仲裁员,则该仲裁员不再担任仲裁员审理本案。上述情形并不表示当事人提出回避的理由成立。

（六）除上述第(五)款规定的情形外,仲裁员是否回避,由仲裁委员会主任作出终局决定并可以不说明理由。

（七）在仲裁委员会主任就仲裁员是否回避作出决定前,被请求回避的仲裁员应当继续履行职责。

第二十七条　替换仲裁员

（一）仲裁员在法律上或事实上不能履行其职责,或者没有按照本规则的要求或在规则规定的期限内履行应尽职责时,仲裁委员会主任有权自行决定将其更换;该仲裁员也可以主动申请不再担任仲裁员。

（二）仲裁员因死亡、除名、回避或者由于自动退出等其他原因不能履行职责时,应按照原选定或者指定该仲裁员的程序,在仲裁委员会规定的期限内选定或者指定替代的仲裁员。

（三）替代的仲裁员选定或者指定后,由仲裁庭决定以前进行过的全部或部分审理是否需要重新进行。

（四）是否替换仲裁员，由仲裁委员会主任作出终局决定并可以不说明理由。

第二十八条　多数仲裁员继续仲裁程序

在最后一次开庭终结后，如果三人仲裁庭中的一名仲裁员因死亡或被除名而不能参加合议及/或作出裁决，另外两名仲裁员可以请求仲裁委员会主任按照第二十七条的规定替换该仲裁员；在征求双方当事人意见并经仲裁委员会主任同意后，该两名仲裁员也可以继续进行仲裁程序，作出决定或裁决。仲裁委员会秘书局应将上述情况通知双方当事人。

第三节　审　理

第二十九条　审理方式

（一）除非当事人另有约定，仲裁庭可以按照其认为适当的方式审理案件。在任何情形下，仲裁庭均应公平和公正地行事，给予各方当事人陈述与辩论的合理机会。

（二）仲裁庭应当开庭审理案件，但经双方当事人申请或者征得双方当事人同意，仲裁庭也认为不必开庭审理的，仲裁庭可以只依据书面文件进行审理。

（三）除非当事人另有约定，仲裁庭可以根据案件的具体情况采用询问式或辩论式审理案件。

（四）仲裁庭可以在其认为适当的地点或以其认为适当的方式进行合议。

（五）除非当事人另有约定，仲裁庭认为必要时可以发布程序指令、发出问题单、举行庭前会议、召开预备庭、制作审理范围书等。

第三十条　开庭通知

（一）仲裁案件第一次开庭审理的日期，经仲裁庭决定后，由秘书局于开庭前20天通知双方当事人。当事人有正当理由的，可以请求延期开庭，但必须在开庭前10天以书面形式向秘书局提出；是否延期，由仲裁庭决定。

（二）第一次开庭审理后的开庭审理日期及延期后开庭审理日期的通知，不受第（一）款中20天的限制。

第三十一条　仲裁地

（一）双方当事人书面约定仲裁地的，从其约定。

（二）如果当事人对仲裁地未作约定，仲裁委员会或其分会所在地为仲裁地。

（三）仲裁裁决应视为在仲裁地作出。

第三十二条　开庭地点

（一）当事人约定了开庭地点的，仲裁案件的开庭审理应当在约定的地点进行，但出现本规则第六十九条第（三）款规定的情形除外。

（二）除非当事人另有约定，由仲裁委员会受理的案件应当在北京开庭审理；如仲裁庭认为必要，经仲裁委员会秘书长同意，也可以在其他地点开庭审理。由仲裁委员会分会受理的案件应当在该分会所在地开庭审理；如仲裁庭认为必要，经该分会秘书长同意，也可以在其他地点开庭审理。

第三十三条　保密

（一）仲裁庭审理案件不公开进行。如果双方当事人要求公开审理，由仲裁庭作出是否公开审理的决定。

（二）不公开审理的案件，双方当事人及其仲裁代理人、证人、翻译、仲裁员、仲裁庭咨询的专家和指定的鉴定人、仲裁委员会秘书局的有关人员，均不得对外界透露案件实体和程序的有关情况。

第三十四条　当事人缺席

（一）申请人无正当理由开庭时不到庭的，或在开庭审理时未经仲裁庭许可中途退庭的，可以视为撤回仲裁申请；如果被申请人提出了反请求，不影响仲裁庭就反请求进行审理，并作出裁决。

（二）被申请人无正当理由开庭时不到庭的，或在开庭审理时未经仲裁庭许可中途退庭的，仲裁庭可以进行缺席审理，并作出裁决；如果被申请人提出了反请求，可以视为撤回反请求。

第三十五条　庭审笔录

（一）开庭审理时，仲裁庭可以制作庭审笔录及/或影音记录。仲裁庭认为必要时，可以制作庭审要点，并要求当事人及/或其代理人、证人及/或其他有关人员在庭审笔录或庭审要点上签字或者盖章。

（二）庭审笔录和影音记录供仲裁庭查用。

第三十六条　举证

（一）当事人应当对其申请、答辩和反请求所依据的事实提供证据加以证明。

（二）仲裁庭可以规定当事人提交证据的期限。当事人应当在规定的期限内提交。逾期提交的，仲裁庭可以不予接受。当事人在举证期限内提交证据材料确有困难的，可以在期限届满前申请延长举证期限。是否延长，由仲裁庭决定。

（三）当事人未能在规定的期限内提交证据，或者虽提交证据但不足以证明其主张的，负有举证责任的当事人承担因此产生的后果。

第三十七条　仲裁庭自行调查

（一）仲裁庭认为必要时，可以自行调查事实，收集证据。

（二）仲裁庭自行调查事实、收集证据时，认为有必要通知双方当事人到场的，应及时通知双方当事人到场。经通知而一方或双方当事人不到场的，仲裁庭自行调查事实和收集证据不受其影响。

（三）仲裁庭自行调查收集的证据,应经仲裁委员会秘书局转交双方当事人,给予双方当事人提出意见的机会。

第三十八条　专家报告及鉴定报告

（一）仲裁庭可以就案件中的专门问题向专家咨询或者指定鉴定人进行鉴定。专家和鉴定人可以是中国或外国的机构或公民。

（二）仲裁庭有权要求当事人,而且当事人也有义务向专家或鉴定人提供或出示任何有关资料、文件或财产、货物,以供专家或鉴定人审阅、检验或鉴定。

（三）专家报告和鉴定报告的副本应送给双方当事人,给予双方当事人对专家报告和鉴定报告提出意见的机会。任何一方当事人要求专家或鉴定人参加开庭的,经仲裁庭同意后,专家或鉴定人可以参加开庭,并在仲裁庭认为必要和适宜的情况下就他们的报告作出解释。

第三十九条　质证

（一）一方当事人提交的证据材料应经仲裁委员会秘书局转交对方当事人。

（二）开庭审理的案件,证据应当在开庭时出示,由当事人质证。

（三）当事人开庭后提交的证据材料,仲裁庭决定接受但不再开庭审理的,可以要求当事人在一定期限内提交书面质证意见。

第四十条　仲裁与调解相结合

（一）当事人在仲裁委员会之外通过协商或调解达成和解协议的,可以凭当事人达成的由仲裁委员会仲裁的仲裁协议和他们的和解协议,请求仲裁委员会组成仲裁庭,按照和解协议的内容作出仲裁裁决。除非当事人另有约定,仲裁委员会主任指定一名独任仲裁员组成仲裁庭,按照仲裁庭认为适当的程序进行审理并作出裁决。具体程序和期限不受本规则其他条款限制。

（二）如果双方当事人有调解愿望,或一方当事人有调解愿望并经仲裁庭征得另一方当事人同意的,仲裁庭可以在仲裁程序进行过程中对其审理的案件进行调解。

（三）仲裁庭可以按照其认为适当的方式进行调解。

（四）仲裁庭在进行调解的过程中,任何一方当事人提出终止调解或仲裁庭认为已无调解成功的可能时,应停止调解。

（五）在仲裁庭进行调解的过程中,双方当事人在仲裁庭之外达成和解的,应视为是在仲裁庭调解下达成的和解。

（六）经仲裁庭调解达成和解的,双方当事人应签订书面和解协议;除非当事人另有约定,仲裁庭应当根据当事人书面和解协议的内容作出裁决书结案。

（七）如果调解不成功,仲裁庭应当继续进行仲裁程序,并作出裁决。

（八）如果调解不成功,任何一方当事人均不得在其后的仲裁程序、司法程序和其他任何程序中援引对方当事人或仲裁庭在调解过程中曾发表的意见、提出的观点、作出的陈述、表示认同或否定的建议或主张作为其请求、答辩或反请求的依据。

第四十一条 撤回申请和撤销案件

（一）当事人可以向仲裁委员会提出撤回全部仲裁请求或全部仲裁反请求。申请人撤回全部仲裁请求的，不影响仲裁庭就被申请人的反请求进行审理和裁决。被申请人撤回全部仲裁反请求的，不影响仲裁庭就申请人的仲裁请求进行审理和裁决。

（二）在仲裁庭组成前撤销案件的，由仲裁委员会秘书长作出决定；在仲裁庭组成后撤销案件的，由仲裁庭作出决定。

（三）当事人就已经撤回的仲裁申请再提出仲裁申请时，由仲裁委员会作出受理或者不受理的决定。

第三章 裁　　决

第四十二条 作出裁决的期限

（一）仲裁庭应当在组庭之日起6个月内作出裁决书。

（二）在仲裁庭的要求下，仲裁委员会主任认为确有正当理由和必要的，可以延长该期限。

第四十三条 裁决的作出

（一）仲裁庭应当根据事实，依照法律和合同规定，参考国际惯例，并遵循公平合理原则，独立公正地作出裁决。

（二）仲裁庭在其作出的裁决中，应当写明仲裁请求、争议事实、裁决理由、裁决结果、仲裁费用的承担、裁决的日期和地点。当事人协议不写明争议事实和裁决理由的，以及按照双方当事人和解协议的内容作出裁决的，可以不写明争议事实和裁决理由。仲裁庭有权在裁决中确定当事人履行裁决的具体期限及逾期履行所应承担的责任。

（三）裁决书应加盖仲裁委员会印章。

（四）由三名仲裁员组成的仲裁庭审理的案件，裁决依全体仲裁员或多数仲裁员的意见作出。少数仲裁员的书面意见应当附卷，并可以附在裁决书后，但该书面意见不构成裁决书的组成部分。

（五）仲裁庭不能形成多数意见时，裁决依首席仲裁员的意见作出。其他仲裁员的书面意见应当附卷，并可以附在裁决书后，但该书面意见不构成裁决书的组成部分。

（六）除非裁决依首席仲裁员意见或独任仲裁员意见作出，裁决应由多数仲裁员署名。持有不同意见的仲裁员可以在裁决书上署名,也可以不署名。

（七）作出裁决书的日期,即为裁决发生法律效力的日期。

（八）裁决是终局的,对双方当事人均有约束力。任何一方当事人均不得向法院起诉,也不得向其他任何机构提出变更仲裁裁决的请求。

第四十四条　中间裁决和部分裁决

如果仲裁庭认为必要或者当事人提出请求经仲裁庭同意时,仲裁庭可以在作出最终仲裁裁决之前的任何时候,就案件的任何问题作出中间裁决或部分裁决。任何一方当事人不履行中间裁决,不影响仲裁程序的继续进行,也不影响仲裁庭作出最终裁决。

第四十五条　裁决书草案的核阅

仲裁庭应在签署裁决书之前将裁决书草案提交仲裁委员会核阅。在不影响仲裁庭独立裁决的情况下,仲裁委员会可以就裁决书的有关问题提请仲裁庭注意。

第四十六条　费用承担

（一）仲裁庭有权在仲裁裁决书中裁定当事人最终应向仲裁委员会支付的仲裁费和其他费用。

（二）仲裁庭有权根据案件的具体情况在裁决书中裁定败诉方应当补偿胜诉方因办理案件而支出的合理的费用。仲裁庭裁定败诉方补偿胜诉方因办理案件而支出的费用是否合理时,应具体考虑案件的裁决结果、复杂程度、胜诉方当事人及/或代理人的实际工作量以及案件的争议金额等因素。

第四十七条　裁决书的更正

任何一方当事人均可以在收到裁决书之日起30天内就裁决书中的书写、打印、计算上的错误或其他类似性质的错误,书面申请仲裁庭作出更正;如确有错误,仲裁庭应在收到书面申请之日起30天内作出书面更正。仲裁庭也可以在发出裁决书后的合理时间内自行以书面形式作出更正。该书面更正构成裁决书的一部分。

第四十八条　补充裁决

如果裁决有漏裁事项,任何一方当事人可以在收到裁决书之日起30天内以书面形式请求仲裁庭就裁决中漏裁的仲裁事项作出补充裁决;如确有漏裁事项,仲裁庭应在收到上述书面申请之日起30天内作出补充裁决。仲裁庭也可以在发出裁决书后的合理时间内自行作出补充裁决。该补充裁决构成原裁决书的一部分。

第四十九条　裁决的履行

（一）当事人应当依照裁决书写明的期限履行仲裁裁决;裁决书未写明履行期限的,应当立即履行。

（二）一方当事人不履行裁决的,另一方当事人可以根据中国法律的规定,向有管辖权的中国法院申请执行;或者根据一九五八年联合国《承认及执行外国仲裁裁决公约》或者中国缔结或参加的其他国际条约,向有管辖权的法院申请执行。

第四章 简易程序

第五十条 简易程序的适用

（一）除非当事人另有约定,凡争议金额不超过人民币50万元的,或争议金额超过人民币50万元,经一方当事人书面申请并征得另一方当事人书面同意的,适用本简易程序。

（二）没有争议金额或者争议金额不明确的,由仲裁委员会根据案件的复杂程度、涉及利益的大小以及其他有关因素综合考虑决定是否适用本简易程序。

第五十一条 仲裁通知

申请人向仲裁委员会提出仲裁申请,经审查可以受理并适用简易程序的,仲裁委员会秘书局或其分会秘书处应向双方当事人发出仲裁通知。

第五十二条 仲裁庭的组成

适用简易程序的案件,依照本规则第二十三条的规定成立独任仲裁庭审理案件。

第五十三条 答辩和反请求

（一）被申请人应在收到仲裁通知之日起20天内向仲裁委员会提交答辩书及有关证明文件;如有反请求,也应在此期限内提交反请求书及有关证明文件。仲裁庭认为有正当理由的,可以适当延长此期限。

（二）申请人应在收到反请求书及其附件后20天内对被申请人的反请求提交答辩。

第五十四条 审理方式

仲裁庭可以按照其认为适当的方式审理案件;可以决定只依据当事人提交的书面材料和证据进行书面审理,也可以决定开庭审理。

第五十五条 开庭审理

（一）对于开庭审理的案件,仲裁庭确定开庭日期后,仲裁委员会秘书局或其分会秘书处应在开庭前15天将开庭日期通知双方当事人。当事人有正当理由的,可以请求延期开庭,但必须在开庭前7天书面向仲裁庭提出。是否延期,由仲裁庭决定。

（二）如果仲裁庭决定开庭审理,仲裁庭只开庭一次,确有必要的除外。

（三）第一次开庭审理后的开庭审理日期及延期后开庭审理日期的通知,不受第(一)款中 15 天的限制。

第五十六条 作出裁决的期限

(一)仲裁庭应当在组庭之日起 3 个月内作出裁决书。

(二)在仲裁庭的要求下,仲裁委员会主任认为确有正当理由和必要的,可以对上述期限予以延长。

第五十七条 程序变更

仲裁请求的变更或反请求的提出,不影响简易程序的继续进行。经变更的仲裁请求或反请求所涉及争议的金额超过人民币 50 万元的,除非当事人约定继续适用简易程序,简易程序变更为普通程序。

第五十八条 本规则其他条款的适用

本章未规定的事项,适用本规则其他各章的有关规定。

第五章 国内仲裁的特别规定

第五十九条 本章的适用

(一)仲裁委员会受理的国内仲裁案件,适用本章规定。

(二)符合本规则第五十条规定的国内仲裁案件,适用第四章简易程序的规定。

第六十条 受理

(一)仲裁委员会收到仲裁申请书后,认为符合本规则第十条规定的受理条件的,应当在 5 天内受理,并通知当事人,也可以当即受理并通知当事人;认为不符合受理条件的,应当书面通知当事人不予受理,并说明理由。

(二)仲裁委员会收到仲裁申请书后,认为仲裁申请书不符合本规则第十条规定的,可以要求当事人在规定的期限内补正。

第六十一条 仲裁庭的组成

仲裁庭应当按照本规则第二十一条、第二十二条、第二十三条和第二十四条的规定组成。

第六十二条 答辩和反请求

(一)被申请人应在收到仲裁通知之日起 20 天内向仲裁委员会提交答辩书及有关证明文件;如有反请求,也应在此期限内提交反请求书及有关证明文件。仲裁庭认为有正当理由的,可以适当延长此期限。

(二)申请人应在收到反请求书及其附件后 20 天内对被申请人的反请求提交答辩。

第六十三条 开庭通知

(一)开庭审理的案件,仲裁委员会秘书局或其分会秘书处应当在开庭前

15 天将开庭日期通知双方当事人。仲裁庭经商双方当事人同意,可以提前开庭。当事人有正当理由的,可以请求延期开庭,但必须在开庭前 7 天书面向仲裁庭提出。是否延期,由仲裁庭决定。

(二)第一次开庭审理后开庭审理的日期及延期后开庭审理日期的通知,不受第(一)款 15 天期限的限制。

第六十四条　开庭笔录

(一)仲裁庭应当将开庭情况简要记入笔录。当事人和其他仲裁参与人认为对自己陈述的记录有遗漏或者有差错的,可以申请补正;仲裁庭不同意其补正的,应当将该申请记录在案。

(二)记录由仲裁员、记录人员、当事人和其他仲裁参与人签名或者盖章。

第六十五条　作出裁决的期限

(一)仲裁庭应当在组庭之日起 4 个月内作出裁决书。

(二)在仲裁庭的要求下,仲裁委员会主任认为确有正当理由和必要的,可以延长该期限。

第六十六条　本规则其他条款的适用

本章未规定的事项,适用本规则其他各章的有关规定。

第六章　附　　则

第六十七条　仲裁语言

(一)当事人约定了仲裁语言的,从其约定。当事人没有约定的,仲裁程序以中文为正式语言。

(二)仲裁庭开庭时,如果当事人或其代理人、证人需要语言翻译,可以由仲裁委员会秘书局或其分会秘书处提供译员,也可以由当事人自行提供译员。

(三)当事人提交的各种文书和证明材料,仲裁庭及/或仲裁委员会秘书局或其分会秘书处认为必要时,可以要求当事人提供相应的中文译本或其他语言译本。

第六十八条　送达

(一)有关仲裁的一切文书、通知、材料等均可以派人或以挂号信或特快专递、传真、电传、电报或仲裁委员会秘书局认为适当的其他方式发送给当事人及/或其仲裁代理人。

(二)向一方当事人及/或其仲裁代理人发送的任何书面通讯,如经当面递交收讯人或投递至收讯人的营业地、注册地、住所地、惯常居住地或通讯地址,或者经对方当事人合理查询不能找到上述任一地点,仲裁委员会秘书局或其分会秘书处以挂号信或能提供投递记录的其他任何手段投递给收讯人最后一个为人所知的营业地、注册地、住所地、惯常居住地或通讯地址,即应视为已经送达。

第六十九条 仲裁费用及实际费用

(一)仲裁委员会除按照其制定的仲裁费用表向当事人收取仲裁费外,可以向当事人收取其他额外的、合理的实际开支费用,包括仲裁员办理案件的特殊报酬、差旅费、食宿费以及仲裁庭聘请专家、鉴定人和翻译等的费用。

(二)当事人选定了需要开支差旅费、食宿费等实际费用的仲裁员,在仲裁委员会规定的期限内未预缴实际费用的,视为其没有选定仲裁员。在此情况下,仲裁委员会主任可以按照本规则第二十二条的规定,代为指定仲裁员。

(三)当事人约定在仲裁委员会所在地之外开庭的,应预缴因此而发生的差旅费、食宿费等实际费用。在仲裁委员会规定的期限内未预缴此实际费用的,则在仲裁委员会所在地开庭。

第七十条 规则的解释

(一)本规则条文标题不用于解释条文含义。

(二)本规则由仲裁委员会负责解释。

第七十一条 规则的施行

本规则自 2005 年 5 月 1 日起施行。在本规则施行前仲裁委员会及其分会受理的案件,仍适用受理案件时适用的仲裁规则;双方当事人同意的,也可以适用本规则。